Index of American Periodical Verse: 1979

by

Sander W. Zulauf

with

Jandra Milkowski

The Scarecrow Press, Inc.
Metuchen, N.J. & London
1981

Library of Congress Catalog Card No. 73-3060

ISBN 0-8108-1389-0

Copyright © 1981 by Sander W. Zulauf and Jandra Milkowski

Manufactured in the United States of America

CONTENTS

PREFACE

The 1979 edition of the Index of American Periodical Verse
records the last poetry of the seventies. The nine completed vol-
umes of the Index record the work of a decade of enormous activity
in poetry and in publishing. This volume welcomes a new editorial
assistant, Ms. Jandra Milkowski, who gracefully insured the publi-
cation of the 1979 Index with all of her diligent indexing. It also
marks the departure of Dr. Edward Cifelli who has been essential
to this publication for the last three volumes.

The format of the Index remains the same as that of its pre-
decessors. The first section lists the title abbreviations of each
publication indexed, the complete name of the magazine, the names
of the editors, the editorial addresses, the issues of the magazines
covered in this Index, and the latest available subscription or single
copy prices.

The main section of the Index is the alphabetical listing of
poets and their published poems. A reference citation which locates
the poem follows each title. This citation includes the underlined
title abbreviation for the magazine--"OhioR" (for Ohio Review); the
volume and/or number of the issue in parentheses--"(3:6)" signifying
volume 3, number 6; "Wint 79" for an issue dated winter 1979; and
the page number--"p. "--on which the poem appears.

Poet Philip Dacey involved 102 contemporary poets in a pro-
ject between 1972 and 1977 which became "The Great American
Poem. " Each poet contributed a line to the poem and the final re-
sult was published in Antaeus. The poets who participated have
"The Great American Poem" listed as one of their published poems
in this volume.

This year special thanks are extended to Mr. and Mrs. Len-
roy Adams of Mt. Arlington, New Jersey, who made this issue pos-
sible; Mrs. Constance Lane, director of the Roxbury Public Library,
Succasunna, N. J.; and Mrs. Dorothy Souchack and the periodicals
staff of the Sherman H. Masten Learning Resources Center at County
College of Morris in Randolph, N. J.

This issue would not exist at all if it weren't for the cooper-
ation of the editors whose names appear in the Periodicals Indexed
section. Through the efforts of each of them, American poetry lives.

Finally, I thank my family--Madeline and Scott Zulauf, and Mary Beth and Michael Stoddard--for all the love they freely give to me.

S. W. Z.

Succasunna, N. J.
August, 1980

ABBREVIATIONS

ad.	adaptation
arr.	arrangement
Back:	back-issue copy price
Ed. (s.)	Editor(s)
Exec.	Executive
(ind.)	price for individuals
(inst.)	price for institutions
(lib.)	price for libraries
p.	page
pp.	pages
Po. Ed.	Poetry Editor
Pub.	Publisher
Sing:	single copy price
SI	Special Issue
(stud.)	price for students
Subs:	subscription price or address
tr.	translation
U	University
w.	with
$9/yr	nine dollars per year
$9/4	nine dollars for four issues
(19)	number 19
(7:9)	volume 7, number 9

Months

Ja	January		Jl	July
F	February		Ag	August
Mr	March		S	September
Ap	April		O	October
My	May		N	November
Je	June		D	December

Seasons

Aut	Autumn, Fall		Spr	Spring
Wint	Winter		Sum	Summer

PERIODICALS ADDED

Black American Literature Forum
Chariton Review
Conditions
Images
Mississippi Review

Osiris
Poultry
Urthkin
West Branch

PERIODICALS DELETED

Aieee
Aphra
Arion's Dolphin
The Ark
Big Deal
Bird Effort
Carousel Quarterly
DeKalb Literary Arts Journal
Epos
Gravida
Hand Book
Juice
La Bas
Ladies' Home Journal
Madrona

Moons and Lion Tailes
New Collage
New River Review
Norwottuck
Perspective
Poet Lore
Remington Review
The Smudge
Stonecloud
Unmuzzled Ox
Waters
Women/Poems
Xanadu
Yale Lit

PERIODICAL TITLE CHANGES

AAUP Bulletin became Academe.

Pikestaff Forum became Pikestaff Review.

AAR
ANN ARBOR REVIEW
Fred Wolven, Ed.
Washtenaw Community College
Ann Arbor, MI 48106
 (29)
 Subs: $6/3
 Sing: $2

Academe
ACADEME: BULLETIN OF
 THE AAUP
R. K. Webb
Ellen Morgenstern, Eds.
Suite 500
One Dupont Circle, N.W.
Washington, DC 20036
 (65:1-8)
 Subs: $24/yr

Agni
AGNI REVIEW
Sharon Dunn
Askold Melnyczuk, Eds.
Box 349
Cambridge, MA 02138
 (10/11)
 Subs: $8/2 yrs
          $4/yr
 Sing: $3.95/double issue
          $2.50

AmerPoR
AMERICAN POETRY REVIEW
Stephen Berg, et al., Eds.
Temple U Center City
1616 Walnut St.
Room 405
Philadelphia, PA 19103
 (8:1-5)
 Subs: $19/3 yrs

          $13/2 yrs
          $7.50/yr
 Sing: $1.50

AmerS
THE AMERICAN SCHOLAR
Joseph Epstein, Ed.
1811 Q Street, N.W.
Washington, DC 20009
 (48:1-4)
 Subs: $24/3 yrs
          $18/2 yrs
          $10/yr
 Sing: $3

AndR
THE ANDOVER REVIEW
William H. Brown, Ed.
Erica Funkhouser, Po. Ed.
Phillips Academy
Andover, MA 01810
 (6:1-2)
 Subs: $6/yr
 Sing: $3

Antaeus
ANTAEUS
Daniel Halpern, Ed.
1 West 30th St.
New York, NY 10001
 (32-35)
 Subs: $14/yr
 Sing: $4

AntR
ANTIOCH REVIEW
Robert S. Fogarty, Ed.
Ralph Dawes
John Giarelli, Po. Assistants
Box 148
Yellow Springs, OH 45387

1

(37:1-4)
Subs:　$10/yr
Sing:　$2.50

ArizQ
ARIZONA QUARTERLY
Albert Frank Gegenheimer, Ed.
U of Arizona
Tucson, AZ 85721
　(35:1-4)
　Subs:　$5/3 yrs
　　　　　$2/yr
　Sing:　$.50

ArkRiv
THE ARK RIVER REVIEW
Jonathan Katz
Anthony Sobin, Eds.
Box 14
Wichita State U
Wichita, KS 67208
　(4:3-4)
　Subs:　$5/4

Ascent
ASCENT
The Editors
English Dept.
U of Illinois
Urbana, IL 61801
　(4:2-3) (5:1)
　Subs:　$3/yr
　Sing:　$1.50

Aspect
ASPECT
Ed Hogan, Ed.
13 Robinson St.
Somerville, MA 02145
　(74/75)
　Subs:　$6/yr
　Sing:　$2.50

Aspen
ASPEN ANTHOLOGY
J. D. Muller, Ed.
Box 3185
Aspen, CO 81611
　(7-8)
　Subs:　$13.50/3 yrs
　　　　　$9/2 yrs
　　　　　$4.50/yr
　Sing:　$2.50

Atl
THE ATLANTIC
Robert Manning, Ed.
Peter Davison, Po. Ed.
8 Arlington St.
Boston, MA 02116
Subs:　Subs Processing Center
　　　　Box 1857
　　　　Greenwich, CT 06830
　(243:1-6) (244:1-6)
　Subs:　$45/3 yrs
　　　　　$33/2 yrs
　Sing:　$1.50

Bachy
BACHY
F. X. Feeney, Prose Ed.
Leland Hackman, Po. Ed.
Papa Bach Paperbacks
11317 Santa Monica Boulevard
West Los Angeles, CA 90025
　(14-15)
　Subs:　$10/yr
　Sing:　$3.50

BallSUF
BALL STATE UNIVERSITY
　FORUM
Merrill & Frances M. Rippy,
　Eds.
Ball State U
Muncie, IN 47306
　(20:1-4)
　Subs:　$5/yr
　Sing:　$1.50

BelPoJ
THE BELOIT POETRY JOURNAL
Robert H. Glauber, et al., Eds.
Box 2
Beloit, WI 53511
　(29:3-4) (30:1-2)
　Subs:　$11/3 yrs
　　　　　$4/yr
　Sing:　$1.50

BerksR
BERKSHIRE REVIEW
Charles Karelis, et al., Eds.
Williams College
Box 633
Williamstown, MA 02167
　(14)

Subs: $1/yr
Sing: $.50

Bits
BITS
Robert Wallace, et al., Eds.
Dept. of English
Case Western Reserve U
Cleveland, OH 44106
(9-10) (chapbook)
Subs: $2/yr
Sing: $1

BlackALF
*BLACK AMERICAN LITERA-
  TURE FORUM
Joe Weixlmann, Ed.
Parsons Hall 237
Indiana State U
Terre Haute, IN 47809
(13:1-4)
Subs: $4/yr
Sing: $1

BlackF
BLACK FORUM
Julia Coaxum, Ed.
Revish Windham
Zandra Holmes, Po. Eds.
Box 1090
Bronx, NY 10451
(3:1)
Subs: $9/3 yrs
          $6/2 yrs
          $3/yr
Sing: $2

BosUJ
BOSTON UNIVERSITY JOURNAL
Paul Kurt Ackermann, Ed.
704 Commonwealth Ave.
Boston, MA 02215
(-)
Subs: $9/yr (inst.)
          $6/yr (ind.)
Sing: $2

Bound
BOUNDARY 2
William V. Spanos, et al.,
  Eds.

Dept. of English
SUNY-Binghamton
Binghamton, NY 13901
(7:2-3) (8:1)
Subs: $15/yr (inst.)
          $10/yr (ind.)
          $7/yr (stud.)
Sing: $7 (double issue)
          $4

CalQ
CALIFORNIA QUARTERLY
Elliot L. Gilbert, Ed.
Sandra M. Gilbert
Kevin Clark, Po. Eds.
100 Sproul Hall
U of California
Davis, CA 95616
(15)
Subs: $5/yr
Sing: $1.50

CarlMis
CARLETON MISCELLANY
Keith Harrison, Ed.
Carleton College
Northfield, MN 55057
(17:2/3) (18:1)
Subs: $10/2 yrs
          $5.50/yr
Sing: $2

CarolQ
CAROLINA QUARTERLY
Dorothy Combs Hill, Ed.
Miriam Marty
Michael McFee, Po. Eds.
Greenlaw Hall 066-A
U of North Carolina
Chapel Hill, NC 27514
(31:1-3)
Subs: $6/yr
Sing: $2
Back: $3

CEACritic
CEA CRITIC
Elizabeth Wooten Cowan, Ed.
Dept. of English
Texas A&M U
College Station, TX 77843

*New titles added to the Index in 1979.

(41:2-4) (42:1)
Subs: $18/yr (lib.)
$12/yr (ind.)

CentR
CENTENNIAL REVIEW
David Mead, Ed.
Linda Wagner, Po. Ed.
110 Morrill Hall
Michigan State U
East Lansing, MI 48824
(23:1-4)
Subs: $5/2 yrs
$3/yr
Sing: $1

CharR
*CHARITON REVIEW
Jim Barnes, Ed.
Div. of Language and Litera-
ture
Northeast Missouri State U
Kirksville, MO 63501
(5:1-2-SI)
Subs: $7/4
Sing: $2

Chelsea
CHELSEA
Sonia Raiziss, Ed.
Box 5880
Grand Central Station
New York, NY 10017
(38)
Subs: $6/2
Sing: $3.50

ChiR
CHICAGO REVIEW
Michael Gorman, et al. , Eds.
U of Chicago
970 E. 58th St. Box C
Chicago, IL 60637
(30:4) (31:1-2)
Subs: $27/3 yrs
$18.50/2 yrs
$10/yr
Sing: $3

Chomo
CHOMO-URI
Box 1057
Amherst, MA 01002

(5:3) (6:1)
Final issue.
Sing: $1.50

Chowder
CHOWDER REVIEW
Ron Slate, Ed.
Floyd Skloot, Associate Ed.
Box 33
Wollaston, MA 02170
or
856 South Park Ave.
Springfield, IL 62704
(12-13)
Subs: $8/3 (inst.)
$7/3 (ind.)
$2.50

ChrC
THE CHRISTIAN CENTURY
James M. Wall, Ed.
407 S. Dearborn St.
Chicago, IL 60605
(96:1-43)
Subs: $45/3 yrs
$30/2 yrs
$18/yr
Sing: $.60

CimR
CIMARRON REVIEW
Neil J. Hackett, Ed.
William Mills, Po. Ed.
208 Life Sciences East
Oklahoma State U
Stillwater, OK 74074
(46-49)
Subs: $10/yr
Sing: $4

ColEng
COLLEGE ENGLISH
Donald Gray, Ed.
Brian O'Neill, Po. Ed.
Dept. of English
Indiana U
Bloomington, IN 47401
Subs: NCTE
1111 Kenyon Rd.
Urbana, IL 61801
(40:5-8) (41:1-4)
Subs: $25/yr
Sing: $2.50

Columbia
COLUMBIA
The Editors
404 Dodge
Columbia U
New York, NY 10027
(3)
Sing: $3

Comm
COMMONWEAL
James O'Gara, Ed.
Rosemary Dean
Marie Ponsat, Po. Eds.
232 Madison Ave.
New York, NY 10016
(106:1-23)
Subs: $35/2 yrs
$20/yr
Sing: $1

ConcPo
CONCERNING POETRY
Ellwood Johnson, Ed.
A. J. Hovde, Po. Ed.
Dept. of English
Western Washington U
Bellingham, WA 98225
(12:1)
Subs: $4/yr
Sing: $2

Cond
*CONDITIONS
Lorraine Bethel
Barbara Smith, Eds.
Box 56
Van Brunt Station
Brooklyn, NY 11215
(5)
Subs: $15/3 (inst.)
$8/3 (ind.)
Sing: $3
Free upon request
to women in pris-
ons and mental
institutions.

Confr
CONFRONTATION
Martin Tucker, Ed.
English Dept.
Brooklyn Center of Long

Island U
Brooklyn, NY 11201
Subs: Ms. Eleanor Feleppa
Director of Public Rela-
tions
Southampton College
Long Island U
Southampton, NY 11968
(18-19)
Subs: $15/3 yrs
$10/2 yrs
$5/yr
Sing: $2

CornellR
CORNELL REVIEW
Baxter Hathaway, Ed.
108 North Plain St.
Ithaca, NY 14850
(5-7)
Final issue.
Sing: $3. 50

CutB
CUTBANK
Don Schofield
Sherman Apt, Eds.
Dept. of English
U of Montana
Missoula, MT 59812
(12-13)
Subs: $7. 50/2 yrs
$4/yr
Sing: $2. 50

DacTerr
DACOTAH TERRITORY
Mark Vinz, Ed.
Moorhead State U
Box 775
Moorhead, MN 56560
(16)
Sing: $2

DenQ
DENVER QUARTERLY
Leland H. Chambers, Ed.
U of Denver
Denver, CO 80208
(14:1-3)
Subs: $14/2 yrs
$8/yr
Sing: $2

Durak
DURAK
Robert Lloyd
D. A. Hoffman, Eds.
RD1   Box 352
Joe Green Road
Erin, NY 14838
(2-3)
Subs: $6/2 yrs
         $3/yr
Sing: $1. 50

EngJ
ENGLISH JOURNAL
Stephen N. Judy, Ed.
B. Jo Kinnick, Po. Ed.
Box 112
E. Lansing, MI 48823
Subs: NCTE
       1111 Kenyon Rd.
       Urbana, IL 61801
(68:5)
Poetry in May issue.
Subs: $25/yr (inst.)
         $20/yr (ind.)

EnPas
EN PASSANT
James A. Costello, Ed.
4612 Sylvanus Dr.
Wilmington, DE 19803
(8-9)
Subs: $11/8
         $6/4
Sing: $1. 75

Epoch
EPOCH
James McConkey
Walter Slatoff, Eds.
245 Goldwin Smith Hall
Cornell U
Ithaca, NY 14853
(28:2-3) (29:1)
Subs: $5/yr
Sing: $2

Falcon
THE FALCON
W. A. Blais, Ed.
Mansfield State College
Mansfield, PA 16933
(18)

Subs: $2/yr
Sing: $1

Field
FIELD
Stuart Friebert
David Young, Eds.
Rice Hall
Oberlin College
Oberlin, OH 44074
(20-21)
Subs: $8/2 yrs
         $5/yr
Sing: $2. 50
Back: $10

Focus
FOCUS/MIDWEST
Charles L. Klotzer, Ed. /Pub.
Dan Jaffe, Po. Ed.
928a N. McKnight
St. Louis, MO 63132
(13:80-84)
Subs: $27/30
         $15. 50/18
         $11. 50/12
         $7/6 (yr)
Sing: $1. 25

FourQt
FOUR QUARTERS
John Christopher Kleis, Ed.
Richard Lautz, Po. Ed.
LaSalle College
20th & Olney Aves.
Philadelphia, PA 19141
(28:2-4) (29:1)
Subs: $7/2 yrs
         $4/yr
Sing: $1

GeoR
GEORGIA REVIEW
Stanley W. Lindberg, Ed.
U of Georgia
Athens, GA 30602
(33:1-4)
Subs: $10/2 yrs
         $6/yr
Sing: $3

Glass
GLASSWORKS

Betty Bressi, Ed.
Box 163
Rosebank Sta.
Staten Island, NY 10305
(-)
Subs: $4.50
Sing: $1.25
Temporarily suspended w.
(3:1/2/3) in 78.

GreenfieldR
THE GREENFIELD REVIEW
Joseph Bruchac III, Ed.
Carol Worthen Bruchac,
Managing Ed.
Greenfield Center
New York 12833
(7:3/4)
Subs: $5/2 double issues
Sing: $3

GRR
GREEN RIVER REVIEW
Raymond Tyner, Ed.
Box 56 SVSC
University Center, MI 48710
(10:1-3)
Subs: $6/yr

HangL
HANGING LOOSE
Robert Hershon, et al., Eds.
231 Wyckoff St.
Brooklyn, NY 11217
(35-36)
Subs: $15/12
$10/8
$5.50/4
Sing: $1.50

Harp
HARPER'S MAGAZINE
Lewis H. Lapham, Ed.
2 Park Ave.
New York, NY 10016
(258:1544-49) (259:1550-55)
Subs: $11.98/yr
Sing: $1.50

HarvAd
HARVARD ADVOCATE
Sarah V. Chace, Pres.
X. Ted Barber, Po. Ed.

Advocate House
21 South St.
Cambridge, MA 02138
(112:2-4)
(113:1/2)
Subs: $10/yr (inst.)
$7.50/yr (ind.)
Sing: $4

Hills
HILLS
Bob Perelman, Ed.
1220 Folsom
San Francisco, CA 94103
(-)
Sing: $2

HiramPoR
HIRAM POETRY REVIEW
David Fratus
Carol Donley, Eds.
Box 162
Hiram, OH 44234
(26)
Subs: $2/yr
Sing: $1

HolCrit
THE HOLLINS CRITIC
John Rees Moore, Ed.
Hollins College
Virginia 24020
(16:1-5)
Subs: $4/yr

Hudson
THE HUDSON REVIEW
Frederick Morgan
Paula Deitz, Eds.
65 E. 55th St.
New York, NY 10022
(32:1-4)
Subs: $10/yr
Sing: $3

Humanist
HUMANIST
Lloyd L. Morain, Ed.
7 Harwood Dr.
Amherst, NY 14226
(39:1-6)
Subs: $12/yr
Sing: $2

Im
*IMAGES
Gary Pacernick, Ed.
Dept. of English
Wright State U
Dayton, OH 45435
  (5:3) (6:1)
  Subs: $1.50
  Sing: $.50

Iowa
IOWA REVIEW
David Hamilton
Frederick Woodard, Eds.
308 EPB
U of Iowa
Iowa City, IA 52242
  (10:1-3)
  Subs: $8/yr (inst.)
         $7/yr (ind.)
  Sing: $2

JnlONJP
JOURNAL OF NEW JERSEY
  POETS
English Dept.
Fairleigh Dickinson U
285 Madison Ave.
Madison, NJ 07940
  (3:2) (4:1)
  Subs: $3/2
  Sing: $1.50

JnlOPC
JOURNAL OF POPULAR
  CULTURE
Ray B. Browne, Ed.
Popular Culture Center
Bowling Green U
Bowling Green, OH 43403
  (12:4) (13:1)
  Subs: $25/2 yrs
         $15/yr
  Sing: $5

KanQ
KANSAS QUARTERLY
Harold Schneider
Ben Nyberg
W. R. Moses, Eds.
Dept. of English
Kansas State U
Manhattan, KS 66506

  (11:1/2-4)
  Subs: $16/2 yrs
         $9/yr
  Sing: $2.50
  Back: $2.50

Kayak
KAYAK
George Hitchcock, Ed.
Marjorie Simon, Associate Ed.
325 Ocean View Ave.
Santa Cruz, CA 95062
  (50-52)
  Subs: $5/4
  Sing: $1

LitR
THE LITERARY REVIEW
Martin Green
Harry Keyishian, Eds.
Fairleigh Dickinson U
285 Madison Ave.
Madison, NJ 07940
  (22:3-4) (23:1-2)
  Subs: $9/yr
  Sing: $3.50

LittleM
THE LITTLE MAGAZINE
Marilyn Hacker
John Silbersack, Eds.
Box 207
Cathedral Station
New York, NY 10025
  (12:1/2)
  Subs: $7/4
  Sing: $1.50

LittleR
THE LITTLE REVIEW
John McKernan
Arne Weingart
W. G. Webster, Eds.
Box 2015
Marshall U
Huntington, WV 25701
  (-)
  Subs: $2.50
  Sing: $1.25

Madem
MADEMOISELLE
Edith Raymond Locke, Ed.

Mary Elizabeth McNichols,
    Po. Ed.
Conde Nast Building
350 Madison Ave.
New York, NY 10017
Subs: Box 5204
        Boulder, CO 80323
    (85:1-12)
    Subs: $10/yr
    Sing: $1.50

MalR
THE MALAHAT REVIEW
Robin Skelton, Ed.
U of Victoria
Box 1700
Victoria, BC
V8W 2Y2
    (49-52)
    Subs: $25/3 yrs
             $10/yr

MassR
THE MASSACHUSETTS RE-
    VIEW
Lee Edwards, et al., Eds.
Memorial Hall
U of Massachusetts
Amherst, MA 01002
    (20:1-4)
    Subs: $27/3 yrs
             $19/2 yrs
             $10/yr
    Sing: $3

MichQR
MICHIGAN QUARTERLY RE-
    VIEW
Laurence Goldstein, Ed.
3032 Rackham Bldg.
The U of Michigan
Ann Arbor, MI 48109
    (18:1-4)
    Subs: $22/3 yrs
             $16/2 yrs
             $9/yr
    Sing: $2.50
    Back: $2

MidwQ
THE MIDWEST QUARTERLY
V. J. Emmett, Jr., Ed.
Michael Heffernan, Po. Ed.

The Midwest Quarterly
Pittsburg State U
Pittsburg, KS 66762
    (20:2-4) (21:1)
    Subs: $4/yr
    Sing: $1.50

MinnR
THE MINNESOTA REVIEW
Roger Mitchell, Ed.
Box 211
Bloomington, IN 47402
    (NS12-NS13)
    Subs: $12/2 yrs (inst.)
             $9/2 yrs (ind.)
             $7/yr (inst.)
             $5/yr (ind.)
    Sing: $2.50

MissR
*MISSISSIPPI REVIEW
Frederick Barthelme, Ed.
The Center for Writers
Box 5144
Hattiesburg, MS 39401
    (22/23-24)
    Subs: $20/3 yrs
             $14/2 yrs
             $8/yr
    Sing: $3
    Back: Prices on request.

MissouriR
MISSOURI REVIEW
Larry Levis
Marcia Southwick, Eds.
Dept. of English
231 Arts & Science
U of Missouri
Columbia, MO 65211
    (2:2/3) (3:1)
    Subs: $10/2 yrs
             $6/yr
    Sing: $2.25

ModernPS
MODERN POETRY STUDIES
Jerry McGuire
Robert Miklitsch, Eds.
207 Delaware Ave.
Buffalo, NY 14202
    (-)
    Subs: $9/3 (inst.)
             $7.50/3 (ind.)

ModR
MODULARIST REVIEW
R. C. Morse, Ed.
Cultural Council Foundation
Wooden Needle Press
175 5th Ave.
New York, NY 10010
  (-)
  Subs: $3
  Sing: $3

Montra
MONTEMORA
Eliot Weinberger, Ed.
Box 336 Cooper Station
New York, NY 10003
  (5-6)
  Subs: $12/3 (inst.)
            $10/3 (ind.)
  Sing: $4

Mouth
MOUTH OF THE DRAGON
Andrew Bifrost, Ed.
Box 957
New York, NY 10009
  (2:1-3)
  Subs: $36/10 (inst.)
            $15/5 (ind.)
  Sing: $3

Mund
MUNDUS ARTIUM
Rainer Schulte, Ed.
U of Texas at Dallas
Box 688
Richardson, TX 75080
  (11:1)
  Subs: $10/2 (inst.)
            $8/2 (ind.)
  Sing: $4

Nat
THE NATION
Victor Navasky, Ed.
Grace Schulman, Po. Ed.
72 Fifth Ave.
New York, NY 10011
  (228:1-25) (229:1-22)
  Subs: $45/2 yrs
            $25/yr
            $17/yr (stud.)
  Sing: $1

NegroHB
NEGRO HISTORY BULLETIN
Dr. J. Rupert Picott, Ed.
1401 14th St. , N.W.
Washington, DC 20005
  (42:1-3)
  Subs: $8/yr
  Sing: $1. 50
  Bound: $12/yr

NewEngR
NEW ENGLAND REVIEW
Sydney Lea, Ed.
Box 170
Hanover, NH 03755
  (1:3-4) (2:1)
  Subs: $10/yr

NewL
NEW LETTERS
David Ray, Ed.
U of Missouri--Kansas City
5346 Charlotte
Kansas City, MO 64110
  (45:3-4) (46:1-2)
  Subs: $40/5 yrs (lib.)
            $25/5 yrs (ind.)
            $18/2 yrs (lib.)
            $12/2 yrs (ind.)
            $10/yr (lib.)
            $8/yr (ind.)
  Sing: $2. 50
  Back: Prices on request.

NewOR
NEW ORLEANS REVIEW
Dawson Gaillard, Ed.
Box 195
Loyola U
New Orleans, LA 70118
  (6:2-4)
  Subs: $19/3 yrs
            $13/2 yrs
            $7/yr
  Sing: $2. 50

NewRena
THE NEW RENAISSANCE
Louise T. Reynolds, Ed.
Stanwood Bolton, Po. Ed.
9 Heath Rd.
Arlington, MA 02174
  (11)

Subs: $6.50/3
Sing: $3

Subs: $4/yr
Sing: $2

NewRep
THE NEW REPUBLIC
Martin Peretz, Ed./Pub.
Robert Pinsky, Po. Ed.
1220 19th St., N.W.
Washington, DC 20036
  (180:1-26) (181:1/2-26)
  Subs: $28/yr
      $17/yr (stud.)
  Sing: $1

NoAmR
NORTH AMERICAN REVIEW
Robley Wilson, Jr., Ed.
Peter Cooley, Po. Ed.
1222 West 27th St.
Cedar Falls, IA 50613
  (264:1-4)
  Subs: $8/yr
  Sing: $2

NewWR
NEW WORLD REVIEW
Marilyn Bechtel, Ed.
Suite 308
156 Fifth Ave.
New York, NY 10010
  (47:1-6)
  Subs: $5/yr
  Sing: $1

Northeast
NORTHEAST
John Judson, Ed.
Juniper Press
1310 Shorewood Dr.
LaCrosse, WI 54601
  (3:7)
  Subs: $15/yr (w. 6 chap-
      books)
  Sing: $2

NewYorker
THE NEW YORKER
Howard Moss, Po. Ed.
25 W. 43rd St.
New York, NY 10036
  Subs: $46/2 yrs
      $28/yr
  Sing: $1

NorthSR
NORTH STONE REVIEW
James Naiden, Ed.
U Station
Box 14098
Minneapolis, MN 55414
  (-)
  Subs: $7.50/3 (inst.)
      $6.50/3 (ind.)
  Sing: $3

NewYRB
THE NEW YORK REVIEW
  OF BOOKS
Robert B. Silvers
Barbara Epstein, Eds.
250 W. 57th St.
New York, NY 10019
Subs: Subs Service Dept.
    Box 940
    Farmingdale, NY 11737
  (26:1-21/22)
  Subs: $16.50/yr
  Sing: $1

NowestR
NORTHWEST REVIEW
John Witte, Ed.
John Addiego
Jay Williams, Po. Eds.
U of Oregon
Eugene, OR 97403
  (17:3/4) (18:1-2)
  Subs: $16/3 yrs
      $11/2 yrs
      $6/yr
      $5/yr (stud.)
  Sing: $2.50

Nimrod
NIMROD
Francine Ringold, Ed.
U of Tulsa
Tulsa, OK 74104
  (23:1)

Obs
OBSIDIAN
Alvin Aubert, Ed.
Dept. of English

Wayne State U
Detroit, MI 48202
  (4:3)
    Subs: $5.50/yr
    Sing: $2

OhioR
OHIO REVIEW
Wayne Dodd, Ed.
Ellis Hall
Ohio U
Athens, OH 45701
  (20:1-2)
    Subs: $25/3 yrs
           $10/yr
    Sing: $3.50

OP
OPEN PLACES
Eleanor M. Bender, Ed.
Box 2085
Stephens College
Columbia, MO 65215
  (27-28)
    Subs: $7/2 yrs
           $4/yr
    Sing: $2

Os
*OSIRIS
Andrea Moorhead, Ed.
Box 297
Deerfield, MA 01342
  (8-9)
    Subs: $4
    Sing: $2

Paint
PAINTBRUSH
Dr. Ben Bennani
Dept. of English
U of Riyadh
Box 2456
Riyadh, Saudi Arabia
Subs: Jelm Mountain Publi-
            cations
          209 Grand Ave.
          Suite 205
          Laramie, WY 82070
  (11-12)
    Subs: $12/2 yrs
           $7/yr
    Sing: $4
    Rates effective 11/15/81.

Pan
PANACHE
David Lenson, Pub.
Box 77
Sunderland, MA 01375
  (20)
  Note: (23) will be a ten year
      retrospective issue.

ParisR
THE PARIS REVIEW
George A. Plimpton, Ed.
Jonathan Galassi, Po. Ed.
541 E. 72nd St.
New York, NY 10021
Subs: 45-39 171 Place
          Flushing, NY 11358
  (75-76)
    Subs: $100/life
           $20/8
           $11/4
    Sing: $3.25

PartR
PARTISAN REVIEW
William Phillips, Ed.
John Ashbery, Po. Ed.
128 Bay State Rd.
Boston, MA 02215
  (46:1-4)
    Subs: $27/3 yrs
           $19/2 yrs
           $10/yr
    Sing: $2.75

Paunch
PAUNCH
Arthur Efron, Ed.
123 Woodward Ave.
Buffalo, NY 14214
  (-)
    Subs: $7/yr (lib.)
           $4/yr (ind.)
           $3/yr (stud.)
    Sing: Prices on request.

Peb
PEBBLE
Greg Kuzma, Ed.
The Best Cellar Press
118 S. Boswell Ave.
Crete, NE 68333
  (17)
    Subs: $10/4 (lib.)

$8/4 (ind.)
Sing: $4/double issue
         $2

Pequod
PEQUOD
David Paradis, Fiction Ed.
Mark Rudman, Po. Ed.
3478 22nd St.
San Francisco, CA 94110
Po.:   817 West End Ave.
       New York, NY 10025
   (3:1-2)
   Subs: $12/3 yrs
            $9/2 yrs
            $5/yr
   Sing: $3

Pig
PIGIRON
Jim Villani, Ed.
Rose Sayre, Assoc. Ed.
Pig Iron Press
Box 237
Youngstown, OH 44501
   (6)
   Subs: $18/3 yrs
            $13/2 yrs
            $7/yr
   Sing: $4

PikeF
PIKESTAFF FORUM
see PIKESTAFF REVIEW
   (2)

PikeR
THE PIKESTAFF REVIEW
James R. Scrimgeour
Robert D. Sutherland, Eds.
Box 127
Normal, IL 61761
   (1)
   Subs: $5/3
   Sing: $2

Playb
PLAYBOY
Hugh M. Hefner, Ed. /Pub.
919 N. Michigan Ave.
Chicago, IL 60611
   (26:1-12)
   Subs: $48/3 yrs

$18/yr
Sing: Varies.

Ploughs
PLOUGHSHARES
DeWitt Henry
Peter O'Malley
Directors
Box 529
Cambridge, MA 02139
   (5:1-4)
   Subs: $10/4
   Sing: $3. 50

Poem
POEM
Robert L. Welker, Ed.
Box 1247
West Station
Huntsville, AL 35807
   (35-37)
   Subs: $5/yr

PoetC
POET AND CRITIC
David Cummings, Ed.
203 Ross Hall
Iowa State U
Ames, IA 50011
Subs: Iowa State U Press
        South State St.
        Ames, IA 50010
   (10:3) (11:1-3)
   Subs: $7/2 yrs
            $4/yr
   Sing: $2

Poetry
POETRY
John Frederick Nims, Ed.
601 S. Morgan St.
Box 4348
Chicago, IL 60680
   (133:4-6) (134:1-6) (135:1-3)
   Subs: $18/yr
   Sing: $2
   Back: $2. 25

PoetryNW
POETRY NORTHWEST
David Wagoner, Ed.
4045 Brooklyn Ave., N. E.
U of Washington

Seattle, WA 98105
(20:1-4)
  Subs: $5/yr
  Sing: $1.50

PoNow
POETRY NOW
E. V. Griffith, Ed./Pub.
3118 K St.
Eureka, CA 95501
(21-25)
  Subs: $19/18
            $13/12
            $7.50/6
  Sing: $1.50
  Back: Bicentennial
  Issue, 200 pp., $5.

PortR
PORTLAND REVIEW
Mark Jones, Ed.
Portland State U
Box 751
Portland, OR 97207
(25)
  Missing (24).
  Sing: $3.95

Poultry
*POULTRY A MAGAZINE OF
  VOICE
Brendan Galvin
George Garrett, Eds.
Box 727
Truro, MA 02666
(1)
  Subs: $2
  Sing: $1

PraS
PRAIRIE SCHOONER
Bernice Slote, Ed.
201 Andrews Hall
U of Nebraska
Lincoln, NE 68588
(53:1-4)
  Subs: $24/3 yrs (ind.)
            $16/2 yrs (ind.)
            $12/yr (lib.)
            $9/yr (ind.)
  Sing: $2.50

QRL
QUARTERLY REVIEW OF

LITERATURE
T. & R. Weiss
26 Haslet Avenue
Princeton, NJ 08540
(21:1/2)
  Subs: $20/2 (cloth)
            $10/2 (paper)
  Sing: $13 (cloth)
            $5.95 (paper)

QW
QUARTERLY WEST
Bruce Weigl, Ed.
Sandra Andrews, Managing Ed.
312 Olpin Union
U of Utah
Salt Lake City, UT 84112
(6-9)
  Subs: $5/yr
  Sing: $2

RusLT
RUSSIAN LITERATURE TRI-
  QUARTERLY
Carl R. Proffer
Ellendea Proffer, Eds.
Ardis Publishers
2901 Heatherway
Ann Arbor, MI 48104
(-)
  Subs: $25/3 (inst.)
            $16.95/3 (ind.)
            $13.95/3 (stud.)
  Back: Prices on request.
  Cloth: Add $10 to each rate.

St. AR
ST. ANDREWS REVIEW
Ronald H. Bayes, Founding Ed.
William Loftus, Exec. Ed.
St. Andrews Presbyterian Col-
  lege
Laurinburg, NC 28352
(5:2-3)
  Subs: $12/2 yrs
            $6/yr
  Sing: $3
Note: (5:2) was unavailable and
was indexed from a photocopy
of the contents page.

Salm
SALMAGUNDI
Robert Boyers, Ed.

Peggy Boyers, Exec. Ed.
Skidmore College
Saratoga Springs, NY 12866
(43-46)
   Subs: $20/2 yrs (inst.)
           $10/2 yrs (ind.)
           $12/yr (inst.)
           $6/yr (ind.)
   Sing: $3

Sam
SAMISDAT
Merritt Clifton
Robin Michelle Clifton, Eds.
Box 231
Richford, VT 05476
(71-80)
   Subs: 3¢ per printed p.
           $15/500 pp.

SeC
SECOND COMING
A. D. Winans, Ed.
Second Coming Press
Box 31249
San Francisco, CA 94131
(6:1-2) (7:1-2) (8:1)
   Subs: $6.50/yr (lib.)
           $4/yr (ind.)

SenR
SENECA REVIEW
James Crenner
Bob Herz, Eds.
Hobart & William Smith Col-
   leges
Geneva, NY 14456
(10:1)
   Subs: $5/yr
   Sing: $3

SewanR
SEWANEE REVIEW
George Core, Ed.
U of the South
Sewanee, TN 37375
(87:1-4)
   Subs: $26/3 yrs (inst.)
           $22/3 yrs (ind.)
           $19/2 yrs (inst.)
           $16/2 yrs (ind.)
           $11/yr (inst.)
           $9/yr (ind.)

Sing: $2.75
Back: $4

Shen
SHENANDOAH
James Boatwright, Ed.
Richard Howard, Po. Ed.
Box 722
Washington and Lee U
Lexington, VA 24450
(30:1-4)
   Subs: $8/2 yrs
           $5/yr
   Sing: $1.50
   Back: $2.50

Sky
SKYWRITING
Martin Grossman, Ed.
511 Campbell Ave.
Kalamazoo, MI 49007
(9)
   Sing: $2.50

SlowLR
SLOW LORIS READER
Patricia Petrosky, Ed.
923 Highview St.
Pittsburgh, PA 15206
(3)
   Subs: $10/4
           $5.50/2
   Sing: $3

SmF
SMALL FARM
Jeff Daniel Marion, Ed.
Route 5 Cline Road
Box 345
Dandridge, TN 37725
(7/8-9/10)
   Subs: $6 (lib.)
           $5 (ind.)
   Sing: $5/double issue

SmPd
SMALL POND
Napoleon St. Cyr, Ed./Pub.
10 Overland Dr.
Stratford, CT 06497
(45-47)
   Subs: $3.75/yr
   Sing: $1.50

SoCaR
SOUTH CAROLINA REVIEW
Robert J. Calhoun
Robert W. Hill, Eds.
Dept. of English
Clemson U
Clemson, SC 29631
    (11:2) (12:1)
    Subs: $5/2 yrs
             $3/yr
    Sing: $2

SoDakR
SOUTH DAKOTA REVIEW
John R. Milton, Ed.
Box 111
U Exchange
Vermillion, SD 57069
    (17:1-4)
    Subs: $10/2 yrs
             $6/yr
    Sing: $1.50

Some
SOME
Alan Ziegler, et al., Eds.
309 W. 104th St.
Apt. 9D
New York, NY 10025
    (-)
    Subs: $9/yr (inst.)
             $5/yr (ind.)
    Sing: $2.50

SouthernHR
SOUTHERN HUMANITIES RE-
  VIEW
Barbara A. Mowat
David K. Jeffrey, Eds.
9088 Haley Center
Auburn U
Auburn, AL 36830
    (13-1-4)
    Subs: $6/yr
    Sing: $2

SouthernPR
SOUTHERN POETRY REVIEW
Robert Grey, Ed.
English Dept.
The U of North Carolina
Charlotte, NC 28223
    (19:1-2)

    Subs: $4/yr
    Sing: $2

SouthernR
SOUTHERN REVIEW
Donald E. Stanford
Lewis P. Simpson, Eds.
Drawer D
U Station
Baton Rouge, LA 70893
    (15:1-4)
    Subs: $13/3 yrs
             $9/2 yrs
             $5/yr
    Sing: $1.50

SouthwR
SOUTHWEST REVIEW
Margaret L. Hartley, Ed.
Southern Methodist U Press
Southern Methodist U
Dallas, TX 75275
    (64:1-4)
    Subs: $12/3 yrs
             $9/2 yrs
             $5/yr
    Sing: $1.50

Sparrow
SPARROW
Felix and Selma Stefanile, Eds.
Sparrow Press
103 Waldron St.
West Lafayette, IN 47906
    (38-39)
    Subs: $6/3
    Sing: $2

Spirit
THE SPIRIT THAT MOVES US
Morty Sklar, Ed.
Box 1585
Iowa City, IA 52240
    (3:1/2-3) (4:1-2/3)
    Subs: $12/2 yrs (lib.)
             $9/2 yrs (ind.)
             $6.50/yr (lib.)
             $5/yr (ind.)
    Sing: $1.75

Stand
STAND
Jon Silkin, Ed.

Jim Kates, American Ed.
16 Forest St.
Norwell, MA 02061
Subs: 19 Haldane Terr.
    Newcastle-upon-Tyne
    England
    NE2 3AN
  (20:1-4)
  Subs: $11.75/2 yrs
          $6/yr
  Sing: $2

StoneC
STONE COUNTRY
Judith Neeld, Ed.
20 Lorraine Rd.
Madison, NJ 07940
  (6:1-3)
  Subs: $4/3
  Sing: $1.75
  Back: $1.50

SunM
SUN & MOON
Douglas Messerli, Literary
  Ed.
4330 Hartwick Road, #418
College Park, MD 20740
  (8)
  Subs: $15/4 (inst.)
          $10/4 (ind.)
  Sing: $4.50

Tele
TELEPHONE
Maureen Owen, Ed.
Box 672
Old Chelsea Station
New York, NY 10011
  (15)
  Subs: $5/2

Tendril
TENDRIL
George E. Murphy, Jr., et
  al., Eds.
Box 512
Green Harbor, MA 02041
  (4-6)
  Subs: $5/yr
  Sing: $2

TexQ
TEXAS QUARTERLY

Miguel González-Gerth, Ed.
U of Texas
Austin, TX 78712
  (21:2-4)
  Final issue.
  Sing: $4

13thM
13th MOON
Ellen Marie Bissert, Ed.
Drawer F
Inwood Station
New York, NY 10034
  (4:2)
  Subs: $12/3 (inst.)
          $6/3 (ind.)
  Sing: $2.25

Thought
THOUGHT
G. Richard Dimler, S.J., Ed.
Fordham U Press
Bronx, NY 10458
  (54:212-215)
  Subs: $12/yr
  Sing: $4

ThRiPo
THREE RIVERS POETRY
  JOURNAL
Gerald Costanzo, Ed.
Box 21
Carnegie-Mellon U
Pittsburgh, PA 15213
  (13/14)
  Subs: $5/4
  Sing: $1.50

TriQ
TRIQUARTERLY
Elliott Anderson
Robert Onopa, Eds.
1735 Benson Ave.
Northwestern U
Evanston, IL 60201
  (44-46)
  Subs: $30/3 yrs
          $20/2 yrs
          $12/yr
  Sing: $5.95
  Back: Prices on request.

Ur
*URTHKIN

Larry Ziman, Ed./Pub.
Box 67485
Los Angeles, CA 90067
(2)
Sing: $3.95

US1
U.S. 1 WORKSHEETS
U.S. 1 Poets' Cooperative
21 Lake Drive
Roosevelt, NJ 08555
(-)
Subs: $4/8
Sing: $.50
Back: Prices on request.

UTR
UT REVIEW
Duane Locke, Ed.
U of Tampa
Tampa, FL 33606
(6:1-3/4)
Subs: $9/4
Sing: $2.50

Vaga
VAGABOND
John Bennett, Ed.
Betti Dempsey, Asst. Ed.
1610 N. Water
Ellensburg, WA 98926
(29-30)
Subs: $6
Sing: $2

VirQR
VIRGINIA QUARTERLY REVIEW
Staige D. Blackford, Ed.
Gregory Orr, Po. Ed.
One West Range
Charlottesville, VA 22903
(55:1-4)
Subs: $15/3 yrs
         $12/2 yrs
         $7/yr
Sing: $2

WebR
WEBSTER REVIEW
Nancy Schapiro, Ed.
Jerred Metz
Pamela Hadas, Po. Eds.
Webster College

Webster Groves, MO 63119
(4:3-4)
Subs: $5/yr
Sing: $1.25

WestB
*WEST BRANCH
Karl Patten
Robert Taylor, Eds.
Dept. of English
Bucknell U
Lewisburg, PA 17837
(4-5)
Subs: $8/2 yrs
         $5/yr
Sing: $2.50

WestHR
WESTERN HUMANITIES RE-
VIEW
Jack Garlington
Franklin Fisher, Eds.
U of Utah
Salt Lake City, UT 84112
(33:1-4)
Subs: $10/yr (inst.)
         $6/yr (ind.)
Sing: $2

Wind
WIND
Quentin R. Howard, Ed.
Route 1
Box 809 K
Pikeville, KY 41501
(32-35)
Subs: $6/4 (inst.)
         $5/4 (ind.)
Sing: $1.25

WindO
THE WINDLESS ORCHARD
Robert Novak, Ed.
English Dept.
Indiana-Purdue U
Fort Wayne, IN 46805
(34-35)
Subs: $20/3 yrs
         $7/yr
         $4/yr (stud.)
Sing: $2

WorldO
WORLD ORDER

Firuz Kazemzadeh, Ed.
415 Linden Ave.
Wilmette, IL 60091
  (13:1-4)
  Subs: $11/2 yrs
           $6/yr
  Sing: $1. 60

WormR
WORMWOOD REVIEW
Marvin Malone, Ed.
Ernest Stranger, Art Ed.
Wormwood Review Press
Box 8840
Stockton, CA 95204
  (73-76)
  Subs: $12/4 (Patron)
           $6/4 (inst.)
           $4. 50/4 (ind.)

YaleR
THE YALE REVIEW
Kai T. Erikson, Ed.
1902A Yale Station
New Haven, CT 06520
  (68:3-4) (69:1-2)
  Subs: $12/yr (inst.)
           $10/yr (ind.)
  Sing: $3
  Back: Prices on request.

YellowBR
YELLOW BRICK ROAD
Robert Matte, Jr.
Paul H. Cook, Eds.
Emerald City Press
Box 40814
Tucson, AZ 85717
  (-)
  Subs: $5. 50/3 (inst.)
           $4/3 (ind.)
  Sing: $1. 50

Zahir
ZAHIR
Diane Kruchkow, Ed.
Box 715
Newburyport, MA 01950
  (10)
  Subs: $6/2 (inst.)
           $4/2 (ind.)
  Sing: $2. 50

THE INDEX

AAL, Katharyn Machan
"Four Minutes Before Midnight. " GreenfieldR (7:3/4) Spr-Sum
79, p. 212.
"The Making of Bread. " PoNow (25) 79, p. 46.
"Myra with the Crimson Mouth. " Paint (11) Spr 79, p. 6.
"Roger. " PoNow (25) 79, p. 1.
"Sundaze. " PoNow (25) 79, p. 1.
"To a Lover." Paint (11) Spr 79, p. 5.
"What it Means to Love You. " Paint (12) Aut 79, p. 18.

AARON, Howard
"Montana Song. " PortR (25) 79, p. 82.
"Unemployment. " PortR (25) 79, p. 83.

ABBE, Cate
"Beside the Ocean. " DenQ (14:2) Sum 79, p. 81.

ABBOTT, Carolyn
"Dressing Poetry. " PoetryNW (20:4) Wint 79-80, pp. 21-22.

ABBOTT, Lee K. , Jr.
"The Cowboys of New Mexico Respond to a Question of Usage. "
PoNow (25) 79, p. 1.
"Love Is Not the Goal of Rhyme. " Bits (9) Ja 79.
"Sweetheart of the Rodeo at the Polling Booth. " KanQ (11:3)
Sum 79, p. 42.

ABBOTT, Nell
"In the Antique Barn. " Poem (36) Jl 79, p. 47.
"The Mothers. " Poem (36) Jl 79, p. 46.
"Postcard to a Husband from a Breakfast Stop. " Poem (36) Jl
79, p. 48.

ABBOTT, Steve
"The Gift of Maldoror. " Mouth (2:1) F 79, p. 25.
"Lines for Panch Aquila, Reza Baraheni and Grennady Trifonov. "
SeC (7:1) 79, p. 35.

ABISSI, Colette E.
"Dead Line. " Paint (11) Spr 79, p. 7.

ABRAMS, Doug
"Climbing. " KanQ (11:1/2) Wint-Spr 79, p. 82.
"Dove Hunt. " Spirit (3:1/2) Aut-Wint 77-78, p. 49.

ABREU, José Vincente
"But All... ". LitR (23:2) Wint 80, p. 176.
"Violence! " LitR (23:2) Wint 80, p. 176.

ABSE, Dannie
"The Doctor. " AmerPoR (8:3) My-Je 79, p. 16.
"Doll Disaster. " AmerPoR (8:3) My-Je 79, p. 16.
"The House Ghost. " AmerPoR (8:3) My-Je 79, p. 16.
"Last Words. " Poetry (133:5) F 79, p. 261.
"Pantomime Diseases. " Poetry (133:5) F 79, p. 264.
"The Power of Prayer. " Poetry (133:5) F 79, p. 263.
"X Ray. " Poetry (133:5) F 79, p. 262.

ABSHER, Tom
"August. " Ploughs (5:1) 79, p. 11.
"Hunting with My Father. " Ploughs (5:1) 79, p. 12.
"Vespers. " Ploughs (5:1) 79, p. 13.

ACKER, Paul
"Near Sestina of Satie and the Sea Cucumber. " Chelsea (38) 79,
    p. 174.

ACKERMAN, Diane
"Freeing the Evergreens. " MichQR (18:4) Aut 79, p. 634.
"Language Lab. " MichQR (18:4) Aut 79, p. 636.
"Ode to the Alien. " MichQR (18:2) Spr 79, p. 218.
"Savonarola. " CarolQ (31:2) Spr-Sum 79, p. 110.

ACKERSON, Duane
"The Big Dinner. " PoNow (22) 79, p. 1.
"Commercial Message. " PoNow (22) 79, p. 1.
"Copyrighting. " PoNow (22) 79, p. 1.
"Dog Days. " PoNow (22) 79, p. 1.
"The Fire Man Leaves. " PoNow (22) 79, p. 1.
"Instant Animal. " PoNow (22) 79, p. 1.
"The Medium. " PoNow (22) 79, p. 1.
"Octopus. " Chelsea (38) 79, p. 171.

ACOSTA, Oscar
"Let Him Not Rest. " LitR (23:2) Wint 80, p. 272.

ACUÑA, René
"Narciso. " GRR (10:2) 79, p. 186.

ADAIR, Linda
"Such Good Friends. " JnlONJP (4:1) 79, p. 20.

ADAMO, Ralph
"Homecoming. " PoNow (25) 79, p. 19.
"How I Got the Girl. " PoNow (25) 79, p. 19.

ADAMS, Betsy
"Choices. " Focus (13:81) My-Je 79, p. 30.
"Ningyo Lady, a Diary. " EnPas (9) 79, p. 36.
"Terminal: 1. and 2. " Im (6:1) 79, p. 3.

ADAMS, Craig
"Bull Run from Quinn, S. D. " GreenfieldR (7:3/4) Spr-Sum 79,
    p. 162.

ADAMS, David
"Direction. " CentR (23:3) Sum 79, p. 294.
"a harbor in three weathers. " St. AR (5:3) Aut-Wint, 79, p. 116.

ADAMS, Michael S.
"Another Day. " NegroHB (42:3) Jl-Ag-S 79, p. 79.

ADCOCK, Betty
"Nothing Happened. " GeoR (33:4) Wint 79, p. 786.

ADDIEGO, John
"Anthem. " PoNow (23) 79, p. 47.
"Twenty-Seven. " CutB (12) Spr-Sum 79, p. 74.

ADLER, Hans
"Protect Me. " ChrC (96:24) 18-25 Jl 79, p. 733.
"Ulster. " ChrC (96:29) 19 S 79, p. 876.

ADY, Endre
"The Poet of the Puszta" (tr. by Bruce Berlind). PoNow (24)
    79, p. 1.

AESCHYLUS
"Aeschylus, Son of Euphorion" (tr. by I. F. Stone). NewYRB
    (26:2) 22 F 79, p. 10.

AGUDELO, Dario Jaramillo
"Love Story" (tr. by Julie Mishkin). Pequod (3:2) 79, p. 87.
"Story" (tr. by Julie Mishkin). Pequod (3:2) 79, p. 88.
"Story of My Brother" (tr. by Julie Mishkin). Pequod (3:2) 79,
    p. 89.

AHARONI, Ada
"Volcanic African Pomona. " Im (5:3) 79, p. 9.

AHERN, Maureen
"Consciousness" (tr. of Rosario Castellanos). 13thM (4:2) 79,
    p. 15.
"Home Economics" (tr. of Rosario Castellanos). 13thM (4:2) 79,
    p. 12.
"Routine" (tr. of Rosario Castellanos). NewL (46:1) Aut 79, p.
    79.
"Silence Near an Ancient Stone" (tr. of Rosario Castellanos).
    13thM (4:2) 79, p. 10.

AI
"Killing Floor. " ParisR (75) Spr 79, pp. 281-282. Corrected
reprint.

AICHINGER, Ilse
"Winter Beginning" (tr. by Cynthia Hogue). AmerPoR (8:4) Jl-
Ag 79, p. 46.

AJAY, Stephen
"The Giraffe. " Chelsea (38) 79, p. 221.
"Knowing Where to Look. " Chelsea (38) 79, p. 195.

AKESSON, Sonja
"A Letter" (tr. by John Matthias). GreenfieldR (7:3/4) Spr-Sum
79, p. 130.

AKHMATOVA, Anna
"Do Not Speak... " (tr. by Irina Zheleznova). PoNow (24) 79,
p. 1.
"I Possess" (tr. by Leonard Opalov). Spirit (3:1/2) Aut-Wint
77-78, p. 9.
"I" (tr. by Marianne Andrea). NewOR (6:2) 79, p. 139.
"II" (tr. by Marianne Andrea). NewOR (6:2) 79, p. 139.

AKIGAWA, Ken
"Zen Men. " Poultry (1) 79, p. 2.

AKMAKJIAN, Alan P.
"A Part of the Past. " Wind (35) 79, p. 34.
"The Passing Image. " Wind (35) 79, p. 33.

ALBERT, Frank J.
"Bus Driver. " Wind (34) 79, p. 36.

ALBERT, Steve
"City Lights: I Took That Picture. " Ploughs (5:2) 79, pp. 127-
128.
"I Always Thought. " Ploughs (5:2) 79, pp. 124-126.

ALBERTI, Rafael
"The Bridge of Breasts" (tr. by Brian Swann). PoNow (24) 79,
p. 1.
"Nocturne" (tr. by Brian Swann). PoNow (24) 79, p. 1.
"Song of the Unlucky Angel" (tr. by Martin Paul). QW (8) Wint
79, p. 92.
"The Wood Is Vast and Lonely... " (tr. by Martin Paul). QW
(8) Wint 79, p. 92.

ALCARO, Marion Walker
"Central Casting. " JnlONJP (3:2) 79, p. 9.

ALCOSSER, Sandra
"The Photographer. " PortR (25) 79, p. 130.
"Salamander. " PortR (25) 79, p. 130.

ALDAN, Daisy
"In a Mljet Monastery. " Mouth (2:1) F 79, p. 33.
"Meeting. " 13thM (4:2) 79, p. 71.

ALDERDICE, Eve
"The Captive. " Wind (33) 79, p. 1.
"The Jellyfish. " Wind (33) 79, p. 1.

ALDRICH, Marcia
"Night Song. " Chelsea (38) 79, p. 195.

ALDRIDGE, Richard
"Rhododendrons. " PoNow (23) 79, p. 18.
"Upon a Marriage. " PoNow (23) 79, p. 18.
"Words and the Man. " PoNow (23) 79, p. 18.

ALEGRIA, Claribel
"Cambric Tamales" (for Eduardo and Helena) (tr. by Darwin
    Flakoll). VirQR (55:2) Spr 79, p. 306.
"Disillusionment" (tr. by Darwin Flakoll). VirQR (55:2) Spr 79,
    p. 306.
"We Were Three--" (for Paco and Rololfo) (tr. by Carolyn
    Forché). VirQR (55:2) Spr 79, p. 304.

ALEIXANDRE, Vicente
"Close to Death" (tr. by Lewis Hyde and David Unger). PoNow
    (24) 79, p. 29.
"Goodbye to the Fields" (tr. by Sarah B. Arsone). Aspen (7)
    Spr 79, p. 92.
"Guitar or Moon" (tr. by Lewis Hyde and David Unger). PoNow
    (24) 79, p. 29.
Seventeen Poems (tr. by Miguel González-Gerth). TexQ (21:4)
    Wint 78, pp. 183-204.
"Song to a Dead Girl" (tr. by Sarah B. Arsone). Aspen (7) Spr
    79, p. 94.
"Surrendered Hand" (tr. by Joseph V. Ricapito). PoNow (24)
    79, p. 2.
"Unity in Her" (tr. by Sarah B. Arsone). Aspen (7) Spr 79, p.
    93.

ALEXANDER, Meena
"Rootedness. " MalR (52) O 79, p. 41.

ALEXANDER, Morgan
"vanilla custard. " Ur (2) 79, p. 1.

ALEXANDER, Paul
"Beginning. " PoNow (25) 79, p. 1.
"Madame Renoir Feeding Her Son. " HiramPoR (26) Spr-Sum 79,
    p. 14.

ALEXANDER, William
"Swansea" (tr. of Roberto Sanesi). PoNow (24) 79, p. 51.
"Toward Winter" (tr. of Roberto Sanesi). PoNow (24) 79, p. 51.

ALFRED, William
"In Memory of My Friend Robert Lowell. " HarvAd (113:1/2)
N 79, p. 40.

ALI, Agha Shahid
"The Butcher. " GreenfieldR (7:3/4) Spr-Sum 79, p. 170.
"The Poet as Refugee. " GreenfieldR (7:3/4) Spr-Sum 79, p.
169.
"Vacating an Apartment. " Ascent (5:1) 79, p. 22.

ALIFERIS, Eudoxia
"A Nietzschian Priest. " Mund (11:1) 79, p. 128.
"Soft Cry. " Mund (11:1) 79, p. 128.

ALLEGRA, Donna
"Before I Dress and Soar Again. " Cond (5) 79, p. 100.
"Up in the Sky. " Cond (5) 79, p. 101.

ALLEN, Dan Dulaney
"Decision. " Mouth (2:1) F 79, p. 42.

ALLEN, Deborah
"Embroidery. " 13thM (4:2) 79, p. 93.

ALLEN, Dick
"Green Pastures. " Poetry (134:3) Je 79, p. 130.
"Small Hotel. " Poetry (134:3) Je 79, pp. 125-126.
"Sunshower. " Poetry (134:3) Je 79, p. 129.
"The Persistence. " Poetry (134:3) Je 79, pp. 127-128.

ALLEN, Gilbert
"At the Factory. " Wind (33) 79, p. 2.
"Extended Forecast. " StoneC (6:1) F 79, p. 16.

ALLEN, John
"Thoughts. " Os (8) 79, p. 24.

ALLEN, Judith
"Aurora Borealis: Hangman Hills. " Tendril (5) Sum 79, p. 11.
"Eastern Washington: August 1978. " Tendril (5) Sum 79, p. 10.

ALLEN, Lee E.
"The Traveller. " Wind (32) 79, p. 13.

ALLGOOD, Steve
"for laura. " St. AR (5:3) Aut-Wint 79, p. 40.

ALLGREN, Joe
"Coming of Age. " Pig (6) 79, p. 75.

ALLMAN, John
"Crazy Horse in 'A Little Flat Place at the Edge of a Few
Trees'--1874. " Chowder (13) Aut-Wint 79, p. 46.

"Dostoevsky at Semyonov Square. " AmerPoR (8:1) Ja-F 79, p.
31.
"Ezra Pound in the Cage, Near Pisa. " PoetryNW (20:2) Sum
79, pp. 4-5.
"Glen Island. " Atl (244:1) Jl 79, p. 59.
"J. Robert Oppenheimer at Alamogordo. " PoetryNW (20:2) Sum
79, pp. 6-7.
"Kaethe Kollwitz Installs Her Statues at Roggevelde Cemetery
1932. " MassR (20:1) Spr 79, p. 73.
"Mao Tse-Tung at Pao An, After the Long March. " PoetryNW
(20:2) Sum 79, pp. 3-4.
"The Scattering. " PoetryNW (20:4) Wint 79-80, pp. 25-26.

ALOFF, Mindy
"Amaryllis. " PortR (25) 79, p. 163.

ALTIZER, Nell
"First Blood. " PraS (53:3) Aut 79, p. 244.
"Haworth Parsonage, 31 March 1855. " PraS (53:3) Aut 79, p.
240.

ALTMAN, Irwin
"Creative Writing Class Combined Class Project Poem. " SeC
(6:1) 78, p. 72.

ALVAREZ, Lynne
"He said all women were whores. " NewL (46:2) Wint 79-80, p.
26.
"La Napa in Church. " NewL (46:2) Wint 79-80, p. 27.
"The Marica. " NewL (46:2) Wint 79-80, p. 26.
"Pipo Gets Well. " NewL (46:2) Wint 79-80, p. 28.

ALWAN, Ameen
"Candle" (tr. of Jaime Sabines). VirQR (55:2) Spr 79, p. 307.
"No quiero decir nada" (tr. of Jaime Sabines). VirQR (55:2)
Spr 79, p. 308.
"Poemas de unas horas misticas" (tr. of Jaime Sabines).
VirQR (55:2) Spr 79, p. 310.
"Si uno pudiera encontrar" (tr. of Jaime Sabines). VirQR (55:2)
Spr 79, p. 309.

AMATO, Michael
"Enough Rope. " Wind (33) 79, p. 4.

AMICHAI, Yehuda
"The Clouds are the First Fatalities" (tr. by Bernhard Frank).
PoNow (24) 79, pp. 2-3.
"The diameter of the bomb was thirty centimeters" (tr. by
Bernhard Frank). PoNow (24) 79, p. 3.
"Lament" (tr. by Shlomo Vinner and Howard Schwartz).
AmerPoR (8:3) My-Je 79, p. 43.
"Letter of Recommendation" (tr. by Yehuda Amichai and Ted
Hughes). PoNow (24) 79, p. 29.

"Since Then" (tr. by Shlomo Vinner and Howard Schwartz).
AmerPoR (8:3) My-Je 79, p. 43.
"Song" (tr. by Yehuda Amichai and Ted Hughes). PoNow (24)
79, p. 29.
"Take Me to the Airport" (tr. by Yehuda Amichai and Ted
Hughes). PoNow (24) 79, p. 29.

AMIR, Aharon
"Cock" (tr. by Bernhard Frank). PoNow (24) 79, p. 3.
"Exodus from the Garden of Delights" (tr. by Bernhard Frank).
PoNow (24) 79, p. 3.

AMIS, Barry D.
"The Rapprochement of the Rainbow. " Obs (4:3) Wint 78, pp.
71-73.

AMMONS, A. R.
"Dry Spell Spiel. " AmerPoR (8:3) My-Je 79, p. 3.
"Easter Morning. " Poetry (134:1) Ap 79, pp. 1-4.
"Enameling. " CornellR (7) Aut 79, p. 74.
"Epistemology. " Epoch (28:2) Wint 79, p. 139.
"Focus. " AmerPoR (8:3) My-Je 79, p. 3.
"Givings. " AmerPoR (8:3) My-Je 79, p. 3.
"The Great American Poem. " Antaeus (32) Wint 79, pp. 82-86.
"An Improvisation for Jerald Bullis. " AmerPoR (8:2) Mr-Ap 79,
p. 48.
"An Improvisation for the Stately Dwelling. " AmerPoR (8:2)
Mr-Ap 79, p. 48.
"In Memoriam Mae Norblitt. " AmerPoR (8:3) My-Je 79, p. 4.
"Keepsake. " AmerPoR (8:3) My-Je 79, p. 3.
"Walking Around in the Evening. " CornellR (7) Aut 79, p. 74.
"Winter Sanctuaries. " AmerPoR (8:3) My-Je 79, p. 3.

AMOROSI, Ray
"Festivals. " NewL (46:1) Aut 79, p. 43.
"Good Hope. " NewL (46:1) Aut 79, p. 43.

AMSEL, Nori
"The Big Bad Wolf. " GreenfieldR (7:3/4) Spr-Sum 79, p. 205.
"Hansel and Gretel. " GreenfieldR (7:3/4) Spr-Sum 79, p. 204.

ANAGNOSTAKIS, Manólis
"The Shipwreck" (tr. by Kimon Friar). AmerPoR (8:1) Ja-F 79,
p. 37.

ANCHEVSKI, Zoran
"Drought" (tr. of Radovan Pavlovski w. Bryce Conrad). CharR
(5:2) Aut 79, p. 8.
"Landscape from the War" (tr. of Radovan Pavlovski w. Bryce
Conrad). CharR (5:2) Aut 79, p. 7.
"Road to the Mountain" (tr. of Radovan Pavlovski w. Bryce Con-
rad). CharR (5:2) Aut 79, p. 6.
"Skin" (tr. of Radovan Pavlovski w. Bryce Conrad). CharR

(5:2) Aut 79, p. 7.
"Sowers" (tr. of Radovan Pavlovski w. Bryce Conrad). CharR
(5:2) Aut 79, p. 5.
"Watchtower" (tr. of Radovan Pavlovski w. Bryce Conrad).
CharR (5:2) Aut 79, p. 5.

ANDERS, Shirley
"crazy lady poem III. " Wind (34) 79, p. 63.

ANDERSDATTER, Karla Margaret
"Old Poet. " SeC (6:1) 78, p. 62.
"Shoshone Father. " SeC (6:1) 78, p. 71.

ANDERSON, Benny
"Just to Be Sure" (tr. by Alexander Taylor). PoNow (24) 79,
   p. 30.
"The Pampered Mermaid" (tr. by Alexander Taylor). PoNow
   (24) 79, p. 30.
"Photographs" (tr. by Alexander Taylor). PoNow (24) 79, p. 30.

ANDERSON, David Earle
"With the Nuns at Cape May Point" (for Kristin). ChrC (96:36)
   7 N 79, p. 1076.

ANDERSON, Douglas
"Hymn to Orpheus. " DenQ (14:2) Sum 79, p. 48.
"Sarabande: Johann Sebastian Bach. " DenQ (14:2) Sum 79, p.
   50.

ANDERSON, Duane
"Another Drink to Go. " PoNow (25) 79, p. 2.

ANDERSON, Gerald
"Midnight. " WindO (35) Aut-Wint 79-80.
"pedaling alone. " WindO (35) Aut-Wint 79-80.

ANDERSON, Jack
"A Calm. " PoNow (22) 79, pp. 3-4.
"Can You Believe It?" PoNow (22) 79, p. 3.
"Commanding a Telephone to Ring. " CharR (5:2) Aut 79, p. 57.
"Departure Gate. " HangL (35) Spr 79, p. 10.
"Faith. " PoNow (23) 79, p. 19.
"From the Memoirs of My Career as a Mountebank in South
   America. " PoNow (22) 79, p. 2.
"Hatred as a Kind of Art. " PoNow (23) 79, p. 9.
"In Distrust of Poetry. " HangL (35) Spr 79, p. 14.
"The Philosophical Background. " HangL (35) Spr 79, p. 12.
"Responsibilities of a Householder. " PoNow (22) 79, pp. 2-3.
"Transcendence of the Pencil. " Mouth (2:3) N 79, p. 5.
"True-or-False Quiz. " PoNow (23) 79, p. 19.
"The Watersheds. " NewL (46:1) Aut 79, p. 10.

ANDERSON, James
"One Night. " Aspen (7) Spr 79, p. 41.

ANDERSON, Jon
  "The Great American Poem. " Antaeus (32) Wint 79, pp. 82-86.
  "The Milky Way. " Field (20) Spr 79, p. 44.

ANDERSON, Ken
  "The Call. " Mouth (2:1) F 79, p. 46.
  "The Dark Field. " Mouth (2:1) F 79, p. 27.
  "Vince. " Mouth (2:2) Je 79, p. 14.

ANDERSON, Kurt
  "Misery Is Pain. " EngJ (68:5) My 79, p. 39.

ANDERSON, Wendy
  "Holiday. " BalPoJ (29:3) Spr 79, p. 23.

ANDRADE, Jorge Carrera
  "Final Invocation to the Word. " LitR (23:2) Wint 80, p. 197.

ANDRE, Michael
  "At Home with John and Gillian Dobbin. " Tele (15) Spr 79, p.
    63.
  "Crumbs for Lytton Strachey. " PoNow (21) 79, p. 34.
  "Parrot. " GreenfieldR (7:3/4) Spr-Sum 79, p. 248.
  "The Seamy Underside of Underwear. " PoNow (21) 79, p. 34.
  "Trials of Eustace. " PoNow (21) 79, p. 34.

ANDREA, Marianne
  "An Autumn Day. " Focus (13:82) Ag 79, p. 31.
  "I" (tr. of Anna Akhmatova). NewOR (6:2) 79, p. 139.
  "II" (tr. of Anna Akhmatova). NewOR (6:2) 79, p. 139.
  "When the Sky Night Enters You. " Confr (18) Spr-Sum 79, p.
    42.

ANDRESEN, Sophia de Mello Breyner
  "Manha de outono num palacio de sintra. " Mund (11:1) 79, p.
    108.
  "Retrato de uma princesa desconhecida. " Mund (11:1) 79, p.
    106.

ANDREWS, Michael
  "And Before That. " Ur (2) 79, p. 2.

ANDREWS, Michael C.
  "The Life of the Sea. " PikeF (2) Wint 78-79, p. 32.

ANGELL, Roger
  "Greetings, Friends!' " NewYorker (55:45) 24 D 79, p. 37.

ANGELOTTI, Mike
  "Night Class. " EngJ (68:5) My 79, p. 30.

ANGOFF, Charles
  "God Is Here Again. " LitR (23:1) Aut 79, p. 4.

ANGST, Bim
   "Building. " WestB (4) 79, p. 67.
   "Red Dress. " Im (5:3) 79, p. 3.
   "Visit to Italy. " WestB (4) 79, p. 67.

ANIAKOR, Chike C.
   Eight poems. BlackALF (13:3) Aut 79, p. 96.

ANNAS, Pam
   "September Requiem. " Chomo (5:3) Spr 79, p. 46.

ANONYMOUS
   "Are your neighbors very bad?" Playb (26:2) F 79, p. 55.
   "As I looked in my/mirror yesterday. " EngJ (68:5) My 79, p.
      44.
   from The Giblet Pye: "Una's Lock. " Playb (26:3) Mr 79, p.
      153.
   "It's been about a year and a half. " EngJ (68:5) My 79, p. 44.
   "Nae Hair On't. " Playb (26:1) Ja 79, p. 257.
   "The next morning" (tr. by Andrew Schelling).   ChiR (31:2) Aut
      79, p. 109.
   "O Western Wind. " Playb (26:1) Ja 79, p. 257.
   "The Rabbit. " Playb (26:1) Ja 79, p. 256.
   "Set beside a fawn-eyed lady" (tr. by Andrew Schelling).   ChiR
      (31:2) Aut 79, p. 110.
   "A Song with Logic. " Playb (26:1) Ja 79, p. 256.
   "This, noble Sabinus, is but a stone" (tr. by I. F. Stone).
      NewYRB (26:2) 22 F 79, p. 10.
   "A Trick. " Playb (26:1) Ja 79, p. 256.
   "Unable to cast a likeness" (tr. by Andrew Schelling).   ChiR
      (31:2) Aut 79, p. 111.
   "A Warning to Virgins and Young Men about a Certain Vile Prac-
      tice" (from a New England Broadside of 1785).   Playb (26:2)
      F 79, p. 141.

ANTHONY, Steven
   "Michelangelo's David. " Mouth (2:1) F 79, p. 22.
   "Seven Years. " Mouth (2:3) N 79, p. 8.

ANTONITUS, Joseph
   "Ultimate Lecture. " Academe (65:1) F 79, p. 111.

APLON, Roger
   "The Great American Poem. " Antaeus (32) Wint 79, pp. 82-86.

APPEL, Dori
   "Alter Ego. " BelPoJ (29:3) Spr 79, p. 29.
   "Bread Line. " BelPoJ (29:3) Spr 79, p. 28.

APPLEMAN, Philip
   "After the Faith Healings. " ColEng (41:2) O 79, p. 185.
   "Always the Others. " Wind (32) 79, p. 1.
   "Nostalgie de la Boue. " Poetry (134:6) S 79, pp. 330-333.
   "A Questionnaire to the Poets of 1926. " Poultry (1) 79, p. 12.

APPLEWHITE, James
  "Autumn Ivy. " MissR (24) Aut 79, p. 12.
  "Blood Ties: for Jan. " MissR (24) Aut 79, p. 15.
  "Building in the Country. " MissR (24) Aut 79, p. 13.
  "The Call. " MissR (24) Aut 79, p. 9.
  "Crossing Over. " SouthernPR (19:1) Spr 79, p. 5.
  "First by the Sea. " CarolQ (31:2) Spr-Sum 79, p. 108.
  "January Farmhouse. " MissR (24) Aut 79, p. 11.
  "The Mary Tapes. " PoNow (23) 79, pp. 4-6.
  "Pamlico River. " MissR (24) Aut 79, p. 10.
  "The Ravine. " SouthernPR (19:1) Spr 79, p. 7.
  "The Visitor. " CarolQ (31:2) Spr-Sum 79, p. 109.

APPOLLINAIRE, Guillaume
  "Palace" (tr. by Patricia O'Callaghan). Pig (6) 79, p. 56.

ARA, Agneta
  "The Girl" (tr. by Lennart Bruce). Spirit (4:2/3) Spr-Sum 79,
      p. 51.
  "We had all the possibilities in the world" (tr. by Lennart Bruce).
      Spirit (4:2/3) Spr-Sum 79, p. 52.

ARAGON, Louis
  "All Alone" (tr. by Christian-Albrecht Gollub and Jean-Luc
      Filoche). Spirit (3:1/2) Aut-Wint 77-78, p. 58.

ARANZON, Leonid
  "Empty Sonnet" (tr. by Richard McKane). Pequod (3:2) 79, p.
      91.
  "In the Hours of Sleeplessness" (tr. by Richard McKane).
      Pequod (3:2) 79, p. 90.

ARCHER, Nuala
  "The Deviant Mantis. " CarlMis (18:1) Wint 79-80, p. 157.
  "Gypsy Asleep. " WindO (34) Spr-Sum 79, p. 20.
  "In a Sauna. " WindO (34) Spr-Sum 79, p. 18.
  "Lovers. " WindO (34) Spr-Sum 79, p. 18.
  "Staying. " WindO (34) Spr-Sum 79, p. 19.
  "Winter Watch. " WindO (34) Spr 79, p. 19.

ARCIDIACONO, Giovanni
  "1" (tr. by Mario Fratti). Wind (33) 79, p. 5.
  "2" (tr. by Mario Fratti). Wind (33) 79, p. 5.
  "3" (tr. by Mario Fratti). Wind (33) 79, p. 5.

ARENA, Adri
  "Within Confusion of Vibration. " StoneC (6:3) O 79, p. 9.

ARIAS, Arnold
  "Union. " Mouth (2:1) F 79, p. 4.

ARIDJIS, Homero
  "Before the Kingdom" (tr. by Brian Swann). PoNow (24) 79, p. 4.

"Burn the Boats" (tr. by Eliot Weinberger).   DenQ (14:1) Spr 79,
    p. 41.
"Chapultapec. " LitR (23:2) Wint 80, p. 164.
"Dream in Tenochtitlán" (tr. by Eliot Weinberger).   DenQ (14:1)
    Spr 79, p. 42.
"Letter from Mexico" (tr. by Eliot Weinberger).   DenQ (14:1)
    Spr 79, p. 44.
"The Prophecy of Man" (tr. by Eliot Weinberger).   DenQ (14:1)
    Spr 79, p. 47.
"Sun Set" (tr. by Eliot Weinberger).   DenQ (14:1) Spr 79, p. 46.
"Teotihuacán. " LitR (23:2) Wint 80, p. 164.
"There are Birds in This Land" (tr. by Eliot Weinberger).
    DenQ (14:1) Spr 79, p. 45.

ARKIN, Frieda
    "Delight's Advice to Her Daughter. " CalQ (15) Wint 79, p. 26.

ARMAND, Octavio
    "Water Color" (tr. by Carol Maier).   NewOR (6:3) 79, p. 197.

ARMBRUSTER, L. S.
    "A Tender Wet Narcissus. " FourQt (28:3) Spr 79, p. 35.

ARMSTRONG, Lewis
    "Tapestry. " GreenfieldR (7:3/4) Spr-Sum 79, p. 73.

ARMSTRONG, Tom C.
    "Extra, Read All About It. " MalR (49) Ja 79, p. 28.

ARNDT, Dorla
    "Candy and Flowers. " GRR (10:1) 79, p. 132.
    "A sonnet for my daughter. " GRR (10:1) 79, p. 130.
    "Tuesday. " GRR (10:1) 79, p. 131.

ARONOFF, Nina
    "new mexico blue. " Chomo (5:3) Spr 79, p. 15.

ARREOLA, Juan Jose
    "Domestic Recipes" (tr. by James Normington).   PoNow (24) 79,
    p. 4.

ARSONE, Sarah B.
    "Goodbye to the Fields" (tr. of Vicente Aleixandre).   Aspen (7)
    Spr 79, p. 92.
    "Song to a Dead Girl" (tr. of Vicente Aleixandre).   Aspen (7)
    Spr 79, p. 94.
    "Unity in Her" (tr. of Vicente Aleixandre).   Aspen (7) Spr 79, p.
    93.

ARTMANN, Hans Carl
    "Transience and Resurrection of the Pastoral Life" (tr. by Emery
    E. George).   ChiR (30:4) Spr 79, pp. 97-101.

ASHBERY, John
"Crazy Weather. " PoNow (21) 79, p. 19.
"Five Pedantic Pieces. " Poetry (134:4) Jl 79, p. 192.
"Flowering Death. " Poetry (134:4) Jl 79, p. 193.
"The Gazing Grain. " PoNow (21) 79, p. 19.
"Haunted Landscape. " NewYorker (55:23) 23 Jl 79, p. 33.
"Histoire Universelle. " NewYRB (26:17) 8 N 79, p. 12.
"Knocking Around. " NewYorker (55:6) 26 Mr 79, p. 40.
"Late Echo. " Poetry (134:4) Jl 79, p. 187.
from Litany: (II). AmerPoR (8:4) Jl-Ag 79, pp. 18-32.
"Many Wagons Ago. " Poetry (134:4) Jl 79, p. 190.
"My Erotic Double. " NewYRB (26:17) 8 N 79, p. 12.
"Not Only/But Also. " Poetry (134:4) Jl 79, p. 189.
"The Sun. " Poetry (134:4) Jl 79, p. 191.
"Tapestry. " NewYorker (55:14) 21 My 79, p. 34.
"Train Rising Out of the Sea. " Poetry (134:4) Jl 79, p. 188.

ASPENSTRÖM, Werner
"At the Corner, on the Way to the Postoffice" (tr. by D. L.
    Emblem). PoNow (24) 79, p. 4.
"Comes May" (tr. by D. L. Emblem). PoNow (23) 79, p. 45.
"Gray Sparrow" (tr. by D. L. Emblem). PoNow (23) 79, p. 45.
"Interpretation of a Dream" (tr by D. L. Emblem). PoNow (24)
    79, p. 4.
"Sunday" (tr. by D. L. Emblem and Siv Cedering Fox). PoNow
    (24) 79, p. 4.
"Theology for a Ruminating Friend" (tr. by D. L. Emblem).
    PoNow (23) 79, p. 45.

ASTLEY, Neil
"Death Telling. " Stand (20:1) 78-79, p. 14.

ASTOR, Susan
"Uncle Huge. " CarlMis (17:2/3) Spr 79, p. 88.
"Urbanization. " PartR (46:3) 79, p. 426.

ATCHITY, Kenneth John
"A Delicate Impasse. " KanQ (11:1/2) Wint-Spr 79, p. 68.
"Point of View. " KanQ (11:1/2) Wint-Spr 79, p. 68.
"Safe Landing. " KanQ (11:1/2) Wint-Spr 79, p. 69.

ATWOOD, Calvin
Poem. St.AR (5:2) 79, p. 17.

ATWOOD, Margaret
"Foretelling the Future. " AmerPoR (8:5) S-O 79, p. 23.
"Four Small Elegies. " AmerPoR (8:5) S-O 79, p. 26.
"The Puppet of the Wolf. " AmerPoR (8:5) S-O 79, p. 26.
"Two-Headed Poems. " AmerPoR (8:5) S-O 79, p. 24.

AUBERT, Jimmy
"Fat" (for my wife). PoetC (11:2) 79, p. 31.
"Home for the Wandering Jew. " PoetC (11:2) 79, p. 31.

AUGUSTINE, Jane
"May Day and All. " Confr (19) Aut 79-Wint 80, p. 87.

AULT, Leslie F.
"The Boulder Shoved Aside. " JnlONJP (4:1) 79, p. 18.
"Picasso: Avignon, 1970. " JnlONJP (4:1) 79, p. 19.

AUSTER, Paul
"XLIV" (tr. of Maurice Sceve). Pequod (3:1) 79, p. 60.
"LIX" (tr. of Maurice Sceve). Pequod (3:1) 79, p. 60.
"LXXIX" (tr. of Maurice Sceve). Pequod (3:1) 79, p. 61.

AUSTIN, F. A.
"Im Abendrot" (for Martha Collins). WestB (4) 79, p. 58.
"Im Abendrot" (for Martha Collins). WestB (5) 79, p. 48.
"Two Scenes and an Envoy. " WestB (4) 79, p. 57.

AUSTIN, Regina M.
"Still Life. " KanQ (11:1/2) Wint-Spr 79, p. 106.

AVALLON, Joanne
"Daughter. " HangL (36) Aut 79, p. 73.
"Five garbed nuns, black silouettes. " HangL (36) Aut 79, p.
   72.

AVERILL, Diane
"Walking the Rails. " PortR (25) 79, p. 137.

AVES, Jonathan
"Dear Me, the Sky Is Falling. " Mouth (2:3) N 79, p. 10.

AVICOLLI, Tommi
"The Deaf Mute's Final Dance. " Mouth (2:3) N 79, p. 26.
"The Secretary. " Mouth (2:3) N 79, p. 50.

AWAD, Joseph
"Going Back. " Poem (36) Jl 79, p. 45.
"Time. " Poem (36) Jl 79, p. 44.

AXELROD, David B.
"Forgetful Oedipus. " NewL (46:2) Wint 79-80, p. 42.
"Tongue Hotel" (for Emily). NewL (46:2) Wint 79-80, p. 41.

AXINN, Donald E.
"Bird-Watching. " Confr (19) Aut 79-Wint 80, p. 164.

AYRES, Noreen
"Pasadena Cafeteria. " DacTerr (16) 79, p. 5.

AZRAEL, Mary
"Glyphs: 1. Birth. " PraS (53:1) Spr 79, p. 34.
"Glyphs: 2. Eclipse. " PraS (53:1) Spr 79, p. 35.
"Lullaby. " PraS (53:1) Spr 79, p. 35.

BBB
"Anniversary in Clintwood Cemetery. " Wind (34) 79, pp. 3-10.

BACHMANN, Ingeborg
"Every Day" (tr. by Ken Fontenot). NewOR (6:2) 79, p. 163.

BACHSTEIN, Michael
"My Mother Asking My Sister When She's Going to Get Married. "
    Nimrod (23:1) Aut-Wint 79, p. 83.
"Shriner's Hospital for Crippled Children, St. Louis. " Nimrod
    (23:1) Aut-Wint 79, p. 84.

BACKSTRAND, Brian E.
"Prayer to the God of Silence. " ChrC (96:31) 3 O 79, p. 950.

BACON, Martha
"An Epitaph for Lovell, Our Dog. " Atl (244:3) S 79, p. 83.

BADGETT, Amanda
"Winter. " StoneC (6:3) O 79, p. 5.

BAGLEY, Anne
"April Morning. " GRR (10:1) 79, p. 120.
"Fire Poem. " GRR (10:1) 79, p. 121.

BAILEY, Larry
"Small Business. " NewRena (11) 79, p. 23.
"With Apologies to Rose. " NewRena (11) 79, p. 21.

BAILIE, Anne
"Encounter with Sirens. " JnlONJP (4:1) 79, p. 15.

BAKAITIS, Vyt
"Slow down and stop. The sentence falls apart" (tr. of Tomas
    Venclova). Pequod (3:1) 79, p. 38.

BAKER, David
"Hermit. " CharR (5:1) Spr 79, p. 56.
"Paths Toward Town. " WindO (34) Spr-Sum 79, p. 6.
"Through the apartment walls. " WindO (34) Spr-Sum 79, p. 5.

BAKER, Prentice
"The Burying. " Wind (34) 79, p. 11.

BAKKEN, Dick
"Cousins. " PoNow (21) 79, p. 39.

BALABAN, John
"Crossing West Nebraska, Looking for Blue Mountain. " PraS
    (53:3) Aut 79, p. 259.
"Hitch-Hiking and Listening to My CB Walkie-Talkie. " NewL
    (46:1) Aut 79, p. 74.

BALAKIAN, Peter
"The Angler. " GreenfieldR (7:3/4) Spr-Sum 79, p. 112.
"Azaleas! Azaleas!" PoetryNW (20:2) Sum 79, p. 43.
"Down the Cliff" (for Bill Worth). Confr (19) Aut 79-Wint 80,
    p. 149.
"Granny, Making Soup. " CarolQ (31:3) Aut 79, pp. 31-35.
"O Little Sister" (for Janet). CarolQ (31:3) Aut 79, p. 27.
"The Only Bear. " PoetryNW (20:2) Sum 79, pp. 42-43.
"Poem for the Holy Week. " WestB (4) 79, p. 28.
"Relief. " GreenfieldR (7:3/4) Spr-Sum 79, p. 113.
"Water for Land" (for Jack Wheatcroft). WestB (4) 79, p. 28.

BALAZS, Mary
"The Dreams About Us. " WebR (4:3) Spr 79, p. 23.
"In Defence of Reticence. " WebR (4:3) Spr 79, p. 25.
"Incident at Mossel Bay. " GRR (10:2) 79, p. 180.
"Mid-Afternoon. " StoneC (6:2) My 79, p. 13.
"Ploys. " Wind (35) 79, p. 3.
"Still-Life: A Metaphor. " Wind (35) 79, p. 4.

BALCOFF, Sophie
"Making Potato Salad. " KanQ (11:3) Sum 79, p. 90.

BALDERSTON, Jean
"Blue Concords. " Bits (10) Jl 79.
"Camels. " Kayak (50) My 79, p. 33. Found poem.
"It Was the Nature of the Era. " PoNow (22) 79, p. 4.

BALDWIN, Neil
"Escapist. " Tele (15) Spr 79, p. 137.
"Morning song. " Tele (15) Spr 79, p. 137.
"Poem for the end of illness. " Tele (15) Spr 79, p. 136.

BALL, Angela
"The Lost Colony. " Ploughs (5:1) 79, p. 14.

BALLANTYNE, Deirdre
"The Long Word. " MalR (49) Ja 79, p. 126.

BANGS, Carol Jane
"Fate. " PoNow (21) 79, p. 4.
"Irreconcilable Differences. " MalR (49) Ja 79, p. 101.

BANKS, Stanley E.
"Uncle Orie. " EngJ (68:5) My 79, p. 29.

BARALE, Michele
"The Interpretation of Dreams. " LittleM (12:1/2) Spr-Sum 78
    (79), p. 60.

BARASOVSKA, Joan
"High Relief. " Tendril (15) Spr 79, p. 9.

BARBER, X. Ted
"Folk Mythology of Turkestan. " HarvAd (112:4) My 79, p. 29.
"Four Examples from the History of Art. " HarvAd (112:2) Mr
   79, p. 13.

BARCIAUSKAS, J.
"What Her Eyes Told Me. " ConcPo (12:1) Spr 79, p. 44.

BARGEN, Walter
"Hard Angel. " KanQ (11:3) Sum 79, p. 61.
"Utterly Gone. " SoDakR (17:2) Sum 79, p. 66.
"Vaporized. " SoDakR (17:2) Sum 79, p. 65.

BARKER, David
Scenes from a Marriage. WormR (75) 79. Entire issue.

BARKER, George
"A Certain Form of Love. " Stand (20:4) 79, p. 4.

BARKER, Max S.
"Soiled Spots on Our Sheets. " Wind (32) 79, p. 31.

BARKER, W. W.
"The Sack" (for Tim and Darka). MalR (52) O 79, p. 48.

BARKER, Wendy
"Expatriate" (to my mother). CalQ (15) Wint 79, p. 50.
"First Memory. " Chomo (5:3) Spr 79, p. 19.
"Hotel Proprietor. " CalQ (15) Wint 79, p. 51.

BARKS, Coleman
"The Flood at Toccoa. " Aspen (7) Spr 79, p. 24.
"The Great American Poem. " Antaeus (32) Wint 79, pp. 82-86.
"In the Woods, You and I. " GeoR (33:1) Spr 79, p. 208.
"Night, Sleep, Death and the Stars. " QW (6) Spr-Sum 78, p. 90.
"Noon or Midnight. " QW (6) Spr-Sum 78, p. 89.
"A Picture in a News Magazine. " QW (6) Spr-Sum 78, p. 89.
"WRFC. " QW (9) Spr-Sum 79, p. 110.
"A Silver Globe. " Aspen (7) Spr 79, p. 25.

BARNARD, Mary
Twelve Poems. NowestR (17:2/3) 79, pp. 234-242.

BARNES, Jane
"Gathering" (for Heather). Ploughs (5:1) 79, p. 15.
"Inventions. " AndR (6:1) Spr 79, p. 48.

BARNES, Jeannette
"At Winter's Edge. " Wind (34) 79, p. 12.

BARNES, Jim
"Above the Harbor of Lindos" (tr. of Dagmar Nick). DenQ
   (14:2) Sum 79, p. 53.

"Accident at Three Mile Island. " NewL (46:2) Wint 79-80, p.
   97.
"The Cruel Month. " QW (6) Spr-Sum 78, p. 112.
"Diluvium" (tr. of Dagmar Nick). PoNow (24) 79, p. 37.
"Exodus" (tr. of Dagmar Nick). DenQ (14:2) Sum 79, p. 55.
"Magpie. " GRR (10:1) 79, p. 47.
"My Father's House. " MissouriR (2:2/3) Spr 79, p. 14.
"Near Crater Lake. " BelPoJ (30:2) Wint 79-80, p. 41.
"On the Mountain: At Bear Den Cave. " GRR (10:1) 79, p. 48.
"Self-Portrait. " GRR (10:1) 79, p. 50.
"Southward" (tr. of Dagmar Nick). DenQ (14:2) Sum 79, p. 54.
"Summons" (tr. of Dagmar Nick). PoNow (24) 79, p. 37.

BARNES, Tim
   "A Good Day for Miles. " PortR (25) 79, p. 165.
   "Pomegranates. " PortR (25) 79, p. 164.
   "Winter Fog Along the Willamette. " CutB (12) Spr-Sum 79, p.
      20.

BARNES, W. D.
   "Child in the Room. " Wind (32) 79, p. 4.
   "Old Poets Never Die. " Wind (32) 79, p. 3.
   "The Pack/for Jerry. " Wind (32) 79, p. 2.

BARNETT, Patricia
   "Break. " PraS (53:4) Wint 79-80, p. 354.

BARNSTONE, Willis
   "Borges. " AmerS (48:2) Spr 79, p. 226.

BARONE, Patricia
   "After the blizzard we meet. " Tendril (4) Wint 79, p. 10.

BARRETT, Carol
   "entering the north field" (w. Anita Skeen). Nimrod (23:1) Aut-
      Wint 79, p. 57.
   "rites of access" (w. Anita Skeen). Nimrod (23:1) Aut-Wint 79,
      p. 58.

BARROWS, Anita
   from The Limits: (1-6). Montra (5) 79, p. 40.

BARRY, Jack
   "The Widow Woman of Listowel. " NewL (46:1) Aut 79, p. 48.

BARRY, Jim
   "Dream Speaker. " SmPd (45) 79, p. 27.

BARRY, Paul
   "Clearance. " KanQ (11:1/2) Wint-Spr 79, p. 196.
   "The House Below the Water. " Poetry (134:6) S 79, p. 339.
   "Reconciliation. " Poetry (134:6) S 79, p. 340.
   "September: The Literary Perspective" (for Julie). Poetry
      (134:6) S 79, p. 341.

BARTH, R. L.
"The Crossing. " SouthernR (15:4) Aut 79, p. 1008.
"Epigram. " SouthernR (15:4) Aut 79, p. 1009.
"The Jeweler" (for the memory of Yvor Winters). SouthernR
    (15:4) Aut 79, p. 1009.
"Night Piece. " SouthernR (15:4) Aut 79, p. 1007.
"Waking Early" (to Susan). SouthernR (15:4) Aut 79, p. 1007.

BARTLETT, Paul Alexander
"His Private Research Facility. " Wind (32) 79, p. 6.
"Mist. " Wind (32) 79, p. 6.

BARTON, Paulé
"The Carnival" (tr. by Howard Norman). VirQR (55:1) Wint 79,
    p. 119.
"Dry Tune. " MichQR (18:1) Wint 79, p. 115.
"Dry Tune" (tr. by Howard Norman). VirQR (55:1) Wint 79, p.
    117.
"Three Paintings of Hers Bélem Saw" (tr. by Howard Norman).
    VirQR (55:1) Wint 79, p. 119.
"Too Many Proverbs" (tr. by Howard Norman). VirQR (55:1)
    Wint 79, p. 118.

BARTOW, Stuart
Poem. St. AR (5:2) 79, p. 59.

BARWELL, Jay
"Cicada's Death. " Aspen (8) Aut 79, p. 42.

BASQUETTE-BAAL, Bill E.
"my little bird E. " Tele (15) Spr 79, p. 33.
"stub yer toes. " Tele (15) Spr 79, p. 33.
"virtue iz my vice. " Tele (15) Spr 79, p. 33.
"weather u like it oar knot. " Tele (15) Spr 79, p. 33.

BASS, Madeline Tiger
"Divorce Poems. " LitR (22:3) Spr 79, p. 349.
"The 3 of Us" (for Toi, After the Reading). LitR (22:3) Spr 79,
    p. 351.

BASSETT, Lee
"Teaching the Mentally Retarded to Swim. " GreenfieldR (7:3/4)
    Spr-Sum 79, p. 33.
"Watermelon. " CutB (12) Spr-Sum 79, p. 50.

BASSO, Eric
"Tattoo #1. " ChiR (30:4) Spr 79, p. 8.

BATES, Peter
"Interview II. " Aspect (74/75) Ja-Ag 79, p. 34.
"Jack Pepper, Junk Shop Owner. " Aspect (74/75) Ja-Ag 79, p.
    35.
"John Miller, Rummy. " Aspect (74/75) Ja-Ag 79, p. 33.

BATKI, John
"April 11" (tr. of Attila József). PoNow (24) 79, p. 22.
"Lullaby" (tr. of Attila József). PoNow (24) 79, p. 22.

BAUER, Steven
"Antigone: Polynice's Version. " DenQ (14:2) Sum 79, p. 76.
"Lust. " DenQ (14:2) Sum 79, p. 77.
"Mobilgas. " PoNow (25) 79, p. 2.
"Raid on the Inarticulate. " CharR (5:2) Aut 79, p. 54.
"Seals in the Damariscotta. " DenQ (14:2) Sum 79, p. 78.
"Stopped in Memphis. " CharR (5:1) Spr 79, p. 32.
"Twins. " DenQ (14:2) Sum 79, p. 80.

BAUMAN, Lawrence P.
"If a Tree Falls in the United Nations. " JnlONJP (3:2) 79, p.
    40.
"The Imposter. " JnlONJP (3:2) 79, p. 39.

BAUMANN, Susan
"Igniting. " Shen (30:2) Wint 79, p. 45.

BAUMGARTNER, John M.
"The Boy. " LittleM (12:1/2) Spr-Sum 78 (79), p. 88.

BAVENCI, Campbell
"History. " PraS (53:2) Sum 79, p. 120.
"Sounding the Silence. " PraS (53:2) Sum 79, p. 120.

BAXTER, Charles
"The Hart Crane Poems. " MinnR (NS13) Aut 79, p. 40.
"The Return of the Repressed. " Poetry (134:2) My 79, pp. 93-
    94.
"Two Theories of the Unconscious. " Poetry (134:2) My 79, p.
    94.

BAYES, Ronald H.
"Polity. " SouthernPR (19:2) Aut 79, p. 51.

BAYLES, Martha
"The New Museum/The Old Museum. " LittleM (12:1/2) Spr-Sum
    78 (79), p. 12.

BAYLEY, Michael
"Last Rites. " Stand (20:1) 78-79, p. 61.

BEAKE, Fred
"Elegy at the Beginning of Spring. " Stand (20:3) 79, p. 6.
"Elegy 1. 10" (tr. of Tibullus). Stand (20:3) 79, p. 7.

BEALL, DeWitt
"15, Rue du sommerard. " Harp (258:1548) My 79, p. 107.

BEAME, Jeffery
"The Bathing House. " Mouth (2:1) F 79, p. 31.

"Grace. " Mouth (2:1) F 79, p. 19.
"Letter. " Mouth (2:3) N 79, p. 27.
"The Silent Speak for You" (to Peter-James).   Mouth (2:1) F 79,
    p. 21.

BEAN, Manya
"Singing the Rotten Blues. " JnlONJP (4:1) 79, p. 9.

BEARDSLEY, Doug
"Love Poem. " MalR (51) Jl 79, p. 92.

BEASLEY, Sherry Hughes
"Poem: Where will it end. " StoneC (6:2) My 79, p. 20.

BEAUSOLEIL, Beau
"Half and Half Again. " SeC (6:2) 78, p. 3.
"Passage # 3. " SeC (6:2) 78, p. 9.
"Poem for a Cuban Brigade of Women Cane Cutters. " SeC (6:2)
    78, p. 4.
"Remain. " SeC (6:2) 78, p. 8.
"Your Thick Hair" (for García Lorca).   SeC (6:2) 78, p. 5.

BECERRA, Jose Carlos
"(The Drowned)" (tr. by Linda Scheer).   PoNow (24) 79, p. 5.

BECHTOL, Beatrice
"Stumbling Franz. " Ur (2) 79, p. 3.

BECK, Gary
"Coma. " PoetryNW (20:3) Aut 79, pp. 45-46.

BECK, John Peter
"Lines. " GRR (10:1) 79, p. 136.

BECKER, Laurence A.
"When we begin to long. " EngJ (68:5) My 79, p. 28.

BECKER, Robin
"A Long Distance" (for Lennie).   Aspect (74/75) Ja-Ag 79, p. 59.

BECKMAN, Megan
"Anise. " ChiR (31:1) Sum 79, p. 58.

BECKWITH, Ruthie-Marie
"Benny's poem" (for R. A.).   Wind (32) 79, p. 8.
"A Chariot for Phaethon. " SouthernPR (19:1) Spr 79, p. 62.
"the crazy boy. " Wind (32) 79, p. 8.
"Sadder songs have been recorded" (for g. m.).   Wind (32) 79,
    p. 7.

BEELER, Janet
"The Photographer's Wife. " OP (28) Aut 79, p. 29.
"The Tightrope Walker. " OP (28) Aut 79, pp. 30-31.

"The Woman Who Was Born on Her Father's Ship. " OP (28)
    Aut 79, p. 32.

BEENE, Rickey
    "At the Fallen Tree. " SmF (7/8) Spr-Aut 79, p. 9.
    "At the Taxidermist's Window. " SmF (7/8) Spr-Aut 79, p. 8.
    "Back Porch. " SmF (7/8) Spr-Aut 78, p. 7.
    "Lug's Vision: The Perfect Carpenter. " SmF (7/8) Spr-Aut 78,
        p. 10.

BEER, Christian
    "A Question of Belonging: Soweto, 1978" (to Wopko Jensma).
        Stand (20:2) 79, p. 73.

BEER, Ralph
    "Riding Line. " CutB (13) Aut-Wint 79, p. 50.

BEGGS-DAVIDSON, Ann
    "Seasons. " Wind (34) 79, p. 49.

BEHM, Richard
    "The Collector" (for Jessica). GreenfieldR (7:3/4) Spr-Sum 79,
        p. 218.
    "Flying. " EnPas (8) 79, p. 16.

BEHRENS, Richard David
    "Frog sitting alone. " Wind (33) 79, p. 36.
    "Neither rafts nor boats. " Wind (33) 79, p. 36.

BEINING, Guy R.
    "Circulation (91). " Mouth (2:2) Je 79, p. 39.
    "Circulation (96). " Mouth (2:2) Je 79, p. 39.
    "Circulation (101). " Mouth (2:2) Je 79, p. 40.
    "Circulation (102) J. R. M. (Flick). " Mouth (2:2) Je 79, p. 40.
    "Circulation (103). " Mouth (2:2) Je 79, p. 41.
    "the headdress of our romance. " Ur (2) 79, p. 4.
    "A Local Street. " Mouth (2:1) F 79, p. 39.
    "Ogden as Texas Traveller. " SeC (6:1) 78, p. 38.
    The Ogden Diary. Zahir (10) 79. Entire issue.
    "Rebirth # 21. " Mouth (2:1) F 79, p. 5.
    "So Close as to Dissolve. " PikeF (2) Wint 78-79, p. 7.
    "Stoma 25. " Pig (6) 79, p. 59.
    "Stoma 258. " StoneC (6:3) O 79, p. 32.

BELITT, Ben
    "The Great American Poem. " Antaeus (32) Wint 79, pp. 82-86.
    "Walker. " SewanR (87:2) Spr 79, p. 219.

BELL, Marvin
    "The Great American Poem. " Antaeus (32) Wint 79, pp. 82-86.

BELLAMY, Joe David
    "Alone in the Gym I Can't Miss. " PoNow (25) 79, p. 2.

"An Ambience Gearing Up" (for George C. Schmidt).   ArkRiv
  (4:3) 79, p. 22.
"Electrical Storm. " PoNow (25) 79, p. 2.
"Mile Run. " PoNow (25) 79, p. 46.

BELLI, Carlos Germán
  "Segregation N. 1. " LitR (23:2) Wint 80, p. 225.
  "Someday Love. " LitR (23:2) Wint 80, p. 226.

BELLI, Giuseppe Gioachino
  "Abraham's Sacrifice: I" (tr. by Miller Williams).   NewOR
    (6:2) 79, p. 122.
  "Abraham's Sacrifice: II" (tr. by Miller Williams).   NewOR
    (6:2) 79, p. 122.
  "Abraham's Sacrifice: III" (tr. by Miller Williams).   NewOR
    (6:2) 79, p. 123.
  "The Builders" (tr. by Miller Williams).   NewOR (6:2) 79, p.
    121.
  "The Circumcision of the Lord" (tr. by Miller Williams).
    CharR (5:1) Spr 79, p. 7.
  "The Creation of the World" (tr. by Miller Williams).   CharR
    (5:1) Spr 79, p. 5.
  "The Flight of the Holy Family" (tr. by Miller Williams).
    CharR (5:1) Spr 79, p. 7.
  "The Letter" (tr. by Miller Williams).   CharR (5:1) Spr 79, p.
    6.
  "The Slaughter of the Innocents" (tr. by Miller Williams).
    CharR (5:1) Spr 79, p. 8.
  "The Universal Flood" (tr. by Miller Williams).   CharR (5:1)
    Spr 79, p. 6.

BELLINGER, Tom
  "Afraid of Those Who Change. " Poem (35) Mr 79, p. 50.
  "Alleged Friend. " Poem (35) Mr 79, p. 49.
  "Your Poised Hand. " Poem (35) Mr 79, p. 48.

BENBOW, Margaret Savides
  "Deadlines" (for A. M.).   BelPoJ (29:3) Spr 79, p. 11.
  "Pizzeria. " AntR (37:3) Sum 79, p. 318.
  "The Tumble. " BelPoJ (29:3) Spr 79, p. 10.
  "Woman Carrying Twins. " AntR (37:3) Sum 79, p. 320.

BENDA, Jan
  "Elegy about a Postal Deliverer" (tr. of Milan Exner w. Clayton
    Eshleman).   Montra (5) 79, p. 152.

BENDER, Sheila
  "Folding. " PoetryNW (20:1) Spr 79, pp. 30-31.

BENEDETTI, David
  "Age. " PoNow (22) 79, p. 21.
  "Bouquet of Weeds. " Tele (15) Spr 79, p. 85.
  "Losing. " PoNow (22) 79, p. 4.

"Lucidity. " PoNow (22) 79, p. 20.
"My Work. " Tele (15) Spr 79, p. 84.
"Recipe. " PoNow (22) 79, p. 21.
"Science Fiction. " PoNow (22) 79, p. 4.

BENEDETTO, Arnaldo di
"Modigliani" (tr. by Sonia Raiziss). PoNow (24) 79, p. 5.

BENEDIKT, Michael
from Dear Alice: "Alice's Ashes. " Agni (10/11) 79, p. 194.
from Dear Alice: "Alice's Wants. " Agni (10/11) 79, pp. 185-
193.
"Establishment of a Community in Brazil" (tr. of Max Jacob).
QW (9) Spr-Sum 79, p. 14.
"For Zekie. " Durak (3) 79, p. 52.
"Gerald Fenchel. " AmerPoR (8:3) My-Je 79, p. 19.
"The Great American Poem. " Antaeus (32) Wint 79, pp. 82-86.
"I Looked. " PoNow (21) 79, p. 8.
"I Saw. " PoNow (21) 79, p. 8.
"I Tried. " PoNow (21) 79, p. 8.
"Letter to Joan Mercuryindividual in Newton Boston from a Fig-
newton near Brookline (actually Back Bay) January 29, 1978. "
MassR (20:4) Wint 79, pp. 662-665.
"The Litany of Lies. " Kayak (51) S 79, p. 20.
"Naming the Language. " QW (9) Spr-Sum 79, p. 13.
"Photo-Album, with Child. " Sky (9) Aut 79, p. 45.
"Truckers and Literary Intellectuals. " Ploughs (5:1) 79, pp. 16-
17.

BENGTSON, David
"My Right Hand Is Gone. " NewL (46:2) Wint 79-80, p. 59.
"Two Men's Rooms--Nine Years Apart. " NewL (46:2) Wint 79-
80, p. 58.

BENGSTON, Paul
"Pee-ay's Song. " Poultry (1) 79, p. 11.

BENJAMIN, Loretta
"Shiney Objects" (for Clifford Glover and Randolph Evans).
NewWR (47:5) S-O 79, p. 17.
"Summertime, Ghetto Summertime. " NewWR (47:5) S-O 79, p.
16.
"Yvonne. " NewWR (47:5) S-O 79, p. 16.

BENJAMIN, Pat
"The Dead Volcano. " SmF (7/8) Spr-Aut 78, p. 14.

BENNANI, Ben
"Camel's Bite. " Paint (12) Aut 79, p. 9.

BENNETT, Bruce
"Bella. " Pequod (3:2) 79, p. 29.
"A Dream of Flying. " PoNow (22) 79, p. 5.

"The Faithful Seed. " PoNow (22) 79, p. 5.
"The Farewell Dinner. " PoNow (22) 79, p. 5.
"Light. " Bits (9) Ja 79.
"Not Wanting to Write Like Everyone Else. " Pequod (3:2) 79,
     p. 27.
"Sort of a Sestina. " Pequod (3:2) 79, p. 28.
"The Strange Animal. " PoNow (22) 79, p. 4.
"The Wall. " PoNow (22) 79, p. 5.

BENNETT, John
   Crazy Girl on the Bus. Vaga (30) 79. Entire issue.
   "Legends and Shadows. " PoNow (21) 79, p. 38.
   "Legends and Shadows. " PoNow (22) 79, p. 5.
   "Non-Marriage Rites in the Ghettoed Suburbs. " Ur (2) 79, p. 7.
   "Postage Due. " PoNow (22) 79, p. 5.
   "Relationships. " PoNow (22) 79, p. 5.
   "TV Sport Spectacular at the New Omni-Coliseum. " Ur (2) 79,
     p. 8.
   "The Very Brief. " Ur (2) 79, p. 9.

BENNETT, Mac
   "Suspension of Disbelief. " Wind (32) 79, p. 9.

BENOIT, Michelle
   "Double Head" (tr. of Henri Michaux w. Tom Whalen). Chelsea
     (38) 79, p. 27.
   "He Writes" (tr. of Henri Michaux w. Tom Whalen). NewOR
     (6:2) 79, p. 151.
   "The Old Vulture" (tr. of Henri Michaux w. Tom Whalen).
     Chelsea (38) 79, p. 27.

BENSKO, John
   "The Children's Committee. " PoetryNW (20:3) Aut 79, p. 8.
   "A Last Look in the Sambre Canal" (for Wilfred Owen).
     PoetryNW (20:3) Aut 79, p. 6.
   "Mail Call. " PraS (53:4) Wint 79-80, p. 325.
   "The Pet Cat. " CarolQ (31:3) Aut 79, p. 69.
   "A Veteran of the Great War. " PoetryNW (20:3) Aut 79, pp. 6-
     8.
   "The Young Woman at Amiens: 1914. " PraS (53:4) Wint 79, p.
     324.

BENSON, Steve
   "A Bundle in the Sun. " PoetC (11:2) 79, p. 6.
   "On a Hillside Facing West. " PoetC (10:3) 79, p. 44.

BENTLEY, Beth
   "At St. Sulpice. " NewEngR (1:4) Sum 79, p. 441.

BERG, Eric Ivan
   "Predators. " Chelsea (38) 79, p. 172.

BERG, Sharon
   "Starting Over. " MalR (51) Jl 79, p. 136.

'We Are This Simple. " MalR (51) Jl 79, p. 134.
"When You Go to the Sage. " MalR (51) Jl 79, p. 138.

BERG, Stephen
    from With Akhmatova at the Black Gates: "Two Free Varia-
        tions. " NewRep (181:26) 29 D 79, p. 25.

BERGE, Carol
    "The Old Ones. " Im (6:1) 79, p. 4.
    "Sunday Music. " Kayak (50) My 79, p. 39.

BERGER, Suzanne E.
    "For the Father. " Ploughs (5:1) 79, p. 18.
    "Your Life: An Invention. " Ploughs (5:1) 79, pp. 19-20.

BERGGOLTS, Olga
    "Days of Shame and Sorrow" (tr. by Vera S. Dunham). Nat
        (229:22) 29 D 79, p. 693.

BERGGREN, Edward
    'My Love Sleeps Through Winter. " Poem (35) Mr 79, p. 4.

BERGMAN, David
    "Doldrums. " VirQR (55:3) Sum 79, p. 507.
    "The Priestess of Apollo. " CimR (46) Ja 79, p. 24.
    'Why I Am Offended by Miracles. " KanQ (11:1/2) Wint-Spr 79,
        p. 31.

BERGMAN, Roger
    "Bears. " PoetC (11:3) 79, p. 16.
    "A Charm for My Daughter on the Occasion of Her First Child-
        hood Accident. " PoetC (11:3) 79, p. 14.

BERKSON, Bill
    'Domino. " SunM (8) Aut 79, p. 3.
    'Voyage to Jericho" (for Steve Emerson). SunM (8) Aut 79, p.
        3.

BERKOWITZ, Shari
    "Sabbath. " Ploughs (5:3) 79, pp. 85-87.

BERLIND, Bruce
    "Defend It" (tr. of Agnes Nemes Nagy). PoNow (21) 79, p. 45.
    "The Horseman" (tr. of Agnes Nemes Nagy). Stand (20:4) 79,
        p. 24.
    "January Thaw. " PoetryNW (20:1) Spr 79, p. 15.
    "The Sleeping Horsemen" (for Lajos Kassak) (tr. of Agnes Nemes
        Nagy). PoNow (24) 79, p. 27.
    "Storm" (tr. of Agnes Nemes Nagy). PoNow (24) 79, p. 27.
    "28" (tr. of Lajos Kassak). PoNow (24) 79, p. 22.

BERLINER, Tom
    "Collapsible Ladies in Collapsible Chairs. " Tele (15) Spr 79, p.
        88.

"Evening Tucks in Her Clouds. " <u>Tele</u> (15) Spr 79, p. 88.

BERNHARDT, Suzanne
"The Man Walking Out of the Fog. " <u>Wind</u> (33) 79, p. 6.
"When There Was Snow. " <u>Wind</u> (33) 79, p. 6.

BERNSTEIN, Carole
"Traveling Without Signs. " <u>HangL</u> (35) Spr 79, p. 15.

BERNSTEIN, Charles
"3 Fifths Equals" (w. Steve McCaffery and Ron Silliman).   <u>SunM</u>
   (8) Aut 79, pp. 162-169.

BERNSTEIN, Michael André
"To Go Beyond. " <u>NewOR</u> (6:2) 79, p. 166.

BERRY, D. C.
"Near the Coffin of Uncle George. " <u>QW</u> (6) Spr-Sum 78, p. 72.

BERRY, John
"The Red Hunter. " <u>BelPoJ</u> (29:3) Spr 79, p. 27.

BERRY, Wendell
"Another Descent. " <u>Hudson</u> (32:1) Spr 79, p. 43.
"The River Bridged and Forgot. " <u>Hudson</u> (32:1) Spr 79, p. 41.
"Ronsard's Lament for the Cutting of the Forest of Gastine. "
   <u>Hudson</u> (32:1) Spr 79, p. 43.
"The Way of Pain. " <u>NewEngR</u> (1:4) Sum 79, p. 440.

BERRYHILL, Lori
"Substitute. " <u>QW</u> (6) Spr-Sum 78, p. 99.

BERSSENBRUGGE, Mei-Mei
"Rabbit, Hair, Leaf. " <u>Pequod</u> (3:1) 79, pp. 54-55.
"Tail. " <u>Pequod</u> (3:1) 79, p. 55.

BERTHELOT, N.
"Indian Summer. " <u>Playb</u> (26:1) Ja 79, p. 256.

BERTOLINO, James
"The Alien. " <u>PartR</u> (46:2) 79, p. 256.
"The Alleged Conception. " <u>PoNow</u> (21) 79, p. 19.
"The Cathedral. " <u>Spirit</u> (3:1/2) Aut-Wint 77-78, p. 8.
"Like a Brain. " <u>PoNow</u> (21) 79, p. 19.
"The Poem About Dust. " <u>Spirit</u> (3:1/2) Aut-Wint 77-78, p. 7.
"Rhubarb at Fall Creek. " <u>PoNow</u> (21) 79, p. 19.

BERTRAM, Diane Marie
"autobiography. " <u>Nimrod</u> (23:1) Aut-Wint 79, p. 66.
"Cat Poem. " <u>Nimrod</u> (23:1) Aut-Wint 79, p. 65.

BERTRAND, Aloysius
"Lepers" (tr. by James Weeks). <u>Field</u> (20) Spr 79, p. 48.

"Messire jean" (tr. by James Weeks). Field (20) Spr 79, p. 47.

BESER, Ya'akov
"In the Beginning My Mother Screeched" (tr. by Bernhard
    Frank). PoNow (24) 79, p. 5.
"Snake Skin" (tr. by Bernhard Frank). PoNow (24) 79, p. 5.

BEST, Zoe
"Building. " Tele (15) Spr 79, p. 118.
"Smelt Run. " Tele (15) Spr 79, p. 118.

BETHEL, Lorraine
"What Chou Mean We, White Girl?" Cond (5) 79, pp. 86-91.

BETT, Stephen
"Anspach, S. --Movie Star. " Tele (15) Spr 79, p. 106.
"A Form of Madness. " Tele (15) Spr 79, p. 107.
"Insane or Busted. " Tele (15) Spr 79, p. 107.
"Magritte in Browns. " Tele (15) Spr 79, p. 106.
"Major Street Looking Down Vister" (for Pam). Tele (15) Spr
    79, p. 108.

BEUM, Robert
"Imperia. " SewanR (87:3) Sum 79, p. 374.

BIALOSZEWSKI, Miron
"A Fin-de-Siècle Myth" (tr. by Andrzej Busza and Bogdan Czay-
    kowski). Durak (2) 79, p. 12.
"I Don't Know How to Write" (tr. by Andrzej Busza and Bogdan
    Czaykowski). Durak (2) 79, p. 13.

BIAMONTE, Edgar L.
"About the Mind to Sing or Not. " StoneC (6:2) My 79, p. 31.

BIASOTTI, Raymond
"The Day Joe Died" (for Mario). SmPd (46) 79, p. 18.

BIDART, Frank
"The Sacrifice. " Ploughs (5:2) 79, pp. 68-69.

BIEN, Peter
"The Moonlight Sonata" (tr. of Yannis Ritsos). NewEngR (1:3)
    Spr 79, p. 301.

BIERDS, Linda
"Freeing the Apes in the New Savannah. " CutB (13) Aut-Wint
    79, p. 10.
"The Haunting. " Chomo (5:3) Spr 79, p. 23.
"Lesson: The Spider's Eighth Eye. " PoetryNW (20:2) Sum 79,
    pp. 16-17.
"One Hot Day in October. " CutB (13) Aut-Wint 79, p. 11.

BIERMANN, Wolf
"Self Portrait on a Rainy Sunday in the City of Berlin" (tr. by
    Almut McAuley). NewOR (6:3) 79, p. 220.

BIG EAGLE, Duane
"Love Charm. " BelPoJ (30:2) Wint 79-80, p. 35.

BIGUENET, John
"Snake's Riddle. " NewOR (6:4) 79, p. 335.

BIGUENET, Marsha
"Almost a Fantasy" (tr. of Eugenio Montale). NewOR (6:2) 79,
    p. 124.

BIJOU, Rachelle
"February 27, 1978. " Tele (15) Spr 79, p. 38.
"Halftone. " Tele (15) Spr 79, p. 39.
"I Know It's Not Good Taste. " Tele (15) Spr 79, p. 36.
"A Sudden Rush of White. " Tele (15) Spr 79, p. 37.
"Woman at the Dior Counter. " Tele (15) Spr 79, p. 38.

BILLET, Bonni
"The Allergy. " Pequod (3:2) 79, p. 54.
"List of Refusals. " Pequod (3:2) 79, p. 55.
"Moving. " Pequod (3:2) 79, pp. 51-52.
"The Nursing Home. " Pequod (3:2) 79, p. 53.

BILLINGS, Philip
"Before Breakfast" (for Marion). WindO (35) Aut-Wint 79-80,
    p. 13.
"Father Explaining a Divorce. " WindO (35) Aut-Wint 79-80, p.
    15.
"That Log. " WindO (35) Aut-Wint 79-80, p. 14.

BILOFSKY, Fred
"all i have left of you. " StoneC (6:3) O 79, p. 17.

BIRTHA, Becky
"At 20, I began to know. " Cond (5) 79, p. 97.
"Maria de las Rosas. " Cond (5) 79, p. 98.

BISHOP, Elizabeth
"North Haven" (in memoriam: R. T. S. L.). HarvAd (113:1/2)
    N 79, p. 25.
"One Art. " Iowa (10:1) Wint 79, p. 76.
"One Art. " Poetry (135:3) D 79, back cover.
"Pink Dog. " NewYorker (55:2) 26 F 79, p. 32.
"Sonnet. " NewYorker (55:37) 29 O 79, p. 38.

BISHOP, Wendy
"The Round Moon. " MassR (20:1) Spr 79, p. 126.
"Tropical Sleep. " Kayak (51) S 79, p. 46.
"To You. " Nimrod (23:1) Aut-Wint 79, p. 12.

BISSERT, Ellen Marie
"Stepfather. " 13thM (4:2) 79, p. 67.

BIXBY, R. J.
"Road Song No. 18. " GRR (10:1) 79, p. 114.
"Rock and Roll. " GRR (10:1) 79, p. 114.

BIZZARO, Patrick
"Keeping a Hold on Himself. " WormR (76) 79, p. 124.
"The Past. " WormR (76) 79, p. 125.
"A Shadow's Love" (for Susan). WormR (76) 79, p. 125.

BLACK, Charles
"All Too Little on Pictures. " ArizQ (35:2) Sum 79, p. 169.
"The King Repairs to His Temple. " DenQ (14:2) Sum 79, p. 46.
"The Reach of Silence. " ArizQ (35:4) Wint 79, p. 372.

BLACKWELL, Will H.
"Tides. " BallSUF (20:1) Wint 79, p. 2.

BLAIN, Alexander, III
"Moon Landing. " MichQR (18:2) Spr 79, p. 176.

BLAISDELL, Harold W.
"The Steel-Toed Kiss. " Mouth (2:3) N 79, p. 48.

BLAISDELL, R. E.
Twelve Poems. WormR (76) 79, p. 127.

BLANKENBURG, Gary
"To My Father. " EngJ (68:5) My 79, p. 31.

BLASING, Randy
"Blur. " PoNow (23) 79, p. 18.
"Elegy for Satan" (tr. of Nazim Hikmet w. Motlu Konuk).
    PoNow (23) 79, p. 46.
"From Sofia" (tr. of Nazim Hikmet w. Motlu Konuk). PoNow
    (24) 79, p. 20.
"Hog Heaven. " PoNow (23) 79, p. 19.
"New Smyrna Beach. " PoNow (23) 79, p. 19.
"Night Music. " VirQR (55:3) Sum 79, p. 513.
"Poem: This year, early fall in the far south" (tr. of Nazim
    Hikmet w. Motlu Konuk). PoNow (24) 79, p. 20.
"Postcard. " DenQ (14:3) Aut 79, p. 98.
"Sailing into Winter. " PoNow (23) 79, p. 18.
"Small Potatoes. " PoNow (23) 79, p. 18.
"Sonora Wildflowers. " WestHR (33:3) Sum 79, p. 203.
"Walt Whitman Speaking. " PoNow (23) 79, p. 19.

BLAUNER, Laurie
"Billiards. " GreenfieldR (7:3/4) Spr-Sum 79, p. 249.
"The Tropics. " GreenfieldR (7:3/4) Spr-Sum 79, p. 250.

BLAZEK, Douglas
  "The Lyric Prince. " PoNow (22) 79, p. 6.
  "The Man Who Killed Himself into Life. " PoNow (22) 79, p. 6.
  "The Robbery. " PoNow (23) 79, p. 20.
  "Snapshot of the Fever. " PoNow (23) 79, p. 20.
  "Special Favors for Reality. " PoNow (23) 79, p. 38.
  "Straightening the Warp. " PoNow (23) 79, p. 20.
  "Woman in an Amber Room. " PoNow (22) 79, p. 6.

BLESSING, Richard
  "Dust Jacket. " PoetryNW (20:2) Sum 79, pp. 22-23.
  "Soccer Practice. " PoetryNW (20:2) Sum 79, pp. 21-22.

BLEVINS, Earl, Jr.
  "Self-Portrait. " Tendril (6) Aut 79, p. 9.

BLOCH, Chana
  "Deep Calleth unto Deep" (tr. of Dahlia Ravikovitch). PoNow
    (24) 79, p. 33.
  "The Tearing" (tr. of Dahlia Ravikovitch). PoNow (24) 79, p.
    33.

BLOCK, Ron
  "Moving from the Farm. " NewL (46:1) Aut 79, p. 49.

BLOOMFIELD, Maureen
  "Gift. " Nat (228:6) 17 F 79, p. 182.

BLOSSOM, Laurel
  "Another Woman. " Pequod (3:2) 79, p. 31.
  "April. " Pequod (3:2) 79, p. 32.
  "Local. " Pequod (3:2) 79, p. 30.
  "Someplace Hot. " Pequod (3:2) 79, p. 33.

BLUE, Jane
  "What the Sybil Saw. " Chomo (6:1) Sum 79, p. 70.

BLUE CLOUD, Peter (Aroniawenrate)
  "A Poet for Dinner. " Montra (5) 79, p. 112.
  "Sixteen Postholes. " BelPoJ (30:2) Wint 79-80, p. 11.

BLUGER, Marianne
  "Easter Poem. " ChrC (96:13) 11 Ap 79, p. 402.

BLUM, Etta
  "The Big Thing. " PoNow (22) 79, p. 6.
  "Retrospective. " PoNow (21) 79, p. 6.

BLY, Robert
  "The Clock Struck... " (tr. of Antonio Machado). MissouriR
    (3:1) Aut 79, p. 12.
  "The Cry Going Out over Pastures. " PoNow (22) 79, p. 21.
  "Feeling at Home in the Body" (for Robert Creeley). GeoR

(33:1) Spr 79, p. 108.
"Galloping Horses. " PoNow (22) 79, p. 21.
"It's Possible That... " (tr. of Antonio Machado).   MissouriR
    (3:1) Aut 79, p. 12.
"Listening to a Friend's Easter Sermon" (for H. Kleven).
    CarlMis (17:2/3) Spr 79, p. 13.
"Prayer Service in an English Church. " GeoR (33:2) Sum 79,
    p. 277.
"Small Poem. " CarlMis (17:2/3) Spr 79, p. 13.

BOBROWSKI, Johannes
"Latvian Songs" (tr. by Almut McAuley).   NewOR (6:3) 79, p.
    219.

BOCK, Frederick
"Champs. " Poetry (133:6) Mr 79, p. 331.
"Hatching. " Ascent (4:2) 79, p. 50.

BOCK, Layeh
"Myths, Most of These. " NewOR (6:3) 79, p. 228.

BOE, Deborah
"Affluence. " HangL (36) Aut 79, p. 4.
"Back Yards. " HangL (36) Aut 79, p. 2.
"Hibernant. " SmPd (45) 79, p. 25.
"Insomnia. " Kayak (52) D 79, p. 53.
"The Left Hand. " Kayak (52) D 79, p. 52.
"Miscarriage. " HangL (36) Aut 79, p. 5.

BOENIG, Robert
"Vaughan Williams. " JnlONJP (3:2) 79, p. 18.

BOESKY, Amy
"Conch. " Harp (258:1547) Ap 79, p. 93.
"Father. " Atl (244:1) Jl 79, p. 60.
"North of Grayling. " Madem (85:8) Ag 79, p. 150.

BOGEN, Don
"Glass Music. " NewRep (180:26) 30 Je 79, p. 34.

BOGEN, Laurel Ann
"27 Years of Madness. " SeC (6:1) 78, p. 22.

BOGIN, George
"Alone in the House. " SouthernHR (13:2) Spr 79, p. 162.

BOHNEN, James
"Drying the Laundry. " Tendril (5) Sum 79, p. 13.
"Girl Scout Round-up Site, 1959. " Tendril (5) Sum 79, p. 12.

BOLAND, Eavan
"On Renoir's 'The Grape Pickers'. " Ploughs (5:1) 79, p. 21.

BOLTON, Charles E.
"Regarding My Father. " SouthernPR (19:2) Aut 79, p. 22.
"Twin. " Shen (30:1) Aut 78, p. 56.

BONAZZI, Alfredo
"I've Dreamed of Escaping" (tr. by Frank Judge). PoNow (24)
    79, p. 6.
"Port Azzurro Prison" (tr. by Frank Judge). PoNow (24) 79,
    p. 6.

BONAZZI, Robert
"Ancient Music. " PoNow (22) 79, p. 6.
"Cat Found Alive in Elevator Shaft. " SouthwR (64:4) Aut 79, p.
    377.
"That Prodigy. " PoNow (22) 79, p. 6.

BOND, Harold
"Love Note. " SouthernPR (19:1) Spr 79, p. 36.
"Swallowing. " Ploughs (5:3) 79, p. 82.

BOND, Pearl
"Poetry Reading. " PoNow (23) 79, p. 32.

BONNER, Carrington
"Untitled 650. " BlackF (3:1) Aut-Wint 79, p. 24.

BONOMO, J.
"Believing the World Is Round. " StoneC (6:2) My 79, p. 22.

BONOMO, Jacquelyn
"Two Modern Men, a Woman, and a Dog: A Short Story. "
    MassR (20:2) Sum 79, p. 243.

BOOKER, Betty
"April in Virginia. " Wind (32) 79, p. 45.

BOOMGAARDEN, Don
"Runners. " TexQ (21:2) Aut 78, p. 125.

BOOTH, Philip
"Before Sleep. " PoetryNW (20:2) Sum 79, p. 47.
"Calendar. " Field (20) Spr 79, p. 8.
"Generation. " MissouriR (3:1) Aut 79, p. 33.
"The Great American Poem. " Antaeus (32) Wint 79, pp. 82-86.
"Hunt. " Ploughs (5:3) 79, p. 34.
"Liv. " NewL (46:1) Aut 79, p. 47.
"Ossipee: November. " NewYorker (55:38) 5 N 79, p. 51.
"Out of the Ordinary. " Field (20) Spr 79, p. 7.
"Predispositions. " Kayak (50) My 79, p. 23.
"Sorting It Out. " Ploughs (5:3) 79, p. 33.
"Thoreau Near Home. " NewYorker (55:15) 28 My 79, p. 40.
"Woman: A Mirror. " GeoR (33:2) Sum 79, p. 422.

BORAKS, Jagna
"The Algonquin of the Lake of Two Rivers. " MalR (49) Ja 79,
p. 96.
"Glass" (tr. of Andrzej Busza). MalR (49) Ja 79, p. 94.
"Witchcraft" (tr. of Andrzej Busza). MalR (49) Ja 79, p. 95.

BORAWSKI, Walta
"Cruising Athletes from a Sunny Window in Lamont. " Mouth
(2:3) N 79, p. 55.
"Didn't That Bother You. " Mouth (2:1) F 79, p. 40.
"For Dorothy Parker, Emily Dickinson, and Charley Shively. "
Mouth (2:1) F 79, p. 26.
"Hunger. " Mouth (2:1) F 79, p. 38.
"Loveability zero. " Mouth (2:3) N 79, p. 44.
"On the Roof. " Mouth (2:3) N 79, p. 42.
"Surprising Kisses" (for Malcolm). Mouth (2:1) F 79, p. 24.
"Three Poems from the Pompeii Exhibit" (for Greg Parks).
Mouth (2:1) F 79, p. 8.
"Voyeur. " Mouth (2:2) Je 79, p. 1.
"Wool-gathering. " Aspect (74/75) Ja-Ag 79, p. 57.

BORDERS, J. B.
"Idling in a Hotbed. " Obs (4:3) Wint 78, pp. 68-69.
"Sway back Boogie Scatter-Brained Blues (or, last year for
heart failure). " Obs (4:3) Wint 78, pp. 66-68.

BORENSTEIN, Emily
"Death Watch. " GreenfieldR (7:3/4) Spr-Sum 79, p. 60.

BORGES, Jorge Luis
"Benares" (tr. by Irvine Frost Upham). TexQ (21:4) Wint 78,
p. 7.
"A Dream" (tr. by Alastair Reid). NewEngR (1:4) Sum 79, p.
469.
"Ein Traum" (tr. by Norman Thomas di Giovanni). SunM (8)
Aut 79, p. 6.
"Of Heaven and Hell" (tr. by Irvine Frost Upham). TexQ (21:4)
Wint 78, p. 9.
"A Prospect (Un Mañana)" (tr. by Irvine Frost Upham). TexQ
(21:4) Wint 78, p. 12.
"Rosas" (tr. by Irvine Frost Upham). TexQ (21:4) Wint 78, p.
6.
"Simón Carbajal" (tr. by Irvine Frost Upham). TexQ (21:4) Wint
78, p. 10.
"Things That Might Have Been" (tr. by Alastair Reid).
NewEngR (1:4) Sum 79, p. 468.
"To a Caesar" (tr. by Irvine Frost Upham). TexQ (21:4) Wint
78, p. 11.
"To Francisco López Merino" (tr. by Irvine Frost Upham).
TexQ (21:4) Wint 78, p. 8.

BORICH, Michael
"A Farmer's Death. " KanQ (11:1/2) Wint-Spr 79, p. 184.
"In This Light. " NewYorker (55:37) 29 O 79, p. 105.

BOSS, Laura
"My Ringless Fingers on the Steering Wheel Tell the Story. "
JnlONJP (4:1) 79, p. 28.
"Overhearing My Thirteen-Year-Old Son Tell the Kid Next Door. "
JnlONJP (3:2) 79, p. 32.
"A Penny For. " JnlONJP (4:1) 79, p. 30.

BOTTOMS, David
"The Drunk Hunter. " PoNow (25) 79, p. 19.
"Jamming with the Band at the VFW. " PoNow (25) 79, p. 19.
"The Orchid. " GreenfieldR (7:3/4) Spr-Sum 79, p. 197.
"A Trucker Breaks Down. " SouthernR (15:2) Spr 79, p. 414.
"Wrestling Angels" (for J. and Diana Stege). Antaeus (33) Spr
79, p. 130.

BOTTRALL, Ronald
"Aspects of Darkness. " Poetry (135:1) O 79, p. 29.

BOUCHEY, Myrna
"Communing at Midnight. " MalR (52) O 79, p. 97.

BOULLATA, Kamal J.
"Color of Memory: Color of Blood" (tr. of Amira al-Zein).
Paint (12) Aut 79, p. 31.

BOWDEN, Michael
"Across the Line. " Tendril (6) Aut 79, p. 12.
"Cuervos Bailan" (para Maria). GreenfieldR (7:3/4) Spr-Sum 79,
p. 82.
"Dancing with the Ghost" (for Marty). GreenfieldR (7:3/4) Spr-
Sum 79, p. 83.
"Photograph: Deer. " Tendril (4) Wint 79, p. 11.
from The River People: "The Farmer's Wife. " Wind (33) 79,
p. 7.
"Skinning the Fox" (for Roger). Tendril (6) Aut 79, p. 10.

BOWEN, James K.
"Debris. " YaleR (69:2) Wint 80, p. 259.
"Feather River Canyon. " YaleR (69:2) Wint 80, p. 260.
"Rain. " KanQ (11:3) Sum 79, p. 74.

BOWEN, Keith
Poem. St. AR (5:2) 79, p. 63.

BOWERS, Neal
"Archetypes. " SouthernPR (19:2) Aut 79, p. 30.
"Saying. " BallSUF (20:1) Wint 79, p. 80.
"Unplanned Design. " BallSUF (20:1) Wint 79, p. 74.

BOWMAN, P. C.
"Our Cook, the Poet" (for Elizabeth Libbey). PoetryNW (20:1)
Spr 79, pp. 24-26.
"Route 95 North: New Jersey. " KanQ (11:1/2) Wint-Spr 79, p.
102.

BOYCHUK, Bohdan
"My Sister, Life" (tr. of Boris Pasternak w. Mark Rudman).
PoNow (24) 79, p. 42.
"The Purpose of Soul" (tr. of Boris Pasternak w. Mark Rud-
man). PoNow (24) 79, p. 42.

BRADD, William
"Five Riders in Cardinal Red. " BelPoJ (30:2) Wint 79-80, p.
35.

BRADHAM, Jo Allen
"Crushing Moths. " Poem (35) Mr 79, p. 30.
"Garden Apartment. " Poem (35) Mr 79, p. 28.
"Maude Again. " Poem (35) Mr 79, p. 29.

BRADLEY, George
"An Arrangement of Sunlight at Hagia Sophia. " Poetry (134:2)
My 79, p. 86.
"Committed to Memory. " Poetry (134:2) My 79, p. 88.
"Escape. " Poetry (134:2) My 79, p. 87.
"In Bed with a River. " ParisR (75) Spr 79, p. 199.
"A Palaeologan Apology. " Shen (30:1) Aut 78, p. 45.
"Swing One, Swing All. " MichQR (18:2) Spr 79, p. 217.

BRADLEY, Sam
"Casual Meeting. " ArizQ (35:4) Wint 79, p. 392.
"Counter-Encounter. " TexQ (21:3) Aut 78, p. 64.
"A Fair Sleeper in an Ancient Grave. " Wind (35) 79, p. 36.
"Gifts. " ChrC (96:10) 21 Mr 79, p. 301.
"Landfall. " SouthernHR (13:1) Wint 79, p. 12.
"A Lifting of Guilt. " SouthwR (64:2) Spr 79, p. 139.
"That Otherness, Never Known. " TexQ (21:3) Aut 78, p. 65.
"Wings That Fly and Yet Remain. " Northeast (3:7) Spr 79, p. 4.

BRADY, Dan
"black hair beaten. " Ur (2) 79, p. 10.

BRADY, Elmer
"Hard Times for Merlin. " GreenfieldR (7:3/4) Spr-Sum 79, p.
161.

BRAMBACH, Rainer
Thirteen Poems (tr. by Stuart Friebert). QW (6) Spr-Sum 78,
pp. 42-46.

BRAND, Alice Glarden
"In the Drizzle. " JnlONJP (3:2) 79, p. 43.
"Keep That Good Eye, Mr. Fritz. " EngJ (68:5) My 79, p. 33.
"Still Life. " JnlONJP (3:2) 79, p. 44.

BRAND, Millen
"About my Brother, Radio Operator. " Im (6:1) 79, p. 7.
"Night Scene, Inside. " HangL (35) Spr 79, p. 16.
"Thirty Childbirths. " Harp (258:1548) My 79, p. 105.

BRANIN, Jeff
"A Billboard in Las Palmas. " WormR (73) 79, p. 13.
"the movie on 29/a farewell to arms. " Ur (2) 79, p. 11.
"My Tho To Saigon. " GreenfieldR (7:3/4) Spr-Sum 79, p. 188.
"Vogelweh BOQ. " Ur (2) 79, p. 12.

BRANTINGHAM, Philip
"Sarentino--South Tyrol. " AmerS (48:3) Sum 79, p. 298.

BRASCH, Thomas
"Song" (tr. by Almut McAuley). NewOR (6:3) 79, p. 225.

BRASFIELD, James
"The Stringer. " Columbia (3) 79, p. 74.

BRASH, Edward
"Les Demoiselles of Piney Woods. " Poetry (134:5) Ag 79, pp.
    285-286.

BRASHERS, Charles
"Poem After a Speech by Chief Seattle, 1855. " DenQ (14:2) Sum
    79, p. 56.

BRAUER, Ann
"Virginia Woolf Walked to the River. " SoDakR (17:2) Sum 79,
    pp. 17-21.

BRAUN, Volker
"Of That Which Is Somehow Living" (tr. by Almut McAuley).
    NewOR (6:3) 79, p. 224.

BREAZEALE, Daniel
"Honeycombs on the Boulevard. " NewL (46:2) Wint 79-80, p. 42.
"Pocketed Hand. " NewL (46:2) Wint 79-80, p. 43.

BREEN, Nancy
"Morning Glories. " WindO (34) Spr-Sum 79, p. 37.

BREHM, Gregory
"The Tides of Day and Night" (for Octavio Paz) (w. Harry Has-
    kell). Mund (11:1) 79, p. 48.

BRENNAN, Matthew
"The First Anniversary. " Wind (35) 79, p. 5.

BRENT, Jonathan
"To A. A. Akhmatova" (tr. of Joseph Brodsky). AmerS (48:1)
    Wint 78-79, p. 81.

BRESLIN, Paul
"Accuser. " Poetry (134:2) My 79, p. 70.
"Meditations on the Field Museum. " Poetry (134:2) My 79, pp.
    63-69.

BRETON, Jean
  "Seul comme une bête. " Mund (11:1) 79, p. 68.
  "Tu es revenue. " Mund (11:1) 79, p. 70.

BRETT, Peter
  "Blue Whale. " Chelsea (38) 79, p. 173.
  "Lopez the proprietor. " Ur (2) 79, p. 13.
  "Night Teeth. " CimR (48) Jl 79, p. 42.
  "Pickers. " Tendril (6) Aut 79, p. 13.
  from Seasons in Mexico: "The Ghost of God. " Wind (35) 79,
     p. 6.
  "Vulture. " Chelsea (38) 79, p. 196.

BREWER, Kenneth
  "How the Outhouse School of Art Fell from Grace. " Spirit (3:3)
     Sum 78, p. 45.
  "Shadows of Danaë. " StoneC (6:3) O 79, p. 24.
  "Woman in the Gallery. " StoneC (6:3) O 79, p. 24.

BRIGHAM, Besmilr
  "Builder Bird, carpintero. " Confr (19) Aut 79-Wint 80, p. 40.
  "Sleeping All Night at Dickinson's Clinic. " SouthwR (64:1) Wint
     79, p. 42.
  "The Young Whip Moccasin. " Confr (18) Spr-Sum 79, p. 92.

BRINGHURST, Robert
  "The Long and the Short of It. " NewOR (6:2) 79, p. 155.

BRINTON, George
  "Admonition for Cathode Ray Computer Terminal. " SouthwR
     (64:4) Aut 79, p. 322.

BRISBY, Stewart
  "Yuletide on 9th St. " Ur (2) 79, p. 14.

BRITT, Alan W.
  "Bedridden, and Not Caring About the Bicentennial. " UTR (6:3/4)
     79, p. 5.
  "Heavy Snow. " UTR (6:3/4) 79, p. 7.
  "Industrial Disease. " UTR (6:3) 79, p. 8.
  from Malaise: (# 44). UTR (6:3/4) 79, p. 4.
  from Malaise: (# 85). UTR (6:3/4) 79, p. 3.
  "Wolf Eyes. " UTR (6:3/4) 79, p. 6.

BRITTON, Donald
  "Capital Life. " SunM (8) Aut 79, p. 103.
  "Plusieurs Jours" (for Bernard Welt). SunM (8) Aut 79, p. 99.

BROADDUS, William
  "The Oldest Woman. " HangL (36) Aut 79, p. 74.

BROCK, Edwin
  "Holy Cow. " Poetry (133:5) F 79, p. 282.

"To His Love in Middle Age. " Poetry (133:5) F 79, pp.
   280-281.

BROCK, Randall
   "as. " SmPd (46) 79, p. 10.
   "the deep: lush. " Wind (33) 79, p. 10.
   "in: a rancid. " Wind (33) 79, p. 10.
   "in: a slice. " Wind (33) 79, p. 10.
   "in: the sore. " Wind (33) 79, p. 19.
   "Poem: in/the. " SmPd (46) 79, p. 10.

BROCK, Van K.
   "The Great American Poem. " Antaeus (32) Wint 79, pp. 82-86.

BROCK-BROIDO, Lucie
   "On the Poem: The Rh Variations. " Shen (30:4) 79, pp. 62-67.

BROCKWAY, Michael
   "wilde. " SmPd (46) 79, p. 13.

BRODSKY, Joseph
   "I Sit by the Window" (tr. by Howard Moss). NewYorker (55:16)
      4 Je 79, p. 34.
   from A Part of Speech. NewYRB (26:20) 20 D 79, p. 15.
   "Plato Elaborated" (tr. by George L. Kline). NewYorker (55:4)
      12 Mr 79, p. 40.
   "San Pietro" (tr. by Barry Rubin). NewYorker (55:11) 30 Ap
      79, p. 38.
   "Six Years Later" (tr. by Richard Wilbur). NewYorker (54:46)
      1 Ja 79, p. 30.
   "To A. A. Akhmatova" (tr. by Jonathan Brent). AmerS (48:1)
      Wint 78-79, p. 81.

BRODSKY, Louis Daniel
   "Buffalo. " BallSUF (20:1) Wint 79, p. 45.
   "Weeding in January. " FourQt (28:2) Wint 79, p. 3.

BROMIGE, David
   "My Career. " PartR (46:3) 79, pp. 423-25.

BRONK, William
   "What Form the World Has. " Montra (5) 79, p. 243.

BROOK, Donna
   "Crazy in Denver" (for Bob Hershon). HangL (36) Aut 79, p. 6.
   "The Deaf and Dumb Café. " Kayak (50) My 79, p. 29.
   "Little House on the Prairie. " HangL (36) Aut 79, p. 8.
   "The Madness of Vegetables. " HangL (36) Aut 79, p. 9.
   "Say What. " Kayak (50) My 79, p. 30.

BROOKS, David
   "From Weilan. " NewEngR (2:1) Aut 79, p. 94.
   "On Durras Beach. " NewEngR (2:1) Aut 79, p. 92.
   "One of the Last Nights. " NewEngR (2:1) Aut 79, p. 93.

BROOKS, Robert A.
"Litany for a Later Day. " Atl (243:1) Ja 79, p. 77.

BROSMAN, Catharine Savage
"At Night, in a Child's Room. " SewanR (87:4) Aut 79, p. 530.
"Postcard. " SewanR (87:4) Aut 79, p. 531.
"St. Armand's Key. " SewanR (87:4) Aut 79, p. 528.

BROUGHTON, T. Alan
"Apple Wine 1975" (for Camm). Chowder (12) Spr-Sum 79, p.
    26.
"The Bather. " SouthernHR (13:1) Wint 79, p. 78.
"Flowers for Elizabeth. " SouthernHR (13:4) Aut 79, p. 308.
"Leaving the Clearing. " Confr (18) Spr-Sum 79, p. 34.
"Love. " PoNow (21) 79, p. 33.
"Sex. " PoNow (21) 79, p. 33.
"To Market to Market. " SouthernHR (13:1) Wint 79, p. 62.

BROUMAS, Olga
"Banner. " 13thM (4:2) 79, p. 22.
"Blockade. " 13thM (4:2) 79, p. 19.
"Body and Soul. " Agni (10/11) 79, p. 44.
"Elegy. " Agni (10/11) 79, p. 45.
"Landscape with Driver" (for Stephen). 13thM (4:2) 79, p. 21.
"Landscape with Mantra. " NowestR (18:2) 79, p. 19.

BROUTHERS, Paul S.
"Lover. " Mouth (2:2) Je 79, p. 4.
"a man enters my life with no fanfare. " Mouth (2:2) Je 79, p.
    4.

BROWN, Allan G.
"Bar Fishing" (for Tony). MalR (49) Ja 79, p. 30.

BROWN, Beth
"Daily Poems. " Obs (4:3) Wint 78, pp. 84-88.
"For Whom It Is Too Late Now. " Obs (4:3) Wint 78, p. 83.

BROWN, Michael R.
"The Hawk. " WormR (73) 79, p. 27.

BROWN, Rebecca
"A Day Saved by Landscape. " Tele (15) Spr 79, p. 124.
"Emily D. " Tele (15) Spr 79, p. 126.
"Memories Won't Buy You Soup. " Tele (15) Spr 79, p. 125.
"To Bill Berkson. " Tele (15) Spr 79, p. 126.
"Wonder If I Could Feel So Good. " Tele (15) Spr 79, p. 123.

BROWN, Russell M.
"Times of Uncertainty. " LitR (22:3) Spr 79, p. 357.

BROWN, Sam
"Ned Ludd and the Dream of the Indian Maiden. " Stand (20:1)
    78-79, p. 23.

BROWN, Spencer
  "Light and Darkness. " SewanR (87:3) Sum 79, p. 375.
  "Punctuation. " Bits (9) Ja 79.

BROWN, Steven Ford
  "Beethoven. " PoNow (22) 79, p. 7.
  "Erections. " PoNow (22) 79, p. 7.
  "I Have Come. " Wind (35) 79, p. 7.
  "Love Song of the Artist to His Model 2. " Wind (35) 79, p. 7.
  "The Story of Two Lovers. " PoNow (22) 79, p. 7.
  "Year of the Snowed-in Moon. " Ur (2) 79, p. 16.

BROWN, Terry W.
  "The Last Fire. " KanQ (11:3) Sum 79, p. 100.
  "The Mountain. " KanQ (11:1/2) Wint-Spr 79, p. 154.
  "Shame. " KanQ (11:1/2) Wint-Spr 79, p. 153.

BROWN, Tom
  from A Collection of Miscellany Poems: "An Epitaph upon the
      Charming Peggy. " Playb (26:4) Ap 79, p. 169.
  from A Collection of Miscellany Poems: "The Claret Drinker's
      Song, or, The Good Fellow's Design. " Playb (26:4) Ap 79,
      p. 169.
  from A Collection of Miscellany Poems: "The Old Fumbler. "
      Playb (26:4) Ap 79, p. 169.
  from A Collection of Miscellany Poems: "The Poet's Condition. "
      Playb (26:4) Ap 79, p. 169.

BROWNE, Michael Dennis
  "The Great American Poem. " Antaeus (32) Wint 79, pp. 82-86.
  "March Day. " Atl (243:4) Ap 79, p. 87.

BROWNING, Stephen
  "And Count Myself a King of Infinite Space. " MichQR (18:2) Spr
      79, p. 343.

BROWNLOW, Timothy
  "Ars Poetica. " MalR (51) Jl 79, p. 99.

BROWNSTEIN, Michael
  "California. " PoNow (22) 79, p. 7.
  from Oracle Night, A Love Poem: "She wanted to be the re-
      ceiver of everything. " SunM (8) Aut 79, pp. 39-47.

BRUCE, Lennart
  "The Girl" (tr. of Agneta Ava). Spirit (4:2/3) Spr-Sum 79, p.
      51.
  "I really want to make love differently" (tr. of Gurli Linden).
      Spirit (4:2/3) Spr-Sum 79, p. 53.
  from The Impossible: (50) (tr. of Goran Sonnevi). PoNow (24)
      79, p. 57.
  from The Impossible: (76) (tr. of Goran Sonnevi). PoNow (24)
      79, p. 57.

from The Impossible: (82) (tr. of Goran Sonnevi).   PoNow (24)
    79, p. 57.
from The Impossible: (83) (tr. of Goran Sonnevi).   PoNow (24)
    79, p. 57.
from The Impossible: (90) (tr. of Goran Sonnevi).   PoNow (24)
    79, p. 57.
from The Impossible: (180) (tr. of Goran Sonnevi).   PoNow (24)
    79, p. 57.
"Motif" (tr. of Par Lagerkvist).   PoNow (24) 79, p. 23.
"The Ride. "   Spirit (4:2/3) Spr-Sum 79, p. 50.
"We had all the possibilities in the world" (tr. of Agneta Ara).
    Spirit (4:2/3) Spr-Sum 79, p. 52.

BRUCHAC, Joseph
"The Burning. "   EnPas (8) 79, p. 15.
"The Buffalo Skull. " SeC (6:1) 78, p. 40.
"Calling Rain. "   SeC (6:1) 78, p. 39.
"Crotalus. "   Chelsea (38) 79, p. 222.
"The Dreaming Place. "   Spirit (3:1/2) Aut-Wint 77-78, p. 20.
"Fort Still, Oklahoma, June 1978. "   VirQR (55:2) Spr 79, p. 302.
"Hearing the River. "   PikeR (1) Sum 79, p. 64.
"Horses in a Field Near Fort Ann. "   StoneC (6:2) My 79, p. 25.
"Killing Chickens. "   Salm (46) Aut 79, p. 93.
"Migration. "   PikeR (1) Sum 79, p. 65.
"Night Flight. "   Nimrod (23:1) Aut-Wint 79, p. 19.
"The Release. "   Bits (10) Jl 79.
"The Star-Nosed Mole. "   EnPas (8) 79, p. 14.
"Sunlight" (for Swift Eagle).   VirQR (55:2) Spr 79, p. 303.
"That Cave. "   WestB (4) 79, p. 50.
"Tonawanda. "   Spirit (3:1/2) Aut-Wint 77-78, p. 21.
"Walking Bear. "   BelPoJ (30:2) Wint 79-80, p. 3.
"Wichita Range Haiku. "   HolCrit (16:4) O 79, p. 20.

BRUNER, Mark
"birthday poem. "   Wind (35) 79, p. 9.

BRUSH, Thomas
"Another Rough Draft. "   PoetryNW (20:4) Wint 79-80, pp. 19-20.
"Don't Go. "   QW (8) Wint 79, p. 99.
"DooDah. "   PoetryNW (20:4) Wint 79-80, pp. 20-21.
"Oakland. "   QW (8) Wint 79, p. 98.

BRYANT, Tammy
"The Deer. "   PikeF (2) Wint 78-79, p. 17.

BUCHANAN, Marian
"In the Spaces of Sleep" (tr. of Robert Desnos).   AmerPoR (8:1)
    Ja-F 79, p. 21.
"No Love Is Not Dead" (tr. of Robert Desnos).   AmerPoR (8:1)
    Ja-F 79, p. 21.

BUCKHOLTS, Claudia
"The Freedom of the Will. "   HiramPoR (26) Spr-Sum 79, p. 15.

BUCKLEY, Christopher
"Amedeo Modigliani. " Antaeus (34) Sum 79, p. 84.
"Flowers. " Poetry (134:4) Jl 79, pp. 210-211.
"For Aunt Tade Ironing in Lexington. " SlowLR (3) 79, p. 66.
"Gangrene (last note to a composition teacher). " Sky (9) Aut 79,
    pp. 21-23.
"Heartland" (for James Riley Miller). SlowLR (3) 79, p. 64.
"The Homeward Star. " SlowLR (3) 79, p. 69.
"January" (for Aunt Shelly). MissouriR (2:2/3) Spr 79, p. 45.
"Last Rites" (for Gary Soto). NewEngR (2:1) Aut 79, p. 54.
"The Letters of Summer. " Poetry (134:4) Jl 79, p. 212.
"On Being Whole. " Chelsea (38) 79, p. 197.
"On Bosch's 'Christ Taken Captive'" (for Sherod Santos).
    NewEngR (2:1) Aut 79, p. 56.
"Other Lives. " CharR (5:2) Aut 79, p. 19.
"Resignation to Patience at the Irvine Bird Refuge. " NewEngR
    (2:1) Aut 79, p. 57.
"To Us, Taken Off by Wind. " Antaeus (34) Sum 79, p. 87.

BUCKNER, Sally
"No Deposit, No Return. " ChrC (96:11) 28 Mr 79, p. 342.

BUDBILL, David
"Abraham Washington Davis. " BelPoJ (30:1) Aut 79, p. 4.
"Antoine on the Bowser Factory, Free Enterprise, Women,
    Love and Loneliness. " BelPoJ (30:1) Aut 79, p. 2.
"Raymond and Ann. " Harp (259:1553) O 79, p. 77.

BUDIN, Sue
"leaves. " AAR (29) 79, p. 39.

BUESA, Jose Angel
"We Walk Between Shadows" (tr. by James Normington). PoNow
    (24) 79, p. 6.

BUGDEN, Roger
"Pastoral History. " Stand (20:1) 78-79, p. 24.
"Prophesy. " Stand (20:1) 78-79, p. 24.

BUISSON, Justine
"Like Roethke, for Instance. " CimR (49) O 79, p. 15.

BUKOWSKI, Charles
"A Boy and His Dog. " SeC (6:1) 78, p. 6.
"Crisscross Under Sideways. " SeC (7:1) 79, p. 1.
"Downtown. " SeC (6:1) 78, p. 1.
"The Great American Poem. " Antaeus (32) Wint 79, pp. 82-86.
"The Immortals. " WormR (76) 79, p. 155.
"The Indian. " SeC (7:1) 79, p. 4.
"Interview. " WormR (74) 79, p. 69.
"The Ladies Who Rip Men Apart. " SeC (6:1) 78, p. 5.
"The Lady With the Dog. " WormR (73) 79, p. 37.
"Nana. " WormR (73) 79, p. 39.

"An Observer. " WormR (76) 79, p. 158.
"The Old Quarterback. " SeC (6:1) 78, p. 3.
"Rock. " WormR (74) 79, p. 73.
"2nd Street, Near Hollister, in Santa Monica. " WormR (76) 79,
     p. 157.
"Sibelius and Etc. " WormR (76) 79, p. 156.
"Silk. " WormR (76) 79, p. 157.
"Social. " WormR (74) 79, p. 68.
"Tongue-Cut. " WormR (74) 79, p. 73.
"Within My Own Madness. " WormR (74) 79, p. 72.

BULLIS, Jerald
"Alpenglow. " CarlMis (17:2/3) Spr 79, p. 168.
"For Fran. " NewEngR (2:1) Aut 79, p. 21.
"Revelation. " Hudson (32:4) Wint 79-80, p. 537.

BUNDY, Elroy L.
"Isthmian 5" (for Phylákidas of Aigína) (tr. of Pindar).
     SouthernR (15:4) Aut 79, p. 1022.
"Olympian 4" (for Psaumis of Kamarina) (tr. of Pindar).
     SouthernR (15:4) Aut 79, p. 1017.
"Olympian 11" (for Hagesidámus of Epizephýrian Lokris) (tr. of
     Pindar). SouthernR (15:4) Aut 79, p. 1019.
"Olympian 12" (for Ergóteles of Himera) (tr. of Pindar).
     SouthernR (15:4) Aut 79, p. 1020.
"Olympian 14" (for Asópikhos of Orchómenos) (tr. of Pindar).
     SouthernR (15:4) Aut 79, p. 1021.

BUNTING, Basil
"Per Che No Spero. " Montra (5) 79, p. 13.
"Snow's on the fellside, look." How deep. " Montra (5) 79, p.
     14.
"You, with my enemy, strolling down my street. " Montra (5)
     79, p. 15.

BURDEN, Jean
"Poem for a Birthday. " TexQ (21:4) Wint 78, p. 89.

BURINE, Claude de
"Montagne. " GRR (10:3) 79, p. 100.

BURKARD, Michael
"Houses at Night. " MissouriR (2:2/3) Spr 79, p. 21.
"The Unbeautiful Banker. " MissouriR (2:2/3) Spr 79, p. 18.

BURKE, Daniel, F. S. C.
"The Bear. " Comm (106:8) 27 Ap 79, p. 230.
"The Teacher to Heloise (After Waddell). " Comm (106:17) 28 S
     79, p. 534.

BURKE, France
"Inpatient Days. " Confr (19) Aut 79-Wint 80, p. 113.

BURLINGAME, Robert
"Common Day. " DacTerr (16) 79, p. 6.
"Listening to the Kansas Wind" (for E. N. B.).   KanQ (11:1/2)
    Wint-Spr 79, p. 218.

BURNES, Carol
"Adoption" (for Sarah).   13thM (4:2) 79, p. 77.

BURNEY, Jeanette
"Magdalena. "   Shen (30:2) Wint 79, p. 49.

BURNHAM, Deborah
"Breathing" (for Paul Desmond).   KanQ (11:3) Sum 79, p. 62.
"Floating in Fairport Harbor. "   AmerPoR (8:2) Mr-Ap 79, p. 43.
"Hypnotist. "   AmerPoR (8:2) Mr. Ap 79, p. 43.
"Nullipara. "   WestB (5) 79, p. 9.

BURNHAM, Philip
"Nine Photographs of Descartes. "   Poetry (135:3) D 79, pp. 137-
    141.

BURNS, Ralph
"Dear Father,. "   Southern PR (19:1) Spr 79, p. 53.
"Everyone Headed for the River. "   ColEng (41:1) S 79, p. 78.
"Revision. "   ColEng (41:1) S 79, p. 77.
"Sensualist. "   SouthernPR (19:1) Spr 79, p. 54.
"Teaching at Oxford Federal Prison. "   GreenfieldR (7:3/4) Spr-
    Sum 79, p. 69.
"Us. "   NowestR (18:2) 79, p. 18.

BURNS, Richard
"Second Death" (for Rini).   SouthernR (15:1) Wint 79, p. 135.
"The Woods. "   MalR (51) Jl 79, p. 116.

BURNS, Robert
"My Girl. "   Playb (26:1) Ja 79, p. 257.

BURNS, Thomas LaBorie
"A Future Archeologist Finds a Beer Can. "   SmPd (45) 79, p. 6.
"Goodbye Poem" (for E.).   SmPd (45) 79, p. 8.
"Lucia Regina at World Famous Copacabana Beach. "   SmPd (45)
    79, p. 9.
"This Knife, for Example. "   SmPd (45) 79, p. 7.

BURR, Gray
"Black Widow. "   PoNow (21) 79, p. 36.
"Indian Summer. "   PoNow (23) 79, p. 34.

BURROWS, E. G.
"Eden Revisited. "   PoNow (21) 79, p. 20.
"The Farm--. "   PoNow (21) 79, p. 20.
"Gulliver. "   PoNow (21) 79, p. 20.
"How Those Stories Got Started. "   Epoch (28:3) Spr-Sum 79, p.
    269.

"Palo Duro. " PoNow (21) 79, p. 20.
Properties: A Play for Voices. QRL (21:1/2) 78, pp. 131-
    164.
"The Tower Above York. " Epoch (28:3) Spr-Sum 79, p. 267.

BURSK, Christopher
"Fed by the Ladies of Distinction. " Im (6:1) 79, p. 9.
"The German Schoolbell. " AntR (37:4) Aut 79, p. 452.
"Goliards. " Im (6:1) 79, p. 9.
"In the Narrow Kitchen. " LitR (22:3) Spr 79, p. 354.
"Keeping Store. " AntR (37:4) Aut 79, p. 448.
"Making Wings. " Im (6:1) 79, p. 8.
"No Hands. " LitR (22:3) Spr 79, p. 352.
"The Quick Harsh German We Spoke to the Crabs. " Im (6:1) 79,
    p. 8.
"The Secret Island of the Teachers. " AntR (37:4) Aut 79, p.
    450.
"Today the Men's Group Will Meet Outside. " Im (6:1) 79, p. 9.
"Tying My Wrists. " PoNow (23) 79, p. 41.

BURT, Don
"The Poolhall. " KanQ (11:1/2) Wint-Spr 79, p. 219.

BURT, John
"After the Thunderstorm. " Spirit (4:1) Aut-Wint 78-79, p. 44.
"Robert Falcon Scott Enters Paradise. " ChiR (30:4) Spr 79, p.
    9.

BURT, Lucile
"After All. " ColEng (40:7) Mr 79, p. 787.
"March. " Tendril (4) Wint 79, p. 12.
"The Memory, the Dream, the Vision. " Tendril (6) Aut 79, p.
    16.
"The Plumed Serpent. " Tendril (4) Wint 79, p. 13.
"Sleeping at the Beach. " Tendril (6) Aut 79, p. 14.
"Uxmal: The Top of the Temple at Daybreak. " Tendril (6) Aut
    79, p. 15.

BURTIS, William
"View from a Third Story Window on a Winter Afternoon. "
    Aspen (8) Aut 79, p. 66.

BURWELL, Rex
"Three Deaf-Mutes. " CimR (47) Ap 79, p. 46.

BUSCH, Trent
"The Church. " SouthernPR (19:1) Spr 79, p. 68.
"Clorice Henry. " CarolQ (31:2) Spr-Sum 79, p. 101.
"Country Church. " SmPd (47) 79, p. 24.
"Romey Davis. " CarolQ (31:2) Spr-Sum 79, p. 100.

BUSH, Barney
"Notes from British Columbia. " BelPoJ (30:2) Wint 79, pp. 25-29.

BUSZA, Andrzej
"Art and the Bitch" (tr. of Kazim'erz Wierzynski w. Bogdan
Czaykowski). Durak (3) 79, p. 14.
"Autumn scattering bitter cinnamon" (tr. of Jaroslaw Iwaszkie-
wicz w. Bogdan Czaykowski). Durak (3) 79, p. 15.
"A Fin-de-Siècle Myth" (tr. of Miron Bialoszewski w. Bogdan
Czaykowski). Durak (2) 79, p. 12.
"Glass" (tr. by Jagna Boraks). MalR (49) Ja 79, p. 94.
"I Don't Know How to Write" (tr. of Miron Bialoszewski w. Bog-
dan Czaykowski). Durak (2) 79, p. 13.
"Rembrandt" (tr. of Bogdan Ostromecki w. Bogdan Czaykowski).
Durak (3) 79, p. 13.
"White" (tr. of Mieczyslaw Jastrun w. Bogdan Czaykowski).
Durak (3) 79, p. 12.
"Witchcraft" (tr. by Jagna Boraks). MalR (49) Ja 79, p. 95.

BUTCHER, Grace
"The Would-Be Hero. " PoNow (22) 79, p. 7.

BUTKIE, Joseph D.
"Getting Hard-ons in Korea. " Mouth (2:2) Je 79, p. 32.
"Inexpensive Perfume. " Mouth (2:3) N 79, p. 51.
"Mid-Town St. Louis: at the Mikado. " Mouth (2:3) N 79, p. 47.
"Pilot. " Mouth (2:3) N 79, p. 46.
"Please. " Mouth (2:2) Je 79, p. 45.

BUTLER, Jack
"Afterglow. " NewYorker (55:27) 20 Ag 79, p. 32.
"Flood Stage. " PoetryNW (20:2) Sum 79, pp. 17-18.
"The Kid Who Wanted to Be a Spaceman. " NewOR (6:4) 79, pp.
332-334.
"Poem. " PoetryNW (20:2) Sum 79, p. 19.
"Two Isn't Much Better Than One or Real Numbers Ain't All In-
tegral. " PoetryNW (20:2) Sum 79, pp. 18-19.

BUTRICK, L. H.
"Getting Clear. " CarlMis (17:2/3) Spr 79, p. 43.

BUTRICK, Lyle
"Audience Participation. " LitR (22:3) Spr 79, p. 368.
"Listen IX. " LitR (22:3) Spr 79, p. 367.

BUTSCHER, Edward
"Keeper of Pigeons. " Confr (19) Aut 79-Wint 80, p. 91.

BUZZATI, Dino
"On the Crest of the Wave" (tr. by Ruth Feldman). Chowder
(12) Spr-Sum 79, p. 8.

BYLANDER, Linda Newmark
"Touch of Music. " SoDakR (17:2) Sum 79, p. 84.

BYNUM, Edward B.
"Poems. " BlackALF (13:1) Spr 79, p. 36.

BYRD, Erin
"The Way She Was. " EngJ (68:5) My 79, p. 39.

BYRNE, Edward
"Miles Davis. " AmerPoR (8:3) My-Je 79, p. 20.
"South of Bleeker. " AmerPoR (8:3) My-Je 79, p. 20.

CABALQUINTO, Luis
"Five Weeks. " Mouth (2:1) F 79, p. 19.
"The Fly. " GreenfieldR (7:3/4) Spr-Sum 79, p. 74.
"When They Come" (for Colette Inez). GreenfieldR (7:3/4) Spr-
    Sum 79, p. 74.

CADER, Teresa
"Sighting the Curlew at Menemsha, Martha's Vineyard. " Tendril
    (5) Sum 79, p. 15.

CADNUM, Michael
"Anatomy of a Giant. " AntR (37:4) Aut 79, p. 455.
"Deer Skull. " AntR (37:4) Aut 79, p. 454.
"Old City. " CentR (23:4) Aut 79, p. 424.
"The Triumph. " AntR (37:4) Aut 79, p. 453.

CADSBY, Heather
"Continuum. " MalR (49) Ja 79, p. 33.
"Poem for a Son. " MalR (49) Ja 79, p. 32.

CAIN, John
"A Dream of Butterflies. " KanQ (11:1/2) Wint-Spr 79, p. 62.

CAIN, Seymour
"Due Date. " ChrC (96:9) 14 Mr 79, p. 279.

CALABRESE, John M.
"Waiting for the Ascension of Grecian Grapes. " Mouth (2:3) N
    79, p. 43.

CALDWELL, Justin
"Sunday Afternoon in Hope, Arkansas. " PoNow (23) 79, p. 17.

CALISCH, Richard
"Moment Before Pole Vaulting. " EngJ (68:5) My 79, p. 29.

CALLAHAN, Bob
Eight Poems. Tele (15) Spr 79, pp. 22-26.

CALLANAN, Dierdre
"Christopher (1967-1977). " HolCrit (16:2) Ap 79, p. 13.

CALLAWAY, Kathy
"As'vamedha. " Antaeus (35) Aut 79, p. 48.
"Black Sabbath. " Antaeus (33) Spr 79, p. 127.
"Farming and Dreaming. " Ploughs (5:1) 79, pp. 22-23.
"Final Notice. " CutB (13) Aut-Wint 79, p. 37.

"Heart of the Garfish. " Iowa (10:2) Spr 79, p. 78.
"It Could Start This Way. " Nat (229:8) 22 S 79, p. 250.
"Mary, Mary. " CutB (13) Aut-Wint 79, p. 39.
"Rivers and History. " Antaeus (33) Spr 79, p. 128.
"The Sleeper. " Ploughs (5:1) 79, p. 24.
"Staple Supplies. " Ploughs (5:1) 79, pp. 25-26.
"Stepping Aside. " Nat (229:1) 7 Jl 79, p. 28.
"The White Horse, 1950. " Iowa (10:3) Sum 79, p. 110.

CALSBEEK, Janine
"At Aunt Mabel's. " WindO (34) Spr-Sum 79, p. 10.

CAMBANIS, Miranda
Poem. St. AR (5:2) 79, p. 118.
Poem. St. AR (5:2) 79, p. 119.

CAMERON, Michael
"February. " Poetry (133:5) F 79, pp. 258-260.

CAMIER, Jamé-Maçeo
"After Braille. " PartR (46:4) 79, p. 603.
"Another Life" (for Raymond Roussel). PartR (46:4) 79, p. 602.

CAMILLO, Victor
"This Evening. " PoetC (11:1) 79, p. 9.

CAMPBELL, Bonnie
"If I peeled you, my dear. " HangL (35) Spr 79, p. 69.
"In the study hall, amid the roar. " HangL (35) Spr 79, p. 68.

CAMPBELL, Christina M.
"Runner. " SmPd (45) 79, p. 26.

CAMPBELL, Douglas
"Sunny Day Special. " Ur (2) 79, p. 17.

CAMPBELL, Larry
"Reflections. " BlackF (3:1) Aut-Wint 79, p. 23.

CAMPBELL, Mitchell
"The Ice. " Poem (36) Jl 79, p. 58.
"Short Echoes. " Poem (36) Jl 79, p. 59.

CAMPBELL, Natalie
"Wind!" " NewL (46:1) Aut 79, p. 96.

CAMPION, Daniel
"The Exile of Andy Granatelli. " Spirit (4:1) Aut-Wint 78-79, p. 45.
"The Trapper Considers" (for George Caleb Bingham). Spirit (4:1) Aut-Wint 78-79, p. 45.

CANNON, Melissa
"Nuptial Molt. " Tendril (6) Aut 79, p. 18.

"The Sisters of the Slaughtered. " Tendril (6) Aut 79, p. 19.
"The Suicide's Daughter. " Tendril (4) Wint 79, p. 16.
"Tumbler. " Tendril (4) Wint 79, p. 14.

CANTALUPO, C.
"The Death of Colin Clout. " JnlONJP (3:2) 79, p. 10.
"The Sharper. " JnlONJP (3:2) 79, p. 12.
"To the Jersey Shore. " JnlONJP (3:2) 79, p. 11.

CANTRELL, Charles
"Around the Snow Fire. " PoNow (25) 79, p. 3.
"Chopping Wood Times Two. " SouthernPR (19:1) Spr 79, p. 51.
"Crazy Glue. " PoNow (25) 79, p. 3.
"The Kitten Drowning. " Wind (33) 79, p. 10.
"The Promontory. " SouthernPR (19:1) Spr 79, p. 49.
"Thanksgiving--1950. " Wind (33) 79, p. 9.
"An Unprayed-for Song. " PoetryNW (20:4) Wint 79-80, pp. 34-
37.

CANTU, Norma
"Eye" (tr. of Alfonsina Storni). PraS (53:3) Aut 79, p. 207.
"Fishermen" (tr. of Alfonsina Storni). PraS (53:3) Aut 79, p.
207.

CAPELLO, Phyllis
"getting my jazz down. " LittleM (12:1/2) Spr-Sum 78 (79), p.
14.

CARDENAL, Ernesto
"Psalm 36. " LitR (23:2) Wint 80, p. 222.
from O Hour: "There was a Nicaraguan in a foreign country"
(tr. by Martin Paul). AmerPoR (8:2) Mr-Ap 79, p. 4.

CARDONA-HINE, Alvaro
"Enough Horses. " Bachy (14) Spr/Sum 79, p. 77.
"Funeral Train Following the Taking of Bilbao" (tr. of César
Vallejo). PoNow (24) 79, p. 36.
"In the Lobby of the Old Hotel. " DacTerr (16) 79, p. 7.
"Masses" (tr. of César Vallejo). PoNow (24) 79, p. 36.
"The Sunlight of the Blind. " Bachy (14) Spr/Sum 79, p. 77.
"Tentative Wine. " Bachy (14) Spr/Sum 79, p. 77.

CARDOZO, Nancy
"Behind the Museum. " Confr (19) Aut 79-Wint 80, p. 24.

CARÊME, Maurice
"Do You Know the Taste" (tr. by Norma Farber). PoNow (21)
79, p. 46.
"Hands Folded Simply" (tr. by Norma Farber). PoNow (24) 79,
p. 7.
"I Could've Been Born a King" (tr. by Norma Farber). PoNow
(24) 79, p. 7.
"Image" (tr. by Norma Farber). PoNow (24) 79, p. 7.
"In the Kitchen the Good Smell" (tr. by Norma Farber). PoNow

(24) 79, p. 7.
"When I Haven't Anything to Say" (tr. by Norma Farber).
PoNow (21) 79, p. 46.
"You Can Get Despondent" (tr. by Norma Farber).   PoNow (24)
79, p. 7.

CARISIO, Justin
"Ecce Ancilla Domini. "   Shen (30:1) Aut 78, p. 88.

CARLILE, Henry
"Flying. "   AmerPoR (8:1) Ja-F 79, p. 47.

CARLISLE, Susan E.
"Questions Concerning the Muse. "   Chomo (5:3) Spr 79, p. 45.

CARLISLE, Susan Goodman
"My Son Has a Necklace. "   AndR (6:2) Aut 79, p. 42.

CARLOS, Peter
"The Preying. "   WebR (4:3) Spr 79, p. 33.

CARNEVALE, Robert
"In the Long Room" (for Skip Kreisell).   Columbia (3) 79, p. 72.

CARNEY, Mary Lou
"Executive Confession. "   Wind (33) 79, p. 13.

CAROTHERS, R. L.
"Tongues. "   DenQ (14:2) Sum 79, p. 93.
"With No Rights. "   DenQ (14:2) Sum 79, p. 92.

CARPENTER, William
"The Yacht: A Meditation on Form. "   Nimrod (23:1) Aut-Wint
79, p. 9.
"The Yacht: A Meditation Poem. "   BelPoJ (29:4) Sum 79, p. 16.

CARPER, Thomas
"The First-Born. "   BelPoJ (29:3) Spr 79, p. 7.

CARR, Jim
"Relics. "   Wind (35) 79, p. 10.

CARR, John
"Jetty Off the Shore of Massachusetts" (for Pat Sims).   HolCrit
(16:2) Ap 79, p. 13.

CARRIER, Lois
"Mesquite. "   BelPoJ (29:3) Spr 79, p. 14.

CARRINGTON, Rae
"Know Yourself. "   BlackF (3:1) Aut-Wint 79, p. 26.

CARROLL, Liz
"Coyote. "   SouthernPR (19:1) Spr 79, p. 34.

CARRUTH, Hayden
"Anima" (for Janet). PoNow (21) 79, p. 4.
"Love Poem. " Hudson (32:4) Wint 79-80, p. 538.
"A Particular Valentine" (for Joanna). Hudson (32:4) Wint 79-80,
    p. 539.

CARSON, Ciarán
"Great-Grandmother. " LitR (22:3) Spr 79, p. 362.

CARSON, Tom
"A Period Piece. " Aspen (7) Spr 79, p. 42.

CARTER, Guy D. L.
"Elegy. " GRR (10:3) 79, p. 97.
"Reclamation. " GRR (10:3) 79, p. 96.

CARTER, Jared
"Don King's Neighborhood. " Spirit (3:3) Sum 78, p. 29.
"The Fire's Dream. " Nimrod (23:1) Aut-Wint 79, p. 39.
"Following the Animals. " SoDakR (17:1) Spr 79, p. 18.
"In the North Pasture. " Im (5:3) 79, p. 3.
"Meditation. " SoDakR (17:1) Spr 79, p. 17.
"Objets d'Art. " SoDakR (17:1) Spr 79, p. 19.
"Second Sheet. " Bits (10) Jl 79.

CARTER, Lynda
"The Stretch. " BlackF (3:1) Aut-Wint 79, p. 26.

CARTER, Rick
"Freeways and Alley Cats. " Mouth (2:2) Je 79, p. 36.
"Reasons. " Mouth (2:2) Je 79, p. 36.
"Room. " Mouth (2:2) Je 79, p. 35.
"Wasted. " Mouth (2:2) Je 79, p. 41.

CARTIGLIA, Joe
"Be bop da. " SmPd (45) 79, p. 19.

CARUSO, Joseph
"Approaching White Water. " PoNow (25) 79, p. 4.
"Two Miles Deep. " PoNow (25) 79, p. 4.

CARVER, Raymond
"The Baker. " Kayak (50) My 79, p. 41.
"Luck. " Kayak (50) My 79, p. 40.

CASEY, Deb
"Old Story. " ChiR (31:2) Aut 79, p. 14.

CASEY, Helen Marie
"Keeping a Promise. " ChrC (96:37) 14 N 79, p. 1121.

CASHMAN, David
"I am at my typewriter. " WindO (34) Spr-Sum 79, p. 4.
"On Balance. " WindO (34) Spr-Sum 79, p. 15.

CASSITY, Turner
"The Great American Poem. " Antaeus (32) Wint 79, pp. 82-86.

CASTAÑO, Wilfredo Q.
"To People Who Pick Food. " SeC (6:1) 78, p. 47.

CASTELLANOS, Rosario
"Economía doméstica. " 13thM (4:2) 79, p. 13.
"Routine" (tr. by Maureen Ahern). NewL (46:1) Aut 79, p. 79.
"Silencio cerca de una piedra antigua. " 13thM (4:2) 79, p. 11.
"Toma de conciencia. " 13thM (4:2) 79, p. 17.

CASTLE, Terry
"Antiochus at the Breakfast Table. " CarlMis (17:2/3) Spr 79,
     p. 47.
"Folk Tale. " CarlMis (17:2/3) Spr 79, p. 47.

CASTO, Robert Clayton
Poem. St.AR (5:2) 79, p. 20.
"Vampire Bessy. " Epoch (28:2) Wint 79, p. 153.

CASWELL, Donald
"The Way Home. " Wind (34) 79, p. 15.

CATE, Hollis
"Reflections. " KanQ (11:4) Aut 79, p. 132.

CATENACCI, Edward N.
"The Overcoat. " JnlONJP (3:2) 79, p. 35.
"The Survivors. " JnlONJP (4:1) 79, p. 22.

CATTAFI, Bartolo
"Hypotheses" (tr. by Rina Ferrarelli). PoNow (24) 79, p. 9.
Nine Poems (tr. by Brian Swann and Ruth Feldman). PoNow
     (24) 79, pp. 8-9.
"Patience" (tr. by Rina Ferrarelli). PoNow (24) 79, p. 9.
"Things" (tr. by Rina Ferrarelli). PoNow (24) 79, p. 9.

CATULLUS, Gaius Valerius
"Furius (No. 23 of the Carmina)" (tr. by Geoffrey Cook). Spirit
     (3:1/2) Aut-Wint 77-78, p. 43.

CAZDEN, David Benjamin
"Instructions to the Young Preacher. " Wind (34) 79, p. 16.

CECIL, Richard
"The Confessions of Saint Augustine's Secretary. " Chelsea (38)
     79, p. 59.
"Daedalus or Icarus?" Chelsea (38) 79, p. 61.
"Home. " AmerPoR (8:4) Jl-Ag 79, p. 13.
"The Prince as King. " Chelsea (38) 79, p. 60.
"Serenade for the Man Downstairs. " PoNow (23) 79, p. 40.

CEDRINS, Inara
"for my godmother" (tr. of Astrid Ivask). Chelsea (38) 79, p.
  84.
"(untitled): In the evening forest a bird sings, perhaps" (tr. of
  Astrid Ivask). Chelsea (38) 79, p. 85.
"K. H. " (tr. of Astrid Ivask). Chelsea (38) 79, p. 85.
"Swimming. " MinnR (NS 12) Spr 79, p. 18.

CENTER, Bill
"It's spring again. " GreenfieldR (7:3/4) Spr-Sum 79, p. 156.
"Muscatel Cousins. " GreenfieldR (7:3/4) Spr-Sum 79, p. 158.

CERVANTES, Francisco
"Pardonless Autumn" (tr. by Sandford Cohen). PoNow (24) 79,
  p. 9.

CERVANTES, James V.
"The Killing of the Rooster. " NewL (46:2) Wint 79-80, p. 61.
"When Something Large Breaks. " NewL (46:2) Wint 79-80, p.
  62.

CERVO, Nathan
"The Heat. " EnPas (8) 79, p. 30.
"Oak, Willow. " EnPas (9) 79, p. 22.
"On Fire Island. " PoNow (21) 79, p. 42.
"Pyramid. " EnPas (9) 79, p. 22.
"The Quiet Things. " EnPas (8) 79, p. 31.

CESAIRE, Aimé
"Annunciation" (to André Breton) (tr. by Joan C. Dayan). Paint
  (12) Aut 79, p. 27.
"Notebook of a Return to the Native Land" (tr. by Clayton Eshle-
  man and Annette Smith). Montra (6) 79, pp. 7-37.

CHACE, Sarah
"The Purgatory Dream. " HarvAd (112:2) Mr 79, p. 21.

CHACE, Susan
"Payne Whitney: Danny's River View. " Pequod (3:2) 79, p. 26.

CHAFFIN, Lillie D.
"Celebration. " SouthernHR (13:1) Wint 79, p. 24.

CHAFIN, Shirley R.
"I Should Have Come Sunday. " EngJ (68:5) My 79, p. 32.

CHAMBERS, Craig
"Departure. " Wind (33) 79, p. 11.
"Midnight After the Snow. " Wind (33) 79, p. 11.

CHAMBERS, Richard
"Nocturne" (tr. of Eugenio Montejo). NewOR (6:2) 79, p. 109.

CHANDLER, Mike
"In the Bathtub Reading Voznesensky. " PoNow (25) 79, p. 3.

CHANDLER, Stephen
"The Missing. " QW (7) Aut 78, p. 62.
"Vacation. " QW (7) Aut 78, p. 63.

CHANDONNET, Ann Fox
"On a Human Scale. " Ploughs (5:1) 79, p. 27.

CHANDRA, G. S. Sharat
"Indian Poet Living in the West. " MalR (51) Jl 79, p. 33.

CHANG, Diana
"Wonder. " Confr (18) Spr-Sum 79, p. 154.

CHAPMAN, Diane
"Heavy. " PoNow (25) 79, p. 46.

CHAPMAN, Robert
"In the Swamp. " StoneC (6:1) F 79, p. 19.
"Offshore II. " StoneC (6:1) F 79, p. 19.
"Timor Mortis Conturbat Me. " StoneC (6:1) F 79, p. 18.

CHAPPELL, Fred
"At the Grave of Virgil Campbell. " QW (8) Wint 79, pp. 119-
125.
"My Grandmother's Dream of Plowing. " Epoch (29:1) Aut 79,
p. 16.

CHARNOCH, Kathleen
"Oral Poem. " SeC (6:1) 78, p. 32.

CHARTERS, Samuel
"Schubertiana" (tr. of Tomas Tranströmer). VirQR (55:1) Wint
79, p. 115.

CHASE, Josiah
"The Corner Lot. " Wind (35) 79, p. 10.
"The Monsoon. " Wind (35) 79, p. 11.

CHASE, Naomi Feigelson
"The Yoga Teacher. " Paint (11) Spr 79, p. 8.

CHASIN, Helen
"S-M. " MissouriR (3:1) Aut 79, p. 28.

CHATAIN, Robert
"Connemara Earth Ode. " Poetry (132:3) Je 79, p. 133.
"Curragh. " Poetry (134:3) Je 79, p. 131.
"Evasions of the Animal Hospital. " Poetry (134:3) Je 79, p.
132.

CHATFIELD, Emily
"Melting 1978. " Ploughs (5:3) 79, p. 81.

CHATFIELD, Hale
"Going to Work for Horace Sondergard. " PoNow (21) 79, p. 40.

CHEDID, Andree
"Chains, Our Freedom" (tr. by Carl Hemey). MalR (49) Ja 79,
    p. 91.
"Lightning in Chains" (tr. by Carl Hemey). MalR (49) Ja 79, p.
    91.

CHERKOVSKI, Neeli
"Notes for a Basterd Angel" (to Harold Norse). SeC (6:2) 78,
    p. 83.
"Thomas Merton" (for John Landry). SeC (6:2) 78, p. 81.

CHERNOFF, Maxine
"A abridged bestiary" (for Peter Kostakis). PoNow (22) 79, p.
    22.
"The Fetus. " PoNow (22) 79, p. 8.
"The Limits of Science. " PoNow (23) 79, p. 15.
"The Man Struck Twenty Times by Lightning. " PoNow (22) 79,
    p. 8.
"The moat. " PoNow (22) 79, p. 22.
"What the Dead Eat. " PoNow (22) 79, p. 8.

CHERRY, Kelly
"The Family. " SouthernPR (19:1) Spr 79, pp. 41-45.
"Letter to a Censor. " GeoR (33:4) Aut 79, p. 784.
"Lines Written on the Eve of a Birthday. " NewOR (6:4) 79, p.
    381.
"Volga Car Song. " NewOR (6:4) 79, p. 382.
"When the Earth Slept Under Snow, and Its Dreams Were of
    Diamond. " NewOR (6:4) 79, p. 380.

CHESTERVILLE, J. B.
"Following with You. " Poultry (1) 79, p. 8.

CHIA Tao
"Gazing at the Clear Evening After Snow" (tr. by Joan Iten Suth-
    erland and Peter Levitt). Bachy (15) Aut 79, p. 28.

CHICHIBABIN, Boris
"Stalin Is Not Dead" (tr. by Vera S. Dunham). Nat (229:22) 29
    D 79, p. 693.

CHIECO, Michael
"A Wedding Gift. " Wind (32) 79, p. 16.

CHIESURA, Giorgio
from The Immobile Zone: "The Action (table of contents)" (tr.
    by Rina Ferrarelli). Hudson (32:2) Sum 79, p. 201.

from The Immobile Zone: "The Immobile Zone" (tr. by Rina
    Ferrarelli). Hudson (32:2) Sum 79, p. 201.
from The Immobile Zone: "The Man with the Handkerchief" (tr.
    by Rina Ferrarelli). Hudson (32:2) Sum 79, p. 204.
from The Immobile Zone: "The Rock" (tr. by Rina Ferrarelli).
    Hudson (32:2) Sum 79, p. 203.
from The Immobile Zone: "The Trees" (tr. by Rina Ferrarelli).
    Hudson (32:2) Sum 79, p. 202.
from The Immobile Zone: "Time (Forecast)" (tr. by Rina Fer-
    rarelli). Hudson (32:2) Sum 79, p. 203.

CHILDERS, David C.
    "For a Woman Not Put Off. " GRR (10:3) 79, p. 60.
    Poem. St. AR (5:2) 79, p. 18.

CHMIELARZ, Sharon
    "In the Woods I Pretend. " EngJ (68:5) My 79, p. 31.

CHRISTENSON, Kathryn
    "Sarah to Hagar. " ChrC (96:25) 1-8 Ag 79, p. 761.

CHRISTIANSEN, Mary Burritt
    Thirteen Poems. SenR (10:1) Spr 79, pp. 79-92.

CHRISTINA, Martha
    "Back on Narragansett Bay. " Tendril (5) Sum 79, p. 16.
    "Through Blue Cellophane. " Tendril (5) Sum 79, p. 17.

CHRISTOPHER, Nicholas
    "Double Solitaire. " NewYorker (55:22) 16 Jl 79, p. 32.
    "Heat. " NewYorker (55:22) 16 Jl 79, p. 32.
    "Nocturne for Miranda. " NewYorker (55:22) 16 Jl 79, p. 32.
    "Providence. " NewYorker (55:22) 16 Jl 79, p. 32.
    "Rimbaud Crossing the Alps. " NewYorker (55:22) 16 Jl 79, p.
    33.

CHUCKWUDI, Obioma
    "Bondage. " Obs (4:3) Wint 78, p. 89.
    "Looking at the Poor. " Obs (4:3) Wint 78, pp. 88-89.

CHUMLEY, Janis
    "The Essential Flow of Blood. " QW (7) Aut 78, p. 91.
    "July 13, 1968 Swimming at Night Near the Cape. " QW (7) Aut
    78, p. 92.

CHURA, David
    "His eyes haven't moved. " Mouth (2:2) Je 79, p. 14.
    "Nova Scotia Night. " Mouth (2:2) Je 79, p. 12.
    "On Being an Uncle for the Second Time. " Mouth (2:2) Je 79,
    p. 18.

CHUTE, Bob
    "Still Life with Fruit. " Northeast (3:7) Spr 79, p. 30.

CIARDI, John
"Apprehendee the Exited Vee-hicle. " Poetry (133:6) Mr 79, p.
341.
"By a Bush in Half Twilight. " Poultry (1) 79, p. 3.
"A Crate of Sterling Silver Loving Cups. " Poetry (133:6) Mr 79,
pp. 344-345.
"No White Bird Sings. " Poetry (133:6) Mr 79, p. 340.
"On the Patio. " Poetry (133:6) Mr 79, pp. 342-343.

CIESZYNSKI, Wladyslaw
"I Want to Take You. " Focus (13:80) Mr. Ap 79, p. 38.
"The Plants Are Flourishing: A Love Poem. " Conf (18) Spr-
Sum 79, p. 87.
"Some Are Flight Summer Fancy. " Focus (13:80) Mr-Ap 79, p.
38.

CIMATTI, Pietro
"Excerpt of a Sonnet on the Population of the Roman Night.
Where the Whores Die" (tr. by Frank Judge). PoNow (24)
79, p. 9.

CISNEROS, Sandra
"South Sangamon. " QW (7) Aut 78, p. 106.

CITINO, David
"The Accident: A Folk Tale. " PoNow (25) 79, p. 5.
"Folk Humor. " PoNow (22) 79, p. 8.
"Glass, Corpse, Eyetooth of a Hog. " SouthernPR (19:1) Spr 79,
p. 32.
"Hen. " Focus (13:82) Ag 79, p. 31.
"Instructions. " LitR (22:3) Spr 79, p. 328.
"Last Rites. " LitR (22:3) Spr 79, p. 327.
"Living on the Border. " SouthwR (64:2) Spr 79, p. 165.
"Map Reading. " WestB (5) 79, p. 71.
"The Martyr. " PoetC (11:1) 79, p. 22.
Poem. St. AR (5:2) 79, p. 64.
Poem. St. AR (5:2) 79, p. 105.
"The Retired Pastor Celebrates Christmas. " PoetC (11:1) 79, p.
20.
"The Sin-Eater. " HiramPoR (26) Spr-Sum 79, p. 16.
"Snow. " HolCrit (16:4) O 79, p. 11.
"To Grow Holy. " Wind (33) 79, p. 13.
"Under the Volcano. " SouthernPR (19:2) Aut 79, p. 8.

CLAFLIN, Lola White
"Let Me Die Falling. " Tendril (4) Wint 79, p. 17.
"Mountain Home. " Tendril (5) Sum 79, p. 18.

CLAIRE, William
"In the South of France. " Chelsea (38) 79, p. 131.
"The Jello Man on the Feast of Circumcision. " Chelsea (38) 79,
p. 130.

CLAMPITT, Amy
"Agreeable Monsters. " Antaeus (33) Spr 79, p. 133.
"The Cormorant in Its Element. " Atl (244:6) D 79, p. 70.
"The Cove. " NewYorker (55:5) 19 Mr 79, p. 44.
"Fog. " Atl (244:2) Ag 79, p. 75.
"Gradual Clearing. " ChiR (31:2) Aut 79, p. 105.
"Ladies' Tresses. " NewYorker (55:13) 14 My 79, p. 153.
"Mysterious Britain. " AmerS (48:4) Aut 79, p. 471.
"On the Disadvantages of Central Heating. " Atl (243:6) Je 79,
    p. 74.

CLARK, Carole
"Grandpa. " EngJ (68:5) My 79, p. 38.

CLARK, Catherine
"Coming Back. " GreenfieldR (7:3/4) Spr-Sum 79, p. 1.
"A Leg at a Time. " GreenfieldR (7:3/4) Spr-Sum 79, p. 1.

CLARK, Constance
"Godspeed. " StoneC (6:3) O 79, p. 23.

CLARK, Gerald
"The naked backs of rainbows. " AAR (29) 79, p. 22.

CLARK, James
"After Last Night. " QW (8) Wint 79, p. 79.
"As the Painter. " QW (8) Wint 79, p. 78.
"Finny. " QW (8) Wint 79, p. 79.

CLARK, Kevin
"The Neighbor. " CutB (12) Spr-Sum 79, p. 55.

CLARK, Tom
"The Great American Poem. " Antaeus (32) Wint 79, pp. 82-86.

CLARK, Naomi
"Dorothy Lake. " PoNow (25) 79, p. 20.
"Dream. " PoNow (25) 79, p. 20.

CLARK, Patricia
"Waking Early. " CutB (13) Aut-Wint 79, p. 36.

CLARKE, Gillian
"Hay-Making. " WebR (4:3) Spr 79, p. 57.

CLAUDEL, Alice Moser
"Snow Geese, Swans, Weather Testing. " CharR (5:1) Spr 79, p.
    51.

CLAUSEN, Jan
"impermanence. " LittleM (12:1/2) Spr-Sum 78 (79), p. 62.

CLEVELAND, Betty
"Cycles. " SmF (7/8) Spr-Aut 78, p. 17.

"Night Roost. " SmF (7/8) Spr-Aut 78, p. 15.
"Pulling Fodder. " SmF (7/8) Spr-Aut 78, p. 16.

CLEWELL, David
  "Dancing Down the Circus. " Chowder (12) Spr-Sum 79, p. 22.
  "Gladiola Hotel. " DacTerr (16) 79, p. 8.
  from Heroes: "The Dogs. " Northeast (3:7) Spr 79, p. 20.
  from Heroes: "The Game. " Northeast (3:7) Spr 79, p. 21.
  "Mormon Graveyard, Utah Night. " Chowder (13) Aut-Wint 79,
    p. 40.

CLIFF, William
  "Adulthood" (tr. by Maxine Kumin and Judith Kumin). PoNow
    (24) 79, p. 10.
  "Childhood" (tr. by Maxine Kumin and Judith Kumin). PoNow
    (24) 79, p. 10.
  "The Messiah" (tr. by Maxine Kumin and Judith Kumin).
    NewEngR (1:3) Spr 79, p. 280.
  "Twins" (tr. by Maxine Kumin and Judith Kumin). PoNow (24)
    79, p. 10.
  "The White Farm" (tr. by Maxine Kumin and Judith Kumin).
    PoNow (24) 79, p. 10.

CLIFTON, Harry
  "Sketches from Berlin. " Stand (20:3) 79, p. 43.

CLIFTON, Merritt
  "Debate, Barnyard, After First Snow. " Sam (72) 79, p. 61.
  "R. I. P. " Sam (72) 79, p. 75.

CLINE, Charles
  "A Boy. " GRR (10:1) 79, p. 140.

CLINTON, Michelle T.
  "Debra. " Cond (5) 79, p. 121.
  "For Strong Women:. " Cond (5) 79, p. 118.

CLINTON, Robert
  "A Malediction on the Artless. " Shen (30:1) Aut 78, p. 48.
  "No Quitters. " LittleM (12:1/2) Spr-Sum 78(79), p. 84.
  "Spring Schedule. " Shen (30:4) 79, p. 17.

CLIPPARD, Dave
  "No Eagle. " Mouth (2:3) N 79, p. 49.

CLOUTIER, Cécile
  "extraits d'un recueil à paraître. " Os (9) 79, pp. 20-24.

CLOUTIER, David
  "Immaculate. " Aspect (74/75) Ja-Ag 79, p. 66.
  "Night has a hand. " Aspect (74/75) Ja-Ag 79, p. 66.

CLOUTIER, Sylvie
  "Habit conjonctif. " Os (8) 79, p. 20.

COBB, Alice S.
"To Erroll Garner. " BlackALF (13:4) Wint 79, p. 149.
"Untitled: Up near Dragoon. " BlackALF (13:4) Wint 79, p. 149.
"A Vision. " BlackALF (13:4) Wint 79, p. 149.

COCHRAN, Jo
"Mask of the Man. " BelPoJ (30:2) Wint 79-80, p. 15.
"Mask of the Woman. " BelPoJ (30:2) Wint 79-80, p. 14.

COCHRANE, Shirley
"Leaving Home. " HolCrit (16:3) Je 79, p. 19.

COCTEAU, Jean
"Cocteau/The Crucifixion" (tr. by Charles Guenther). WebR
(4:4) Aut 79, pp. 9-19.

COFFIN, Lyn
"The Bank of America. " AndR (6:2) Aut 79, p. 23.
"A Little Girl's Drawing. " MichQR (18:4) Aut 79, p. 617.
"The Plane and the Watcher. " Iowa (10:2) Spr 79, p. 79.

COGGESHALL, Rosanne
"Berryman. " SoCaR (12:1) Aut 79, p. 54.
"For Ross. " SoCaR (12:1) Aut 79, p. 53.
"Houdini. " SouthernR (15:2) Spr 79, p. 385.
"Mission. " SoCaR (12:1) Aut 79, p. 55.
"Shifts: In Time" (for AF & PS). SouthernR (15:2) Spr 79, p.
382.
"Swim. " SoCaR (12:1) Aut 79, p. 54.
"Whirling. " SouthernR (15:2) Spr 79, p. 384.

COHEN, Jay
"Plantagenet, Etc. " Poem (36) Jl 79, p. 28.
"Sonnet at Winter's End. " Poem (36) Jl 79, p. 27.

COHEN, Rosetta M.
"The Town of Insomniacs. " CarolQ (31:3) Aut 79, p. 70.

COHEN, Sandford
"Pardonless Autumn" (tr. of Francisco Cervantes). PoNow (24)
(24) 79, p. 9.

COHL, Izora Corpman
"Loretta. " AntR (37:3) Sum 79, p. 323.
"Sitting with Mother on the Screened Porch. " AntR (37:3) Sum
79, p. 322.

COHRS, Tomothy
"Because I Am Broke and Returned. " Epoch (28:2) Wint 79, p.
183.
"Election Day. " BelPoJ (29:3) Spr 79, p. 18.
"The Escalator/Birth Poem. " BelPoJ (29:3) Spr 79, p. 20.
"Why I Am Not a New Yorker (the Chicago School of Architec-
ture). " Epoch (28:2) Wint 79, p. 184.

COKER, Clark
"Going Winter. " KanQ (11:3) Sum 79, p. 89.

COKER, David
"Breaking in Place" (for John Clare). ChiR (31:1) Sum 79, p.
  55.
"Her Queerest Footprints. " ChiR (31:1) Sum 79, p. 56.

COLBY, Joan
"Apparitions of Earth. " KanQ (11:3) Sum 79, p. 49.
"Black Flowers. " NewRena (11) 79, p. 36.
"The Circus Rider. " Chowder (12) Spr-Sum 79, p. 21.
"Epidemics. " Ascent (5:1) 79, p. 16.
"Grandfather. " Ur (2) 79, p. 18.
"History of the World. " NewRena (11) 79, p. 35.
"The House of Death. " WestB (4) 79, p. 27.
"The Hue of the Animal. " NewRena (11) 79, p. 33.
"Kisses. " HolCrit (16:5) D 79, p. 14.
"Kittens. " NewRena (11) 79, p. 34.
"The Morgue. " ArkRiv (4:3) 79, p. 20.
"The Old Nudists. " PortR (25) 79, p. 120.
"The Quality That Reflects No Light. " WestB (4) 79, p. 26.
"Taking My Medicine. " PortR (25) 79, p. 121.
"That Old Woman, That Enchantress. " Tele (15) Spr 79, p. 89.
"Writing the Egg" (for Christine). WestB (4) 79, p. 24.

COLBY, Wendelin
"Final Resolution. " PikeF (2) Wint 78-79, p. 16.
"A Word. " PikeF (2) Wint 78-79, p. 16.

COLE, Henri R.
"Mother's Dream. " BelPoJ (30:1) Aut 79, p. 37.

COLE, Jane Coil
"Anne Sexton. " JnlONJP (4:1) 79, p. 25.
"Answering Your Letter. " JnlONJP (4:1) 79, p. 26.

COLE, Richard
"Muromachi Folding Screen. " ChiR (30:4) Spr 79, p. 26.

COLEMAN, Wanda
"The African Queen Meets Her Match. " Bachy (14) Spr/Sum 79,
  p. 18.
"At Vital Statistics. " PartR (46:4) 79, p. 598.
"Flight of the California Condor/Wind Sistuh Blooded Eyes/Mind
  Full of Flesh. " Bachy (14) Spr/Sum 79, p. 15.
"the head of my baby. " Bachy (14) Spr/Sum 79, p. 19.
"Jerry 1967. " PartR (46:4) 79, p. 601.
"Last Grave at Dimbaza. " BlackALF (13:1) Spr 79, p. 34.
"Lessons. " PartR (46:4) 79, p. 599.
"Luz. " Bachy (14) Spr/Sum 79, p. 20.
"Men Lips. " PartR (46:4) 79, p. 597.
"1 War. " GreenfieldR (7:3/4) Spr-Sum 79, p. 293.
"Queen of Sinking Sand. " PartR (46:4) 79, p. 600.

"Somewhere There's an Alley with My Name On It. "   BlackALF
(13:1) Spr 79, p. 35.
"Under Arrest. "   Bachy (14) Spr/Sum 79, p. 17.
"Under Arrest (2). "   Bachy (14) Spr/Sum 79, p. 18.

COLEMAN, Willie M.
"Among the Things That Use to Be. " Cond (5) 79, p. 59.

COLES, Don
"Recluse. " Poetry (134:2) My 79, p. 89.

COLES, Gladys Mary
"In Praising Darkness. " Os (8) 79, p. 8.

COLGAN, Helen Hope
"Concerning the Disposition of Property. " WormR (74) 79, p.
67.
"Hooked on Rugs. " WormR (74) 79, p. 67.
"Rockhounding. " WormR (74) 79, p. 68.

COLGAN, Robert
"After Parra: Need. " Pequod (3:2) 79, p. 20.
"Eaten. " Pequod (3:2) 79, p. 25.
"Nora Barnacle: Maybe Mine Will Make Us Some Money. "
Pequod (3:2) 79, p. 24.
"Nurse's Testimony. " Pequod (3:2) 79, p. 21.
"Personal: Night Flight Bomber Pilot. " Pequod (3:2) 79, p. 23.
"Woman in the Oven. " Pequod (3:2) 79, p. 22.

COLLIER, Carol J.
"Midnight and Rain. " SmF (7/8) Spr-Aut 78, p. 41.

COLLINS, Billy
"A Symbology of Growling. " Spirit (3:1/2) Aut-Wint 77-78, p.
60.

COLLINS, Martha
"Beneath the Skin. " SouthernR (15:1) Wint 79, p. 115.
"Descent. " WestB (5) 79, p. 50.
"In Argentina. " Agni (10/11) 79, p. 135.
"A Single Woman of a Certain Age. " SouthernR (15:1) Wint 79,
p. 116.
"Somewhere Is Susan. " CarlMis (17:2/3) Spr 79, p. 89.

COLOBIALE, James V.
Poem. St. AR (5:2) 79, p. 111.
Poem. St. AR (5:2) 79, p. 112.

COLQUITT, Betsy
"Photographing the Facade--San Miguel de Allende. " ChrC (96:13)
11 Ap 79, p. 398.
"Schliemann in Eden. " ChrC (96:33) 17 O 79, p. 1010.

COLT, George Howe
"Falling Through Clouds. " PoNow (25) 79, p. 4.
"First Drunk. " PoNow (25) 79, p. 4.

COMBS, Bruce
"Urgent Request. " Sam (72) 79, p. 53.

CONALLIS, Martha
"Friends. " BelPoJ (30:2) Wint 79-80, p. 16.
"Highway 1-40 East. " BelPoJ (30:2) Wint 79-80, p. 17.

CONDEE, Nancy
"The Arsonist's Aesthetic: A Treatise on Beautiful Women. "
    PoNow (22) 79, p. 10.
"The Differences Between the Intellectual and the Doughnut. "
    PoNow (22) 79, p. 10.
"Mrs. Charles Sanders Pierce, or The Solution to the Universe. "
    PoNow (22) 79, p. 10.

CONDINI, N. E.
"Printemps. " Mouth (2:2) Je 79, p. 27.
"The Thirteenth Game. " Mouth (2:2) Je 79, p. 42.

CONDIT, David L.
"The Consumptive Poet Hunts Like Ahab for Air. " Tendril (5)
    Sum 79, p. 19.

CONGDON, Kirby
"Hero. " PoNow (22) 79, p. 9.
"The Lighthouse. " PoNow (22) 79, p. 9.
"The Motorcycle Social Club. " PoNow (22) 79, p. 22.
"The Speed Track. " PoNow (22) 79, p. 22.
"Thousand Cats Hill. " PoNow (22) 79, p. 9.
"The Tower. " PoNow (22) 79, p. 9.

CONLEY, Robert J.
"The Hills of Tsa La Gi" (for Gene LeRoy Hart). BelPoJ (30:2)
    Wint 79-80, p. 39.

CONNELL, Kim
"Sleep. " Tendril (4) Wint 79, p. 18.

CONNER, Shirley
"Early Morning Weather Report. " KanQ (11:1/2) Wint-Spr 79,
    p. 82.

CONNOLLY, James F.
"Going Thirty. " Aspect (74/75) Ja-Ag 79, p. 53.
"The Undertakers: My Mother, My Father. " Tendril (5) Sum
    79, p. 20.

CONQUEST, Robert
"Breathings. " Stand (20:3) 79, p. 31.

CONRAD, Bryce
"Drought" (tr. of Radovan Pavlovski w. Zoran Anchevski).
CharR (5:2) Aut 79, p. 8.
"Landscape from the War" (tr of Radovan Pavlovski w. Zoran
Anchevski). CharR (5:2) Aut 79, p. 7.
"Road to the Mountain" (tr of Radovan Pavlovski w. Zoran
Anchevski). CharR (5:2) Aut 79, p. 6.
"Skin" (tr. of Radovan Pavlovski w. Zoran Anchevski). CharR
(5:2) Aut 79, p. 7.
"Sowers" (tr. of Radovan Pavlovski w. Zoran Anchevski).
CharR (5:2) Aut 79, p. 5.
"Watchtower" (tr. of Radovan Pavlovski w. Zoran Anchevski).
CharR (5:2) Aut 79, p. 5.

CONRAD, Karen
"On a Name." Ploughs (5:3) 79, pp. 122-123.

CONSTANTINI, Humberto
"Algebra." LitR (23:2) Wint 80, p. 207.
"Gardel." LitR (23:2) Wint 80, p. 206.
"Immortality." LitR (23:2) Wint 80, p. 205.

CONTOSKI, Victor
"Biting My Fingernails." PoNow (21) 79, p. 32.
"Game 23." PoNow (21) 79, p. 32.
"Paper Poem." PoNow (23) 79, p. 31.

CONTRAIRE, A. U.
Eleven Poems. WindO (35) Aut-Wint 79-80.

CONTRERAS, Melinda
"The Crucifixion." Obs (4:3) Wint 78, pp. 75-76.
"Maisha." Obs (4:3) Wint 78, pp. 73-74.
"Revolucion." Obs (4:3) Wint 78, p. 75.

COOK, Geoffrey
"Furius (No. 23 of the Carmina)" (tr. of Gaius Valerius Catul-
lus). Spirit (3:1/2) Aut-Wint 77-78, p. 43.

COOK, Paul H.
"Fail-Safe:" (for Arlene). QW (7) Aut 78, p. 44.
"The Fifth Wheel." Spirit (3:1/2) Aut-Wint 77-78, p. 33.
"Grandmother Loved Mahler." GeoR (33:1) Spr 79, p. 64.
"Late to Work." Ur (2) 79, p. 22.
"Little League." QW (8) Wint 79, p. 63.
"Living in Small Animals." CarolQ (31:2) Spr-Sum 79, p. 51.
"Looking for Clues." SouthernPR (19:2) Aut 79, p. 29.
"The Whisker of Hercules." Ur (2) 79, p. 20.

COOK, William W.
"Hudson Hornet." NewEngR (1:4) Sum 79, p. 444.

COOKE, Michael G.
"The Foxhole. " YaleR (69:2) Wint 80, p. 256.
"An Unseen Fire. " YaleR (69:2) Wint 80, p. 257.

COOLEY, Peter
"After Terror. " NewOR (6:4) 79, p. 357.
"Coda to a Poetry Reading. " CalQ (15) Wint 79, p. 23.
"The Great American Poem. " Antaeus (32) Wint 79, pp. 82-86.
"Magnolia Tree. " NewOR (6:4) 79, p. 358.
"The Momentary Fiction. " PoNow (23) 79, p. 11.
"The Other. " NewYorker (55:4) 12 Mr 79, p. 125.
"Within the Rooms of Summer. " PoNow (23) 79, p. 11.

COOPER, Dennis
"At One of Life's Parties. " PoNow (25) 79, p. 5.
"Billy McCall's Summer. " Spirit (3:1/2) Aut-Wint 77-78, p. 50.
"Full Speed Ahead. " Ur (2) 79, p. 23.
"My Type" (for Mike Robarts). PoNow (25) 79, p. 5.
"My Grandmother Grows. " Ur (2) 79, p. 24.
"The Tenderness of the Wolves. " Bachy (15) Aut 79, p. 122.

COOPER, Jane
"The Blue Anchor. " Pequod (3:1) 79, p. 31.

COOPER, Wyn
"The Coast. " QW (9) Spr-Sum 79, p. 13.
"The Man and the Moon. " QW (9) Spr-Sum 79, p. 12.

COOPERMAN, Stanley
"Redemption. " SouthwR (64:3) Sum 79, p. 289.

COREY, Stephen
"Sitting on Each Other's Laps" (for my daughter). SouthernPR
    (19:2) Aut 79, p. 25.

CORKERY, Christopher Jane
"Metamorphosis to Punta Gorda. " AntR (37:4) Aut 79, p. 456.
"The Painter Speaks of Blue and His Beginnings. " AndR (6:2)
    Aut 79, p. 64.
"Water. " AntR (37:4) Aut 79, p. 458.

CORLEY, Elisabeth Lewis
"Glow. " CarolQ (31:1) Wint 79, p. 49.

CORMAN, Cid
"1. " Ploughs (5:3) 79, p. 128.
"2. " Ploughs (5:3) 79, p. 129.
"3. " Ploughs (5:3) 79, p. 129.

CORN, Alfred
"Cornwall. " Poetry (135:3) D 79, pp. 145-147.
"Gloze. " PartR (46:3) 79, p. 430.
"Grass. " NewYorker (55:8) 9 Ap 79, p. 129.

"The Great American Poem. " Antaeus (32) Wint 79, pp. 82-86.
"Herb Garden. " Nat (228:20) 26 My 79, p. 612.
"Terrier. " NewRep (181:7) 18 Ag 79, p. 28.
"Town Center in December. " NewRep (180:7) 17 F 79, p. 33.

CORNETT, Fran
"Hide and Seek. " Wind (34) 79, p. 58.

CORNISH, Sam
"General. " PoNow (21) 79, p. 20.
"Harriet Tubman, Harriet Tubman. " PoNow (21) 79, p. 20.
"I Smell Death. " PoNow (21) 79, p. 20.
"Slave Ship. " PoNow (21) 79, p. 20.

CORRIGAN, Paul
"The Boss Machine-Tender After Losing a Son. " GreenfieldR
    (7:3/4) Spr-Sum 79, p. 4.
"Canadian Woodcutters in Our Townships. " GreenfieldR (7:3/4)
    Spr-Sum 79, p. 3.
"Complaint of the Dam Tender's Wife. " CutB (12) Spr-Sum 79,
    p. 72.
"Midnight on the Stacker Chain. " GreenfieldR (7:3/4) Spr-Sum
    79, p. 2.
"Old Woodpolers. " GreenfieldR (7:3/4) Spr-Sum 79, p. 3.

CORTAZAR, Julio
"After Such Pleasures" (tr. by Calvin Harlan, Manuel Merán and
    Beatriz Varela). NewOR (6:2) 79, p. 103.
"Commission" (tr. by Calvin Harlan, Manuel Menán and Beatriz
    Varela). NewOR (6:2) 79, p. 105.
"Gains and Losses" (tr. by Calvin Harlan, Manuel Menán and
    Beatriz Varela). NewOR (6:2) 79, p. 104.
"Happy New Year" (tr. by Calvin Harlan, Manuel Menán and
    Beatriz Varela). NewOR (6:2) 79, p. 104.
"Restitution" (tr. by Calvin Harlan, Manuel Menán and Beatriz
    Varela). NewOR (6:2) 79, p. 102.

CORTEZ, Ricardo
"Five Red Sisters. " MissR (22/23) Wint-Spr 79, p. 35.

CORWIN, Phillip
"Achilles. " KanQ (11:1/2) Wint-Spr 79, p. 63.

COSCA, Laurie
"Children with Secrets. " PoetC (11:3) 79, p. 11.
"Gardenias. " PoetC (11:3) 79, p. 10.
"Perfect as a Flute. " PoetC (11:2) 79, p. 5.
"Those Russians. " PoetC (11:3) 79, p. 8.

COSTANZO, Gerald
"The Great American Poem. " Antaeus (32) Wint 79, pp. 82-86.

COSTELLO, James
"Underbelly Poem. " EnPas (8) 79, p. 34.

COTT, Jonathan
"Dew. " PartR (46:2) 79, p. 257.

COTTON, John
"Fragments. " Poetry (134:3) Je 79, p. 156.

COTTONWOOD, Sally
"Bread. " PraS (53:1) Spr 79, p. 70.
"Jeanne. " PraS (53:4) Wint 79, p. 352.
"Men and Women. " PraS (53:4) Wint 79-80, p. 353.

COUNCILMAN, Emily Sargent
"As One. " ArizQ (35:4) Wint 79, p. 391.
"Between the Tides. " ArizQ (35:1) Spr 79, p. 24.
"Satellite. " ArizQ (35:2) Sum 79, p. 182.

COURT, Wesli
"The Corpse of Urien. " Iowa (10:3) Sum 79, p. 100.
"Epigrams from the Gaelic. " Bits (9) Ja 79.
"Love in Exile. " Iowa (10:3) Sum 79, p. 99.
"A Winter Song. " SouthernHR (13:3) Sum 79, p. 220.

COURSEN, H. R.
"Fall Again. " SmPd (47) 79, p. 9.

COUSENS, Mildred
"Once I Looked Deep Into the Trees. " Paint (11) Spr 79, p. 9.

COVINO, Michael
"The Legacy. " Kayak (51) S 79, p. 6.

COWARD, John
"At Sunset in Kodak. " SmF (7/8) Spr-Aut 78, p. 45.
"In this corner of Sevier County. " SmF (7/8) Spr-Aut 78, p. 44.

COWING, Sheila
"After Love in August. " JnlONJP (3:2) 79, p. 34.
"The End of Summer. " StoneC (6:3) O 79, p. 29.
"The Legacy. " JnlONJP (3:2) 79, p. 33.
"The Old Woman. " Wind (34) 79, p. 33.

COX, Carol
"The Orange Cloth Hung with Mirrors. " HangL (35) Spr 79, p.
    20.
"A Poem About Will (The Stone Inside the Arm). " HangL (35)
    Spr 79, p. 19.
"Three Flower Stories. " HangL (35) Spr 79, p. 22.

COX, Kathleen Lawless
"I wake up early. " HangL (36) Aut 79, p. 10.

CRAMER, Scott D.
"apple-skin still stuck. " WindO (34) Spr-Sum 79, p. 4.

CRAMER, Steven
"Haymarket Street." Ploughs (5:1) 79, p. 28.
"Thirty-Three and a Third." OhioR (20:2) Spr-Sum 79, pp. 38-39.
"Two Women with Mangoes." CutB (12) Spr-Sum 79, p. 62.
"The Youngest Son." OhioR (20:2) Spr-Sum 79, pp. 39-40.

CRASE, Douglas
"Felix Culpa Returns from France." Shen (30:4) 79, p. 45.
"Sagg Beach." Nat (229:7) 15 S 79, p. 214.
"Toronto Means the Meeting Place." NewYorker (55:46) 31 D 79, p. 36.

CRAWFORD, Jack Jr.
"Carrying His Head Under His Arm." PoetryNW (20:3) Aut 79, pp. 32-33.
"Through the Looking Glass." PoetryNW (20:4) Wint 79-80, pp. 22-23.

CRENSHAW, Brad
from The Husbandman: "We stood off before them." ChiR (31:1) Sum 79, pp. 22-26.

CREOLE
"The Wave Seller" (tr. by Howard Norman). MichQR (18:1) Wint 79, p. 116.

CREW, Louie
"Fay." Mouth (2:1) F 79, p. 44.

CREWE, Jennifer
"Seeds." Ploughs (5:1) 79, p. 29.

CREWS, Jacquelyn
"Auguries for Three Women." Tendril (6) Aut 79, p. 22.
"Back Water." Tendril (6) Aut 79, p. 20.
"Todd Carter." Ploughs (5:2) 79, pp. 32-33.

CREWS, Judson
"Resemblances." PoNow (23) 79, p. 37.
"Your Buck." SeC (7:1) 79, p. 11.

CRIDER, Sheila A.
"Black Widow." GreenfieldR (7:3/4) Spr-Sum 79, p. 57.
"Tri-Angle." GreenfieldR (7:3/4) Spr-Sum 79, p. 57.

CRISCI, Pat J.
"Song: I've Caught a Sunfish." SmPd (45) 79, p. 16.

CRITES, B. A.
Poem. St. AR (5:2) 79, p. 63.
Poem. St. AR (5:2) 79, p. 64.

CROM, Elizabeth
"Midnight Poem. " BelPoJ (29:3) Spr 79, p. 1.

CROOKER, Barbara
"Brass Section. " Chomo (5:3) Spr 79, p. 14.

CROW, Mary
"After a Certain Number of Years, the Light Changes. " Ploughs
   (5:1) 79, pp. 30-31.
"Foreign Streets. " AmerPoR (8:2) Mr-Ap 79, p. 40.
"Girl Floating on Air. " NewL (46:2) Wint 79-80, p. 33.
"A Walk-on Rather Than a Speaking Part. " NewL (46:2) Wint
   79-80, p. 34.

CROWELL, Doug
"The Gaping Pig. " Epoch (28:2) Wint 79, p. 190.

CSOORI, Sándor
"At a Wake" (tr. by Nicholas Kolumban). Pequod (3:1) 79, p.
   101.

CULLUM, J. W.
"The December Breakfast Poems. " MidwQ (20:4) Sum 79, p.
   363.
"Hungover Blues: A Riff for the American Academy of Religion. "
   MidwQ (20:4) Sum 79, p. 362.
"Studies in Twilight Landscape" (for Celest Miller). MidwQ
   (20:2) Wint 79, p. 187.

CUMMING, Robert
"Lesson. " Wind (34) 79, p. 17.

CUMMINGS, David
"The Cook's Tale" (parody of Chaucer, w. William Zaranka).
   PoetC (10:3) 79, pp. 4-21.

CUMMINGS, Melissa
"Oblique. " Os (9) 79, p. 9.
"Public Landing. " Os (9) 79, p. 8.

CUMMINS, Eric
"Bone Gates. " Spirit (4:2/3) Spr-Sum 79, p. 59.

CUMMINS, Judith
"Mrs. Dooley. " JnlONJP (3:2) 79, p. 36.
"Two Thursdays. " JnlONJP (3:2) 79, p. 36.

CUNNINGHAM, Carl
"One of a Kind. " DacTerr (16) 79, p. 9.
"A World Aboriginal Model. " KanQ (11:1/2) Wint-Spr 79, p. 67.

CUNNINGHAM, Jo An
"At the Broken Bit. " PoetC (11:1) 79, p. 34.

CUNNINGHAM, Patricia
"Pianist. " PikeF (2) Wint 78-79, p. 26.
"Poet. " PikeF (2) Wint 78-79, p. 27.

CURRAN, Mary Doyle
"Bubbles. " Ploughs (5:2) 79, p. 123.
"No Fear. " MassR (20:1) Spr 79, p. 46.
"Prayer On My 62nd Birthday" (to Andrew Goodman). MassR
    (20:3) Aut 79, p. 416.

CURRY, Laurie
"Paraphernalia. " EngJ (68:5) My 79, p. 38.

CURTIS, Jack
"The Stonemason. " StoneC (6:3) O 79, p. 20.

CURTIS, Lucy
"My Granny Raised Eight Children. " Chomo (5:3) Spr 79, p. 42.

CURTIS, Tony
"Letter Found, Undated, in a Packet of Welsh Correspondence. "
    Kayak (52) D 79, p. 21. Found poem.
"To My Father. " MalR (52) O 79, p. 133.

CURZON, David
"Munch's Scream. " SewanR (87:1) Wint 79, p. 49.
"Three Old Symbols. " SewanR (87:1) Wint 79, p. 49.

CUSACK, Anne E.
"Raritan. " JnlONJP (3:2) 79, p. 19.

CUSH, Cathie
"Catching Hedgehogs. " JnlONJP (3:2) 79, p. 6.
"Collaboration. " JnlONJP (3:2) 79, p. 6.

CUTLER, Bruce
"Comforts of an Egg. " PraS (53:3) Aut 79, p. 258.
"From the Doctrine of Selective Depravity. " NewL (45:3) Spr
    79, p. 18.
from The Doctrine of Selective Depravity: "The Incident in the
    Light Blue Lounge: Sgt. Pete Kudirka vs. The Losers. "
    MidwQ (20:3) Spr 79, p. 264.
"Results of a Scientific Survey. " NewL (45:3) Spr 79, p. 15.
"Three Images from an Italian Summer. " NewL (45:3) Spr 79,
    p. 15.
"Tin Miners. " NewL (45:3) Spr 79, p. 17.

CZAYKOWSKI, Bogdan
"Art and the Bitch" (tr. of Kazimierz Wierzynski w. Andrzej
    Busza). Durak (3) 79, p. 14.
"Autumn scattering bitter cinnamon" (tr. of Jaroslaw Iwaszkie-
    wicz w. Andrzej Busza). Durak (3) 79, p. 15.
"A Fin-de-Siècle Myth" (tr. of Miron Bialoszewski w. Andrzej

Busza). Durak (2) 79, p. 12.
"I Don't Know How to Write" (tr. of Miron Bialoszewski w.
Andrzej Busza). Durak (2) 79, p. 13.
"Rembrandt" (tr. of Bogdan Ostromecki w. Andrzej Busza).
Durak (3) 79, p. 13.
"White" (tr. of Mieczyslaw Jastrun w. Andrzej Busza). Durak
(3) 79, p. 12.

CZECHOWSKI, Heinz
"Love Talk" (tr. by Almut McAuley). NewOR (6:3) 79, p. 225.

DAANE, Jane F.
"PB and J. " EngJ (68:5) My 79, p. 36.

DABNEY, Janice
"Afternoon at the Zoo. " PoetryNW (20:3) Aut 79, pp. 40-41.
"Concert: A Dwelling" (for R. N.). SmPd (45) 79, p. 11.
"Father's Boots. " SmPd (45) 79, p. 10.
"Responsive Remarks. " PoetryNW (20:3) Aut 79, pp. 39-40.
Found poem.

DACEY, Philip
"The Amputee. " PoNow (21) 79, p. 21.
"The Boy Under the Bed. " Ascent (4:2) 79, p. 16.
"Brazil, Yes. " WebR (4:3) Spr 79, p. 39.
"The Condom. " QW (7) Aut 78, p. 108.
"Coupon Love. " PoetryNW (20:3) Aut 79, pp. 36-37.
"The Fish of His Woman. " PoNow (21) 79, p. 21.
"The Great American Poem" (compiled by Philip Dacey). Antaeus
(32) Wint 79, pp. 82-86.
"The Green Machine. " Chowder (13) Aut-Wint 79, p. 34.
"Hortatory. " Epoch (28:2) Wint 79, p. 138.
"How I Escaped from the Labyrinth. " PoNow (21) 79, p. 21.
"Manus Minus. " PoNow (22) 79, p. 10.
"Memento Prophylactico. " Chowder (13) Aut-Wint 79, p. 32.
"The No. " Iowa (10:3) Sum 79, p. 103.
"Not Correcting His Name Misspelled on the Mailing Label. "
GreenfieldR (7:3/4) Spr-Sum 79, p. 34.
"Praiseful Mouths. " Poetry (135:3) D 79, p. 153.
"Proofreading. " GreenfieldR (7:3/4) Spr-Sum 79, p. 35.
"The Racing Form. " SouthernPR (19:2) Aut 79, p. 5.
"The Rules. " DacTerr (16) 79, p. 10.
"The Sitting. " CarolQ (31:1) Wint 79, p. 88.
from Thin Men, Thinner Angels: A Hopkins Triptych: "Angel
Hopkins. " Nimrod (23:1) Aut-Wint 79, p. 100.
"Thumb. " PoNow (21) 79, p. 21.
"Travel Note. " PoNow (22) 79, p. 10.
"Waiting for the Mail. " PoetryNW (20:3) Aut 79, pp. 35-36.
"X on Tour. " Chowder (13) Aut-Wint 79, p. 91.

DADOURIAN, Aharon
"From the Notebook of the Mad Man" (tr. by Diana Der Hovanes-
sian). PoNow (24) 79, p. 11.

DAIGON, Ruth
"Main Street. " Tendril (5) Sum 79, p. 22.

DAILEY, Joel
"Qualms. " PoNow (22) 79, p. 11.

DALE, Kathleen
"Fragmentation. " Chomo (5:3) Spr 79, p. 20.

DALLMAN, Elaine
"From the Dust. " Paint (11) Spr 79, p. 10.

DALTON, Roque
"Poet in Jail. " LitR (23:2) Wint 80, p. 258.

DALVEN, Rae
"First Rain" (tr. of Yannis Ritsos). PoNow (24) 79, p. 34.
"The Heard and the Unheard" (tr. of Yannis Ritsos). PoNow
 (24) 79, p. 34.
"In the Barracks" (tr. of Yannis Ritsos). PoNow (24) 79, p. 34.

DANA, Robert
"Discord for a Dream Piano. " PoNow (22) 79, p. 11.
"Horses. " Spirit (3:3) Sum 78, p. 36.
"The Lives of the Saints. " QW (6) Spr-Sum 78, pp. 62-66.
"Small Game" (for Peg and Moose). QW (6) Spr-Sum 78, p. 66.
"The Way We Live Now. " AmerPoR (8:3) My-Je 79, p. 11.
"Your Own. " QW (6) Spr-Sum 78, p. 68.

DANE, David
"Saturday. " QW (9) Spr-Sum 79, p. 50.
"Simplicity. " QW (9) Spr-Sum 79, p. 49.

DANEKER, Jojo
"On St. Valentine's Day. " GreenfieldR (7:3/4) Spr-Sum 79, p.
 220.
"School. " GreenfieldR (7:3/4) Spr-Sum 79, p. 220.

DANGEL, Leo
"Plowing at Full Moon. " Comm (106:6) 30 Mr 79, p. 181.

DANIEL, Judy
"Against Too Much Illumination. " CarlMis (17:2/3) Spr 79, p.
 153.
"The New Land. " CarlMis (17:2/3) Spr 79, p. 152.

DANIELS, Guy
"Dry Spell" (tr. of Andrei Voznesensky). PoNow (24) 79, p. 36.

DANIELS, Jim
"Back to the Basics. " WormR (74) 79, p. 49.
"Factory Love. " PoNow (25) 79, p. 5.
"For a Woman Hired in with Me. " WormR (74) 79, p. 48.

"Heat Doctor. " WormR (74) 79, p. 49.
"Parking Lot in July. " WormR (74) 79, p. 48.
"Work Shoes # 2. " CarolQ (31:2) Spr-Sum 79, p. 6.

DANIELS, Kate
"Black Lions" (for Thomas Minton). SeC (6:1) 78, p. 48.

DANKLEFF, Richard
"Blizzard. " CarolQ (31:1) Wint 79, p. 36.
"Mountain Camp. " NewRep (180:1) 6 Ja 79, p. 34.

DANTE
"Purgatory: Canto II" (tr. by Mark Musa). NewL (46:2) Wint
    79-80, pp. 87-92.

DANTE, Robert
"Amy. " EnPas (8) 79, p. 23.
"Petit Mort. " EnPas (8) 79, p. 24.
"7 A. M. " EnPas (8) 79, p. 23.

DARIO, Rubén
"Nocturne II" (tr. by Jan Pallister). PoNow (24) 79, p. 11.

DARLINGTON, Robert
"In Articulo Mortis" (to Richard Brian Apthorp). Poem (36) Jl
    79, p. 63.
"Our Last Meeting. " Poem (36) Jl 79, p. 62.
"Swans. " Poem (36) Jl 79, p. 60.
"This Woman. " Poem (36) Jl 79, p. 61.

DARR, Ann
"Hope Keeps Popping Up Like Toadstools in the Grass. " PoNow
    (21) 79, p. 35.
"I Gave My Love A. " PoNow (23) 79, p. 20.
"Insight Number 76. " PoNow (23) 79, p. 20.
"Late Afternoon Near Sligo. " PoNow (21) 79, p. 35.
"Relative Matter. " PoNow (23) 79, p. 20.

DARYUSH, Elizabeth
"Armistice. " SouthernR (15:4) Aut 79, p. 1001.

DAUMAL, Rene
"Disappointments" (tr. by Jan Pallister). PoNow (24) 79, p. 11.
"The Four Cardinal Times of Day" (tr. by Jan Pallister).
    PoNow (24) 79, p. 11.
"I Am Dead... " (tr. by Jan Pallister). PoNow (24) 79, p. 11.

DAUNT, Jon
"Circles of the City. " Wind (32) 79, p. 51.
"Daybreak at a Pennsylvania Highway. " GRR (10:1) 79, p. 135.
"The Empty Rifle. " GRR (10:1) 79, p. 134.
"Outcasts. " HiramPoR (26) Spr-Sum 79, p. 17.

DAVID, Almitra
"Just About to Become. " Chomo (6:1) Sum 79, p. 5.
"Unburying Mother. " BelPoJ (29:4) Sum 79, p. 2.
"Winter in Cazenovia, New York. " StoneC (6:3) O 79, p. 10.

DAVIDSON, Jean Heaton
"The Chameleon Within. " CharR (5:2) Aut 79, p. 51.

DAVIDSON, Tommie
"Salvation. " EnPas (8) 79, p. 19.

DAVIE, Donald
"Having No Ear. " AmerS (48:4) Aut 79, p. 470.
"Irene Haigh. " Stand (20:2) 79, p. 43.
"Worship. " NewRep (181:5/6) 4-11 Ag 79, p. 44.

DAVIS, H. L.
from The Selected Poems of H. L. Davis: "The River People. "
    NowestR (17:2/3) 79, p. 121.

DAVIS, Lloyd
"Driving into Buffalo at Six O'Clock. " GreenfieldR (7:3/4) Spr-
    Sum 79, p. 206.
"Gribble and I. " PoNow (25) 79, p. 6.
"Just West of Bovina, Colorado. " GreenfieldR (7:3/4) Spr-Sum
    79, p. 206.

DAVIS, Pam
"Life Study. " SmPd (47) 79, p. 10.

DAVIS, Paul
"Sunday Morning Television. " ChrC (96:32) 10 O 79, p. 971.

DAVIS, Susan
"The Doll at State Fair. " CutB (13) Aut-Wint 79, p. 56.
"The Doll in the Sheepfield. " CutB (13) Aut-Wint 79, p. 55.

DAVIS, Thadious M.
"Asante sana, Te Te. " BlackALF (13:3) Aut 79, p. 100.
"Double Take at Relais de L'espadon. " BlackALF (13:3) Aut 79,
    p. 100.
"Emergence: For Gerry, A Neo-New Yorker. " BlackALF
    (13:3) Aut 79, p. 101.
"A Greeting on Tabaski. " BlackALF (13:3) Aut 79, p. 100.
"In Mordiop's Room: Rue Mohamed V, Dakar. " BlackALF
    (13:3) Aut 79, p. 100.

DAVIS, William Virgil
"Box. " PoNow (22) 79, p. 11.
"Breakfast as a Last Resort. " CharR (5:2) Aut 79, p. 18.
"The Chandelier as Protagonist. " SouthernPR (19:1) Spr 79, p.
    26.
"The Death of the Grandfather Clock. " PoNow (22) 79, p. 11.

"Letter to My Brothers. " MalR (52) O 79, p. 120.
"The Missing Book. " SouthernPR (19:1) Spr 79, p. 25.
"The Oxygen Tent. " SouthernPR (19:2) Aut 79, p. 48.
"A Short History of Misunderstanding. " CharR (5:2) Aut 79, p. 18.
"Short Treatise on the Hand. " GeoR (33:3) Aut 79, p. 568.
"Still Life: Winter in Ohio. " Poem (35) Mr 79, p. 5.
"Telegram. " PoNow (22) 79, p. 11.
"This Winter. " PoetC (11:2) 79, p. 29.
"The Visitor. " Wind (34) 79, p. 18.
"Why I Am Blind in One Eye and Have Only One Hand. "
    SouthernPR (19:1) Spr 79, p. 25.

DAVISON, Peter
"Il se sauve. " NewEngR (2:1) Aut 79, p. 62.
"July Meeting. " Poetry (134:4) Jl 79, p. 205.
"My Lady the Lake. " Harp (258:1547) Ap 79, p. 93.
"Paradise as a Garden" (for Elizabeth Moynihan).   NewEngR
    (2:1) Aut 79, p. 61.
"Untuned String. " AmerS (48:1) Wint 78-79, p. 60.

DAWSON, Gene
"The One with My Number on It" (for Allan).   KanQ (11:1/2)
    Wint-Spr 79, p. 155.
"When a Body" (for _____).   KanQ (11:1/2) Wint-Spr 79, p.
    154.

DAWSON, Hester Jewell
"Divorce. " JnlONJP (3:2) 79, p. 42.
"Listen. " JnlONJP (3:2) 79, p. 42.

DAWSON, Richard G.
"We Listened to Our Hearts. " Wind (35) 79, p. 13.

DAYAN, Joan C.
"Annunciation" (to André Breton) (tr. of Aimé Césaire).   Paint
    (12) Aut 79, p. 27.

DAYTON, David
"Poem Appended to a Gift. " Tendril (5) Sum 79, p. 23.
"Round Trip to the Lake Isle. " SouthernPR (19:2) Aut 79, p. 27.

DAYTON, Irene
Poem.   St. AR (5:2) 79, p. 59.

DEAGON, Ann
"Arte Vitraria--The Glassmaker's Trade. " NewL (46:1) Aut 79,
    p. 91.
"Sex-Specific. " NewL (46:1) Aut 79, p. 93.

DEAL, Susan
"Daguerreotype. " PoNow (25) 79, p. 46.
"Daguerreotype. " EnPas (8) 79, p. 33.

DEAN, C.
"On Board the Maid of the Mist. " NewL (46:1) Aut 79, p. 51.

DEAN, John
"Going Nowhere Fast. " MalR (52) O 79, p. 42.
"Schedules. " MalR (52) O 79, p. 43.

DeANGELIS, Jacqueline
"Interior Improvisations. " Bachy (15) Aut 79, p. 64.

DeARAUJO, Virginia
"Last Child. " BelPoJ (29:3) Spr 79, p. 26.

DeBOLT, William Walter
"Fringe Benefits. " ChrC (96:23) 4-11 Jl 79, p. 693.
"Misers of Inaction. " ChrC (96:8) 7 Mr 79, p. 244.
"Response. " KanQ (11:3) Sum 79, p. 81.
"Underdog. " ChrC (96:30) 26 S 79, p. 919.

DEBRAVO, Jorge
"Silences. " LitR (23:2) Wint 80, p. 226.

DECHAR, Lorie
"Like the Soft Laughter of Hard Bells. " Tendril (5) Sum 79, p. 24.

DeCHAZAL, Malcolm
from Sens Magique: Fourteen poems (tr. by Irving Weiss).
    Chelsea (38) 79, p. 20.

DeCORMIER-SHEKERJIAN, R.
"On the eighth we listen to a mix of Charles Ives. " Tendril (4)
    Wint 79, p. 21.
"Sunday, the first. " Tendril (4) Wint 79, p. 20.
"Winter. " Tendril (4) Wint 79, p. 19.

DEEM, George
"Aanababcac. " SunM (8) Aut 79, p. 170.

DEETER, Kay
"In Sickness and in Health. " FourQt (28:3) Spr 79, p. 36.

DeFINA, Allan
"the cloud shrinks earth curse the world shrinks. " Mouth (2:3)
    N 79, p. 45.
"For David. " Mouth (2:3) N 79, p. 47.

DeFOE, Mark
"The Abandoned Farm--An Inventory. " CarlMis (17:2/3) Spr 79,
    p. 119.
"Bringing Home Breakfast: Buckhannon, W. Va. " PoNow (25)
    79, p. 6.
"Deep Winter. " Confr (18) Spr-Sum 79, p. 57.
"Euphoria, Euphoria. " CarlMis (17:2/3) Spr 79, p. 120.

DeFORD, Sara
Poem. St. AR (5:2) 79, p. 18.
Poem. St. AR (5:2) 79, p. 46.
"So Be It. " ArizQ (35:1) Spr 79, p. 41.
"Teacher. " ArizQ (35:4) Wint 79, p. 356.

DeFREES, Madeline
"Birthday Poem. " MissouriR (3:1) Aut 79, p. 19.
"Imaginary Ancestors: What Makes or Breaks Them. " MassR
    (20:4) Wint 79, p. 683.
"Ulysses S. Grant (1822-1885). " MassR (20:4) Wint 79, p. 684.

DeGRAVELLES, Charles
"Night Out, Tom Cat" (for John). PoNow (25) 79, p. 6.

DeGRAZIA, Emilio
"Professor of Desire. " CarlMis (17:2/3) Spr 79, p. 46.

DELANEY, Douglas
"After and Before There Was Anything. " Ploughs (5:3) 79, pp.
    124-125.
"Thank You Note. " Ploughs (5:3) 79, p. 126.
"Tired Eyes. " MissouriR (2:2/3) Spr 79, p. 33.

De la TORRIENT, Donna Duesel
"The Pathetic Man?" Tele (15) Spr 79, p. 147.
"The Pickle Jar. " Tele (15) Spr 79, p. 146.

DeLAURENTIS, Louise Budd
"Letter to the Man in the Moon. " KanQ (11:3) Sum 79, p. 76.
"Travel for Water-Bearing Clouds. " Wind (33) 79, p. 14.

DeLEON, Ulálume González
"Décalages" (tr. by Sara Nelson). DenQ (14:1) Spr 79, p. 31.
"L'esprit de la langue" (tr. by Sara Nelson). DenQ (14:1) Spr
    79, p. 30.
"The Familiar Sheets" (tr. by Sara Nelson). DenQ (14:1) Spr
    79, p. 28.
")Parentheses(" (tr. by Sara Nelson). DenQ (14:1) Spr 79, p. 27.
"Words" (tr. by Sara Nelson). DenQ (14:1) Spr 79, p. 32.

DELP, Michael
"The Leaving. " PoNow (22) 79, p. 12.
"Power. " PoNow (22) 79, p. 12.
"Rain. " PoNow (22) 79, p. 12.
"River. " PoNow (22) 79, p. 12.
"Warning. " PoNow (22) 79, p. 12.

DeMARIS, Ron
"Fiddler Crab. " SouthernPR (19:1) Spr 79, p. 24.

DeMOTT, Robert
"The Deaths That Stay with Us. " QW (9) Spr-Sum 79, p. 95.

"Trout Fishing, West Branch of the Saugatuck. " SouthernPR
(19:2) Aut 79, p. 49.

DEMPSTER, Barry
"The Boy in the Middle of the Land. " GreenfieldR (7:3/4) Spr-
Sum 79, p. 267.
"Clea. " CarlMis (17:2/3) Spr 79, p. 91.
"Cottage Country. " Poem (35) Mr 79, pp. 24-27.
"Havelock Hotel. " EnPas (8) 79, p. 22.
"The Lion's Dream. " EnPas (9) 79, p. 19.
"Post-Operative. " WindO (34) Spr-Sum 79, p. 12.
"Role Playing. " StoneC (6:2) My 79, p. 30.
"71 Yearbook, 78. " GreenfieldR (7:3/4) Spr-Sum 79, p. 268.
"The Snake and the Dinosaur. " Poem (35) Mr 79, pp. 22-23.
"Three Approaches. " WindO (34) Spr-Sum 79, p. 13.
"Titanic. " WindO (34) Spr-Sum 79, p. 11.
"The Unexpected Sorrow of a Logical Man. " MalR (51) Jl 79,
p. 132.

DEN BOER, James
"Appaloosa Mule. " PortR (25) 79, pp. 51-55.
"Weeds. " PortR (25) 79, p. 55.

DENIS, Philippe
"A l'amarre de ton sang. " Mund (11:1) 79, p. 40.
"A la place du vent. " Mund (11:1) 79, p. 42.
"A vivre comme respirer. " Mund (11:1) 79, p. 42.
"Living not living--" (tr. by Mark Irwin). PoNow (24) 79, p. 12.
"La maison tremble parfois. " Mund (11:1) 79, p. 40.
"Le monde est déjà loin derrière. " Mund (11:1) 79, p. 40.
"Sentier. " Mund (11:1) 79, p. 42.

DENNING, T. A.
"A Football Injury, A Mourning Haze. " BelPoJ (29:3) Spr 79,
p. 5.

DENNIS, Carl
"Backyard Guidebook. " PoetryNW (20:1) Spr 79, pp. 6-7.
"The Band. " VirQR (55:3) Sum 79, p. 501.
"The Embassy. " NewRep (180:9) 3 Mr 79, p. 35.
"Fiction. " PoetryNW (20:1) Spr 79, pp. 4-5.
"Igor. " PoetryNW (20:1) Spr 79, pp. 3-4.
"In Belmerton. " NewRep (180:15) 14 Ap 79, p. 53.
"In the West. " VirQR (55:3) Sum 79, p. 502.
"Oyez! Oyez! " AmerPoR (8:5) S-O 79, p. 46.
"The Reunion. " PoetryNW (20:1) Spr 79, pp. 7-8.
"Where Have You Been?" PoetryNW (20:1) Spr 79, pp. 5-6.

DeOCA, Marco Antonio Montes
"Francis Ponge's District" (tr. by Lysander Kemp). DenQ (14:1)
Spr 79, p. 110.
"Green Light for the Yellow Light" (tr. by Lysander Kemp).
DenQ (14:1) Spr 79, p. 109.

"The Poet Doesn't Want to Wake Up" (tr. by Lysander Kemp).
DenQ (14:1) Spr 79, p. 112.
"Traveling Balcony" (tr. by Lysander Kemp). DenQ (14:1) Spr
79, p. 111.

DePAOLA, Daniel
"Separation. " Poem (37) N 79, p. 59.

DEPTA, Victor M.
"Civilized Rooms. " PoetC (11:2) 79, p. 26.
"The Couple. " PoetC (11:2) 79, p. 25.

DerHOVANESSIAN, Diana
"Burst if you wish, cry if you will" (tr. of Hamo Sahian).
PoNow (24) 79, p. 51.
"From the Notebook of the Mad Man" (tr. of Aharon Dadourian).
PoNow (24) 79, p. 11.
"The Hanum" (tr. of Vahan Tekeyan). PoNow (24) 79, p. 59.
"My ideas" (tr. of Hamo Sahian). PoNow (24) 79, p. 51.
"The Poet to His Nation" (tr. of Vahan Tekeyan). PoNow (21)
79, p. 45.
"Spanish Guitar. " Paint (11) Spr 79, p. 25.
"Vision" (tr. of Hamo Sahian). PoNow (24) 79, p. 51.
"Your Unripe Love" (tr. of Payour Sevak). PoNow (24) 79, p.
54.

DeROSA, Elaine
"Alone Like a Beast" (tr. of Jean Breton). Mund (11:1) 79, p.
69.
"You Grow New" (tr. of Jean Breton). Mund (11:1) 79, p. 71.

DERR, Mark B.
"Days of Rain. " KanQ (11:1/2) Wint-Spr 79, p. 103.

DERRICK, Curtis
"Metamorphosis. " Wind (35) 79, p. 14.

DERRICOTTE, Toi
"For a Godchild, Regina, on the Occasion of Her First Love. "
Cond (5) 79, p. 109.

DESNOS, Robert
"Devil's Day" (tr. by Perry Oldham). Kayak (52) D 79, p. 67.
"In the Spaces of Sleep" (tr. by Marion Buchanan). AmerPoR
(8:1) Ja-F 79, p. 21.
"Men" (tr. by Perry Oldham). EnPas (9) 79, p. 30.
"No Love Is Not Dead" (tr. by Marian Buchanan). AmerPoR
(8:1) Ja-F 79, p. 21.
"The Ox and the Rose" (tr. by Perry Oldham). Kayak (52) D
79, p. 66.
"Les Quatre Sans Cou" (tr. by John Glassco). MalR (49) Ja 79,
p. 122.
"To Those Without any Heads" (tr. by Perry Oldham). EnPas
(9) 79, p. 28.

DESSI, Gigi
"All Will Hear" (tr. by Mario Fratti). Wind (33) 79, p. 15.
"I'm Empty" (tr. by Mario Fratti). Wind (33) 79, p. 15.
"I'm Not a Fisherman" (tr. by Mario Fratti). Wind (33) 79, p. 15.
"on the rope" (tr. by Dominick Lepore). St. AR (5:3) Aut-Wint 79, p. 123.

DEUTSCH, Babette
"The Aged Woman to Her Sons. " Paint (11) Spr 79, p. 11.

DEVANANDASHAM, Jnana
"Don't Bury the Part of History You Don't Like--Hang It Out to Dry. " SeC (7:1) 79, p. 15.
"Worne Houses Puckered Haymounds Westron Barns Garland the Wind. " SeC (7:1) 79, p. 18.

DeVAUL, Diane
"I Want You. " PoetC (11:1) 79, p. 28.

DeVEAUX, Alexis
"The Sisters. " Cond (5) 79, p. 31.

DeVRIES, Carrow
"A Pink Lady. " WindO (35) Aut-Wint 79-80, p. 16.

DeVRIES, Rachel
"Anniversary Poem. " PoNow (25) 79, p. 6.
"My Mother's Demons. " PoNow (25) 79, p. 7.

DEY, Richard Morris
from Wind Against the Tide: "Airport 1/5/76. " Poetry (133:4) Ja 79, p. 205.
from Wind Against the Tide: "Fog 9/76. " Poetry (133:4) Ja 79, pp. 206-207.
from Wind Against the Tide: "Wind Against the Tide 5/9/77. " Poetry (133:4) Ja 79, pp. 207-210.
from Wind Against the Tide: "China Royal Restaurant 11/13/77. " Poetry (133:4) Ja 79, pp. 210-212.

DeYOUNG, Robert
"My Son's Uncle Bill. " Confr (18) Spr-Sum 79, p. 110.

DiCICCO, Pier Giorgio
"Pushing It. " MalR (49) Ja 79, p. 35.
"Words to the Wind. " MalR (49) Ja 79, p. 34.

DICKEY, James
"A Saying of Farewell. " NewRep (181:16) 20 O 79, p. 36.

DICKEY, R. P.
"Big Attack Dogs. " PoNow (23) 79, p. 14.
"The Black Egret of New Zealand. " PoNow (22) 79, p. 13.

"A Covey of Quails. " PoNow (22) 79, p. 13.
"The Great American Poem. " Antaeus (32) Wint 79, pp. 82-86.
"Meringue. " PoNow (23) 79, p. 14.

DICKEY, William
    "Another Given: The Last Day of the Year. " NewEngR (1:3)
        Spr 79, p. 356.
    "Aubrey's Brief Lives. " Poetry (134:6) S 79, pp. 344-352.
    "Bare Feet in the Wrong Household. " Chowder (13) Aut-Wint
        79, p. 8.
    "The Great American Poem. " Antaeus (32) Wint 79, pp. 82-86.
    "Hand-Made Animals and the Great Depression. " NewEngR (2:1)
        Aut 79, p. 125.
    "Happiness. " PoNow (23) 79, p. 21.
    "Miss Mabel Mercer at 78. " PoNow (21) 79, p. 9.
    "Moment of Waking. " NewEngR (2:1) Aut 79, p. 122.
    "Old People. " Chowder (13) Aut-Wint 79, p. 6.
    "The Rainbow Grocery. " PoNow (23) 79, p. 20.

DICKINSON, Patric
    "Our Living John. " Stand (20:1) 78-79, p. 4.

DICKINSON, Simonne
    "Bread and Butter Letter" (Tribute to Eve Triem). Wind (35)
        79, p. 15.
    "The Empty Chair. " StoneC (6:1) F 79, p. 24.

DIGBY, Joan
    "September Gray. " Confr (19) Aut 79-Wint 80, p. 176.

DiGIOVANNI, Norman Thomas
    "Ein Traum" (tr. of Jorge Luis Borges). SunM (8) Aut 79, p.
        7.

DINER, Steven
    "The Death of All These Things. " Chelsea (38) 79, p. 204.

DiPASQUALE, E.
    "Mid-March. " PoNow (23) 79, p. 34.

DiPIERO, W. S.
    "Aurelio. " Ploughs (5:1) 79, pp. 34-35.
    "City Lights" (for Mary Jane). SouthernR (15:3) Sum 79, p.
        638.
    Fifteen Poems (tr. of Sandro Penna). PoNow (24) 79, pp. 42-44.
    "I live today. " SouthernR (15:3) Sum 79, p. 642.
    "It was September. People were back" (tr. of Sandro Penna).
        PoNow (21) 79, p. 45.
    "A living. " SouthernR (15:3) Sum 79, p. 641.
    Nine Poems (tr. of Leonardo Sinisgalli). PoNow (24) 79, pp.
        55-56.
    "O cemetery lights, don't tell me" (tr. of Sandro Penna).
        PoNow (21) 79, p. 45.

"Steerage. " Ploughs (5:1) 79, pp. 32-33.
"There was no one in the porter's lodge" (tr. of Sandro Penna).
    PoNow (21) 79, p. 45.
"Too much at once. " SouthernR (15:3) Sum 79, p. 640.
"The Tracking Shot. " Chelsea (38) 79, p. 215.
"Two Things. " Agni (10/11) 79, p. 145.
"Under the April sky this peace of mine" (tr. of Sandro Penna).
    PoNow (21) 79, p. 45.
"View" (tr. of Christian J. Van Geel w. Emilie Peech).   PoNow
    (24) 79, p. 61.
"The White Horses of Dawn. " Chelsea (38) 79, p. 186.
"Wildwood by the Sea. " SouthernR (15:3) Sum 79, p. 639.
"Wind is always driving, wind" (tr. of Christian J. Van Geel w.
    Emilie Peech). PoNow (24) 79, p. 61.

DiPRIMA, Diane
    "Uptown Motel. " DacTerr (16) 79, p. 12.
    "Waking at Josie's. " DacTerr (16) 79, p. 11.

DiPRISCO, Joseph
    "The Party. " Kayak (50) My 79, p. 22.

DISCH, Tom
    "The Childhood of Language" (for Chip and Iva).   LittleM (12:1/2)
        Spr-Sum 78 (79), p. 21.
    "A Concise History of Music. " PartR (46:1) 79, p. 103.
    "The Forbidden Children. " OP (27) Spr 79, p. 52.
    "Songs of the Rooftops. " OP (27) Spr 79, pp. 47-48.
    "Symbols of Love and Death. " Shen (30:2) Wint 79, p. 91.
    "Vespers. " OP (27) Spr 79, pp. 49-51.
    "What it was like. " PartR (46:1) 79, p. 102.

DISTLER, Bette
    "cousin" (In memorial: Dr. Peter Lake). NewL (46:2) Wint 79-
        80, p. 48.
    "growth. " NewL (46:2) Wint 79-80, p. 49.
    "I put my body. " NewL (46:2) Wint 79-80, p. 50.

DITSKY, John
    "Advice to a Young Man. " Spirit (3:1/2) Aut-Wint 77-78, p. 57.
    "Cutting the Roots. " Poem (37) N 79, p. 44.
    "Epithalamium. " Poem (37) N 79, p. 46.
    "Growl. " KanQ (11:1/2) Wint-Spr 79, p. 50.
    "A Single Dip Is Enough. " HolCrit (16:4) O 79, p. 12.
    "Student Power. " WindO (35) Aut-Wint 79-80, p. 11.
    "Sunstroke. " MalR (49) Ja 79, p. 38.
    "Vacation. " CarlMis (18:1) Wint 79-80, p. 57.
    "The Wager. " Poem (37) N 79, p. 45.

DIXON, Melvin
    "Autumn Leaving" (for Didier). Mouth (2:3) N 79, p. 19.

DJANIKIAN, Gregory
    "After the First Snow. " Confr (18) Spr-Sum 79, p. 55.

DLUGOS, Tim
"In London" (for Michael Chaplin). SunM (8) Aut 79, p. 31.

DOBBERSTEIN, Michael
"China Nights. " WestHR (33:3) Sum 79, p. 252.
"Church of Christ, West Texas. " CharR (5:2) Aut 79, p. 73.
"Junior Lopez. " QW (8) Wint 79, p. 62.
"New Moon. " QW (6) Spr-Sum 78, p. 91.
"Snow. " SouthwR (64:1) Wint 79, p. 85.

DOBRIN, Arthur
"Father and Son. " Chelsea (38) 79, p. 133.
"Fever. " Confr (18) Spr-Sum 79, p. 94.
"Politics, as Usual. " Chelsea (38) 79, p. 132.

DOBYNS, Stephen
"Fear. " VirQR (55:3) Sum 79, p. 510.
"Night Song. " Kayak (52) D 79, p. 48.
"Pablo Neruda. " NoAmR (264:4) Wint 79, p. 79.
"The Poem as Actor in Three Parts for Michael Ryan. " Kayak
    (52) D 79, p. 49.
"Separations. " Ploughs (5:1) 79, pp. 36-38.
"Song of Basic Necessities" (for E. F.). VirQR (55:3) Sum 79,
    p. 511.
"Song of Four Dancers. " Kayak (51) S 79, p. 40.
"Song of the Drowned Boy. " Kayak (51) S 79, p. 41.

DODD, Wayne
from The General Mule Poems: A Selection: "Of Characters. "
    GeoR (33:3) Aut 79, p. 598.
from The General Mule Poems: A Selection: "Of Chopping
    Wood. " GeoR (33:3) Aut 79, p. 596.
from The General Mule Poems: A Selection: "Of Journeys. "
    GeoR (33:3) Aut 79, p. 594.
from The General Mule Poems: A Selection: "Of Killing. "
    GeoR (33:3) Aut 79, p. 595.
from The General Mule Poems: A Selection: "Of Legends. "
    GeoR (33:3) Aut 79, p. 597.
from The General Mule Poems: A Selection: "Of Sitting Bear. "
    GeoR (33:3) Aut 79, p. 600.
from The General Mule Poems: A Selection: "Of Sunlight. "
    GeoR (33:3) Aut 79, p. 599.
"Of Silence. " Nat (229:11) 13 O 79, p. 342.

DODMAN, Martin
"Passages. " Montra (5) 79, p. 191.

DOLAN, John D.
"I cruise the bar with a practiced eye. " Mouth (2:3) N 79, p.
    42.

DONAHUE, Jack
"Dominion over the Design of Daily Life. " Im (6:1) 79, p. 11.

DONAHUE, Joe
"Returning. " Columbia (3) 79, p. 75.

DONEGAN, Ann W.
"From the Diary of Noe's Wife. " Tendril (4) Wint 79, p. 22.

DONEHOWER, Bruce
"The Emerald Tablet. " GreenfieldR (7:3/4) Spr-Sum 79, p. 246.
"Hands. " GreenfieldR (7:3/4) Spr-Sum 79, p. 247.

DONOVAN, Brad
"More Facts About Socks. " GreenfieldR (7:3/4) Spr-Sum 79, p.
    117.
"The White Road. " GreenfieldR (7:3/4) Spr-Sum 79, p. 115.

DONOVAN, Susan
"The Born Bride. " Kayak (51) S 79, p. 27.
"Last Wishes. " NewL (46:1) Aut 79, p. 99.
"Song of a Figurehead. " NewL (46:1) Aut 79, p. 98.

DORESKI, William
"After Blake, An All-Night Stand. " Ur (2) 79, p. 26.
"The Blue Angel. " MissR (24) Aut 79, p. 25.
"The Blue Dress. " MissR (24) Aut 79, p. 19.
"Coastal Storm. " MissR (24) Aut 79, p. 21.
"The Dudley Murders. " Ploughs (5:3) 79, pp. 153-155.
"Not a Love Letter. " MissR (24) Aut 79, p. 27.
"The Old Garden Swing Rehung for Sexual Gymnastics. " MissR
    (24) Aut 79, p. 23.

DORMAN, Sonya
"The Crows. " NoAmR (264:3) Aut 79, p. 67.
"Dear Jane Doe. " PoNow (22) 79, p. 13.
"The Death of the Night Nurse. " WestB (4) 79, p. 51.
"Maps. " PoNow (22) 79, p. 13.
"An Old Movie. " WestB (4) 79, p. 52.

DOTY, M. R.
"Come the Revolution. " Kayak (50) My 79, p. 58.
"For His Cat. " Nimrod (23:1) Aut-Wint 79, p. 63.
"Night Work. " PoNow (25) 79, p. 7.
"Owls. " GreenfieldR (7:3/4) Spr-Sum 79, p. 173.
"Questions Answered About Birds. " Tendril (4) Wint 79, p. 24.
"Remembering You. " Nimrod (23:1) Aut-Wint 79, p. 61.
"Roots. " GreenfieldR (7:3/4) Spr-Sum 79, p. 175.
"Thistles and Ears. " Nimrod (23:1) Aut-Wint 79, p. 62.
"Towers. " Tendril (5) Sum 79, p. 25.
"Variations. " GreenfieldR (7:3/4) Spr-Sum 79, p. 174.

DOUBIAGO, Sharon
"1730. " BelPoJ (30:2) Wint 79-80, p. 40.

DOUGHERTY, Mary
"A Dry Wind Flies. " CalQ (15) Wint 79, p. 62.

"I Was the First and Not Planned But O. " CalQ (15) Wint 79,
  p. 60.
"What Cowgirls Say. " CalQ (15) Wint 79, p. 63.

DOUGHERTY, Mary Ellen
"Early Autumn. " ChrC (96:32) 10 O 79, p. 975.

DOUGLAS, Ann
"Not Going Out Today. " GeoR (33:4) Wint 79, p. 900.

DOUSKEY, Franz
"Bardo. " GreenfieldR (7:3/4) Spr-Sum 79, p. 202.
"Burning the Gypsies. " GreenfieldR (7:3/4) Spr-Sum 79, p. 203.
"Clear Moonlight. " GeoR (33:1) Spr 79, p. 84.
"Everything Is Ready. " Chelsea (38) 79, p. 218.
"Hell's Kitchen. " GreenfieldR (7:3/4) Spr-Sum 79, p. 200.
"It's Getting Late Earlier. " Ur (2) 79, p. 25.
"The Sleep Collector. " GeoR (33:1) Spr 79, p. 85.
"The Tragedy of Beasts. " Kayak (52) D 79, p. 47.

DOVE, Rita
"Beauty and the Beast. " NoAmR (264:4) Wint 79, p. 47.
"Champagne. " OhioR (20:2) Spr-Sum 79, p. 36.
"David Walker (1785-1830). " MissouriR (2:2/3) Spr 79, p. 56.
"Ö. " OhioR (20:2) Spr-Sum 79, p. 37.
"Small Town. " GeoR (33:4) Wint 79, p. 805.

DOW, Philip
"Divorce. " SlowLR (3) 79, p. 45.
"Ghazals. " Pequod (3:1) 79, pp. 8-9.
"Potlatch. " Pequod (3:1) 79, pp. 1-7.
"Sacre du Printemps. " Kayak (50) My 79, p. 38.   Found poem.

DOWD, Jeanne
"Divining Rod. " Ploughs (5:1) 79, p. 39.

DOYLE, James
"The Prescience. " Wind (33) 79, p. 16.
"The Visit. " Wind (33) 79, p. 16.

DOYLE, Mike
"Klee and Kandinsky at Dessau. " MalR (51) Jl 79, p. 131.

DOYLE, Suzanne
"Near Dark. " SouthernR (15:4) Aut 79, p. 1014.
"November Walk. " SouthernR (15:4) Aut 79, p. 1014.
"A Simple Privacy. " SouthernR (15:4) Aut 79, p. 1010.
"This Shade. " SouthernR (15:4) Aut 79, p. 1013.
"The Unforgiving. " SouthernR (15:4) Aut 79, p. 1012.
"The Wasp. " SouthernR (15:4) Aut 79, p. 1011.

DRAKE, Barbara
"Bus Fare. " PoNow (25) 79, p. 20.
"The Man Who Invented One. " PoNow (25) 79, p. 20.

"Roses Are Heavy Feeders. " PoNow (25) 79, p. 20.
"The Woman Gets Restless. " PoNow (25) 79, p. 20.

DRENDEL, Denise
"There Is a Difference. " EngJ (68:5) My 79, p. 37.

DREW, George
"A Death on Campus. " PoNow (25) 79, p. 7.

DRISCOLL, Jack
"The Accidents of Dreams. " SouthernPR (19:1) Spr 79, p. 23.
"Ice. " SouthernPR (19:1) Spr 79, p. 21.
"Instructions for Diving Under the Ice. " SouthernPR (19:1) Spr
    79, p. 22.
"January: Hunting Ducks in the Dark. " BelPoJ (30:1) Aut 79,
    p. 1.
"The Mailman. " PoetryNW (20:2) Sum 79, pp. 29-30.
"Snowblinded While Hunting. " PoetryNW (20:2) Sum 79, pp. 28-
    29.

DRURY, John
"Chestnuts. " SouthernPR (19:1) Spr 79, p. 71.
"Decoys. " Poetry (134:4) Jl 79, pp. 218-220.
"Ransom Note. " Shen (30:1) Aut 78, p. 47.

DRUSKA, John
"This Evening. " Bits (10) Jl 79.

DUBELYEW, Didi Susan
"Illuminations. " Tele (15) Spr 79, p. 86.
"Oatmeal and Other Mush. " Tele (15) Spr 79, p. 87.
"Poem: on waking up. " Tele (15) Spr 79, p. 87.

DUBIE, Norman
"Coleridge Crossing the Plain of Jars: 1833" (for Sherod San-
    tos). Field (20) Spr 79, p. 9.
"Einstein's Exile in an Old Dutch Winter. " NewYorker (55:38)
    5 N 79, p. 46.
"Elsinore in the Late Ancient Autumn. " GeoR (33:1) Spr 79, p.
    149.
"The Mystery of Six Empty Places: Confucius and the Raven
    Haired Daughter:. " QW (7) Aut 78, p. 57.
"Spirit Pond. " QW (7) Aut 78, p. 59.

DUBIE, William
"The Burned Barn. " Wind (32) 79, p. 10.

DUBROFF, Susanne
"With Boris Pasternak. " Tendril (4) Wint 79, p. 26.

DUCKWORTH, Mark
"Bubble Gum Addiction Clinic. " HangL (35) Spr 79, p. 69.
"Summer and Cinnamon. " HangL (35) Spr 79, p. 70.
"Teaching After Hours. " HangL (35) Spr 79, p. 70.

DUDDY, Patrick
"Garden in Sidari. " Paint (12) Aut 79, p. 14.

DUDIS, Ellen Kirvin
"Authors. " PortR (25) 79, p. 104.
"Stroke. " CarlMis (17:2/3) Spr 79, p. 106.

DUEMER, Joseph
"The Burning of the Ozark Hotel. " DacTerr (16) 79, p. 13.
"Curses. " CarolQ (31:1) Wint 79, p. 48.
"The Gazelles. " PoetryNW (20:4) Wint 79-80, p. 33.
"Whisky Bottle Found on the Beach. " PoNow (25) 79, p. 47.

DUERN, Darlene Nowlan
"From a Blue Notebook. " Os (8) 79, p. 27-31.

DUFAULT, Peter Kane
"Evensong. " Atl (243:5) My 79, p. 79.

DUGAN, Alan
"The Great American Poem. " Antaeus (32) Wint 79, pp. 82-86.

DUKES, Thomas
"June 31. " KanQ (11:1/2) Wint-Spr 79, p. 183.

DUNCAN, Michael
"The Latin Hustle. " Mouth (2:3) N 79, p. 41.

DUNHAM, Vera S.
"Children of the Cult" (tr. of Andrei Voznesensky). Nat (229:22)
    29 D 79, p. 692.
"Days of Shame and Sorrow" (tr. of Olga Berggolts). Nat
    (229:22) 29 D 79, p. 693.
"Saga" (tr. of Andrei Voznesensky w. William Jay Smith).
    PoNow (24) 79, p. 36.
"Stalin Is Not Dead" (tr. of Boris Chichibabin). Nat (229:22) 29
    D 79, p. 693.

DUNLOP, Donna
"To My Great Aunt Edie Liddiard-Vincent. " MalR (52) O 79, p.
    119.
"Wolf Print. " MalR (52) O 79, p. 118.

DUNLOP, Lane
"I am taking the train with you to the ballpark. Then you. "
    PoNow (22) 79, p. 13.

DUNMORE, Helen
"The Marshalling Yard. " Stand (20:4) 79, p. 47.

DUNN, Millard
"Choirmaster. " PoetryNW (20:1) Spr 79, pp. 32-33.

DUNN, Robert
"A Ghost. " Aspect (74/75) Ja-Ag 79, p. 41.
"New England town. " Aspect (74/75) Ja-Ag 79, p. 40.

DUNN, Sharon
"Anna. " WestB (5) 79, p. 64.
"The Falcon's Back. " WestB (5) 79, p. 65.
"Mail Order. " CutB (12) Spr-Sum 79, p. 22.
"Working Mother. " Confr (19) Aut 79-Wint 80, p. 90.

DUNN, Stephen
"After Losses" (for J. P.).   MissouriR (2:2/3) Spr 79, p. 26.
"Amidst the Faltering. " QW (8) Wint 79, p. 56.
"Checklist. " NowestR (18:2) 79, p. 16.
"The Clarities. " QW (8) Wint 79, p. 57.
"Currents. " CutB (13) Aut-Wint 79, p. 43.
"The Great American Poem. " Antaeus (32) Wint 79, pp. 82-86.
from The Monastery of Work and Love: "A Worker's Creed. "
    OhioR (20:2) Spr-Sum 79, p. 31.
from The Monastery of Work and Love: "From an Upstairs
    Window. " MissouriR (2:2/3) Spr 79, p. 25.
from The Monastery of Work and Love: "Second Prelude to the
    Monastery. " OhioR (20:2) Spr-Sum 79, p. 32.
from The Monastery of Work and Love: 'Watching the News:
    First Prelude to the Monastery. " OhioR (20:2) Spr-Sum 79,
    p. 30.
from The Monastery of Work and Love: 'With No Experience in
    Such Matters. " OhioR (20:2) Spr-Sum 79, p. 31.
"Money. " QW (7) Aut 78, p. 115.
"Monologue for the Man Who Is Always Next Door. " PoetryNW
    (20:3) Aut 79, pp. 37-38.
"Movements. " CutB (13) Aut-Wint 79, p. 44.
"Outfielder. " Bits (9) Ja 79.
"Sentience. " PoetryNW (20:3) Aut 79, pp. 38-39.
"Something. " QW (8) Wint 79, p. 57.
"Truckstop: Minnesota. " DacTerr (16) 79, p. 14.

DUNNE, Carol
"Nursing the Hide. " Poem (35) Mr 79, p. 9.
"Opportunist. " Poem (35) Mr 79, pp. 6-7.
"Provender. " Poem (35) Mr 79, p. 8.

DUNNING, Stephen
"About the Grave of Emily. " CharR (5:2) Aut 79, p. 77.
"Checking In. " CutB (12) Spr-Sum 79, p. 11.
"Gathering Light. " HiramPoR (26) Spr-Sum 79, p. 18.
"Kisses or Hugs. " CarlMis (17:2/3) Spr 79, p. 184.
"A Little Poem. " Wind (32) 79, p. 11.
"Player. " NewL (46:1) Aut 79, p. 42.
"Slants. " Wind (32) 79, p. 12.
"Springtime, swallowing gently. " SouthernPR (19:2) Aut 79, p.
    10.
"Surprise, like a fly. " SouthernPR (19:2) Aut 79, p. 11.

DuPLESSIS, Rachel Blau
"Medusa. " Montra (5) 79, p. 22.

DUPREE, Thomas
"Evening. " LittleM (12:1/2) Spr-Sum 78 (79), p. 45.

DuPRIEST, Travis
from Kentucky Tone Poems: "Carpet. " Wind (33) 79, p. 17.
from Kentucky Tone Poems: "Home. " Wind (33) 79, p. 17.
from Kentucky Tone Poems: "Vision. " Wind (33) 79, p. 17.
"Myth. " Wind (33) 79, p. 18.
"Visit to the Grave of Victor Hammer, Pisgah Church, Late
    Easter Morning, 1977. " Wind (33) 79, p. 17.

DUPUIS, Gilbert
"Parfois la vie. " Os (8) 79, p. 6.

DURAK, Carol
"Graveyard. " Wind (34) 79, p. 19.

DURAN, Jorge Gaitán
"Canto XV. " LitR (23:2) Wint 80, p. 256.
"Lovers. " LitR (23:2) Wint 80, p. 257.

DUREN, Francis
"The Incongruous. " CarlMis (18:1) Wint 79-80, p. 155.

DUVAL, Quinton
"The First Dog" (tr. of Jules Supervielle w. Andrew Grossbardt).
    QW (8) Wint 79, p. 83.
"The Last Time I Say Heart. " CutB (13) Aut-Wint 79, p. 34.
"Letter. " QW (7) Aut 78, p. 124.
"The Morning Comes Early. " QW (7) Aut 78, p. 125.
"Out of Touch. " QW (7) Aut 78, p. 124.
"The Port at Cameroon. " PoNow (22) 79, p. 13.
"Sonnet to Pilar" (tr. of Jules Supervielle w. Andrew Grossbardt).
    QW (8) Wint 79, p. 82.
"The Story of Spring. " QW (7) Aut 78, p. 125.
"The Trouble with Love. " CutB (13) Aut-Wint 79, p. 35.

DWORZAN, Hélène
"In the Pyrenees. " Chelsea (38) 79, p. 223.

DWYER, David
from Ariana Olisvos: Posthumous Verses and Letters: "Vanes-
    sa. " Agni (10/11) p. 53.
"Cold Comfort" (a vision for Carol Keller). Agni (10/11) 79, p.
    52.

DWYER, Frank
"On the Edge" (for Frank O'Hara). CentR (23:4) Aut 79, p. 427.
"Santayana's Maxim: A Corollary. " AntR (37:3) Sum 79, p. 317.

DYBEK, Stuart
"Dreams. " Sky (9) Aut 79, pp. 48-49.
"Groom. " PoNow (22) 79, p. 14.
"Kiddie Corner. " Poetry (135:1) O 79, p. 18.
"New Year's, Mingo Cay. " WestB (5) 79, p. 49.
"Stumps. " PoNow (21) 79, p. 8.
"To Acquire a Beautiful Body. " PoNow (22) 79, p. 14.
"Traveling Salesman. " PoNow (22) 79, p. 14.
"Two Fishermen. " WestB (5) 79, p. 50.
"Visibility. " WestB (5) 79, p. 49.

DYER, Thomas
"Fence Fruit. " EnPas (8) 79, p. 4.

EADES, Joan
"The Explorer. " PikeF (2) Wint 78-79, p. 22.
"The Writer's Conference. " PikeF (2) Wint 78-79, p. 27.

EARLE, Jean
"The Heart Tattoo. " Stand (20:3) 79, p. 4.
"One Man's Answer. " Stand (20:3) 79, p. 5.

EASTMAN, Jon
"An Old Man Scavenging in the Park. " SouthernPR (19:2) Aut
    79, p. 47.
"Working the Skeet House. " CharR (5:1) Spr 79, p. 65.

EATON, Charles Edward
"The Admissible Evidence of Autumn. " Poem (35) Mr 79, p. 2.
"Architectural Visions. " Paint (12) Aut 79, p. 16.
"Collected Works of an Erotic Author. " HolCrit (16:2) Ap 79,
    p. 19.
"In Search of the Sunbather as a Very Safe Thing. " Poem (35)
    Mr 79, p. 1.
"Inland Without Letters in Autumn. " SewanR (87:4) Aut 79, p.
    532.
"Interrupted Images. " SouthernPR (19:1) Spr 79, p. 9.
"The Paper weight. " SouthernHR (13:4) Aut 79, p. 330.
"Red. " Poem (35) Mr 79, p. 3.
"the search warrant. " St. AR (5:3) Aut-Wint 79, p. 123.
"Seascape with Bookends. " ArizQ (35:3) Aut 79, p. 196.
"Sleeping Nude. " SouthernPR (19:2) Aut 79, p. 71.

EATON, Philip
"The Field Hands: Phoenix, 1954. " PoetC (10:3) 79, p. 32.
"The Young Poet. " PoetC (11:2) 79, p. 33.

EBERHART, Richard
"Fog. " NewRep (181:11) 15 S 79, p. 28.
"Offering to the Body. " Poetry (134:6) S 79, pp. 342-343.
"Speculative Nature Note. " Poetry (134:6) S 79, p. 343.

EBERLY, David
"Mangaka. " Mouth (2:1) F 79, p. 6.

ECKMAN, Frederick
"Kieferville Cemetery. " Bits (9) Ja 79.

EDDY, Darlene Mathis
"Drifting. " GRR (10:1) 79, p. 123.
"Fire Woods. " GRR (10:1) 79, p. 124.
"In Early November. " GRR (10:1) 79, p. 122.

EDDY, Gary
"After Reading Lu Yu. " SlowLR (3) 79, p. 53.
"Borrowing My House from Insects. " SlowLR (3) 79, p. 51.
"Fishing with Buddies. " SlowLR (3) 79, p. 50.
"Widower's Guitar. " SlowLR (3) 79, p. 54.

EDELMAN, Ane
"Picture from a Sunday Supplement--The 1930's. " Madem (85:3)
Mr 79, p. 138.

EDGE, Donald
"Solstice. " JnlONJP (4:1) 79, p. 17.

EDKINS, Anthony
"Flower Piece. " Chelsea (38) 79, p. 128.
"Never and Always. " Chelsea (38) 79, p. 128.
"One of Those Summer Days When Everything Shimmers. "
Chelsea (38) 79, p. 129.

EDSON, Russell
"The Banker's Children. " PoNow (22) 79, Backcover.
"The Barking Dog. " Durak (3) 79, p. 20.
"The Bread Music. " Falcon (18) Spr 79, p. 52.
"By Candle Light. " PoNow (22) 79, p. 16.
"The Colleagues. " PoNow (22) 79, p. 15.
"The Conspiracy. " PoNow (22) 79, p. 23.
"The Dinner Monkey. " PoNow (22) 79, p. 16.
"The Fishermen. " Falcon (18) Spr 79, p. 51.
"The General and Mary Sue. " Durak (3) 79, p. 21.
"The Gingerbread Crime. " PoNow (22) 79, p. 23.
"The Great American Poem. " Antaeus (32) Wint 79, pp. 82-86.
"How It All Gets Kind of Fluttery. " Durak (2) 79, p. 10.
"The Inconvenienced Farmer. " PoNow (22) 79, p. 16.
"The Maggot. " PoNow (22) 79, p. 15.
"A Man Who Makes Tears. " PoNow (22) 79, p. 23.
"The Master's Nap. " PoNow (21) 79, p. 38.
"Mr. San Marino's Underwear. " Falcon (18) Spr 79, p. 54.
"No Poison in the House. " PoNow (22) 79, p. 16.
"The Old Grandfather Counting His Fingers. " PoNow (22) 79, p.
15.
"An Old Man's Fascination. " Durak (2) 79, p. 11.
"On the Cooking of Old Men. " Durak (3) 79, p. 19.
"A Piggyback Ride to the Slaughterhouse. " PoNow (23) 79, p.
14.
"The Royal Navy. " Falcon (18) Spr 79, p. 55.
"The Terrible Ape. " PoNow (21) 79, p. 38.

"The Two Isidores. " Agni (10/11) 79, p. 157.
'What the Talking-Doll Said. " PoNow (23) 79, p. 14.
'Why the Dean Needs His Smelling Salts. " Falcon (18) Spr 79,
    p. 53.

EERSEL, Eugenie
"Amsterdam No. 1. " GreenfieldR (7:3/4) Spr-Sum 79, p. 63.
"Brother. " GreenfieldR (7:3/4) Spr-Sum 79, p. 65.
'Wayana Man. " GreenfieldR (7:3/4) Spr-Sum 79, p. 64.

EGAN, Desmond
'My Second in Kentucky. " Confr (18) Spr-Sum 79, p. 109.
'Woodcutter. " Confr (18) Spr 79, p. 108.

EGEMO, Constance
"Professional Woman Room 309. " DacTerr (16) 79, p. 15.
'Welcoming Committee: Seaside Hotel. " DacTerr (16) 79, p.
    16.

EGGERTH, Chuck
'Much of Me. " KanQ (11:1/2) Wint-Spr 79, p. 202.

EHRENBURG, Ilya
"Once Upon a Time" (tr. by Leonard Opalov). Spirit (4:1) Aut-
    Wint 78-79, p. 17.

EHRHART, W. D.
"Peary & Henson Reach the North Pole. " Sam (72) 79, p. 34.
'Wilbur Wright. " Sam (79) 79, p. 84.

EHRLICH, Shelley
"Job's Wife. " Chowder (13) Aut-Wint 79, p. 26.
"On Linden Street. " Chowder (13) Aut-Wint 79, p. 28.
'The Swimming Lesson. " Northeast (3:7) Spr 79, p. 18.

EICH, Günter
"Present Time" (tr. by Betty Falkenberg). PoNow (24) 79, p.
    12.
"Unsigned" (tr. by Betty Falkenberg). PoNow (24) 79, p. 12.
'Where I Live" (tr. by Betty Falkenberg). PoNow (24) 79, p.
    12.

EICHHORN, Douglas
"And to Think We Could Have... " (tr. of Ramon Lopez Velarde).
    PoNow (24) 79, p. 23.
'My Heart Is Honored... " (tr. of Ramon Lopez Velarde). PoNow
    (24) 79, p. 23.
'The Purple Blemish" (tr. of Ramon Lopez Velarde). PoNow
    (24) 79, p. 23.

EIGNER, Larry
"Leaves. " SunM (8) Aut 79, p. 123.

EISENBERG, Edward
"Identity Pieces. " Mouth (2:3) N 79, p. 38.

ELDER, Gary
"Wolf House" (for James E. Sisson). Pig (6) 79, p. 29.

ELDER, Karl
"Standing in Line for Popcorn. " KanQ (11:3) Sum 79, p. 90.

ELIOT, Eileen
"A Perfect Mother. " SmPd (45) 79, p. 29.

ELKIND, Sue Saniel
"Battered. " BelPoJ (30:1) Aut 79, p. 34.
"Frustrations. " Wind (35) 79, p. 16.
"Sister and Brother. " Wind (35) 79, p. 16.

ELLEDGE, Jim
"At Home in Sodom. " Mouth (2:2) Je 79, p. 10.

ELLIOTT, Bill
"Letter to My Father-in-Law I. " PartR (46:2) 79, pp. 252-254.

ELLIOTT, Harley
"All the Heroes" (for Sean Flynn). Aspen (7) Spr 79, p. 74.
"Anonymous Strangers" (for Ron Slate). Aspen (7) Spr 79, p.
   73.
"Blue Wind. " Spirit (3:1/2) Aut-Wint 77-78, p. 19.
"Dream of the Kiowa. " HangL (36) Aut 79, p. 11.
"Flowery Words. " NewL (46:1) Aut 79, p. 37.
"For Farmers. " NewL (46:1) Aut 79, p. 36.
"The Iris" (for my father). Spirit (4:2/3) Spr-Sum 79, p. 6.
"John's Light" (for John Gill). HangL (36) Aut 79, p. 17.
"Men Hug Trees. " Spirit (4:2/3) Spr-Sum 79, p. 7.
"Old Man Finds the Spot. " Northeast (3:7) Spr 79, p. 7.
"Old Man Pitting Dates. " HangL (36) Aut 79, p. 16.
"Smoky Red Lights" (for Jim Nuhlicek). HangL (36) Aut 79, p.
   15.
"Stopping to Piss at Night" (for RVZ). Aspen (7) Spr 79, p. 74.
"Straight Man to the Muse. " HangL (36) Aut 79, p. 19.
"Ten Point Back to Nature Program. " HangL (36) Aut 79, p.
   12.
"To the Redbird. " HangL (36) Aut 79, p. 18.
"The Vacuum Cleaner Salesmen of America. " Northeast (3:7)
   Spr 79, p. 6.

ELLIOTT, William D.
"Hotel in Melbourne. " DacTerr (16) 79, p. 17.

ELLIOTT, William I.
"Five Minutes Into Sleep. " CarlMis (18:1) Wint 79-80, p. 73.

ELLIS, Don
"Lennie. " SmPd (46) 79, p. 5.

ELLIS, Kate
"All Night Cafeteria. " Tele (15) Spr 79, p. 100.
"The Patron Saint of Telegraph Avenue" (for Julia Vinograd).
13thM (4:2) 79, p. 75.

ELLIS, Patricia
"Monk's Song. " EnPas (8) 79, p. 20.

ELLIS, Rebecca
"Gardens. " HangL (35) Spr 79, p. 25.
"Night After Night Your Life. " HangL (35) Spr 79, p. 24.
"Small Reminders. " HangL (35) Spr 79, p. 23.

ELLIS, Reuben
"The Lone Volcano. " Wind (33) 79, p. 19.

ELLISON, Jessie T.
"The Cat Calendar Cats. " Poem (37) N 79, p. 65.
"The Chinese Cemetery. " WindO (35) Aut-Wint 79-80, p. 20.
"In the Summer Pond. " WindO (34) Spr-Sum 79, p. 23.
"The Newborn. " WindO (34) Spr-Sum 79, p. 22.
"The Touch of Frost. " WindO (34) Spr-Sum 79, p. 21.
"Waikiki Disco Dancer. " WindO (35) Aut-Wint 79-80, p. 21.

ELLMAN, Dennis
Thirteen Poems. Bachy (15) Aut 79, pp. 51-57.

ELMSLIE, Kenward
"The Great American Poem. " Antaeus (32) Wint 79, pp. 82-86.

ELON, Florence
"Generations. " SewanR (87:2) Spr 79, p. 221.
"The Match. " SewanR (87:2) Spr 79, p. 222.

ELSON, Virginia
"Not Being Wise. " LitR (23:2) Spr 79, p. 326.

ELVARD, Paul
"Nurse" (tr. by Richard Lebovitz). PoNow (24) 79, p. 12.

ELVIN, Frank
"Heard Poem. " PoNow (25) 79, p. 7.

ELYTES, Odysseus
"Medical Examiner's Report" (for Pasos Lignades) (tr. by Yiannis Petropoulos). HarvAd (112:4) My 79, p. 16.

EMANUEL, James A.
"For Young Blacks, The Lost Generation. " BlackALF (13:3)
Aut 79, p. 87.
"Stiff Roses Bring Their Simple Wish. " BlackALF (13:3) Aut
79, p. 88.

EMANUEL, Lynn
"Robinson Crusoe Who Was a Poet. " MissouriR (2:2/3) Spr 79,
    p. 44.

EMBLEM, D. L.
"At the Corner, on the Way to the Postoffice" (tr. of Werner
    Aspenström). PoNow (24) 79, p. 4.
"Comes May" (tr. of Werner Aspenström). PoNow (23) 79, p.
    45.
"Gray Sparrow" (tr. of Werner Aspenström). PoNow (23) 79,
    p. 45.
"Interpretation of a Dream" (tr. of Werner Aspenström).
    PoNow (24) 79, p. 4.
"Sunday" (tr. of Werner Aspenström w. Siv Cedering Fox).
    PoNow (24) 79, p. 4.
"Theology for a Ruminating Friend" (tr. of Werner Aspenström).
    PoNow (23) 79, p. 45.

EMERSON, Dorothy
"Imagined Girl. " Poetry (133:4) Ja 79, p. 217.
"Space Divides. " Poetry (133:4) Ja 79, p. 216.

EMIN, Gevorg
"And I Understood" (tr. by Martin Robbins). PoNow (24) 79, p.
    13.
"Dialogue" (tr. by Martin Robbins). PoNow (23) 79, p. 46.
"Doesn't It Seem to You, " (tr. by Martin Robbins). PoNow (24)
    79, p. 14.
"The Piano" (tr. by Martin Robbins). PoNow (24) 79, pp. 13-14.
"Winter Scene" (tr. by Martin Robbins). PoNow (24) 79, p. 13.

EMMETT, Elaine
"The Prodigals at Sunset. " SouthernHR (13:2) Spr 79, p. 164.

ENDER, Alison
"The Right Diet. " QW (9) Spr-Sum 79, p. 121.

ENGEL, Mary
"Apparition in the Afternoon. " NewRena (11) 79, p. 44.

ENGELS, John
"Adam Signing. " Agni (10/11) 79, p. 139.
"Bay Settlement, 1938. " NewEngR (1:3) Spr 79, p. 268.
"Bullhead. " Harp (258:1547) Ap 79, p. 83.
"Cerrita Buczkowski. " PoNow (21) 79, p. 42.
"The Crows. " Salm (46) Aut 79, p. 96.
"The Electric Fence Game. " Antaeus (34) Sum 79, p. 50.
"The Guardian of the Lakes at Notre Dame. " SewanR (87:3)
    Sum 79, p. 378.
"In Cedar Grove Cemetery. " SewanR (87:3) Sum 79, p. 377.
"In Panama. " Chowder (13) Aut-Wint 79, pp. 20-24.
"Instances of Blood in Iowa. " Iowa (10:1) Wint 79, p. 39.
"Mahler Waiting. " Salm (46) Aut 79, p. 97.

"The Mothwing, Ice at Dawn. " <u>Antaeus</u> (34) Sum 79, p. 54.
"The Reliquiarium in Sacred Heart Church. " <u>SewanR</u> (87:3) Sum
  79, p. 376.
"Saying the Names. " <u>Antaeus</u> (34) Sum 79, p. 52.
"Wilbur on the Trampoline. " <u>Iowa</u> (10:2) Spr 79, p. 80.

ENGLE, Paul
  "Dancer: Four Poems" (for Lan-Lan King).   <u>Poetry</u> (133:6) Mr
  79, p. 339.

ENGLER, Robert Klein
  "Dichterliebe. " <u>KanQ</u> (11:4) Aut 79, p. 54.
  "Hands. " <u>FourQt</u> (28:3) Spr 79, p. 18.
  "White Sky" (for Paul T.).   <u>WindO</u> (35) Aut-Wint 79-80, p. 9.

ENGMAN, John
  "The Absence of the Cabbage Moth. " <u>Iowa</u> (10:1) Wint 79, p. 59.
  "Poem with Sedative Effect. " <u>Iowa</u> (10:1) Wint 79, p. 57.

ENRIGHT, D. J.
  "Shopping at the Palace. " <u>AmerS</u> (48:1) Wint 78-79, p. 35.

ENSLER, Eve
  "Not Quite What It Seems. " <u>ChiR</u> (30:4) Spr 79, p. 82.

ENTREKIN, Charles
  "A Day's Work. " <u>WestB</u> (5) 79, p. 9.

ENZENSBERGER, Hans Magnus
  "Out-of-the-Way-House" (tr. by Nicholas Kolumban).   <u>PoNow</u> (24)
  79, p. 14.

EPLING, Kathy
  "Answering the Wild Iris" (for Rick Landry).   <u>Kayak</u> (51) S 79,
  p. 25.
  "Eye of the Doe. " <u>DenQ</u> (14:2) Sum 79, p. 104.
  "Garth's Lullaby. " <u>Kayak</u> (51) S 79, p. 26.
  "He Has Sky to Dance. " <u>Kayak</u> (51) S 79, p. 26.
  "Three Years After. " <u>Kayak</u> (51) S 79, p. 24.

EPSTEIN, Daniel Mark
  "Climbing. " <u>AmerS</u> (48:2) Spr 79, p. 209.
  "The Sentry of Portoferraio. " <u>NewYorker</u> (55:34) 8 O 79, p. 46.

EPSTEIN, Elaine
  "Something Ugly. " <u>Pequod</u> (3:1) 79, pp. 56-57.

EPSTEIN, Richard
  "For a Class Reunion. " <u>DenQ</u> (14:2) Sum 79, p. 40.
  "Homer Was Not. " <u>DenQ</u> (14:2) Sum 79, p. 41.

EQUI, Elaine
  "Waiting for a Letter from NY. " <u>Tele</u> (15) Spr 79, p. 43.

ERBA, Luciano
"La Grande Jeanne" (tr. by Lawrence R. Smith). PoNow (24)
    79, p. 14.

ERDRICH, Louise
"The Lesky Girls. " CarolQ (31:3) Aut 79, p. 29.
"Neighbors. " WebR (4:3) Spr 79, p. 32.
"The Stripper. " WebR (4:3) Spr 79, p. 31.
"Turtle Mountain Reservation 1977. " Shen (30:2) Wint 79, p. 46.

ESHLEMAN, Clayton
"Elegy about a Postal Deliverer" (tr. of Milan Exner, w. Jan
    Benda). Montra (5) 79, p. 152.
"Frida Kahlo's Release. " Montra (5) 79, p. 155.
"Notebook of a Return to the Native Land" (tr. of Aimé Césaire,
    w. Annette Smith). Montra (6) 79, pp. 7-37.

ESPOSITO, Nancy
"On Cognition" (for Ellen Strenski). CarolQ (31:3) Aut 79, p. 44.
"The Storyteller Tells His Story. " Nat (229:2) 14-21 Jl 79, p.
    58.
"Watching Off Provincetown. " Nat (228:20) 26 My 79, p. 611.

ESPRIU, Salvador
"Sure Prey" (tr. by Nathaniel B. Smith). Paint (12) Aut 79, p.
    31.

ESTAVER, Paul
"Bulkheader. " StoneC (6:2) F 79, p. 14.

ESTESS, Sybil P.
"Evacuation. " SouthernPR (19:2) Aut 79, p. 38.

ESTROFF, Nadine
"Blue Song for a Captain" (for Walter). CarlMis (18:1) Wint 79-
    80, p. 156.
"Dark Angels. " KanQ (11:3) Sum 79, p. 75.
"Washing Rocks Madison County, N.C. " Ur (2) 79, p. 28.

ETTER, Dave
"The Apple Trees of Bible Grove. " PoNow (21) 79, p. 21.
"Barn Dreams. " AAR (29) 79, p. 61.
"Billboard. " PraS (53:2) Sum 79, p. 160.
"Central Standard Time. " PoNow (21) 79, p. 21.
"The Depot Hotel. " DacTerr (16) 79, p. 19.
"Downtown. " AAR (29) 79, p. 66.
"Emmylou. " AAR (29) 79, p. 64.
"Empty Beer Can. " PoNow (23) 79, p. 21.
"Father and Son. " PraS (53:2) Sum 79, p. 159.
"Flowers and Smoke. " AAR (29) 79, p. 62.
"Four Rows of Sweet Corn. " AAR (29) 79, p. 65.
"The Great American Poem. " Antaeus (32) Wint 79, pp. 82-86.
"Great-Grandmother's Speech on Christmas Eve. " AAR (29) 79,

p. 63.
"Hotel Tall Corn. " DacTerr (16) 79, p. 18.
"Jack-O'-Lanterns. " Im (6:1) 79, p. 11.
"Jane's Blue Jeans. " Poetry (134:2) My 79, p. 98.
"Living in the Middle. " Poetry (134:2) My 79, p. 98.
"Nature Studies. " PoNow (23) 79, p. 6.
"Old King Coal. " PoNow (21) 79, p. 37.
"Orange. " PoNow (23) 79, p. 21.
"Pickle Puss. " Im (6:1) 79, p. 11.
"Rose Petals. " PraS (53:2) Sum 79, p. 160.
"Say, What's Going on Here?" Im (6:1) 79, p. 11.
"Three for the Month of March. " Im (6:1) 79, p. 11.
"Three Sparrows. " PoNow (23) 79, p. 6.
"Time and Tomatoes. " PoNow (23) 79, p. 21.
"Yellow-Belly. " PoNow (23) 79, p. 21.
"You. " PoNow (21) 79, p. 21.

EUGSTER, Carla
"Applause for Rachel. " Sam (79) 79, p. 29.
"The Legacy. " Sam (79) 79, p. 29.

EVANS, David Allan
"The Great American Poem. " Antaeus (32) Wint 79, pp. 82-86.
"Pigs. " CharR (5:1) Spr 79, p. 60.
"Swan Hotel. " DacTerr (16) 79, p. 20.

EVANS, Elisabeth Murawski
"Gulf Sign and Moon. " SouthwR (64:1) Wint 79, p. 43.

EVANS, Jean
"The Old Engine Show. " HiramPoR (26) Spr-Sum 79, p. 19.

EVARTS, Prescott Jr.
"Apology. " StoneC (6:1) F 79, p. 10.

EVE, Barbara
"New Orleans, 1900. " PoNow (21) 79, p. 9.

EVERSON, William
"Kingfisher Flat. " Kayak (52) D 79, p. 36.
from The Waldport Poems: "One. " NowestR (17:2/3) 79, p. 272.
from The Waldport Poems: "Three. " NowestR (17:2/3) 79, p. 273.
from The Waldport Poems: "Seven. " NowestR (17:2/3) 79, p. 273.
from The Waldport Poems: "Eight. " NowestR (17:2/3) 79, p. 274.
from The Waldport Poems: "Eleven. " NowestR (17:2/3) 79, p. 275.

EWING, Patricia Renee
"The Beautiful Butcher. " St. AR (5:3) Aut-Wint 79, p. 109.
"the other land. " St. AR (5:3) Aut-Wint 79, p. 109.

EXNER, Milan
"Elegy about a Postal Deliverer" (tr. by Jan Benda and Clayton
Eshleman). Montra (5) 79, p. 152.

EXNER, Richard
"A Chimney Sweep's Remarks" (tr. of Günter Bruno Fuchs).
Mund (11:1) 79, p. 11.

EVATT, Julia
"The Calving. " Poem (37) N 79, p. 39.
"Digging Up Roots. " Poem (37) N 79, p. 43.
"The Planting. " Poem (37) N 79, p. 42.
"Quilting. " Poem (37) N 79, pp. 40-41.

FABRIS, Dino
"I Am Pleased" (tr. of Pier Paolo Pasolini). PoNow (24) 79,
p. 41.
"Lied" (tr. of Pier Paolo Pasolini). PoNow (24) 79, p. 41.
"Rain Beyond Everything II" (tr. of Pier Paolo Pasolini).
PoNow (24) 79, p. 41.
"The True Christ Will Come" (tr. of Pier Paolo Pasolini).
PoNow (24) 79, p. 41.

FAGAN, Robert
"Paragraph. " Tele (15) Spr 79, p. 57.
"The Seasons. " Tele (15) Spr 79, p. 54.
from Stepping Out: (6). Tele (15) Spr 79, p. 56.

FAHEY, Sister Miriam Daniel
"The Hills" (tr. of Carlos Pellicer). MalR (49) Ja 79, p. 92.

FAHEY, W. A.
"Aiming for the Moon" (for Léon-Felipe). Confr (18) Spr-Sum
79, p. 122.
"The Asparagus. " PoNow (22) 79, p. 17.
"Garlic. " PoNow (22) 79, p. 17.

FAHY, Christopher
"Class Reunion. " PoNow (25) 79, p. 21.
"I Saw an Old Cat, Toothless. " PoNow (25) 79, p. 21.
"Miss Hipple. " PoNow (25) 79, p. 21.

FAINLIGHT, Ruth
"Seven Sibyls. " MassR (20:1) Spr 79, p. 98.
"Weeds. " SouthernR (15:1) Wint 79, p. 112.

FAIR, Ronald
from Voices: The Afro-Americans: "civil war too. " BlackALF
(13:3) Aut 79, p. 94.
from Voices: The Afro-Americans: "disremember when i first. "
BlackALF (13:3) Aut 79, p. 93.
, from Voices: The Afro-Americans: "slavery ain't just no word. "
BlackALF (13:3) Aut 79, p. 95.

from Voices: The Afro-Americans: "story's too long. "
BlackALF (13:3) Aut 79, p. 93.

FAIRFAX, John
"Mirrored. " MalR (51) Jl 79, p. 123.
"Robert Stephen Hawker Vicar of Morwenstow, 1804-1875. "
MalR (51) Jl 79, p. 122.
"September 12th. " MalR (51) Jl 79, p. 120.

FAIZ, Faiz Ahmed
"Five Poems from the Pakistani" (tr. by Naomi Lazard).   Kayak
(51) S 79, p. 63.

FALK, Marcia
"The First Day. " Sky (9) Aut 79, p. 14.
"The Household Poems. " Sky (9) Aut 79, pp. 15-16.
"Sheep in a Field. " Sky (9) Aut 79, p. 17.

FALKENBERG, Betty
"How I Was Her Kitchen Boy" (tr. of Günter Grass).   PoNow
(24) 79, p. 17.
"Present Time" (tr. of Günter Eich).   PoNow (24) 79, p. 12.
"Unsigned" (tr. of Günter Eich).   PoNow (24) 79, p. 12.
"Where I Live" (tr. of Günter Eich).   PoNow (24) 79, p. 12.

FALLIS, L. S.
"Appointment in Samarra: J. F. K. -Kolombangara Island, New
Georgia Archipelago (August, 1943)--Dallas, Texas (Novem-
ber, 1963). " Ur (2) 79, p. 29.

FALLON, Teresa
"Learning. " PoetC (11:2) 79, p. 19.
"A New Development. " PoetC (11:3) 79, p. 12.
"Recipe for Cheese Soup. " PoetC (11:2) 79, p. 20.

FANDEL, John
"Derelict. " Confr (19) Aut 79-Wint 80, p. 53.
"Tribute. " Bits (10) Jl 79.
"Views. " Bits (9) Ja 79.

FARBER, Norma
"Begging the Question. " Wind (34) 79, p. 21.
"Cagework. " CEACritic (41:3) Mr 79, p. 25.
"Do You Know the Taste" (tr. of Maurice Carême).   PoNow (21)
79, p. 46.
"Every Time. " CEACritic (41:3) Mr 79, p. 30.
"For My Flightless Cormorant. " Wind (34) 79, p. 22.
"Hands Folded Simply" (tr. of Maurice Carême).   PoNow (24)
79, p. 7.
"I Could've Been Born a King" (tr. of Maurice Carême).   PoNow
(24) 79, p. 7.
"Image" (tr. of Maurice Carême).   PoNow (24) 79, p. 7.
"In the Kitchen the Good Smell" (tr. of Maurice Carême).   PoNow

(24) 79, p. 7.
"Judas, Joyous Little Son." ChrC (96:13) 11 Ap 79, p. 404.
"Reconciliations." CEACritic (41:3) Mr 79, p. 31.
"The Rime of the Man Who Sold His Shadow." CEACritic (41:3)
    Mr 79, pp. 26-30.
"Toward Darkness." Wind (34) 79, p. 21.
"The Trees Stand Witness." CEACritic (41:3) Mr 79, p. 24.
"Vulture Faith." Wind (34) 79, p. 20.
"When I Haven't Anything to Say" (tr. of Maurice Carême).
    PoNow (21) 79, p. 46.
"You Can Get Despondent" (tr. of Maurice Carême). PoNow (24)
    79, p. 7.

FARINELLA, Salvatore
"Nothing Up Your Sleeve." Mouth (2:2) Je 79, p. 1.

FARISS, Aislinn
"Saying." StoneC (6:3) O 79, p. 8.

FARMER, Harold
"Hearing the News." SewanR (87:1) Wint 79, p. 52.
"Victoria Falls." SewanR (87:1) Wint 79, p. 50.

FARMER, Ruth
"The Dream." Cond (5) 79, p. 96.

FARQUHARSON, Jan
"Overtaken." Stand (20:1) 78-79, p. 17.
"Pyramid." Stand (20:1) 78-79, p. 17.

FARRANT, Elizabeth
"Objects Which by Their Nature." Poem (37) N 79, p. 10.
"The Reason for This Place." Poem (37) N 79, p. 9.
"Ten Thousand Angels Dancing." Poem (37) N 79, p. 8.

FARRELL, Kate
"It's Not Only That a Person Is Born." MissR (22/23) Wint-Spr
    79, pp. 89-104.

FARRELL, Mary Ann
Poem. St.AR (5:2) 79, p. 36.

FAULKNER, Margherita Woods
"The Beehive." Spirit (3:1/2) Aut-Wint 77-78, p. 35.
"Old Man Wishing He'd Shaved." Spirit (3:1/2) Aut-Wint 77-78,
    p. 35.
"Wishes." Spirit (3:1/2) Aut-Wint 77-78, p. 36.

FAULWELL, Dean
"The Confession." PoNow (22) 79, p. 17.
"Nocturne." AmerPoR (8:5) S-O 79, p. 44.
"The Surprise." AmerPoR (8:5) S-O 79, p. 44.
"Two of Them." PoNow (22) 79, p. 17.

FAY, Steve
"On Archetypes. " PoetC (11:2) 79, p. 15.

FEDO, David
"For My Mother in the Ambulance, Dying, Perhaps Dead. "
    CarlMis (17:2/3) Spr 79, p. 107.

FEHLER, Gene
"Sunday Morning, After Poker. " Wind (33) 79, p. 20.

FEIN, Cheri
"For Elizabeth. " Pequod (3:2) 79, p. 44.
"Gold Rush. " Pequod (3:2) 79, p. 43.
"The Home Base. " Pequod (3:2) 79, p. 41.
"32 N. Main. " Pequod (3:2) 79, p. 42.

FEIRSTEIN, Frederick
"Heliotropes. " BelPoJ (30:1) Aut 79, p. 10.
"Sitting with David. " BelPoJ (30:1) Aut 79, p. 12.

FELDMAN, Irving
"Elegies. " Shen (30:2) Wint 79, pp. 15-24.
"Family History. " NewRep (180:4) 27 Ja 79, p. 31.
"Naming the Parts. " Confr (18) Spr-Sum 79, p. 44.
"Rowing on the Acheron. " NewRep (180:14) 7 Ap 79, p. 30.

FELDMAN, Ruth
"bystander. " GRR (10:3) 79, p. 26.
"Christmas" (tr. of Rocco Scotellaro w. Brian Swann). Os (8)
    79, p. 5.
"The Compass" (tr. of Luciano Marrucci w. Martin Robbins).
    PoNow (24) 79, p. 25.
"The Eaves" (tr. of Rocco Scotellaro w. Brian Swann). Os (8)
    79, p. 3.
"Eye of the Beholder. " GRR (10:3) 79, p. 25.
"For a Foreign Woman Who Is Leaving" (tr. of Rocco Scotellaro
    w. Brian Swann). PoNow (21) 79, p. 46.
"Freezing Point. " GRR (10:3) 79, p. 22.
"The Friar's Boundary-Wall" (tr. of Rocco Scotellaro w. Brian
    Swann). PoNow (21) 79, p. 46.
"a lot of give. " GRR (10:3) 79, p. 27.
"Mother" (tr. of Luciano Marrucci w. Martin Robbins). PoNow
    (24) 79, p. 25.
"Night Trees" (tr. of Luciano Marrucci w. Martin Robbins).
    PoNow (24) 79, p. 25.
Nine Poems (tr. of Bartolo Cattafi w. Brian Swann). PoNow (24)
    79, pp. 8-9.
"Nocturne: Homage to Whistler. " GRR (10:3) 79, p. 23.
"On the Crest of the Wave" (tr. of Dino Buzzah). Chowder (12)
    Spr-Sum 79, p. 8.
"Rival. " GRR (10:3) 79, p. 28.
Twenty-two Poems (tr. of Rocco Scotellaro w. Brian Swann).
    PoNow (24) 79, pp. 52-54.
"Waiting Game. " GRR (10:3) 79, p. 24.

FELLOWES, Peter
"Alewife Harvest. " YaleR (69:2) Wint 80, p. 259.
"Release. " YaleR (69:2) Wint 80, p. 258.

FELSENTHAL, Peter
"Father Puzzle. " SmPd (46) 79, p. 10.

FENNELL, Derrick
"Bones. " EngJ (68:5) My 79, p. 37.

FENSTERMAKER, Vesle
"Click!' " KanQ (11:4) Aut 79, p. 4.

FENTON, Elizabeth
"The Days After New Year. " PartR (46:3) 79, pp. 419-420.
"Saturn Song. " PartR (46:3) 79, pp. 420-421.

FEREN, David
"The Artist. " Mouth (2:2) Je 79, p. 5.
"August Scar. " Mouth (2:2) Je 79, p. 5.
"It Is Night, Moonless. " Mouth (2:2) Je 79, p. 8.
"Piscean. " KanQ (11:1/2) Wint-Spr 79, p. 70.
"Shirtless in Summer. " Mouth (2:2) Je 79, p. 7.

FERICANO, Paul F.
"The After" (for marty). SeC (6:2) 78, p. 171.
"Borderline. " SeC (6:2) 78, p. 173.
"A Closer Look. " Wind (32) 79, p. 14.
"Collage of Us in May Windows" (for Katherine). SeC (6:2) 78,
    p. 175.
"Dark in Winters on Road 88. " SeC (6:1) 78, p. 20.
"Learning from America. " Wind (32) 79, p. 15.
"San Francisco Pier Poems. " SeC (6:2) 78, p. 177.
"Upstairs in C Ward. " SeC (6:1) 78, p. 18.

FERLINGHETTI, Lawrence
"At the Bodega. " PoNow (21) 79, p. 22.
"Seascape with Sun and Eagle. " PoNow (21) 79, p. 22.

FERLITA, Ernest
"Quetzal. " NewOR (6:2) 79, pp. 144-147.

FERNANDEZ, Pablo Armando
"Complaint" (tr. by Stuart Friebert). WestB (4) 79, p. 47.

FERRARELLI, Rina
Eight Poems (tr. of Salvatore Quasimodo). PoNow (24) 79, pp.
    46-47.
"Hypotheses" (tr. of Bartolo Cattafi). PoNow (24) 79, p. 9.
from The Immobile Zone: "The Action (table of contents)" (tr.
    of Giorgio Chiesura). Hudson (32:2) Sum 79, p. 201.
from The Immobile Zone: "The Immobile Zone" (tr. of Giorgio
    Chiesura). Hudson (32:2) Sum 79, p. 201.

from The Immobile Zone: "The Man with the Handkerchief" (tr.
of Giorgio Chiesura). Hudson (32:2) Sum 79, p. 204.
from The Immobile Zone: "The Rock" (tr. of Giorgio Chiesura).
Hudson (32:2) Sum 79, p. 203.
from The Immobile Zone: "The Trees" (tr. of Giorgio Chie-
sura). Hudson (32:2) Sum 79, p. 202.
from The Immobile Zone: "Time (Forecast)" (tr. of Giorgio
Chiesura). Hudson (32:2) Sum 79, p. 203.
"Things" (tr. of Bartolo Cattafi). PoNow (24) 79, p. 9.

FERRELL, William
"Finding the Owl." PortR (25) 79, p. 141.

FERRY, David
"Evening News I." Ploughs (5:2) 79, p. 171.
"Evening News II." Ploughs (5:2) 79, p. 172.
"Graveyard." NewRep (180:3) 20 Ja 79, p. 35.
"Rereading Old Writing." Ploughs (5:2) 79, p. 174.
"Sculptures by Dimitri Hadzi." Ploughs (5:2) 79, p. 173.
"To Sestius." NewRep (181:23) 8 D 79, p. 26.

FET, Afanasii
"I will not tell you anything" (tr. by Maria Pupko). AmerPoR
(8:3) My-Je 79, p. 27.

FEWELL, Richard
"The 'Duke' and the 'Count.'" GreenfieldR (7:3/4) Spr-Sum 79,
p. 195.

FIALKOWSKI, Barbara
"Out of Our Element" (for Chris). NoAmR (264:4) Wint 79, p.
73.
"To Sleep." OhioR (20:2) Spr-Sum 79, p. 67.

FIEDLER, William A.
"Holiday Visit" (tr. of Behcet Necatigil w. Dionis Coffin Riggs
and Ozcan Yalim). StoneC (6:1) F 79, p. 28.

FIELD, Edward
"Nostalgie du Pays." PoNow (23) 79, p. 22.
"Sonja Henie Sonnet." PoNow (23) 79, p. 22.

FIELD, Matt
"Farm Wife." BallSUF (20:4) Aut 79, p. 2.
"Foxborough Raceway." PoNow (25) 79, p. 7.
"Instructional." Tendril (5) Sum 79, p. 26.

FIELDS, Kenneth
"The Great American Poem." Antaeus (32) Wint 79, pp. 82-86.

FIERRO, Armando Cervantes
"For Chuck." StoneC (6:2) My 79, p. 8.

FIFER, Ken
"April 4. " PartR (46:2) 79, p. 261.
"Betsy's Vegetable Ghazal. " WestB (5) 79, p. 26.
"Vegetable Love. " Wind (35) 79, p. 19.

FILES, Meg
"To the Other Woman. " Focus (13:81) My-Je 79, p. 31.

FILOCHE, Jean-Luc
"All Alone" (tr. of Louis Aragon w. Christian-Albrecht Gollub).
    Spirit (3:1/2) Aut-Wint 77-78, p. 58.

FINALE, Frank
"City Girls. " JnlONJP (4:1) 79, p. 14.

FINCKE, Gary
"Cold Snap. " GreenfieldR (7:3/4) Spr-Sum 79, p. 211.
"Dancing on My Birthday. " EnPas (9) 79, p. 21.
"Greeter. " CutB (13) Aut-Wint 79, p. 23.
"The Princess, Rescued. " SouthernPR (19:2) Aut 79, p. 26.
"Principal. " PoNow (22) 79, p. 17.
"The Talking Woman. " PoNow (22) 79, p. 17.

FINE, Warren
"The Confederate Soldier at the Battle of Fredericksburg Said. "
    PraS (53:4) Wint 79-80, p. 333.

FINEMAN, Michal
"The Moon" (tr. of Federico García Lorca w. Marianne Loyd).
    EnPas (9) 79, p. 31.
"St. Gabriel" (tr. of Federico García Lorca w. Marianne Loyd).
    EnPas (9) 79, p. 32.
"St. Michael" (tr. of Federico García Lorca w. Marianne Loyd).
    EnPas (9) 79, p. 34.

FINK, Jon-Stephen
"Chaldea The Story of Inanna, Sumeria c 3000 B. C. " Chelsea
    (38) 79, pp. 46-52.
"Shiphrah, Her House in the Treasure City. " ChiR (30:4) Spr
    79, pp. 27-31.

FINKEL, Donald
"Another Matter. " MassR (20:4) Wint 79, p. 747.
"The Dolphin and the Lady. " PoetryNW (20:1) Spr 79, pp. 45-
    46.
"The Great American Poem. " Antaeus (32) Wint 79, pp. 82-86.
"Her Coat of Hair. " PoetryNW (20:1) Spr 79, pp. 43-44.
"Hound Song. " PoNow (21) 79, p. 8.
"How Things Fall. " Kayak (50) My 79, p. 56.
"It Was Someone. " Kayak (50) My 79, p. 57.
"Lives of a Cell. " Kayak (52) D 79, p. 41.
"MMMMMM. " PoetryNW (20:1) Spr 79, pp. 46-47.
"The One-Eyed Cat. " PoNow (21) 79, p. 8.

"Quarrel. " Kayak (52) D 79, p. 41.
"A Question of Memory. " Ascent (5:1) 79, p. 43.
"SHHH. " PoetryNW (20:1) Spr 79, p. 47.
"The Strange One. " MassR (20:4) Wint 79, p. 745.
"The Taste of Ashes. " Ascent (5:1) 79, p. 42.
"The Work of an Instant. " PoetryNW (20:1) Spr 79, pp. 44-45.

FINKELSTEIN, Caroline
"How Random. " LittleM (12:1/2) Spr-Sum 78 (79), p. 86.
"In the Country of Marquez. " LittleM (12:1/2) Spr-Sum 78 (79),
    p. 87.

FINLAYSON, Logan
"Cow Contours Outline Inscape Escape Out of Line After the
    Rain. " Tele (15) Spr 79, p. 96.
"Mother Coca. " Tele (15) Spr 79, p. 95.

FINLEY, C. Stephen
"An Empty House. " SouthernHR (13:4) Aut 79, p. 311.
"Found After a Storm. " SouthernHR (13:4) Aut 79, p. 344.
"October Dusk. " CarolQ (31:1) Wint 79, p. 66.

FINLEY, Jeanne
"The Dead of the World. " CentR (23:3) Sum 79, p. 293.
"Lazarus. " CutB (12) Spr-Sum 79, p. 52.

FINLEY, Mike
"Accident. " GreenfieldR (7:3/4) Spr-Sum 79, p. 292.
"Hippopotamus. " Northeast (3:7) Spr 79, p. 12.

FINNE, Diderik
"Apollo 113. " MichQR (18:2) Spr 79, p. 265.
"Jacques Derrida on St. Helene. " SewanR (87:4) Aut 79, p. 536.

FISCHER, Aaron
"The Eel Grounds. " NewYorker (55:23) 23 Jl 79, p. 75.
"Lockjaw. " Poetry (134:2) My 79, p. 95.
"Three Versions. " Poetry (134:2) My 79, pp. 96-97.

FISCHER, William
"I and the Night (New York City). " PortR (25) 79, p. 88.

FISHER, David
"The Amorous Poet. " Kayak (52) D 79, p. 43.
"The Deaf Man. " Kayak (52) D 79, p. 42.
"Harvest Poem. " Kayak (51) S 79, p. 18.
"The Pastor Speaks Out. " Kayak (51) S 79, p. 19.

FISHER, David L.
"The Land of Cockaigne. " MassR (20:4) Wint 79, p. 800.

FISHER, Gary
"A Friend's Death" (for Bert Meyers). Kayak (52) D 79, p. 63.

FISHER, George William
"After You're Declared the World's Greatest Lover. " SeC (6:1)
   78, p. 25.

FISHER, Harrison
"1839 A.D. " PikeR (1) Sum 79, p. 66.
"Genius Without Madness. " PikeR (1) Sum 79, p. 67.

FISHER, Vardis
from The Antelope Sonnets (1927): "Susan Hemp. " NowestR
   (17:2/3) 79, p. 164.

FISHMAN, Charles
"For Life. " Confr (19) Aut 79-Wint 80, p. 118.

FITZGERALD, Doreen
"thinking. " Focus (13:80) Mr-Ap 79, p. 38.

FITZGERALD, Neil
Poem. St. AR (5:2) 79, p. 75.

FITZPATRICK, Kevin
"Photograph of a Famous Person--Age 11--with Classmates
   (1887). " PikeF (2) Wint 78-79, p. 3.

FITZPATRICK, Vincent
"Rimbaud Walks on Foot. " Mouth (2:3) N 79.   Front cover.

FITZPATRICK, W. P.
"Among Schoolchildren. " SouthernHR (13:1) Wint 79, p. 83.

FIXMER, Clyde
"A Bedlam Ballad. " PoNow (25) 79, p. 21.
"The Hunger. " PoNow (25) 79, p. 21.

FLAKOLL, Darwin
"Cambric Tamales" (for Eduardo and Helena) (tr. of Claribel
   Alegría). VirQR (55:2) Spr 79, p. 306.
"Disillusionment" (tr. of Claribel Alegría). VirQR (55:2) Spr 79,
   p. 306.

FLANDERS, Jane
"Air for Elizabeth. " CarolQ (31:2) Spr-Sum 79, p. 121.
"Dandelion Greens. " MassR (20:4) Wint 79, p. 754.
"The Death of Will Rogers and Wiley Post. " Confr (19) Aut 79-
   Wint 80, p. 116.
"The Experiment. " Nat (228:6) 17 F 79, p. 184.
"Encounter at Harper's Ferry. " PoetC (10:3) 79, p. 30.
"The Incurables. " PoetC (10:3) 79, p. 29.
"The Love Letters of Sigmund Freud. " AmerPoR (8:2) Mr-Ap
   79, p. 15.
"Moss. " Nat (228:20) 26 My 79, p. 610.
"Roses. " MassR (20:3) Aut 79, p. 520.

"The Snake Hunters. " PoetC (11:1) 79, p. 14.
"The Tipsy Woman (after Manet). " NewRep (181:22) 1 D 79, p. 30.
"The Students of Snow. " Chowder (12) Spr-Sum 79, p. 4.
"Wild Asters. " Poetry (134:5) Ag 79, p. 259.
"When She Puts on the Hat. " Chowder (12) Spr-Sum 79, p. 5.

FLECK, Anne
"The Quiet Light. " Paint (11) Spr 79, p. 12.

FLEMING, Harold
"Elegy for Juan. " Wind (34) 79, p. 23.
"A Punch and Judy Act. " StoneC (6:2) My 79, p. 24.

FLEMING, Ray
"Aretha. " BlackALF (13:1) Spr 79, p. 35.
"Bakke's Law, or Lateral Movement. " BlackALF (13:1) Spr 79, p. 35.
"Summertime. " BlackALF (13:1) Spr 79, p. 35.

FLETCHER, Ralph J. Jr.
"at Davenport Beach, California" (for Jim V.). Wind (32) 79, p. 17.

FLEU, Richard
"Absence. " StoneC (6:3) O 79, p. 12.
"The Mockingbird. " StoneC (6:3) O 79, p. 13.

FLOCK, Miriam
"Skymarks. " KanQ (11:3) Sum 79, p. 41.
"Taking Orders: A Sestina. " Salm (46) Aut 79, p. 88.
"Variations on a Theme. " KanQ (11:3) Sum 79, p. 40.

FLOWERS, Betty
"Medium. " NewL (45:3) Spr 79, p. 20.

FLOWERS, Yvonne A.
"The Nightmare Is. " Cond (5) 79, p. 112.

FLYNN, Elizabeth
"After Grave Deliberation. " LitR (22:3) Spr 79, p. 284.
"Sonnet at Solstice. " EngJ (68:5) My 79, p. 29.

FLYNN, Tony
"Jessica Drew's Married Son. " Stand (20:4) 79, p. 55.

FOERSTER, Richard
"Concentrics. " StoneC (6:1) F 79, p. 25.
"Medusas. " StoneC (6:1) F 79, p. 25.

FOGEL, Daniel Mark
"Régime. " AmerS (48:2) Spr 79, p. 154.

131 FOLEY

FOLEY, M. J.
"Animus. " Poem (37) N 79, pp. 31-36.

FOLKESTAD, Marilyn
"Glass Beach. " PortR (25) 79, p. 93.
"Letter to Sandy from San Juan. " CutB (12) Spr-Sum 79, p. 76.
"Potato Pie. " PoetryNW (20:3) Aut 79, pp. 43-44.

FOLKS, Jeffrey
"Flower Lady. " Wind (35) 79, p. 12.
"The Writing Lab." ConcPo (12:1) Spr 79, p. 75.

FOLLAIN, Jean
from D'Après Tout: Eleven Poems (tr. by Heather McHugh).
ParisR (76) Aut 79, pp. 155-159.
from Exister: "Le Pain" (tr. by Geoffrey Gardner). Nimrod
(23:1) Aut-Wint 79, p. 60.
from Territoires: "Police" (tr. by Geoffrey Gardner). Nimrod
(23:1) Aut-Wint 79, p. 59.
Twelve Poems (tr. by Heather McHugh). Pequod (3:2) 79, pp.
92-97.

FOLTZ-GRAY, Dorothy
"Gifts for a Dig, 5000 A.D. " MissR (24) Aut 79, p. 38.
"A History as Told By. " MissR (24) Aut 79, p. 31.
"Long Past Me. " MissR (24) Aut 79, p. 34.
"Niagara Falls. " MissR (24) Aut 79, p. 35.
"The Second Caller. " MissR (24) Aut 79, p. 33.
"Travelers. " MissR (24) Aut 79, p. 36.

FONTENOT, Ken
"Every Day" (tr. of Ingeborg Bachmann). NewOR (6:2) 79, p.
163.

FOOTE, Lyn
"Tribute. " JnlONJP (3:2) 79, p. 8.

FORBES, Dora
"Kitchen Countertop: A Terrible Sonnet. " Poultry (1) 79, p. 10.

FORCHE, Carolyn
"Departure. " Antaeus (34) Sum 79, p. 65.
"Letter from Prague 1968-1978. " Atl (244:6) D 79, p. 82.
"Photograph of My Room. " Antaeus (34) Sum 79, p. 66.
"The Visitor. " Atl (243:6) Je 79, p. 67.
"We Were Three--" (for Paco and Rodolfo) (tr. of Claribel Aleg-
ría). VirQR (55:2) Spr 79, p. 304.

FORD, Agatha
from Marsiglia and Agostino: "Agostino at 9: Messina, Sicily. "
GRR (10:2) 79, p. 172.
from Marsiglia and Agostino: "Paper Cuts and Splinters. " GRR
(10:2) 79, p. 170.

FORD, Dan
"Love Is Loathing and Why." ConcPo (12:1) Spr 79, p. 76.

FORD, Robert
"The Edge" (tr. of Andrei Voznesensky). PoNow (24) 79, p. 36.

FORD, Theresa
"Scene on a Metrobus." BlackALF (13:4) Wint 79, p. 150.

FORD, William
"Baudelaire's Pipe." ColEng (41:3) N 79, p. 308.
"Children's War." ColEng (41:3) N 79, p. 309.
"Finding Out About the Dodgers." ColEng (41:3) N 79, p. 308.
"The Weightlifter." KanQ (11:1/2) Wint-Spr 79, p. 105.

FORTINI, Franco
"The English Cemetery" (tr. by Lawrence R. Smith). PoNow
(24) 79, p. 15.

FOSTER, Carolyn
"6 Ways of Looking at the Act of a Poem." Wind (33) 79, p. 21.

FOSTER, Linda Nemec
"Family Pose." Tendril (5) Sum 79, p. 29.
"Sestina: Grandma." Chowder (13) Aut-Wint 79, p. 38.
"Throwing Old Things Away." Tendril (5) Sum 79, p. 28.

FOSTER, Michaelene K.
"Bouquet." SouthernR (15:1) Wint 79, p. 131.
"The Glass Hunter." SouthernR (15:1) Wint 79, p. 128.
"Thick Light, White Light." SouthernR (15:1) Wint 79, p. 130.

FOURTOUNI, Eleni
"Eurydice I." LitR (22:3) Spr 79, p. 343.
"Eurydice II." LitR (22:3) Spr 79, p. 344.
"Eurydice III." LitR (22:3) Spr 79, p. 345.

FOWLER, Barbara
"Journey to the End of My Life, 1948." LittleM (12:1/2) Spr-
Sum 78 (79), p. 59.

FOWLER, Russell T.
"In Blanco Country." SoCaR (11:2) Spr 79, p. 69.

FOX, Connie
"Black bug." Tele (15) Spr 79, p. 83.
"I become." Tele (15) Spr 79, p. 83.
"My/our pencil-arms." Tele (15) Spr 79, p. 82.
"She." Tele (15) Spr 79, p. 82.

FOX, Hugh
"51." Spirit (3:1/2) Aut-Wint 77-78, p. 41.
"Orchids in the Tree Opposite the Balcony at Polly's Restaurant."

GreenfieldR (7:3/4) Spr-Sum 79, p. 75.
"Salario Minimo 1. " GreenfieldR (7:3/4) Spr-Sum 79, p. 76.

FOX, Hugo
"The Bard. " Im (5:3) 79, p. 3.

FOX, Siv Cedering
"In the Taxidermist's Shop. " GeoR (33:4) Wint 79, p. 899.
"Sunday" (tr. of Werner Aspenström w. D. L. Emblem).
    PoNow (24) 79, p. 4.

FRANCIS, Pat Therese
"Cape Cod, 1958. " 13thM (4:2) 79, p. 72.
"Father and Daughter. " Chomo (6:1) Sum 79, p. 32.
"Men Touch Me. " EnPas (9) 79, p. 23.
"Poem for a Neighbor. " Tendril (6) Aut 79, p. 24.
"Post Card. " Chomo (6:1) Sum 79, p. 29.
"Running at Forty-One. " Chomo (6:1) Sum 79, p. 34.
"The Snowman Realizes Who He Is. " Tendril (5) Sum 79, p. 30.
"Your Body" (for Karen Silkwood). Chomo (6:1) Sum 79, p. 30.

FRANK, Bernhard
"After the Guests Departed" (tr. of Tsfrirar Gar). PoNow (24)
    79, p. 16.
"Air drips from rock" (tr. of Yehuda Offen). PoNow (24) 79, p.
    38.
"Armchairs" (tr. of Dan Pagis). PoNow (24) 79, p. 41.
"Balloons" (tr. of Dan Pagis). PoNow (24) 79, p. 40.
"A Citizen's Dissertation on His Neighborhood" (tr. of Avraham
    Shlonsky). PoNow (24) 79, p. 55.
"The Clouds Are the First Fatalities" (tr. of Yehuda Amichai).
    PoNow (24) 79, pp. 2-3.
"Cock" (tr. of Aharon Amir). PoNow (24) 79, p. 3.
"The diameter of the bomb was thirty centimeters" (tr. of Yehuda
    Amichai). PoNow (24) 79, p. 3.
"Etruscan Statue" (tr. of Ester Ra'av). PoNow (24) 79, p. 47.
"Exodus from the Garden of Delight" (tr. of Aharon Amir).
    PoNow (24) 79, p. 3.
"Heat Spell in Venice" (tr. of Leah Goldberg). PoNow (24) 79,
    p. 17.
"Hide and Seek" (tr. of Dan Pagis). PoNow (24) 79, p. 40.
"Impromptu Heart" (tr. of Dan Pagis). PoNow (24) 79, p. 40.
"In the Beginning My Mother Screeched" (tr. of Ya'akov Beser).
    PoNow (24) 79, p. 5.
"Inwards" (tr. of Yehuda Offen). PoNow (24) 79, p. 38.
"My Best Clothes" (tr. of Eli Nester). PoNow (24) 79, p. 28.
"Night Walk" (tr. of Eli Nester). PoNow (24) 79, p. 28.
"On the Hazards of Smoking" (tr. of Leah Goldberg). PoNow (24)
    79, p. 17.
"On the River Lookout" (tr. of Hamar Ya'oz-Kest). PoNow (24)
    79, p. 63.
"Quarry" (tr. of Hamar Ya'oz-Kest). PoNow (24) 79, p. 63.
"Seeing the Light" (tr. of Tsfrirar Gar). PoNow (24) 79, p. 16.

"Snake Skin" (tr. of Ya'akov Beser). PoNow (24) 79, p. 5.
"Stones Are Undone by the River" (tr. of Yonah Wallach).
  PoNow (24) 79, p. 62.
"Tin Toys" (tr. of Tsfrirar Gar). PoNow (24) 79, p. 16.
"The Two-Legged Kind" (tr. of Dan Pagis). PoNow (21) 79, p.
  46.

FRANK, Peter
"Air Peel. " SunM (8) Aut 79, p. 5.
"Sample Textures" (for Maureen Sullivan). SunM (8) Aut 79, p.
  4.

FRATTI, Mario
"All Will Hear" (tr. of Gigi Dessi). Wind (33) 79, p. 15.
"Angel face. " Wind (33) 79, p. 25.
"I'm Empty" (tr. of Gigi Dessi). Wind (33) 79, p. 15.
"I'm Not a Fisherman" (tr. of Gigi Dessi). Wind (33) 79, p. 15.
"Old Rose" (tr. of Miriam Shastri). Wind (33) 79, p. 48.
"1" (tr. of Giovanni Arcidiacono). Wind (33) 79, p. 5.
"Only Love" (tr. of Antonio Magnifico). Wind (33) 79, p. 48.
"Pink. " Wind (33) 79, p. 26.
"A Summer Morning" (tr. of Antonio Magnifico). Wind (33) 79,
  p. 48.
"3" (tr. of Giovanni Arcidiacono). Wind (33) 79, p. 5.
"2" (tr. of Giovanni Arcidiacono). Wind (33) 79, p. 5.

FRATUS, David
"O Feathered Denizen of Night. " HiramPoR (26) Spr-Sum 79, p.
  13.

FREEMAN, William T.
"Chekhov Comes to Mind at Harvard. " GreenfieldR (7:3/4) Spr-
  Sum 79, p. 26.
"Fleshing Out. " GreenfieldR (7:3/4) Spr-Sum 79, p. 27.

FREIS, Richard
"Tornado Warning. " SouthernR (15:1) Wint 79, p. 140.

FRENAUD, Andre
"Freeing the Bodies" (tr. by William Kulik). AmerPoR (8:3) My-
  Je 79, p. 28.

FREUD, Rita
"evening flute. " WindO (34) Spr-Sum 79, p. 7.

FRIAR, Kimon
"The Earth's Attraction" (tr. of Yannis Ritsos w. Kostas Myrsi-
  ades). Chelsea (38) 79, p. 82.
"Erotic Tank" (tr. of Leftéris Poúlios). Durak (3) 79, p. 56.
"Imitation of Cephalonia" (tr. of Nikos Phocás). Durak (3) 79,
  p. 51.
"Lightless" (tr. of Yannis Ritsos w. Kostas Myrsiades). Chelsea
  (38) 79, p. 81.

"Secret Audience" (tr. of Yannis Ritsos w. Kostas Myrsiades).
Chelsea (38) 79, p. 83.
"The Shipwreck" (tr. of Manólis Anagnostákis).   AmerPoR (8:1)
Ja-F 79, p. 37.

FRIBERG, Gosta
"The Growing" (tr. by John Matthias).   GreenfieldR (7:3/4) Spr-
Sum 79, p. 125.

FRIEBERT, Stuart
"Achilles and the Turtle" (tr. of Miroslav Holub w. Dana Háb-
ová).   WestB (5) 79, p. 23.
"The Age of the Butcher. "   CentR (23:2) Spr 79, p. 157.
"Annunciation" (tr. of Miroslav Holub w. Dana Hábová).   Field
(21) Aut 79, p. 70.
"Autumn" (tr. of Miroslav Holub w. Dana Hábová).   Field (21)
Aut 79, p. 74.
"Brief Reflection on Dwarves" (tr. of Miroslav Holub w. Dana
Hábová).   Field (21) Aut 79, p. 69.
"Complaint" (tr. of Pablo Armando Fernandez).   WestB (4) 79,
p. 47.
"Crocheting" (tr. of Miroslav Holub w. Dana Hábová).   Field
(21) Aut 79, p. 72.
"Even More on Stealing. "   DenQ (14:2) Sum 79, p. 44.
"Eye of the Storm. "   QW (8) Wint 79, p. 77.
"Fever. "   DenQ (14:2) Sum 79, p. 45.
"First Person. "   CentR (23:2) Spr 79, p. 156.
"The Garden of Old People" (tr. of Miroslav Holub w. Dana
Hábová).   WestB (5) 79, p. 25.
"Geese" (tr. of Miroslav Holub w. Dana Hábová).   WestB (5) 79,
p. 24.
"He Saved My Life. "   PoetryNW (20:2) Sum 79, p. 35.
"I've Always Lived in Cuba" (tr. of Heberto Padilla).   WestB
(4) 79, p. 46.
"Let the Laugh" (tr. of Karl Krolow).   Durak (2) 79, p. 55.
"Love that Travels. "   Durak (3) 79, p. 11.
"Mother and Me, Inside, Drinking. "   QW (8) Wint 79, p. 77.
"On Never Seeing Your Menstrual Blood Though You Have a New
Apartment in Bologna and the Only Cut-Class Candy Dish
They Export from Prague, I Wrapped It All by Myself. "
Durak (2) 79, p. 49.
"On Not Commanding What We Adore. "   CutB (13) Aut-Wint 79,
p. 59.
"On the Origin of Fatherhood" (tr. of Miroslav Holub w. Dana
Hábová).   Field (21) Aut 79, p. 73.
"On the Origin of the Contrary" (tr. of Miroslav Holub w. Dana
Hábová).   Field (21) Aut 79, p. 75.
"On Writing Poems" (tr. of Heberto Padilla).   WestB (4) 79, p.
47.
"Saneness/Accident" (tr. of Miroslav Holub w. Dana Hábová).
WestB (5) 79, p. 26.
"Der Schwanendreher. "   Durak (2) 79, p. 48.
"Several Very Smart People" (tr. of Miroslav Holub w. Dana

Hábová). WestB (5) 79, p. 23.
"Soldier" (tr. of Miroslav Holub w. Dana Hábová). Field (21)
Aut 79, p. 71.
Ten Poems (tr. of Giovanni Raboni w. Vinio Rossi). QW (8)
Wint 79, pp. 72-76.
Thirteen Poems (tr. of Rainer Brambach). QW (6) Spr-Sum 78,
pp. 42-46.
"Time Passing" (tr. of Karl Krolow). MalR (52) O 79, p. 134.
"View/Prospect" (tr. of Karl Krolow). Durak (2) 79, p. 54.
"Wishing Well." WestB (4) 79, p. 13.

FRIED, Philip
"Unwatched Birds." PartR (46:3) 79, pp. 427-428.

FRIEDMAN, Barton
"Angelo." Wind (34) 79, p. 24.
"Hemingway." Wind (34) 79, p. 24.

FRIEND, Barbara
"Hardware." NewEngR (2:1) Aut 79, p. 117.

FROST, Carol
"An Adolescent Girl." PraS (53:2) Sum 79, p. 161.
"Early Blizzard." HiramPoR (26) Spr-Sum 79, p. 20.
"A Good Cafeteria." DacTerr (16) 79, p. 21.
"Klimt's Baby." PoNow (21) 79, p. 43.
"Klimt's Baby." PoNow (23) 79, p. 22.
"Liar's Dice." PoNow (23) 79, p. 22.
"Ode to the Horseshoe Crab." PraS (53:2) Sum 79, p. 162.
"Our Night." Shen (30:4) 79, p. 95.
"The Salt Lesson." PoNow (23) 79, p. 22.
"The Scar." Shen (30:4) 79, p. 94.
"Unfinished Song." Madem (85:7) Jl 79, p. 154.

FRUMKIN, Gene
"California Christmas." MalR (52) O 79, p. 19.
"El Conquistador: The Seventh Floor." DacTerr (16) 79, p. 22.
"The Garden of Technology." MalR (52) O 79, p. 23.
"The Great American Poem." Antaeus (32) Wint 79, pp. 82-86.
"Loops II." MalR (52) O 79, p. 20.
"New Name." PoNow (21) 79, p. 16.
"Stopping at the Ramada Inn in Kingman, Arizona." DacTerr (16)
79, p. 23.
"A Whiskey Bottle, A Manila Folder." PraS (53:2) Sum 79, p.
174.

FRY, Susie
"One Small Inspiration." SouthernPR (19:2) Aut 79, p. 28.
"Passage." StoneC (6:2) My 79, p. 28.

FRYDMAN, Anne
"394" (tr. of Osip Mandelstam w. Jean Valentine). AmerPoR
(8:2) Mr-Ap 79, p. 11.

FUCHS, Günter Bruno
"Bemerkungen eines Schornsteinfegers. " Mund (11:1) 79, p. 10.

FUERTES, Gloria
"I Think Table and I Say Chair" (tr. by Ada Cong and Philip
Levine). MissouriR (3:1) Aut 79, p. 9.
"Instructions" (tr. by Ada Long and Philip Levine). MissouriR
(3:1) Aut 79, p. 11.
"Society of Friends and Protectors" (tr. by Ada Long and Philip
Levine). MissouriR (3:1) Aut 79, p. 10.

FULANI, Richard
"Consider Further. " Obs (4:3) Wint 78, p. 70.
"Poets of Our People. " Obs (4:3) Wint 78, p. 70.
"A Real Black Wind. " Obs (4:3) Wint 78, pp. 69-70.

FULLER, Ethel Romig
from White Peaks and Green (1928): "A Song for Churning. "
NowestR (17:2/3) 79, p. 163.
from White Peaks and Green (1928): "Slippers. " NowestR (17:
2/3) 79, p. 162.
from White Peaks and Green (1928): "Wind Is a Cat. " NowestR
(17:2/3) 79, p. 161.
from White Peaks and Green (1928): "Winter Orchard. "
NowestR (17:2/3) 79, p. 162.

FULLEN, George
"Elegy for Allyn. " Wind (32) 79, p. 18.

FULTON, Alice
"Agoraphobia. " LittleM (12:1/2) Spr-Sum 78 (79), p. 103.
"The Endangered. " PoetC (11:2) 79, p. 2.
"Intense Dude, Heavy Brother. " Ur (2) 79, p. 30.
"Sestina for Janis Joplin. " Ur (2) 79, p. 33.
"Sex with Someone Who Resembles Hemingway, Disguised. " Ur
(2) 79, p. 34.
"Sheets. " Ur (2) 79, p. 35.
"This November, Your Lyrical Lies. " PoetC (11:2) 79, p. 4.

FUNK, Allison
"Georgia Power. " PoetryNW (20:4) Wint 79-80, p. 42.
"Trestle. " GeoR (33:4) Wint 79, p. 847.
"Twin Lakes. " PoetryNW (20:4) Wint 79-80, pp. 41-42.

FUNKHOUSER, Erica
"Hand Saw. " Ploughs (5:3) 79, p. 31.
"Plane. " Ploughs (5:3) 79, p. 32.

FURTNEY, Diane
"Working Out. " PoetryNW (20:4) Wint 79-80, pp. 24-25.

GABIROL, Solomon ibn
from The Crown of Kingdom: (X-XXXII) (tr. by Harris Lenowitz).
Montra (5) 79, pp. 218-229.

GAESS, Roger
"Gifts. " Ur (2) 79, p. 36.

GAFFORD, Charlotte
"Quills. " SouthernPR (19:2) Aut 79, p. 38.

GAIK, Frank
"I Am Not an Orange. " PoNow (25) 79, p. 8.
"Questions to Francis Bacon. " BallSUF (20:4) Aut 79, p. 72.
"Show Me the Way to Go Home. " PoNow (25) 79, p. 8.
"Whatever Is, Is Right. " BallSUF (20:4) Aut 79, p. 71.

GALLAGHER, Tess
"Bird-Window-Flying. " NewYorker (55:7) 2 Ap 79, p. 108.
"I Save Your Coat but You Lose It Later. " AmerPoR (8:5) S-O
    79, p. 19.
"I Take Care of You: A Lantern Dashes by in the Grass. "
    AmerPoR (8:3) My-Je 79, p. 11.
"Some with Wings, Some with Manes. " AmerPoR (8:5) S-O 79,
    p. 19.
"You Talk on Your Telephone; I Talk on Mine. " AmerPoR (8:3)
    My-Je 79, p. 12.

GALLANT, Suzanne
"Housing the Monster. " AndR (6:2) Aut 79, p. 13.

GALLER, David
"The Great American Poem. " Antaeus (32) Wint 79, pp. 82-86.
"The Progress of Anger. " Confr (19) Aut 79-Wint 80, p. 118.
Third Poems: 1965-1978 (for Thelma Jurgrau, Karen McLaugh-
    lin, Robert Stock, and to the memory of Alfred Schick).
    QRL (21:1/2) 78, pp. 229-282.

GALOS, Jennifer
"Canyons of Winter. " Mund (11:1) 79, p. 104.
"darkness is refracted. " Mund (11:1) 79, p. 105.
"Winter Solstice at Dog Theater. " Mund (11:1) 79, p. 104.

GALVIN, Brendan
"Bear's Spring, The Way It Comes. " QW (8) Wint 79, p. 31.
"Becoming a Dump Keeper. " QW (9) Spr-Sum 79, p. 115.
"Climacteric. " Poem (35) Mr 79, p. 52.
"Defending the Provinces. " QW (8) Wint 78, p. 29.
"Great Horned Owls. " QW (6) Spr-Sum 78, p. 74.
"Green Woods Pool. " Poem (35) Mr 79, p. 53.
"The Gnats. " PoetryNW (20:2) Sum 79, pp. 27-28.
"The Migrants. " QW (6) Spr-Sum 78, p. 77.
"Netsilik. " QW (6) Spr-Sum 78, p. 78.
"Old Map of Barnstable County. " GeoR (33:3) Aut 79, p. 622.
"The Old Trip by Dream Train. " GeoR (33:1) Spr 79, p. 43.
"Scallops. " CalQ (15) Wint 79, p. 68.
"Though. " QW (6) Spr-Sum 78, p. 76.
"A Triptych for Snowlight. " CharR (5:1) Spr 79, p. 50.

"Trying to Flatter Twelve Mile River. " PoetryNW (20:2) Sum
    79, p. 26-27.

GALVIN, James
    "Airbrush. " Iowa (10:2) Spr 79, p. 81.
    "Fool's Errand. " Agni (10/11) 79, p. 62.
    "Hematite Lake. " Antaeus (34) Sum 79, p. 71.
    "A Man's Vocation Is Nobody's Business. " GeoR (33:3) Aut 79,
        p. 657.
    "Rendezvous. " Agni (10/11) 79, p. 60.
    "Three Songs of the One-Man-Band. " AmerPoR (8:3) My-Je 79,
        p. 12.
    "Watershed. " Antaeus (35) Aut 79, p. 89.

GALVIN, Martin
    "Heron's Bay. " Comm (106:17) 28 S 79, p. 534.

GAMSON, Rosanna
    "Changing Weather. " Columbia (3) 79, p. 40.

GAR, Tsfrirar
    "After the Guests Departed" (tr. by Bernhard Frank). PoNow
        (24) 79, p. 16.
    "Seeing the Light" (tr. by Bernhard Frank). PoNow (24) 79, p.
        16.
    "Tin Toys" (tr. by Bernhard Frank). PoNow (24) 79, p. 16.

GARCIA-DUES, Ann
    "Jacobo's Sun. " GRR (10:2) 79, p. 198.

GARDIVER, Doll
    Poem.   St. AR (5:2) 79, p. 100.
    Poem.   St. AR (5:2) 79, p. 101.

GARDNER, Geoffrey
    from Exister: "Bread" (tr. of Jean Follain). Nimrod (23:1) Aut-
        Wint 79, p. 60.
    from Territoires: "Police" (tr. of Jean Follain). Nimrod (23:1)
        Aut-Wint 79, p. 59.

GARDNER, Ruth
    "Alarm. " CutB (12) Spr-Sum 79, p. 65.
    "Behind Us. " CutB (12) Spr-Sum 79, p. 64.

GARDNER, Stephen
    "Another Cross. " StoneC (6:2) My 79, p. 15.

GARDNER, Thomas
    "The Mime, Speaking. " PoetryNW (20:1) Spr 79, pp. 19-21.
    "Plowing" (for my father). WestB (4) 79, p. 53.

GARIN, Marita
    "Crow. " SmF (7/8) Spr-Aut 78, p. 47.

"Dry Spell. " Poem (35) Mr 79, p. 47.
"Touch-Me-Not. " Poem (35) Mr 79, p. 46.
"Weather Diviner. " SmF (7/8) Spr-Aut 78, p. 48.

GARMON, John
"Light Morning Snow, We Wait for a Warmer Season. " SouthernHR
    (13:2) Spr 79, p. 113.

GARTON, Victoria
"Spring Song. " CharR (5:1) Spr 79, p. 68.

GARVER, Dan
"The Deaf-Mute, Just Escaped After Thirty Years in a Mental
    Hospital, Takes a Piss in the River. " QW (7) Aut 78, p.
    64.

GARRETSON, Pete
"The Girl Down the Lane. " PoNow (25) 79, p. 8.
"The Workoholic. " PoNow (25) 79, p. 8.

GARRISON, Joseph
"An Album. " WormR (73) 79, p. 4.
"At the Contractors' Ball. " WormR (73) 79, p. 4.
"A Dream with a Knife in It. " SouthernPR (19:2) Aut 79, p. 31.
"Keeping Fit. " PoNow (25) 79, p. 9.
"This Man Has Nothing to Do. " SouthernPR (19:2) Aut 79, p. 32.
"Through a Glass, Darkly. " PoetryNW (20:1) Spr 79, p. 37.

GARRISON, Philip
"Stumps. " PoNow (25) 79, p. 9.

GATENBY, Greg
"A Death Alone. " LitR (22:3) Spr 79, p. 366.
"Girl Asleep. " LitR (22:3) Spr 79, p. 365.

GATTI-TAYLOR, Marisa
"And, then, remember, life is only this much" (tr. of Nico
    Naldini w. Jan Pallister). PoNow (24) 79, p. 28.
"Between the real and the unreal" (tr. of Nico Naldini w. Jan
    Pallister). PoNow (24) 79, p. 27.
"Comisso, de Pisi, Sandro Penna" (to the great Alfred) (tr. of
    Nico Naldini w. Jan Pallister). PoNow (24) 79, p. 28.
"It was still a trifle cold" (tr. of Nico Naldini w. Jan Pallister).
    PoNow (24) 79, p. 27.
"A shadow upon the unmade bed" (tr. of Nico Naldini w. Jan
    Pallister). PoNow (24) 79, p. 27.

GAUGER, Jan
"The Chickasaw Quarry. " CarlMis (17:2/3) Spr 79, p. 34.

GAWORSKI, Kate
"I would be the sun. " Confr (19) Aut 79-Wint 80, p. 89.

GEHM, John
"If simple man be simple passion's slave. " Poem (35) Mr 79,
   p. 58.
"The summer cusp is poised again on summer love. " Poem (35)
   Mr 79, p. 59.

GEIGER, Geoff
"Death of Burns. " Sam (79) 79, p. 56.

GEIST, Anthony
"A Prison (1936)" (tr. of Jorge Guillén, w. Reginald Gibbons).
   NewEngR (1:3) Spr 79, p. 344.

GEISTMAN, Harold
"Beth. " GRR (10:2) 79, p. 178.
"Ojibway Island. " GRR (10:2) 79, p. 179.
"Seasons. " GRR (10:2) 79, p. 176.

GELINEAU, Christine Marie
"Gelding the Two Year Old. " PoNow (21) 79, p. 47.

GELMAN, Juan
"Maria the Servant Girl. " LitR (23:2) Wint 80, p. 223.

GENEGA, Paul
"Postcards from Silence. " Epoch (28:2) Wint 79, p. 142.

GENSLER, Kinereth
"The Traveller and the Elephant. " VirQR (55:3) Sum 79, p. 514.

GEORGE, Anne
"After the Funeral. " EngJ (68:5) My 79, p. 32.

GEORGE, Emery
"Circling, the eagle plies his trade in the sky; deep down on the"
   (tr. of Miklós Radnóti). PoNow (23) 79, p. 45.
"84. " (tr. of Osip Mandelstam). Spirit (3:3) Sum 78, p. 30.
"Elegy" (tr. of Miklós Radnóti). MinnR (NS 12) Spr 79, p. 22.
"Essay. " KanQ (11:3) Sum 79, p. 22.
"48. Admiralty Building" (tr. of Osip Mandelstam). Spirit (3:3)
   Sum 78, p. 30.
"Friday" (tr. of Osip Mandelstam). Spirit (3:3) Sum 78, p. 32.
"Montenegro Elegy" (tr. of Miklós Radnóti). PoNow (23) 79, p.
   45.
"On the Way Home" (tr. of Miklós Radnóti). MinnR (NS 12) Spr
   79, p. 23.
"Poem in Autumn" (tr. of Miklós Radnóti). PoNow (24) 79, p.
   47.
"The Ragged Robin Opens" (tr. of Miklós Radnóti). MichQR
   (18:3) Sum 79, p. 408.
"To Be Poor" (tr. of Otto Orban). PoNow (24) 79, p. 38.
"Transience and Resurrection of the Pastoral Life" (tr. of Hans
   Carl Artmann). ChiR (30:4) Spr 79, pp. 97-101.

"Twenty-Eight Years" (tr. of Miklós Radnóti).   MinnR (NS 12)
    Spr 79, p. 20.
"Youth" (tr. of Miklós Radnóti).   MichQR (18:3) Sum 79, p. 408.

GEORGE, Stefan
    "The Antichrist" (tr. of Peter Viereck).   PoNow (24) 79, p. 16.
    "Homecoming" (tr. by Peter Viereck).   PoNow (24) 79, p. 16.
    "A Last Letter" (tr. by Peter Viereck).   PoNow (24) 79, p. 17.
    "Southern Strand: Bay" (tr. by Peter Viereck).   PoNow (24) 79,
    p. 17.
    "The Stranger" (tr. by Peter Viereck).   PoNow (24) 79, p. 44.

GERBER, Dan
    "Making Time. "   PoNow (21) 79, p. 18.

GERBERICK, M. E.
    "The Swamp Doll. "   BelPoJ (29:3) Spr 79, p. 16.

GERMAIN, Valerie
    "Not That Thing." "   Kayak (50) My 79, p. 32.   Found poem.

GERNEAUX, Robert
    "The Fifth Is Reality. "   Wind (33) 79, p. 22.
    "Mon Musse de Toi. "   Wind (33) 79, p. 22.

GERNES, Sonia
    "Auction. "   NewEngR (2:1) Aut 79, p. 60.
    "Genus, Species. "   PoetryNW (20:1) Spr 79, p. 41.
    "The Nun. "   Bits (10) Jl 79.
    "Water Witch. "   PoetryNW (20:1) Spr 79, pp. 40-41.

GERTLER, Pesha
    "The Mermaids and the Seated Women. "   PoetryNW (20:3) Aut
    79, pp. 25-26.

GERY, John
    "Charlemagne in Milwaukee. "   SoDakR (17:1) Spr 79, p. 42.
    "Edifice Rex. "   SoDakR (17:1) Spr 79, p. 39.
    "The Macula. "   SoDakR (17:1) Spr 79, p. 44.

GESSEL, Michael
    "Mickey Jogs. "   JnlONJP (4:1) 79, p. 6.
    "Mickey Khayham. "   JnlONJP (4:1) 79, p. 7.
    "Opening. "   JnlONJP (4:1) 79, p. 8.

GETSI, Manon
    "A Dream to Go. "   PikeF (2) Wint 78-79, p. 16.

GETTY, Sarah
    "Mother Visit. "   Tendril (4) Wint 79, p. 27.
    "October, Crows. "   Tendril (5) Sum 79, p. 31.
    "A Sleep Song for My Father. "   Tendril (5) Sum 79, p. 33.

GHIGNA, Charles
  "The Alabama Elm. " Poem (35) Mr 79, p. 37.
  "Brothers Travel. " Poem (35) Mr 79, p. 36.
  "A Lesson of Night. " Ur (2) 79, p. 37.
  "When Grandpa Danced on the Water. " Poem (35) Mr 79, p. 38.
  "You and the Lady with the Hat. " Ur (2) 79, p. 38.

GHISELIN, Brewster
  "Poetry. " Poetry (135:2) N 79, pp. 89-90.
  "Reading the Rose. " WestHR (33:3) Sum 79, p. 202.
  "Rite De Passage. " WestHR (33:3) Sum 79, p. 254.
  "Rose of the Winds: A Wreath for Allen. " Poetry (135:2) N 79,
      p. 88.

GHITELMAN, David
  "The Story of One Who Set Out to Study Fear. " CutB (13) Aut-
      Wint 79, p. 30.

GIANOLI, Paul
  "Bank Swallows. " WebR (4:3) Spr 79, p. 55.

GIBB, Robert
  "The Convert. " PraS (53:4) Wint 79-80, p. 323.
  "Entering the Oven. " CarolQ (31:3) Aut 79, pp. 45-50.
  "Entering Time in a House Photographed by Walker Evans. "
      NewL (46:1) Aut 79, p. 32.
  "Genesis. " PraS (53:4) Wint 79-80, p. 321.
  "Insomnia. " Tendril (6) Aut 79, p. 27.
  "Snapshots. " Chowder (12) Spr-Sum 79, p. 32.
  "Snowfall on Washington's Birthday. " PraS (53:4) Wint 79-80, p.
      322.
  "The Vultures. " Tendril (6) Aut 79, p. 26.

GIBBONS, Reginald
  "The Foreigner. " Mund (11:1) 79, p. 77.
  "Luckies. " NewRep (181:19) 10 N 79, p. 38.
  "A Prison (1936)" (tr. of Jorge Guillén, w. Anthony Geist).
      NewEngR (1:3) Spr 79, p. 344.
  Roofs, Voices, Roads (for Ginny). QRL (21:1/2) 78, pp. 167-
      226.
  "A Transcription. " Mund (11:1) 79, p. 77.

GIBSON, Margaret
  "Ice Storm. " Tendril (4) Wint 79, p. 28.
  "The Onion. " MinnR (NS 12) Spr 79, p. 19.
  from Signs: A Progress of the Soul: "Cold. An unreasonable
      mist. " SouthernR (15:1) Wint 79, p. 125.
  from Signs: A Progress of the Soul: "Dark, dark, dark. "
      SouthernR (15:1) Wint 79, p. 126.
  from Signs: A Progress of the Soul: "The sycamore blows. "
      SouthernR (15:1) Wint 79, p. 124.
  "Still Life. " SouthernPR (19:1) Spr 79, p. 14.

GIBSON, Sandra
   "Didactic Poem from Jeffers Country. " ArkRiv (4:3) 79, p. 33.
   "The Egg People. " CarolQ (31:1) Wint 79, p. 45.
   "From a Recipe of Emily Dickinson's. " CarolQ (31:1) Wint 79,
      p. 44.
   "The Moment. " ArkRiv (4:3) 79, p. 32.

GIBSON, Stephen M.
   "The Dance. " KanQ (11:4) Aut 79, p. 144.

GILBERT, Celia
   "The Book of Revelations. " PartR (46:3) 79, p. 428.

GILBERT, Jack
   "Quinlan. " Kayak (50) My 79, p. 48.
   "Sestina. " Kayak (50) My 79, p. 48.

GILBERT, James
   "The Words of Praise You So Desperately Need. " Mouth (2:3)
      N 79, p. 30.

GILBERT, Marie
   "The Beast. " GRR (10:1) 79, p. 138.
   "The Beast. " GRR (10:3) 79, p. 126.   Corrected version.
   "Choice. " GRR (10:3) 79, p. 106.
   "Gravitation. " GRR (10:3) 79, p. 106.

GILBERT, Sandra M.
   "Beets. " PoetryNW (20:3) Aut 79, pp. 26-27.
   "Still Life: Woman Cooking. " ColEng (41:4) D 79, p. 410.
   "Vampire. " PoNow (21) 79, p. 36.

GILBERT, Virginia
   "The Great American Poem. " Antaeus (32) Wint 79, pp. 82-86.

GILBOA, Amir
   from Gazelle, I'll Send You: "A bouquet--to scatter its flowers
      on the floor and the table" (tr. by Shirley Kaufman and
      Shlomith Rimmon). WebR (4:3) Spr 79, p. 9.
   from Gazelle, I'll Send You: "Finally I go to the man who set
      traps for the birds" (tr. by Shirley Kaufman and Shlomith
      Rimmon). WebR (4:3) Spr 79, p. 8.
   from Gazelle, I'll Send you: "How would I stand then, what side
      of my face expose to the light" (tr. by Shirley Kaufman and
      Shlomith Rimmon). WebR (4:3) Spr 79, p. 8.
   from Gazelle, I'll Send You: "Standing on tiptoe shutting my eyes
      so I won't see what's going on in the yard" (tr. by Shirley
      Kaufman and Shlomith Rimmon). WebR (4:3) Spr 79, p. 8.

GILCHRIST, Ellen
   "Dad I'm in Conway, Arkansas, Writing About You. " CalQ (15)
      Wint 79, p. 28.
   "For the Head Cheerleader as She Hits Forty-Eight. " CalQ (15)

Wint 79, p. 29.
"Sharecropper. " CalQ (15) Wint 79, p. 27.

GILDNER, Gary
"4th Base. " PoNow (21) 79, p. 22.
"The Great American Poem. " Antaeus (32) Wint 79, pp. 82-86.
"Last Articles. " PoNow (21) 79, p. 22.
"Mammals. " PoNow (23) 79, p. 3.
"Mulligan on His Death, His Women. " PoNow (23) 79, p. 3.
"Old Farm in Northern Michigan. " PoNow (21) 79, p. 6.
"Then. " PoNow (21) 79, p. 22.

GILL, Evalyn P.
"Arcosanti. " GRR (10:3) 79, p. 98.
"Mountain" (tr. of Claude de Burine). GRR (10:3) 79, p. 101.
"The Red Cabbage" (tr. of Gabrielle Marquet). GRR (10:3) 79,
    p. 103.
"Tulips. " GRR (10:3) 79, p. 105.
"Where Darkness Meets Light. " GRR (10:3) 79, p. 99.

GILLESPIE, Robert
"The Husband. " Epoch (28:2) Wint 79, p. 156.

GILLETT, Michelle
"First Generation. " PoetryNW (20:3) Aut 79, pp. 11-12.
"Flesh and Blood. " PoetryNW (20:3) Aut 79, pp. 9-10.
"In My Mother's House. " PoetryNW (20:3) Aut 79, pp. 10-11.
"Nothing I Could Name as Loss. " PoetryNW (20:3) Aut 79, pp.
    12-13.
"The Shell-Collector ... Miquelon. " Wind (33) 79, p. 24.

GINGERICH, Alina
"Atlantic April" (tr. of Guillermo Sucre, w. Willard Gingerich).
    Mund (11:1) 79, p. 57.
"In Idleness" (tr. of Guillermo Sucre, w. Willard Gingerich).
    Mund (11:1) 79, p. 57.
"Just Silence" (tr. of Guillermo Sucre, w. Willard Gingerich).
    Mund (11:1) 79, p. 55.
"The Other Sun" (tr. of Guillermo Sucre, w. Willard Gingerich).
    Mund (11:1) 79, p. 59.
"Proscripted, 1930" (to G. Y. B.) (tr. of Guillermo Sucre, w.
    Willard Gingerich). Mund (11:1) 79, p. 59.
"Stone of Scandal" (tr. of Guillermo Sucre, w. Willard Gingerich).
    Mund (11:1) 79, p. 55.

GINGERICH, Willard
"Atlantic April" (tr. of Guillermo Sucre, w. Alina Gingerich).
    Mund (11:1) 79, p. 57.
"In Idleness" (tr. of Guillermo Sucre, w. Alina Gingerich).
    Mund (11:1) 79, p. 57.
"Just Silence" (tr. of Guillermo Sucre, w. Alina Gingerich).
    Mund (11:1) 79, p. 55.
"The Other Sun" (tr. of Guillermo Sucre, w. Alina Gingerich).

Mund (11:1) 79, p. 59.
"Proscripted, 1930" (to G. Y. B.) (tr. of Guillermo Sucre w.
Alina Gingerich). Mund (11:1) 79, p. 59.
"Stone of Scandal" (tr. of Guillermo Sucre, w. Alina Gingerich).
Mund (11:1) 79, p. 55.

GINSBERG, Allen
"Contest of Bards. " Hudson (32:1) Spr 79, pp. 36-40.
Eight Poems. AmerPoR (8:3) My-Je 79, pp. 21-26.

GIOIA, Dana
"Long Distance. " SouthernR (15:1) Wint 79, p. 109.
"Song for the End of Time. " SouthernR (15:1) Wint 79, p. 108.

GIOVANNI, Nikki
"Cotton Candy on a Rainy Day. " Paint (11) Spr 79, p. 13.

GIRRI, Alberto
"Lyric. " LitR (23:2) Wint 80, p. 277.
"Poem from Kierkegaard. " LitR (23:2) Wint 80, p. 279.
"Quartet in F Minor ('Serioso'). " LitR (23:2) Wint 80, p. 278.

GITLIN, Todd
"A Few Freedoms. " ChiR (30:4) Spr 79, p. 34.
"Invocation to Ocean. " CarlMis (18:1) Wint 79-80, p. 144.
"Love Includes Irony, Irony Not Love. " CarlMis (18:1) Wint 79-
80, p. 143.
"Some Facts, Some Uprising. " CarlMis (18:1) Wint 79, p. 144.
"Without Ends. " CarlMis (17:2/3) Spr 79, p. 94.

GITZEN, Julian
"Apprehensions on a Winter Night. " Poem (35) Mr 79, p. 62.
"Canada Geese. " Poem (35) Mr 79, p. 63.
"Saturday at the Salebarn. " Poem (35) Mr 79, p. 64.

GLASER, Elton
"At the Children's Home for the Criminally Insane. " PoNow (22)
79, p. 18.
"Escape Artist. " PoNow (22) 79, p. 18.
"Figure and Ground. " NowestR (18:1) 79, p. 75.
"In Medias Res. " PoetryNW (20:3) Aut 79, p. 22.
"In the Sex Hotel. " PoNow (22) 79, p. 18.
"Six Dances in Bulgarian Rhythms. " PoetryNW (20:3) Aut 79,
pp. 21-22.
"Scraping Our Boot Soles. " PoNow (22) 79, p. 18.

GLASER, Michael S.
"Dustballs. " Poem (35) Mr 79, p. 51.
"The Garden. " ChrC (96:7) 28 F 79, p. 205.

GLASS, Malcolm
"The Boy; or, Son of Rip-Off. " Poultry (1) 79, p. 2.
"The Letter (A Poem for Two Voices). " MichQR (18:4) Aut 79,

p. 618.
"A Wheelbarrow of Rocks. " Poultry (1) 79, p. 2.

GLASSCO, John
    "Les Quatre Sans Cou" (tr. of Robert Desnos). MalR (49) Ja
        79, p. 122.

GLASSER, Carole
    "You Were Her. " PartR (46:3) 79, p. 422.

GLAZE, Andrew
    "Boy. " PoNow (21) 79, p. 23.
    "Concert at the Station" (tr. of Osip Mandelstam). PoNow (24)
        79, p. 24.
    "Eyes of the Heart. " PoNow (21) 79, p. 23.
    "I Am the Jefferson County Courthouse. " DenQ (14:2) Sum 79,
        p. 94.
    "I will search in the Romany camp of the darkened street" (tr.
        of Osip Mandelstam). PoNow (24) 79, p. 24.
    "Leningrad" (tr. of Osip Mandelstam). PoNow (23) 79, p. 44.
    "Luck. " PoNow (21) 79, p. 37.
    "Please Take the Joy of It" (tr. of Osip Mandelstam). PoNow
        (24) 79, p. 24.
    "So Well Aware. " PoNow (21) 79, p. 23.
    "Twilight of Freedom" (tr. of Osip Mandelstam). PoNow (24)
        79, p. 24.

GLAZIER, Lyle
    "Bus Ride: Ankara. " Mouth (2:1) F 79, p. 47.

GLEN, Emilie
    "Sadly Out Over. " Spirit (4:2/3) Spr-Sum 79, p. 34.
    "Smother Sting. " Tele (15) Spr 79, p. 91.
    "So I Sculptured. " StoneC (6:3) O 79, p. 31.

GLENN, Karen
    "The Seal. " GreenfieldR (7:3/4) Spr-Sum 79, p. 221.

GLOVER, Jon
    "Letters and Fictions. " Stand (20:2) 79, p. 57.
    "Nature. " Stand (20:2) 79, p. 58.

GLOWNEY, John
    "Before Starting Out for Michigan, I Deliver Holly and Poinsettias
        Across the Mississippi, Christmas Eve, 1977. " Antaeus (33)
        Spr 79, p. 131.
    "A Recent Convert. " Northeast (3:7) Spr 79, p. 27.
    "Traverse City Poem for Mike and Carolyn. " Northeast (3:7)
        Spr 79, p. 26.

GLÜCK, Louise
    "Aphrodite. " NewYorker (55:1) 19 F 79, p. 131.
    "Autumnal. " Salm (46) Aut 79, p. 84.

"Grandmother. " Salm (46) Aut 79, p. 85.
"The Great American Poem. " Antaeus (32) Wint 79, pp. 82-86.
"Portrait. " Salm (46) Aut 79, p. 84.

GOBA, Ron
"recollection 2. " Tendril (4) Wint 79, p. 29.
"recollection 3. " Tendril (4) Wint 79, p. 30.

GOEBEL, Ulf
"His Age. " KanQ (11:3) Sum 79, p. 82.
"In the Face of Old Mountains. " KanQ (11:3) Sum 79, p. 81.

GOEDICKE, Patricia
"All the Princes of Heaven. " AmerPoR (8:4) Jl-Ag 79, p. 43.
"The Arrival of the Egrets. " NewL (46:1) Aut 79, p. 62.
"Asparagus. " PoetryNW (20:3) Aut 79, pp. 28-29.
"The Coexistence. " QW (9) Spr-Sum 79, p. 56.
"Counting the Waves. " Hudson (32:2) Sum 79, p. 225.
"The Dog That Was Barking Yesterday. " Confr (18) Spr-Sum 79,
     p. 24.
"The Egrets Again. " NewL (46:1) Aut 79, p. 65.
"George Dying. " Chowder (13) Aut-Wint 79, p. 50.
"Hands That Have Waved Farewell. " AmerPoR (8:4) Jl-Ag 79,
     p. 44.
"The Hotel Buena Vista. " DacTerr (16) 79, p. 24.
"The Husband and Wife Team. " ThRiPo (13/14) 79, p. 26.
"In San Miguel de Allende. " NewL (46:1) Aut 79, p. 67.
"In the Middle of the Kitchen Smiling. " NewL (46:1) Aut 79, p.
     61.
"In the Waiting Room. " ThRiPo (13/14) 79, p. 17.
"Making a Double Angel. " Hudson (32:2) Sum 79, p. 226.
"Moonscape. " QW (9) Spr-Sum 79, p. 56.
"My Father. " NewL (46:1) Aut 79, p. 59.
"One More Time. " ThRiPo (13/14) 79, p. 19.
"Over Our Dead Bodies. " ThRiPo (13/14) 79, p. 20.
"Recreo # 108. " Agni (10/11) 79, p. 141.
"The Rings of All That Is Possible. " AmerPoR (8:4) Jl-Ag 79,
     p. 44.
"Rose" (for Leonard Wallace Robinson). ThRiPo (13/14) 79, p.
     24.
"Surrounded by Sadness, Escaping" (for my sister, Jean-Marie
     McKenna Cook). ThRiPo (13/14) 79, p. 15.
"The Tree Itself. " Ascent (4:3) 79, p. 47.
"What Are You Doing Here. " OhioR (20:2) Spr-Sum 79, pp. 90-
     92.
"What's Friendship?" ThRiPo (13/14) 79, p. 22.

GÖMÖRI, George
"Letter to My Wife" (tr. of Miklós Radnóti w. Clive Wilmer).
     SouthernR (15:1) Wint 79, p. 143.
"The Third Eclogue" (tr. of Miklós Radnóti w. Clive Wilmer).
     SouthernR (15:1) Wint 79, p. 144.

GOFEN, Ethel
"Credo. " KanQ (11:4) Aut 79, p. 132.

GOLD, Edward
"At Hebrew School. " CimR (48) Jl 79, p. 40.
"Heaven of Cowboys. " PoNow (25) 79, p. 9.

GOLD, Herman
"Jewboy. " PoNow (22) 79, p. 18.
"The Postcard. " Confr (19) Aut 79-Wint 80, p. 165.

GOLD, Sid
"Berry Takes Rye in December. " CimR (49) O 79, p. 46.

GOLDBARTH, Albert
"Animal Functionsong. " PoetryNW (20:2) Sum 79, p. 11.
"Basics, in Landscape. " DenQ (14:3) Aut 79, p. 20.
"Cross-Country, and Motif Appears. " PraS (53:2) Sum 79, p.
   178.
"A Definition. " PraS (53:2) Sum 79, p. 179.
"For Children Six to Sixty" (from his notebooks). MidwQ (20:3)
   Spr 79, p. 258.
"For Some of Us. " GeoR (33:2) Sum 79, p. 380.
"Fuse/Jan. 31/Shereema. " VirQR (55:1) Wint 79, p. 112.
"The Great American Poem. " Antaeus (32) Wint 79, pp. 82-86.
"The Greed Song. " KanQ (11:1/2) Wint-Spr 79, p. 32.
"How It Works. " DenQ (14:3) Aut 79, p. 24.
"Math Song. " Columbia (3) 79, p. 56.
"Monday, February 26, 1979. " NoAmR (264:3) Aut 79, p. 55.
"My Law for Little Hope in Retrospect. " VirQR (55:1) Wint 79,
   p. 113.
"NYC/Curbing" (homage a Pound). PoNow (21) 79, p. 5.
"note from an exhibition. " Salm (46) Aut 79, p. 87.
"Object Functionsong. " PoetryNW (20:2) Sum 79, pp. 11-12.
"Of Secret. " VirQR (55:1) Wint 79, p. 114.
"A Percussionist's Wife. " Bits (10) Jl 79.
"Poem with a Quote from Ross Macdonald. " Iowa (10:2) Spr 79,
   p. 82.
"Resemblance Song. " KanQ (11:1/2) Wint-Spr 79, p. 31.
"Scroll. " Chowder (12) Spr-Sum 79, p. 13.
"Shattuck. " Salm (46) Aut 79, p. 86.
"The Shape. " ArkRiv (4:3) 79, p. 5.
"Song Up and Down. " DenQ (14:3) Aut 79, p. 22.
"The Spirit. " CutB (12) Spr-Sum 79, p. 8.
"The Story of the Giant Panda a wedding service in 9 parts. "
   BelPoJ (30:1) Aut 79, pp. 14-23.
"Then I put on slow music, and dimmed the lamp, and just. "
   PoNow (22) 79, p. 18.
"Therefore I Ams. " DenQ (14:2) Aut 79, p. 23.
"To Rest. " Epoch (29:1) Aut 79, p. 20.
"Vermont Notebook. " CarolQ (31:2) Spr-Sum 79, pp. 53-58.
"Wonders Occult and Fantasia. " ArkRiv (4:3) 79, p. 4.

GOLDBERG, Beckian Fritz
"The Last Man. " NewL (46:2) Wint 79-80, p. 45.
"Your Mother's Laboratory. " NewL (46:2) Wint 79-80, p. 47.

GOLDBERG, Leah
"Heat Spell in Venice" (tr. by Bernhard Frank). PoNow (24) 79,
    p. 17.
"On the Hazards of Smoking" (tr. by Bernhard Frank). PoNow
    (24) 79, p. 17.

GOLDBERG, Natalie
"Been Here Once. " DacTerr (16) 79, p. 26.

GOLDEN, Renny
"For Jeanette Piccard Ordained at 79. " ChrC (96:16) 2 My 79,
    p. 484.

GOLDENSOHN, Barry
"After the Revolution. " Salm (46) Aut 79, p. 91.
"During the Time of the Executions. " Salm (46) Aut 79, p. 90.

GOLDENSOHN, Lorrie
"Beauty and the Beast. " Ploughs (5:1) 79, pp. 41-42.
"Joseph. " Ploughs (5:1) 79, pp. 40-41.
"The Plains of Heaven. " AmerPoR (8:2) Mr-Ap 79, p. 41.
"Suite. " AmerPoR (8:2) Mr-Ap 79, p. 41.

GOLDINER, Jim
"Even Royalty Finds It Rough Going Sometimes. " Spirit (3:3)
    Sum 78, p. 44.

GOLDSBERRY, Steven
"At Puako, Kohala. " NewYorker (55:37) 29 O 79, p. 149.

GOLDSBY, Marcie
"If Your Real Father Drove the Car for Bonnie and Clyde. "
    CutB (13) Aut-Wint 79, p. 31.
"Stopping by the Side of the Road. " PortR (25) 79, p. 72.

GOLDSTEIN, Jonas
"On Philosophy. " BallSUF (20:4) Aut 79, p. 24.

GOLDSTEIN, Laurence
"A Masterpiece Apparently Destroyed. " SouthernR (15:3) Sum 79,
    p. 643.
"Reunion at 35. " SouthernR (15:3) Sum 79, p. 644.

GOLEMBIEWSKI, Alison
"The Sense of Sin. " GeoR (33:3) Aut 79, p. 621.

GOLLUB, Christian-Albrecht
"All Alone" (tr. of Louis Aragon w. Jean-Luc Filoche). Spirit
    (3:1/2) Aut-Wint 77-78, p. 58.

GOMEZ, Manuel
"Chicano in Resonance. " PraS (53:2) Sum 79, p. 118.

GONZALEZ, Ray
"Laughing at the Border Patrol. " GreenfieldR (7:3/4) Spr-Sum
79, p. 31.
"The Spirals of Dawn. " GreenfieldR (7:3/4) Spr-Sum 79, p. 30.

GONZALEZ-GERTH, Miguel
Seventeen Poems (tr. of Vicente Aleixandre). TexQ (21:4) Wint
78, pp. 183-204.

GOOD, Ruth
"The American Woman at the Club de Corresponsales Who Always
Wanted to Cry at Four O'Clock. " NewRena (11) 79, p. 15.

GOODENOUGH, J. B.
"Sleepwalkers. " HiramPoR (26) Spr-Sum 79, p. 21.

GOODMAN, Deborah
"Dialogue with Herself. " CutB (12) Spr-Sum 79, p. 18.
"The Tour Guide's Speech: Eagles at Fish Creek. " CutB (13)
Aut-Wint 79, p. 53.
"Until I Was Older, I Believed Swimming Was Learning to
Breathe in the Womb. " CutB (12) Spr-Sum 79, p. 17.

GOODMAN, Mark
"The acorns crack. " WindO (34) Spr-Sum 79, p. 47.
"Autumn evening--. " WindO (34) Spr-Sum 79, p. 47.
"July twilight, ". WindO (34) Spr-Sum 79, p. 47.
"September night. " WindO (34) Spr-Sum 79, p. 47.
"The snow finally melted. " WindO (34) Spr-Sum 79, p. 47.

GOODMAN, Ryah Tumarkin
"Do the Dead Eat? " GRR (10:1) 79, p. 133.

GOODRICH, Chip
"In the night garden. " PortR (25) 79, p. 166.

GOODSON, Michael
"A Creation-of-the-World Poem. " Ploughs (5:2) 79, pp. 120-
122.

GOODWIN, Aly
"Rendezvous. " Iowa (10:2) Spr 79, p. 83.

GORDETT, Marea
"Anastasia. " PraS (53:4) Wint 79-80, p. 318.
"The Child Weeds. " DenQ (14:2) Sum 79, p. 67.
"Family Living in Abandoned Cave. " Nat (228:20) 26 My 79, p.
611.
"The Fishwife. " DenQ (14:2) Sum 79, p. 66.
"Marriage. " DenQ (14:2) Sum 79, p. 68.

"1943. " ChiR (31:1) Sum 79, p. 54.
"Potato Grower and Child. " DenQ (14:2) Sum 79, p. 69.

GORDON, Don
  "Autobiography. " GreenfieldR (7:3/4) Spr-Sum 79, p. 210.
  "Deadfalls. " PoetC (11:3) 79, p. 18.
  "Free Fall. " GreenfieldR (7:3/4) Spr-Sum 79, p. 209.
  "In the Hospital. " StoneC (6:2) My 79, p. 7.
  "In the Real World. " PoetC (11:3) 79, p. 17.

GORDON, Donna
  "Lyric. " CarlMis (18:1) Wint 79-80, p. 164.

GORDON, Kirpal Singh
  "Catfish of the Eggcream. " WindO (34) Spr-Sum 79, p. 29.
  "The Lake. " Pig (6) 79, p. 87.
  "Not Returning. " WindO (34) Spr-Sum 79, p. 27.
  "100 Years in Yucca Valley. " Pig (6) 79, p. 55.
  "The Retreat. " Pig (6) 79, p. 32.
  "What Fingers Do. " WindO (34) Spr-Sum 79, p. 28.

GORDON, Robert
  "Canzoni. " StoneC (6:1) F 79, p. 17.
  "Sea-Letter. " JnlONJP (4:1) 79, p. 27.
  "Trauma. " JnlONJP (3:2) 79, p. 14.

GOREN, Judith
  "October. " CentR (23:4) Aut 79, p. 423.

GORHAM, Sarah
  "Mother in the Garden. " Ploughs (5:1) 79, pp. 44-45.
  "October. " Ploughs (5:1) 79, p. 43.
  "Sampler. " Ploughs (5:1) 79, p. 47.
  "Verondrye: A Waterway to the West. " Ploughs (5:1) 79, p. 46.

GORMAN, Michael
  "Job's Prayer. " MalR (49) Ja 79, p. 59.
  "Triad. " MalR (49) Ja 79, p. 59.

GOTO, Miyoko
  "Four Tanka Poems" (tr. by Reiko Tsukimura). MalR (52) O
    79, p. 24.

GOULD, Roberta
  from American Indian Portraits: "Mrs. Frank Corndropper--
    Domeshehe: Osage. " StoneC (6:3) O 79, p. 15.

GOULD, Stephen
  "Place of Drowning Birds. " Aspect (74/75) Ja-Ag 79, p. 80.
  "Recognitions. " Aspect (74/75) Ja-Ag 79, p. 82.

GOUMAS, Yannis
  "On the National Health. " Mund (11:1) 79, p. 98.

GOVAN, Bob
"The Web. " Bits (9) Ja 79.

GRABILL, Jim
Eight Poems. Bachy (15) Aut 79, p. 61.

GRABMAN, Richard
"Three Poems About Pigeons. " WindO (35) Aut-Wint 79-80, p. 7.

GRAHAM, David
"Cow Country. " NewEngR (2:1) Aut 79, p. 91.
"Longing to Be State Animal. " Poultry (1) 79, p. 9.
"The Magic Monkey" (for Russell Edson). Poultry (1) 79, p. 9.
"Snowbound Between Thaws" (for Charles Wright). Poultry (1) 79, p. 9.
"They Feed They Face" (for Philip Levine). Poultry (1) 79, p. 9.
"Wasteyard Valediction" (for Seamus Heaney). Poultry (1) 79, p. 9.

GRAHAM, Jorie
"An Artichoke for Montesquieu. " NewEngR (1:4) Sum 79, p. 400.
"Cross-Stitch. " Paint (11) Spr 79, p. 15.
"A Feather for Voltaire. " Antaeus (34) Sum 79, p. 74.
"For Mark Rothko. " Iowa (10:2) Spr 79, p. 85.
"The Geese. " Iowa (10:2) Spr 79, p. 84.
"Hybrids of Plants and of Ghosts. " VirQR (55:2) Spr 79, p. 297.
"I Was Taught Three. " Ploughs (5:1) 79, pp. 48-49.
"In High Waters. " Ploughs (5:1) 79, pp. 49-50.
"It Begins, What I Can Hear. " PoetryNW (20:1) Spr 79, pp. 9-10.
"Mirrors. " ParisR (75) Spr 79, pp. 208-209.
"Netting. " Nat (228:11) 24 Mr 79, p. 317.
"Now the Sturdy Wind. " Agni (10/11) 79, p. 65.
"One in the Hand. " MissouriR (2:2/3) Spr 79, p. 32.
"Pearls. " Antaeus (34) Sum 79, p. 72.
"Taking Possession. " Agni (10/11) 79, p. 63.
"Tennessee June. " PoetryNW (20:1) Spr 79, p. 8.
"To Paul Eluard. " VirQR (55:2) Spr 79, p. 298.
"Whore's Bath. " Shen (30:2) Wint 79, p. 95.

GRAHAM, Philip
"A Great Moment in Sports. " PoNow (22) 79, p. 23.
"Origins. " PoNow (22) 79, p. 23.
"Ronald McDonald. " PoNow (22) 79, p. 23.
"Travelogue. " PoNow (22) 79, p. 19.

GRAHAM, W. S.
"Dear Bryan Wynter. " Antaeus (34) Sum 79, p. 125.
"Language Ah Now You Have Me. " Antaeus (34) Sum 79, p. 114.
"The Night City. " Antaeus (34) Sum 79, p. 121.
"A Note to the Difficult One. " Antaeus (34) Sum 79, p. 113.

"The Stepping Stones. " Antaeus (34) Sum 79, p. 124.
"Ten Shots of Mister Simpson. " Antaeus (34) Sum 79, pp. 116-120.
"To Alexander Graham. " Antaeus (34) Sum 79, p. 123.

GRAHN, Judy
"A Woman Is Talking to Death. " AmerPoR (8:3) My-Je 79, pp. 34-39.

GRASS, Günter
"How I Was Her Kitchen-Boy" (tr. by Betty Falkenberg). PoNow (24) 79, p. 17.

GRATHWOHL, Susan
"In Defense of Inez Garcia. " AmerPoR (8:2) Mr-Ap 79, p. 41.

GRAUER, Priscilla June
"Monody. " SmPd (46) 79, p. 27.

GRAVELLE, Barbara
"Moon into Capricorn. " SeC (6:2) 78, p. 150.
"My Daddy Read Luke Short, Baby. " SeC (6:2) 78, pp. 152-158.
"Port Arthur Riddle. " SeC (6:2) 78, p. 149.

GRAVES, Steven
"The Graveyard of Small Children. " KanQ (11:1/2) Wint-Spr 79, p. 118.

GRAY, Elizabeth
"Ghazal I" (tr. of Hafiz-i Shirazi). Antaeus (33) Spr 79, p. 138.
"Ghazal II" (tr. of Hafiz-i Shirazi). Antaeus (33) Spr 79, p. 139.
"Ghazal III" (tr. of Hafiz-i Shirazi). Antaeus (33) Spr 79, p. 140.
"Ghazal IV" (tr. of Hafiz-i Shirazi). Antaeus (33) Spr 79, p. 141.
"Ghazal V" (tr. of Hafiz-i Shirazi). Antaeus (33) Spr 79, p. 142.
"Ghazal VI" (tr. of Hafiz-i Shirazi). Antaeus (33) Spr 79, p. 143.
Ten Ghazals (tr. of Hafiz-i Shirazi). Falcon (18) Spr 79, pp. 3-14.

GRAY, Pat
"Grandfather. " SmF (7/8) Spr-Aut 78, p. 11.

GRAY, Patrick Worth
"Death in Arnett. " Pig (6) 79, p. 11.
"Everlasting Song of the Sad Skiny Poopoohead. " Poultry (1) 79, p. 5.
"Father at Midcareer. " SouthwR (64:3) Sum 79, p. 228.
"Firing Range No. 4, Fort Hood, 1971. " CornellR (6) Sum 79, p. 42.
"The First Step. " KanQ (11:3) Sum 79, p. 97.
"For My Grandmothers. " PoetC (11:1) 79, p. 35.
"The Longest Journey. " StoneC (6:3) O 79, p. 6.

"Matron and Men. " TexQ (21:4) Wint 78, p. 90.
"Night by the Washita. " Poem (37) N 79, p. 13.
"She Wakes at Morning" (for Joyce). Poem (37) N 79, p. 12.
"Spring Begins as Yellow Crocuses Arch to Me. " KanQ (11:3)
    Sum 79, p. 98.
"Spring Thaw in Arnett, Oklahoma. " Poem (37) N 79, p. 11.
"Thirteen Warnings Find a Feminist Poet and Jump Up and Down
    on Her Pudgy Prostrate Body. " Poultry (1) 79, p. 5.
"Today. " Im (5:3) 79, p. 6.
"TV with My Daughter. " ChrC (96:39) 28 N 79, p. 1184.
"Us. " MalR (52) O 79, p. 52.

GRAZIANO, Frank
"Absolution. " GreenfieldR (7:3/4) Spr-Sum 79, p. 226.
"Ars Poetica: The Notebooks of Christopher Bisojo. " QW (9)
    Spr-Sum 79, p. 114.
"The Cell. " BelPoJ (29:4) Sum 79, pp. 6-12.
"Cook Ting: Ars Poetica. " GreenfieldR (7:3/4) Spr-Sum 79, p.
    226.
"The Honeymoon. " CharR (5:1) Spr 79, p. 64.

GREALISH, Gerard
"Four Oranges. " PikeR (1) Sum 79, pp. 36-37.
"The Work. " PikeR (1) Sum 79, p. 35.

GREEN, Samuel
"On Being Questioned About a Bank Robbery Beneath My Office. "
    PoNow (25) 79, p. 22.
"Poem for Graciano Jauregui's Twenty-first Birthday, Papeete,
    Tahiti. " PoNow (25) 79, p. 22.
"Wind: Three Letters to Melinda Mueller. " PoetryNW (20:2)
    Sum 79, pp. 12-15.

GREENBERG, Alvin
"today is just today. " ChiR (31:1) Sum 79, p. 51.

GREENBERG, Barbara L.
"Alarm. " PoetryNW (20:2) Sum 79, p. 46.
"The Armless Legless Deafmute Acrobat. " PoNow (23) 79, p.
    36.
"Art Lesson One. " PoNow (23) 79, p. 36.
"Attachments. " Ploughs (5:1) 79, p. 55.
"Class of 1953. " PoetryNW (20:2) Sum 79, p. 45.
"The Claustrophobe. " WestB (4) 79, p. 24.
"Destinations. " WestB (4) 79, p. 23.
"How It Is. " Ploughs (5:1) 79, p. 53.
"Son. " Ploughs (5:1) 79, p. 54.

GREENBURG, Candace
"Yom Hazzikkaron. " CutB (13) Aut-Wint 79, p. 57.

GREENE, Jeffrey
"The Extended Night. " Ploughs (5:1) 79, pp. 51-52.

GREENE, Jonathan
"Going Thru Night Together." Confr (18) Spr-Sum 79, p. 43.

GREGER, Debora
Fourteen Poems. SenR (10:1) Spr 79, pp. 10-24.
"Graces." GeoR (33:4) Wint 79, p. 848.
"Harvest." VirQR (55:2) Spr 79, p. 296.
"Letter: The Half of It." NewL (45:3) Spr 79, p. 97.
"Painted Desert." Antaeus (33) Spr 79, p. 129.
"The Painter's Model." NewL (45:3) Spr 79, p. 96.
"Physical Pleasures." GeoR (33:3) Aut 79, p. 565.
"Sea Change." AmerPoR (8:3) My-Je 79, p. 27.

GREGERSON, Linda
"Fire in the Conservatory." Field (20) Spr 79, p. 18.
"Man Sitting in the Sun." OhioR (20:2) Spr-Sum 79, p. 33.
"Russia, Morocco, Peru." Ploughs (5:1) 79, p. 56.
"Vladimir Horowitz, Clementi's Sonata Quasi Concerto, Opus
    33." QW (9) Spr-Sum 79, p. 67.
"Without You." OhioR (20:2) Spr-Sum 79, p. 33.

GREGG, Linda
"Goethe's Death Mask." NewYorker (55:24) 30 Jl 79, p. 32.
"Not Wanting Myself." 13thM (4:2) 79, p. 89.

GREGOR, Arthur
"The Great American Poem." Antaeus (32) Wint 79, pp. 82-86.

GREGORY, Carole Clemmons
"Love Letter." Cond (5) 79, p. 64.
"Revelation." Cond (5) 79, p. 61.

GREGORY, Carolyn Holmes
"Like Grain, We Grow." PikeR (1) Sum 79, p. 34.

GREGORY, Cynde
"jane mecrowley, my." Ur (2) 79, p. 40.
"visiting grandmother." GreenfieldR (7:3/4) Spr-Sum 79, p. 21.

GREGORY, Horace
"Balquhidder at Morning." Poetry (134:3) Je 79, pp. 134-135.

GREGORY, R. D.
"Lullaby." Mund (11:1) 79, p. 19.
"Recollections." Mund (11:1) 79, p. 19.

GREVE, Ludwig
"Hannah Arendt" (tr.). PartR (46:2) 79, p. 317.

GRIERSON, Patricia
"On the Details of Life." Spirit (3:1/2) Aut-Wint 77-78, p. 64.

GRIFFIN, Jonathan
Nine Poems. GRR (10:3) 79, pp. 87-95.

Nine poems. <u>Montra</u> (5) 79, p. 212.
Ten poems (tr. of Pierre de Ronsard). <u>Montra</u> (5) 79, p. 163.

GRIFFIN, Larry D.
"She Was Wearing Red Overalls. " <u>PikeF</u> (2) Wint 78-79, p. 19.
"The Thanksgiving Poems. " <u>PikeR</u> (1) Sum 79, pp. 7-11.

GRIFFITH, Benjy
"Hold Your Fire. " <u>FourQt</u> (28:2) Wint 79, p. 21.

GRIFFITH, Jonathan
"In the Beginning. " <u>NewL</u> (46:1) Aut 79, p. 76.

GRIFFITH, Margaret
"Uncle John. " <u>Ur</u> (2) 79, p. 39.

GRIFFITHS, Steve
"Suffering does for the character. " <u>Stand</u> (20:1) 78-79, p. 7.

GRIMES, Michael
"An Endorsement for Pudding. " <u>Spirit</u> (3:1/2) Aut-Wint 77-78,
    p. 39.

GRIMES, Nikki
"For Gwendolyn Brooks on Mother's Day. " <u>GreenfieldR</u> (7:3/4)
    Spr-Sum 79, p. 14.
"Niks: # 1. " <u>GreenfieldR</u> (7:3/4) Spr-Sum 79, p. 14.
"Niks: # 2. " <u>GreenfieldR</u> (7:3/4) Spr-Sum 79, p. 15.
"Who Raps for the Dead Lecturer (in seance). " <u>GreenfieldR</u>
    (7:3/4) Spr-Sum 79, p. 17.
"The Women in My Life. " <u>GreenfieldR</u> (7:3/4) Spr-Sum 79, p.
    16.

GRINDAL, Gracia
"Dance of the Fall Fields. " <u>Epoch</u> (28:2) Wint 79, p. 158.
"Mother Tongue. " <u>Epoch</u> (28:2) Wint 79, p. 160.
"Rosy Orient. " <u>ChrC</u> (96:2) 17 Ja 79, p. 36.
"Ruth. " <u>Epoch</u> (28:2) Wint 79, p. 159.

GRINYER, Mark
"In Satan's Place" (for G. K.). <u>KanQ</u> (11:1/2) Wint-Spr 79, p.
    9.

GROSHOLZ, Emily
"Letter from Germany. " <u>Hudson</u> (32:3) Aut 79, p. 398.
"The Metaphysicians. " <u>Hudson</u> (32:3) Aut 79, p. 399.

GROSS, Bonnie
"Night Swim. " <u>PoNow</u> (25) 79, p. 9.

GROSS, Jim
"the linkage. " <u>GreenfieldR</u> (7:3/4) Spr-Sum 79, p. 292.

GROSSBARDT, Andrew
"The First Dog" (tr. of Jules Supervielle w. Quinton Duval).
QW (8) Wint 79, p. 83.
"Jogging at Dusk. " AmerS (48:2) Spr 79, p. 208.
"Sonnet to Pilar" (tr. of Jules Supervielle w. Quinton Duval).
QW (8) Wint 79, p. 82.

GROSSMAN, Allen
"By the Pool. " ParisR (75) Spr 79, p. 77.
"The Book of Father Dust" (for Louis, my father).   Ploughs
(5:2) 79, pp. 152-154.
"The Comet. " ParisR (75) Spr 79, p. 80.
"The Department. " Ploughs (5:2) 79, pp. 148-151.
"The Field, Her Pleasure. " ParisR (75) Spr 79, pp. 78-79.
"The Holdout. " Poetry (134:3) Je 79, p. 157.
"The Loss of the Beloved Companion. " Ploughs (5:2) 79, pp.
156-158.
"The Room. " NewRep (180:11) 17 Mr 79, p. 30.
"The Thrush Relinquished. " Ploughs (5:2) 79, p. 155.
"Victory. " ParisR (75) Spr 79, pp. 81-82.
"The Woman on the Bridge Over the Chicago River. " ParisR
(75) Spr 79, pp. 75-76.

GROSSMAN, Martin
"A Field of Apple Trees. " PoNow (22) 79, p. 19.

GROSSMAN, Richard
"Behavior. " Tele (15) Spr 79, p. 139.
"Business Trip. " DacTerr (16) 79, p. 27.
"The Devil. " Chelsea (38) 79, p. 152.
"Drama. " Tele (15) Spr 79, p. 139.
"Gorilla. " ArkRiv (4:3) 79, p. 18.
"Great Hornbill. " ArkRiv (4:3) 79, p. 19.
"Harmony. " Tele (15) Spr 79, p. 140.
"The Pit. " Chelsea (38) 79, p. 153.
"Starfish. " SouthernPR (19:2) Aut 79, p. 58.
"The Way. " Chelsea (38) 79, p. 151.

GROVE, T. N.
"The Merman Episode. " CEACritic (41:4) My 79, p. 19.

GRUTZMACHER, Harold M.
"Guenevere. " BallSUF (20:3) Sum 79, p. 11.

GUBERNAT, Susan
"Pancho Villa Enter Auschwitz" (by Aiiieee).   Poultry (1) 79, p.
2.

GUENTHER, Charles
"Cocteau/The Crucifixion" (tr. of Jean Cocteau).   WebR (4:4)
Aut 79, pp. 9-19.

GUERNSEY, Bruce
"Deer Stand. " Tendril (6) Aut 79, p. 28.
"Tracks. " Tendril (6) Aut 79, p. 30.

GUILLEN, Jorge
"A Prison (1936)" (tr. by Anthony Geist and Reginald Gibbons).
NewEngR (1:3) Spr 79, p. 344.

GULLANS, Charles
"Many Houses. " SouthernR (15:3) Sum 79, pp. 617-626.

GUNDERSON, Andy
"In Midsummer. " StoneC (6:2) My 79, p. 21.
In the Park. Sam (75) 79. Entire issue.

GUNDERSON, Keith
from The Book of Light/The Book of Water (tr. of Heraclitus).
CarlMis (17:2/3) Spr 79, p. 15.
from The Book of Light/The Book of Water (tr. of Thales).
CarlMis (17:2/3) Spr 79, p. 14.

GUNN, Thom
"The Great American Poem. " Antaeus (32) Wint 79, pp. 82-86.
"Sweet Things. " ParisR (75) Spr 79, pp. 238-239.

GUNNISON-WISEMAN, John
"American Pastoral. " Ploughs (5:2) 79, p. 31.

GUPTA, Sudheer
"A Donkey's Tail. " GreenfieldR (7:3/4) Spr-Sum 79, p. 50.
"Goat's Eat . . . . " GreenfieldR (7:3/4) Spr-Sum 79, p.
49.
"My Eyes Dangle by, My Sides . . . . " GreenfieldR (7:3/4)
79, p. 47.

GURLEY, George H. Jr.
"Heart Attack on Music Creek. " PoetryNW (20:2) Sum 79, pp.
20-21.

GURNIS, Peter
"Barbara. " Ploughs (5:3) 79, pp. 63-64.
"Periplum. " Ploughs (5:3) 79, p. 65.

GUTHRIE, Woody
Eight Poems. NowestR (17:2/3) 79, pp. 184-195.

GWILLIM, Joy
"I Wept When Horses Bit Me" (for Katie Pawley). Poetry (134:2)
My 79, p. 90.
"It Covers Me. " Poetry (134:2) My 79, p. 91.
"Poem for My Whip" (to Johnny Wink). QW (7) Aut 78, p. 107.
"The Ritual. " Poetry (134:2) My 79, p. 92.

GYURKOVICS, Tibor
   "Psalm Entering Jerusalem" (tr. by Nicholas Kolumban).   TexQ
      (21:4) Wint 78, p. 33.
   "Shadows" (tr. by Nicholas Kolumban).   PoNow (24) 79, p. 18.

HA, Chung
   "Shyness. "   PikeF (2) Wint 78-79, p. 18.

HAAKE, Katharine Koss
   "To Leo. "   HangL (36) Aut 79, pp. 20-27.

HAAS, Jan E. M.
   "down and out in apartment 5-d. "   Ur (2) 79, p. 42.

HABOVA, Dana
   "Achilles and the Turtle" (tr. of Miroslav Holub w. Stuart Frie-
      bert).   WestB (5) 79, p. 23.
   "Annunciation" (tr. of Miroslav Holub w. Stuart Friebert).   Field
      (21) Aut 79, p. 70.
   "Autumn" (tr. of Miroslav Holub w. Stuart Friebert).   Field (21)
      Aut 79, p. 74.
   "Brief Reflection on Dwarves" (tr. of Miroslav Holub w. Stuart
      Friebert).   Field (21) Aut 79, p. 69.
   "Crocheting" (tr. of Miroslav Holub w. Stuart Friebert).   Field
      (21) Aut 79, p. 72.
   "The Garden of Old People" (tr. of Miroslav Holub w. Stuart
      Friebert).   WestB (5) 79, p. 25.
   "Geese" (tr. of Miroslav Holub w. Stuart Friebert).   WestB
      (5) 79, p. 24.
   "On the Origin of Fatherhood" (tr. of Miroslav Holub w. Stuart
      Friebert).   Field (21) Aut 79, p. 73.
   "On the Origin of the Contrary" (tr. of Miroslav Holub w. Stuart
      Friebert).   Field (21) Aut 79, p. 75.
   "Saneness/Accident" (tr. of Miroslav Holub w. Stuart Friebert).
      WestB (5) 79, p. 26.
   "Several Very Smart People" (tr. of Miroslav Holub w. Stuart
      Friebert).   WestB (5) 79, p. 23.
   "Soldier" (tr. of Miroslav Holub w. Stuart Friebert).   Field (21)
      Aut 79, p. 71.

HACKENBRUCH, Carol R.
   "Ceramic Frogs. "   SmPd (47) 79, p. 13.

HACKER, Marilyn
   "Adult Entertainment. "   PartR (46:3) 79, p. 432.
   "Five Meals" (for Sandy).   MissouriR (3:1) Aut 79, p. 17.
   "For Getting Started in a New Place. "   Confr (19) Aut 79-Wint
      80, p. 27.
   "From a Sequence for My Daughter. "   Ploughs (5:1) 79, p. 57.
   "The Hang-Glider's Daughter" (for Catherine Logan).   Poetry
      (135:3) D 79, pp. 133-134.
   "Home, and I've" (for Sandy).   OP (27) Spr 79, pp. 6-7.
   "Ordinary Women. "   Confr (19) Aut 79-Wint 80, p. 26.

"Part of a Letter. " Salm (44/45) Spr-Sum 79, p. 152.
"Poem: Matte brandy bottle, adjacent voices, skin. " Salm
    (44/45) Spr-Sum 79, p. 153.
"Prayer for My Daughter. " OP (27) Spr 79, p. 3.
"Sonnet Ending with a Film Subtitle" (for Judith Landry). Salm
    (44/45) Spr-Sum 79, p. 153.
'To Iva, Two-and-a-Half. " OP (27) Spr 79, p. 8.
"Why We Are Going Back to Paradise Island. " OP (27) Spr 79,
    pp. 4-5.

HACKETT, Philip
"Red Currents. " Ur (2) 79, p. 43.

HADAS, Pamela White
"Plain Lisa" (for Alice Quinn). Poetry (133:4) Ja 79, pp. 222-
    226.

HADAS, Rachel
"Blaue Stunde. " PraS (53:4) Wint 79-80, p. 320.
"Cleaning Fish in the Sea. " PraS (53:4) Wint 79-80, p. 319.
"Fall Foliage. " PraS (53:1) Spr 79, p. 79.
"Fog. " Agni (10/11) 79, pp. 152-156.
"Hill. " PartR (46:1) 79, p. 104.
'Island. " NewEngR (2:1) Aut 79, p. 90.
"Mountain. " VirQR (55:3) Sum 79, p. 512.
"Moving. " Pequod (3:1) 79, pp. 58-59.

HAGEN, Cecelia
"Leaving, She Speaks Out. " GreenfieldR (7:3/4) Spr-Sum 79, p.
    253.

HAGERUP, Inger
"Emily Dickinson. " Paint (11) Spr 79, p. 16.

HAINES, John
"The Billboards in Exile. " MichQR (18:1) Wint 79, p. 100.
"The Chase. " PoNow (21) 79, p. 23.
"Cicada. " PoNow (21) 79, p. 23.
"The Great American Poem. " Antaeus (32) Wint 79, pp. 82-86.
"In the House of Wax. " Kayak (52) D 79, p. 44.
"Red Trees in the Wind. " PoNow (21) 79, p. 23.

HAIRSTON, Andrea
from We Are Institutionalized: "Slavery Now." " Chomo (6:1)
    Sum 79, p. 12.
from We Are Institutionalized: "Tylenol and Cope. " Chomo
    (6:1) Sum 79, p. 11.

HALE, Dorinda
"Disorientation and the Weather. " Aspect (74/75) Ja-Ag 79, p.
    52.

HALE, Frances
"In the Belly of a Whale. " Paint (12) Aut 79, p. 23.

"Persephone's Lament. " Poem (37) N 79, p. 6.
"To a Son Dying Young. " Poem (37) N 79, p. 7.

HALEY, Vanessa
"Lessons for the Solitary. " SouthernPR (19:1) Spr 79, p. 52.

HALL, David
"Memento Mori. " SmPd (45) 79, p. 14.

HALL, Donald
"Adultery at Forty. " Poetry (133:5) F 79, p. 279.
"Apology for Old Clothes. " Poetry (133:5) F 79, p. 279.
"For an Early Retirement. " Poetry (133:5) F 79, p. 279.
"The Great American Poem. " Antaeus (32) Wint 79, pp. 82-86.
"Poem Beginning with a Line of Wittgenstein. " Poetry (133:5)
    F 79, p. 279.
"Twenty-five Years. " Ploughs (5:1) 79, p. 58.

HALL, Hazel
Thirteen Poems. NowestR (17:2/3) 79, pp. 104-111.

HALL, James Baker
"At first they appear. " Hudson (32:1) Spr 79, p. 65.
"Earl Camp, call the operator please, all those. " QW (8) Wint
    79, p. 117.
"from where I am now. " Hudson (32:1) Spr 79, p. 64.
"Going to School. " PoNow (21) 79, p. 31.
"Her Hand. " Poetry (134:4) Jl 79, p. 201.
"The idea. " AmerS (48:1) Wint 78-79, p. 100.
"In the check-out line, carton of half-and-half, bag. " QW (8)
    Wint 79, p. 115.
"The inner workings are hidden. " SouthernPR (19:2) Aut 79, p.
    14.
"Let me try again to be. " Hudson (32:1) Spr 79, p. 66.
"The people who use the body to obtain. " AmerPoR (8:1) Ja-F
    79, p. 22.
"A Thin Strip of Bright Light Falls. " Poetry (134:4) Jl 79, p.
    202.
"This is a love poem to you. " Hudson (32:1) Spr 79, p. 67.
"We should know. " Hudson (32:1) Spr 79, p. 68.
"Whenever He Leaves. " Poetry (134:4) Jl 79, p. 200.

HALL, Jim
"The Dead at the Picnic. " Ploughs (5:1) 79, p. 59.
"The Hair Contest. " Ploughs (5:1) 79, p. 60.
"The Hair Contest. " Wind (34) 79, p. 26.
"Maybe Dats Your Pwoblem Too. " BelPoJ (29:3) Spr 79, p. 31.
"My Acceptance Speech. " BelPoJ (29:3) Spr 79, p. 30.
"Nana in Her Hudson Wasp. " PoetryNW (20:3) Aut 79, pp. 4-5.
"Replica. " PoetryNW (20:3) Sum 79, p. 5.

HALL, Joan Joffe
"In Place. " MassR (20:2) Sum 79, p. 237.

"Matthew at Thirteen. " MinnR (NS 12) Spr 79, p. 43.
'The Occupation. " SouthernPR (19:2) Aut 79, p. 54.
from Painting the House: "The Document. " GeoR (33:4) Wint
    79, p. 803.
from Painting the House: 'The Homeless. " GeoR (33:4) Wint
    79, p. 802.
"Reinventing the Wherewithal. " MinnR (NS 12) Spr 79, p. 42.
'The Stories. " BelPoJ (29:3) Spr 79, p. 15.
'Traffic. " MinnR (NS 12) Spr 79, p. 40.
'Watching" (for Judy). MassR (20:2) Sum 79, p. 240.

HALL, Judith
"The Bedroom. " Shen (30:2) Wint 79, p. 50.

HALL, Richard
"Previous Lives. " Mouth (2:2) Je 79, p. 15.

HALL, Steven
"A Valentine. " PartR (46:2) 79, p. 258.
'The Wooden Sky. " PartR (46:2) 79, p. 257.

HALL, Susan Grove
'In an English Churchyard 1976. " PoetC (11:2) 79, p. 18.
"Sheep Eat Wordsworth's Garden. " PoetC (11:2) 79, p. 16.

HALL, Thelma R.
'The Winner. " Poem (35) Mr 79, p. 21.

HALL, Theodore
'Water Sestina. " AndR (6:1) Spr 79, p. 18.

HALL, Walter
"Absence of Trail. " OP (28) Aut 79, p. 24.
'The Hat. " OP (28) Aut 79, p. 21.
"Passing Through. " OP (28) Aut 79, pp. 22-23.
'That Brings Us to the Woodstove in the Wilds, at Night. " OP
    (28) Aut 79, p. 20.

HALLEY, Anne
"Starting Over. " Ploughs (5:2) 79, pp. 97-98.

HALLIDAY, Mark
"An Artist Is An Alien And Plans Poorly. " KanQ (11:3) Sum
    79, p. 80.
"Blue Spruce. " Ploughs (5:2) 79, pp. 9-12.
"Five Notes on Sex. " Ploughs (5:2) 79, pp. 19-21.
"Functional Poem. " Ploughs (5:2) 79, pp. 16-18.
"Get It Again. " NewRep (180:12) 24 Mr 79, pp. 36-37.
'Western North Carolina. " Ploughs (5:2) 79, pp. 13-15.

HALPERIN, Mark
"April 1945. " Poetry (134:1) Ap 79, p. 5.
"Fasting on Yom Kippur. " Iowa (10:3) Sum 79, p. 96.

"A Servant. " Poetry (134:1) Ap 79, p. 6.
"Voltairine de Cleyre at St. John's. " Iowa (10:3) Sum 79, p. 97.

HALPERN, Daniel
"Dawn. " Madem (85:3) Mr 79, p. 138.
"Distance. " PoNow (21) 79, p. 9.
"The Great American Poem. " Antaeus (32) Wint 79, pp. 82-86.
"The Hermit. " AmerPoR (8:4) Jl-Ag 79, p. 45.
"Life Among Others. " PoNow (23) 79, p. 23.
"Return, Starting Out. " NewYorker (55:17) 11 Je 79, p. 36.
"Sunset Tattoo" (for D. Schmitz). PoNow (21) 79, p. 9.
"White Contact. " PoNow (23) 79, p. 23.
"White Field. " NewYorker (55:44) 17 D 79, p. 50.

HALPERN, Mark
"Playing with the Children" (for Dianna and John Rengstorff).
QW (7) Aut 78, p. 114.
"Sal. " QW (7) Aut 78, p. 113.

HAMBURGER, Michael
"Variations: In Suffolk. " Poetry (133:5) F 79, pp. 283-285.
"Willow. " Pequod (3:1) 79, p. 30.

HAMEL, Guy F. Claude
"Burglaries. " BlackF (3:1) Aut-Wint 79, p. 23.

HAMES, Carl Martin
"Reading Groups. " AndR (6:2) Aut 79, p. 31.

HAMILL, Sam
"The Wakening. " CutB (12) Spr-Sum 79, p. 57.

HAMILTON, Alfred Starr
"Awesome. " NewL (46:1) Aut 79, p. 94.
"Rain. " NewL (46:1) Aut 79, p. 94.

HAMILTON, David
"Aubade. " PoetryNW (20:2) Sum 79, p. 40.
"A Fable. " PoetryNW (20:2) Sum 79, pp. 39-40.

HAMILTON, Elizabeth
"Canto villano" (tr. of Blanca Varela). Field (21) Aut 79, p. 54.
"A Game" (tr. of Blanca Varela). Field (21) Aut 79, p. 51.
"Persona" (tr. of Blanca Varela). Field (21) Aut 79, p. 53.

HAMILTON, Horace
"Displacement. " SouthernR (15:2) Spr 79, p. 412.

HAMLIN, Garry
"Settling In. " GRR (10:1) 79, p. 119.

HAMM, Timothy
"Finding a Friend Home" (for Todd). SouthernPR (19:1) Spr 79,
p. 57.

HAMMER, Patrick Jr.
"Deadline into N. " JnlONJP (4:1) 79, p. 25.
"Once I Lived. " JnlONJP (4:1) 79, p. 24.

HAMMOND, Karla M.
"Odysseus. " CharR (5:1) Spr 79, p. 55.
"paper moon jungle. " St. AR (5:3) Aut-Wint 79, p. 39.
"snow burial. " St. AR (5:3) Aut-Wint 79, p. 38.

HAMMOND, Mac
"An Indian Miniature. " Poetry (133:6) Mr 79, p. 322.

HAMPL, Patricia
"Blue Bottle. " Iowa (10:1) Wint 79, p. 61.
"The Car in the Picture. " PoNow (25) 79, p. 22.
"Fortune-Tellers. " PoNow (25) 79, p. 22.
"Ice Age. " PoNow (25) 79, p. 22.

HAND, J. C.
"In Praise of Babies. " NewL (46:2) Wint 79-80, p. 40.
"Junkyard Madam" (for David and Donald). NewL (46:2) Wint
    79-80, p. 38.

HANDKE, Peter
from Fantasies and Prejudices: Ten Poems. ParisR (75) Spr
    79, pp. 95-106.

HANDLEY, Sandy
"My Husband's Oldest Daughter. " 13thM (4:2) 79, p. 45.

HANDLIN, Jim
"The Calliope. " Bits (10) Jl 79.
"her hair pin. " WindO (34) Spr-Sum 79, p. 7.
"suddenly. " WindO (34) Spr-Sum 79, p. 7.

HANLEY, Katherine, C. S. J.
"After Vacation. " ChrC (96:31) 3 O 79, p. 947.

HANSEN, Carol Baker
"The Arrangement. " MissR (24) Aut 79, p. 43.
"The Musical Offering. " MissR (24) Aut 79, p. 44.
"Photograph. " MissR (24) Aut 79, p. 49.
"Thorn. " Ploughs (5:1) 79, pp. 61-63.
"Tongue. " Ploughs (5:1) 79, p. 63.
"Tryst. " MissR (24) Aut 79, p. 48.
"Two Bird Dreams at Seventeen. " MissR (24) Aut 79, p. 41.
"The Witness. " MissR (24) Aut 79, p. 45.

HANSEN, Jon
"Buoy Light. " FourQt (28:3) Spr 79, p. 28.

HANSEN, Tom
"The City of Voluptuaries. " CimR (47) Ap 79, p. 32.

"Dead Fly. " BallSUF (20:2) Spr 79, p. 2.
"Dead Ringer. " MinnR (NS 12) Spr 79, p. 47.
"Father's Head. " KanQ (11:1/2) Wint-Spr 79, p. 8.
"Night Voice. " PoNow (22) 79, p. 19.
"Stone Man. " PoetryNW (20:2) Sum 79, p. 41.

HANSON, Charles D.
"Grandfather. " PoetC (11:2) 79, p. 22.
"Mexico City. " PoetC (11:2) 79, p. 24.

HANSON, Harold P.
"The Deepest Bow" (tr. of Marie Takuam). Paint (11) Spr 79,
   p. 75.
"From Another Reality" (tr. of Gunvor Hofmo). Paint (11) Spr
   79, p. 21.
"Words About Gates" (tr. of Halldis Moren Vesaas). Paint (11)
   Spr 79, p. 79.

HANSON, Howard G.
"As Rocks Rooted. " ArizQ (35:2) Sum 79, p. 128.
"That Is Not Indifference. " ArizQ (35:4) Wint 79, p. 302.

HANSON, Jim
"The Instructions. " Spirit (3:1/2) Aut-Wint 77-78, p. 61.

HANZLICEK, C. G.
"Among Mountain Men. " PoNow (21) 79, p. 24.
"Belief. " PoNow (21) 79, p. 24.
"Midnight in the Garden. " QW (9) Spr-Sum 79, p. 87.
"Prophecy. " QW (9) Spr-Sum 79, p. 88.
"Room for Doubt. " QW (6) Spr-Sum 78, p. 96.
"We Didn't Know Where. " QW (6) Spr-Sum 78, p. 97.
"What I Want Is. " PoNow (21) 79, p. 24.

HANZLIK, Josef
"The Rubbish Dump" (tr. by Ewald Osers). Stand (20:1) 78-79,
   p. 21.

HARALSON, Carol
"How to Grow Roses. " Nimrod (23:1) Aut-Wint 79, p. 7.
"Watching for Deer. " Nimrod (23:1) Aut-Wint 79, p. 5.

HARASYMOWICZ, Jerzy
"Before Dawn in March" (tr. by John Pijewski). Field (20) Spr
   79, p. 13.
"The Land of November" (tr. by John Pijewski). Field (20) Spr
   79, p. 14.
"The Myth of St. George" (tr. by John Pijewski). Field (20)
   Spr 79, p. 11.
"Twilight" (tr. by John Pijewski). Field (20) Spr 79, p.
   15.

HARCHICK, D. R.
"Graduates. " EngJ (68:5) My 79, p. 32.

HARCOURT, Ethelinde
"With Them. " Poultry (1) 79, p. 8.

HARDIE, Doris
"Fighting Back. " SouthernPR (19:1) Spr 79, p. 16.

HARDING, Gunnar
from Starnberger See: "For seven years, she was my kingdom
of snow" (tr. by Anselm Hollo). Spirit (4:2/3) Spr-Sum 79,
p. 57.
from Starnberger See: "I changed myself into a deer" (tr. by
Anselm Hollo). Spirit (4:2/3) Spr-Sum 79, p. 56.
from Starnberger See: "In the reform school, the children lie"
(tr. by Anselm Hollo). Spirit (4:2/3) Spr-Sum 79, p. 54.
from Starnberger See: "Reality never repeats itself" (tr. by
Anselm Hollo). Spirit (4:2/3) Spr-Sum 79, p. 58.
from Starnberger See: "The first world within this one" (tr. by
Anselm Hollo). Spirit (4:2/3) Spr-Sum 79, p. 55.
from Starnberger See: "The mad king's only children" (tr. by
Anselm Hollo). Spirit (4:2/3) Spr-Sum 79, p. 54.

HARJO, Joy
"Cuchillo. " BelPoJ (30:2) Wint 79-80, p. 2.

HARLAN, Calvin
"After Such Pleasures" (tr. of Julio Cortázar w. Manuel Menán
and Beatriz Varela). NewOR (6:2) 79, p. 103.
"Commission" (tr. of Julio Cortázar w. Manuel Menán and Beatriz
Varela). NewOR (6:2) 79, p. 105.
"Gains and Losses" (tr. of Julio Cortázar w. Manuel Menán and
Beatriz Varela). NewOR (6:2) 79, p. 104.
"Happy New Year" (tr. of Julio Cortázar w. Manuel Menán and
Beatriz Varela). NewOR (6:2) 79, p. 104.
"Restitution" (tr. of Julio Cortázar w. Manuel Menán and Beatriz
Varela). NewOR (6:2) 79, p. 102.

HARMON, James
"Tutor. " EngJ (68:5) My 79, p. 33.

HARMON, William
"Occidental Domestication Comedies. " Agni (10/11) 79, pp. 5-11.
"One Ode. " SouthernPR (19:1) Spr 79, p. 27.
"Target Practice. " Kayak (52) D 79, p. 60.
"The 3-Min. War. " CarolQ (31:2) Spr-Sum 79, pp. 85-91.

HARNED, Susan
"Hurricane. " JnlONJP (3:2) 79, p. 46.
"Instructions to Her Daughter at Bedtime. " JnlONJP (3:2) 79, p.
45.

HARO, Rodrigo de
"The Old King" (tr. by Alexis Levitin). PoNow (24) 79, p. 18.

HARPER, Michael
"The Great American Poem. " Antaeus (32) Wint 79, pp. 82-86.

HARRIS, Jana
"Glitter Box. " SeC (6:2) 78, p. 144.
"Hannah to Anthony, Blowin Out the Flame Wick of a Kerosene
    Lamp. " NewL (46:2) Wint 79-80, p. 22.
"The Lady Analyst and the Little Green Room. " SeC (6:2) 78,
    p. 142.
"Pin Money. " SeC (6:2) 78, pp. 137-141.
"Song of the Sitka Wind, Southeast Wailing. " NewL (46:2) Wint
    79-80, p. 25.

HARRIS, John
"The Bullet Holes in My Left Leg. " Ur (2) 79, p. 44.

HARRIS, John S.
"Handball Gloves. " WebR (4:3) Spr 79, p. 38.
"Rain at the Japanese Garden. " WebR (4:3) Spr 79, p. 37.

HARRIS, Joseph
"love song of an old man. " St. AR (5:3) Aut-Wint 79, p. 115.
"the man who died by lightning. " St. AR (5:3) Aut-Wint 79, p.
    114.
"a psalm of the sixties. " St. AR (5:3) Aut-Wint 79, p. 112.

HARRIS, Michael
"The Ice Castle. " Atl (243:3) Mr 79, p. 122.

HARRIS, William J.
"Oh, Noble Cat. " Epoch (28:2) Wint 79, p. 186.
"The Polyester Coat Runs Off. " Epoch (28:2) Wint 79, p. 187.

HARRISON, James
"Easier. " MalR (51) Jl 79, p. 37.
"Sea Changes. " MalR (51) Jl 79, p. 34.

HARRISON, Steve
"Down by the Moors. " SouthernHR (13:4) Aut 79, p. 342.
"Jabbo Stokes. " SoCaR (11:2) Spr 79, p. 30.

HARRISON, Tony
"A Question of Sentences. " Stand (20:2) 79, p. 3.
from The School of Eloquence: "Next Door. " Stand (20:2) 79,
    p. 2.
"Stalely Home. " Stand (20:2) 79, p. 4.

HARROLD, William
"4040 Sunrise. " Wind (32) 79, p. 19.

HARSHMAN, Marc
"Berries. " PoNow (25) 79, p. 10.
"Stories. " Wind (33) 79, p. 26.
"Turning Out the Stones. " PoNow (25) 79, p. 10.

HART, Henry
"Apples. " TexQ (21:4) Wint 78, p. 62.
"Tumbledown Mountain. " NewEngR (2:1) Aut 79, p. 58.

HART, James
"Blemishes. " CharR (5:2) Aut 79, p. 25.
"Hosannah. " CharR (5:2) Aut 79, p. 24.
"Remembering Arthur's Seat, Edinburgh. " CharR (5:1) Spr 79,
    p. 66.

HARTBARGER, Greg
"Mrs. Susie. " StoneC (6:3) O 79, p. 5.

HARTLEY, Lodwick
"Levee. " SewanR (87:4) Aut 79, p. 526.

HARTMAN, Charles O.
"The Fruit. " CarolQ (31:2) Spr-Sum 79, p. 130.
"Over a Cup of Tea" (for Meredith). Poetry (135:3) D 79, pp.
    135-136.
"The Soul Is Corrigible by Sleep. " CarolQ (31:2) Spr-Sum 79,
    p. 124.
"Theme and Variations" (for Chuck and Kathy Wolterink).
    CarolQ (31:2) Spr-Sum 79, p. 122.
"Trading Chicago. " CarolQ (31:2) Spr-Sum 79, p. 123.
"Two Poems About Grass. " Poetry (135:3) D 79, p. 136.

HARTMAN, Yuki
"At a Bar. " Tele (15) Spr 79, p. 5.
"Now. " Tele (15) Spr 79, p. 5.

HARVEY, Gayle Elen
"17 Summers. " SouthernPR (19:2) Aut 79, p. 73.
"We Are Found Out. " EnPas (8) 79, p. 38.

HARWOOD, Lee
"Wish You Were Here" (for Tony Lopez). Montra (5) 79, p. 184.

HASKELL, Harry
"The Tides of Day and Night" (for Octavio Paz) (w. Gregory
    Brehm). Mund (11:1) 79, p. 48.

HASKELL, Philip
"Castle Contagious. " Shen (30:1) Aut 78, p. 44.

HASKINS, Lola
"A Note on the Acquisition by American Medical Schools of Skele-
    tons from India. " BelPoJ (30:1) Aut 79, p. 26.

HASSE, Margaret
"At Thirteen, She Begins. " Northeast (3:7) Spr 79, p. 13.
"Strangers. " DacTerr (16) 79, p. 28.

HASSELSTROM, Linda M.
"Midnight in Missouri. " MidwQ (20:4) Sum 79, p. 365.
"Nude, 1978. " MidwQ (20:4) Sum 79, p. 366.
"Rankin Ridge: Only an Ancient Moon. " MidwQ (20:4) Sum 79,
    p. 365.
"Sky Ranch: Coming Back. " Spirit (4:2/3) Spr-Sum 79, p. 35.

HASSLER, Donald M.
"The End of the Seventies. " BallSUF (20:4) Aut 79, p. 80.

HASTINGS, Tom
"hidden indian. " WindO (35) Aut-Wint 79-80, p. 4.

HASTY, Palmer
"The Silence. " Confr (18) Spr-Sum 79, p. 72.

HASWELL, Rich
"Autumn and the Sea" (tr. of Javier Heraud). Mund (11:1) 79,
    p. 21.
"Poem: A eucalyptus, tall" (tr. of Javier Heraud). Mund (11:1)
    79, p. 21.
"Poem: Tarma valley" (tr. of Javier Heraud). Mund (11:1) 79, p. 23.

HATHAWAY, James
"Accuracy & Detail. " PoNow (25) 79, p. 23.
"Nephew. " PoNow (25) 79, p. 23.

HATHAWAY, Jeanine
"Conversation with God. " NewOR (6:3) 79, p. 242.
"Difference in Ages. " OhioR (20:2) Spr-Sum 79, p. 28.
"The Hermit Woman. " KanQ (11:3) Sum 79, p. 56.
"Sometimes the Coming of Babies. " OhioR (20:2) Spr-Sum 79,
    p. 28.
"What the Hermit Mutters at the Mouth of Her Cave. " PoetryNW
    (20:1) Spr 79, pp. 38-39.
"World Enough. " CarolQ (31:1) Wint 79, p. 65.

HATHAWAY, Lodene Brown
"His Is the Highway. " ChrC (96:34) 24 O 79, p. 1030.

HATHAWAY, William
"The American Poet--'But Since It Came to Good. '" Im (6:1)
    79, p. 4.
"Fishing Without Beer" (for John Dillon). Im (6:1) 79, p. 4.
"The Initiation. " NewL (46:1) Aut 79, p. 70.
"Lysistrata. " PoNow (21) 79, p. 16.

HATLEN, Burton
"For Michael. " BelPoJ (30:1) Aut 79, p. 7.

"In November the Mind Can Touch Bottom. " BelPoJ (30:1) Aut
    79, p. 8.

HATTERSLEY, Michael
    "Death Watch. " PoetC (11:1) 79, p. 16.

HAUG, James
    "House Moving. " GreenfieldR (7:3/4) Spr-Sum 79, p. 190.

HAUK, Barbara
    "The Frustrated Husband. " PoNow (23) 79, p. 47.
    "How to Dress. " KanQ (11:1/2) Wint-Spr 79, p. 156.

HAVLIK, Helen
    "After the Heat of Struggle Is a Resolution of Cool Water. "
        KanQ (11:1/2) Wint-Spr 79, p. 79.

HAWKINS, Hunt
    "My Brother's Face. " CarlMis (17:2/3) Spr 79, p. 36.
    "Pessimism in a Burger King in Minneapolis. " CarlMis (17:2/3)
        Spr 79, p. 35.
    "Subzero Weather. " CarlMis (17:2/3) Spr 79, p. 36.

HAWKINS, Tom
    "I Don't Know if You've Ever Seen a Shark. " PikeR (1) Sum 79,
        p. 58.
    "Incarnation Recalled at Night. " Wind (35) 79, p. 21.
    "The Night Walker's Golden Age. " Chelsea (38) 79, p. 148.
    "Pandora as in Pandemonium. " PikeF (2) Wint 78-79, p. 27.
    "Relinquishing. " Ur (2) 79, p. 45.
    "Uncle Hank. " Chelsea (38) 79, p. 149.

HAWKSWORTH, Marjorie
    "Daylight. " KanQ (11:1/2) Wint-Spr 79, p. 127.
    "Geology Text. " TexQ (21:3) Aut 78, p. 91.
    "The Ingrown Tiger. " CarlMis (17:2/3) Spr 79, p. 118.
    "Knowing How Easily. " CarlMis (17:2/3) Spr 79, p. 118.
    "Recovery. " KanQ (11:1/2) Wint-Spr 79, p. 126.

HAWLEY, Richard A.
    "Aloft. " Comm (106:15) 31 Ag 79, p. 461.
    "January. " Comm (106:1) 19 Ja 79, p. 19.

HAYDEN, Robert
    "Theory of Evil. " WorldO (13:2) Wint 78-79, p. 23.
    "The Year of the Child" (for my Grandson). WorldO (13:4) Sum
        79, p. 44.

HAYNA, Lois
    "Lux Aeterna. " Chowder (12) Spr-Sum 79, p. 29.

HEAD, Gwen
    "Blond Mahogany. " PoetryNW (20:4) Wint 79-80, pp. 5-6.

"Digitalis. "   PoetryNW (20:4) Wint 79-80, pp. 3-4.
"Hawthorns, Late Spring. " Chowder (13) Aut-Wint 79, p. 29.
"Rubato. " PoetryNW (20:4) Wint 79-80, pp. 4-5.

HEALY, Eloise Klein
"Dark. " Bachy (14) Spr/Sum 79, p. 71.
"Entries: L.A. Dog. " Bachy (14) Spr/Sum 79, p. 72.
"Poem for My Youth/Poem for Young Women. " Bachy (14)
    Spr/Sum 79, p. 72.
"She Was My Friend, Too" (for Shen).   Bachy (14) Spr/Sum 79,
    p. 73.
"This Is Not Making Love. " Bachy (14) Spr/Sum 79, p. 74.
"The Words Begin Again. " Bachy (14) Spr/Sum 79, p. 71.

HEANEY, Seamus
"An Afterwards. " NewRep (181:8) 25 Ag 79, p. 30.
"Casualty. " NewYorker (55:7) 2 Ap 79, p. 38.
"Field Work. " Antaeus (33) Spr 79, p. 22.
"The Gutteral Muse. " NewYorker (55:19) 25 Je 79, p. 28.
"High Summer. " HarvAd (112:4) My 79, p. 9.
"In Memoriam Francis Ledwidge. " NewRep (181:1/2) 7-14 Jl
    79, p. 32.
from Inferno, Cantos XXXII and XXXIII: "Ugolino. " Antaeus
    (33) Spr 79, p. 29.
"A Kite for Michael and Christopher. " Ploughs (5:3) 79, p. 23.
"Leavings. " ParisR (75) Spr 79, p. 233.
"Near Anahorish. " Ploughs (5:3) 79, p. 24.
"The Otter. " Antaeus (33) Spr 79, p. 25.
"Polder. " HarvAd (112:4) My 79, p. 6.
"Polder. " ParisR (75) Spr 79, p. 234.
"Song. " Antaeus (33) Spr 79, p. 24.
"Sonnet. " NewYorker (55:2) 26 F 79, p. 38.
"The Strand at Lough Beg" (in memory of Colum McCartney).
    Antaeus (33) Spr 79, p. 20.
"The Toome Road. " NewYRB (26:14) 27 S 79, p. 8.
"Triptych. " Antaeus (33) Spr 79, p. 26.

HEARST, James
"An Account of Failures. " WestB (4) 79, p. 65.
"Do People Care for People?" WormR (73) 79, p. 32.
"The Great American Poem. " Antaeus (32) Wint 79, pp. 82-86.
"Hang On to the Grab Bar. " KanQ (11:3) Sum 79, p. 71.
"Hard Way to Learn. " Poetry (134:1) Ap 79, p. 17.
"The Insatiable Demand. " NewRena (11) 79, p. 45.
"No Nightingales, No Nymphs. " Poetry (134:1) Ap 79, p. 18.
"No Word for the Wise. " SouthwR (64:4) Aut 79, p. 393.
"Not to Be Overlooked. " PoNow (23) 79, p. 23.
"Off Limits. " PoNow (23) 79, p. 11.
"Shove It, Brother, Shove It. " NoAmR (264:2) Sum 79, p. 26.
"Small Thorns. " WormR (73) 79, p. 33.
"The Way It Is. " PoNow (23) 79, p. 23.
"Wheelchair Blues. " NoAmR (264:2) Sum 79, p. 26.

HEAVNER, Wendy
"The New Neighbors. " EngJ (68:5) My 79, p. 36.

HEBALD, Carol
"Eve with Son. " KanQ (11:1/2) Wint-Spr 79, p. 30.
"The Moon Leaks Red. " NoAmR (264:1) Spr 79, p. 72.

HECHT, Anthony
"Auspices. " NewRep (180:6) 10 F 79, p. 33.
"The Grapes. " AmerS (48:1) Wint 78-79, p. 61.
"The Great American Poem. " Antaeus (32) Wint 79, pp. 82-86.
"Invective Against Denise, a Witch" (tr. of Pierre de Ronsard).
    AmerS (48:4) Aut 79, p. 499.
"Still Life. " Antaeus (33) Spr 79, p. 61.

HEDIN, Mary
"Inheritance: In a Churchyard in Sweden. " WorldO (13:1) Aut
    78, p. 39.
"Stanislaus. " WorldO (13:2) Wint 78-79, p. 14.

HEDIN, Robert
"On the Edge at Douz. " GreenfieldR (7:3/4) Spr-Sum 79, p.
    270.
"Rattlesnake Bluff. " PoNow (25) 79, p. 10.
"The Wreck of the Great Northern. " GreenfieldR (7:3/4) Spr-
    Sum 79, p. 272.

HEFFERNAN, Beth
"The Man Who Loved Oranges. " EngJ (68:5) My 79, p. 35.

HEFFERNAN, Michael
"A Canticle of the Stars. " AmerPoR (8:4) Jl-Ag 79, p. 42.
"Daffodils. " CarolQ (31:1) Wint 79, p. 43.
"Dreaming of Women. " Chowder (13) Aut-Wint 79, p. 18.
"A Figure of Plain Force. " PoNow (25) 79, p. 23.
"The Four Things. " PoNow (25) 79, p. 23.
"In Praise of It. " KanQ (11:3) Sum 79, p. 11.
"The Lives of the Just. " Chowder (13) Aut-Wint 79, p. 19.
"Naked War. " Poultry (1) 79, p. 11.
"Of Those Dear to Him. " KanQ (11:3) Sum 79, p. 11.
"Putting on My Shoes I Hear the Floor Cry Out Beneath Me. "
    Poultry (1) 79, p. 11.
"The Return. " AmerPoR (8:4) Jl-Ag 79, p. 41.
"St. Ambrose and the Bees. " CarlMis (17:2/3) Spr 79, p. 171.
"The Saint and the Lady. " CarlMis (17:2/3) Spr 79, p. 172.
"The Ugly Reality. " PoetryNW (20:3) Aut 79, pp. 18-19.

HEFFERNAN, Thomas
"Easter Monday. " SouthernPR (19:1) Spr 79, p. 66.

HEINEMAN, W. F.
"the vision. " St. AR (5:3) Aut-Wint 79, p. 16.

HELLER, Janet Ruth
"Jana Spurned. " Paint (11) Spr 79, p. 17.

HELLER, Michael
"Father Studies. " NewL (46:2) Wint 79-80, p. 50.
"Finding the Wave" (for J. A.). NewL (46:2) Wint 79-80, p. 54.
"Visitor at Acabonac. " Confr (18) Spr-Sum 79, p. 71.

HELLEREN, Maureen
"They Say God Has His Hands in His Pockets. " MassR (20:3)
Aut 79, p. 472.

HELMES, Scott
"Assimilate. " Tele (15) Spr 79, p. 53.
"High systems and orange juices. " Tele (15) Spr 79, p. 53.

HEMEY, Carl
"Chains, Our Freedom" (tr. of Andree Chedid). MalR (49) Ja
79, p. 91.
"Lightning in Chains" (tr. of Andree Chedid). MalR (49) Ja 79,
p. 91.

HEMLEY, Robin Cecil
"The Postman. " Confr (19) Aut 79-Wint 80, p. 54.

HEMPHILL, Essex C.
"Vows" (for Mel). Mouth (2:1) F 79, p. 37.

HEMSCHEMEYER, Judith
"All These Things. " Hudson (32:3) Aut 79, pp. 333-342.
"In Camp I Am Fed. " ArkRiv (4:3) 79, p. 9.
"Mahler's Symphony # 2. " ArkRiv (4:3) 79, p. 10.

HENDERSON, Jock
"Feeling the Heat's Pyrotechnics. " Comm (106:23) 21 D 79, p.
726.

HENDERSON, Lew Alan
"Over and Over. " BlackF (3:1) Aut-Wint 79, p. 30.

HENDERSON, Riley
"On Races. " Spirit (3:1/2) Aut-Wint 77-78, p. 17.

HENDLER, Earl
"Legacy. " SouthernHR (13:3) Sum 79, p. 214.

HENDRY, Diana
"Bank Holiday Sunday on the Canal. " Poetry (134:2) My 79, p.
77.
"Trespassing. " Poetry (134:2) My 79, p. 76.

HENNESSY, Madeline
"Here and There. " GreenfieldR (7:3/4) Spr-Sum 79, p. 237.

"Letter to My Mother. " Ploughs (5:1) 79, p. 64.
"Red Easter. " GreenfieldR (7:3/4) Spr-Sum 79, p. 237.
"Tattoo. " GreenfieldR (7:3/4) Spr-Sum 79, p. 236.

HENRY, Raymond
"Old Woman at Tenement Window. " Confr (19) Aut 79-Wint 80,
   p. 54.

HENSON, David
"The Last Atlantean. " PikeF (2) Wint 78-79, p. 32.
"One Size Fits All. " PoNow (25) 79, p. 11.
"Uncomfortable in Suits, My Father and His Two Brothers Sip
   Coffee, Smoke Cigarettes and Talk About Dogs. " PikeF (2)
   Wint 78-79, p. 32.

HENSON, James
"Watch Fires. " NewYorker (55:15) 28 My 79, p. 96.

HENSON, Lance
"for white antelope. " BelPoJ (30:2) Wint 79-80, p. 8.
"impressions of the cheyenne way. " BelPoJ (30:2) Wint 79-80,
   p. 8.
"in early september. " Nimrod (23:1) Aut-Wint 79, p. 102.

HERACLITUS
from The Book of Light/The Book of Water (tr. by Keith Gunder-
   son). CarlMis (17:2/3) Spr 79, p. 15.

HERAUD, Javier
"I Do Not Laugh at Death. " LitR (23:2) Wint 80, p. 238.
"El otono y el mar. " Mund (11:1) 79, p. 20.
"Poema: El valle de. " Mund (11:1) 79, p. 22.
"Poema: Un eucalipto, alto. " Mund (11:1) 79, p. 20.

HERBERT, Anne
"Music" (tr. by Jan Pallister). PoNow (24) 79, p. 18.

HERBERT, F. John
"An Opinion for a Card. " SunM (8) Aut 79, p. 67.
"Hello Neil and Buzz from Omaha. " SunM (8) Aut 79, p. 68.
"It Is My Duty (II). " SunM (8) Aut 79, p. 65.

HERBERT, George
Ten Poems. SouthernHR (13:4) Aut 79, p. 326.

HERBERT, Zbigniew
"Mr. Cogito and the Pearl" (tr. by Laurie Schneider). QW (7)
   Aut 78, p. 112.
"The two legs of Mr. Cogito" (tr. by Laurie Schneider). QW
   (7) Aut 78, p. 111.

HERMAN, Jack
"Sweet Fifteen and Falling in Love. " Mouth (2:3) N 79, p. 20.
"Tell Me About It, You Said. " Mouth (2:3) N 79, p. 23.

HERMANS, Theo
"Albi" (tr. of H. C. tenBerge w. Paul Vincent). ChiR (31:2)
Aut 79, p. 27.
"Andes" (tr. of H. C. tenBerge w. Paul Vincent). ChiR (31:2)
Aut 79, p. 25.
"Brassem povy" (tr. of H. C. tenBerge w. Paul Vincent). ChiR
(31:2) Aut 79, p. 21.
"Lübeck" (tr. of H. C. tenBerge w. Paul Vincent). ChiR (31:2)
Aut 79, p. 22.
"Nemrud dagh" (tr. of H. C. tenBerge w. Paul Vincent). ChiR
(31:2) Aut 79, p. 24.
"Swartkrans" (tr. of H. C. tenBerge w. Paul Vincent). ChiR
(31:2) Aut 79, p. 20.
"Water and shadow, shadow and water" (tr. of H. C. tenBerge
w. Paul Vincent). ChiR (31:2) Aut 79, p. 28.

HERNANDEZ, Francisco
"Negative" (tr. by Linda Scheer). PoNow (24) 79, p. 19.
"The Old Man and the Gunpowder" (tr. by Linda Scheer). PoNow
(24) 79, p. 19.
"Street" (tr. by Linda Scheer). PoNow (24) 79, p. 19.

HERNANDEZ, Miguel
"Cancion Primera" (tr. fr. the Spanish by Mary L. Schreiner).
MalR (49) Ja 79, p. 99.
"Cancion Ultima" (tr. by Mary L. Schreiner). MalR (49) Ja 79,
p. 100.
"Casida del Sediento" (tr. by Mary L. Schreiner). MalR (49)
Ja 79, p. 98.

HERRICK, Robert
"Upon the Nipples of Julia's Breast. " Playb (26:1) Ja 79, p.
256.

HERRON, Elizabeth
"The Setting. " PikeF (2) Wint 78-79, p. 7.
"Your Letter for Lisette. " Chomo (5:3) Spr 79, p. 41.

HERRSTROM, David Sten
"Between the Lines. " StoneC (6:2) My 79, p. 12.
from Marysuite: "Courante. " Nimrod (23:1) Aut-Wint 79, p. 8.

HERSHEY, Kara-Paige
"Terminal. " PikeF (2) Wint 78-79, p. 17.

HERSHON, Elizabeth
"The crows. " HangL (35) Spr 79, p. 71.

HERSHON, Robert
"A Blue Shovel. " PoetryNW (20:3) Aut 79, pp. 3-4.
"The Fifth of July. " PoetryNW (20:1) Spr 79, pp. 22-23.
"Last Night the Wind Came in. " Chowder (12) Spr-Sum 79, p.
14.

"May Comma Merry Month Of. " PoetryNW (20:1) Spr 79, p. 22.
"Popularity. " PoNow (23) 79, p. 32.

HESTER, M. L.
  "The Drill Press Operator. " Northeast (3:7) Spr 79, p. 16.
  "Poem to Cow. " WestB (5) 79, p. 10.
  "Poem to Slug. " WestB (5) 79, p. 10.
  "The Pool Lifeguard. " PoNow (23) 79, p. 15.
  "To a Fat Cat. " Northeast (3:7) Spr 79, p. 17.
  "With Byrd at the South Pole. " WestB (4) 79, p. 21.
  "With Crockett at the Alamo. " WestB (4) 79, p. 20.
  "With the Curies in the Laboratory. " WestB (4) 79, p. 20.

HESTER, Mark L.
  "My Father Knew. " GRR (10:1) 79, p. 39.

HEWITT, Geof
  "Moonlight. " Harp (259:1553) O 79, p. 115.
  "Some of My Dearest Friends. " Harp (259:1553) O 79, p. 115.
  "This Ego in the Wilderness. " Harp (258:1548) My 79, p. 102.

HEY, Phil
  "Elsie's Cafe in Aurelia Iowa. " DacTerr (16) 79, p. 29.

HEYD, Michael
  "Father. " WestB (4) 79, p. 76.

HEYEN, William
  "The Buffalo. " Poetry (135:3) D 79, p. 127.
  "The Flowers. " SouthernR (15:1) Wint 79, p. 120.
  "Mantle. " Poetry (135:3) D 79, p. 127.
  "Redwings. " Poetry (135:3) D 79, p. 128.
  "Ryó Kan. " OhioR (20:2) Spr-Sum 79, p. 66.
  "Stories. " NewYorker (55:21) 9 Jl 79, p. 32.
  "A Story from Chekhov. " Poetry (135:3) D 79, p. 126.

HEYM, Georg
  "Demons of the Cities" (tr. by Peter Viereck). PoNow (24) 79,
      p. 19.
  "Final Vigil" (tr. by Peter Viereck). PoNow (24) p. 20.
  "High Over Roofs He Comes" (tr. by Peter Viereck). MichQR
      (18:3) Sum 79, p. 406.
  "Prayer" (tr. by Peter Viereck). MichQR (18:3) Sum 79, p. 405.
  "War" (tr. by Peter Viereck). MichQR (18:3) Sum 79, p. 404.
  "With the Ships of Passage" (tr. by Peter Viereck). PoNow (21)
      79, p. 44.

HEYNEN, Jim
  "Who Built a Lot of Sheds. " PoNow (22) 79, p. 20.
  "Who Had Six Toes. " PoNow (22) 79, p. 20.
  "Who Made Such Good Pies. " PoNow (22) 79, p. 20.

HICKMAN, Leland
  from Tiresias I:9:B: Great Slave Lake Suite: "Part Two. "

<u>Bachy</u> (14) Spr/Sum 79, pp. 120-130.
from Tiresias I:9:B: Great Slave Lake Suite: "Part Three. "
<u>Bachy</u> (15) Aut 79, pp. 135-139.

HIERRO, José
"First Prayer" (tr. by Robert Mezey). <u>Durak</u> (2) 79, p. 50.

HIGASHI, Rose Anna
"Mendocino. " <u>CalQ</u> (15) Wint 79, p. 52.
"The New Year. " <u>CalQ</u> (15) Wint 79, p. 53.

HIGGINS, Dick
"Eight Year Snowflake" (for e. w.). <u>Mouth</u> (2:1) F 79, front
cover.

HIGGINS, Frank
"Henry Hatter Cymbals in Hand. " <u>KanQ</u> (11:1/2) Wint-Spr 79,
p. 64.

HIGGS, Ted
"From Mistra: A Prospect. " <u>ArizQ</u> (35:3) Aut 79, p. 244.

HIKMET, Nazim
"Elegy for Satan" (tr. by Randy Blasing and Motlu Konuk).
<u>PoNow</u> (23) 79, p. 46.
"From Sofia" (tr. by Randy Blasing and Motlu Konuk). <u>PoNow</u>
(24) 79, p. 20.
"Poem: This year, early fall in the far south" (tr. by Randy
Blasing and Motlu Konuk). <u>PoNow</u> (24) 79, p. 20.

HILBERRY, Conrad
"Headlights. " <u>NewL</u> (45:3) Spr 79, p. 71.
"House-Marks. " <u>MissouriR</u> (3:1) Aut 79, pp. 20-26.
"Man in the Attic. " <u>PoNow</u> (23) 79, p. 40.

HILDEBIDLE, John
"The Mastery of the Knuckleball" (for W. C. Williams and Hoyt
Wilhelm). <u>Ploughs</u> (5:2) 79, p. 147.

HILL, Brian Merrikin
"Pietà. " <u>Stand</u> (20:1) 78-79, p. 15.

HILL, Robert
"When Black Men Laugh. " <u>NegroHB</u> (42:3) Jl-Ag-S 79, p. 79.

HILLMAN, Brenda
"Ballet. " <u>Iowa</u> (10:1) Wint 79, p. 47.
"Storm Clouds. " <u>CalQ</u> (15) Wint 79, p. 22.
"Through a Window Filled with Rain" (for Nan). <u>Madem</u> (85:5)
My 79, p. 228.

HILTON, David
"The Filipino Farmer. " <u>NewL</u> (46:1) Aut 79, p. 78.
"See the Live Bear, Cherokee, N. C. " <u>PoNow</u> (23) 79, p. 12.

HIND, Steven
"This Time. " KanQ (11:3) Sum 79, p. 30.

HINDLEY, Norman
"Escape" (for Mike Nasif). PraS (53:2) Sum 79, p. 116.
"New York, New York. " PoNow (25) 79, p. 11.

HINDS, Jeanette
"Memo to God. " ChrC (96:8) 7 Mr 79, p. 247.
"Oblique Confession. " ChrC (96:30) 26 S 79, p. 909.

HINER, James
"Signatures. " DenQ (14:3) Aut 79, p. 87.

HINRICHSEN, Dennis
"On the Attraction of Heavenly Bodies. " Agni (10/11) 79, p. 70.

HINSHAW, Dawn
"One. " Paint (11) Spr 79, p. 18.
"The Other. " Paint (11) Spr 79, p. 19.
"Not-Knowing" (for Matisse's Blue Nude). Paint (11) Spr 79, p.
   20.
"Two Old Friends or Adversaries. " Paint (11) Spr 79, p. 18.

HIRSCH, Edward
"At the Grave of Marianne Moore. " SouthernR (15:1) Wint 79,
   p. 113.
"A Chinese Vase. " Agni (10/11) 79, p. 100.
"Christopher Smart. " Agni (10/11) 79, p. 98.
"Equinox. " SewanR (87:2) Spr 79, p. 223.
"Impressions: Monet. " NewYorker (55:33) 1 O 79, p. 42.
"Insomnia. " SewanR (87:2) Spr 79, p. 224.
"Little Political Poem. " Sky (9) Aut 79, p. 34.
"Poets, Children, Soldiers. " Agni (10/11) 79, p. 102.
"Reminiscence of Carrousels and Civil War. " Agni (10/11) 79,
   p. 96.
"Sonata" (for Janet). NewRep (181:17) 27 O 79, p. 38.
"Still Life: An Argument. " DenQ (14:2) Sum 79, p. 70.
"Strike While the Iron Is Hot." Chelsea (38) 79, p. 226.
"The Sweatshop Poem. " Agni (10/11) 79, p. 103.
"Transfigured Night, Come Down to Me, Slowly. " Agni (10/11)
   79, p. 105.
"A True Account of the Fabulous Ascent of a Unicorn with a Re-
   tarded Girl in New York City Last Night. " BelPoJ (29:3)
   Spr 79, p. 8.
"With Isaac Babel in Odessa. " Agni (10/11) 79, p. 94.

HIRSHMAN, Rose
"Edge of Words. " StoneC (6:2) My 79, p. 21.

HITCHCOCK, George
"The Great American Poem. " Antaeus (32) Wint 79, pp. 82-86.

HOAGLAND, William
  "After the Auction. "   Bits (10) Jl 79.
  "After Wordsworth. "   Spirit (3:3) Sum 78, p. 26.
  "I Said. "   Spirit (3:3) Sum 78, p. 25.
  "The Idiot Asleep. "   CarolQ (31:1) Wint 79, p. 46.
  "Poem: A rat blunders through heating pipes. "   Spirit (3:3) Sum
      78, p. 26.
  "Sympathy for the buddha. "   Spirit (3:3) Sum 78, p. 24.
  "When Travelling. "   Spirit (3:3) Sum 79, p. 27.

HOBEN, Sandra
  "Fishing. "   QW (9) Spr-Sum 79, p. 54.

HOBSON, Geary
  "Barbara's Land Revisited--August 1978. "   BelPoJ (30:2) Wint
      79-80, p. 6.
  "Meeting Andrew Jackson in an Albuquerque Bar. "   BelPoJ (30:2)
      Wint 79-80, p. 5.

HODGE, Marion
  "Three Birds. "   SmF (7/8) Spr-Aut 78, p. 46.

HODGES, Karen
  "Black Snake in My Room. "   BelPoJ (30:1) Aut 79, p. 33.
  "Pandora's Box. "   BelPoJ (30:1) Aut 79, p. 33.

HOEFT, Robert D.
  "For Eric. "   KanQ (11:3) Sum 79, p. 10.
  "A Poem Is Not. "   ArizQ (35:1) Spr 79, p. 48.

HOEY, Allen
  "Moving Again. "   Wind (34) 79, p. 27.
  "Pulled from Sleep by a Dream of Names. "   StoneC (6:3) O 79,
      p. 22.
  "Snake Night. "   Tendril (5) Sum 79, p. 34.

HOFFMAN, Carla
  "Edward. "   PoNow (21) 79, p. 47.

HOFFMAN, Daniel
  "The Great American Poem. "   Antaeus (32) Wint 79, pp. 82-86.
  "Halflives. "   NewRep (180:20) 19 My 79, p. 33.
  "Ode to Joy. "   SouthernR (15:4) Aut 79, p. 998.

HOFFMAN, Jerome A.
  "Flat Water. "   PraS (53:1) Spr 79, p. 81.

HOFMO, Gunvor
  "From Another Reality" (tr. by Harold P. Hanson).   Paint (11)
      Spr 79, p. 21.

HOGAN, Linda
  "Daughters Sleeping. "   BelPoJ (30:2) Wint 79-80, p. 33.

"Half-Life. " SmPd (47) 79, p. 21.
from The Trees: "1978 Mississippi. " BelPoJ (30:2) Wint 79-80,
    p. 34.
"What's Living?" SmPd (47) 79, p. 22.

HOGAN, Michael
    "Golden. " PoNow (22) 79, p. 24.
    "Water, Water. " PoNow (22) 79, p. 24.

HOGUE, Cynthia
    "Winter Beginning" (tr. of Ilse Aichinger). AmerPoR (8:4) Jl-
        Ag 79, p. 46.

HOLBROOK, John
    "AH. " PoetryNW (20:4) Wint 79-80, pp. 40-41.

HOLDEN, Jonathan
    "Crusade. " Chelsea (38) 79, p. 209.
    "Fixing the Deep-Well Jet Pump. " MidwQ (20:2) Wint 79, p. 189.
    "I Lie Awake on Top of the Sheets. " OhioR (20:2) Spr-Sum 79,
        pp. 70-71.
    "The Kite. " CimR (48) Jl 79, p. 10.
    "Liberace. " MidwQ (20:2) Wint 79, p. 192.
    "Nesting. " MidwQ (20:2) Wint 79, p. 191.
    "Oz. " WestHR (33:1) Wint 79, p. 54.
    "Politics. " Chelsea (38) 79, p. 198.
    "The Sorrow of Captain Hook. " MidwQ (20:2) Wint 79, p. 188.
    "Three Poems on Bernoulli's Principle. " MidwQ (20:2) Wint 79,
        p. 193.
    "To a Boyhood Friend: How We Changed. " CharR (5:1) Spr 79,
        p. 88.
    "Toilers of the Sea: Albert Pinkham Ryder. " WestHR (33:1)
        Wint 79, p. 16.

HOLDT, David
    "The Black Duck. " Chelsea (38) 79, p. 200.

HOLLAMAN, Keith
    "A Thousand Times" (tr. of Benjamin Péret). Kayak (50) My 79,
        p. 55.
    "To Wait on the Street Corner" (tr. of Benjamin Péret). Field
        (20) Spr 79, p. 20.
    "Tortured Girls" (tr. of Benjamin Péret). Kayak (50) My 79, p.
        54.

HOLLAND, John
    "Two Sound-Poems: I. " Agni (10/11) 79, p. 160.
    "Two Sound-Poems: II. " Agni (10/11) 79, p. 161.

HOLLANDER, Jean
    "Etruscan Discoveries. " NewEngR (1:3) Spr 79, p. 359.
    "The Making of a Saint. " SewanR (87:4) Aut 79, p. 533.

HOLLANDER, John
"An Old Engraving. " NewYRB (26:14) 27 S 79, p. 16.
"The Great American Poem. " Antaeus (32) Wint 79, pp. 82-86.

HOLLANDER, Martha
"Telling Tales. " Shen (30:4) 79, p. 93.

HOLLANDER, Robert
"Cornelia. " SouthernR (15:2) Spr 79, p. 400.
"Ice Cream in Paradise" (for J. A. M.). SouthernR (15:2) Spr
79, p. 401.
"Roman Holiday. " CimR (46) Ja 79, p. 56.

HOLLEY, Margaret
"The Dark Horses. " Wind (32) 79, p. 20.
"The Spiders. " Tendril (4) Wint 79, p. 31.
"Wind at Midnight. " Wind (32) 79, p. 20.

HOLLO, Anselm
"The Great American Poem. " Antaeus (32) Wint 79, pp. 82-86.
from Starnberger See: "For seven years, she was my kingdom of
snow" (tr. of Gunnar Harding). Spirit (4:2/3) Spr-Sum 79, p. 57.
from Starnberger See: "I changed myself into a deer" (tr. of
Gunnar Harding). Spirit (4:2/3) Spr-Sum 79, p. 56.
from Starnberger See: "In the reform school, the children lie"
(tr. of Gunnar Harding). Spirit (4:2/3) Spr-Sum 79, p. 54.
from Starnberger See: "Reality never repeats itself" (tr. of
Gunnar Harding). Spirit (4:2/3) Spr-Sum 79, p. 58.
from Starnberger See: "The first world within this one" (tr. of
Gunnar Harding). Spirit (4:2/3) Spr-Sum 79, p. 55.
from Starnberger See: "The mad king's only children" (tr. of
Gunnar Harding). Spirit (4:2/3) Spr-Sum 79, p. 54.

HOLLOWAY, John
"Speaking, Telling, Knowing. " Hudson (32:1) Spr 79, p. 74.

HOLMES, Charlotte
"Slow Motion. " PoetryNW (20:3) Aut 79, pp. 13-14.

HOLMES, Zandra
"Loneliness. " BlackF (3:1) Aut-Wint 79, p. 16.

HOLMGREN, Mark
"nu apartment. " SmPd (46) 79, p. 4.

HOLSCHUR, Rory
"Copperhead. " ColEng (40:6) F 79, p. 663.

HOLSHOUSER, W. L.
"Turning Point. " ChrC (96:42) 19 D 79, p. 1261.

HOLT, Helen
"I am not a child of our times--. " EngJ (68:5) My 79, p. 32.

HOLTZ, Barry
"The Fish. " EngJ (68:5) My 79, p. 28.

HOLUB, Miroslav
"Achilles and the Turtle" (tr. by Dana Hábová and Stuart Frie-
bert). WestB (5) 79, p. 23.
"Annunciation" (tr. by Dana Hábová and Stuart Friebert). Field
(21) Aut 79, p. 70.
"Autumn" (tr. by Dana Hábová and Stuart Friebert). Field (21)
Aut 79, p. 74.
"Brief Reflection on Dwarves" (tr. by Dana Hábová and Stuart
Friebert). Field (21) Aut 79, p. 69.
"Crocheting" (tr. by Dana Hábová and Stuart Friebert). Field
(21) Aut 79, p. 72.
"The Garden of Old People" (tr. by Dana Hábová and Stuart Frie-
bert). WestB (5) 79, p. 25.
"Geese" (tr. by Dana Hábová and Stuart Friebert). WestB (5)
79, p. 24.
"On the Origin of Fatherhood" (tr. by Dana Hábová and Stuart
Friebert). Field (21) Aut 79, p. 73.
"On the Origin of the Contrary" (tr. by Dana Hábová and Stuart
Friebert). Field (21) Aut 79, p. 75.
"Saneness/Accident" (tr. by Dana Hábová and Stuart Friebert).
WestB (5) 79, p. 26.
"Several Very Smart People" (tr. by Dana Hábová and Stuart
Friebert). WestB (5) 79, p. 23.
"Soldier" (tr. by Dana Hábová and Stuart Friebert). Field (21)
Aut 79, p. 71.

HOLZMAN, Dennis
"Daguerreoman. " Ur (2) 79, p. 49.
"A Global Vocabulary for my nephew. " Ur (2) 79, p. 48.

HOMER, Art
"Anthem to a Little Known River. " CharR (5:1) Spr 79, p. 57.
"Port Townsend in Good Time. " PortR (25) 79, p. 125.
"What We Did After Rain. " Antaeus (34) Sum 79, p. 82.
"Winter Afternoon Ramble. " PortR (25) 79, p. 124.

HONECKER, George J.
from Storybook Fossils: "Inside the heart of. " Chelsea (38) 79,
p. 228.

HONGO, Garrett Kaoru
"Who Among You Knows the Essence of Garlic?" Antaeus (35)
Aut 79, p. 86.

HONIG, Edwin
"Being Somebody. " PoNow (23) 79, p. 8.
"Casida of the Boy Wounded by Water" (tr. of Federico García
Lorca). PoNow (24) 79, p. 30.
"Five Erotics for Jack's Fiftieth. " PoNow (21) 79, p. 14.
"For His Mother Flying into Her Seventy-seventh. " SouthwR

(64:4) Aut 79, p. 379.
"Gacela of Love Unforeseen" (tr. of Federico García Lorca).
  PoNow (24) 79, p. 30.
"It Might Have Been Sunday. " PoNow (21) 79, p. 14.
"Old Boat. " NewRep (181:9/10) 1-8 S 79, p. 39.
"The Spinster at Mass" (tr. of Federico García Lorca). PoNow
  (24) 79, p. 30.
"Starting the Hostilities. " NewRep (181:9/10) 1-8 S 79, p. 39.

HOOD, Ernest A.
"A Love Poem. " Mouth (2:3) N 79, p. 28.
"Tonight. " Mouth (2:3) N 79, p. 25.

HOOKER, Renel
"Sandpiper. " Wind (32) 79, p. 22.

HOOPER, Patricia
"9:00. " CentR (23:3) Sum 79, p. 290.
"Other Lives. " CentR (23:3) Sum 79, p. 290.

HOOVER, Paul
"Lesson of the Monocle Thugs. " PoNow (22) 79, p. 24.
"Lesson of the Billboard Dogs. " PoNow (22) 79, p. 24.
"The Nature Poem. " ChiR (30:4) Spr 79, p. 5.

HOOVER, Robert
"Bound for Europe. " Mouth (2:3) N 79, p. 36.
"Head Over Heels. " Mouth (2:3) N 79, p. 33.
"Wanting to Dance. " Mouth (2:3) N 79, p. 32.

HOPES, David
"First Thaw: A Refutation. " Salm (44/45) Spr-Sum 79, p. 161.
"'Gazelle Drinking From One of the Rivers of Paradise' Balti-
  more Museum of Art. " Epoch (29:1) Aut 79, p. 14.
"The Night Way. " StoneC (6:3) O 79, p. 19.
"The Pileated Woodpecker" (Dryocapus pileatus). KanQ (11:4)
  Aut 79, p. 124.
"The Walking Fern" (Camptosorus rhizophyllus). KanQ (11:4)
  Aut 79, p. 124.
"The Woodwoman. " KanQ (11:4) Aut 79, p. 104.

HOPPER, Paul
"The smoke of night. " Os (9) 79, p. 7.

HOROVITZ, Sari
"Rituals. " Paint (11) Spr 79, p. 24.
"Witness. " Paint (11) Spr 79, p. 22.

HORTON, Barbara
"Untitled: I have unfolded myself. " SmPd (46) 79, p. 31.

HORVATH, John
"Brad Hamilton's Daughter. " Poem (36) Jl 79, pp. 29-31.

"Growing Season. " Poem (36) Jl 79, p. 33.
'The Man Who Called Phone Numbers Found in Bathrooms. "
    Poem (36) Jl 79, p. 32.

HORVATH, John Jr.
    "A Veteran's Twelve Stories. " Aspect (74/75) Ja-Ag 79, p. 52.

HORVATH, Lou
    "Could have been Phoenix. " Tele (15) Spr 79, p. 141.
    "For You. " Tele (15) Spr 79, p. 142.
    "The Head. " Tele (15) Spr 79, p. 141.

HOUGH, N. C.
    'The Black Diaries of Roger Casement. " Mouth (2:1) F 79, pp.
        10-14.

HOUSE, Thomas
    "a synopsis. " Wind (35) 79, p. 20.
    'To the Bitter End. " EnPas (9) 79, p. 14.

HOWARD, Ben
    "Criminal. " NoAmR (264:2) Sum 79, p. 32.
    'Migration. " CarolQ (31:3) Aut 79, p. 82.
    "R. S. V. P. " NoAmR (264:2) Sum 79, p. 32.

HOWARD, Jim
    "Newspaper Hats. " NewL (46:2) Wint 79-80, p. 102.

HOWARD, Richard
    "A Commission. " NewRep (180:3) 20 Ja 79, p. 30.
    "George Sand" (The Portrait by Nadar). Nat (228:17) 5 My 79,
        p. 510.
    "Giuseppe Verdi" (for William Weaver). NewRep (181:14) 6 O
        79, p. 32.
    'The Great American Poem. " Antaeus (32) Wint 79, pp. 82-86.
    'Honoré Daumier. " Ploughs (5:2) 79, pp. 43-44.
    'Nadar" (for Rosalind Krauss). Antaeus (33) Spr 79, p. 68.
    "Saintly Hermits in a Landscape. " NewYorker (54:52) 12 F 79,
        p. 34.

HOWARTH, William
    "Aspen Grove. " KanQ (11:4) Aut 79, p. 48.

HOWE, Fanny
    'Me and Mine. " Tele (15) Spr 79, p. 40.
    "St. Mary of Egypt. " Ploughs (5:3) 79, pp. 72-77.

HOWE, Susan
    "Childbed Mumming. " Tele (15) Spr 79, p. 18.

HOWELL, Christopher
    "Chimes. " PortR (25) 79, p. 129.
    "Cinnamon Is the Secret. " CutB (12) Spr-Sum 79, p. 6.

"Devil-Mere. " PoetryNW (20:1) Spr 79, p. 34.
"The Dreamers Future. " CarlMis (18:1) Wint 79-80, p. 27.
"The Dreams of Cellos. " CutB (12) Spr-Sum 79, p. 7.
"Drum. " ChiR (31:2) Aut 79, p. 106.
"Ling Wei and the Good Warrior. " PortR (25) 79, p. 128.
"Ling Wei Hungry. " CarlMis (18:1) Wint 79-80, p. 27.
"The Sarcasm. " PortR (25) 79, p. 129.
"Sentence Applauding the Trees" (for Gregory Polakou). CarlMis
    (18:1) Wint 79-80, p. 27.
"The Stone that Fell in Love. " ChiR (31:2) Aut 79, p. 107.
"Voice of the Jade Carving. " PortR (25) 79, p. 128.
"Winter Sequence. " PoetryNW (20:1) Spr 79, p. 33.

HOWES, Barbara
    "Barn-Razing in Pownal. " Poetry (135:1) O 79, p. 34.
    "Old Age: A Tableau. " Paint (11) Spr 79, p. 26.
    "A Thanksgiving Guernsey" (for Robert). Poetry (135:1) O 79,
    p. 35.

HUCHEL, Peter
    "Snow" (tr. by Almut McAuley). NewOR (6:3) 79, p. 221.
    Twenty-one Poems (tr. by Eveline Kanes and Rich Ives). DenQ
    (14:2) Sum 79, pp. 3-26.
    "Weeds" (tr. by Rika Lesser). NewYRB (26:20) 20 D 79, p. 33.

HUDDLE, David
    "Bill Spraker's Store, or the Day Geronimo Couldn't Find the
    Scoop. " Harp (258:1549) Je 79, p. 34.
    "What Pig Clemons Told My Mother. " Harp (258:1549) Je 79,
    p. 34.

HUDGINS, Andrew
    "After the Tornado. " CharR (5:1) Spr 79, p. 21.
    "Ghosting. " SouthernPR (19:2) Aut 79, p. 35.
    "Two Worlds of Sleep. " PoetryNW (20:3) Aut 79, pp. 24-
    25.
    "The Venus of the Living Room. " SouthernPR (19:2) Aut 79, p.
    37.

HUDSON, Frederick B.
    "My Relatives for the Most. " MassR (20:2) Sum 79, p.
    311.

HUERTA, David
    "Nine Years Later. " LitR (23:2) Wint 80, p. 227.

HUERTA, Efrain
    "Eunice" (tr. by James Normington). PoNow (24) 79, p. 20.

HUEY, Mark
    "Burglary. " Mouth (2:2) Je 79, p. 17.
    "Calisthenics I. " Mouth (2:2) Je 79, p. 17.
    "Coming of Age: Downproofing. " Mouth (2:2) Je 79, p. 20.

"Fishing the Housatonic. " Mouth (2:2) Je 79, p. 2.
"The Hostage. " Mouth (2:3) N 79, p. 7.
"The Late Show. " Mouth (2:2) Je 79, p. 26.
"Merton College Pinnacle. " Mouth (2:2) Je 79, p. 32.
"Overhearing Someone Else's Dream. " Mouth (2:3) N 79, p. 13.
"The Pig Farmer. " Mouth (2:3) N 79, p. 54.
"Pin-ups. " Mouth (2:3) N 79, p. 31.
"The Unmarried Uncle. " Mouth (2:2) Je 79, p. 18.

HUFF, Robert
"The Great American Poem. " Antaeus (32) Wint 79, pp. 82-86.

HUFFSTICKLER, Albert
"Creature. " Mund (11:1) 79, p. 37.

HUGHES, Barbara
"Dust from a Moth's Wing. " Bachy (14) Spr/Sum 79, p. 23.
"Learning to Pray. " Bachy (14) Spr/Sum 79, p. 22.
"Moving to Minnesota. " Bachy (14) Spr/Sum 79, p. 21.

HUGHES, Sophie
"Cow Moon. " Chelsea (38) 79, p. 213.
"St. George Diary/Two Weeks in the Country. " Chelsea (38) 79,
    p. 212.

HUGHES, Ted
"Children. " NewYorker (55:28) 27 Ag 79, p. 35.
"Letter of Recommendation" (tr. of Yehuda Amichai). PoNow
    (24) 79, p. 29.
"Song" (tr. of Yehuda Amichai). PoNow (24) 79, p. 29.
"Take Me to the Airport" (tr. of Yehuda Amichai). PoNow (24)
    79, p. 29.

HUGO, Richard
"Ayr. " Field (20) Spr 79, p. 45.
"The Cairn in Loch an Duin. " NewRep (180:21) 26 My 79, p. 40.
"Cantina Iannini. " DacTerr (16) 79, p. 30.
"Clachard. " NewEngR (1:4) Sum 79, p. 399.
"The Clouds of Uig" (for Johan Ross). Hudson (32:2) Sum 79, p.
    188.
"Duntulm Castle. " Hudson (32:2) Sum 79, p. 186.
"Ferniehirst Castle" (for Chester Kerr). Poetry (134:1) Ap 79,
    p. 21.
"The Great American Poem. " Antaeus (32) Wint 79, pp. 82-86.
"In Your Young Dream. " PoNow (21) 79, p. 24.
"Letter to Bell from Missoula. " PoNow (21) 79, p. 24.
"Langaig. " NewRep (181:21) 24 N 79, p. 32.
"Mecox Bay" (for Stanley and Jane Moss). Poetry (134:1) Ap 79,
    p. 22.
"Mill at Romesdal" (for Dr. Calum MacRae). Poetry (134:1) Ap
    79, pp. 19-20.
"Piping to You on Skye from Lewis" (for Iain MacLain).
    NewEngR (1:4) Sum 79, p. 397.

"Pizzeria S. Biagio" (for Biagio Avigliano). DacTerr (16) 79,
   p. 31.
"The Right Madness on Skye. " Atl (244:5) N 79, p. 56.
"St. Clement's Church: Harris: Outer Hebrides. " NewYorker
   (55:42) 3 D 79, p. 40.
"Uig Registrar" (for Chatta MacLean). NewEngR (1:4) Sum 79,
   p. 398.
"Villager. " Atl (243:2) F 79, p. 62.
"What the Brand New Freeway Won't Go By. " DacTerr (16) 79,
   p. 32.

HULETT, Ruth
   "A Quick Study of a Slow Afternoon. " PoetryNW (20:1) Spr 79,
   pp. 13-14.

HULL, Gloria T.
   "Poem: What you said" (for Audre). Cond (5) 79, p. 4.

HUMES, Harry
   "Four Men in a Field. " Kayak (50) My 79, p. 61.
   "The Owl in the Refrigerator. " HiramPoR (26) Spr-Sum 79, p.
   22.
   "The Turtle in the Living Room. " Kayak (50) My 79, p. 60.

HUMMA, John
   "Dandelions. " Poem (37) N 79, p. 4.
   "The Insect World. " Poem (37) N 79, p. 5.

HUMMER, T. R.
   "Calf. " SouthernPR (19:2) Aut 79, p. 20.
   "Looking in His Rearview Mirror, The Rural Carrier Thinks He
      Catches a Glimpse of the Angel of Death, Hanging Over
      George Gillespie's Mailbox. " SouthernPR (19:2) Aut 79, p.
      21.
   "The Motion of Returning. " WestHR (33:2) Spr 79, p. 138.
   "Night Burning. " WestHR (33:2) Spr 79, p. 139.
   "Snowlines" (to my daughter). WestHR (33:2) Spr 79, pp. 113-
      117.
   "Without Guilt, the Rural Carrier Reads a Postcard. " SouthernPR
      (19:2) Aut 79, p. 19.

HUMMER, Terry
   "Elijah Edwards Meets the Angel out on Star Route #1. " CimR
      (49) O 79, p. 27.

HUNG, Ko
   "Chao Ch'ü" (tr. by William F. McNaughton). Chelsea (38) 79,
      p. 77.

HUNT, Barbara
   "Indian Gift. " KanQ (11:1/2) Wint-Spr 79, p. 141.

HUNT, Julie
   from Lifespace (tr. of Eduardo Mitre). NewOR (6:2) 79, p. 132.

HUNT, Kenneth
"The Little Peach Tree. " Humanist (39:6) N-D 79, p. 48.

HUNT, Nan
"A Palsied Girl Goes to the Beach. " Bachy (15) Aut 79, p. 98.
"Strange Heavenly Things for Kenneth Rexroth on His Seventy-
    First Birthday. " Bachy (15) Aut 79, p. 96.
'That Which Gives Us Belonging. " Bachy (15) Aut 79, p. 97.
"Yosemite: El Capitan. " Bachy (15) Aut 79, p. 96.

HUNT, William
"Awakening Within the Storm Within. " Salm (43) Wint 79, p.
    101.
'The Initial Vision. " Salm (43) Wint 79, p. 100.
"Looking the Other Way for Frederick Delius. " Salm (43) Wint
    79, p. 99.

HUNTER, Paul
"Some Hillbilly Machiavelli. " NoAmR (264:1) Spr 79, p. 25.

HUNTLEY, Daniel
"Omie's Home Fire. " SouthernPR (19:1) Spr 79, p. 46.

HUTCHINSON, Robert
"On Seeing a Woman with Two Colors of Hair Near the Palais
    Royal. " SoDakR (17:2) Sum 79, p. 36.

HUTCHISON, Joseph
"The Climber. " Aspen (7) Spr 79, p. 43.
"One Evening Early in the New Year. " Aspen (7) Spr 79, p. 44.
"This Year. " OhioR (20:2) Spr-Sum 79, p. 72.

HYDE, Lewis
"Close to Death" (tr. of Vicente Aleixandre w. David Unger).
    PoNow (24) 79, p. 29.
"Guitar or Moon" (tr. of Vicente Aleixandre w. David Unger).
    PoNow (24) 79, p. 29.
"Street Money. " ParisR (75) Spr 79, pp. 242-243.

HYETT, Barbara Helfgott
"At the Seawall. " Tendril (6) Aut 79, p. 31.

HYNES, Chris
"In the Way. " EngJ (68:5) My 79, p. 34.

IGNATOW, David
"Above Everything" (to Tony Ostroff). PortR (25) 79, p. 32.
"Addendum. " Kayak (51) S 79, p. 17.
"The Air Is Filled. " PoNow (22) 79, p. 29.
"As the train door opens I am hoping. " PoNow (21) 79, p. 5.
"The Building. " Poetry (134:5) Ag 79, p. 269.
"Death of a Lawn Mower. " PoNow (23) 79, p. 24.
"The Forest Warden. " PoNow (23) 79, p. 24.
"The Great American Poem. " Antaeus (32) Wint 79, pp. 82-86.

"I Love to Fly. " Poetry (134:5) Ag 79, p. 270.
"In Peace. " NewL (46:1) Aut 79, p. 6.
"In this poem I am a cripple, with my two arms hanging down. "
    NewL (46:1) Aut 79, p. 7.
"Live It Through. " Poetry (134:5) Ag 79, p. 271.
"Lovers. " PoNow (22) 79, p. 29.
"A Memory. " NewL (46:1) Aut 79, p. 6.
"On Censorship. " PoNow (22) 79, p. 29.
"On Hollow Legs. " Ploughs (5:3) 79, pp. 157-158.
"On Quantitive Analysis. " PoNow (22) 79, p. 29.
"On Writing. " PoNow (22) 79, p. 29.
"Peace. " Im (6:1) 79, p. 3.
"The steam hammer pounds with a regularity on steel that. "
    NewL (46:1) Aut 79, p. 5.
"Subway. " Ploughs (5:3) 79, p. 159.
"Thus Truly. " NewL (46:1) Aut 79, p. 5.
"Tomorrow. " Pequod (3:1) 79, p. 27.
"Wallace Stevens. " CentR (23:3) Sum 79, p. 287.
"Walls. " Kayak (51) S 79, p. 17.
"Who Is Very Famous. " PoNow (22) 79, p. 29.
"With the Sun's Fire. " PoNow (23) 79, p. 24.

IKAN, Ron
"Commerce. " MinnR (NS 13) Aut 79, p. 22.
"Natural Selection. " SoDakR (17:2) Sum 79, p. 62.
"Orange Was the Color of Her Dress, then Blue Silk. " MinnR
    (NS 13) Aut 79, p. 23.
"Twister. " SoDakR (17:2) Sum 79, p. 63.

IKEDA, Patricia
"Games. " NowestR (18:1) 79, p. 76.

ILLYES, Gyula
"Consent" (tr. by Nicholas Kolumban). PoNow (24) 79, p. 21.
"Night Watch" (tr. by Nicolas Kolumban). PoNow (24) 79, p. 21.

INEZ, Colette
"Buffalo Sam. " PoNow (21) 79, p. 25.
"Daze of the Week. " PoetryNW (20:4) Wint 79-80, pp. 38-39.
"Dogdays. " PoetryNW (20:4) Wint 79-80, p. 38.
"The Great American Poem." Antaeus (32) Wint 79, pp. 82-86.
"In a Country of Condolences" (for a foster mother). Paint (12)
    Aut 79, p. 10.
"In a Country of Condolences" (for a foster mother dead at thirty-
    two). Paint (11) Spr 79, p. 27.
"Light Takes Eight. " VirQR (55:1) Wint 79, p. 110.
"My Priest Father's Words. " Ploughs (5:3) 79, p. 127.
"November Lord. " PoNow (21) 79, p. 25.
"Pears, Flies in an Interval. " VirQR (55:1) Wint 79, p. 109.
"Small Horses Ride in a Measure of Time. " MissouriR (3:1)
    Aut 79, p. 15.

INGLE, David
"The Gliberjok. " EngJ (68:5) My 79, p. 35.

INMAN, P.
   from Platin: (# 1).   SunM (8) Aut 79, p. 175.
   from Platin: (# 3).   SunM (8) Aut 79, p. 176.
   from Platin: (# 9).   SunM (8) Aut 79, p. 177.

IRION, Mary Jean
   "Invocation from a Lawn Chair. "   ChrC (96:21) 6-13 Je 79, p.
      638.
   "This Strangest Dancing" (for Vassar Miller).   ChrC (96:6) 21
      F 79, p. 185.

IRWIN, Mark
   "The house trembles sometimes. "   Mund (11:1) 79, p. 41.
   "The Invention of the Snowman. "   Shen (30:4) 79, p. 97.
   "Living not living--" (tr. of Phillipe Denis).   PoNow (24) 79, p.
      12.
   "Moored to your blood" (tr. of Philippe Denis).   Mund (11:1) 79,
      p. 41.
   "Path" (tr. of Philippe Denis).   Mund (11:1) 79, p. 43.
   "To live as to breathe" (tr. of Philippe Denis).   Mund (11:1) 79,
      p. 43.
   "The world is already far behind. "   Mund (11:1) 79, p. 41.
   "Where the wind was" (tr. of Philippe Denis).   Mund (11:1) 79,
      p. 43.

ISE, Lady
   Eleven poems.   Montra (5) 79, p. 133.

ISELY, Helen Sue
   "I Fingered Floating Wings. "   KanQ (11:3) Sum 79, p. 41.

ISSENHUTH, Jean-Pierre
   "Botticelli. "   Os (9) 79, p. 11.
   "Le bois sans vie. "   Os (9) 79, p. 12.
   "Le jardinier. "   Os (9) 79, p. 13.
   "Septembre. "   Os (9) 79, p. 13.

ISTEL, John
   "One Morning. "   NewL (46:2) Wint 79-80, p. 30.
   "To the Memory of a Mother. "   NewL (46:2) Wint 79-80, p. 29.

IVASK, Astrid
   from Elukogu (Life Collections):   "Create until the end" (tr. of
      Ivar Ivask).   Nimrod (23:1) Aut-Wint 79, p. 52.
   "for my godmother" (tr. by Inara Cedrins).   Chelsea (38) 79, p.
      84.
   "K. H. " (tr. by Inara Cedrins).   Chelsea (38) 79, p. 85.
   "(untitled):   In the evening forest a bird sings, perhaps" (tr. by
      Inara Cedrins).   Chelsea (38) 79, p. 85.

IVASK, Ivar
   from Elukogu (Life Collections):   "Create until the end" (tr. by
      author and Astrid Ivask).   Nimrod (23:1) Aut-Wint 79, p. 52.
   from A Summer in Haikus: Eleven Poems (for Martti and Liisa).

Nimrod (23:1) Aut-Wint 79, p. 53.
"To sense again snow." Nimrod (23:1) Aut-Wint 79, p. 54.

IVES, Rich
"Leaving the North Country." Epoch (28:2) Wint 79, p. 137.
"The Mysteries" (for Joaquim Cardozo). Epoch (28:2) Wint 79,
    p. 135.
"Notes from the Water Journals." CharR (5:1) Spr 79, pp. 11-
    17.
"Photographs of Our Former Lives" (for Roseann). GreenfieldR
    (7:3/4) Spr-Sum 79, p. 81.
"Poetry and Domestic Life." GreenfieldR (7:3/4) Spr-Sum 79,
    p. 81.
"Potatoes." Epoch (28:2) Wint 79, p. 136.
"Some Winters the Wolves Return." CutB (12) Spr-Sum 79, p.
    75.
Twenty-one poems (tr. of Peter Huchel w. Eveline Kanes).
    DenQ (14:2) Sum 79, pp. 3-26.

IWASZKIEWICZ, Jaroslaw
"Autumn scattering bitter cinnamon" (tr. by Andrzej Busza and
    Bogdan Czaykowski). Durak (3) 79, p. 15.

IZUMI, Lady
"Elegies For Her Daughter, Ko-Shikibu, Who Died In November,
    1025" (tr. by Hiroaki Sato). Montra (5) 79, p. 140.
"Elegies For Prince Atsumichi, Who Died On October 2, 1007"
    (tr. by Hiroaki Sato). Montra (5) 79, p. 139.
"On Love" (tr. by Hiroaki Sato). Montra (5) 79, p. 137.
"Other Subjects" (tr. by Hiroaki Sato). Montra (5) 79, p. 141.

JABES, Edmond
"Water" (tr. by Anthony Rudolf). Stand (20:2) 79, p. 45.
from Yael: "Fear of Time" (tr. by Rosemarie Waldrop).
    Montra (6) 79, p. 63.
from Yael: "My Characters In and Outside the Book" (tr. by
    Rosemarie Waldrop). Montra (6) 79, p. 56.
from Yael: "The Light of the Sea" (tr. by Rosemarie Waldrop).
    Montra (6) 79, p. 61.

JACKOWAY, Jon
"Innuendo." CarlMis (17:2/3) Spr 79, p. 25.

JACKSON, Acy L.
"Untitled: My aunt told me." BlackF (3:1) Aut-Wint 79, p. 37.

JACKSON, Haywood
An Act of God. Sam (74) 79. Entire issue.
"The Great Gang Bang, 1939." Ur (2) 79, p. 50.
"I See the Rocks of Connemara." Sam (72) 79, p. 49.
"My Buddies." Sam (72) 79, p. 50.
"Older Now, And" (for Linda King). Aspect (74/75) Ja-Ag 79,
    p. 65.

"On the Way to the Forum. " PoNow (25) 79, p. 11.
"The Reader of Poetry, December 1977. " Poultry (1) 79, p. 3.
"Tit for Tat. " Ur (2) 79, p. 51.

JACKSON, Henry
"Café de Banzo. " NewYorker (55:28) 27 Ag 79, p. 46.

JACKSON, Richard
"Brevity. " SmF (7/8) Spr-Aut 78, p. 36.
"Pantomimes" (for Mary). SmF (7/8) Spr- Aut 78, p. 37.

JACOB, Max
"Establishment of a Community in Brazil" (tr. by Michael Bene-
    dikt). QW (9) Spr-Sum 79, p. 14.

JACOBS, Clarence
"Free Mouse. " GreenfieldR (7:3/4) Spr-Sum 79, p. 155.

JACOBS, Lucky
"Boundaries. " SeC (7:1) 79, p. 10.
"Jasper, Indiana. " DacTerr (16) 79, p. 33.
"Poets in the Farmhouse. " SouthernPR (19:1) Spr 79, p. 37.

JACOBS, Maria
"Embroidery. " MalR (49) Ja 79, p. 60.

JACOBSEN, Josephine
"The Great American Poem. " Antaeus (32) Wint 79, pp. 82-86.

JACOBSON, Bonnie
"In Which Disciplinary Action Is Taken. " PraS (53:3) Aut 79, p.
    260.

JACOBY, Jay
"Sidewalk Art" (for Marlon H_____s). EnPas (8) 79, p. 28.

JACOBY, Stan
"The Possessed. " Wind (33) 79, p. 27.

JACOX, Lynn C.
"Sunday Afternoon. " SouthernPR (19:2) Aut 79, p. 12.

JAECH, Stephen
"Five on Waking. " Wind (35) 79, p. 22.

JAEGER, Sharon Ann
"Akashics. " StoneC (6:3) O 79, p. 25.
"The ghosts you meet head-on. " StoneC (6:3) O 79, p. 25.
"Mrs. Bovary (Au Red Book). " CimR (48) Jl 79, p. 64.

JAFFE, Dan
"In the Red Lion Inn. " DacTerr (16) 79, p. 34.
"Postscript. " DacTerr (16) 79, p. 35.

JAHNS, T. R.
  "Emily, Again. " PoetC (10:3) 79, p. 24.
  "Explaining to the Child. " PoetC (11:1) 79, p. 24.
  "Mistakes Are Forever. " PoetC (11:1) 79, p. 23.

JALLAIS, Denise
  "Lullaby for My Dead Child" (tr. by Maxine Kumin and Judith
    Kumin). PoNow (23) 79, p. 46.
  "The Time of Mirages" (tr. by Judith Kumin and Maxine Kumin).
    PoNow (24) 79, p. 21.

JAMES, Billie Jean
  "Clam Nectar. " GreenfieldR (7:3/4) Spr-Sum 79, p. 187.
  "Fortune Village. " GreenfieldR (7:3/4) Spr-Sum 79, p. 185.

JAMES, David
  "Autumn in Terms of My Boys, My Wife. " EnPas (9) 79, p. 17.
  "The Crazy Lady. " PoNow (25) 79, p. 12.
  "The Famous Outlaw Stops in for a Drink. " PoNow (25) 79, p.
    12.
  "The Fantasy of an Idiot. " PoNow (22) 79, p. 30.
  "Forgetting. " EnPas (9) 79, p. 16.
  "Going Back for Nothing. " EnPas (9) 79, p. 18.
  "Medusa's Half Brother. " PoNow (25) 79, p. 12.
  "The Rose Case. " PoNow (22) 79, p. 30.

JAMES, E. R.
  "Untitled: I watched. " Mouth (2:1) F 79, p. 20.

JAMES, Elizabeth Ann
  "Floods: Columbus, Ohio, 1913. " HiramPoR (26) Spr-Sum 79,
    p. 23.

JAMES, Nancy Esther
  "Emily Dickinson's Room. " Wind (33) 79, p. 28.

JAMES, Sibyl
  "Night Watch on the Millie" (for Steve). Tendril (4) Wint 79,
    p. 32.

JANIK, Carolyn L.
  "Landscape. " StoneC (6:2) My 79, p. 8.

JANKOWSKI, Theodora A.
  "Lido. " Im (5:3) 79, p. 7.

JANOSCO, Beatrice
  "Inner City Teacher. " EngJ (68:5) My 79, p. 30.

JARLSSON, Rolf
  "Fire Island, the Pines. " Mouth (2:2) Je 79, p. 31.
  "My Brother and I. " Mouth (2:2) Je 79, p. 46.
  "Runaway Boy, Rimbaud's First Trip to Paris. " Mouth (2:2) Je
    79, p. 11.

JARMAN, Mark
"Address to the Devil. " Chowder (13) Aut-Wint 79, p. 12.
"Cross. " Chowder (13) Aut-Wint 79, p. 13.
"Either It Will Rain or It Will Not Rain. " Durak (3) 79, p. 10.
"A Ghost Story" (for Katie). AmerPoR (8:5) S-O 79, p. 44.
"Greensleeves. " Chowder (13) Aut-Wint 79, p. 14.
"Lower Rooms. " PoetryNW (20:4) Wint 79-80, pp. 16-17.
"My Parents Have Come Home Laughing. " PoNow (25) 79, p. 24.
"Neighbors. " Durak (3) 79, p. 8.
"Pet Marjorie. " PoNow (23) 79, p. 43.
"Sedative. " PoNow (25) 79, p. 24.
"To Answer Your Question. " PoetryNW (20:4) Wint 79-80, pp. 18-19.
"When You Give It God's Name. " PoetryNW (20:4) Wint 79-80, pp. 17-18.

JARRETT, Brent
"Thinking Backwards. " CarolQ (31:3) Aut 79, p. 55.

JASON, Philip K.
"Skin. " GreenfieldR (7:3/4) Spr-Sum 79, p. 37.
"Suppose They Came Unbuttoned. " FourQt (28:4) Sum 79, p. 33.

JASTRUN, Mieczyslaw
"White" (tr. by Andrzej Busza and Bogdan Czaykowski). Durak (3) 79, p. 12.

JAUSS, David
"First Blizzards. " PoetryNW (20:1) Spr 79, pp. 36-37.
"How to Hit a Home Run. " PoNow (25) 79, p. 13.
"Oliver Johnson Comes Back to Bed the Morning After the Ice Storm and Tells His Wife Why. " PoNow (25) 79, p. 13.

JEAN, Denis-Jacques
Poem. St.AR (5:2) 79, p. 99.
Poem. St.AR (5:2) 79, p. 100.

JELLEMA, Rod
"Cutting Paper with Matisse. " Columbia (3) 79, p. 20.

JENKINS, Louis
"Driftwood. " Ascent (4:2) 79, p. 41.
"The House at the Lake. " Ascent (4:2) 79, p. 38.
"November. " Ascent (4:2) 79, p. 39.
"Palisade Head. " Ascent (4:2) 79, p. 40.
"A Photograph. " CarlMis (17:2/3) Spr 79, p. 24.
"Sergeant Norquist. " Ascent (4:2) 79, p. 42.
"Tamaracks. " CarlMis (17:2/3) Spr 79, p. 25.

JENKINS, Paul
"Night Song. " MassR (20:1) Spr 79, p. 143.
"The Train That Sang All Day Through the Bush. " MassR (20:1) Spr 79, p. 140.

JENNER, E. A. B.
"The Spring of Ibykos. " Stand (20:1) 78-79, p. 58.
"Sulpicius Lupercus Servasius Junior: Reconstruction from the
    life (IV). " Stand (20:1) 78-79, p. 57.

JENNINGS, Kate
"The First Person Poems. " SouthernPR (19:1) Spr 79, p. 18.
"Late August. " Wind (34) 79, p. 29.
"Man on a Car" (for R. F. K.). Atl (244:1) Jl 79, p. 61.
"Poem for Jeanna. " Wind (34) 79, p. 30.
"She Describes the View. " SouthernPR (19:1) Spr 79, p. 19.
"Theatrics" (for David). CarolQ (31:3) Aut 79, p. 26.

JENSEN, Laura
"At the Greenhouse. " PoetryNW (20:2) Sum 79, pp. 9-10.
"The Clean One. " Field (21) Aut 79, p. 68.
"The Cutting Back. " PoetryNW (20:2) Sum 79, p. 9.
"The Dream Book. " PoetryNW (20:2) Sum 79, pp. 7-8.
"The Kiss. " NewYorker (54:46) 1 Ja 79, p. 57.
"Lipstick. " Iowa (10:1) Wint 79, p. 63.
"Starlings. " Iowa (10:1) Wint 79, p. 64.

JEVREMOVIC, George
"At the Crossroads" (tr. of Vasko Popa). Durak (2) 79, p. 46.
"Lifting Our Arms" (tr. of Vasko Popa). Durak (2) 79, p. 45.

JIMENEZ, Juan Ramon
"adolescence" (tr. by Joel Zeltzer). Wind (34) 79, p. 31.

JNANA
"Maple. " Wind (34) 79, p. 14.
"The Prophecy. " Wind (34) 79, p. 14.

JOENS, Harley
"Snow. " PoetC (11:1) 79, p. 27.

JOHNS, Bethany
"Apologetic. " Spirit (4:1) Aut-Wint 78-79, p. 8.
"Five Weeks in Little Tibet. " Spirit (4:1) Aut-Wint 78-79, p. 8.

JOHNSON, David Owen
"Hester Cuts Boards. " CarolQ (31:1) Wint 79, p. 85.

JOHNSON, Denis
"The Boarding. " Poetry (134:2) My 79, p. 103.
"Now. " MissouriR (2:2/3) Spr 79, p. 42.
"Nude. " Poetry (134:2) My 79, pp. 105-106.
"The Story. " Poetry (134:2) My 79, pp. 101-102.
"Surreptitious Kissing. " Poetry (134:2) My 79, p. 104.

JOHNSON, Don
Nine Poems. Tendril (6) Aut 79, pp. 42-55.
"Renovation" (for Bud Gerber). Tendril (4) Wint 79, p. 33.

JOHNSON, Greg
"Bad News. " Poem (37) N 79, p. 16.
"Landscapes of Feeling. " KanQ (11:1/2) Wint-Spr 79, p. 78.
"The Night Bird. " Poem (37) N 79, pp. 14-15.

JOHNSON, Honor
"Ninja. " ThRiPo (13/14) 79, p. 30.
"Preparing the Silk. " MassR (20:2) Sum 79, p. 324.

JOHNSON, Jane McPhetres
"One Day. " Tendril (5) Sum 79, p. 35.

JOHNSON, Jon
"interlude. " St. AR (5:3) Aut-Wint 79, p. 40.

JOHNSON, Karen
"The Beach at Night. " Tendril (5) Sum 79, p. 37.
"Pleasures. " SouthernPR (19:2) Aut 79, p. 56.

JOHNSON, Marilyn
"The Probe. " Field (20) Spr 79, p. 6.
"V. " Field (20) Spr 79, p. 5.

JOHNSON, Mark
"Letter to a Health Insurance Company. " PoNow (21) 79, p. 41.

JOHNSON, Mary
"The Barn Owl's Love. " Poem (36) Jl 79, p. 36.
"Hunters in Hell. " Poem (36) Jl 79, p. 35.

JOHNSON, Michael L.
"Early Morning in Tuscon" (for Donna Mae). Wind (32) 79, p. 23.
"Frozen Lake" (for L. W.). GRR (10:1) 79, p. 139.
"On Beauty. " Poem (37) N 79, p. 62.
"On Gainsborough's The Morning Walk (1785). " KanQ (11:3) Sum 79, p. 48.
"On the Dates of Poets. " KanQ (11:3) Sum 79, p. 48.
"On the Japanese Warships Sunk in the Truk Lagoon. " Poem (37) N 79, p. 63.
"Party. " Wind (32) 79, p. 23.
"Sublimation. " GRR (10:1) 79, p. 85.

JOHNSON, Nate
"About 5 Blocks of D. C. " Epoch (28:3) Spr-Sum 79, p. 270.

JOHNSON, Paul
"i have junkie love. " Focus (13:81) My-Je 79, p. 30.
"in the Tulsa library. " Nimrod (23:1) Aut-Wint 79, p. 15.
"orthopaedic shoes for Oedipus. " Focus (13:81) My-Je 79, p. 30.

JOHNSON, Rita
"The Corner. " GeoR (33:2) Sum 79, p. 421.

JOHNSON, Sam F.
"After/Word: Berryman, Sexton, Plath et al. " MalR (49) Ja
    79, p. 36.
"Three Songs of Stone. " MalR (49) Ja 79, p. 37.

JOHNSON, Steve
"After the Interstate Crash. " PoNow (25) 79, p. 14.

JOHNSON, Thomas
"Garage. " Confr (18) Spr-Sum 79, p. 64.
"The Ice Futures. " PoNow (23) 79, p. 24.
"The New Architecture. " PoNow (23) 79, p. 24.
"Scald. " PoNow (23) 79, p. 39.

JOHNSON, Tom
"Gabriel Fauré. " SewanR (87:3) Sum 79, p. 381.
"Whether Art Passes, or Should Pass, or Endures. " AmerS
    (48:1) Wint 78-79, p. 9.
"The World Without Metaphor. " SewanR (87:3) Sum 79, p. 380.

JOKL, Vivian
"First Holes Are Fresh. " GreenfieldR (7:3/4) Spr-Sum 79, p.
    23.
"Ricochet. " Paint (11) Spr 79, p. 28.
"Seeing with Sound. " GreenfieldR (7:3/4) Spr-Sum 79, p. 22.

JONES, Andrew McCord
"UNO-Numeral. " GRR (10:1) 79, p. 40.

JONES, Anne G.
"Apple Jelly. " HolCrit (16:3) Je 79, p. 14.

JONES, Cheryl
"I'm Not that Lonely. " Cond (5) 79, p. 71.

JONES, Daryl
"Don't Be an Object. " Kayak (50) My 79, back cover.   Found
    poem.

JONES, Nancy
"The Teacher. " EngJ (68:5) My 79, p. 31.

JONES, Patricia
"I've been thinking of Diana Sands. " Cond (5) 79, p. 26.
"November Poem" (for Maureen). Tele (15) Spr 79, p. 29.
"Table Water. " Tele (15) Spr 79, p. 28.

JONES, Paul
"Native African Revolutionaries. " CarolQ (31:2) Spr-Sum 79, p.
    5.
"voice at the grave of yukio mishima. " St. AR (5:3) Aut-Wint 79,
    p. 33.

JONES, Richard
"Writing Poetry on Black Paper. " Columbia (3) 79, p. 53.

JONES, Robert
"Kansas Poem. " CarlMis (17:2/3) Spr 79, p. 12.

JONES, Robert L.
"I Sleep. " BlackF (3:1) Aut-Wint 79, p. 20.
"Taken. " BlackF (3:1) Aut-Wint 79, p. 27.

JONES, Rodney
"American Forest. " SmF (7/8) Spr-Aut 78, p. 34.
"Bean Station, Late Twenties: A Letter to Fred Chappell. "
    SmF (7/8) Spr-Aut 78, p. 25.
"Chain Saw. " SmF (7/8) Spr-Aut 78, p. 33.
"Dulcimer. " SmF (7/8) Spr-Aut 78, p. 32.
"Going Ahead, Looking Back" (for John Allison).   SmF (7/8)
    Spr-Aut 78, p. 28.
"Measurements of Gravity. " SmF (7/8) Spr-Aut 78, p. 31.
"On Leaving the Farm. " SmF (7/8) Spr-Aut 78, p. 30.

JONES, Sandra F.
"A Water-Colored Tomorrow. " BlackF (3:1) Aut-Wint 79, p. 16.

JONES, Stephen
"On Making a Dream. " Wind (32) 79, p. 39.

JONES, Tom
"Blackout. " Ur (2) 79, p. 54.
"Heresies" (for Louis Boucher).   GreenfieldR (7:3/4) Spr-Sum
    79, p. 114.
"Jonah in Bedlam" (for Zack).   Wind (35) 79, p. 25.
"Rilke's Angels. " Wind (35) 79, p. 23.
"Taking Fire. " Wind (35) 79, p. 24.

JORDAN, Suzanne Britt
"Mother's Place and Mine. " DenQ (14:2) Sum 79, p. 43.

JOSEPH, Jenny
"The Inland Sea. " Stand (20:3) 79, p. 19.

JOYCE, William
"At the White Tower Restaurant During a Freeze. " WestB (4)
    79, p. 68.
"In Homestead, Pennsylvania. " PoNow (21) 79, p. 17.
"Lewisburg, Pa. " NewL (45:3) Spr 79, p. 73.
"Small Town. " NewL (45:3) Spr 79, p. 74.

JOZSEF, Attila
"April 11" (tr. by John Batki).   PoNow (24) 79, p. 22.
"Attila József" (tr. by Nicholas Kolumban).   TexQ (21:4) Wint
    78, p. 28.
"Lullaby" (tr. by John Batki).   PoNow (24) 79, p. 22.

"She Gets Up at Dawn Like Bakers" (tr. by Nicholas Kolumban).
TexQ (21:4) Wint 78, p. 27.

JUDA, Joseph
"Night Nurse. " Sam (79) 79, p. 83.

JUDGE, Frank
"Excerpt of a Sonnet on the Population of the Roman Night.
Where the Whores Die" (tr. of Pietro Cimatti). PoNow (24)
79, p. 9.
"I've Dreamed of Escaping" (tr. of Alfredo Bonazzi). PoNow
(24) 79, p. 6.
"Port Azzurro Prison" (tr. of Alfredo Bonazzi). PoNow (24)
79, p. 6.

JUDSON, John
"4 December 76" (for George Ellison). NoAmR (264:1) Spr 79,
p. 50.
"Gisselle Martin at the Window of Max's Cafe. " DacTerr (16)
79, p. 36.
"March 11, 1977" (for Bill ... Sweet William). NoAmR (264:1)
Spr 79, p. 51.
"North of Athens. " BelPoJ (30:1) Aut 79, p. 24.
"Township and Range. " Confr (18) Spr-Sum 79, p. 35.

JUSTICE, Donald
from Bad Dreams: "Epilogue: To the Morning Light. " Antaeus
(35) Aut 79, p. 45.
"Childhood. " Antaeus (33) Spr 79, pp. 62-67.
"The Furies. " Antaeus (35) Aut 79, p. 47.
"The Great American Poem. " Antaeus (32) Wint 79, pp. 82-86.
"Sonnet: An Old-Fashioned Devil. " Antaeus (35) Aut 79, p. 42.
"The Summer Anniversaries. " Antaeus (35) Aut 79, p. 43.
"Thinking About the Past. " NewEngR (2:1) Aut 79, p. 25.

KALASZ, Marton
"Maiden" (tr. by Jascha Kessler). Spirit (3:3) Sum 78, p. 40.

KALLAS, Anthony C.
"The White Collar Worm's Response to a Blue Collar Worm's
Complaint. " SouthernPR (19:1) Spr 79, p. 60.

KALLET, Marilyn
"Limitation. " NewL (46:2) Wint 79-80, p. 63.
"Return. " GreenfieldR (7:3/4) Spr-Sum 79, p. 199.

KAMINSKY, Daniel
"The Ghibli Cantos. " Pig (6) 79, pp. 60-71.

KANDINSKY, Carla
"I Hold the Scent. " PikeF (2) Wint 78-79, p. 7.

KANE, Katherine
"Song. " CutB (12) Spr-Sum 79, p. 33.

KANES, Eveline
Twenty-one poems (tr. of Peter Huchel w. Rich Ives). DenQ
(14:2) Sum 79, pp. 3-26.

KANFER, Allen
"lili and the captain of sunburn. " St. AR (5:3) Aut-Wint 79, p.
34.
"a new-found authority. " St. AR (5:3) Aut-Wint 79, p. 34.
"the prestidigitator" (for Vi). St. AR (5:3) Aut-Wint 79, p. 33.

KAPLAN, Edward
"Ground Rules. " Wind (34) 79, p. 32.
"On X's On Calendars. " Tele (15) Spr 79, p. 90.
"Since We Live Here Now. " Tele (15) Spr 79, p. 90.
"Woman with a Crow. " Tele (15) Spr 79, p. 91.

KARLINSKY, Simon
"Letter from Prison" (tr. of Gennady Trifanov). PoNow (24)
79, p. 60.

KARP, Vickie
"The Last Farmer in Queens. " NewYorker (54:47) 8 Ja 79, p.
38.
"Sitting on the Beach with Nachman. " NewYorker (55:8) 9 Ap
79, p. 42.

KARR, Mary
"Beyond Freedom and Dignity" (for Walt Mink). PoetryNW (20:4)
Wint 79-80, pp. 26-27.

KASA, Lady
Eighteen poems. Montra (5) 79, p. 123.

KASHNER, Samuel
"eyes. " HangL (35) Spr 79, p. 31.
"my love does not understand. " HangL (35) Spr 79, p. 26.
"You. " HangL (35) Spr 79, p. 32.
"you have chased me. " HangL (35) Spr 79, p. 29.
"you who dance on the shadow of the moon. " HangL (35) Spr 79,
p. 34.
"your hands are the female equivalent of snow. " HangL (35) Spr
79, p. 35.
"your tongue grows like a leaf. " HangL (35) Spr 79, p. 30.

KASKA, Karen
"Lighthouse Sunday. " WindO (34) Spr-Sum 79, p. 31.
"Snow Shovels Wake You. " WindO (34) Spr-Sum 79, p. 32.

KASPER, M.
"In the epileptic's apartment, everything is. " WormR (76) 79,
p. 151.
"System all Run Down. " WormR (76) 79, p. 152.

KASS, Jerry
"Fidelity. "   KanQ (11:1/2) Wint-Spr 79, p. 155.

KASSAK, Lajos
"28" (tr. by Bruce Berlind).   PoNow (24) 79, p. 22.

KATES, J.
"Life Story" (for Jeff Schwartz).   MassR (20:3) Aut 79, p. 435.
"Moving Out, A Restless Farewell."   StoneC (6:2) My 79, p. 6.
"Orientation. "   MassR (20:3) Aut 79, p. 435.

KATES, Jim
"New Jersey. "   Stand (20:3) 79, p. 53.

KATZ, Menke
from Two Friends: "Return to Genesis" (w. Harry Smith).
    KanQ (11:1/2) Wint-Spr 79, p. 142.
from Two Friends: "To Genesis and Back" (w. Harry Smith).
    KanQ (11:1/2) Wint-Spr 79, p. 143.

KATZ, Susan A.
"The Dart Man. "   CarlMis (18:1) Wint 79, p. 59.
"The Unbending. "   Ur (2) 79, p. 55.

KATZ-LEVINE, Judy
Ten poems.   OP (27) Spr 79, pp. 9-15.

KAUFFMAN, Janet
"Driving. "   MissR (24) Aut 79, p. 59.
"Ghost of a Second Shift Mother. "   MissR (24) Aut 79, p. 53.
"Mennonite Farm Wife. "   MissR (24) Aut 79, p. 56.
"Postcard I: Match. "   MissR (24) Aut 79, p. 58.
"Rally. "   MissR (24) Aut 79, p. 57.
"Summer. "   MissR (24) Aut 79, p. 60.

KAUFMAN, Bob
"Cocoa Morning. "   SeC (6:2) 78, p. 21.
"Geneology. "   SeC (6:2) 78, p. 26.
"I Wish.... "   SeC (6:2) 78, p. 24.
"Michaelangelo the Elder. "   SeC (6:2) 78, p. 25.
"Night Song Sailor's Prayer. "   SeC (6:2) 78, p. 23.
"Suicide. "   SeC (6:2) 78, p. 22.

KAUFMAN, Shirley
from Gazelle, I'll Send You: "A bouquet--to scatter its flowers
    on the floor and the table" (tr. of Amir Gilboa w. Shlomith
    Rimmon).   WebR (4:3) Spr 79, p. 9.
from Gazelle, I'll Send You: "Finally I go to the man who set
    traps for the birds" (tr. of Amir Gilboa w. Shlomith Rim-
    mon).   WebR (4:3) Spr 79, p. 8.
from Gazelle, I'll Send You: "How would I stand then, what side
    of my face expose to the light" (tr. of Amir Gilboa w.
    Shlomith Rimmon).   WebR (4:3) Spr 79, p. 8.

from Gazelle, I'll Send You: "Standing on tiptoe shutting my
eyes so I won't see what's going on in the yard" (tr. of
Amir Gilboa w. Shlomith Rimmon). WebR (4:3) Spr 79, p.
8.

KAUFMAN, Stuart
   "Meditations on American Feet. " Tele (15) Spr 79, p. 103.
   "Stolen Flowers. " Tele (15) Spr 79, p. 102.

KAUPPI, Sherry
   "Into Fresh Water. " GRR (10:1) 79, p. 117.

KAY, Hillary
   "Behold, the Woman. " Cond (5) 79, p. 145.
   "I'm a Womon. " Cond (5) 79, p. 147.

KAZIN, Cathrael
   "Three Photographs. " Confr (19) Aut 79-Wint 80, p. 41.

KEARNEY, Lawrence
   "Cuba. " NewL (46:2) Wint 79-80, p. 64.
   "The Heaven of Full Employment" (for my grandfather). NewL
      (46:2) Wint 79-80, pp. 66-70.
   "A Little Onion Music. " MissouriR (2:2/3) Spr 79, p. 48.
   "Someone Else's Story. " MissouriR (2:2/3) Spr 79, p. 46.
   "Water. " MichQR (18:3) Sum 79, p. 495.
   "West Texas. " ChiR (30:4) Spr 79, p. 46.

KEATING, Charles
   "Fate. " Sam (72) 79, p. 83.

KEATING, Diana
   "Moondays. " MalR (52) O 79, p. 50.

KEELER, Greg
   "American Falls. " PraS (53:4) Wint 79, p. 358.
   "At a Grain Elevator in Salt Fork, Oklahoma. " EngJ (68:5) My
      79, p. 28.
   "Bait for the Traps. " PraS (53:4) Wint 79-80, p. 356.

KEELEY, Edmund
   "After Each Death" (tr. of Yannis Ritsos). AmerPoR (8:2) Mr-
      Ap 79, p. 33.
   "Aphrodite Rising" (tr. of Angelos Sikelianos, w. Philip Sher-
      rard). MalR (52) O 79, p. 98.
   "Attack" (tr. of Yannis Ritsos). AmerPoR (8:2) Mr-Ap 79, p.
      33.
   "Because I Deeply Praised" (tr. of Angelos Sikelianos w. Philip
      Sherrard). MalR (52) O 79, p. 100.
   "Current Events" (tr. of Yannis Ritsos). Pequod (3:1) 79, p. 81.
   "Daedalus" (tr. of Angelos Sikelianos w. Philip Sherrard). MalR
      (52) O 79, p. 101.
   "Doubtful Stature" (tr. of Yannis Ritsos). Pequod (3:1) 79, p. 81.

"Insomnia" (tr. of Yannis Ritsos). AmerPoR Mr. Ap 79, p. 33.
"The Only" (tr. of Yannis Ritsos). Pequod (3:1) 79, p. 80.
"Prayer" (tr. of Angelos Sikelianos, w. Philip Sherrard). MalR
(52) O 79, p. 99.
"Sketch" (tr. of Yannis Ritsos). Pequod (3:1) 79, p. 80.
"Triplet" (tr. of Yannis Ritsos). Pequod (3:1) 79, p. 80.
"The Two Sides" (tr. of Yannis Ritsos). AmerPoR (8:2) Mr-Ap
79, p. 33.
"With the Unapproachable" (tr. of Yannis Ritsos). Pequod (3:1)
79, p. 81.
"A Wreath" (tr. of Yannis Ritsos). Pequod (3:1) 79, p. 80.

KEENAN, Deborah
"The Other Lover. " SoDakR (17:2) Sum 79, p. 34.
"Stainless Steel. " PoetryNW (20:2) Sum 79, pp. 44-45.
"What Will Last. " SoDakR (17:2) Sum 79, p. 32.
"The Yearning. " DacTerr (16) 79, p. 38.

KEENAN, Keith
Poem. St. AR (5:2) 79, p. 121.

KEIS, Vitalij
"Christopher Columbus" (tr. of Vladimir Mayakovsky w. Harry
Lewis). Confr (19) Aut 79-Wint 80, pp. 7-23.

KEITHLEY, George
"What She Knew. " Nimrod (23:1) Aut-Wint 79, p. 80.

KEIZER, Garret
"A Confession. " CarlMis (18:1) Wint 79-80, p. 58.
"Epitaph for a Civilization. " CarlMis (18:1) Wint 79-80, p. 58.
"Homer. " CarlMis (18:1) Wint 79, p. 59.
"And Naked Shall I Return. " CarlMis (18:1) Wint 79-80, p. 58.
"War Came to Mind. " CarlMis (18:1) Wint 79-80, p. 58.

KELLER, David
"Diccionario. " Spirit (3:1/2) Aut-Wint 77-78, p. 14.
"In the Dream of the Body. " CutB (12) Spr-Sum 79, p. 63.
"Money Is a Kind of Poetry. " Spirit (3:1/2) Aut-Wint 77-78, p.
15.
"Threads of August. " Ploughs (5:2) 79, p. 145.
"Workmen. " PoNow (25) 79, p. 14.

KELLER, Paul
"Before Tractors. " ChiR (30:4) Spr 79, p. 48.
"For the Baby Shark. " ChiR (30:4) Spr 79, p. 49.

KELLEY, Shannon Keith
"Jigsaw. " KanQ (11:3) Sum 79, p. 10.
"That Man in Manhattan. " KanQ (11:3) Sum 79, p. 9.

KELLY, Conor
"Nocturne: Lake Huron. " SouthernR (15:1) Wint 79, p. 132.

KELLY, Dave
"A Culinary History of the Flesh-Eating Horse. " PoNow (23)
    79, p. 42.
"Eight Miles South of Grand Heaven. " AmerPoR (8:2) Mr-Ap
    79, p. 42.
"Prayer for Drowned Souls. " AmerPoR (8:2) Mr-Ap 79, p. 42.

KELLY, David B.
"July 6. " KanQ (11:1/2) Wint-Spr 79, p. 168.

KELLY, Donald
Poem. St. AR (5:2) 79, p. 18.
Poem. St. AR (5:2) 79, p. 36.
Poem. St. AR (5:2) 79, p. 72.

KEMNITZ, Charles
"Russian Orthodox Cross. " CimR (46) Ja 79, p. 34.

KEMP, Lysander
"Francis Ponge's District" (tr. of Marco Antonio Montes de Oca).
    DenQ (14:1) Spr 79, p. 110.
"Green Light for the Yellow Light" (tr. of Marco Antonio Montes
    de Oca). DenQ (14:1) Spr 79, p. 109.
"The Poet Doesn't Want to Wake Up" (tr. of Marco Antonio
    Montes de Oca). DenQ (14:1) Spr 79, p. 112.
"Traveling Balcony" (tr. of Marco Antonio Montes de Oca).
    DenQ (14:1) Spr 79, p. 111.

KEMPHER, Ruth Moon
"Hilda Halfheart's Notes to the Milkman: #2. " Tele (15) Spr
    79, p. 116.
"Hilda Halfheart's Notes to the Milkman: #27. " Tele (15) Spr
    79, p. 113.
"Mother-in-Law's Tongue. " HiramPoR (26) Spr-Sum 79, p. 24.
"Saturday Started Early, 2 A. M. " BallSUF (20:1) Wint 79, p.
    73.
"Sylvia Savage, Fugitive, Writes Letter #11 to Adam, While
    Sitting by the Fire. " Tele (15) Spr 79, p. 112.
"Sylvia Savage Writes the 7 Millionth Letter to Adam. " Tele
    (15) Spr 79, p. 115.
"Terms: For Al, Who Drove into a Motel Sign and Then Went
    to Tampa and Disappeared Leaving His Good Friends Jesus
    Belmonte and Me Behind, Wondering. " Tele (15) Spr 79, p.
    114.

KENDRICK, Katherine
"Haiku. " PikeF (2) Wint 78-79, p. 17.

KENISON, Gloria
Thirteen Poems. WormR (76) 79, p. 123.

KENNEDY, David
Poem. St. AR (5:2) 79, p. 53.

KENNEDY, Terry
"An Easy Poem" (for Elizabeth). HolCrit (16:1) F 79, p. 15.
"For My Sister on Her 5th Wedding Anniversary. " SeC (6:1)
    78, p. 64.
"The Nun. " Ur (2) 79, p. 56.
"Waiting. " Ur (2) 79, p. 57.

KENNEDY, X. J.
"The Great American Poem. " Antaeus (32) Wint 79, pp. 82-86.

KENNEY, Richard
"In April. " NewYorker (55:9) 16 Ap 79, p. 44.

KENNY, Adele
"morning. ... " JnlONJP (4:1) 79, p. 31.

KENNY, Douglas
"They Had Words/There Were Words Between Them" (w. Sara
    Miles). LittleM (12:1/2) Spr-Sum 78 (79), p. 50.
"We Meet in Veracruz" (w. Sara Miles). LittleM (12:1/2) Spr-
    Sum 78 (79), p. 51.

KENNY, Maurice
"Among the Mohawks. " GreenfieldR (7:3/4) Spr-Sum 79, p. 68.
"Aroniateka. " GreenfieldR (7:3/4) Spr-Sum 79, p. 66.
"Bear. " GreenfieldR (7:3/4) Spr-Sum 79, p. 67.
"Hoanatteniate. " GreenfieldR (7:3/4) Spr-Sum 79, p. 67.
"Yaikni. " BelPoJ (30:2) Wint 79-80, p. 9.

KENT, Margaret
"Limits. " Poetry (134:2) My 79, p. 73.
"The Stammerers. " Poetry (134:2) My 79, p. 71.
"The Uneasy. " Poetry (134:2) My 79, p. 72.
"Where It Came From. " ParisR (75) Spr 79, p. 237.

KENYON, Jane
"From Room to Room. " PoNow (25) 79, p. 24.
"Rain in January. " Ploughs (5:2) 79, p. 57.
"The Shirt. " PoNow (25) 79, p. 24.
"This Morning. " PoNow (25) 79, p. 24.
"What Came to Me. " Ploughs (5:2) 79, p. 56.
"What It's Like. " Ploughs (5:2) 79, p. 58.

KERTESZ, Louise
"Autumnal and Rejoinders. " Im (5:3) 79, p. 9.

KESH, David
Poem. St.AR (5:2) 79, p. 106.

KESSLER, Clyde
"Cruden. " Im (5:3) 79, p. 12.
"Holiday Greeting. " Im (5:3) 79, p. 12.
"Nichol's Creek. " Im (5:3) 79, p. 12.

KESSLER, Jascha
"Apocalypse: II. " CentR (23:3) Sum 79, p. 291.
"Maiden" (tr. of Marton Kalasz). Spirit (3:3) Sum 78, p. 40.
"No Denying" (tr. of Mihalyi Ladanyi). Spirit (3:3) Sum 78, p.
  38.
"Root" (tr. of Miklós Radnóti). MichQR (18:3) Sum 79, p. 407.

KESSLER, Milton
"Bit. " PoNow (23) 79, p. 7.
"Sketching Pain. " PoNow (23) 79, p. 7.
"Thanks Forever. " PoNow (23) 79, p. 7.

KESSLER, Stephen
"Ballad of a Thin Man. " Bachy (14) Spr/Sum 79, p. 82.
"Brazen Overture. " Bachy (14) Spr/Sum 79, p. 83.
"Slow: Prisoners Escaping. " Bachy (14) Spr/Sum 79, p. 81.

KIEFER, Rita Brady
"Shadows. " SouthernPR (19:1) Spr 79, p. 65.
"Until I Know About Dreams. " SouthernPR (19:1) Spr 79, p. 64.

KIEFFABER, Alan
"Easter Egg. " ChrC (96:13) 11 Ap 79, p. 402.

KILMER, Nicholas
"Naked Swimmers. " PoNow (25) 79, p. 14.

KING, Cynthia
"Contrapunctal. " Tendril (4) Wint 79, p. 35.
"Heroines. " Tendril (4) Wint 79, p. 34.

KING, James F.
"Morning. With Coffee. " StoneC (6:1) F 79, p. 24.

KING, Kenneth
"Word Raid" (tongue twisters, etc. for e. e. cummings). ParisR
  (76) Aut 79, pp. 210-217.

KING, Pamela
"Rainbow. " StoneC (6:3) O 79, p. 5.

KING, Robert S.
"Fable of the Bootsfools. " Wind (34) 79, p. 34.
"Forever Walking to the Greater Fire. " Wind (34) 79, p. 35.
"I've Found I Can Whistle with My New False Teeth. " Wind (34)
  79, p. 34.
"Rapunzel Placing a Headstone on the Well. " Wind (34) 79, p.
  35.

KING, Ruth
"Sunflower. " Paint (11) Spr 79, p. 29.
"Unseasonal Weather. " Paint (11) Spr 79, p. 30.

KINNELL, Galway
"The Choir. " NewYorker (55:3) 5 Mr 79, p. 38.
"Fisherman. " Iowa (10:1) Wint 79, p. 38.
"There Are Things I Tell to No One but to the Poem. " Harp
     (259:1552) S 79, p. 82.

KINZIE, Mary
"Allegory. " Salm (43) Wint 79, p. 11.
"Claude Lorrain's 'Herdsman, " 1655. " Salm (43) Wint 79, p. 7.
"Ghiberti's Eve. " SouthernR (15:2) Spr 79, p. 415.
"A Guide to the Fallen Country. " Salm (43) Wint 79, pp. 3-5.
"Ira et Studio. " Salm (43) 79, p. 10.
"Lightning Has Once Hit Near Me. " NewRep (181:24) 15 D 79,
     p. 26.
"List. " Salm (46) Aut 79, p. 92.
"Modern Love. " SouthernR (15:2) Spr 79, p. 417.
"The Quest" (for Mary Etta Knapp). NewRep (181:15) 13 O 79,
     p. 38.
"Scenes from the Liturgy. " Salm (43) Wint 79, p. 8.
"To God Who Gets Away with Things" (for Ruth Limmer). Salm
     (43) Wint 79, p. 5.
"Van Eyck's 'Madonna of Nicholas Rolin, ' 1435. " Salm (43)
     Wint 79, p. 6.

KIPP, Allan F.
"Cubist Blues in Poltergeist Major. " ChrC (96:33) 17 O 79, p.
     1003.

KIRBY, David
"The Fat Planet. " SouthernPR (19:1) Spr 79, p. 31.

KIRCHER, Pamela
"In the Small Boats of Their Hands. " GeoR (33:1) Spr 79, p.
     117.
"The Intimate Earth. " GeoR (33:1) Spr 79, p. 116.

KIRK, Norman Andrew
"Sanctuary. " Wind (33) 79, p. 29.

KIRSCH, Sarah
"Legend of Lilya" (tr. by Almut McAuley). NewOR (6:3) 79, p.
     222.
"Seven Skins" (tr. by Almut McAuley). NewOR (6:3) 79, p. 223.

KIRSCHEN, Mark
"Barcelona. " Montra (5) 79, p. 32.
"Education of the Virgin. " Montra (5) 79, p. 31.
"The Ice Age. " Montra (5) 79, p. 30.
"Pier's End. " Montra (5) 79, p. 34.

KIZER, Carolyn
"Children. " Poetry (134:1) Ap 79, pp. 23-25.

KLAPPERT, Peter
  "Dr. O and the New U. " Agni (10/11) 79, p. 78.
  "Evereux Burning, Louviers Burning, Rouen Burning. " MissouriR
    (2:2/3) Spr 79, p. 49.
  from The Idiot Princess of the Last Dynasty: "Doctor O'Connor
    and the Laughter of War. " Poetry (133:6) Mr 79, pp. 312-
    318.
  from The Idiot Princess of the Last Dynasty: "Pontius O'Con-
    nor. " Poetry (133:6) Mr 79, pp. 311-312.
  from The Idiot Princess of the Last Dynasty: "Saint Matthew
    the Paranoiac. " Poetry (133:6) Mr 79, pp. 318-320.
  "Internal Foreigners. " GreenfieldR (7:3/4) Spr-Sum 79, p. 140.
  "J'Accuse. " Antaeus (35) Aut 79, p. 90.
  "Matthew's Other Love Song. " ParisR (76) Aut 79, pp. 114-116.
  "Les Places Numerotees. " GreenfieldR (7:3/4) Spr-Sum 79, p.
    143.
  "A Sentimental Journey. " GreenfieldR (7:3/4) Spr-Sum 79, p.
    144.
  "Sero Medicina. " CornellR (5) Wint 79, pp. 54-62.
  "The Thinking Hand That Shapes the Human Form. " GreenfieldR
    (7:3/4) Spr-Sum 79, p. 146.

KLAUCK, D. L.
  "Amerika 1976--Memoirs of the Bicentennial. " SeC (7:1) 79, p.
    22.
  "Another October in Prison" (for H. L. Van Brunt). GeoR (33:3)
    Aut 79, p. 624.
  "Dirty Joke. " Nat (228:19) 19 My 79, p. 576.
  "Einstein's Father. " Confr (18) Spr-Sum 79, p. 41.
  "A Farewell A Bit of Egotism and a Modest Display of Self-
    Pity. " SeC (7:1) 79, p. 27.
  "In the Desert" (for Richard Shelton). GreenfieldR (7:3/4) Spr-
    Sum 79, p. 172.
  "These Days.... " GreenfieldR (7:3/4) Spr-Sum 79, p. 171.

KLEIN, James
  "In South Dakota, Pheasant Was the Usual Dish. " JnlONJP (3:2)
    79, p. 17.
  "Lady on the Couch, Half Nude. " PikeF (2) Wint 78-79, p. 21.

KLEIN, Jim
  "Block of Wood. " WormR (73) 79, p. 8.
  "The Cigarette Game. " WormR (73) 79, p. 11.
  "Dad your dying. " WormR (73) 79, p. 12.
  "The Match Game. " WormR (73) 79, p. 9.
  "Take Cotton Candy. " WormR (73) 79, p. 10.

KLEIN, Jodi
  "A wisping wind blowing. " EngJ (68:5) My 79, p. 35.

KLEIN, Melanie
  "The Red Dog. " PikeF (2) Wint 78-79, p. 16.

KLINE, George L.
"Plato Elaborated" (tr. of Joseph Brodsky). NewYorker (55:4)
   12 Mr 79, p. 40.

KLOEFKORN, William
"Crazy Horse: Final Reflection # 7. " MidwQ (20:2) Wint 79,
   p. 195.
"Final Projection No. 13. " PoetC (11:3) 79, p. 22.
"First Storm. " HiramPoR (26) Spr-Sum 79, p. 26.
"Honeymoon. " CutB (12) Spr-Sum 79, p. 29.
"Loony Starts the Day off Shining Bright. " DacTerr (16) 79, p.
   42.
"Monkey Nipples. " MidwQ (20:2) Wint 79, p. 197.
"My Love for All Things Warm and Breathing. " HiramPoR (26)
   Spr-Sum 79, p. 25.
"On the Road" (for Michelle). DacTerr (16) 79, p. 40.
"Out-and-Down Pattern. " Chowder (12) Spr-Sum 79, p. 24.
"Words for a Long Mid-Winter Night. " MidwQ (20:2) Wint 79,
   p. 196.

KNIGHT, Arthur Winfield
"After Hearing Gary Snyder Read. " Tele (15) Spr 79, p. 138.
"Anniversary. " SeC (6:1) 78, p. 34.
"The Dying Gerbil. " PikeF (2) Wint 78-79, p. 7.
"The Nap. " Tele (15) Spr 79, p. 138.

KNIGHT, Etheridge
"Welcome Back, Mr. Knight: Love of My Life. " AmerPoR (8:1)
   Ja-F 79, p. 20.

KNIGHT, Kit
"An Armful of Future. " SeC (6:1) 78, p. 33.

KNOEPFLE, John
"The Great American Poem. " Antaeus (32) Wint 79, pp. 82-86.
"Winter Poems 1970: 1-31. " CharR (5:SI) 79, pp. 11-29.

KNOLL, Michael A.
"4 Grns. Morphine Sulfate/Jan. '76. " GreenfieldR (7:3/4) Spr-
   Sum 79, p. 196.

KNOTT, Bill
"Remembered Message. " Antaeus (34) Sum 79, p. 58.
"Talk to Me. " Antaeus (34) Sum 79, p. 59.

KNOX, Caroline
"The Crybaby at the Library. " Poetry (133:6) Mr 79, pp. 333-
   334.
"Green Animals. " Poetry (133:6) Mr 79, pp. 335-336.
"The Painting. " MinnR (NS 12) Spr 79, p. 46.
"The Phoenix. " Poetry (133:6) Mr 79, p. 337.
"Sports. " Poetry (133:6) Mr 79, p. 338.

KNUEPFEL, George M.
"Narcissus. " Mouth (2:3) N 79, p. 31.

KOCH, Claude
"Morning Thoughts. " FourQt (28:4) Sum 79, p. 12.

KOCH, Kenneth
"The Simplicity of the Unknown Past. " NewYRB (26:12) 19 Jl
79, p. 33.

KOCH, Tom
"To a Government Economist. " Playb (26:12) D 79, p. 273.
"To a Male Striptease. " Playb (26:12) D 79, p. 272.
"To Fred Silverman. " Playb (26:12) D 79, p. 273.
"To Mexico's National Leaders. " Playb (26:12) D 79, p. 273.
"To the Engineers at NASA. " Playb (26:12) D 79, p. 272.

KOEN, S. W.
"The Inheritance. " KanQ (11:1/2) Wint-Spr 79, p. 192.

KOEPPEL, Fredric
"Melancholia" (for Gary Witt). SouthernHR (13:2) Spr 79, p. 136.
"October. " SouthernHR (13:2) Spr 79, p. 137.

KOERTGE, Ronald
"The Bear Is Ill. " PoNow (21) 79, p. 25.
"Bull's Eye. " WormR (73) 79, p. 34.
"The Conversion. " PoNow (23) 79, p. 33.
"Cycle Poem. " Ur (2) 79, p. 58.
"Dear John. " PoNow (21) 79, p. 33.
"Demands of the Molars. " Spirit (4:1) Aut-Wint 78-79, p. 20.
"Dope. " WormR (76) 79, p. 153.
"Excerpts from God's Secret Diary. " HiramPoR (26) Spr-Sum
79, p. 27.
"The Fan. " PoNow (22) 79, p. 31.
"Gretel. " PoNow (21) 79, p. 32.
"The Haunted Aisle. " Spirit (4:1) Aut-Wint 78-79, p. 20.
"Inventing America's Favorite Pastime. " PoNow (22) 79, p. 30.
"Life on the Edge of the Continent. " PoNow (23) 79, p. 25.
"Lilith. " PoNow (21) 79, pp. 32-33.
"A Man in Alabama Fights the Dryness. " WormR (76) 79, p.
154.
"The Mind of the Box Boy. " PoNow (21) 79, p. 33.
"Mutiny. " PoNow (22) 79, p. 31.
"The Mystery of the Mass Drowning of the Senior Class of Hoyle
High School Heretofore Unexplained Finally and Conclusively
Solved. " WormR (73) 79, p. 33.
"Nancy Drew. " PoNow (22) 79, p. 31.
"Old People. " PoNow (23) 79, p. 25.
"Panty Hose. " WormR (76) 79, p. 153.
"Plus Ça Change. " WormR (73) 79, p. 34.
"Points of Interest. " PoNow (22) 79, p. 30.
"Q. Where Can I Meet Girls?

A. Laundromats Are Full of Them. " WormR (73) 79, p. 33.
"Sex Object. " PoNow (23) 79, p. 25.
"Sleeping Beauty. " WormR (73) 79, p. 34.
"Strange Customs of the Natives. " PoNow (23) 79, p. 25.
"To Impress the Girl Next Door. " PoNow (21) 79, p. 25.
"12 Photographs of Yellowstone. " PoNow (21) 79, p. 25.
"Urban Renewal. " PoNow (22) 79, p. 30.
"A Well-Dressed Man. " WormR (76) 79, p. 153.

KOESTENBAUM, Phyllis
"I have looked at them. " Nimrod (23:1) Aut-Wint 79, p. 13.

KOHLER, Sandra
"The Wedding. " MassR (20:2) Sum 79, p. 310.

KOLAR, Linda
"The Ballroom. " EngJ (68:5) My 79, p. 35.

KOLLAR, Sybil
"Cat. " Chelsea (38) 79, p. 192.
"Night Watch. " Chelsea (38) 79, p. 192.

KOLUMBAN, Nicholas
"At a Wake" (tr. of Sandor Csoori). Pequod (3:1) 79, p. 101.
"Attila József" (tr. of Attila József). TexQ (21:4) Wint 78, p.
    28.
"Consent" (tr. of Gyula Illyes). PoNow (24) 79, p. 21.
"Foolish Mirror" (tr. of Lövine Szabó). TexQ (21:4) Wint 78, p.
    35.
"My Poem" (tr. of Sandor Weöres). PoNow (24) 79, p. 62.
"Night Watch" (tr. of Gyula Illyes). PoNow (24) 79, p. 21.
"One of Us" (tr. of István Vas). TexQ (21:4) Wint 78, p. 29.
"Out-of-the-Way-House" (tr. of Hans Magnus Enzensberger).
    PoNow (24) 79, p. 14.
"A Photograph" (tr. of Katalin Mezey). TexQ (21:4) Wint 78, p.
    30.
"Psalm on Entering Jerusalem" (tr. of Tibor Gyurkovics). TexQ
    (21:4) Wint 78, p. 33.
"Resume. " GreenfieldR (7:3/4) Spr-Sum 79, p. 273.
"Shadows" (tr. of Tibor Gyurkovics). PoNow (24) 79, p. 18.
"She Gets Up at Dawn Like Bakers" (tr. of Attila József). TexQ
    (21:4) Wint 78, p. 27.
"The Tomb of the Kennedys" (tr. of Sandor Weöres). PoNow (24)
    79, p. 62.
"The Visit. " GreenfieldR (7:3/4) Spr-Sum 79, p. 275.
"Waiting for the Bus" (tr. of Katalin Mezey). TexQ (21:4) Wint
    78, p. 32.
"Your Time. " GreenfieldR (7:3/4) Spr-Sum 79, p. 274.

KOMACHI, Ono No
Nineteen Poems. Montra (5) 79, p. 128.

KOMUNYAKAA, Yusef
"After Talks with Robert Peters. " SeC (6:1) 78, p. 37.

"Corrigenda. " Kayak (50) My 79, p. 27.
"Death Threat Note. " Kayak (50) My 79, p. 28.
"Falling Down Song. " Kayak (52) D 79, p. 56.
"In the Background of Silence. " Kayak (52) D 79, p. 57.
"The Thorn Merchant. " Durak (3) 79, p. 17.
"Woman, I Got the Blues. " Kayak (50) My 79, p. 26.

KONUK, Motlu
  "Elegy for Satan" (tr. of Nazim Hikmet w. Randy Blasing).
      PoNow (23) 79, p. 46.
  "From Sofia" (tr. of Nazim Hikmet w. Randy Blasing). PoNow
      (24) 79, p. 20.
  "Poem: This year, early fall in the far south" (tr. of Nazim
      Hikmet w. Randy Blasing). PoNow (24) 79, p. 20.

KOOPMAN, Mireya Urquidi
  "Anniversary of a Vision. " UTR (6:3/4) 79, p. 12.
  "Duendes/Llamas of the Andes. " UTR (6:3/4) 79, p. 11.
  "La Paz, Again. " UTR (6:3/4) 79, p. 10.

KOOSER, Ted
  "The Death of the Dentist. " PoNow (21) 79, p. 26.
  "Dynamiting the Old Hotel. " PoetryNW (20:1) Spr 79, pp. 28-29.
  "Fort Robinson. " PoNow (21) 79, p. 26.
  "The Great American Poem. " Antaeus (32) Wint 79, pp. 82-86.
  "A Hairnet with Stars. " DacTerr (16) 79, p. 43.
  "Late September in Nebraska. " PoNow (21) 79, p. 26.
  "The Salesman. " PoetryNW (20:1) Spr 79, pp. 29-30.
  "A Widow. " PoNow (21) 79, p. 26.

KOPELKE, Kendra
  "For My Grandfather. " FourQt (28:3) Spr 79, p. 10.
  "Hardly Sleeping. " SouthernPR (19:1) Spr 79, p. 70.

KOPLAND, Rutger
  "G" (tr. by Ria Leigh-Loohuizen). AmerPoR (8:1) Ja-F 79, p.
      44.

KOPP, Karl
  "Edgar Gevaert, Painter. " CharR (5:1) Spr 79, p. 31.

KORNBLUM, Allan
  "Done. " Spirit (4:2/3) Spr-Sum 79, p. 48.

KOSMICKI, Greg
  "Putting Up the Storm Windows. " KanQ (11:1/2) Wint-Spr 79, p.
      12.

KOSTINER, Eileen
  "Poem on a Line by Elizabeth Bowen. " Paint (11) Spr 79, p. 31.

KOUWENAAR, Gerrit
  Eight poems. Montra (5) 79, p. 196.

KOWIT, Steve
"Amen" (tr. of Jaime Sabines). PoNow (24) 79, p. 51.
"Bad Advice. " WormR (74) 79, p. 46.
"Canvassing. " WormR (74) 79, p. 45.
"Four After the Sanskrit. " WormR (74) 79, p. 43.
"I Will Not Be Silent" (tr. of Pablo Neruda). PoNow (24) 79, p. 32.
"Morning Raga. " Ur (2) 79, p. 59.
"Never" (tr. of Pablo Neruda). PoNow (24) 79, p. 32.
"No, Never" (tr. of Pablo Neruda). PoNow (24) 79, p. 32.
"Pedemonte Taught Philosophy" (tr. of Luis Suardiaz). PoNow (24) 79, p. 58.
"Phone Call. " WormR (74) 79, p. 46.
"Satori. " WormR (74) 79, p. 45.
"Small Business Boom. " Ur (2) 79, p. 60.
"Those of Yesterday" (tr. of Pablo Neruda). PoNow (24) 79, p. 32.

KRAMER, Aaron
"back. " St. AR (5:3) Aut-Wint 79, p. 96.
"pasts. " St. AR (5:3) Aut-Wint 79, p. 94.
"Now, Before Shaving. " CarlMis (18:1) Wint 79-80, p. 163.

KRAPF, Norbert
"Arriving on Paumanok. " PoNow (21) 79, p. 17.
"The Carousel" (tr. of Rainer Maria Rilke). PoNow (24) 79, p. 48.
"Entrance" (tr. of Rainer Maria Rilke). PoNow (21) 79, p. 44.
"Evening" (tr. of Rainer Maria Rilke). PoNow (21) 79, p. 44.
"Fall Day" (tr. of Rainer Maria Rilke). PoNow (21) 79, p. 44.
"For an Old Friend. " AmerS (48:4) Aut 79, p. 513.
"From a Childhood" (tr. of Rainer Maria Rilke). PoNow (24) 79, p. 48.
"In the Back Seat of a Fast-Moving Car. " PoNow (22) 79, p. 31.
"Somewhere in Southern Indiana. " PoNow (22) 79, p. 31.

KRAUSS, Ruth
"I Look. " Tele (15) Spr 79, p. 46.
"When I First Saw. " PoNow (23) 79, p. 13.

KREDA, Avis
"After School. " Poem (36) Jl 79, p. 8.
"Briseis Speaks. " Poem (36) Jl 79, pp. 10-11.
"Two Winter Poems. " Poem (36) Jl 79, p. 9.

KRESH, David
"Antique Old Lady. " Poem (37) N 79, p. 61.
"Look, You Were Saying. " Wind (33) 79, p. 30.
"Opening. " CimR (49) O 79, p. 26.
"Pisces, April 8. " Wind (33) 79, p. 30.
"Shape Changing. " SouthernPR (19:2) Aut 79, p. 66.
"Stir Crazy. " Poem (37) N 79, p. 60.
"View of Spring Garden Street. " Spirit (3:3) Sum 78, p. 11.

KRETZ, Thomas
"Figure in the Red Balloon. " KanQ (11:1/2) Wint-Spr 79, p. 219.

KRIDLER, David
"The Great Blue Heron. " AntR (37:3) Sum 79, p. 321.

KRIEGER, Ian
"Conceptual Snapshot. " Tele (15) Spr 79, p. 4.
"Drugstore. " KanQ (11:1/2) Wint Spr 79, p. 117.
"Fashion" (for Carol). Tele (15) Spr 79, p. 3.
"Fashion (11)" (for Carol). " Im (5:3) 79, p. 12.

KRIEL, Margot
"Florence Nightingale Receives a Visitor. " Iowa (10:3) Sum 79, p. 109.

KRISAK, Len
"Lower Peninsula. " PoetC (11:2) 79, p. 8.

KRISTOFCO, John P.
"America Passes. " Poem (37) N 79, pp. 18-19.
"In a Summer Morning. " Poem (37) N 79, p. 17.
"To One Who Sees the Sun Rise in the West. " Poem (37) N 79, pp. 20-22.

KROGFUS, Miles
"From the Virginia Colony. " CarlMis (18:1) Wint 79-80, p. 37.

KROLL, Ernest
"Aftermath. " Poem (36) Jl 79, p. 16.
"As in a Glass, Clearly. " HiramPoR (26) Spr-Sum 79, p. 28.
"The Barn Owl. " HiramPoR (26) Spr-Sum 79, p. 28.
"Brownstone Dusk. " StoneC (6:3) O 79, p. 14.
"Diehard. " Focus (13:81) My-Je 79, p. 30.
"Domestic. " WebR (4:3) Spr 79, p. 26.
"Eros in a City Park. " Poem (36) Jl 79, p. 15.
"Expectations. " PoNow (22) 79, p. 33.
"Greenbrier Winter. " Wind (35) 79, p. 27.
"The Hard Life in Cockiagne (Venezuela). " Im (6:1) 79, p. 3.
"Ignorance. " PoNow (22) 79, p. 32.
"Interview. " PoNow (22) 79, p. 32.
"Life in the Warehouse District. " PoNow (23) 79, p. 15.
"Mountain Mail. " WebR (4:3) Spr 79, p. 28.
"Newburyport Custom House (1834). " Wind (35) 79, p. 27.
"The Picture Show. " PoNow (22) 79, p. 32.
"Pine and Salt (Winter Vacations). " WebR (4:3) Spr 79, p. 27.
from Songs from the Playing Fields of Delores County: "Prudence. " Northeast (3:7) Spr 79, p. 39.
"The Street. " PoNow (22) 79, p. 32.
"Sundown. " Wind (35) 79, p. 27.
"The Taunting. " Wind (35) 79, p. 27.
"Thomas Hardy. " Chowder (12) Spr-Sum 79, p. 77.
"Too Young for Prudence. " PoNow (22) 79, pp. 32-33.

KROLL, Judith
"At a Time of the Year. " Ploughs (5:1) 79, pp. 75-76.
"The Death of the Racing Car Driver. " NewEngR (1:3) Spr 79,
    p. 345.
"Hotel Metropole. " Poetry (134:5) Ag 79, pp. 274-277.
"Om Kanneshwara Temple. " CarlMis (18:1) Wint 79, p. 160.
"Report to the Dead. " Poetry (134:5) Ag 79, pp. 278-280.

KROLOW, Karl
"In Peacetime" (tr. by J. Michael Yates).   NewOR (6:2) 79, p.
    152.
"Let the Laugh" (tr. by Stuart Friebert).   Durak (2) 79, p. 55.
"My Life. " QW (8) Wint 79, p. 80.
"Time Passing" (tr. by Stuart Friebert).   MalR (52) O 79, p.
    134.
"View/Prospect" (tr. by Stuart Friebert).   Durak (2) 79, p. 54.
"Weiss" (tr. by Paul Morris).   NowestR (18:2) 79, p. 68.
"Where a Ship Belongs. " SlowLR (3) 79, p. 48.

KRONENBERG, Susan
"Hotel Boule Rock. " Tele (15) Spr 79, p. 60.
"San Francisco--Yes and No. " Tele (15) Spr 79, p. 58.
from Simultaneous Occurrences: "Epilogue. " Tele (15) Spr 79,
    p. 61.

KRUCHKOW, Diane
"July 4. " PikeF (2) Wint 78-79, p. 32.
"Jr. Olympics. " PoNow (25) 79, p. 14.

KRUSOE, James
"Claude Lorrain Is Painting Los Angeles. " PoNow (25) 79, p.
    25.
"Ohio. " PoNow (25) 79, p. 25.

KRYSL, Marilyn
"Daughter Melon Elephant Me. " LittleM (12:1/2) Spr-Sum 78
    (79), p. 18.
"Legs. " Aspen (7) Spr 79, p. 39.
"Politics. " Field (20) Spr 79, p. 16.
"Sestina Extolling the Pleasure of Creation. " LittleM (12:1/2)
    Spr-Sum 78 (79), p. 15.
"The Wife of the Nobel Lecturer in Physics Solves the Equation
    That Makes Him Famous. " LittleM (12:1/2) Spr-Sum 78
    (79), p. 17.
"Words Words Words. " Aspen (7) Spr 79, p. 40.

KUBACH, David
"Regent Street Upstream. " PikeF (2) Wint 78-79, p. 23.

KUBY, Lolette
"Door and Passageways. " MinnR (NS 12) Spr 79, p. 13.
"Instructions on Giving Still Birth. " CarlMis (17:2/3) Spr 79, p.
    98.

KUDAKA, Geraldine
"Death Is a Second Cousin Dining with Us Tonight. " NewL (46:2)
    Wint 79-80, p. 36.
"Gambling with Husbands and God. " NewL (46:2) Wint 79-80, p.
    35.

KULIK, William
"Freeing the Bodies" (tr. of Andre Frenaud). AmerPoR (8:3)
    My-Je 79, p. 28.

KULKARNI, Venkatesh Srinivas
"Epiphany. " Wind (35) 79, p. 29.
"Lying in the Sun with a Spanish Beauty. " GreenfieldR (7:3/4)
    Spr-Sum 79, pp. 38-42.
"Unreal City. " GreenfieldR (7:3/4) Spr-Sum 79, p. 43.

KUMAR, Skiv K.
"At the Ghats of Banaras. " GreenfieldR (7:3/4) Spr-Sum 79, p.
    53.
"My Right Hand. " GreenfieldR (7:3/4) Spr-Sum 79, p. 54.
"The Taj. " GreenfieldR (7:3/4) Spr-Sum 79, p. 53.

KUMIN, Judith
"Adulthood" (tr. of William Cliff w. Maxine Kumin). PoNow (24)
    79, p. 10.
"Childhood" (tr. of William Cliff w. Maxine Kumin). PoNow (24)
    79, p. 10.
"Lullaby for My Dead Child" (tr. of Denise Jallais w. Maxine
    Kumin). PoNow (23) 79, p. 46.
"The Messiah" (tr. of William Cliff, w. Maxine Kumin).
    NewEngR (1:3) Spr 79, p. 280.
"The Miracles" (tr. of Robert Sabatier w. Maxine Kumin).
    PoNow (24) 79, p. 50.
"The Time of Mirages" (tr. of Denise Jallais w. Maxine Kumin).
    PoNow (24) 79, p. 21.
"The Track" (tr. of Therese Plantier w. Maxine Kumin). PoNow
    (24) 79, p. 45.
"Twins" (tr. of William Cliff w. Maxine Kumin). PoNow (24)
    79, p. 10.
"The White Farm" (tr. of William Cliff w. Maxine Kumin).
    PoNow (24) 79, p. 10.

KUMIN, Maxine
"Adulthood" (tr. of William Cliff w. Judith Kumin). PoNow (27)
    79, p. 10.
"Childhood" (tr. of William Cliff w. Judith Kumin). PoNow (24)
    79, p. 10.
"The Excrement Poem. " PoNow (23) 79, p. 25.
"July, Against Hunger. " PoNow (23) 79, p. 25.
"Lullaby for My Dead Child" (tr. of Denise Jallais w. Judith
    Kumin). PoNow (23) 79, p. 46.
"The Messiah" (tr. of William Cliff, w. Judith Kumin). NewEngR
    (1:3) Spr 79, p. 280.

"The Miracles" (tr. of Robert Sabatier w. Judith Kumin). PoNow
(24) 79, p. 50.
"Poem, Found in the New Hampshire Department of Agriculture
Weekly Market Bulletin. " Agni (10/11) 79, p. 151.
"Regret. " Iowa (10:1) Wint 79, p. 43.
"The Time of Mirages" (tr. of Denise Jallais w. Judith Kumin).
PoNow (24) 79, p. 21.
"The Track" (tr. of Therese Plantier w. Judith Kumin). PoNow
(24) 79, p. 45.
"Twins" (tr. of William Cliff w. Judith Kumin). PoNow (24) 79,
p. 10.
"The White Farm" (tr. of William Cliff w. Judith Kumin).
PoNow (24) 79, p. 10.

KUNAT, Barbara
"March. " Confr (18) Spr-Sum 79, p. 57.

KUNITZ, Stanley
"The Catch. " Atl (243:1) Ja 79, p. 83.
"The Crystal Cage" (for Joseph Cornell). Nat (228:18) 12 My
79, p. 544.
"The Great American Poem. " Antaeus (32) Wint 79, pp. 82-86.
"The Layers. " AmerPoR (8:1) Ja-F 79, p. 48.
"My Sisters. " Atl (243:1) Ja 79, p. 83.
"The Quarrel. " Atl (243:1) Ja 79, p. 83.
"Route Six. " NewEngR (1:3) Spr 79, p. 361.
"Signs and Portents. " NewYorker (55:1) 19 F 79, p. 38.
"Silence" (from Bella Akhmadulina). NewEngR (1:3) Spr 79, p.
362.
"The Unquiet Ones. " Atl (243:1) Ja 79, p. 83.

KUNZE, Reiner
"Refuge Even Behind Refuge Itself" (for Peter Huchel) (tr. by
Almut McAuley). NewOR (6:3) 79, p. 227.
"The Small Car" (tr. by Almut McAuley). NewOR (6:3) 79, p.
226.

KURKA, Mira Teru
"Under which heading does all this information go?" HangL (35)
Spr 79, p. 36.

KUTCHINS, Laurie
"Body. " CarlMis (17:2/3) Spr 79, p. 154.
"Into April. " CarlMis (17:2/3) Spr 79, p. 155.
"The Milkman. " CarlMis (17:2/3) Spr 79, p. 154.

KUUSENJUURI, Jean
"Jade Coast. " Mouth (2:3) N 79, p. 2.

KUZMA, Greg
"Among Friends. " SouthernR (15:1) Wint 79, p. 134.
"China and Greece" (for Richard Eberhart). PraS (53:1) Spr 79,
pp. 17-21.

'The Dog. " PoNow (21) 79, p. 41.
"A Person in My Life. " PraS (53:1) Spr 79, p. 14.
"Untitled: Will you suggest a title for this poem. " PraS (53:1)
    Spr 79, p. 13.
Village Journal (for George P. Elliott). Peb (17) 79. Entire
    issue.
'What Is It, Now That the Day Has Aged. " PraS (53:1) Spr 79,
    p. 11.

KVAM, Wayne
'The Welcome Bar. " PoNow (25) 79, p. 14.

LaBARE, M.
"Bottom of the ninth. " Aspect (74/75) Ja-Ag 79, p. 50.
'Teeth. " Aspect (74/75) Ja-Ag 79, p. 49.

LaBELLE, Jean
"Nevermore.' " WindO (34) Spr-Sum 79, p. 24.
"Prayer. " WindO (34) Spr-Sum 79, p. 24.

LADANYI, Mihalyi
"No Denying" (tr. by Jascha Kessler). Spirit (3:3) Sum 78, p.
    38.

LAGERKVIST, Par
"Motif" (tr. by Lennart Bruce). PoNow (24) 79, p. 23.

LAGIER, Gary
"A Certificate Told. " SeC (7:1) 79, p. 39.
'How Quickly Dust to Dust. " SeC (6:1) 78, p. 70.
"Poet in Search of a Publisher. " SeC (7:1) 79, p. 43.
"Undeveloped Film. " SeC (7:1) 79, p. 42.

LAHEY-DOLEGA, Christine
"Les Roses" (tr. of Rainer Maria Rilke). GRR (10:1) 79, p. 99.

LAKE, Paul
"Summer. " PoNow (25) 79, p. 15.

LAKIDES, Lucy
"Persephone. " Sam (72) 79, p. 61.
"Veteran. " Sam (79) 79, p. 54.

LAKIN, R. D.
'Rich I Come. " KanQ (11:1/2) Wint-Spr 79, p. 49.

LaLOMBARD, Joan
'Rome. " PraS (53:2) Sum 79, p. 155.
"Silence. " PraS (53:2) Sum 79, p. 157.
'There Is China. " PraS (53:2) Sum 79, p. 158.

LAMPHEAR, Paul A.
"Season Splitting. " Paint (12) Aut 79, p. 15.

LAMPMAN, Ben Hur
    from At the End of the Car Line (1942):   "My Traveled Uncle
        Jim. " NowestR (17:2/3) 79, p. 225.

LAMPORT, Felicia
    "Exxon Sunnyside Up. " NewRep (181:20) 17 N 79, p. 19.

LANDGRAF, Susan
    "First Day at the Alternative School. " Wind (33) 79, p. 32.
    "Storyteller. " Tendril (6) Aut 79, p. 32.

LANE, Donna
    "Letter to Rilke. " SeC (6:1) 78, p. 27.

LANE, Mervin
    Poem. St. AR (5:2) 79, p. 102.

LANE, William
    "Distances, Silences, Circles" (for D. B.).   HangL (35) Spr 79,
        p. 40.
    "Driving Toward Peabody, Kansas. " PoNow (25) 79, p. 15.
    "Nights Without You. " HangL (35) Spr 79, p. 37.
    "Sister Animal" (for C. R.).   HangL (36) Aut 79, p. 28.
    "II. " HangL (36) Aut 79, p. 32.

LANG, George
    "Tchewan-Geist. " BelPoJ (30:1) Aut 79, p. 35.

LANG, Jon
    "The Hunt. " CimR (49) O 79, p. 25.
    "Key. " CharR (5:1) Spr 79, p. 52.
    "Winter Moon. " PoNow (25) 79, p. 15.

LANG, Richard G.
    "No, I will not be. " StoneC (6:1) F 79, p. 12.

LANGE, Art
    "Poem: Reading for the. " SunM (8) Aut 79, p. 29.

LANGLAND, Joseph
    "Upon Hearing His High Sweet Tenor Again. " Epoch (29:1) Aut
        79, p. 12.

LANGTON, Daniel J.
    "Seizure" (tr. of Jules Supervielle).   Spirit (3:3) Sum 78, p. 10.

LANGTON, Roger W.
    "After a Day Teaching Anthropology. " SeC (6:1) 78, p. 56.

LANG-WESCOTT, Martha
    "Cold Teas. " Tendril (4) Wint 79, p. 36.

LAPE, Sue
    "Land Magic. " Wind (35) 79, p. 31.

LAPIDUS, Jacqueline
  "Betrayal. " HangL (35) Spr 79, p. 44.
  "Breakfast, October. " HangL (35) Spr 79, p. 43.
  "Healing. " 13thM (4:2) 79, p. 44.
  "L/F-Gyn: Case Herstory. " 13thM (4:2) 79, p. 41.

LARDAS, Konstantinos
  "All. " Nimrod (23:1) Aut-Wint 79, p. 22.

LARSEN, Carl
  "Love Among the Silverware. " PoNow (21) 79, p. 41.

LARSEN, Elizabeth
  "Here, in the middlewest. " Northeast (3:7) Spr 79, p. 31.
  "Nightmares for Henry's Dream Songs. " CarlMis (17:2/3) Spr
     79, p. 172.

LARSON, R. A.
  "Old 'Meat in the Pot'. " PoNow (22) 79, p. 33.

LaSALLE, Peter
  "Model Homes. " KanQ (11:4) Aut 79, p. 46.

LASNIER, Rina
  "Lumieres paralleles. " Os (8) 79, p. 10.
  "Ne parle pas a dieu.... " Os (8) 79, p. 9.
  "Quand le corps.... " Os (8) 79, p. 11.

LAST, Jim
  "At Boot Lake. " StoneC (6:3) O 79, p. 27.

LATEEF, Noel
  "Heiwa no koen" (to Y. K.). HarvAd (112:3) Ap 79, p. 29.

LATTA, John
  "Notes for a Definition of Myself. " CornellR (7) Aut 79, p. 95.
  "Poem (Via Piccola). " Epoch (28:2) Wint 79, p. 140.

LATTIMORE, Richmond
  "Coastal Stuff. " Poetry (134:5) Ag 79, p. 256.
  "Sliding Scales. " Poetry (134:5) Ag 79, p. 257.
  "Western Ways. " Poetry (134:5) Ag 79, p. 258.

LAUBER, Peg Carlson
  "45° North: Information and Instruction. " Wind (35) 79, p. 32.

LAUCHLAN, Michael F.
  "Coquinas. " BelPoJ (29:4) Sum 79, p. 29.

LAURIE, Peter
  "On the Death of the Poet. " Poetry (134:4) Jl 79, pp. 213-215.

LAUTERMILCH, Steven
  "At the Home of the History Professor. " TexQ (21:4) Wint 78,

p. 63.
"Christmas Morning. " CentR (23:1) Wint 79, p. 62.
Eight Poems (tr. of Rainer Maria Rilke). TexQ (21:4) Wint 78,
   pp. 22-26.
"For My Wife. " CentR (23:1) Wint 79, p. 62.
Poem.   St. AR (5:2) 79, p. 108.

LAVERY, John
   "Lenz-Imbolic" (to Bea Maria Anna). GRR (10:1) 79, pp. 56-82.

LaVOIE, Steven
   "Curtain Call" (for Keith Abbott). Tele (15) Spr 79, p. 75.
   "Don't You Think. " Tele (15) Spr 79, p. 76.
   "Fear. " Tele (15) Spr 79, p. 74.
   "Something Better Change. " Tele (15) Spr 79, p. 74.
   "You Bet Your Life for Walt Whitman. " Tele (15) Spr 79, p. 75.

LAWLOR, Joanne
   "Cyclist on the Near Horizon. " SmPd (47) 79, p. 23.

LAWN, Beverly
   "No Difference. " NewL (46:2) Wint 79-80, p. 44.
   "Stranger. " NewL (46:2) Wint 79-80, p. 44.

LAWNER, Lynne
   from Cracked Obelisk at Aswan: Nine Poems. Poetry (134:5)
      Ag 79, pp. 249-252.

LAWRENCE, Terry
   "The Harvester. " CentR (23:2) Spr 79, p. 154.
   "Migrants. " CentR (23:2) Spr 79, p. 154.

LAWSON, Todd S. J.
   "For James Earl Carter. " SeC (6:2) 78, p. 181.
   "On the Fifth Day of Easter. " SeC (6:2) 78, p. 183.
   "On the First Day of Easter. " SeC (6:2) 78, p. 182.
   "On the Fourteenth Day of Easter. " SeC (6:2) 78, p. 184.
   "On the Twenty-first Day of Easter. " SeC (6:2) 78, p. 185.

LAWTON, Susan
   "The Hydrocephalic Girl Next Door. " SeC (6:1) 78, p. 12.

LAZARD, Naomi
   "Five Poems from the Pakistani" (tr. of Faiz Ahmed Faiz).
      Kayak (51) S 79, p. 63.
   "The Map of the Double World. " Kayak (52) D 79, p. 20.
   "Mortal Love. " Kayak (52) D 79, p. 18.
   "Ritual at Midnight. " CutB (13) Aut-Wint 79, p. 33.

LAZER, Hank
   "Clean Clothes. " PoNow (22) 79, p. 33.
   "The Job. " PoNow (22) 79, p. 33.
   "Smart Lady" (for M). PoNow (22) 79, p. 33.

LEA, Sydney
"For Don C., Against a Proverb. " Hudson (32:4) Wint 79-80,
    p. 532.
"Recalling the Horseman Billy Farrell from an Airplane in Ver-
    mont. " Hudson (32:4) Wint 79-80, p. 531.
"Respect for Your Elders. " Iowa (10:2) Spr 79, p. 89.
"Salad and Simile: A Defense of Cultivation. " Iowa (10:2) Spr
    79, p. 87.
"To Our Son. " Hudson (32:1) Spr 79, p. 71.
"The Train Out. " NewYorker (55:29) 3 S 79, p. 30.
"Vermont: August Fever" (for Jim Cox). VirQR (55:3) Sum 79,
    p. 503.
"Young Man Leaving Home (1960). " PraS (53:4) Wint 79-80, p.
    326.

LEACH, Chet
"Circumstantial Evidence. " WestB (4) 79, p. 29.

LEAKE, Brent T.
"Mountains. " Wind (32) 79, p. 42.

LEALE, B. C.
"At the Cabaret Voltaire, Zurich (1916). " Kayak (50) My 79, p.
    10.
"Has Anyone Found My Siesta?" Kayak (50) My 79, p. 9.
"Taxidermist Extraordinaire. " Kayak (50) My 79, p. 11.
"What Has Happened to the Week Before Last?" Kayak (50) My
    79, p. 9.

LEAMON, Marlene
"The Exercise. " PoetryNW (20:2) Sum 79, p. 38.
"In the Land of Fathers. " PoetryNW (20:2) Sum 79, pp. 37-38.
"Invitation. " PoetryNW (20:2) Sum 79, pp. 38-39.

LEBOVITZ, Richard
"At the Circus" (tr. of Geo Norge). PoNow (24) 79, p. 38.
"Nurse" (tr. of Paul Eluard). PoNow (24) 79, p. 12.
"The Penknife" (tr. of Geo Norge). PoNow (24) 79, p. 38.
"Sky" (tr. of Geo Norge). PoNow (24) 79, p. 38.

LECHLITNER, Ruth
"Pacific Cove: Salt Point. " HolCrit (16:1) F 79, p. 12.

LECKIUS, Ingemar
"Paul Klee" (tr. by John Matthias). GreenfieldR (7:3/4) Spr-
    Sum 79, p. 120.

LeCOUNT, David E.
"Outside the Pioneer Market. " Wind (35) 79, p. 34.

LEE, Al
"The Great American Poem. " Antaeus (32) Wint 79, pp. 82-86.

LEE, Ann
"The Bacchants. " Wind (32) 79, p. 25.
"Light all Night. " ChrC (96:42) 19 D 79, p. 1267.

LEE, L. L.
"Eastbourne" (tr. of Eugenio Montale). WebR (4:3) Spr 79, p.
    5.

LEE, Lance
"August Storm. " Poem (36) Jl 79, pp. 38-39.
"Los Angeles. " Poem (36) Jl 79, p. 37.

LEE, Li-Young
"As You Leave" (for my older brother). Wind (34) 79, p. 38.
"Early in the Morning. " AmerPoR (8:2) Mr-Ap 79, p. 43.
"For Eric, Who Is Mentally Retarded. " Wind (34) 79, p. 37.
"For the Indian Girl Called Nephew. " Wind (34) 79, p. 39.

LEE, Mark
"Hudson Bay 1611. " SewanR (87:4) Aut 79, p. 537.

LEFCOWITZ, Barbara F.
"Matrushka. " PraS (53:4) Wint 79-80, p. 360.
"The Mirrors of Jerusalem. " WebR (4:3) Spr 79, p. 29.

LEFEVERE, André
"Fever Tune" (tr. of Karel Van de Woestijne). Paint (12) Aut
    79, p. 26.
"A Sequence of Absences: Prose Poems About the Tao" (for
    Pat). Paint (12) Aut 79, p. 24.

LeFEVRE, Adam
"Calling. " Ploughs (5:1) 79, p. 66.
"Coeymans. " Ploughs (5:1) 79, pp. 66-67.
"Ice Storm. " Ploughs (5:1) 79, p. 65.
"The Lost Astronaut. " PoNow (25) 79, p. 25.
"Love Takes Heartland. " PoNow (25) 79, p. 25.
"Sequence: Brady at Cold Harbor. " PoNow (25) 79, p. 25.

LEGLER, Philip
"First Snow. " PoetryNW (20:4) Wint 79-80, pp. 14-15.
"Green Thumb. " Bits (9) Ja 79.

LEHMAN, David
"In Praise of Robert Penn Warren. " Poetry (135:2) N 79, p.
    85.
"The Last Laugh. " PartR (46:1) 79, p. 104.
"Ode. " Poetry (135:2) N 79, p. 86.
"The Three Angels" (for Stefanie). NewL (46:1) Aut 79, p. 73.

LEHMANN, Karen
"Love in the Autumn. " Wind (32) 79, p. 26.

LEIGH, Michael G.
"City Skip. " Ur (2) 79, p. 62.

LEIGH-LOOHUIZEN, Ria
"G" (tr. of Rutger Kopland). AmerPoR (8:1) Ja-F 79, p. 44.

LEISER, Dorothy
"The Migrations of People. " ChrC (96:14) 18 Ap 79, p. 441.

LEITHAUSER, Brad
"An Expanded Want Ad. " NewYorker (55:29) 3 S 79, p. 38.
"The Return to a Cabin. " NewRep (180:25) 23 Je 79, p. 28.

LeMASTER, J. R.
"April" (tr. of Claude Vigée). Mund (11:1) 79, p. 93.
"Epilogue" (tr. of Claude Vigée). Mund (11:1) 79, p. 93.
"I Do Not Deny the Night Too Much Loved" (tr. of Claude Vigée).
   Mund (11:1) 79, p. 95.
"Nunc Dimittis" (tr. of Claude Vigée). Mund (11:1) 79, p. 97.
"The Play-Actor of Heaven" (tr. of Claude Vigée). Mund (11:1)
   79, p. 97.

LENNE, N. N.
"Moving Out. " PoetC (11:2) 79, p. 34.

LENOWITZ, Harris
from The Crown of Kingdom: (X-XXXII) (tr. of Solomon ibn
   Gabirol). Montra (5) 79, pp. 218-229.

LENSE, Edward
"EEG. " GRR (10:1) 79, p. 127.
"The Music Room. " GRR (10:1) 79, p. 126.
"Shopping for a Camera. " GreenfieldR (7:3/4) Spr-Sum 79, p.
   80.
"Snow. " KanQ (11:4) Aut 79, p. 131.
"Vanishing Poem. " GRR (10:1) 79, p. 125.

LEONARD, Byron
"Dog. " CalQ (15) Wint 79, p. 63.
"Five Portraits" (tr. of Benjamin Péret). MalR (51) Jl 79, p.
   54.
"Having Grown Old the Devil Became a Hermit" (tr. of Benjamin
   Péret). Chelsea (38) 79, p. 26.
"Lizard. " CalQ (15) Wint 79, p. 69.
"My Latest Misfortunes" (tr. of Benjamin Péret). Chelsea (38)
   79, p. 25.
"Reform" (tr. of Benjamin Péret). Chelsea (38) 79, p. 24.

LEONHARDT, Gay
"The Extra Touch. " Epoch (28:2) Wint 79, p. 134.

LEPORE, Dominick J.
"Northward. " ArizQ (35:2) Sum 79, p. 164.

"on the rope" (tr. of Gigi Dessi). St. AR (5:3) Aut-Wint 79, p. 123.
Poem. St. AR (5:2) 79, p. 76.

LERNER, Linda
"Halloween. " GreenfieldR (7:3/4) Spr-Sum 79, p. 207.
"Holiday Warnings. " TexQ (21:4) Wint 78, p. 115.
"A Lady and Her Photographer. " Chelsea (38) 79, p. 101.
"Paper-Lives. " GreenfieldR (7:3/4) Spr-Sum 79, p. 208.

LESLIE, Lynne
"Bishop Jones Ordains His First Woman. " ChrC (96:38) 21 N
79, p. 1148.

LESNIAK, Rose
"At the People's Cultural Celebration" (to Amiri Baraka). Tele
(15) Spr 79, p. 34.
"for P. P. " Tele (15) Spr 79, p. 35.
"Perambulating Two's. " Tele (15) Spr 79, p. 35.

LESS, Sam
"Cow Bones. " Mouth (2:2) Je 79, p. 7.
"Fire. " Mouth (2:2) Je 79, p. 19.

LESSER, Rika
from Etruscan Things: "A Handle on Things. " PraS (53:4) Wint
79-80, p. 362.
from Etruscan Things: "Sarcophagus. " NewRep (181:25) 22 D
79, p. 26.
"527 Cathedral Parkway. " NewYorker (55:4) 12 Mr 79, p. 46.
"Weeds" (tr. of Peter Huchel). NewYRB (26:20) 20 D 79, p. 33.

LESSING, Karin
Ten poems. Montra (5) 79, p. 54.

LESTER, M. L.
"Latham Park. " PoetC (11:3) 79, p. 28.

LEUTY, Barbara
"The instruments of your life. " SeC (6:1) 78, p. 60.
"Old Poet. " SeC (6:1) 78, p. 61.

LEVENDOSKY, Charles
"The Rustic Bar Pool Shark. " DacTerr (16) 79, p. 44.

LEVERING, Donald
"After Illness. " WestHR (33:2) Spr 79, p. 117.
"Circumambulating Crystal Mountain (Nepal). " PortR (25) 79, p.
131.
"Discovery of a Star. " PortR (25) 79, p. 132.

LEVERTOV, Denise
"Heights, Depths, Silence, Unceasing Sound of the Surf. "

SouthernPR (19:2) Aut 79, p. 39.
"Psalm: People Power at the Die-in. " NewL (46:2) Wint 79-80,
    p. 98.

LEVI, Jan Heller
    "Legacy" (for H. S.). Pequod (3:1) 79, pp. 77-78.
    "Missing in Action. " Pequod (3:1) 79, pp. 76-77.

LEVI, Toni Mergentime
    "To My Husband at 36. " Poem (36) Jl 79, p. 52.
    "Visit to My Mother's. " Poem (36) Jl 79, p. 53.

LEVIN, Arthur
    "An Astrolabe in Red Letters, Said to Be Chaucer's Own Hand. "
    LittleM (12:1/2) Spr-Sum 78 (79), p. 104.

LEVIN, John
    "alone. " Tele (15) Spr 79, p. 110.

LEVIN, Phillis
    "Clearing Over Clouds. " DenQ (14:3) Aut 79, p. 96.
    "Everything Has Its History. " DenQ (14:2) Aut 79, p. 97.

LEVINE, Ellen
    "Aubade. " SeC (6:1) 78, p. 44.
    "Monkey of the Inkpot. " HolCrit (16:3) Je 79, p. 20.

LEVINE, Miriam
    "Coarse Flower. " Ploughs (5:3) 79, pp. 130-131.
    "For a Poem. " ParisR (75) Spr 79, p. 213.
    "Return. " CarolQ (31:3) Aut 79, p. 71.

LEVINE, Norm
    "Tangling with Confucius. " Tendril (4) Wint 79, p. 37.

LEVINE, Philip
    "Buying Earth. " Poetry (134:6) S 79, pp. 320-321.
    "The First Truth. " Poetry (134:6) S 79, p. 313.
    "The Fox. " NewYorker (55:37) 29 O 79, p. 43.
    "The Great American Poem. " Antaeus (32) Wint 79, pp. 82-86.
    "I Think Table and I Say Chair" (tr. of Gloria Fuertes w. Ada
       Long). MissouriR (3:1) Aut 79, p. 9.
    "I Was Born in Lucerne. " NewYorker (55:37) 29 O 79, p. 42.
    "I Won, You Lost. " MissouriR (3:1) Aut 79, p. 7.
    "Instructions" (tr. of Gloria Fuertes w. Ada Long). MissouriR
       (3:1) Aut 79, p. 11.
    "My Life Like Any Other. " MissouriR (3:1) Aut 79, p. 8.
    "My Name. " Poetry (134:6) S 79, pp. 311-312.
    "On My Own. " NewYorker (55:37) 29 O 79, p. 42.
    "One for the Rose. " NewYorker (54:46) 1 Ja 79, p. 36.
    "The Poem of Flight. " NewYorker (55:37) 29 O 79, p. 43.
    "Salt. " Poetry (134:6) S 79, pp. 314-315.
    "Society of Friends and Protectors" (tr. of Gloria Fuertes w.

Ada Long). MissouriR (3:1) Aut 79, p. 10.
"The Suit. " NewYorker (55:37) 29 O 79, p. 42.
"That Day. " Poetry (134:6) S 79, pp. 316-317.
"The Voice. " Field (20) Spr 79, p. 62.
"To Cipriano, In the Wind. " Poetry (134:6) S 79, pp. 318-319.

LEVIS, Larry
"For Miguel Hernandez in His Sleep and in His Sickness: Spring,
1942, Madrid. " Antaeus (34) Sum 79, p. 60.
"Silk. " Ploughs (5:3) 79, pp. 145-146.
"Some Ashes Drifting Above Piedra, California. " Antaeus (34)
Sum 79, p. 62.
"The Wish to Be Picked Clean. " GeoR (33:3) Aut 79, p. 641.

LEVITIN, Alexis
"An Autumn Morning in a Palace at Sintra" (tr. of Sophia de
Mello Breyner Andresen). Mund (11:1) 79, p. 109.
"The Blind" (tr. of Alexandre O'Neill). PoNow (24) 79, p. 38.
"The Old King" (tr. of Rodrigo de Haro). PoNow (24) 79, p. 18.
"Portrait of an Unknown Princess" (tr. of Sophia de Mello Brey-
ner Andresen). Mund (11:1) 79, p. 107.
"The Yoke" (tr. of Carlos Nejar). PoNow (24) 79, p. 28.

LEVITT, Peter
from A Book of Light: "Part I. " Bachy (14) Spr/Sum 79, pp.
24-28.
"Gazing at the Clear Evening After Snow" (tr. of Chia Tao w.
Joan Iten Sutherland). Bachy (15) Aut 79, p. 28.
"Spending the Night on Wu-Yang Stream" (tr. of Meng Hao-Jan
w. Joan Iten Sutherland). Bachy (15) Aut 79, p. 28.
"To the Tune: Hsiao Ch'ung" (tr. of Li Ch'ing Chao w. Joan
Iten Sutherland). Bachy (15) Aut 79, p. 29.
"To the Tune: Ju Meng Ling" (tr. of Li Ch'ing Chao w. Joan
Iten Sutherland). Bachy (15) Aut 79, p. 29.
"To the Tune: P'u Sa Man" (tr. of Li Ch'ing Chao w. Joan Iten
Sutherland). Bachy (15) Aut 79, p. 29.

LEVITZ, Linda
"Tulip Leaves. " SmPd (45) 79, p. 16.

LEVY, Howard
"clarities. " SlowLR (3) 79, p. 22.
"For My Father: On Looking at a Robert Capa Photograph. "
CutB (12) Spr-Sum 79, p. 66.
"Strange Town. " SlowLR (3) 79, p. 20.

LEVY, Larry
"The Cold Room" (for my mother). PoetC (11:3) 79, p. 20.
"In the Plaza San Martín. " PoetC (11:2) 79, p. 10.
"The Orphan. " PoetC (11:2) 79, p. 9.

LEVY, Martin
"The Old Lot. " Ur (2) 79, p. 61.

LEVY, Max
'Why I Won't Wash Busses. " Wind (35) 79, p. 38.

LEWANDOWSKI, Steve
"Field. " HangL (35) Spr 79, p. 46.
"Fit. " Northeast (3:7) Spr 79, p. 22.
"Letter to Josie from Ithaca. " Wind (32) 79, p. 27.
'Mists. " Wind (32) 79, p. 27.
'Without Words-El Joglars. " HangL (35) Spr 79, p. 45.

LEWIS, Carol
"Jennifer. " Ur (2) 79, p. 64.
'Mahogany: A Sestina. " Bachy (15) Aut 79, p. 94.
"On My Deafness. " Bachy (15) Aut 79, p. 92.
'War Games" (to my son). Ur (2) 79, p. 66.
'Why I Don't Take Pictures of You" (for my son Tony). Bachy
   (15) Aut 79, p. 93.

LEWIS, Harry
"Christopher Columbus" (tr. of Vladimir Mayakovsky w. Vitaly
   Keis). Confr (19) Aut 79-Wint 80, pp. 7-23.
"A Joining in an Early Summer's Day" (for Armand, Peggy and
   Jonathan). Tele (15) Spr 79, p. 93.
from Some Poems for Paul Metcalf on the Nature of a Particular
   Jaguar: "Jaguar's Friend" (for David Frankle). Tele (15)
   Spr 79, p. 92.
from Some Poems for Paul Metcalf on the Nature of a Particular
   Jaguar: "Jaguar's Night. " Tele (15) Spr 79, p. 92.

LEWIS, Janet
'Hummingbird, Los Altos. " NewRep (181:20) 17 N 79, p. 38.
'In a Convalescent Hospital. " NewRep (181:12) 22 S 79, p. 44.

LEWIS, Larry
"Story. " PoNow (21) 79, p. 42.

LEWIS, Nancy Sherman
"At Dusk, Your Child Is Asleep in the Grass. " Ploughs (5:1)
   79, p. 69.
'Home Birth. " Ploughs (5:1) 79, p. 68.
"She Sweeps the Floor. " Bits (9) Ja 79.
'To a Man of Science. " LittleM (12:1/2) Spr-Sum 78(79), p.
   89.
'Weeds. " Ploughs (5:1) 79, p. 70.

LEWIS, Steven
'The Name of the River" (for Clover). MinnR (NS 13) Aut 79,
   p. 25.

LEWISOHN, James
"Cemetery. " GreenfieldR (7:3/4) Spr-Sum 79, p. 71.
'Minimum Security. " GreenfieldR (7:3/4) Spr-Sum 79, p. 72.

LEWTER, John
'The Beautiful Boy. " Wind (32) 79, p. 28.
"Dorothy Rising. " Wind (32) 79, p. 28.

LI Ch'ing-Chao
'To the Tune: Hsiao Ch'ung" (tr. by Joan Iten Sutherland and
   Peter Levitt). Bachy (15) Aut 79, p. 29.
'To the Tune: Ju Meng Ling" (tr. by Joan Iten Sutherland and
   Peter Levitt). Bachy (15) Aut 79, p. 29.
'To the Tune: P'u Sa Man" (tr. by Joan Iten Sutherland and
   Peter Levitt). Bachy (15) Aut 79, p. 29.

LIANG, Cecilia
Twelve Folk Poems (tr. from the Chinese). WebR (4:4) Aut 79,
   p. 5.

LIBBEY, Elizabeth
'The Exile. " MissouriR (2:2/3) Spr 79, p. 17.
"How She Can Sing. " PoNow (25) 79, p. 26.
"Leda in the Suburbs. " MissouriR (2:2/3) Spr 79, p. 16.
"Leda in the Suburbs. " PoNow (25) 79, p. 26.

LIEBERMAN, David
"Locus. " HolCrit (16:4) O 79, p. 13.

LIEBERMAN, Laurence
"God's Measurements. " NewYorker (55:12) 7 My 79, p. 48.
'The Great American Poem. " Antaeus (32) Wint 79, pp. 82-86.
'In Pursuit of the Angel. " Hudson (32:3) Aut 79, pp. 364-368.
"Interview. " NewEngR (2:1) Aut 79, p. 114.
"Nara Park: Twilight Deer Feeding. " NewYorker (55:36) 22 O
   79, p. 42.
'The Sea Caves of Dogashima" (for Charles and Norma Rogers).
   AmerPoR (8:2) Mr-Ap 79, p. 45.
'The Washroom Ballet. " NewYorker (55:39) 12 N 79, p. 52.
"Yoshino: False Dawn of the Cherry Blossom. " NewEngR (2:1)
   Aut 79, p. 115.

LIETZ, Robert
"Bad Child. " KanQ (11:4) Aut 79, p. 18.
from Hansel in the West: "if there are two hiding there are
   two disguises somewhere. " Pequod (3:1) 79, p. 28.
'In Preparation for the Child's Birth" (for Arlene Noelle). Agni
   (10/11) 79, p. 132.
'The Inheritor Looking Back. " Agni (10/11) 79, p. 130.
"A Last Elegy for A. B. " Pequod (3:1) 79, p. 29.
"Monologue from a Boarded House: A Survivor. " CharR (5:1)
   Spr 79, p. 63.
"Noel. " CharR (5:2) Aut 79, p. 75.
'The Photograph Album: Page 16. " QW (9) Spr-Sum 79, p. 93.
"Photograph of an Urban Cemetery. " CharR (5:1) Spr 79, p. 61.
'The Predicament of Being German. " Agni (10/11) 79, p. 128.
"Urban Transplant. " ArkRiv (4:3) 79, p. 31.
'The Woodworker. " Agni (10/11) 79, p. 134.

LIFSHIN, Lyn
"After 8 Years of the Panic Bees Swarming Making Hives. "
    HangL (36) Aut 79, p. 34.
"At Night in the House Next Door. " GreenfieldR (7:3/4) Spr-
    Sum 79, p. 264.
"Being Jewish in a Small Town. " Epoch (28:2) Wint 79, p. 189.
"Blue Sunday. " HolCrit (16:5) D 79, p. 10.
"Boston May 1976. " WormR (74) 79, p. 53.
"The Candidate. " Ur (2) 79, p. 67.
"The Candidate. " CentR (23:1) Wint 79, p. 66.
"Cape Cod, 1970. " CalQ (15) Wint 79, p. 44.
"Cape Cod, 1976. " CalQ (15) Wint 79, p. 45.
"Cape Cod 1976: I'm brown getting. " WormR (74) 79, p. 53.
"Cape Cod 1976: 20 years ago i sat. " WormR (74) 79, p. 53.
"Channuka Madonna. " NewL (45:3) Spr 79, p. 49.
"Dove Tailed Madonna. " NewL (45:3) Spr 79, p. 49.
"The Fear Bee. " CalQ (15) Wint 79, p. 46.
"Friday. " WormR (73) 79, p. 7.
"Going Thru the Park in Middlebury. " HangL (36) Aut 79, p. 36.
"The Great American Poem. " Antaeus (32) Wint 79, pp. 82-86.
"Hanging on Madonna. " HangL (36) Aut 79, p. 38.
"I Hate the Way You. " WormR (73) 79, p. 7.
"High Flying. " WormR (73) 79, p. 5.
"Then I Go Down in the Cellar Dream of Dark Snow. "
    GreenfieldR (7:3/4) Spr-Sum 79, p. 265.
"I Learned How to Fight I'm Thinking as My Mother Tells Me
    What My Sister Got from Her. " WormR (73) 79, p. 7.
"If I Ask You to Say The. " SeC (7:1) 79, p. 8.
"In Spite of the Strangeness. " WindO (35) Aut-Wint 79-80, p.
    12.
"It Was Like. " SeC (7:1) 79, p. 7.
"Jealousy. " NewL (45:3) Spr 79, p. 50.
"Julys in the Rose Light House. " Ploughs (5:1) 79, pp. 73-74.
"Listen to the.... " MidwQ (20:4) Sum 79, p. 367.
"Loss; or: One Thing My Mother and I Have in Common. "
    WormR (74) 79, p. 54.
"Model Home. " Paint (12) Aut 79, p. 8.
"Mother and Daughter Photographs. " Ploughs (5:1) 79, p. 72.
"My Mother and the Bed. " CentR (23:1) Wint 79, p. 65.
"My Mother Was Watching. " NewL (45:3) Spr 79, p. 48.
from Naked Charm: "If I Had a Daughter. " PikeR (1) Sum 79,
    p. 4.
from Naked Charm: "Waking Up in the Cold. " PikeR (1) Sum
    79, p. 5.
"1919. " CalQ (15) Wint 79, p. 43.
"Not Letting You See What You Don't Want To. " Paint (11) Spr
    79, p. 33.
"Oh Yes. " WormR (74) 79, p. 54.
"Old Woman in Venice. " WormR (73) 79, p. 5.
"Poison Ivy Madonna. " WormR (73) 79, p. 5.
"Reading Tour. " WormR (73) 79, p. 6.
from Remember the Ladies: (3). NoAmR (264:2) Sum 79, p.
    37.
from Remember the Ladies: (16). NoAmR (264:2) Sum 79, p.

37.
from Remember the Ladies: (27). NoAmR (264:2) Sum 79, p.
     37.
"Sad Blues Mad Blues and Jealous Blues. " PoNow (21) 79, p.
     18.
"Saturday. " WormR (74) 79, p. 54.
"Soap Opera. " GreenfieldR (7:3/4) Spr-Sum 79, p. 263.
"Sorting the Poems Out. " WindO (34) Spr-Sum 79, p. 8.
"Thursday Night. " WormR (74) 79, p. 53.
"Valentine Love Potion. " HangL (36) Aut 79, p. 37.
"Wait. " Paint (11) Spr 79, p. 32.
"When My Teeth Rot. " HangL (36) Aut 79, p. 39.
"Wild Horses Dying Where the Land Becomes a Desert. " Chelsea
     (38) 79, p. 189.
"Wine Apple Smoke and Windchimes. " Ur (2) 79, p. 68.

LIFSON, Martha Ronk
"Ghost-Dreams from the Sea. " MassR (20:2) Sum 79, p. 335.

LIGGETT, Rosy
"Letter to Hugh O'Neill. " Aspen (7) Spr 79, p. 72.
"The Obsession. " Aspen (7) Spr 79, p. 71.

LIGNELL, Kathleen
"Retreat. " PoNow (25) 79, p. 15.
"Still Life with Honeysuckle. " AntR (37:4) Aut 79, p. 459.

LILLY, Othelia
"How Sweetly Odd. " ChrC (96:27) 29 Ag-5 S 79, p. 812.

LILLY, Paul
"Our Beach Is Across from Vigo, Spain. " CalQ (15) Wint 79,
     p. 71.

LIMA, Robert
"Lorca. " LitR (23:2) Wint 80, p. 255.
"Peripatetic. " LitR (23:2) Wint 80, p. 254.
"Persona. " LitR (23:2) Wint 80, p. 254.

LIN, Tan
"Regret--The Dead Man Speaks to His Wife. " Madem (85:8) Ag
     79, p. 154.

LINDEMAN, Jack
"Directions. " SouthernPR (19:1) Spr 79, p. 35.
"Memory Speaks" (for Billie Boothe). KanQ (11:3) Sum 79, p.
     50.

LINDEN, Gurli
"I really want to make love differently" (tr. by Lennart Bruce).
     Spirit (4:2/3) Spr-Sum 79, p. 53.

LINDNER, Carl
"Christmas Day in School." SouthwR (64:1) Wint 79, p. 67.
"Mismatch." SouthwR (64:3) Sum 79, p. 229.

LINDO, Hugo
"Solo la voz." GRR (10:2) 79, p. 190.

LINDSAY, Fran
"The Fifth Season." Ploughs (5:1) 79, p. 71.
"No One Believes." Wind (35) 79, p. 35.
"Snow White and Rose Red." ColEng (40:8) Ap 79, p. 928.

LINDSAY, Frannie
"God Finds Woman." PraS (53:2) Sum 79, p. 164.
"The Harp of the First Day." PraS (53:2) Sum 79, p. 163.

LINDSKOOG, Kathryn
"Light Showers of Light." ChrC (96:24) 18-25 Jl 79, p. 730.

LINDSTROM, Naomi
"Close by in the night, just a little off" (tr. of Jaime Sabines).
      CharR (5:1) Spr 79, p. 19.
"Here" (tr. of Octavio Paz). PoNow (24) 79, p. 42.
"I Stuck a Head on Your Shoulders" (tr. of Jaime Sabines).
      CharR (5:1) Spr 79, p. 18.
"If Someone Tells You It Isn't True" (tr. of Jaime Sabines).
      CharR (5:1) Spr 79, p. 19.
"No One" (tr. of Nicanor Parra). DenQ (14:2) Sum 79, p. 90.
"The noise from the heater in the next room is like an army"
      (tr. of Jaime Sabines). CharR (5:1) Spr 79, p. 20.
"To turn on the stars, press the blue button" (tr. of Jaime
      Sabines). CharR (5:1) Spr 79, p. 20.
"Touch" (tr. of Octavio Paz). PoNow (24) 79, p. 42.

LINETT, Deena
"Towards Atlantic City." JnlONJP (3:2) 79, p. 7.

LINKHORN, René
"Bois." Os (9) 79, p. 14.

LINSALATA, C. R.
"1978-1938: For Catherine." GRR (10:3) 79, p. 108.

LINTON, Deborah
"Jack Kerouac." SeC (6:1) 78, p. 74.

LIPMAN, Joel
"The Case for the Cheap Broadside." MinnR (NS 13) Aut 79, p.
      8.

LIPSCOMB, James
"Fog at a Drive-in Movie." PoNow (25) 79, p. 15.

LIPSITZ, Lou
"Brooklyn Summer. " NewRep (181:8) 79, p. 38.

LIST, Steve
"Fabulous Fish. " LittleM (12:1/2) Spr-Sum 78 (79), p. 37.

LISTMANN, Thomas
"Joaquin Murieta Died Here Arroyo de Cantua. " Wind (32) 79,
    p. 30.
"Saxophones. " Wind (32) 79, p. 30.

LITTLE, Carl
"An Ascent in February. " Columbia (3) 79, p. 24.
"Water Lily. " Columbia (3) 79, p. 23.

LITTLE, Geraldine C.
"Hollyhocks and Other Mallow: Traveling Music. " JnlONJP (4:1)
    79, p. 5.
"how the lake. " WindO (35) Aut-Wint 79-80.
Separation: Seasons in Space. Sparrow (39) 79. Entire issue.

LIU, Stephen Shu Ning
Eleven Poems. SenR (10:1) Spr 79, pp. 63-76.
"Lines. " SouthernPR (19:1) Spr 79, p. 10.
"My Three Aunts. " LitR (22:3) Spr 79, p. 342.

LIVINGSTON, James
"A City and a Tower" (for Pipard Linda Cole). BelPoJ (30:1)
    Aut 79, p. 30.
"Sevilla. " BelPoJ (30:1) Aut 79, p. 29.

LLOYD, David T.
"On Presbyterianism. " Poem (35) Mr 79, p. 34.

LOCKE, Duane
"A Beginning, with an Interruption, That Will Never Have an
    End. " UTR (6:3/4) 79, p. 13.
"Inscriptions on Tombstones Without Graves in an Unseen Ceme-
    tery. " UTR (6:3/4) 79, p. 18.
"Mankind After the Extinction of Bald Eagles, Coyotes, Panthers,
    Etc. " UTR (6:3/4) 79, p. 16.
"The Shore Revisited. " AAR (29) 79, p. 101.

LOCKLIN, Gerald
"the bride of the hound of the baskervilles. " Ur (2) 79, p. 69.
"The Fish Man. " LitR (22:3) Spr 79, p. 323.
"Fish nor Fowl. " WormR (74) 79, p. 76.
"Gunfighter. " LitR (22:3) Spr 79, p. 324.
"He Probably Would Have Been Easier to Get Along with than
    Bella Abzug. " WormR (73) 79, p. 37.
"High Seriousness. " WormR (74) 79, p. 75.
"A Hole in the Head. " WormR (73) 79, p. 35.
"The Mind Is Selective, and I Guess I Just Have a Better Mind

for Wine than for Churches. " WormR (73) 79, p. 35.
"Minimalism. " WormR (74) 79, p. 77.
"A Peece of the Continent. " WormR (73) 79, p. 36.
"People Are Going Crazy in Bakersfield. " WormR (73) 79, p.
    36.
Some Toad Songs: Twenty seven Poems. WormR (76) 79, p.
    133-148.
"Truer Words Were Never Spoken. " WormR (74) 79, p. 76.
"Why I'm Better off Skipping Meetings." WormR (74) 79, p. 75.
"Yellow Incisor. " WormR (74) 79, p. 77.

LOCKWOOD, Margo
    "The August Field. " Ploughs (5:2) 79, pp. 34-35.
    "A Boy. " Ploughs (5:2) 79, p. 38.
    "Roadmap. " Ploughs (5:2) 79, pp. 36-37.

LOEB, Karen
    "The Man Who Is Stingy. " PoNow (25) 79, p. 16.
    "The Man Who Tells Me That Mushrooms Are Filled with Lun-
        acy. " PoNow (25) 79, p. 16.

LOEWE, Ron
    "Dark Nights. " EngJ (68:5) My 79, p. 30.

LOGAN, John
    "The Great American Poem. " Antaeus (32) Wint 79, pp. 82-86.
    "The Library. " Poetry (134:3) Je 79, pp. 144-145.

LOGAN, William
    "A Different Light. " NewL (46:1) Aut 79, p. 8.
    "En Route. " NewL (46:1) Aut 79, p. 9.
    "Leaving August" (for Marlene Dietrich). QW (8) Wint 79, p.
        34.
    "Maelstrom. " NewYorker (55:25) 6 Ag 79, p. 30.
    "The Mantis. " NewYorker (55:25) 6 Ag 79, p. 30.
    "The Storm That Is Your Sleep. " QW (8) Wint 79, p. 32.
    "Wine. " NewYorker (55:25) 6 Ag 79, p. 30.
    "Winter Garden. " NewYorker (55:25) 6 Ag 79, p. 30.
    "You Asleep: Odysseus at the Mast. " QW (8) Wint 79, p. 33.

LOGUE, Christopher
    "30 Out of 600. " NewYRB (26:15) 11 O 79, p. 42.

LOMBARDY, Anthony
    "For the Waitress Bringing Water. " NewYorker (55:25) 6 Ag 79,
        p. 69.
    "Swans. " NewYorker (55:18) 18 Je 79, p. 40.

LONDON, Jonathan
    "Batches of New Leaves" (for Maureen). Wind (33) 79, p. 34.
    "Nonpareils (or--The Sweet Tooth of Nostalgia)" (for Nana).
        Wind (33) 79, p. 33.
    "The Would-Be Bodhisatva. " Wind (33) 79, p. 33.

LONG, Ada
"I Think Table and I Say Chair" (tr. of Gloria Fuertes w. Philip
    Levine). MissouriR (3:1) Aut 79, p. 9.
"Instructions" (tr. of Gloria Fuertes w. Philip Levine).
    MissouriR (3:1) Aut 79, p. 11.
"Society of Friends and Protectors" (tr. of Gloria Fuertes w.
    Philip Levine). MissouriR (3:1) Aut 79, p. 10.

LONG, Robert
"April Again. " NewYorker (55:10) 23 Ap 79, p. 48.
"Montauk Point. " NewYorker (55:14) 14 My 79, p. 40.
"Snowed In. " HangL (35) Spr 79, p. 47.
from The Sonnets: (34). Aspen (8) Aut 79, p. 61.
from The Sonnets: (35). Aspen (8) Aut 79, p. 61.
from The Sonnets: (36). Aspen (8) Aut 79, p. 62.
"What's So Funny 'Bout Peace, Love and Understanding?" Aspen
    (8) Aut 79, p. 60.

LONGWOLF, Tony
"Eating (with 'Don't Give a Damn') in the Prison Messhall. "
    GreenfieldR (7:3/4) Spr-Sum 79, p. 160.
"Hate. " GreenfieldR (7:3/4) Spr-Sum 79, p. 159.
"I Know I Can Do These Three Things. " GreenfieldR (7:3/4)
    Spr-Sum 79, p. 158.

LOOS, Dorothy Scott
"Ancestral Burden" (tr. of Alfonsina Storni). PoNow (24) 79, p.
    58.
"Funeral Notices" (tr. of Alfonsina Storni). PoNow (24) 79, p.
    58.
"The Hoax" (tr. of Alfonsina Storni). PoNow (24) 79, p. 58.
"Tear" (tr. of Alfonsina Storni). PoNow (24) 79, p. 58.
"The Train" (tr. of Alfonsina Storni). PoNow (24) 79, p. 58.

LOPES, Michael
"The Pure Poet. " PoNow (22) 79, p. 34.

LORCA, Federico García
"Casida of the Boy Wounded by Water" (tr. by Edwin Honig).
    PoNow (24) 79, p. 30.
"Gacela of Love Unforeseen" (tr. by Edwin Honig). PoNow (24)
    79, p. 30.
"The Moon" (tr. by Michal Fineman and Marianne Loyd). EnPas
    (9) 79, p. 31.
"St. Gabriel" (tr. by Michal Fineman and Marianne Loyd).
    EnPas (9) 79, p. 32.
"St. Michael" (tr. by Michal Fineman and Marianne Loyd).
    EnPas (9) 79, p. 34.
"The Spinster at Mass" (tr. by Edwin Honig). PoNow (24) 79,
    p. 30.

LORD, Gigi
"Running Water. " PoNow (25) 79, p. 16.
"Storm Swell. " PoNow (25) 79, p. 16.

LOTT, Clarinda Harriss
"Debate: Mortar and Pestle. " LitR (22:3) Spr 79, p. 347.
"Red Toenails. " LitR (22:3) Spr 79, p. 348.

LOUDON, Michael
"Indiana Looking South" (for J. D. Howell). Wind (34) 79, p. 41.

LOURIE, Dick
"forty. " HangL (36) Aut 79, p. 42.
"September 1978. " HangL (36) Aut 79, p. 44.
"ten answers chosen at random to the question 'why do you write
so many political poems?'" HangL (36) Aut 79, p. 40.

LOURIE, Iven
"Reading Poemas Humanos in Cleveland, Ohio. " Spirit (3:1/2)
Aut-Wint 77-78, p. 62.

LOUTHAN, Robert
"The Divorce. " Kayak (52) D 79, p. 46.
"Elegy for My Father. " Ploughs (5:2) 79, p. 55.
"One Thing About High School. " PoNow (25) 79, p. 16.
"Provisions in a Will. " PartR (46:2) 79, p. 251.
"Seasonal. " Kayak (52) D 79, p. 46.
"The Weather Here" (for Heather McHugh). PartR (46:2) 79, p.
252.
"Your Debut Recital" (for Alan Nagel). NewRep (181:16) 20 O
79, p. 39.

LOVELL, Barbara
Poem. St. AR (5:2) 79, p. 27.
Poem. St. AR (5:2) 79, p. 35.

LOWE, Frederick
"When You Were Young. " BelPoJ (29:4) Sum 79, p. 1.

LOWE, Lisa
"concubine. " Nimrod (23:1) Aut-Wint 79, p. 20.

LOWELL, Robert
"For the Union Dead. " HarvAd (113:1/2) N 79, p. 13.
"Three Poems for Kaddish. " Ploughs (5:2) 79, pp. 70-73.
"Waking Early Sunday Morning. " HarvAd (113:1/2) N 79, p. 34.

LOWENSTEIN, Robert
"Peek-a-Boo. " SmPd (47) 79, p. 16.

LOWERY, Mike
"The Family Dancer. " PoNow (23) 79, p. 39.

LOWRY, Betty
Poem. St. AR (5:2) 79, p. 28.

LOWRY, John
"Digital Readouts. " PoNow (21) 79, p. 38.

from Digital Readouts: (3).   PoNow (22) 79, p. 34.
from Digital Readouts: (4).   PoNow (22) 79, p. 34.
from Digital Readouts: (8).   PoNow (22) 79, p. 34.
from Digital Readouts: (9).   PoNow (22) 79, p. 34.

LOYD, Marianne
"Berieth's Tale. " StoneC (6:2) My 79, p. 18.
'The Cat's Dream. " StoneC (6:2) My 79, p. 19.
'The Moon" (tr. of Federico García Lorca w. Michal Fineman).
    EnPas (9) 79, p. 31.
"Niagara Falls. " NewL (46:1) Aut 79, p. 49.
"St. Gabriel" (tr. of Federico García Lorca w. Michal Fineman).
    EnPas (9) 79, p. 32.
"St. Michael" (tr. of Federico García Lorca w. Michal Fine-
    man). EnPas (9) 79, p. 34.

LUCAS, Marie B.
"Listless Lethargy. " Wind (35) 79, p.39.
"Renewal. " Wind (35) 79, p. 39.

LUCHT, Dave
"Broke Branches Over Head. " WormR (73) 79, p. 3.
'Neighbors. " WormR (73) 79, p. 2.

LUCIANI, Frederick
'The Branch" (tr. of José Emilio Pacheco). DenQ (14:1) Spr 79,
    p. 90.
"Fire" (tr. of José Emilio Pacheco). DenQ (14:1) Spr 79, p. 89.

LUCINA, Sister Mary
'Half a Sandwich. " Spirit (3:1/2) Aut-Wint 77-78, p. 18.
"Kathy. " Wind (33) 79, p. 35.
'Rain. " ChrC (96:19) 23 My 79, p. 582.
'To Frances with Sympathy. " Wind (33) 79, p. 35.

LUDVIGSON, Susan (Bartels)
"Absolution" (for my sister). Epoch (28:2) Wint 79, p. 164.
"Before the Recital. " GreenfieldR (7:3/4) Spr-Sum 79, p. 55.
'The Child's Dream. " GeoR (33:2) Sum 79, p. 344.
"Definition of Time. " SouthernHR (13:3) Sum 79, p. 231.
"Enemy. " NewOR (6:2) 79, p. 175.
"Etta. " SoCaR (11:2) Spr 79, p. 35.
'Homage to the Artist. " SouthernHR (13:3) Sum 79, p. 230.
'Minnie. " SoCaR (11:2) Spr 79, p. 34.
'Motherhood. " GeoR (33:4) Wint 79, p. 850.
"On Learning that Certain Peat Bogs Contain Perfectly Preserved
    Bodies. " Atl (244:1) Jl 79, p. 60.
'Trainer's Temper Bars Him from His Beloved Elephants. "
    SouthernPR (19:2) Aut 79, p. 13.
'Victoria. " SoCaR (11:2) Spr 79, p. 32.
'Wilma. " SoCaR (11:2) Spr 79, p. 33.

LUDWIN, Peter
"Shinin' Times" (for Mark Arnold). Spirit (3:3) Sum 78, p. 43.

LUETCHENS, Jane
'The Farmer. " EngJ (68:5) My 79, p. 34.

LUHRMANN, Tom
"Approaching Spring. " GeoR (33:1) Spr 79, p. 46.
"A Change of Season. " Pequod (3:1) 79, p. 97.
'Moving Horizons. " Pequod (3:1) 79, p. 98.
"Outside. " Pequod (3:1) 79, p. 100.
'Riverside. " PartR (46:2) 79, p. 255.
"Untitled. " Pequod (3:1) 79, p. 96.

LULL, Janis
'The Answer, in Part. " BelPoJ (30:1) Aut 79, p. 8.

LUM, Anna
'The Edge. " WebR (4:3) Spr 79, p. 60.
'The Ritual. " WebR (4:3) Spr 79, p. 61.

LUNDE, David
"Dodo. " PoNow (22) 79, p. 34.
'The Roof Sags. " PoNow (22) 79, p. 34.

LUSK, Daniel
"Understudy. " DacTerr (16) 79, p. 45.

LUTTINGER, Abigail
"After the Decapitation. " SeC (6:1) 78, p. 55.
"Going Loco. " CalQ (15) Wint 79, p. 73.

LUX, Thomas
"At the Moment of Death. " Field (20) Spr 79, p. 54.
"Elegy for Frank Stanford. " Antaeus (33) Spr 79, p. 98.
from Field Talk: "Nautilus. " Field (20) Spr 79, p. 50.
'Inventory. " Field (20) Spr 79, p. 50.
from Ladies From Hell: "Place on a Grave. " Field (20) Spr
    79, p. 49.
'The Milkman and His Son. " Ploughs (5:3) 79, pp. 149-150.
'Tarantulas on the Lifebuoy. " Ploughs (5:3) 79, pp. 147-148.
'Teacher Talking Too Much" (for Kathy Wallach). QW (9) Spr-
    Sum 79, p. 34.

LUZ, Helen
Poem. St. AR (5:2) 79, p. 54.

LYLES, Peggy Willis
'Heart wood. " WindO (35) Aut-Wint 79-80.
'Midnight. " WindO (35) Aut-Wint 79-80.
'No wind. " WindO (34) Spr-Sum 79, p. 4.
'The Shadow Lady Encounters Static Electricity. " Im (5:3) 79,
    p. 10.
'The Shadow Lady Walks in Her Sleep. " Im (5:3) 79, p. 10.
"A thread. " WindO (35) Aut-Wint 79-80.

LYNCH, Charles
"Glutton Without a Head. " Tele (15) Spr 79, p. 68.
"jam fa jamaica. " Ur (2) 79, p. 70.
"Soft Wheel. " Tele (15) Spr 79, p. 69.

LYNCH, Gail
"Virginia Woolf. " Madem (85:9) S 79, p. 152.

LYNCH, Priscilla
"The Time When the Silence of Little Girls. " Chomo (6:1) Sum
    79, p. 15.

LYNSKEY, Edward C.
"Eighteen. " SmPd (45) 79, p. 12.
"Wrought Iron. " HiramPoR (26) Spr-Sum 79, p. 29.

LYON, George Ella
"Discoveries. " PoetC (10:3) 79, p. 34.
"The Edge of Night. " HiramPoR (26) Spr-Sum 79, p. 30.

LYON, W.
"Cave at Lascaux. " SmPd (47) 79, p. 11.
"Knifethrower. " BelPoJ (30:1) Aut 79, p. 9.
"The Politics of Moving. " SmPd (47) 79, p. 12.

LYONS, Richard
"Motel. " DacTerr (16) 79, p. 46.

LYONS, Richard J.
"The Amulet. " Epoch (28:3) Spr-Sum 79, p. 265.
"Balance" (for L. S.). Bits (9) Ja 79.
"The Burning of Emile Murray, 1665. " Epoch (28:3) Spr-Sum
    79, p. 264.
"Chalmette Settlement Fishermen. " PortR (25) 79, p. 61.
"Dream Hiatus. " Epoch (28:3) Spr-Sum 79, p. 266.
"Electrical Storm, 1951. " GreenfieldR (7:3/4) Spr-Sum 79, p.
    34.
"Procrastination. " Wind (35) 79, p. 44.
"A Provincial Woman Thinks of the World. " SouthernPR (19:2)
    Aut 79, p. 46.
"A Revision. " Wind (35) 79, p. 43.
"Testimony of John Travers. " NewOR (6:4) 79, p. 325.
"Titus, son of Rembrandt: 1665. " Salm (46) Aut 79, p. 89.

MacAFEE, Norman
"The Ashes of Gramsci" (tr. of Pier Paolo Pasolino, w. Luciano
    Martinengo). ParisR (76) Aut 79, pp. 34-46.

McAFEE, Tom
"Seattle. " PoNow (23) 79, p. 17.

McALEAVY, David
"Celestation. " Chowder (13) Aut-Wint 79, p. 36.

"Driving; Driven. " Poetry (134:3) Je 79, p. 146.
"Hunger. " DenQ (14:2) Sum 79, p. 87.
"Looking In. " PoNow (23) 79, p. 10.
"On the Fall Line. " PoNow (23) 79, p. 10.
"Tristesse. " PoNow (23) 79, p. 10.
"Watching a thunderstorm from a stony hill. " DenQ (14:2) Sum
    79, p. 86.

McALLISTER, Bruce
"The Accident. " QW (9) Spr-Sum 79, p. 72.

McALLISTER, Catherine
"Love Poem in Five Parts. " Sam (79) 79, p. 70.

McAULEY, Almut
"Latvian Songs" (tr. of Johannes Bobrowski). NewOR (6:3) 79,
    p. 219.
"Legend of Lilya" (tr. of Sarah Kirsch). NewOR (6:3) 79, p.
    222.
"Love Talk" (tr. by Almut McAuley). NewOR (6:3) 79, p. 225.
"Of That Which Is Somehow Living" (tr. of Volker Braun).
    NewOR (6:3) 79, p. 224.
"Refuge Even Behind Refuge Itself" (for Peter Huchel) (tr. of
    Reiner Kunze). NewOR (6:3) 79, p. 227.
"Self Portrait on a Rainy Sunday in the City of Berlin" (tr. of
    Wolf Biermann). NewOR (6:3) 79, p. 220.
"Seven Skins" (tr. of Sarah Kirsch). NewOR (6:3) 79, p. 223.
"The Small Car" (tr. of Reiner Kunze). NewOR (6:3) 79, p. 226.
"Snow" (tr. of Peter Huchel). NewOR (6:3) 79, p. 221.
"Song" (tr. of Thomas Brasch). NewOR (6:3) 79, p. 225.

McAULEY, James J.
"Directions. " PoNow (23) 79, p. 16.
"My Ugly Friend. " PoNow (23) 79, p. 16.

McBAIN, Donald J.
"Life: My Life. " JnlONJP (3:2) 79, p. 34.

McBRIDE, Mekeel
"The Evidence. " Kayak (50) My 79, p. 52.
"The Going Under of the Evening Land" (for Joel Noe). Aspen
    (8) Aut 79, p. 8.
"Jack, Patron Saint of Lawyers. " Chelsea (38) 79, p. 63.
"Jack, Saint of Storytellers. " Chelsea (38) 79, p. 62.
"Light, Desire and the Law. " Agni (10/11) 79, p. 58.
"Living Where You Want to: From the Veterinarian's Journal"
    (for Jack Titolo). Aspen (8) Aut 79, p. 9.
"Private Notice. " Aspen (8) Aut 79, p. 7.
"Real Life Unlike the Cinema. " Kayak (50) My 79, p. 53.
"The Story of a Woman as Indescribable as Dawn. " Chowder
    (12) Spr-Sum 79, p. 18.
"The Unidentified Saints of Misperception. " Iowa (10:3) Sum 79,
    p. 108.
"The Will to Live. " Iowa (10:3) Sum 79, p. 107.

McCABE, Victoria
"On His Low Self-Esteem:". NewL (46:1) Aut 79, p. 97.
"Running Head American Heritage Dictionary. " NewL (46:1) Aut
   79, p. 97.

McCAFFERY, Steve
"3 Fifths Equals" (w. Charles Bernstein and Ron Silliman).
   SunM (8) Aut 79, pp. 162-169.

McCAFFREY, Phillip
"Doubles. " Wind (34) 79, p. 44.

McCALLA, Deidre D.
"Billy de Lye. " Cond (5) 79, p. 152.

McCANN, David
"New Year's Prayer: 1976" (tr. of So Chongju). NewL (46:1)
   Aut 79, p. 68.
"The Old Country. " GreenfieldR (7:3/4) Spr-Sum 79, p. 241.
"Skipping Stones. " GreenfieldR (7:3/4) Spr-Sum 79, p. 240.
"Wedding Night. " Epoch (28:3) Spr-Sum 79, p. 250.

McCANN, Janet
"The Gardener. " WindO (34) Spr-Sum 79, p. 14.

McCARRISTON, Linda
"The cleaving. " Ploughs (5:1) 79, p. 79.
"Desire. " Ploughs (5:1) 79, p. 78.
"Eve. " Ploughs (5:1) 79, p. 78.
"Intent. " Ploughs (5:1) 79, p. 80.
"Moon in Aquarius. " Ploughs (5:1) 79, p. 77.
"Rat. " PoetryNW (20:1) Spr 79, p. 36.

McCARTHY, Eugene J.
"Courage at Sixty. " Harp (258:1544) Ja 79, p. 85.
"Ground Fog and Night. " Harp (258:1544) Ja 79, p. 85.
"Handwriting. " Harp (258:1544) Ja 79, p. 85.
"Mouse. " Harp (258:1544) Ja 79, p. 84.
"No Country for the Young. " Harp (258:1544) Ja 79, p. 84.

McCARTHY, Gerald
"The End of the World, Etc. " Ploughs (5:3) 79, p. 114.

McCARTIN, James T.
"Proleek Dolmen. " JnlONJP (4:1) 79, p. 16.

McCLANAHAN, Tom
"After Her Divorce. " LitR (22:3) Spr 79, p. 363.

McCLANE, Kenneth A.
"Meeting. " Wind (34) 79, p. 28.

McCLATCHY, J. D.
"Late Autumn Walk. " YaleR (68:3) Spr 79, p. 398.
"A Month in the Country. " FourQt (28:4) Sum 79, p. 10.

McCLEERY, Nancy
"Monarchs. " CutB (12) Spr-Sum 79, p. 71.

McCLOSKEY, Mark
"At the Height of Her Career. " PoNow (21) 79, p. 31.
"Blessings in the Village of Dim. " PoetryNW (20:3) Aut 79, pp.
    46-47.
"The Body of Coney Island. " PoNow (21) 79, p. 26.
"The History of Your Ex-Lover. " PoNow (23) 79, p. 42.
"Ideas. " PoNow (21) 79, p. 31.
"The Last Delaware Is a Bellydancer. " Ur (2) 79, p. 77.
"One in a Million. " Ur (2) 79, p. 76.
"Our Sense Is Not in Countries. " PoNow (21) 79, p. 26.

McCLURE, Michael
"Despair in the Morning. " PoNow (23) 79, p. 26.
"On Reading Paterson Aloud. " PoNow (23) 79, p. 26.
"The Rains of February. " PoNow (23) 79, p. 26.
"Watching the Stolen Rose. " PoNow (23) 79, p. 3.

McCLUSKEY, Sally
"Dixon County: Bitter Water. " HiramPoR (26) Spr-Sum 79, p.
    31.
"Incident: Nebraska, 1931. " HiramPoR (26) Spr-Sum 79, p. 32.

McCOLL, Mike
"Her Light. " Bits (9) Ja 79.

McCORD, David
"Afternoon of a Toad. " Poetry (134:5) Ag 79, p. 281.
"Early Warning. " Poetry (134:5) Ag 79, p. 282.
"Look Alive. " Poetry (134:5) Ag 79, p. 284.
"One of Two, Three of Four, One of Eight. " Poetry (134:5) Ag
    79, p. 283.

McCORD, Howard
"The Great American Poem. " Antaeus (32) Wint 79, pp. 82-86.

McCOWN, Clint
"change and immortality. " St. AR (5:3) Aut-Wint 79, p. 92.
"deja vu. " St. AR (5:3) Aut-Wint 79, p. 93.
"hamlet. " St. AR (5:3) Aut-Wint 79, p. 92.
"ou sont les neiges d'antan. " St. AR (5:3) Aut-Wint 79, p. 90.
"rate of exchange. " St. AR (5:3) Aut-Wint 79, p. 91.

McCOY, Maureen
"Hardrock Kid. " Spirit (4:1) Aut-Wint 78-79, p. 47.

McCRAY, Chirlane
"I used to think. " Cond (5) 79, p. 29.

McCULLEY, Marilyn Mann
"Norton County, Kansas. " KanQ (11:3) Sum 79, p. 47.

McCULLOUGH, Ken
"Isle of Palms. " NewL (46:1) Aut 79, p. 12.

MACDIARMID, Hugh
"The Eemis Stane. " MassR (20:1) Spr 79, p. 3.

McDONAGH, Michael
"Celebration. " Mouth (2:3) N 79, p. 1.
"Reminiscence. " Mouth (2:3) N 79, p. 9.

McDONALD, Agnes
"Getaway. " SouthernPR (19:2) Aut 79, p. 62.

McDONALD, Barry
"Backroad Lovesongs. " Wind (32) 79, p. 34.
"Downpour. " GreenfieldR (7:3/4) Spr-Sum 79, p. 197.
"Winter Crossing. " GreenfieldR (7:3/4) Spr-Sum 79, p. 198.

MACDONALD, Cynthia
"Beads in a Red Box. " Field (21) Aut 79, p. 64.

McDONALD, D.
"Double Dip Cone. " Kayak (52) D 79, p. 65.
"Iggledy Piggledy. " Kayak (52) D 79, p. 64.

McDONALD, Daniel
"Women. " SouthernHR (13:3) Sum 79, p. 196.

McDONALD, Jim
"Exode VII Cycle III (North of Hibbing, Minnesota). " PikeF (2)
    Wint 78-79, p. 19.

McDONALD, Walter
"The Barefoot Lady" (for James Alan McPherson). GreenfieldR
    (7:3/4) Spr-Sum 79, p. 219.
"Drying Up. " Ascent (4:2) 79, p. 29.
"Evolution. " CEACritic (41:4) My 79, p. 32.
"The Father. " CEACritic (41:4) My 79, p. 31.
"Finding the Right Channel. " CEACritic (41:4) My 79, p. 32.
"Ice Cream Man. " KanQ (11:3) Sum 79, p. 72.
"The Lifeguard. " Ascent (4:2) 79, p. 28.
"Sangre de Cristo, July 18: The Holy Mountain. " CEACritic
    (41:4) My 79, p. 30.
"When You Feel It Most. " KanQ (11:3) Sum 79, p. 72.
"The White-Haired Trial Judge Deliberates. " CEACritic (41:4)
    My 79, p. 31.

McDONOUGH, Kaye
"Dialogue on the Panning of Zelda Sayre Fitzgerald. " SeC (6:2)
    78, p. 65.
"For Frank. " SeC (6:2) 78, p. 63.
"Janice Blue (Poet-Woman). " SeC (6:2) 78, p. 64.

McDOWELL, Robert
"At the House of the Tin Man. " Hudson (32:1) Spr 79, p. 72.
"Black-Out. " Kayak (52) D 79, p. 32.
"Farming in Palmdale. " Chowder (12) Spr-Sum 79, p. 7.
"Flip Side. " Kayak (52) D 79, p. 35.
"Is There Anyone on the Air? " Kayak (52) D 79, p. 33.
"The Joshua Tree and the Lady. " Kayak (50) My 79, p. 46.
"Not Dead, Just Asleep. " Durak (3) 79, p. 50.
"Their Fate. " Kayak (50) My 79, p. 47.
"A Vacant Lot Addresses the Enemy. " Kayak (52) D 79, p. 34.
"What I Will Do. " Durak (3) 79, p. 49.

MACER-STORY, Eugenia
from Myric of a Simple Journey: "Shell Piece. " Tele (15) Spr
    79, p. 16.
from Myric of a Simple Journey: "The Calling. " Tele (15) Spr
    79, p. 8.
from Myric of a Simple Journey: "The Hole in the Sky. " Tele
    (15) Spr 79, p. 12.

McFALL, Gardner
"After Thanksgiving. " Ploughs (5:1) 79, p. 82.
"Shrimp boat. " Ploughs (5:1) 79, p. 81.

McFARLAND, Ron
"At Wakulla Springs. " SouthernPR (19:2) Aut 79, p. 52.
"Fonk's Goes Under. " QW (6) Spr-Sum 78, p. 118.
"Variations on a Logger Stalked by a Cougar. " FourQt (29:1)
    Aut 79, p. 24.
"Young Leda Feeds the Gulls. " ConcPo (12:1) Spr 79, p. 80.

McFEE, Michael
"Christening. " ChrC (96:42) 19 D 79, p. 1261.
"Easter Monday. " ChrC (96:13) 11 Ap 79, p. 407.
"On the Porch. " SouthernPR (19:1) Spr 79, p. 39.
Poem. St.AR (5:2) 79, p. 35.

McGOUGH, Roger
"The Identification. " WestB (4) 79, p. 70.
"Vegetarians. " WestB (4) 79, p. 71.

McGOWAN, James
"The Scholar's Room Well Lit. " PikeF (2) Wint 78-79, p. 23.

McGRAIL, John
"Eastertide at Detox. " GRR (10:1) 79, p. 45.
"Homage to Thomas Carew. " GRR (10:1) 79, p. 46.

McGRATH, Kristina
"Approaching the Rumor of Your Childhood. " YaleR (68:4) Sum
79, p. 547.
"Black Mountain. " LittleM (11:1/2) Spr-Sum 78 (79), p. 33.
"Futures for a Child and a Man. " Chelsea (38) 79, p. 105.
"Just in Case You Should Come by Again Thinking There's Some-
thing Between Now and Then. " Chelsea (38) 79, p. 108.
"The Removals. " LittleM (12:1/2) Spr-Sum 78 (79), p. 35.

McGRATH, Thomas
"Christmas Poem" (Section from Letter to an Imaginary Friend,
an on-going long poem). Kayak (50) My 79, p. 3.
"The Great American Poem. " Antaeus (32) Wint 79, pp. 82-86.
"John Carey's Second Song. " DacTerr (16) 79, p. 47.

MACHADO, Antonio
"The Clock Struck... " (tr. by Robert Bly). MissouriR (3:1) Aut
79, p. 12.
"It's Possible That... " (tr. by Robert Bly). MissouriR (3:1)
Aut 79, p. 12.

McHALE, Karen B.
"Black Diamond. " CarlMis (17:2/3) Spr 79, p. 132.

McHUGH, Heather
"Anniversary Song. " NewYorker (55:2) 26 F 79, p. 89.
"Breath. " Aspen (7) Spr 79, p. 8.
from D'Après Tout: Eleven poems (tr. of Jean Follain). ParisR
(76) Aut 79, pp. 155-159.
"The Fence. " Aspen (7) Spr 79, p. 10.
"Goods. " Aspen (7) Spr 79, p. 11.
"Message at Sunset for Bishop Berkeley. " Ploughs (5:1) 79, p.
83.
"Missing Person. " Aspen (7) Spr 79, p. 9.
"On Time. " CarlMis (18:1) Wint 79-80, p. 7.
Twelve Poems (tr. of Jean Follain). Pequod (3:2) 79, pp. 92-97.
"Vacation. " Aspen (7) Spr 79, p. 9.
"What Believing Is. " Madem (85:2) F 79, p. 176.
"Woosh. " Aspen (8) Aut 79, p. 11.

McINTOSH, Joan
"Aspects of a Marriage IV In Which, Years After Purchase, We
Have a Dialogue About the Bed. " SmPd (45) 79, p. 30.
"Where Two Trails Meet. " Spirit (3:3) Sum 78, p. 42.

MACK, Rick
"Country Homecoming. " Wind (35) 79, p. 45.
"Time to Go. " Wind (35) 79, p. 44.

MACK, Sister Anna Marie
"after thirty years. " EngJ (68:5) My 79, p. 25.

McKANE, Richard
"Empty Sonnet" (tr. of Leonid Aranzon). Pequod (3:2) 79, p. 91.

"In the Hours of Sleeplessness" (tr. of Leonid Aranzon). Pequod
(3:2) 79, p. 90.

MACKAY, Bruce
"Climbing Rock. " Mouth (2:1) F 79, p. 23.
"Conch. " Mouth (2:2) Je 79, p. 3.
"Pretty Teeth for CSD. " Mouth (2:2) Je 79, p. 9.
"With Assistance from the Phone Company, Arguing Grief. "
Mouth (2:2) Je 79, p. 24.

McKAY, Matthew
"Girl in the Park. " Nimrod (23:1) Aut-Wint 79, p. 40.
"The Man Like Admiral Byrd's Fire" (for Z). PoetC (11:2)
79, p. 12.
"Mine of the Lost Oak. " ChiR (31:2) Aut 79, pp. 40-50.
"Miwok Trail. " Nimrod (23:1) Aut-Wint 79, p. 41.
"Parable of the Perfect Fields. " Nimrod (23:1) Aut-Wint 79, p.
39.
"The Road to Where You Will Live. " Nimrod (23:1) Aut-Wint 79,
p. 43.
"The Speeches So Small. " PoetC (11:2) 79, p. 14.
"Still Life. " Nimrod (23:1) Aut-Wint 79, p. 42.
"Whatever Fortune They Can Stand. " Confr (18) Spr-Sum 79, p.
65.

McKEAN, James
"Elegy for an Old Boxer. " PraS (53:3) Aut 79, p. 262.
"Fat Lady. " PoNow (23) 79, p. 47.

MacKENZIE, Ginny
"Accidentally in Kansas. " CarlMis (17:2/3) Spr 79, p. 184.
"For Robbie Taft, Killed January 17, 1978 at the Age of 14. "
PoNow (25) 79, p. 16.
"From the Poetry Teacher. " Aspen (7) Spr 79, p. 45.
"Ossabow Island, Georgia, April 4th" (for my aunt). Ploughs
(5:3) 79, p. 115.
"Reunion. " CarlMis (17:2/3) Spr 79, p. 183.
"Speaking of Possibility" (for Carol Muske). CarlMis (17:2/3)
Spr 79, p. 182.

McKEOWN, Tom
"Early Morning of Another World. " YaleR (68:3) Spr 79, p. 396.
"The Heat at Noon. " YaleR (68:3) Spr 79, p. 397.
"Impressions. " MinnR (NS 13) Aut 79, p. 24.

MCKERNAN, John
"The Mirrors. " KanQ (11:1/2) Wint-Spr 79, p. 64.

MACKIE, J.
"At the Potter's Wheel" (for Ted). KanQ (11:3) Sum 79, p. 124.

McKIM, Elizabeth
"Betty Gordon's Broad Song. " Ploughs (5:3) 79, pp. 120-121.
"The Long Repetitions. " Ploughs (5:3) 79, p. 119.

McKINNEY, Irene
"Cassandra. " QW (6) Spr-Sum 78, p. 61.
"The Dance. " CimR (49) O 79, p. 17.
"Sunday Morning, 1950. " WestHR (33:4) Aut 79, p. 326.
"The Woman in the Test Pattern. " WestHR (33:4) Aut 79, p.
    298.
"Writing on Leaves. " QW (9) Spr-Sum 79, p. 73.

McKINNEY, Sandy
"Bird Watching. " Tendril (4) Wint 79, p. 38.
"Cityscape. " Aspen (8) Aut 79, p. 36.
"The Looney. " Tendril (4) Wint 79, p. 39.
"The Mute Boy. " Tendril (6) Aut 79, p. 34.

MACKLIN, Elizabeth
"A Married Couple Discovers Irreconcilable Differences. "
    NewYorker (55:8) 9 Ap 79, p. 48.

McLANAHAN, Penny
"The Counterpart. " ArizQ (35:4) Wint 79, p. 340.

McLAUGHLIN, Joe-Anne
"After the Circus My Son Makes Me Promise Not to Say Bear. "
    NewL (46:1) Aut 79, p. 46.
"Another Mother and Child. " NewL (46:1) Aut 79, p. 45.

McLAUGHLIN, Joseph
"Station 15. " Confr (18) Spr-Sum 79, p. 110.

McLAUGHLIN, William
"The Farmer Takes a Life. " SouthwR (64:1) Wint 79, p. 60.

McLELLAND, Chris
"Writing Where the Barn Used to Stand. " AAR (29) 79, p. 90.

McLEOD, J. B. Thornton
Poem. St. AR (5:2) 79, p. 22.

McMAHON, Lynne
"Bargain Harvest. " WestHR (33:4) Aut 79, p. 327.
"Break in Transit, Wedding Bells. " QW (9) Spr-Sum 79, p. 85.
"Deet Sleeter. " WestHR (33:4) Aut 79, p. 328.
"For My Sister. " Paint (11) Spr 79, p. 39.
"Poem Out of You. " QW (7) Aut 78, p. 62.

McMAHON, Michael
"A Drowning in the Merrimack River. " EnPas (8) 79, p. 7.
"Flood. " EnPas (8) 79, p. 10.
"New England Light. " EnPas (8) 79, p. 6.
"The Sad Horses of the Ram. " EnPas (8) 79, p. 5.
"Wearing My Black Suit to the Funeral of a Friend. " StoneC
    (6:2) My 79, p. 28.

McMICHAEL, James
"The Great American Poem. " <u>Antaeus</u> (32) Wint 79, pp. 82-86.
"Three Sections from a Book-Length Poem. " <u>Ploughs</u> (5:2) 79,
pp. 47-54.

McMILLEN, William
"Going to the Mailbox at Midnight, I Confront Bigfoot. " <u>PoNow</u>
(21) 79, p. 36.

McMURRAY, Earl Jr.
"Dance. " <u>PoetC</u> (11:1) 79, p. 11.
"Right of Aubaine. " <u>PoetC</u> (11:1) 79, p. 10.

McNAMARA, Bob
"Domestic Animals. " <u>MassR</u> (20:2) Sum 79, p. 259.
"Naming the Weeds. " <u>SmPd</u> (46) 79, p. 17.
"A Piece of Fruit. " <u>Epoch</u> (28:2) Wint 79, p. 162.

McNAMARA, Eugene
"Eheu. " <u>TexQ</u> (21:3) Aut 78, p. 124.

McNAUGHTON, William F.
"Chao Ch'ü" (tr. of Ko Hung). <u>Chelsea</u> (38) 79, p. 77.

McNEILL, Anthony
"Mountain/3. " <u>PartR</u> (46:4) 79, pp. 589-590.
"Mountain/5. " <u>PartR</u> (46:4) 79, pp. 590-591.
"Mountain/10. " <u>PartR</u> (46:4) 79, pp. 591-592.

McPHERSON, Sandra
"Answers: To Myself in Another Year. " <u>Agni</u> (10/11) 79, p.
149.
"Bitch (1). " <u>Field</u> (20) Spr 79, p. 56.
"Bitch (2). " <u>Field</u> (20) Spr 79, p. 56.
"Blue-Black Image" (for Pam Durban). <u>Field</u> (20) Spr 79, p. 58.
"The Clown" (for Arthur Hamilton Smith). <u>Poetry</u> (133:5) F 79,
pp. 249-250.
"Corresponding. " <u>Poetry</u> (133:5) F 79, pp. 256-257.
"For Johannes Bobrowski. " <u>ChiR</u> (31:1) Sum 79, p. 8.
"Flat Light. " <u>NewYorker</u> (54:51) 5 F 79, p. 120.
"Games. " <u>Field</u> (20) Spr 79, p. 57.
"He, Like Everyone. " <u>Poetry</u> (133:5) F 79, pp. 252-253.
"Loneliness. " <u>Agni</u> (10/11) 79, p. 148.
"Veteran. " <u>Poetry</u> (133:5) F 79, p. 251.
"Writing to a Prisoner. " <u>Poetry</u> (133:5) F 79, pp. 254-255.

McPHERSON, William
"Music Lesson. " <u>SunM</u> (8) Aut 79, p. 105.
"October 6, 1977. " <u>SunM</u> (8) Aut 79, p. 107.

McQUILKIN, Rennie
"March 4. " <u>SmPd</u> (46) 79, p. 32.
"Tobacco Barn. " <u>Poem</u> (36) Jl 79, p. 42.
"Training the Wilderness. " <u>Poem</u> (36) Jl 79, p. 43.

MADDEN, David
"Surfaces. " KanQ (11:1/2) Wint-Spr 79, p. 28.

MADDOX, Everette
"Of Fashion. " Kayak (51) S 79, p. 53.

MADONICK, Michael David
"for robert ardrey. " ChiR (31:1) Sum 79, p. 50.

MAGILL, Arthur
"Grandfather. " SoCaR (11:2) Spr 79, p. 43.

MAGNIFICO, Antonio
"Only Love" (tr. by Mario Frath). Wind (33) 79, p. 48.
"A Summer Morning" (tr. by Mario Frath). Wind (33) 79, p. 48.

MAGORIAN, James
"November Night. " Ur (2) 79, p. 72.
Revenge. Sam (80) 79. Entire issue.
"Summer evening at. " WindO (34) Spr-Sum 79, p. 4.

MAGOWAN, Robin
"Kite for Kate. " Kayak (50) My 79, p. 63.

MAHAPATRA, Jayanta
"Grandfather. " SewanR (87:1) Wint 79, p. 29.
"The Skies of Night. " SewanR (87:1) Wint 79, p. 31.
"Woman in Love. " SewanR (87:1) Wint 79, p. 33.

MAHER, James
"The Hermit of Clinch Mountain. " SlowLR (3) 79, p. 61.

MAHNKE, John
"Horse. " QW (7) Aut 78, p. 109.
"Miss Shock. " QW (7) Aut 78, p. 110.
"Romanticism Square. " QW (9) Spr-Sum 79, p. 37.

MAHON, Derek
"The Poet in Residence. " Ploughs (5:3) 79, pp. 25-28.

MAHON, Robert Lee
"Portraits of Helen. " WebR (4:4) Aut 79, pp. 63-80.

MAHONEY, Lizabeth Fairclough
"The White Pages of Calendars. " UTR (6:3/4) 79, pp. 20-26.

MAHONY, Phillip
"Danny and the Can. " PoNow (25) 79, p. 17.

MAIER, Carol
"Water Color" (tr. of Octavio Armand). NewOR (6:3) 79, p. 197.

MAILMAN, Leo
"Birth Poem: Summer 1977. " WormR (74) 79, p. 50.

MAKUCK, Peter
"After Friends. " CarlMis (18:1) Wint 79-80, p. 163.
"The Alchemist. " SouthernHR (13:1) Wint 79, p. 44.
"Dépaysé (2). " DenQ (14:2) Sum 79, p. 84.
"Lapidary. " CarlMis (18:1) Wint 79-80, p. 162.

MALANGA, Gerard
"The Great American Poem. " Antaeus (32) Wint 79, pp. 82-86.

MALARKEY, Susannah P.
"Above the Wall. " AmerS (48:3) Sum 79, p. 403.
"Two Elm Trees. " AmerS (48:3) Sum 79, p. 308.

MALINOWITZ, Michael
"Clouds. " PartR (46:1) 79, p. 103.

MALLARME, Stephane
"A Faun's Afternoon. " SoDakR (17:1) Spr 79, p. 60.

MALLORY, Norman
"Scroll. " Tendril (6) Aut 79, p. 33.

MALONEY, John Owen
"Portrait D'Une Femme. " PoetryNW (20:3) Aut 79, pp. 15-16.
"Running by Water" (for Anika). PoetryNW (20:2) Aut 79, pp.
   16-17.
"The Serious Dreamers. " PoetryNW (20:3) Aut 79, pp. 14-15.

MALOUF, David
"Snow. " NewYorker (55:6) 26 Mr 79, p. 125.

MALTMAN, Kim
"Crocodiles. " CutB (12) Spr-Sum 79, p. 28.

MAN
"My father is a hubcap. " Ur (2) 79, p. 73.

MANDEL, Charlotte
"Dipping In. " WestB (5) 79, p. 73.
"I'm Lucky. " WestB (5) 79, p. 72.

MANDELSTAM, Osip
"A cold spring in starving Old Crimea" (tr. by Bernard Meares).
   PoNow (24) 79, p. 31.
"Concert at the Station" (tr. by Andrew Glaze). PoNow (24) 79,
   p. 24.
"84. " (tr. by Emery George). Spirit (3:3) Sum 78, p. 30.
"48. Admiralty Building" (tr. by Emery George). Spirit (3:3)
   Sum 78, p. 30.
"Friday" (tr. by Emery George). Spirit (3:3) Sum 78, p. 32.

"Hagia Sophia" (tr. by Bernard Meares). PoNow (24) 79, p. 31.
"I will search in the Romany camp of the darkened street" (tr.
    by Andrew Glaze). PoNow (24) 79, p. 24.
"Leningrad" (tr. by Andrew Glaze). PoNow (23) 79, p. 44.
"Please Take the Joy of It" (tr. by Andrew Glaze). PoNow (24)
    79, p. 24.
"394" (tr. by Jean Valentine and Anne Frydman). AmerPoR
    (8:2) Mr-Ap 79, p. 11.
"Twilight of Freedom" (tr. by Andrew Glaze). PoNow (24) 79,
    p. 24.

MANESS, Sandra
"The Acrophobe. " SouthernHR (13:3) Sum 79, p. 232.
"Requiem. " SouthernHR (13:3) Sum 79, p. 232.

MANFRED, Freya
"Male Poets. " PoNow (23) 79, p. 26.
"There Is Something Worse. " Field (21) Aut 79, p. 62.
"The Too-Young All-Man. " PoNow (23) 79, p. 26.
"Woman at Seven Corners, Minneapolis, Minnesota. " PoNow (23)
    79, p. 26.
"You Can Get Men at the General Store. " PoNow (23) 79, p. 40.

MANGAN, Kathy
"Absence. " GeoR (33:4) Wint 79, p. 783.
"The Fireworks. " FourQt (28:2) Wint 79, p. 33.

MANN, Charlotte
"The Ultimate Axis. " ChrC (96:25) 1-8 Ag 79, p. 750.

MANNER, George
"What I Would Say to You. " PoNow (25) 79, p. 17.

MANUS, Fay Whitman
"Windows. " Paint (12) Aut 79, p. 21.

MARANO, Russell
"Nocturnal Pamperings. " PoNow (25) 79, p. 17.

MARCUS, Mordecai
"Classic Lines. " Im (5:3) 79, p. 8.
"Talisman. " Spirit (3:1/2) Aut-Wint 77-78, p. 47.
"Three Arrows. " Im (5:3) 79, p. 8.

MARCUS, Morton
"Meditations on My Fingerprints. " PoNow (22) 79, p. 35.
"The Moment for Which There Is No Name. " Durak (2) 79, p.
    53.
"Scenes from the Life of the Wandering Jew. " Kayak (50) My
    79, p. 12.
"The Spider" (in memoriam, Anthony Ostroff). PortR (25) 79,
    p. 30.
"Stone Hut. " PoNow (22) 79, p. 35.
"Sub-Division. " Durak (2) 79, p. 52.

MARGOLIS, Gary
"Burning Back the Field. " PoNow (25) 79, p. 17.
"The Visit. " Poetry (134:2) My 79, p. 78.

MARGORIAN, James
"Spelunking. " StoneC (6:2) My 79, p. 26.

MARGULIES, Phillip
"Vanishing Act. " PoNow (21) 79, p. 47.

MARIAH, Paul
"A Folk Tale for Another Guy. " PoNow (21) 79, p. 27.
"Journee. " PoNow (21) 79, p. 27.
"Poem for Cavafy. " PoNow (21) 79, p. 27.

MARIANI, Paul
from Cliometrics: frame 32: "The Historian as Intruder. "
    Agni (10/11) 79, p. 250.
from Cliometrics: frame 83: "History as Procession. " Agni
    (10/11) 79, p. 255.
"The Lost Father. " Agni (10/11) 79, p. 244.
"The Scavengers" (for Barry Moser). Agni (10/11) 79, p. 248.
"Sunday Morning. " Agni (10/11) 79, p. 252.
"Torcello: Last Judgement. " Agni (10/11) 79, p. 246.

MARINO, Michael Paul
"Astoria. " PortR (25) 79, p. 135.

MARION, Jeff Daniel
"Lichen. " CarolQ (31:1) Wint 79, p. 38.
"A Morning in April" (for George Scarbrough). SmF (7/8) Spr-
    Aut 78, p. 35.
"Winter Watch" CarolQ (31:1) Wint 79, p. 37.

MARION, Paul F.
"Blood Alley, Fat City. " Aspect (74/75) Ja-Ag 79, p. 60.

MARKO, Jim
"lift your arm lovely boy. " Mouth (2:2) Je 79, p. 33.
"Untitled: I keep seeing your. " Mouth (2:1) F 79, p. 36.

MARLIS, Stefanie
"Then Passes. " Aspen (7) Spr 79, p. 6.
"Like the Oil of the Aloe Vera. " Aspen (7) Spr 79, p. 7.

MARMORI, Giancarlo
"He Was Always Nursing Some Human Wound of His" (tr. by
    Lawrence R. Smith). PoNow (24) 79, p. 25.

MARQUET, Gabrielle
"Le chou rouge. " GRR (10:3) 79, p. 102.
"Les tulipes. " GRR (10:3) 79, p. 104.

MARRUCCI, Luciano
"The Compass" (tr. by Ruth Feldman and Martin Robbins).
PoNow (24) 79, p. 25.
"Mother" (tr. by Ruth Feldman and Martin Robbins). PoNow
(24) 79, p. 25.
"Night Trees" (tr. by Ruth Feldman and Martin Robbins). PoNow
(24) 79, p. 25.

MARSDEN, Carolyn
"Butterfly. " HangL (35) Spr 79, p. 49.
"Defending Ourselves, Karate at the Women's Center. " HangL
(35) Spr 79, p. 50.
"The Hidden. " Iowa (10:3) Sum 79, p. 102.

MARSH, Richard
"Advice by the Ocean (South Beach, Key West, Florida). " Wind
(32) 79, p. 33.
"Entrances and Exits. " Wind (32) 79, p. 32.

MARSHALL, Teresa
"Warning. " KanQ (11:3) Sum 79, p. 82.

MARSHALL, Quitman
"Smoking. " PoNow (25) 79, p. 18.

MARTEAU, Robert
"Royauté. " Poetry (134:1) Ap 79, p. 34.

MARTENSON, Sue
"Bach. " Northeast (3:7) Spr 79, p. 5.

MARTIN, Connie
"Wood Work. " VirQR (55:4) Aut 79, pp. 644-652.

MARTIN, D. Roger
"No Dreams for Sale. " Sam (79) 79, p. 73.
"Turner's House. " Sam (79) 79, p. 72.

MARTIN, Jim
"Comment on an Older Poet. " SeC (6:1) 78, p. 67.

MARTIN, Joan
notes from: "Update on Feminist Resources. " BlackALF (13:4)
Wint 79, p. 150.
"Untitled: it is Sunday. " BlackALF (13:4) Wint 79, p. 150.
"Untitled: shadows. " BlackALF (13:4) Wint 79, p. 150.

MARTIN, Melvin
"Image. " NewRena (11) 79, p. 43.

MARTINENGO, Luciano
"The Ashes of Gramsci" (tr. of Pier Paolo Pasolino, w. Norman
MacAfee). ParisR (76) Aut 79, pp. 34-46.

MARTINO, Mark C.
"Song Lyric. " Mouth (2:2) Je 79, p. 34.
"What Difference. " Mouth (2:2) Je 79, p. 43.

MARTINSON, David
"Three Seasons Journey to the Same Place. " PoNow (21) 79, p. 43.

MARTONE, Michael
"Bypass. " WindO (35) Aut-Wint 79-80, p. 6.
"Hillman's China. " WindO (35) Aut-Wint 79-80, p. 5.

MARTRESS, Eileen
"Gemini. " JnlONJP (3:2) 79, p. 15.

MARZAN, Julio
"After We Swim. " NewL (46:2) Wint 79-80, p. 74.
"Epitaph. " NewL (46:2) Wint 79-80, p. 73.

MASARIK, Al
"A Cathouse in Cincinnati. " SeC (6:2) 78, p. 77.
"Deathwatch. " SeC (6:2) 78, p. 73.
"Dividing the Spoils. " SeC (6:2) 78, p. 75.
"eight arms with suckers. " Vaga (29) 79, p. 19.
"fossil. " Vaga (29) 79, p. 16.
"Marilyn Monroe. " SeC (6:2) 78, p. 71.
"monarch. " Vaga (29) 79, p. 17.
"Spring Training. " SeC (6:2) 78, p. 78.
"They Think Maybe I'm an Old Ford Rusting in a New Mexico
    Arroyo as They Speed by in Their Airconditioned Amtrak. "
    SeC (6:1) 78, p. 13.
"white pelicans in october. " Vaga (29) 79, p. 18.

MASKALERIS, Thanasis
"The Crows of Hakone. " Kayak (52) D 79, p. 55.
"Sun Moon Lake. " Kayak (52) D 79, p. 55.

MASON, Richard
"Liza. " BlackF (3:1) Aut-Wint 79, p. 43.

MASTERMAN, Gwenn
"Gypsy Symphony. " HangL (35) Spr 79, p. 72.

MASTERS, Carol
"First Shower. " AAR (29) 79, p. 74.

MASTERS, Dexter
"Graffiti for a Particle Accelerator. " GeoR (33:2) Sum 79, p. 297.

MASTERS, Greg
"The Coast Is Clear" (for Rene Ricard) (w. Tom Weigel). Tele
    (15) Spr 79, p. 66.

"Holly in the Heart. " Tele (15) Spr 79, p. 65.
"Muse Call. " Tele (15) Spr 79, p. 64.
"To Fritz Lang" (w. Tom Weigel). Tele (15) Spr 79, p. 67.
"Video Bust" (w. Tom Weigel). Tele (15) Spr 79, p. 66.

MASTERSON, Dan
"An Office with a View. " PoNow (25) 79, p. 26.
"Seed. " PoNow (25) 79, p. 26.
"To My Patients. " PoNow (25) 79, p. 26.

MATHIS, Cleopatra
"The Gift. " VirQR (55:3) Sum 79, p. 515.
"Journey in the Snow Season. " Columbia (3) 79, p. 42.
"Peaches: For My Mother. " PoNow (23) 79, p. 39.
"Riding on Empty. " AmerPoR (8:3) My-Je 79, p. 27.
"Stars in Water. " Ploughs (5:3) 79, p. 156.

MATTE, Robert Jr.
"Gas Masks in the Attic. " Vaga (29) 79, p. 28.
"The Painter. " SeC (6:1) 78, p. 29.
"The Poet. " SeC (6:1) 78, p. 21.
"The Policeman. " SeC (6:1) 78, p. 28.
"Train. " Ur (2) 79, p. 74.

MATTESON, Fredric
"Caretaker. " NowestR (18:1) 79, p. 31.
"Sumner's Birds" (for my brother). NowestR (18:1) 79, p. 29.

MATTHEWS, William
"An Airline Breakfast. " Antaeus (33) Spr 79, p. 96.
"E. P. " PortR (25) 79, p. 60.
"Foul Shots: A Clinic. " QW (7) Aut 78, p. 104.
"The Great American Poem. " Antaeus (32) Wint 79, pp. 82-86.
"A Late Movie. " Durak (2) 79, p. 20.
"Restorations. " Durak (3) 79, p. 42.
"A Roadside Near Ithaca, NY. " QW (7) Aut 78, p. 105.
"A Wedding Invitation. " Aspen (7) Spr 79, p. 28.
"Well, Then, What Is It?" PortR (25) 79, p. 60.

MATTHIAS, John
"Baltic Seas III" (tr. of Tomas Transtromer). GreenfieldR
(7:3/4) Spr-Sum 79, p. 123.
"Broendal" (tr. of Goran Printz-Pahlson). GreenfieldR (7:3/4)
Spr-Sum 79, p. 121.
"Evening Song. " GreenfieldR (7:3/4) Spr-Sum 79, p. 118.
"The Fen Birds' Cry. " GreenfieldR (7:3/4) Spr-Sum 79, p. 119.
"From Dresden" (tr. of Lars Noren). GreenfieldR (7:3/4) Spr-
Sum 79, p. 129.
"The Growing" (tr. of Gosta Friberg). GreenfieldR (7:3/4) Spr-
Sum 79, p. 125.
"I Burn My Lamp in the Meadow" (tr. of Lars Noren).
GreenfieldR (7:3/4) Spr-Sum 79, p. 129.
"In Columbus, Ohio. " Salm (43) Wint 79, p. 44.

"A Letter" (tr. of Sonja Akesson). GreenfieldR (7:3/4) Spr-Sum
   79, p. 130.
"Man Made Monster Surreptitiously Regarding Idyllic Scene in
   Swiss Hermitage, a Copy of Goethe's 'Werther' Resting in
   Its Lap" (tr. of Goran Printz-Pahlson). GreenfieldR (7:3/4)
   Spr-Sum 79, p. 121.
"On the Death of Benjamin Britten. " Salm (43) Wint 79, p. 45.
"Paul Klee" (tr. of Ingemar Leckius). GreenfieldR (7:3/4) Spr-
   Sum 79, p. 120.
"The Sphere of the Roads" (tr. of Lars Noren). GreenfieldR
   (7:3/4) Spr-Sum 79, p. 129.
"U. S. I. S. Lecturer. " Salm (43) Wint 79, p. 43.

MATTISON, Alice
   "The Angel in the Playground. " LittleM (12:1/2) Spr-Sum 78
      (79), p. 85.
   "Husband. " Ploughs (5:2) 79, pp. 24-25.
   "Raspberries in New Hampshire. " Ploughs (5:2) 79, pp. 29-30.
   "Secret Animals. " Ploughs (5:2) 79, pp. 22-23.
   "Three Novembers. " Ploughs (5:2) 79, pp. 26-28.

MAURA, Sister
   "A Short History of the Teaching Profession. " ChrC (96:5) 7-14
      F 79, p. 129.

MAXSON, Gloria
   "Critic. " ChrC (96:29) 19 S 79, p. 876.
   "Handicapped. " ChrC (96:41) 12 D 79, p. 1239.
   "Retiree. " ChrC (96:43) 26 D 79, p. 1282.
   "Pragmatist. " ChrC (96:19) 23 My 79, p. 586.

MAXSON, H. A.
   "The Last Arrowhead" (for John Ower). KanQ (11:3) Sum 79, p.
      46.
   "When It Rains" (for Sara and Bob). KanQ (11:3) Sum 79, p. 47.

MAXSON, Harry
   "Stone Attends Jesus '78. " Poultry (1) 79, p. 11.
   "Stone Counts His Toes. " Poultry (1) 79, p. 11.
   "Stone Eats Some Barbed Wire. " Poultry (1) 79, p. 11.
   from Walker in the Storm: Ten Poems. QW (8) Wint 79, pp.
      58-62.

MAXWELL, Margo
   "Hot Weather Number: July 1, 1918. " ChiR (30:4) Spr 79, p.
      78.

MAY, Alyson
   "mournful november. " EngJ (68:5) My 79, p. 35.

MAYAKOVSKY, Vladimir
   "Christopher Columbus" (tr. by Harry Lewis and Vitalij Keis).
      Confr (19) Aut 79-Wint 80, pp. 7-23.

MAYHALL, Jane
    "Hermits Are Selfish. " SouthernHR (13:3) Sum 79, p. 221.
    "Poems of Rebellion. " SouthernHR (13:3) Sum 79, p. 222.
    "Surfaces. " NewYorker (54:50) 29 Ja 79, p. 34.
    "Twilight on the Long Island Expressway. " SouthernHR (13:3)
        Sum 79, p. 221.

MAYROCKER, Friederike
    "Plot of a Belief" (tr. by Derk Wynand).   MalR (52) O 79, p.
        138.

MAZUR, Gail
    "The Adirondacks. " PoNow (25) 79, p. 27.
    "Anomie. " NewRep (180:13) 31 Mr 79, p. 36.
    "Seeing Bats in Cambridge. " PoNow (25) 79, p. 27.
    "The Social Life of the Baboon. " Ploughs (5:2) 79, pp. 99-100.
    "Hurricane Watch. " Ploughs (5:2) 79, pp. 101-102.

MAZZARO, Jerome
    "Fall Colors. " Hudson (32:4) Wint 79-80, p. 535.
    "Laguna Beach: The Settlement. " Hudson (32:4) Wint 79-80, p.
        536.
    "Legends/OAHU. " NewL (46:2) Wint 79-80, p. 57.
    "Pacific Beach. " Hudson (32:4) Wint 79-80, p. 535.
    "The Shrine. " NewL (46:2) Wint 79-80, p. 56.

MAZZOCCO, Robert
    "All Night. " NewYorker (54:48) 15 Ja 79, p. 32.
    "Ceremony. " NewYRB (26:7) 3 My 79, p. 6.
    "Dreams. " VirQR (55:4) Aut 79, pp. 708-712.
    "Papeete. " NewYorker (55:17) 11 Je 79, p. 42.
    "Years. " NewYorker (55:6) 26 Mr 79, p. 34.

MBEMBE (Milton Smith)
    "Did They Help Me at the State Hospital for the Criminally In-
        sane?" NewL (46:1) Aut 79, p. 40.

MEADE, Mary Ann
    "In Distrust of Hunting. " PoetC (11:3) 79, p. 6.
    "Spring in the Ukraine, 1943. " PoetC (11:3) 79, p. 5.

MEADS, Kathy
    "Seascape. " StoneC (6:1) F 79, p. 8.

MEARES, Bernard
    "A cold spring in starving Old Crimea" (tr. of Osip Mandelstam).
        PoNow (24) 79, p. 31.
    "Hagia Sophia" (tr. of Osip Mandelstam).   PoNow (24) 79, p. 31.

MEARS, Charlotte
    "Pentimento. " HolCrit (16:4) O 79, p. 14.

MEATS, Stephen
    "Common Loon. " UTR (6:3/4) 79, p. 30.

"Fossils. " UTR (6:3/4) 79, p. 28.
"In the Space Between. " UTR (6:3/4) 79, p. 31.
"(In Dark Places). " UTR (6:3/4) 79, p. 32.
"Mother. " UTR (6:3/4) 79, p. 29.
"Paths. " UTR (6:3/4) 79, p. 33.
"A Time When the World Was All One Color" (for my father).
    UTR (6:3/4) 79, p. 27.

MEDINA, Pablo
    "In the Old Times. " Spirit (4:1) Aut-Wint 78-79, p. 16.

MEEK, Jay
    "At the Relocation of the Aliens. " CimR (47) Ap 79, p. 58.
    "The Hours Before Leaving. " VirQR (55:3) Sum 79, p. 505.

MEEKER, Steven
    "Veterans. " NewYorker (54:48) 15 Ja 79, p. 93.

MEEKS, Dodie
    "There Goes a Girl Walking. " WindO (35) Aut-Wint 79-80, p.
    10.

MEIER, Sandra D.
    "End of a Season. " Wind (34) 79, p. 42.

MEINERS, R. K.
    "Going Dark. " Wind (35) 79, p. 40.
    "In the Snow. " CentR (23:3) Sum 79, p. 287.
    "Marginal Music. " CentR (23:3) Sum 79, p. 288.

MEIRELLES, Cecilia
    "Away From You" (tr. by Harriet Zinnes). PoNow (24) 79, p.
    25.

MEISSNER, William
    "Clown With a Handful of Confetti. " PoetryNW (20:3) Aut 79, pp.
    44-45.
    "The Contortionist. " NewOR (6:2) 79, p. 154.
    "The Drowner. " SouthernPR (19:2) Aut 79, p. 53.
    "The Fisherman's Last Cast. " KanQ (11:1/2) Wint-Spr 79, p.
    164.
    "The Leap of the Horse. " Chelsea (38) 79, p. 187.
    "Seven A. M. Snowlot. " KanQ (11:1/2) Wint-Spr 79, p. 165.
    "The UFO in Iowa. " PoNow (23) 79, p. 41.

MELENDEZ, Sir Jesus Papoleto
    "Ballerina's War. " GreenfieldR (7:3/4) Spr-Sum 79, p. 19.
    "Guatiao. " GreenfieldR (7:3/4) Spr-Sum 79, p. 17.
    "Night Walkers. " GreenfieldR (7:3/4) Spr-Sum 79, p. 20.
    "Open Poetry Reading. " GreenfieldR (7:3/4) Spr-Sum 79, p. 18.

MELLO, Bruce
    "Like the Last Time. " StoneC (6:3) O 79, p. 7.

MELLOTT, Leland
"The Climber. " SmPd (46) 79, p. 11.

MELNYCZUK, Askold
"Descartes: Final Notes" (for Stuart and Mercedes). Chelsea
(38) 79, p. 64.
"The Grasshopper. " Chelsea (38) 79, p. 206.

MELTON, Keith
"The RH Babies. " KanQ (11:3) Sum 79, p. 112.

MELVIN, Gregg
"Sitting on a Kansas Rocker. " PoNow (25) 79, p. 18.

MEMMOTT, David R.
"Catching Nightcrawlers. " QW (9) Spr-Sum 79, p. 55.

MENAN, Manuel
"After Such Pleasures" (tr. of Julio Cortázar w. Calvin Harlan
and Beatriz Varela). NewOR (6:2) 79, p. 103.
"Commission" (tr. of Julio Cortázar w. Calvin Harlan and Beatriz
Varela). NewOR (6:2) 79, p. 105.
"Gains and Losses" (tr. of Julio Cortázar w. Calvin Harlan and
Beatriz Varela). NewOR (6:2) 79, p. 104.
"Happy New Year" (tr. of Julio Cortázar w. Calvin Harlan and
Beatriz Varela). NewOR (6:2) 79, p. 104.
"Restitution" (tr. of Julio Cortázar w. Calvin Harlan and Beatriz
Varela). NewOR (6:2) 79, p. 102.

MENASHE, Samuel
"Norway. " Confr (19) Aut 79-Wint 80, p. 53.

MENDOZA, Maryann
"On Bringing Andrew Marvell Outside. " FourQt (29:1) Aut 79,
p. 2.

MENEBROKER, Ann
"8:15 P. M. " PoNow (23) 79, p. 41.

MENG Hao-Jan
"Spending the Night on Wu-Yang Stream" (tr. by Joan Iten Suther-
land and Peter Levitt). Bachy (15) Aut 79, p. 28.

MENKITI, Ifeanyi
"A Poem for Winnipeg. " Ploughs (5:3) 79, p. 116.

MERCER, R. Scott
"Sea Dog. " EngJ (68:5) My 79, p. 39.

MERCER, Rose
"Dark Feature. " SouthernPR (19:2) Aut 79, p. 17.
"Walking for the Mail. " SouthernPR (19:2) Aut 79, p. 18.

MEREDITH, William
"The Great American Poem. " Antaeus (32) Wint 79, pp. 82-86.

MERRILL, James
"Gabriel's Second Lesson. " AmerPoR (8:5) S-O 79, p. 7.
"The Great American Poem. " Antaeus (32) Wint 79, pp. 82-86.
"The House in Athens. " NewRep (180:2) 13 Ja 79, pp. 32-33.
"Michael's Fete. " Ploughs (5:2) 79, pp. 59-67.
"Peter's Tattoos. " NewYorker (55:44) 17 D 79, p. 44.
"Samos. " NewYorker (55:33) 1 O 79, p. 36.
"A Sample Seance: The Excursion to Ephesus. " NewYRB (26:7)
    3 My 79, p. 13.

MERRILL, Lee
"Indian Paint Brushes. " PoNow (23) 79, p. 43.

MERRILL, Lynn
"Steady Rain. " SouthernPR (19:1) Spr 79, p. 15.

MERWIN, W. S.
"Apparitions. " AmerPoR (8:4) Jl-Ag 79, p. 3.
"Direction. " Atl (244:2) Ag 79, p. 83.
"Nothing Began as It Is. " PoNow (22) 79, p. 25.
"The Oars. " NewYorker (55:28) 27 Ag 79, p. 38.
"Shaving Without a Mirror. " NewYorker (55:13) 14 My 79, p. 38.
"Sheridan. " AmerPoR (8:4) Jl-Ag 79, p. 4.
"Sunset Water. " NewYorker (55:28) 27 Ag 79, p. 38.
"To Dana for Her Birthday. " AmerPoR (8:4) Jl-Ag 79, p. 3.
"A Tree. " PoNow (22) 79, p. 25.

MESCH, Beverly
"I Wrote My Sister.... " PoNow (25) 79, p. 18.

MESZAROS, Robert
"Spring. " EnPas (8) 79, p. 39.

METHENY, Gary
"Eyeglasses. " Wind (33) 79, p. 37.
"In a Pet Shop. " SmPd (47) 79, p. 5.

METRAS, Gary
"The Fog Follows Me. " EnPas (9) 79, p. 26.
from The Ruins of Dreams: (4). StoneC (6:3) O 79, p. 18.

METZ, Jerred
"The Amored Turnips. " Pig (6) 79, p. 72.
"A Flock of Cranes. " Pig (6) 79, p. 72.
"Honey. " LittleM (12:1/2) Spr-Sum 78 (79), p. 106.
"The Raven Fish. " Pig (6) 79, p. 72.

METZ, Roberta
"A-Frame. " KanQ (11:4) Aut 79, p. 47.
"Cat 22. " Chelsea (38) 79, p. 193.

"Dancer. " Ur (2) 79, p. 78.
"Demons. " KanQ (11:4) Aut 79, p. 47.
"Kaddish. " Ur (2) 79, p. 80.
"Lemon Boy. " PikeR (1) Sum 79, p. 38.
"Middle Ages. " Confr (18) Spr-Sum 79, p. 85.
"Mother's Day. " ColEng (40:8) Ap 79, p. 928.
"There Is a Season. " PikeR (1) Sum 79, p. 39.
"Widow. " PikeR (1) Sum 79, pp. 40-41.
"Zeyde. " PikeF (2) Wint 78-79, p. 22.

METZGER, Deena
"Erato-7-The Elements Are Those Which Open" (for Bruce).
    Bachy (14) Spr-Sum 79, p. 31.
"Erato-3-Even the Still Air Needs Something to Carry. " Bachy
    (14) Spr-Sum 79, p. 29.
"Erato-6-She Said We'd Never Fall in Love Again. " Bachy (14)
    Spr-Sum 79, p. 30.
from Poems for Xochmilco: "Mating. " Bachy (14) Spr-Sum 79,
    p. 33.

MEYERS, Bert
Twelve Poems. Bachy (15) Aut 79, pp. 8-12.

MEZEY, Katalin
"A Photograph" (tr. by Nicholas Kolumban). TexQ (21:4) Wint
    78, p. 30.
"Waiting for the Bus" (tr. by Nicholas Kolumban). TexQ (21:4)
    Wint 78, p. 32.

MEZEY, Robert
"First Prayer" (tr. of José Hierro). Durak (2) 79, p. 50.
"The Great American Poem. " Antaeus (32) Wint 79, pp. 82-86.
"Trying to Begin. " MissouriR (3:1) Aut 79, p. 30.

MICHAELS, Michaelann
"Midwest Rooming House in the Bicentennial Year. " Sam (79)
    79, p. 59.

MICHAUX, Henri
"Double Head" (tr. by Michelle Benoit and Tom Whalen).
    Chelsea (38) 79, p. 27.
"He Writes" (tr. by Michelle Benoit and Tom Whalen). NewOR
    (6:2) 79, p. 151.
"The Old Vulture" (tr. by Michelle Benoit and Tom Whalen).
    Chelsea (38) 79, p. 27.

MICHELINE, Jack
"Ballad of Benny Roads Number 65943. " SeC (6:2) 78, p. 46.
"Jenny Lee. " SeC (6:2) 78, p. 50.
"The Last of the Bohemians. " SeC (6:2) 78, p. 43.
"Zero Is Nothing. " SeC (6:2) 78, p. 52.

MICHELSON, Richard
from A Birthday Card from My Father: (II). PikeR (1) Sum 79,
   p. 6.

MICKENS, Geneva
'I Need You. " BlackF (3:1) Aut-Wint 79, p. 45.

MIDDLETON, Bill
"Cops and Robbers. " KanQ (11:1/2) Wint-Spr 79, p. 144.

MIELE, Frank
"Your. " PoNow (25) 79, p. 18.

MIKLITSCH, Robert
'The Beginning. " SouthernPR (19:1) Spr 79, p. 63.
"Dreaming in a World of Words. " KanQ (11:3) Sum 79, p. 76.

MILBURY-STEEN, John
'Have Already Eaten. " Shen (30:1) Aut 78, p. 70.

MILES, Josephine
"Doll. " NewEngR (2:1) Aut 79, p. 19.
"Easter. " Ascent (4:3) 79, p. 28.
'The Great American Poem. " Antaeus (32) Wint 79, pp. 82-86.
'Trade Center. " NewEngR (2:1) Aut 79, p. 20.

MILES, Sara
"Arithmetic. " LittleM (12:1/2) Spr-Sum 78 (79), p. 49.
"Letter Without Heart. " LittleM (12:1/2) Spr-Sum 78 (79), p.
   50.
"Postcard from California. " LittleM (12:1/2) Spr-Sum 78 (79),
   p. 48.
'They Had Words/There Were Words Between Them" (w. Doug-
   las Kenny). LittleM (12:1/2) Spr-Sum 78 (79), p. 50.
'We Meet in Veracruz" (w. Douglas Kenny). LittleM (12:1/2)
   Spr-Sum 78 (79), p. 51.

MILLARD, Bob
"Bury Our Faces. " KanQ (11:3) Sum 79, p. 12.
"Gestalt and Pepper. " KanQ (11:3) Sum 79, p. 12.

MILLER, A. McA.
"Or Would You Kiss Me Like. " Ascent (5:1) 79, p. 15.

MILLER, Brown
'Mother-in-Law Came. " Spirit (3:1/2) Aut-Wint 77-78, p. 54.

MILLER, Chuck
"As if a Chorus of Voices. " Spirit (4:1) Aut-Wint 78-79, p. 6.
"Smoking Alone. " Spirit (4:1) Aut-Wint 78-79, p. 7.
"snow caked black. " Spirit (4:2/3) Spr-Sum 79, p. 8.
"winter. " Spirit (4:2/3) Spr-Sum 79, p. 9.

MILLER, E. Ethelbert
  "Bajan" (for Marie). Obs (4:3) Wint 78, p. 78.
  "The Next Letter You Get Will Be Lonely" (for Anwar Sadat).
      Obs (4:3) Wint 78, pp. 80-83.
  "Silk. " Obs (4:3) Wint 78, pp. 79-80.
  "Solidarity" (for Roberto Vargas). Obs (4:3) Wint 78, p. 79.

MILLER, E. G.
  "Only the Voice" (tr. of Hugo Lindo). GRR (10:2) 79, p. 191.

MILLER, Edmund
  "Beach Boy. " Mouth (2:1) F 79, p. 42.

MILLER, Errol
  "Constellation. " WestB (4) 79, p. 64.
  "The Forever Walk. " WestB (4) 79, p. 63.
  "The Tough Ones. " HolCrit (16:3) Je 79, p. 15.

MILLER, Eugene
  "Ad Hoc Poem. " Tele (15) Spr 79, p. 77.
  "Drawn Curtains. " Tele (15) Spr 79, p. 76.

MILLER, Hollace
  "Prairie Road. " SoDakR (17:2) Sum 79, p. 67.

MILLER, J. L.
  "A Rubens Nude Descending the Staircase. " BallSUF (20:4) Aut
      79, p. 60.

MILLER, Jane
  "Blue Nude. " MissR (24) Aut 79, p. 70.
  "Circuitous Routes. " MissR (24) Aut 79, p. 67.
  "A Dream of Broken Glass. " Ploughs (5:1) 79, p. 85.
  "Eavesdropping at the Swim Club, 1934. " Ploughs (5:1) 79, p.
      84.
  "Glimpse of a Recluse, South of France. " MissR (24) Aut 79,
      p. 68.
  "The Heart Climbs Devilishly Back into the Body; or, Field of
      Red Thistles. " Columbia (3) 79, p. 54.
  "I Saw the Sun Rise in the West Today, ". MissR (24) Aut 79,
      p. 66.
  "Many Junipers, Heartbeats. " MissR (24) Aut 79, p. 69.
  "The Passenger. " MissR (24) Aut 79, p. 63.
  "Scene. " Ploughs (5:1) 79, p. 87.
  "View at the Window" (for Jeanne Hebuterne). MissR (24) Aut
      79, p. 65.
  "A Winter of Love Letters and a Morning Prayer. " Agni (10/11)
      79, pp. 211-221.
  "Without a Name for This. " Ploughs (5:1) 79, p. 86.

MILLER, Jim Wayne
  Eleven Poems. GRR (10:3) 79, pp. 5-21.

MILLER, John N.
"Unburied. " SmPd (45) 79, p. 13.

MILLER, Joren
"Norm's. " Wind (33) 79, p. 38.

MILLER, Kathy
"Some Ancient Myths. " WindO (34) Spr-Sum 79, p. 17.

MILLER, Laura D.
"Virgin Lost, Virgin Found. " NewOR (6:3) 79, p. 200.

MILLER, Leslie Adrienne
"The Boyfriend. " OP (28) Aut 79, p. 34.
"Circle. " OP (28) Aut 79, p. 35.
"Coyote Hunt. " Chelsea (38) 79, p. 216.
"Intersections. " OP (28) Aut 79, pp. 36-37.
"Thief. " OP (28) Aut 79, p. 33.

MILLER, Mark Crispin
"Before It Gets Late. " SouthernR (15:1) Wint 79, p. 122.
"'Tis of Thee. " SouthernR (15:1) Wint 79, p. 123.

MILLER, Michael
"The Bear. " Confr (19) Aut 79-Wint 80, p. 92.
"The Young Soldier. " KanQ (11:1/2) Wint-Spr 79, p. 200.

MILLER, Philip
"Kansas City Christmas Carol. " KanQ (11:3) Sum 79, p. 91.

MILLER, Rob Hollis
"Daydreams" (tr. of Hans Verhagen). Durak (3) 79, p. 18.

MILLER, Stephen Paul
from Living with You Is a Community, March 1977, May 1977:
    "A Springtime Presentation. " Tele (15) Spr 79, p. 143.
from Living with You Is a Community, March 1977, May 1977:
    "Careen. " Tele (15) Spr 79, p. 144.
from Living with You Is a Community, March 1977, May 1977:
    "Jackson. " Tele (15) Spr 79, p. 143.
from Living with You Is a Community, March 1977, May 1977:
    "Nuts. " Tele (15) Spr 79, p. 145.

MILLER, Vassar
"Aborted. " PoNow (21) 79, p. 2.
"Against Daylight Savings Time. " PoNow (21) 79, p. 2.
"Aubade for Rose Grace. " Paint (11) Spr 79, p. 50.
"The Book of Common Prayer. " ChrC (96:4) 31 Ja 79, p. 99.
"Christmas Meditation. " KanQ (11:1/2) Wint-Spr 79, p. 29.
"A Constant Greenness. " SewanR (87:2) Spr 79, p. 226.
"The Dead of Night. " PoNow (21) 79, p. 2.
"Love Song for a Sunday Morning. " PoNow (21) 79, p. 2.
"One Morning. " KanQ (11:1/2) Wint-Spr 79, p. 29.

"Perplexed. " PoNow (23) 79, p. 36.
"Surrender. " SewanR (87:2) Spr 79, p. 225.
"To a Role Model: Dorothy L. Richardson. " Paint (11) Spr 79,
        p. 49.
"Welcome Mat. " KanQ (11:1/2) Wint-Spr 79, p. 30.

MILLER, Wayne
        "For General Arana Osorio of Guatemala. " SeC (6:2) 78, p. 114.
        "For Josephina. " SeC (6:2) 78, p. 113.
        "For Monique Graham. " SeC (6:2) 78, p. 112.
        "Last Cigarette" (for Alejandro Webelman). SeC (6:2) 78, p. 115.
        "Poem for Elizabeth. " SeC (6:2) 78, p. 111.
        "Tree Perjury. " SeC (6:2) 78, p. 116.

MILLETT, John
        "Totem. " StoneC (6:2) My 79, p. 20.

MILLIGAN, Estelle
        "Car Enters Canal, Driver Missing. " PoNow (25) 79, p. 18.
        "Fat Lady. " PoetC (11:2) 79, p. 30.

MILLIGAN, Thomas
        "Seeking the Owls. " WestB (5) 79, p. 29.

MILLIKEN, Patrick
        "Althouse Ridge. " Agni (10/11) 79, p. 54.

MILLIN, Julie
        "At the Drugstore. " EngJ (68:5) My 79, p. 37.

MILLIS, Christopher
        "Hope Street, Stamford. " Tendril (4) Wint 79, p. 40.
        "Migration (Marshfield, Massachusetts). " Tendril (4) Wint 79, p.
        41.
        "Still Life. " Tendril (5) Sum 79, p. 37.

MILLNER, Gloria A.
        "Black Man. " NegroHB (42:3) Jl-Ag-S 79, p. 79.

MILLS, Ralph J. Jr.
        "March Light. " NewL (46:2) Wint 79-80, p. 70.
        "Midsummer Rain. " NewL (46:2) Wint 79-80, p. 72.
        "On a Birthday. " NewL (46:2) Wint 79-80, p. 71.

MILLS, William
        "Nursery Rhyme. " QW (8) Wint 79, p. 10.
        "On Being Asked to Write More Humorous Poetry" (for Les
                Phillabaum). QW (8) Wint 79, p. 8.
        "A Philosophical Evening in Louisiana" (for Albert and Karola
                Waterson). QW (8) Wint 79, p. 11.
        "Since the Blond Lady Decided to Leave Me to Look for Her In-
                dividuality. " QW (8) Wint 79, p. 9.
        "Wedington Woods. " QW (8) Wint 79, p. 5.

MILNER, Darlene
"Rhythms of a Dream-Song. " Nimrod (23:1) Aut-Wint 79, p. 21.

MILOSZ, Czeslaw
"Readings" (tr. by Czeslaw Milosz and Lillian Vallee). PoNow
(24) 79, p. 31.
"Study of Loneliness" (tr. by Czeslaw Milosz and Lillian Vallee).
PoNow (24) 79, p. 31.

MINAR, Scott A.
"That Same Whirling Motion of the Thrower. " FourQt (28:3)
Spr 79, p. 2.

MINARD, Michael D.
"A Musician Returning from a Cafe Audition. " KanQ (11:1/2)
Wint-Spr 79, p. 80.
"New Year's Day: Oystering. " KanQ (11:1/2) Wint-Spr 79, p.
80.

MINARIK, John Paul
"A Letter from Home. " NewOR (6:3) 79, p. 258.

MINASSIAN, Michael
"The Last Time. " Wind (34) 79, p. 64.
"Running. " Wind (34) 79, p. 43.

MINCZESKI, John
"How to Be a Butterfly" (w. Ms. Martinson's 2nd graders).
CarlMis (17:2/3) Spr 79, p. 150.
"Old Ego Song. " KanQ (11:1/2) Wint-Spr 79, p. 102.
"Why Does the Moon Follow Me Every Time I Go Someplace"
(w. Ms. Heuer's 2nd graders at Maxfield Elementary School).
CarlMis (17:2/3) Spr 79, p. 150.

MINER, Michael
"The Dead Wife. " PikeF (2) Wint 78-79, p. 7.

MINER, Virginia Scott
"Autobiography. " NewL (45:3) Spr 79, p. 35.
"The Blessing. " KanQ (11:1/2) Wint-Spr 79, p. 116.
"Nichols Fountain (Kansas City). " NewL (45:3) Spr 79, p. 34.
"Portrait of Two Poets. " KanQ (11:1/2) Wint-Spr 79, p. 116.

MINOCK, Dan
"Attempted Consolation for Animals. " PoetryNW (20:3) Aut 79,
pp. 19-20.
"Potato. " PoetryNW (20:3) Aut 79, pp. 20-21.

MINOR, John Starr
"Fishing in Night. " Tendril (5) Sum 79, p. 39.
"Strata. " Tele (5) Sum 79, p. 38.

MINTON, Helena
"Etiquette in a Panic." WestB (4) 79, p. 66.
"Lessons." QW (9) Spr-Sum 79, p. 50.

MINTY, Judith
"Letters to My Daughters: 11." Paint (11) Spr 79, p. 51.
"Letters to My Daughters: 12." Paint (11) Spr 79, p. 52.
"Letters to My Daughters: 13." Paint (11) Spr 79, p. 53.
"Letters to My Daughters: 14." Paint (11) Spr 79, p. 54.
from Yellow Dog Journal: "Fall." Poetry (135:1) O 79, pp. 9-
13.

MIRABELLI, Eugene
"Hot." GreenfieldR (7:3/4) Spr-Sum 79, p. 194.

MIRACULA, Nancy Lea
"Peddler." StoneC (6:2) My 79, p. 17.

MIRANDA, Gary
"Deception Pass." PoetryNW (20:2) Sum 79, p. 25.
"The News from Moons." Atl (244:1) Jl 79, p. 73.
"Somewhere, Anywhere, Somewhere." PoetryNW (20:2) Sum 79,
pp. 24-25.
"Witnessing" (for Patty). Atl (244:1) Jl 79, p. 73.

MISHKIN, Julia
"Autumn in New England." VirQR (55:4) Aut 79, p. 713.
"Constraint." CutB (13) Aut-Wint 79, p. 28.

MISHKIN, Julie
"Love Story" (tr. of Dario Jaramillo Agudelo). Pequod (3:2) 79,
p. 87.
"Story" (tr. of Dario Jaramillo Agudelo). Pequod (3:2) 79, p. 88.
"Story of My Brother" (tr. of Dario Jaramillo Agudelo). Pequod
(3:2) 79, p. 89.

MISHLER, Richard
"Wound Factory." Sam (79) 79, p. 45.

MISTRAL, Gabriela
"the cradling" (tr. by Joel Zeltzer). Wind (34) 79, p. 44.

MITCHELL, Adrian
"Question Time in Ireland." Stand (20:4) 79, p. 6.
"Written During the Night Waiting for the Dawn." Stand (20:4)
79, p. 6.

MITCHELL, Garry
"Aunt Clara." Poem (36) Jl 79, p. 55.
"Brief Glance." Poem (36) Jl 79, p. 56.
"The Crowd That Shows Up on Sunday Morning." Poem (36) Jl
79, p. 54.

MITCHELL, Homer
"Breath of the One Animal. " StoneC (6:2) My 79, p. 10.

MITCHELL, Karen L.
"Birmingham, Alabama: 1963. " OP (27) Spr 79, pp. 32-33.
"For Michael. " OP (27) Spr 79, p. 37.
"Returning. " OP (27) Spr 79, pp. 34-35.
"Tree Stillness. " OP (27) Spr 79, p. 36.

MITCHELL, Mark
"St. Peter in the Garden. " Kayak (52) D 79, p. 30.

MITCHELL, Roger
"The Choice. " PoetryNW (20:4) Wint 79-80, pp. 32-33.
"Now. " PoetryNW (20:4) Wint 79-80, pp. 31-32.
"On San Michele. " PoetryNW (20:4) Wint 79-80, p. 31.

MITCHELL, Susan
"The Picture over Our Bed. " Kayak (51) S 79, p. 52.
"The Visit. " NewYorker (55:38) 5 N 79, p. 54.
"The Yard Geese. " Nat (228:20) 26 My 79, p. 611.

MITCHELL, Thomas
"The Affair. " CalQ (15) Wint 79, p. 30.
"Open Range. " CharR (5:2) Aut 79, p. 78.
"Soldiers. " QW (9) Spr-Sum 79, p. 94.
"We Who Need Sorrow. " QW (9) Spr-Sum 79, p. 94.

MITRE, Eduardo
from Lifespace (tr. by Julie Hunt). NewOR (6:2) 79, p. 132.

MITSIOS, Helen
"The Sea Before Departure. " Chowder (12) Spr-Sum 79, p. 30.

MITTELLS, Tim
"Episodes in a Sexual History: creation of impression. " Mouth
   (2:3) N 79, p. 49.
"Episodes in a Sexual History: scouts. " Mouth (2:3) N 79, p. 53.
"Jud. " Mouth (2:3) N 79, p. 4.

MIZEJEWSKI, Linda
"Going Home. " Harp (258:1545) F 79, p. 42.
"Parked in the Country. " Harp (258:1545) F 79, p. 42.
"Sisters Again. " SouthernPR (19:2) Aut 79, p. 34.

MLADINIC, Peter
"A Poem for Egomaniacs. " Spirit (3:1/2) Aut-Wint 77-78, p. 63.

MOFFETT, Judith
"After Shelley. " QW (9) Spr-Sum 79, p. 86.
"From Chapter X, 'Female Song, Duetting, and Corporate Song'
   (pp. 178-9), in A Study of Bird Song by Edward A. Arm-
   strong (London: Oxford University Press, 1963). " Kayak

(50) My 79, p. 36. Five found poems.
"Gingerbread Ladies. " Shen (30:4) 79, p. 96.
"Going to Press. " Poetry (133:4) Ja 79, p. 198.
"The Great American Poem. " Antaeus (32) Wint 79, pp. 82-86.
"Whinny Moor Crossing. " CarolQ (31:2) Spr-Sum 79, pp. 103-107.

MOFFITT, John
"Who Is the Child?" ChrC (96:42) 19 D 79, p. 1263.

MOHR, William
"Candles/Wishes. " Bachy (14) Spr/Sum 79, p. 13.
"The Hitchhiker" (for Marshall Davis). Bachy (14) Spr/Sum 79, p. 12.
"The Kites" (for Anna Kirkland and Pat Zeitlin). Bachy (14) Spr/Sum 79, p. 11.
"The Language of Sleeping Lovers. " Bachy (14) Spr/Sum 79, p. 9.
"(Untitled) My name is Pedro Salinas. " Bachy (14) Spr/Sum 79, p. 9.

MOLESWORTH, Charles
"Mr. Thoreau Sells His Boat--Fall, 1842. " NewEngR (1:4) Sum 79, p. 471.
from Saving the Appearance: "Jung's Dream. " Confr (18) Spr-Sum 79, p. 93.

MOLL, Ernest G.
from Campus Sonnets (1934): "Examination in Romantic Poets. " NowestR (17:2/3) 79, p. 222.
from Campus Sonnets (1934): "On Asking a Class to Read Jeffers. " NowestR (17:2/3) 79, p. 223.
from Campus Sonnets (1934): "Pronouns and Spring. " NowestR (17:2/3) 79, p. 222.
from Campus Sonnets (1934): "Robinson Jeffers. " NowestR (17:2/3) 79, p. 224.

MOLLAND, Michael
"February 13, 1977. " CarlMis (18:1) Wint 79-80, p. 55.

MOLTON, Warren Lane
"Old Man Waiting. " ChrC (96:37) 14 N 79, p. 1110.

MOMADAY, N. Scott
"The Great American Poem. " Antaeus (32) Wint 79, pp. 82-86.

MONTAG, Tom
"Farm Auction. " Northeast (3:7) Spr 79, p. 45.
Letters Home. Sparrow (38) 79. Entire issue.

MONTALE, Eugenio
"Almost a Fantasy" (tr. by Marsha Biguenet). NewOR (6:2) 79, p. 124.

"Eastbourne" (tr. by L. L. Lee). WebR (4:3) Spr 79, p. 5.
"Erase If You Will" (tr. by Jan Pallister). PoNow (24) 79, p.
    26.
"The Lemon-Yellow Rooster" (tr. by Charles Wright). PoNow
    (24) 79, p. 32.
"Life's Evil" (tr. by Jan Pallister). PoNow (24) 79, p. 26.
"Motet" (tr. by Jan Pallister). PoNow (24) 79, p. 26.
"Seaside" (tr. by Charles Wright). PoNow (24) 79, p. 32.
"Spellbound" (tr. by Charles Wright). PoNow (24) 79, p. 32.

MONTEJO, Eugenio
"Nocturne" (tr. by Richard Chambers). NewOR (6:2) 79, p. 109.

MONTEMAYOR, Carlos
"Beth" (tr. by Nigel Grant Sylvester). DenQ (14:1) Spr 79, p.
    63.
"Fifth Ode, Broken" (tr. by Nigel Grant Sylvester). DenQ (14:1)
    Spr 79, p. 66.
"Heth" (tr. by Nigel Grant Sylvester). DenQ (14:1) Spr 79, p.
    64.
"Teth" (tr. by Nigel Grant Sylvester). DenQ (14:1) Spr 79, p.
    65.

MONTERROSO, Augusto
"The Dinosaur" (tr. by Linda Scheer). Chelsea (38) 79, p. 231.

MONTGOMERY, George
"Things Could Be Worse." PoNow (23) 79, p. 37.

MONTIE, Denise
"Departure." QW (9) Spr-Sum 79, p. 89.

MONTLLOR, Peter
"Peapack Road" (for D. Ryan). JnlONJP (4:1) 79, p. 11.
"You had other dreams. Say a gravel driveway." JnlONJP
    (4:1) 79, p. 10.

MOODY, Rodger
"It Pops Off." PoNow (25) 79, p. 31.
"Turning Stars into Deep Snow." Nimrod (23:1) Aut-Wint 79, p.
    16.

MOODY, Shirley
"Candle Making." SouthernPR (19:2) Aut 79, p. 24.
"life after life: an explanation." St. AR (5:3) Aut-Wint 79, p.
    124.

MOON, Sheila
"Existence." ChrC (96:19) 23 My 79, p. 580.

MOONEY, James
"The Day I Turned the Volume Way Down." PortR (25) 79, p.
    136.

MOORE, Elizabeth
  "For Gene Crenshaw. " SmF (7/8) Spr-Aut 78, p. 18.

MOORE, Lynette
  "Haiku. " PikeF (2) Wint 78-79, p. 18.

MOORE, Richard
  "Apology. " SouthernR (15:1) Wint 79, p. 103.
  "The Visitors. " SouthernR (15:1) Wint 79, p. 106.

MOORE, Rosalie
  "Double Fault. " PoNow (21) 79, p. 7.

MOORE, Thomas
  "The Difficult Choice. " Playb (26:1) Ja 79, p. 256.

MOORE, Todd
  "Grandmother Cheating. " PikeF (2) Wint 78-79, p. 22.
  "She's Telling. " PikeF (2) Wint 78-79, p. 7.

MOORE, Tom
  "Frogs. " ColEng (40:6) F 79, p. 664.

MOORHEAD, Andrea
  "crossed light. " Os (9) 79, p. 19.
  "imprint. " Os (8) 79, p. 23.
  "new summer snow. " Os (9) 79, p. 4.
  "poultice of light and heat. " GRR (10:1) 79, p. 17.
  "Print of Snow. " Os (9) 79, p. 18.
  "root to the sea. " Os (8) 79, p. 22.
  "shade of a bee. " GRR (10:1) 79, p. 129.
  "touch of skin. " Os (8) 79, p. 23.
  "Wet Leaves. " GRR (10:1) 79, p. 18.
  "white bloom. " Os (8) 79, p. 21.
  "Winter Landscape IV. " StoneC (6:2) My 79, p. 11.

MOOS, Michael
  "Dipping for Minnows. " Ur (2) 79, p. 81.
  "The Monastery. " Ur (2) 79, p. 83.
  "Piece of the Day. " Ur (2) 79, p. 82.
  "The Unfinished Room. " Ur (2) 79, p. 84.
  "The Waitress. " Ur (2) 79, p. 85.

MOOSE, Ruth
  Poem. St. AR (5:2) 79, p. 59.

MORAFF, Barbara
  "I sit alone. " WormR (76) 79, p. 155.
  "I'll give you. " WormR (73) 79, p. 14.
  "there is in me. " WormR (76) 79, p. 154.
  "you breathe out. " WormR (76) 79, p. 154.
  "you go through. " WormR (76) 79, p. 155.

MORAN, Stephanie
"Pausing Between Sighs, and Then. " Aspen (8) Aut 79, p. 63.

MOREHEAD, Maureen
"Before the Guests Arrive. " KanQ (11:1/2) Wint-Spr 79, p. 81.
"It Is What Makes a Woman Not Want to Save Her Own Life. "
    CalQ (15) Wint 79, p. 67.

MORELAND, Jane P.
"The Argument. " Poetry (134:5) Ag 79, p. 268.
"Child at the Window. " SouthernPR (19:2) Aut 79, p. 26.
"My Mother Reads My Poems. " PoetC (10:3) 79, p. 28.
"Remember. " PoNow (25) 79, p. 31.
"Serapes, Jugs, Owls. " PoetC (10:3) 79, p. 26.
"Tuesday. " KanQ (11:3) Sum 79, p. 74.

MORGAN, Alex
"Untitled: So, they say, lock up the house. " Mouth (2:1) F 79,
    p. 28.

MORGAN, Colin
"Cultivated responses. " Stand (20:4) 79, p. 56.

MORGAN, Elizabeth
"At a Lecture. " PraS (53:4) Wint 79-80, p. 336.

MORGAN, Frederick
"At Midnight. " Nat (229:5) 25 Ag-1 S 79, p. 152.
"Breath. " Nat (229:13) 27 O 79, p. 410.
"Canandaigua. " Poetry (134:3) Je 79, pp. 136-138.
"Century Poem" (for A. R. Ammons). Hudson (32:2) Sum 79, pp.
    167-174.
"Do you seek a door?" Confr (18) Spr-Sum 79, p. 146.
"The End. " SouthernR (15:3) Sum 79, p. 634.
"February 11, 1977" (to my son John). AmerS (48:1) Wint 78-
    79, p. 108.
"History. " SouthernR (15:3) Sum 79, p. 633.
"In Mexico. " NewEngR (1:3) Spr 79, p. 332.
"Lucky black man in my dream... " (for Rosemary Felton).
    NewYRB (26:18) 22 N 79, p. 50.
"Orpheus to Eurydice. " NewEngR (1:3) Spr 79, p. 327.
"Paul Verlaine: Ariettes oubliées IV" (tr.). VirQR (55:3) Sum
    79, p. 506.
"President Poem. " NewYorker (55:9) 16 Ap 79, p. 38.
"Samson. " Kayak (50) My 79, p. 16.
"The Summit. " Nat (229:17) 24 N 79, p. 540.
"The Turtle. " AmerS (48:3) Sum 79, p. 382.
"Writing is simplicity.... " SouthernR (15:3) Sum 79, p. 632.

MORGAN, Jean
"Ice Poem. " SouthernPR (19:1) Spr 79, p. 55.

MORGAN, John
  "The Adulterer. " Chelsea (38) 79, p. 154.
  "Listen. " Poetry (133:4) Ja 79, p. 221.
  "Modern Times. " AmerPoR (8:4) Jl-Ag 79, p. 10.
  "Sonnet of the Lost Labor. " PoNow (21) 79, p. 15.
  "To Our Customers. " PoNow (21) 79, p. 15.
  "The Vortex. " Chelsea (38) 79, p. 155.
  "The Wildness of Wild Animals. " Poetry (133:4) Ja 79, p. 220.

MORGAN, Robert
  "Clay Eaters. " Durak (2) 79, p. 9.
  "Earth Closet. " Poetry (135:1) O 79, p. 4.
  "Feed Room. " PoNow (21) 79, p. 27.
  "Horace Kephart. " Poetry (135:1) O 79, p. 2.
  "Humus. " CornellR (6) Sum 79, pp. 93-100.
  "Lake Summit. " Poetry (135:1) O 79, p. 3.
  "Land Diving. " PoNow (21) 79, p. 27.
  "Pig Dream. " Durak (2) 79, p. 8.
  "Possum. " CarolQ (31:3) Aut 79, p. 19.
  "Rattlesnake Treasure. " Durak (2) 79, p. 7.
  "Spirit Level. " Poetry (135:1) O 79, p. 1.
  "Subsoiling. " CarolQ (31:3) Aut 79, p. 15.
  "Turpentine the Dog. " PoNow (21) 79, p. 27.
  "Wedding Party. " Poetry (135:1) O 79, pp. 6-8.
  "Zircon Pit. " Poetry (135:1) O 79, p. 5.

MORICE, Dave
  "The Bookseller. " Tele (15) Spr 79, p. 81.
  "Double Triple Quadruple Quintuple Sextuple Septuple Octuple. "
      SunM (8) Aut 79, p. 140.
  "The No-Parking Sign. " Tele (15) Spr 79, p. 81.
  "Single Solitary Heaps. " SunM (8) Aut 79, p. 139.
  "Super Superb Super Superb. " SunM (8) Aut 79, p. 137.

MORIN, Edward
  "Expressway Dogs. " PoNow (22) 79, p. 35.
  "Induction. " PoNow (22) 79, p. 35.

MORIN, Gerald
  "Poem to the Woman with the Violent Husband Who Chose to Stay
      the Weekend. " Wind (35) 79, p. 46.

MORITZ, Albert Frank
  "Birth of the Symbol. " PoetC (11:1) 79, p. 30.
  "The Dead. " PoetC (10:3) 79, p. 40.
  "Stabbing. " DenQ (14:2) Sum 79, p. 82.

MORLEY, Hilda
  "Lucky. " Harp (259:1555) D 79, p. 64.
  "The Rose. " Harp (259:1555) D 79, p. 65.
  "The Seaweed. " Harp (259:1555) D 79, p. 64.
  "The Shirt. " Harp (259:1555) D 79, p. 65.

MORRIS, Herbert
"Coming Home in the Dark." Kayak (52) D 79, p. 50.
"How to Improve Your Personality." NewEngR (1:4) Sum 79, p. 402.
"Knowing What the House Is Made Of." Agni (10/11) 79, p. 81.
"These Are Lives." ParisR (75) Spr 79, pp. 235-236.

MORRIS, Patricia Ann
"Lazarus." StoneC (6:2) My 79, p. 16.

MORRIS, Paul
"Washing the Corpse" (tr. of Rainer Maria Rilke). WebR (4:3) Spr 79, p. 7.
"White" (tr. of Karl Krolow). NowestR (18:2) 79, p. 68.

MORRIS, Richard
"The Pearly Gates." Spirit (3:1/2) Aut-Wint 77-78, p. 38.

MORRISON, Madison
"The Twentieth Century, II." Spirit (3:1/2) Aut-Wint 77-78, p. 42.

MORSE, Samuel French
from A Handful of Beach Glass: (I). Paint (12) Aut 79, p. 12.
from A Handful of Beach Glass: (II). Paint (12) Aut 79, p. 13.

MORTON, Bruce
"The American Dental Society." StoneC (6:3) O 79, p. 31.

MORTON, W. C.
"A Full Moon." SouthernPR (19:2) Aut 79, p. 57.
"Grapefruit." SouthernPR (19:2) Aut 79, p. 57.

MOSBY, George Jr.
"lines from a letter from jpw." HangL (35) Spr 79, p. 51.
"Now." Im (5:3) 79, p. 5.
"On the Other Side of the Mirror Reflecting Creation." Im (5:3) 79, p. 5.
"prison poem 15." HangL (35) Spr 79, p. 51.

MOSBY, Katherine
"Correspondents." Poetry (134:6) S 79, p. 328.
"Three Readings of Catullus XI." Poetry (134:6) S 79, pp. 326-327.
"Watercolor." Poetry (134:6) S 79, p. 329.

MOSES, W. R.
"After a Winter Thaw." Bits (9) Ja 79.
"Between the Food and the Water." PoNow (21) 79, p. 3.
"By the Mackenzie." Northeast (3:7) Spr 79, p. 11.
"Cruelest Month." Northeast (3:7) Spr 79, p. 8.
"North/Cold." Northeast (3:7) Spr 79, p. 10.
"Rhapsody on an Owl." PoNow (21) 79, p. 3.
"Two Images." Northeast (3:7) Spr 79, p. 9.

MOSS, Howard
"A Fall. " NewYorker (55:32) 24 S 79, p. 40.
"The Great American Poem. " Antaeus (32) Wint 79, pp. 82-86.
"I Sit by the Window" (tr. of Joseph Brodsky). NewYorker (55:
    16) 4 Je 79, p. 34.
"The Night Express. " NewYorker (55:20) 2 Jl 79, p. 30.
"Remains. " NewYorker (55:11) 30 Ap 79, p. 45.
"The Repetitions. " NewYorker (55:5) 19 Mr 79, p. 40.
"Rilke's Childhood. " NewYorker (55:35) 15 O 79, p. 51.
"The Sleeper. " NewYorker (54:50) 29 Ja 79, p. 30.
"Stars" (for James Merrill). Antaeus (34) Sum 79, pp. 43-47.

MOSS, Stanley
"Clouds. " AmerPoR (8:1) Ja-F 79, p. 36.
"The Dog. " AmerPoR (8:1) Ja-F 79, p. 36.
"An Exchange of Hats. " AmerPoR (8:1) Ja-F 79, p. 36.

MOTT, Michael
"Cloud Climber. " MissouriR (3:1) Aut 79, p. 16.
"The Knot. " DenQ (14:2) Sum 79, p. 57.
"Meadow Grass" (for Marie Mellinger). Poetry (134:1) Ap 79,
    pp. 15-16.
"Patterson Gap Falls" (for Mary Nikas). SouthernPR (19:1) Spr
    79, p. 8.
"The Pierce Poems. " GRR (10:3) 79, pp. 29-34.

MOUL, Keith
"After the Robbery. " Wind (33) 79, p. 39.
"The Motion. " KanQ (11:1/2) Wint-Spr 79, p. 47.

MOVIUS, Geoffrey
"Bodybuilder. " Ploughs (5:3) 79, p. 70.
"He Undergoes a Peculiar Metamorphosis. " Ploughs (5:3) 79, p.
    71.

MUELLER, Lisel
"Another Version. " PoNow (21) 79, p. 4.
"Asylum. " ChiR (31:1) Sum 79, p. 13.
"Daughter. " PoNow (21) 79, p. 4.
"Escape Artist. " ChiR (31:1) Sum 79, p. 12.
"The Plot. " ArkRiv (4:3) 79, p. 13.
"Signs. " ArkRiv (4:3) 79, p. 12.
"Talking to Helen. " SouthernR (15:2) Spr 79, pp. 376-381.
"Testimony. " ChiR (31:1) Sum 79, p. 10.
"The Weaver. " ChiR (31:1) Sum 79, p. 11.

MUEZLER, John
"The Meal of Love and Art Is Over. " SeC (6:1) 78, p. 57.

MULLEN, Harryette
"A Black Woman Never Faints" (for Gertrude Wilks). GreenfieldR
    (7:3/4) Spr-Sum 79, p. 25.
"Cold Storage. " BlackALF (13:4) Wint 79, p. 149.

"Madonna. " GreenfieldR (7:3/4) Spr-Sum 79, p. 25.
"No More Arguments, No More Anything. " BlackALF (13:4)
     Wint 79, p. 149.
"Roadmap. " GreenfieldR (7:3/4) Spr-Sum 79, p. 24.
"To a Woman. " BlackALF (13:4) Wint 79, p. 149.

MULLEN, Richard E.
"Three Teacher Jokes. " HolCrit (16:4) O 79, p. 14.

MULLIGAN, J. B.
The Stations of the Cross. Sam (78) 79. Entire issue.

MUMFORD, Enka
"Eightieth Birthday" (for Margie). GRR (10:1) 79, p. 24.
"Fisher King. " GRR (10:1) 79, p. 26.
"Ghazal. " GRR (10:1) 79, p. 28.
"In the Grove. " GRR (10:1) 79, p. 21.
"Island Picnic. " GRR (10:1) 79, p. 20.
"Metamorphoses" (for my Father). GRR (10:1) 79, p. 22.
"Narcissus. " GRR (10:1) 79, p. 19.

MURAWSKI, Elisabeth
"Birthstone. " CarolQ (31:1) Wint 79, p. 64.
"Desert. " SouthernHR (13:4) Aut 79, p. 342.
"Elegy. " SouthernPR (19:2) Aut 79, p. 55.
"The Entire Conjugation. " SouthernHR (13:4) Aut 79, p. 292.
"Medicine Man. " PoetC (11:1) 79, p. 36.
"Navajo Woman. " PoetC (11:1) 79, p. 37.
"West Virginia Variations. " LitR (22:3) Spr 79, p. 321.

MURDOCK, Caleb
"Concerned not for any comfort save yours, ". Mouth (2:2) Je
     79, p. 23.

MURDY, Anne Elizabeth
"Dionysus. " PikeF (2) Wint 78-79, p. 16.

MURPHY, Aidan
"Bending Rivers. " GRR (10:3) 79, p. 35.

MURPHY, George E. Jr.
"Conestoga. " GreenfieldR (7:3/4) Spr-Sum 79, p. 105.
"Early Gravity. " WindO (34) Spr-Sum 79, p. 34.
"Marsh Wine. " PoetC (11:3) 79, p. 2.
"The Naming of Bears. " WindO (34) Spr-Sum 79, p. 33.
"Passion. " PoetC (11:3) 79, p. 4.
"A Programmed Lesson on the Acquisition of Commitments and
     the Imposition of the Literary Experience on This Particular
     Moment. " Aspect (74/75) Ja-Ag 79, p. 48.

MURPHY, Mardy
"The Danger of Plastic Nipples" (for the Nestlé boycott). 13thM
     (4:2) 79, p. 37.

"The First Time. " 13thM (4:2) 79, p. 35.
"My Afternoon at Maude's" (for Pat). 13thM (4:2) 79, p. 39.

MURPHY, Peter E.
"After Hours. " Confr (19) Aut 79-Wint 80, p. 187.

MURPHY, Richard
"Tony White. " NewYRB (26:15) 11 O 79, p. 12.

MURPHY, Romaine
"Silkworm. " KanQ (11:3) Sum 79, p. 99.

MURPHY, Sheila E.
"Waiting for You to Come Home. " Paint (11) Spr 79, p. 58.

MURPHY, Sister Ellen
"Elm Tree and Other Shadows. " Comm (106:15) 31 Ag 79, p.
461.

MURRAY, C. E.
Poem. St. AR (5:2) 79, p. 53.

MURRAY, G. E.
from Sequels to an Uncollected Winter: "The Certainties. "
ChiR (31:1) Sum 79, p. 53.
"Shelby County, Indiana. February 1977. " NewL (45:3) Spr 79,
p. 72.
"Shelby County, Ohio. November 1974. " NewL (45:3) Spr 79,
p. 72.
"Southern Exposures. " ChiR (31:1) Sum 79, p. 52.

MURRAY, Joan
"Crocus. " Harp (258:1548) My 79, p. 107.

MURRAY, Philip
"Kitsune-Gami (Wicked Fox Deity). " MichQR (18:1) Wint 79, p.
71.
"O-Ta-No-Kami (Deity of the Wet Rice Fields). " MichQR (18:1)
Wint 79, p. 70.
"They Were Dancing. " AmerS (48:1) Wint 78-79, p. 33.

MURRIAGUI, Alfonso
"I the Uninhabited. " LitR (23:2) Wint 80, p. 220.

MUSA, Mark
"Purgatory: Canto II" (tr. of Dante). NewL (46:2) Wint 79-80,
pp. 87-92.

MUSKE, Carol
"Coincidence" (for Tom). Ploughs (5:3) 79, p. 132.
"The Fault. " MissouriR (2:2/3) Spr 79, p. 8.
"The Great American Poem. " Antaeus (32) Wint 79, pp. 82-86.
"Idolatry" (for Delmira Augustini). AmerPoR (8:4) Jl-Ag 79, p.

11.
"Real Estate. " Ploughs (5:3) 79, p. 133.
"Semaphore. " PortR (25) 79, p. 71.
"War Crimes. " NewYorker (55:19) 25 Je 79, p. 38.

MUTIS, Alvaro
"Amen" (tr. by James Normington). PoNow (24) 79, p. 26.

MYERS, Jack
"Hand-Me-Downs" (in memory of Louis Cohen). QW (6) Spr-Sum
     78, p. 33.
"The Instinct. " AmerPoR (8:3) My-Je 79, p. 40.
"It Hurts Everywhere. " QW (6) Spr-Sum 78, p. 33.
"Light Sips on Nothingness. " GeoR (33:3) Aut 79, p. 531.
"Saved. " AmerPoR (8:3) My-Je 79, p. 41.
"Taking a Refrain from the Dance We Do. " CharR (5:1) Spr 79,
     p. 30.
"What's Left. " AmerPoR (8:3) My-Je 79, p. 40.

MYERS, Joan Rohr
"Evolution. " StoneC (6:1) F 79, p. 15.
"Passages. " Wind (35) 79, p. 67.

MYERS, Neil
"My Father's Tales. " PoNow (25) 79, p. 31.
"Terrace. " CharR (5:1) Spr 79, p. 24.

MYHAN, L. L.
"The Crossing. " StoneC (6:1) F 79, p. 23.

MYRSIADES, Kostas
"The Earth's Attraction" (tr. of Yannis Ritsos w. Kimon Friar).
     Chelsea (38) 79, p. 82.
"Lightless" (tr. of Yannis Ritsos w. Kimon Friar). Chelsea (38)
     79, p. 81.
"Secret Audience" (tr. of Yannis Ritsos w. Kimon Friar).
     Chelsea (38) 79, p. 83.

NADEL, Alan
"Spring Skiing. " ParisR (75) Spr 79, p. 87.
"To March. " PartR (46:2) 79, p. 256.
"To October. " PartR (46:3) 79, p. 429.
"To Summer. " ParisR (75) Spr 79, p. 86.

NAGAI, Tomi
"The Calligrapher. " MissouriR (2:2/3) Spr 79, p. 55.
"Collecting White Radish. " MissouriR (2:2/3) Spr 79, p. 53.
"The Rabbit in the Moon. " MissouriR (2:2/3) Spr 79, p. 52.

NAGY, Agnes Nemes
"Defend It" (tr. by Bruce Berlind). PoNow (21) 79, p. 45.
"The Horseman" (tr. by Bruce Berlind). Stand (20:4) 79, p. 24.
"The Sleeping Horsemen" (to Lajos Kassak) (tr. by Bruce Ber-

lind).   PoNow (24) 79, p. 27.
"Storm" (tr. by Bruce Berlind).   PoNow (24) 79, p. 27.

NALDINI, Nico
"And, then, remember, life is only this much" (tr. by Jan Pal-
    lister and Marisa Gatti-Taylor).   PoNow (24) 79, p. 28.
"Between the real and the unreal" (tr. by Jan Pallister and
    Marisa Gatti-Taylor).   PoNow (24) 79, p. 27.
"Comisso, de Pisi, Sandro Penna" (to the great Alfred) (tr. by
    Jan Pallister and Marisa Gatti-Taylor).   PoNow (24) 79, p.
    28.
"It was still a trifle cold" (tr. by Jan Pallister and Marisa Gatti-
    Taylor).   PoNow (24) 79, p. 27.
"A shadow upon the unmade bed" (tr. by Jan Pallister and Marisa
    Gatti-Taylor).   PoNow (24) 79, p. 27.

NAPLACHOWSKI, Stephanie
"Bronzed. "   NewOR (6:2) 79, p. 143.

NAPORA, Joseph
"From U. S. Government Printing Office, PT-26, Polish Intro-
    ductory Material. "   Kayak (50) My 79, p. 34.   Found poem.
"Sore Eros. "   Bits (9) Ja 79.

NASH, Harriet
"Orange. "   PikeF (2) Wint 78-79, p. 18.

NATHAN, Leonard
"Callings. "   MassR (20:3) Aut 79, p. 500.
"The Fourth Dimension. "   GeoR (33:3) Aut 79, p. 592.
"Lighting Up. "   Chowder (13) Aut-Wint 79, p. 42.
"Morning Song. "   PraS (53:1) Spr 79, p. 75.
"One for Mouse. "   Bits (9) Ja 79.
"Rebecca. "   Chowder (13) Aut-Wint 79, p. 43.
"Shelving. "   Bits (10) Jl 79.
"View from the Mid-Fifties. "   MassR (20:2) Sum 79, p. 392.
"Yours Truly. "   PoNow (23) 79, p. 9.

NATHAN, Norman
"Collectors. "   Poem (35) Mr 79, p. 45.
"Myself. "   SouthernHR (13:2) Spr 79, p. 126.
"One Night Stand. "   SouthernHR (13:2) Spr 79, p. 125.
"Photography Class with a Nude in a Wooded Garden. "   SoCaR
    (11:2) Spr 79, p. 51.
"Substrata. "   Poem (35) Mr 79, p. 44.

NATHAN, Terry
"Lamenting the Frogs near Moorhead, Minnesota. "   Focus (13:81)
    My-Je 79, p. 31.
"The Pig Farms Outside Griswold, Iowa" (for R. P. Chambers).
    Focus (13:82) Ag 79, p. 31.

NATKIE, John L.
"Reflections of a Prison Guard. " SeC (6:1) 78, p. 51.
"A Ten Minute Poem" (for A. D.). SeC (6:1) 78, p. 49.

NAVA, Thelma
"Poem to Che. " LitR (23:2) Wint 80, p. 259.

NAYER, Louise
"Trying to Make Myself Clear. " Ur (2) 79, p. 86.

NAYLOR, James Ball
"King David and King Solomon. " Playb (26:1) Ja 79, p. 256.

NECATIGIL, Behcet
"Bayram Ziyareh. " StoneC (6:1) F 79, p. 28.
"Holiday Visit" (tr. by Dionis Coffin Riggs, Ozcan Yalim and
    William A. Fiedler). StoneC (6:1) F 79, p. 28.

NEEL, Dorothy I.
Poem. St. AR (5:2) 79, p. 88.

NEELD, Judith
"After Seven Days and Seven Nights. " Im (5:3) 79, p. 4.
from Scripts for a Life in Three Parts: "Winter: In the Fort-
    ress. " PikeR (1) Sum 79, p. 32.
from Scripts for a Life in Three Parts: "On Balance. " PikeR
    (1) Sum 79, p. 33.
"storm the day after. " St. AR (5:3) Aut-Wint 79, p. 108.
"Watching Dogs Walked. " Im (5:3) 79, p. 4.

NEIDERBACH, Shelley
"Correspondence. " StoneC (6:3) O 79, p. 22.

NEIMARK, Jill
"Judy and the Real-Estate Agent. " MassR (20:4) Wint 79, p. 751.
"The Pallet. " MassR (20:4) Wint 79, p. 752.

NEISBERG, Arthur
"Calm" (tr. of Giuseppe Ungaretti w. Jan Pallister). PoNow (24)
    79, p. 61.
"Night" (tr. of Giuseppe Ungaretti w. Jan Pallister). PoNow
    (24) 79, p. 61.
"Nostalgia" (tr. of Giuseppe Ungaretti w. Jan Pallister). PoNow
    (24) 79, p. 61.

NEJAR, Carlos
"The Yoke" (tr. by Alexis Levitin). PoNow (24) 79, p. 28.

NELSON, Eric
"Watering Horses in Winter. " EnPas (9) 79, p. 13.

NELSON, Howard
"Reading 'Crossing Brooklyn Ferry' on a Summer Morning. "
    MissouriR (2:2/3) Spr 79, p. 57.

NELSON, Jay
"Lines Upon Seeing a Domesticated Lover. " KanQ (11:1/2) Wint-
    Spr 79, p. 50.

NELSON, Joyce
"Trying to Keep You Living. " MalR (51) Jl 79, p. 38.

NELSON, Laura
"meditation: december. " Ascent (4:2) 79, p. 52.

NELSON, Nils
"He remembers. " PoNow (25) 79, p. 31.

NELSON, Paul
"The Bat in His Room" (for my brother). Ploughs (5:1) 79, p.
    88.
"The Lost World. " Ploughs (5:1) 79, p. 89.
"The Mind Speaks of the Body. " OhioR (20:2) Spr-Sum 79, p.
    63.

NELSON, Rodney
"Anabasis. " SoDakR (17:4) Wint 79-80, p. 44.

NELSON, Sandie
"Feast Day. " BelPoJ (30:2) Wint 79-80, p. 36.

NELSON, Sara
"Décalages" (tr. of Ulálume González de Leon). DenQ (14:1)
    Spr 79, p. 31.
"L'esprit de la langue" (tr. of Ulálume González de Leon).
    DenQ (14:1) Spr 79, p. 30.
"The Familiar Sheets" (tr. of Ulálume González de Leon). DenQ
    (14:1) Spr 79, p. 28.
")Parentheses(" (tr. of Ulálume González de Leon). DenQ (14:1)
    Spr 79, p. 27.
"Words" (tr. of Ulálume González de Leon). DenQ (14:1) Spr 79,

NEMEROV, Howard
"By Al Lebowitz's Pool. " NewRep (180:10) 10 Mr 79, pp. 30-31.
"Coming Home to New York When It Was Said to Be Going Down
    the Drain. " Poetry (134:1) Ap 79, p. 11.
"A Christmas Storm. " NewYorker (55:45) 24 D 79, p. 42.
"During a Solar Eclipse. " NewYorker (55:15) 28 My 79, p. 44.
"The Little Aircraft. " Atl (243:5) My 79, p. 65.
"Monet. " Poetry (134:1) Ap 79, p. 10.
"Pomp. " Poetry (134:1) Ap 79, p. 9.
"Remembering Ford Madox Ford and Parade's End" (for Sondra
    Stang). Poetry (134:1) Ap 79, p. 8.
"The Revenants (After a Movie). " Poetry (134:1) Ap 79, p. 7.
"The Three Towns. " GeoR (33:3) Aut 79, p. 530.

NERONI, Rosalind
"Collecting. " Ur (2) 79, p. 87.

NERUDA, Pablo
"The Human Condition" (tr. by Alastair Reid). NewEngR (2:1)
    Aut 79, p. 119.
"I Will Not Be Silent" (tr. by Steve Kowit). PoNow (24) 79, p.
    32.
"Never" (tr. by Steve Kowit). PoNow (24) 79, p. 32.
"No, Never" (tr. by Steve Kowit). PoNow (24) 79, p. 32.
from Las piedras del cielo: (XXV). GRR (10:1) 79, p. 92.
from Las piedras del cielo: (XXVII). GRR (10:1) 79, p. 94.
from Las piedras del cielo: (XXVIII). GRR (10:1) 79, p. 96.
"The School of Winter" (tr. by Alastair Reid). NewEngR (2:1)
    Aut 79, p. 118.
from Stones of the Sky: (IV) (tr. by James Nolan). NewOR (6:2)
    79, p. 111.
from Stones of the Sky: (V) (tr. by James Nolan). NewOR (6:2)
    79, p. 112.
from Stones of the Sky: (VIII) (tr. by James Nolan). NewOR
    (6:2) 79, p. 112.
from Stones of the Sky: (XV) (tr. by James Nolan). NewOR
    (6:2) 79, p. 113.
"Those of Yesterday" (tr. by Steve Kowit). PoNow (24) 79, p.
    32.

NESTER, Eli
"My Best Clothes" (tr. by Bernhard Frank). PoNow (24) 79, p.
    28.
"Night Walk" (tr. by Bernhard Frank). PoNow (24) 79, p. 28.

NESTOR, Richard
"Dune Grass" (for Bert Yarborough). Ploughs (5:1) 79, p.
    95.
"Meeting with Snakes. " Ploughs (5:1) 79, pp. 90-91.
"Ulysses Simpson Grant 1822-1885. " Ploughs (5:1) 79, p.
    94.
"William Harrison Slusher 1889-1961. " Ploughs (5:1) 79, pp.
    92-93.

NEWBY, Rich
"Letter to Oregon, from Montana" (for Jack Wendel). CutB (13)
    Aut-Wint 79, p. 8.
"Manifesto" (for Rene Char). CutB (13) Aut-Wint 79, p. 5.
"Montana Pastoral. " CutB (13) Aut-Wint 79, p. 7.

NEWMAN, Felice
"Hiroshima. " MinnR (NS 12) Spr 79, p. 45.

NEWMAN, P. B.
"Mr. Cherry. " SoCaR (12:1) Aut 79, p. 10.
"science and poetry. " St. AR (5:3) Aut-Wint 79, p. 122.
"Stained Glass. " KanQ (11:3) Sum 79, p. 20.
"Tryon Palace, 1791: Washington as Count Dracula. " CarolQ
    (31:1) Wint 79, p. 86.

NEWQUIST, Greta
"New Music. " PikeF (2) Wint 78-79, p. 17.
"Passages in Data. " PikeF (2) Wint 79, p. 17.

NEWTH, Rebecca
"Haying. " PoNow (23) 79, p. 27.
"Rain. " PoNow (23) 79, p. 27.
"To the Owner of the Orchard. " PoNow (23) 79, p. 27.

NEWTON, Debbi
"'my song. '" NegroHB (42:3) Jl-Ag-S 79, p. 78.

NIATUM, Duane
"The Art of Clay. " CharR (5:1) Spr 79, p. 54.
"For Those Women Friends at Whitman College. " CharR (5:1)
    Spr 79, p. 53.
"The Great American Poem. " Antaeus (32) Wint 79, pp. 82-86.
"The Passenger. " NewEngR (1:4) Sum 79, p. 401.
"Sky of Departing. " BelPoJ (30:2) Wint 79-80, p. 13.

NIBBELINK, Cynthia
Fifteen Poems. GRR (10:3) 79, pp. 37-53.

NICHOLSON, Joseph
"At the Supermarket. " PoNow (22) 79, p. 25.
"Fingernails. " Durak (2) 79, p. 47.
"Out of the Old Rock" (for J. Frank Dobie). PoNow (22) 79, p.
    25.

NICK, Dagmar
"Above the Harbor of Lindos" (tr. by Jim Barnes). DenQ (14:2)
    Sum 79, p. 53.
"Diluvium" (tr. by Jim Barnes). PoNow (24) 79, p. 37.
"Exodus" (tr. by Jim Barnes). DenQ (14:2) Sum 79, p. 55.
"Southward" (tr. by Jim Barnes). DenQ (14:2) Sum 79, p. 54.
"Summons" (tr. by Jim Barnes). PoNow (24) 79, p. 37.

NICKELL, Joe
"All. " Wind (35) 79, p. 48.
"The Ghost Watcher. " Wind (35) 79, p. 49.
"The Gambler to His Lady. " Wind (35) 79, p. 50.
"The Girl in the Story. " Wind (35) 79, p. 47.
"Look. " Wind (35) 79, p. 47.
"There Is this Fame" (for Ezra Pound). Wind (35) 79, p. 51.
"Waking. " Wind (35) 79, p. 49.

NICKERSON, Sheila
"At the Sharp-All Shop. " Bits (9) Ja 79.
"The News from Nikolai. " Bits (10) Jl 79.

NICOL, Alfred
"I Spend the Morning's First Hour Looking for Things I've Lost. "
    AndR (6:2) Aut 79, p. 40.
"The Inheritance. " NewEngR (1:3) Spr 79, p. 269.

NIDITCH, B. Z.
"At Emily Dickinson's House. " Im (5:3) 79, p. 11.
"Conrad Aiken's Boston (in Memoriam 1889-1978). " Im (5:3) 79,
    p. 11.
"The Festival of Weeks. " Spirit (3:3) Sum 78, p. 34.
"Franz Kafka. " Im (5:3) 79, p. 11.
"The Jews of Salonika. " GreenfieldR (7:3/4) Spr-Sum 79, p. 260.
"The Kid Next Door. " CimR (47) Ap 79, p. 64.
"The Kid Next Door. " Ur (2) 79, p. 92.
"Lower Manhattan. " GreenfieldR (7:3/4) Spr-Sum 79, p. 262.
"Moscow's Rain" (for Anna Akhmatova). Im (6:1) 79, p. 10.
"On Indian Lake. " Os (9) 79, p. 6.
"Rimbaud. " Im (6:1) 79, p. 10.
"A Summer Evening. " WindO (34) Spr-Sum 79, p. 38.
"To Allen Tate. " Poem (36) Jl 79, p. 57.
"Warsaw's Sink. " GreenfieldR (7:3/4) Spr-Sum 79, p. 261.

NIEHOFF, Marilee S.
"What I Would Like to Know. " PikeF (2) Wint 78-79, p. 27.

NIFLIS, Michael
"Ephemera. " ChrC (96:28) 12 S 79, p. 849.

NIJMEIJER, Peter
Eight poems (tr. of Gerrit Kouwenaar). Montra (5) 79, p. 197.
"Homage to Singer" (tr. of Paul van Ostaijen). Montra (5) 79,
    p. 149.

NIMMO, Kurt
"Life in the Littles. " SeC (7:1) 79, p. 38.
"Standing in the Bathroom Naked. " SeC (7:1) 79, p. 37.
"The Women Poets. " Sam (79) 79, p. 82.

NIMNICHT, Nona
"Letters from Troy. " CalQ (15) Wint 79, p. 47.
"Ulysses. " QW (7) Aut 78, p. 119.

NIMTZ, Steve
"Indoors. " Wind (35) 79, p. 53.
"jersey shore. " St. AR (5:3) Aut-Wint 79, p. 86.
"1978. " Wind (35) 79, p. 52.

NIST, John
"The Aging Light" (for Marisa). ArizQ (35:4) Wint 79, p. 292.
"Made to See. " ArizQ (35:1) Spr 79, p. 56.

NIXON, David Michael
"Tomorrow Morning with Tennessee Williams. " SmPd (46) 79,
    p. 19.

NIXON, John Jr.
"Gone. " Comm (106:17) 28 S 79, p. 530.
"Why You Never Inhabit My Prayers. " ChrC (96:36) 7 N 79, p.
    1087.

NOEL, Marie
"When down upon us come, some evening" (tr. by Jan Pallister).
PoNow (24) 79, p. 37.

NOGRADY, Maureen
"For Anne Sexton. " EngJ (68:5) My 79, p. 34.

NOLAN, James
"Downtown, New Year's Eve. " NewL (46:1) Aut 79, p. 14.
"Love Poem to a Lady UFO. " PoNow (23) 79, p. 13.
"The Mannequin. " PoNow (23) 79, p. 13.
"Mr. Rock. " Poetry (134:2) My 79, p. 100.
from Stones of the Sky: (IV) (tr. of Pablo Neruda).   NewOR
   (6:2) 79, p. 111.
from Stones of the Sky: (V) (tr. of Pablo Neruda).   NewOR (6:2)
   79, p. 112.
from Stones of the Sky: (VIII) (tr. of Pablo Neruda).   NewOR
   (6:2) 79, p. 112.
from Stones of the Sky: (XV) (tr. of Pablo Neruda).   NewOR
   (6:2) 79, p. 113.
from Stones of the Sky: (XXV) (tr. of Pablo Neruda).   GRR
   (10:1) 79, p. 93.
from Stones of the Sky: (XXVII) (tr. of Pablo Neruda).   GRR
   (10:1) 79, p. 95.
from Stones of the Sky: (XXVIII) (tr. of Pablo Neruda).   GRR
   (10:1) 79, p. 97.
"Undercurrent. " NewL (46:1) Aut 79, p. 13.
"The Widow. " Poetry (134:2) My 79, p. 99.

NOLAN, Pat
"Kicking the Gong Around" (for Michael-Sean Lazarchuk).   Tele
   (15) Spr 79, p. 30.
"Poem: Transparent Buds of Spring's. " Tele (15) Spr 79, p.
   32.
"Pretty Basic. " Tele (15) Spr 79, p. 32.

NORD, Arthur
"Waking. " Wind (34) 79, p. 47.

NORDBRANDT, Henrik
"Gesture" (tr. by Alexander Taylor).   PoNow (24) 79, p. 37.
"Roads" (tr. by Alexander Taylor).   PoNow (24) 79, p. 37.

NORDHAUS, Jean
"Along This Corridor, ".   GreenfieldR (7:3/4) Spr-Sum 79, p.
   243.
"Erica Jong Is Singing a Song. " Ploughs (5:2) 79, pp. 117-118.
"Painting the Room: Pink. " WestB (4) 79, p. 54.
"Painting the Room Yellow. " WestB (4) 79, p. 54.
"Pre-Historic Voyages. " WestB (4) 79, p. 55.
"Sleeping Out. " PraS (53:1) Spr 79, p. 72.
"Smiles: at the embassy. " GreenfieldR (7:3/4) Spr-Sum 79, p.
   242.
"Tell Me Color. " Chowder (12) Spr-Sum 79, p. 20.

NOREN, Lars
"From Dresden" (tr. by John Matthias). GreenfieldR (7:3/4)
    Spr-Sum 79, p. 129.
"I Burn My Lamp in the Meadow" (tr. by John Matthias).
    GreenfieldR (7:3/4) Spr-Sum 79, p. 129.
"The Sphere of the Roads" (tr. by John Matthias). GreenfieldR
    (7:3/4) Spr-Sum 79, p. 129.

NORGE, Geo
"At the Circus" (tr. by Richard Lebovitz). PoNow (24) 79, p.
    38.
"The Penknife" (tr. by Richard Lebovitz). PoNow (24) 79, p. 38.
"Sky" (tr. by Richard Lebovitz). PoNow (24) 79, p. 38.

NORMAN, Howard
"The Carnival" (tr. of Paulé Bartón). VirQR (55:1) Wint 79, p.
    119.
"Dry Tune" (tr. of Paulé Bartón). VirQR (55:1) Wint 79, p. 117.
"Three Paintings of Hers Bélem Saw" (tr. of Paulé Bartón).
    VirQR (55:1) Wint 79, p. 119.
"Too Many Proverbs" (tr. of Paulé Bartón). VirQR (55:1) Wint
    79, p. 118.
"The Wave Seller" (tr. from the Creole). MichQR (18:1) Wint
    79, p. 116.

NORMINGTON, James
"Amen" (tr. of Alvaro Mutis). PoNow (24) 79, p. 26.
"Domestic Recipes" (tr. of Juan Jose Arreola). PoNow (24) 79,
    p. 4.
"Eunice" (tr. of Efrain Huerta). PoNow (24) 79, p. 20.
"Poem: semen is an angelblast. " PoNow (25) 79, p. 31.
"We Walk Between Shadows" (tr. of Jose Angel Buesa). PoNow
    (24) 79, p. 6.

NORRIS, Gunilla Brodde
"Capriccio. " SouthernPR (19:1) Spr 79, p. 17.
"Lessons. " CarlMis (17:2/3) Spr 79, p. 90.
"A Pause in the Desert. " NewEngR (1:3) Spr 79, p. 270.

NORRIS, John N.
"The Autobiography. " GeoR (33:2) Sum 79, p. 377.
"My Children's Book. " GeoR (33:2) Sum 79, p. 379.

NORTH, Gloria
"Nothing But the Truth. " Sam (79) 79, p. 80.
"Shopping. " Sam (79) 79, p. 81.
"The Woman Whose Name Was Love Me. " Kayak (51) S 79, p.
    45.

NORTH, Susan
"Chains. " Spirit (3:1/2) Aut-Wint 77-78, p. 10.
"Encore. " OP (28) Aut 79, p. 15.
"Love. " OP (28) Aut 79, pp. 18-19.

'What I Have. " OP (28) Aut 79, p. 17.
'Where I Am Now. " OP (28) Aut 79, p. 16.

NORTHUP, Harry E.
"the bedroom" (for holly prado). Bachy (15) Aut 79, p. 116.
"my mother. " Bachy (15) Aut 79, p. 117.
"one knife. " Bachy (15) Aut 79, p. 115.
"some Love could make me kill. " Bachy (15) Aut 79, p. 116.

NOSTRAND, Jennifer
"Untitled: Least expected comes the rush. " KanQ (11:3) Sum
   79, p. 91.

NOVAK, Robert
"To the Hansens, Our Most Generous Patrons. " WindO (35)
   Aut-Wint 79-80, p. 3.

NOVEMBER, Sharyn
"Androgyne. " Wind (33) 79, p. 23.
"Florida Manicure. " QW (7) Aut 78, p. 46.
'Night Driving. " Agni (10/11) 79, p. 147.

NYE, Naomi Shihab
"Coming into Cuzco. " PraS (53:4) Wint 79-80, p. 350.
'Madison Street. " PraS (53:4) Wint 79-80, p. 349.

NYHART, Nina
'Vocation. " AndR (6:1) Spr 79, p. 82.

NYSTEDT, Bob
"Nocturne 50. " StoneC (6:1) F 79, p. 13.

OANDASAN, William
'The Janitor" (for John Nims). BelPoJ (30:2) Wint 79-80, p. 24.
'New Day Chant. " BelPoJ (30:2) Wint 79-80, p. 24.

OATES, Joyce Carol
"Back Country. " GeoR (33:4) Wint 79, p. 876.
"Last Things. " VirQR (55:4) Aut 79, p. 713.
"Leavetaking. " Hudson (32:2) Sum 79, p. 190.
'Moving Out. " Hudson (32:2) Sum 79, p. 189.
'Mythology. " ParisR (75) Spr 79, p. 244.
"Painting the Balloon Face. " ParisR (75) Spr 79, pp. 245-246.
'The Present Tense. " Atl (244:5) N 79, p. 81.
"A Report to an Academy. " ParisR (75) Spr 79, pp. 246-247.

OBEJAS, Achy
"Come the Fox. " BelPoJ (30:1) Aut 79, p. 39.

O'BRIEN, M. K.
"Accoutrements de Guerre. " PoNow (22) 79, p. 26.
'The Glad Woman. " PoNow (22) 79, p. 26.
"Parental Pride. " PoNow (22) 79, p. 26.

OBSTFELD, Raymond
"The Typist. " Confr (18) Spr-Sum 79, p. 159.

O'CALLAGHAN, Patricia
"Palace" (tr. of Guillaume Appollinaire). Pig (6) 79, p. 56.

OCAMPO, Silvina
"Dolphins. " LitR (23:2) Wint 80, p. 233.
"Epitaph of a Mariner" (tr. by Jason Weiss). NewEngR (1:4)
    Sum 79, p. 432.
"In Front of the Seine, Recalling the Rio de la Plata" (for Octa-
    vio Paz) (tr. by Jason Weiss). NewEngR (1:4) Sum 79, p.
    431.
"Infinite Horses" (tr. by Jason Weiss). PraS (53:3) Aut 79, p.
    210.
"My Distant Feet. " LitR (23:2) Wint 80, p. 234.
"Sleepless Palinurus" (tr. by Harriet Zinnes). PoNow (24) 79,
    p. 38.
"Sleep's Persuasion" (tr. by Jason Weiss). PraS (53:3) Aut 79,
    p. 211.
"Song of the Ferocious Cradle. " LitR (23:2) Wint 80, p. 233.
"To My Desperation" (tr. by Jason Weiss). PraS (53:3) Aut 79,
    p. 209.
"Towns" (for Dominga). LitR (23:2) Wint 80, p. 235.

OCHESTER, Ed
"The Bride of Frankenstein. " PoNow (21) 79, p. 36.
"Western Pa. " PoNow (23) 79, p. 17.

O'CONNOR, Mark
"Frigate-Birds. " Nat (228:9) 10 Mr 79, p. 282.

ODAM, Joyce
"The Hen. " CimR (47) Ap 79, p. 57.
"That Undeciphered. " StoneC (6:2) My 79, p. 31.

ODOM, Doug
How He Got the Mule. Sam (77) 79. Entire issue.

O'DONNELL, Mark
"The Diner. " Columbia (3) 79, p. 55.

O'DONOGHUE, Gregory
"A Gift. " LitR (22:3) Spr 79, p. 359.
"Legend. " LitR (22:3) Spr 79, p. 361.
"Russian Song, 1938. " LitR (22:3) Spr 79, p. 360.

OFFEN, Yehuda
"Air drips from rock" (tr. by Bernhard Frank). PoNow (24) 79,
    p. 38.
"Inwards" (tr. by Bernhard Frank). PoNow (24) 79, p. 38.

O'GARA, Phyllis
  "When the River Froze Over" (for Grandmother Hayes).   PortR
  (25) 79, p. 77.

O'GRADY, Tom
  "Eastern State Hospital. " Aspect (74/75) Ja-Ag 79, p. 51.

O HEHIR, Diana
  "Anima. " Kayak (50) My 79, p. 45.
  "Artificial Light. " Chowder (12) Spr-Sum 79, p. 39.
  "Blame. " Shen (30:4) 79, p. 68.
  "The First Death of the Season. " Kayak (50) My 79, p. 44.
  "The House in the Secret Part of the City. " Kayak (50) My 79,
    p. 43.
  "I Search for My Mother, Who Died When I Was Four. "
    PoetryNW (20:1) Spr 79, pp. 27-28.
  "Manuscript Decoded from a Lost Language. " PoetryNW (20:1)
    Spr 79, p. 27.
  "Night Twin. " Chowder (12) Spr-Sum 79, p. 38.
  "The People in My Walled-Up House. " Kayak (50) My 79, p. 44.

OJAIDE, Tanure
  "Kukawa. " NewL (46:1) Aut 79, p. 50.
  "They Are Many. " NewL (46:1) Aut 79, p. 50.
  "Thought in a Bus. " NewL (46:1) Aut 79, p. 50.

OKAI, Atukwei
  from Rhododendrons in Donkeydom: "Fanfare for Ododuwa. "
    Spirit (4:2/3) Spr-Sum 79, pp. 21-33.

O'KEEFE, Richard
  "Sunflowers in Moonlight. " Chowder (12) Spr-Sum 79, p. 6.

OLDENBURG, Patty
  "Get Lost. " Tele (15) Spr 79, p. 80.
  "Live Stock. " Tele (15) Spr 79, p. 78.
  "We were going to chop off her head. " Tele (15) Spr 79, p. 79.

OLDHAM, Perry
  "Devil's Day" (tr. of Robert Desnos). Kayak (52) D 79, p. 67.
  "Men" (tr. of Robert Desnos). EnPas (9) 79, p. 30.
  "The Ox and the Rose" (tr. of Robert Desnos). Kayak (52) D
    79, p. 66.
  "To Those Without Any Heads" (tr. of Robert Desnos). EnPas
    (9) 79, p. 28.

OLDKNOW, Antony
  "Dakota Hotel Ode. " DacTerr (16) 79, p. 48.
  "Spanish Ladies. " MinnR (NS 12) Spr 79, p. 48.
  "You Are Now Living in a New Past. " CharR (5:2) Aut 79, p.
    74.

OLDS, Sharon
  "Airport Hotel. " MissR (24) Aut 79, p. 73.

"Bad Marriage. " CarlMis (17:2/3) Spr 79, p. 117.
"The Death of Marilyn Monroe. " PoNow (25) 79, p. 45.
"Encounter" (for Betty). SoCaR (12:1) Aut 79, p. 10.
"The End of World War One. " MassR (20:4) Wint 79, p. 666.
"Feared Drowned. " MissR (24) Aut 79, p. 78.
"Late. " MissR (24) Aut 79, p. 80.
"Leningrad Cemetery, Winter of 1941. " NewYorker (55:46) 31 D
   79, p. 51.
"Nurse Whitman. " CarlMis (17:2/3) Spr 79, p. 116.
"The Other Life. " MissR (24) Aut 79, p. 76.
"The Perfect Lady Takes Her Opportunity. " Paint (11) Spr 79,
   p. 60.
"Photograph of the Girl. " MissouriR (2:2/3) Spr 79, p. 58.
"Solitary" (for Muriel Rukeyser). Paint (11) Spr 79, p. 59.
"Tricks. " MissR (24) Aut 79, p. 74.
"Visiting In-laws in the Extreme North. " SoCaR (12:1) Aut 79,

O'LEARY, Dawn
   "Rust. " JnlONJP (3:2) 79, p. 20.
   "The Visit. " JnlONJP (3:2) 79, p. 20.

OLES, Carole
   "Now, While We Have the Body Before Us. " PoetryNW (20:2)
      Sum 79, p. 34.

OLIVER, Louis
   from The Sleep Maker: "In Taskigi I was born, ". BelPoJ (30:2)
      Wint 79-80, p. 37.

OLIVER, Mary
   "At the Cove. " AmerS (48:2) Spr 79, p. 286.
   "The Black Snake. " Ploughs (5:1) 79, p. 98.
   "Chippewa Jack, the Mayor, and Jimmy McFee. " GeoR (33:4)
      Wint 79, p. 896.
   "Crow. " Bits (9) Ja 79.
   "Listening. " Ploughs (5:1) 79, pp. 96-97.
   "Mushrooms. " NewYorker (55:34) 8 O 79, p. 99.
   "Something. " PraS (53:2) Sum 79, p. 117.
   "Web. " OhioR (20:2) Spr-Sum 79, p. 29.
   "The Well. " Comm (106:13) 6 Jl 79, p. 405.
   "Wolf Moon. " Atl (243:4) Ap 79, p. 51.

OLIVER, Merrill
   "To the Horizon. " VirQR (55:4) Aut 79, p. 715.

OLIVER, William
   "The Rhythms of Blackness" (for my man Genie James).
      BlackALF (13:1) Spr 79, p. 35.

OLIVEROS, Chuck
   "Elegy. " Poem (37) N 79, p. 28.
   "Violence in Chicago. " Poem (37) N 79, p. 29.

OLSEN, William
  "Always the Same. " CarlMis (18:1) Wint 79-80, p. 73.
  "Boundary. " Wind (34) 79, p. 45.
  "Farm. " CarolQ (31:3) Aut 79, p. 83.
  "Her Recurrent Dream About Auschwitz. " CharR (5:2) Aut 79,
     p. 79.
  "How to Sell Eggs in the City. " GreenfieldR (7:3/4) Spr-Sum
     79, p. 189.

OLSON, Charles
  "Blue. " PoetC (11:3) 79, p. 24.

OLSON, Elder
  "The Russian Doll. " NewYorker (55:24) 30 Jl 79, p. 77.

O'NEILL, Alexandre
  "The Blind" (tr. by Alexis Levitin). PoNow (24) 79, p. 38.

O'NEILL, Brian
  "Pike Through the Ice. " ColEng (40:5) Ja 79, p. 522.
  "Warren. " ColEng (40:5) Ja 79, p. 523.

O'NEILL, Patrick
  "Down by the Seaside. " Ur (2) 79, p. 90.

OPALOV, Leonard
  "I Possess" (tr. of Anna Akhmatova). Spirit (3:1/2) Aut-Wint
     77-78, p. 9.
  "Once Upon a Time" (tr. of Ilya Ehrenburg). Spirit (4:1) Aut-
     Wint 78-79, p. 17.

OPENGART, Bea
  "Driving Through Nebraska. " Ploughs (5:1) 79, p. 99.
  "Migrations. " CutB (12) Spr-Sum 79, p. 10.
  "Seven Boys Fishing by Moonlight. " QW (9) Spr-Sum 79, p. 113.
  "Speak. " CarolQ (31:1) Wint 79, p. 63.

OPPENHEIMER, Joel
  "Changes. " St. AR (5:3) Aut-Wint 79, p. 31.
  "the four fathers. " St. AR (5:3) Aut-Wint 79, p. 24.
  "summer songs. " St. AR (5:3) Aut-Wint 79, p. 25.
  "a village poem. " St. AR (5:3) Aut-Wint 79, p. 27.

ORBAN, Otto
  "To Be Poor" (tr. by Emery George). PoNow (24) 79, p. 38.

ORELLI, Giorgio
  "The Man Who Walks in the Woods" (tr. by Lawrence Venuti).
     PoNow (24) 79, p. 39.
  "A Short Walk with Lucia in Autumn" (tr. by Lawrence Venuti).
     PoNow (24) 79, p. 39.
  "Summer" (tr. by Lawrence Venuti). PoNow (24) 79, p. 39.
  "To a Philologist" (tr. by Lawrence Venuti). PoNow (24) 79, p.
     39.

ORGEL, Irene
"Scuba Diving. " AndR (6:1) Spr 79, p. 74.

ORLEN, Steve
"Because of Degas. " Antaeus (33) Spr 79, p. 100.
"The Blind Man and the Blind Man's Son. " SenR (10:1) Spr 79,
    p. 33.
"The Drunken Man. " PoNow (21) 79, p. 28.
"The First Day. " SenR (10:1) Spr 79, p. 26.
"Fruit. " SenR (10:1) Spr 79, p. 35.
"The Great Wall of China. " SenR (10:1) Spr 79, p. 29.
"No Way. " SenR (10:1) Spr 79, p. 37.
"Porcupine. " MissouriR (2:2/3) Spr 79, p. 29.
"Tobacco Farms. " PoNow (21) 79, p. 28.
"What He Saw. " SenR (10:1) Spr 79, p. 31.

ORLOCK, C.
"Signature. " GreenfieldR (7:3/4) Spr-Sum 79, p. 216.
"talk (the vulgate). " Tendril (5) Sum 79, p. 40.

ORR, Ed
"The Critic. " PoNow (23) 79, p. 37.

ORR, Gregory
"After the Guest" (for my brother). Poetry (135:3) D 79, p. 142.
"Nightpoem. " NewEngR (1:4) Sum 79, p. 428.
"Song: Deaths of the Innocent. " NewEngR (1:4) Sum 79, p. 429.
"Then. " Poetry (135:3) D 79, p. 144.
"Two Songs of the River. " Poetry (135:3) D 79, p. 143.
"The Visitor. " NewEngR (1:4) Sum 79, p. 430.

ORR, Thomas
"A Friendly Game. " KanQ (11:1/2) Wint-Spr 79, p. 51.

ORREGO, Carmen
"From Afar" (tr. by author and Howard Schwartz). WebR (4:3)
    Spr 79, p. 40.

ORTEGA, Martinez
"Words Before the End. " LitR (23:2) Wint 80, p. 236.

ORTIZ, Simon J.
"The Polka Dot Kid Tells All About Squeeze. " BelPoJ (30:2)
    Wint 79-80, p. 45.

ORTLEB, Charles
"Every Boy. " Mouth (2:1) F 79, p. 15.
"4 A.M. " Mouth (2:1) F 79, p. 27.

OSBORNE-McKNIGHT, Juilene
"You Stand in the Doorway. " EngJ (68:5) My 79, p. 31.

OSERS, Ewald
from Prohibited Man: "Again I am inaudible, inaudible as light"

(tr. of Jan Skácel).   Stand (20:1) 78-79, p. 20.
"The Rubbish Dump" (tr. of Josef Hanzlik).   Stand (20:1) 78-79,
   p. 21.

OSTRIKER, Alicia
   "After the Shipwreck. "   Poetry (134:4) Jl 79, p. 198.
   "Anxiety about Dying. "   Poetry (134:4) Jl 79, p. 199.
   "Ceremony of the Bathtub. "   LittleM (12:1/2) Spr-Sum 78 (79),
      p. 81.
   "The Diver. "   GreenfieldR (7:3/4) Spr-Sum 79, p. 215.
   "The End of the Line. "   Poetry (134:4) Jl 79, p. 196.
   "Fisherman. "   Poetry (134:4) Jl 79, p. 197.
   "Moon and Earth. "   LittleM (12:1/2) Spr-Sum 78 (79), p. 83.
   "The Raven of Death. "   AmerPoR (8:3) My-Je 79, p. 20.
   "The Voices. "   LittleM (12:1/2) Spr-Sum 78 (79), p. 82.
   "Woman with Pocketbook. "   AmerPoR (8:3) My-Je 79, p. 20.

OSTROFF, Anthony
   "Summer and the Radar Base on Mount Hebo. "   PortR (25) 79,
      p. 17.

OSTROMECKI, Bodgan
   "Rembrandt" (tr. by Andrzej Busza and Bogdan Czaykowski).
      Durak (3) 79, p. 13.

OTT, Tom
   "Introduction. "   FourQt (28:2) Wint 79, p. 22.

OVERTON, Ron
   "Admirals' Lobby. "   PoNow (22) 79, p. 36.
   "Albers. "   Shen (30:2) Wint 79, p. 42.
   "American Light Homage to Hopper. "   Salm (44/45) Spr-Sum 79,
      p. 148.
   "1895. "   HangL (36) Aut 79, p. 47.
   "School. "   Shen (30:2) Wint 79, p. 42.

OWEN, Sue
   "The Spell. "   PoetryNW (20:4) Wint 79-80, pp. 29-30.

OWENS, Rochelle
   from Constructs: "Chariots in Subways. "   13thM (4:2) 79, p. 91.
   from Constructs: "On a Center of a Blue-White Sea. "   13thM
      (4:2) 79, p. 92.
   from Constructs: "Winters North. "   13thM (4:2) 79, p. 91.

OWER, John
   "A Death-Sequence. "   SouthernHR (13:3) Sum 79, p. 209.
   "An Epigrammist Savors His Martini. "   GRR (10:1) 79, p. 85.
   "The Gingerbread House. "   KanQ (11:1/2) Wint-Spr 79, p. 70.
   "A Pride of Craft. "   GRR (10:1) 79, p. 84.
   "Refugees. "   Wind (34) 79, p. 46.
   "The Sorceress. "   GRR (10:1) 79, p. 83.

OZAKI, Hōsai
"Big Sky" (tr. by Hiroaki Sato). Pequod (3:2) 79, pp. 85-86.
Free Verse Haiku from Big Sky: "At Shodo Island" (tr. by
    Hiroaki Sato). PartR (46:1) 79, pp. 92-101.

OZAROW, Kent Jorgensen
"Trespass. " StoneC (6:2) My 79, p. 32.

PACE, Rosella
from The Children: (I-III). Bachy (15) Aut 79, pp. 58-60.
"Rain When You're Older. " Bachy (15) Aut 79, p. 60.

PACERNICK, Gary
"Babel. " AmerPoR (8:5) S-O 79, p. 32.
"Jersey City. " PoNow (21) 79, p. 17.
"Portrait. " Spirit (3:1/2) Aut-Wint 77-78, p. 46.
"Walking with Kafka. " StoneC (6:2) My 79, p. 9.

PACHECO, José Emilio
"The Branch" (tr. by Frederick Luciani). DenQ (14:1) Spr 79,
    p. 90.
"Chronicle from the Indies" (tr. by Alastair Reid). PoNow (24)
    79, p. 33.
"Eyes of the Fish" (tr. by Michael Rieman). PoNow (24) 79, p.
    40.
"Fire" (tr. by Frederick Luciani). DenQ (14:1) Spr 79, p. 89.
"A Lecture on Crabs" (tr. by Ernesto Trejo). Chelsea (38) 79,
    p. 178.
"Mosquitoes" (tr. by Alastair Reid). PoNow (24) 79, p. 33.
"Physiology of the Slug" (tr. by Ernesto Trejo). Chelsea (38)
    79, p. 177.
"pompeii" (tr. by Joel Zeltzer). Wind (34) 79, p. 47.
"Turner's Landscape" (tr. by Alastair Reid). PoNow (24) 79, p.
    33.

PACK, Robert
"The Great American Poem. " Antaeus (32) Wint 79, pp. 82-86.
"The Stained Glass Window. " PraS (53:1) Spr 79, p. 32.
"Waking to My Name. " Antaeus (32) Wint 79, p. 59.

PACZKOWSKI, Susan
"For Window-Peekers. " Madem (85:6) Je 79, p. 48.

PADGETT, Ron
"The Great American Poem. " Antaeus (32) Wint 79, pp. 82-86.

PADHI, Bibhu Prasad
"Puri. " WebR (4:3) Spr 79, p. 58.
"Summer Afternoon in Cuttack. " WebR (4:3) Spr 79, p. 59.

PADILLA, Heberto
"I've Always Lived in Cuba" (tr. by Stuart Friebert). WestB
    (4) 79, p. 46.

"On Writing Poems" (tr." by Stuart Friebert). WestB (4) 79, p. 47.

"Overboard" (tr. by Alastair Reid). NewYRB (26:16) 25 O 79, p. 16.

"Self-Portrait of the Other" (tr. by Alastair Reid). NewYRB (26:16) 25 O 79, p. 16.

"To Pablo Armando Fernandez" (tr. by Alastair Reid). NewYRB (26:16) 25 O 79, p. 16.

PAGE-YORK, Gary
"Footloose Elias Blind. " StoneC (6:1) F 79, p. 17.

PAGIS, Dan
"Armchairs" (tr. by Bernhard Frank). PoNow (24) 79, p. 41.
"Balloons" (tr. by Bernhard Frank). PoNow (24) 79, p. 40.
"Hide and Seek" (tr. by Bernhard Frank). PoNow (24) 79, p. 40.
"Impromptu Heart" (tr. by Bernhard Frank). PoNow (24) 79, p. 40.
"The Two-Legged Kind" (tr. by Bernhard Frank). PoNow (21) 79, p. 46.

PAINTER, An
Poem. St. AR (5:2) 79, p. 19.

PALCHI, Alfredo de
"The moth staggers against the glass panes" (tr. by Sonia Raiziss). PoNow (24) 79, p. 41.
"Spring is a pigeon picking at" (tr. by Sonia Raiziss). PoNow (24) 79, p. 41.

PALLISTER, Jan
"And, then, remember, life is only this much" (tr. of Nico Naldini w. Marisa Gatti-Taylor). PoNow (24) 79, p. 28.
"Between the real and the unreal" (tr. of Nico Naldini w. Marisa Gatti-Taylor). PoNow (24) 79, p. 27.
"Calm" (tr. of Giuseppe Ungaretti w. Arthur Neisberg). PoNow (24) 79, p. 61.
"Disappointments" (tr. of Rene Daumal). PoNow (24) 79, p. 11.
"Erase if You Will" (tr. of Eugenio Montale). PoNow (24) 79, p. 26.
"The Fawn" (tr. of Jules Supervielle). PoNow (24) 79, p. 59.
"The Four Cardinal Times of Day" (tr. of Rene Daumal). PoNow (24) 79, p. 11.
"I Am Dead... " (tr. of Rene Daumal). PoNow (24) 79, p. 11.
"In Arles" (tr. of Jean-Paul Toulet). PoNow (24) 79, p. 59.
"It was still a trifle cold" (tr. of Nico Naldini w. Marisa Gatti-Taylor). PoNow (24) 79, p. 27.
"Life's Evil" (tr. of Eugenio Montale). PoNow (24) 79, p. 26.
"Motet" (tr. of Eugenio Montale). PoNow (24) 79, p. 26.
"Music" (tr. of Anne Herbert). PoNow (24) 79, p. 18.
"My Poetry" (tr. of Sandro Penna). PoNow (24) 79, p. 45.
"Night" (tr. of Giuseppe Ungaretti w. Arthur Neisberg). PoNow (24) 79, p. 61.

"Nocturne II" (tr. of Rubén Darío). PoNow (24) 79, p. 11.
"Nostalgia" (tr. of Giuseppe Ungaretti w. Arthur Neisberg).
    PoNow (24) 79, p. 61.
"Prophecy" (for Jean Cassou) (tr. of Jules Superveille). PoNow
    (24) 79, p. 59.
"A shadow upon the unmade bed" (tr. of Nico Haldini w. Marisa
    Gatti-Taylor). PoNow (24) 79, p. 27.
(to the great Alfred) "Comisso, de Pisi, Sandro Penna:" (tr. of
    Nico Naldini w. Marisa Gatti-Taylor). PoNow (24) 79, p. 28.
"When down upon us come, some evening" (tr. of Marie Noel).
    PoNow (24) 79, p. 37.

PALMER, Leslie
"Quietly Done. " SmPd (46) 79, p. 33.

PALMER, Opal
"Impressions of a Great Grand Aunt. " Wind (34) 79, p. 48.

PALMER, William
"With Moon Eyes She Talks of Her Husband. " Bits (9) Ja 79.

PALMER, Winthrop
."The Unmelted Eye. " Confr (19) Aut 79-Wint 80, p. 6.

PAPE, Greg
"At the Edge of the River. " QW (9) Spr-Sum 79, p. 47.
"Black Branches" (for W. Eugene Smith). Antaeus (35) Aut 79,
    p. 49.
"A Man in the Street. " PoNow (25) 79, p. 27.
"Naming Winners. " PoNow (25) 79, p. 27.
"Part of an Old Story. " QW (9) Spr-Sum 79, p. 45.
"Self-Pity at Seven. " PoNow (25) 79, p. 27.
"Stanley. " QW (6) Spr-Sum 78, p. 92.

PARATTE, Henri-Dominique
"Juillet. " Os (9) 79, p. 15.

PARHAM, Robert
"The Cultist. " Wind (32) 79, p. 36.
"Sunday in South Carolina. " SouthwR (64:2) Spr 79, p. 138.

PARINI, Jay
"The Lackawanna at Dusk. " Agni (10/11) 79, p. 138.
"This Scrying. " NewRep (180:22) 2 Je 79, p. 32.

PARISI, Philip
"Niagara Falls. " NewL (46:1) Aut 79, p. 46.

PARKER, Christopher W.
"A Father's Plea for His Muscular Dystrophic Child. " JnlONJP
    (3:2) 79, p. 37.
"Letter to My Apartment Window Woman. " JnlONJP (3:2) 79, p.
    38.

PARKER, Mary
"Linda in Love. "   PikeF (2) Wint 78-79, p. 3.
'The Lion Dream After You Left Me. "   PikeR (1) Sum 79, p. 42.
"Subway Rider. "   PikeF (2) Wint 78-79, p. 3.

PARKER, Pat
"Where Will You Be?"   Cond (5) 79, pp. 128-132.

PARKERSON, Michelle
"(Observations at a Poetry Reading, Women's Detention Center,
    Summer '75). "   Cond (5) 79, p. 68.
"Resumé. "   Cond (5) 79, p. 65.

PARKS, Patricia
"Wandering Still. "   GRR (10:1) 79, p. 115.

PARRA, Nicanor
"No One" (tr. by Naomi Lindstrom).   DenQ (14:2) Sum 79, p. 90.

PARRY, D. W.
'The Japanese Haiku: 23 Imitations. "   DenQ (14:2) Sum 79, p.
    63.

PASCHEN, Elise
"In the Fields. "   HarvAd (112:4) My 79, p. 21.

PASOLINI, Pier Paolo
"The Ashes of Gramsci" (tr. by Norman MacAfee and Luciano
    Martinengo).   ParisR (76) Aut 79, pp. 34-46.
'I Am Pleased" (tr. by Dino Fabris).   PoNow (24) 79, p. 41.
"Lied" (tr. by Dino Fabris).   PoNow (24) 79, p. 41.
"Rain Beyond Everything II" (tr. by Dino Fabris).   PoNow (24)
    79, p. 41.
'The True Christ Will Come" (tr. by Dino Fabris).   PoNow (24)
    79, p. 41.

PASTAN, Linda
"After Minor Surgery. "   Poetry (135:3) D 79, p. 149.
"Attempt at Dialogue. "   NewRep (180:24) 16 Je 79, p. 26.
"Barbecue. "   PoNow (21) 79, p. 35.
"Dreams. "   Poetry (135:3) D 79, p. 150.
"End of Summer: Leaving. "   PoNow (23) 79, p. 34.
"Epilogue" (for J. I.).   GeoR (33:4) Wint 79, p. 800.
"Ethics. "   Poetry (135:3) D 79, p. 151.
"Eyes Only. "   VirQR (55:2) Spr 79, p. 299.
'Her Lover Speaks. "   NewRep (181:12) 22 S 79, p. 46.
"Instructions to the Reader. "   MissouriR (3:1) Aut 79, p. 31.
'It Is Raining on the House of Anne Frank. "   PoNow (23) 79, p.
    27.
"My Achilles Son. "   Poetry (135:3) D 79, pp. 148-149.
"Preparing for an Audit by the IRS. "   Paint (11) Spr 79, p. 61.
"Prologue. "   GeoR (33:4) Wint 79, p. 801.
"Prose Poem. "   PoNow (22) 79, p. 36.

"Secrets. " Atl (243:4) Ap 79, p. 93.
"25th Anniversary. " NewYorker (55:14) 21 My 79, p. 130.
"25th High School Reunion. " PoNow (23) 79, p. 27.
"The Vanishing Point. " CarolQ (31:2) Spr-Sum 79, p. 49.
"The War Between Desire and Dailiness. " NewL (46:1) Aut 79,
   p. 95.
"When the Moment Is Over. " GeoR (33:1) Spr 79, p. 115.
"whom do you visualize as your reader?" PoNow (23) 79, p. 27.
"Why Not?" NewL (46:1) Aut 79, p. 96.
"Widow's Walk, Somewhere Inland. " Poetry (135:3) D 79, p. 152.

PASTERNAK, Boris
"My Sister, Life" (tr. by Mark Rudman and Bohdan Boychuk).
   PoNow (24) 79, p. 42.
"The Purpose of Soul" (tr. by Mark Rudman and Bohdan Boy-
   chuk). PoNow (24) 79, p. 42.

PASTOR, Ricardo
"Narcissus" (tr. of René Acuña). GRR (10:2) 79, p. 187.

PATERSON, Evangeline
"Parting from My Son. " NewEngR (1:3) Spr 79, p. 358.

PATTEN, Brian
"Advice from the Original Gatecrasher to the Recently Dead. "
   WestB (4) 79, p. 74.
"The Mule's Favourite Dream. " WestB (4) 79, p. 72.
"The Right Mask. " WestB (4) 79, p. 72.

PATTEN, Karl
"January 11, 1977: Three News Items. " GreenfieldR (7:3/4)
   Spr-Sum 79, p. 191.
"Memories Fire Clouds" (for my father). FourQt (29:1) Aut 79,
   p. 22.

PATTERSON, Thomas
"The Battle for Hill Sixteen: Meyers on KP. " CalQ (15) Wint
   79, p. 49.

PATTON, Patti
"Cup. " SmPd (46) 79, p. 12.

PATTON, Rob
"Going Confessional. " GreenfieldR (7:3/4) Spr-Sum 79, p. 59.

PAUL, James
"Silhouette. " QW (7) Aut 78, p. 81.

PAUL, Jay S.
"Beds Over the River's Kitchen. " PikeR (1) Sum 79, p. 60.
"I Come Back to Talk Your Talk, Mary Haber. " Wind (33) 79,
   p. 40.
"Leaning into the Wind. " StoneC (6:1) F 79, p. 22.

PAUL, Martin
    from O Hour: "There was a Nicaraguan in a foreign country"
        (tr. of Ernesto Cardenal). AmerPoR (8:2) Mr-Ap 79, p. 4.
    "Song of the Unlucky Angel" (tr. of Raphael Alberti). QW (8)
        Wint 79, p. 92.
    "The Wood Is Vast and Lonely... " (tr. of Raphael Alberti). QW
        (8) Wint 79, p. 92.

PAU-LLOSA, Ricardo
    "Links. " Epoch (29:1) Aut 79, p. 13.

PAULUS
    "seed. " St. AR (5:3) Aut-Wint 79, p. 116.

PAVLICH, Walter
    "The Return" (for Paul). CutB (13) Aut-Wint 79, p. 22.

PAVLOVSKI, Radovan
    "Drought" (tr. by Zoran Anchevski and Bryce Conrad). CharR
        (5:2) Aut 79, p. 8.
    "Landscape from the War" (tr. by Zoran Anchevski and Bryce
        Conrad). CharR (5:2) Aut 79, p. 7.
    "Road to the Mountain" (tr. by Zoran Anchevski and Bryce Con-
        rad). CharR (5:2) Aut 79, p. 6.
    "Skin" (tr. by Zoran Anchevski and Bryce Conrad). CharR (5:2)
        Aut 79, p. 7.
    "Sowers" (tr. by Zoran Anchevski and Bryce Conrad). CharR
        (5:2) Aut 79, p. 5.
    "Watchtower" (tr. by Zoran Anchevski and Bryce Conrad).
        CharR (5:2) Aut 79, p. 5.

PAYACK, Peter
    "Body Language. " PoNow (22) 79, p. 36.
    "How We Built the Matterhorn. " PoNow (22) 79, p. 36.
    "The New Random Dictionary. " PoNow (22) 79, p. 36.

PAYNE, John Burnett
    "Family Reunion. " Wind (33) 79, p. 42.

PAYNE, Nina
    "Anecdote of the Stolen Coins. " Ploughs (5:1) 79, pp. 100-102.
    "Grazing. " Ploughs (5:1) 79, p. 103.

PAZ, Octavio
    "Between Leaving and Staying" (tr. by Mark Strand). NewYorker
        (55:10) 23 Ap 79, p. 43.
    "Black and White Stone" (tr. by Eliot Weinberger). Nat (229:10)
        6 O 70, p. 316.
    "Concert in the Garden" (for Carmen Figueroa de Meyer) (tr. by
        Eliot Weinberger). Nat (228:23) 16 Je 79, p. 733.
    "A Draft of Shadows" (tr. by Eliot Weinberger). Montra (6) 79,
        p. 85.
    "Epitaph for No Stone" (tr. by Eliot Weinberger). DenQ (14:1)

Spr 79, p. 14.
"Golden Lotuses (3)" (tr. by Eliot Weinberger). Nat (229:9) 29
S 79, p. 282.
"Here" (tr. by Naomi Lindstrom). PoNow (24) 79, p. 42.
"Immemorial Landscape" (for José de la Colina) (tr. by Eliot
Weinberger). Nat (228:23) 16 Je 79, p. 732.
"In the Middle of This Phrase" (tr. by Eliot Weinberger).
ParisR (75) Spr 79, pp. 24-28.
"Light Holds" (to the Painter, Balthus) (tr. by Mark Strand).
NewYorker (55:10) 23 Ap 79, p. 42.
"Nightfall" (tr. by Eliot Weinberger). Nat (228:24) 23 Je 79, p.
764.
"Small Variation" (tr. by Mark Strand). NewYorker (55:10) 23
Ap 79, p. 42.
"A Tale of Two Gardens" (tr. by Eliot Weinberger). Montra (5)
79, p. 64.
"Touch" (tr. by Naomi Lindstrom). PoNow (24) 79, p. 42.
"Waking" (tr. by Mark Strand). NewYorker (55:10) 23 Ap 79, p.
42.
"Wind and Water and Stone" (tr. by Mark Strand). NewYorker
(55:10) 23 Ap 79, p. 42.
"With Eyes Closed" (tr. by Eliot Weinberger). Nat (229:5) 25
Ag-1 S 79, p. 154.

PEACOCK, Molly
"Anno Domini." Shen (30:1) Aut 78, p. 20.
"Little Portrait." MissR (24) Aut 79, p. 86.
"Peacock's Superette." MissR (24) Aut 79, p. 83.
"Safe, Safe" (for Corrine, Marc, Nancy and Phil). MissR (24)
Aut 79, p. 88.
"Two Figures." EnPas (9) 79, p. 24.
"Two Flowers." EnPas (9) 79, p. 25.

PEARLSON, F. S.
"Sea-Crazy (Night Sounds)." CalQ (15) Wint 79, p. 72.

PEASE, Deborah
"Casualty." PoNow (25) 79, p. 32.
"Did You Know?" Salm (44/45) Spr-Sum 79, p. 155.
"Displacement." Salm (44/45) Spr-Sum 79, p. 157.
"Martyr under a Cathedral Ceiling." PoNow (25) 79, p. 32.
"Natural Selection." Salm (44/45) Spr-Sum 79, p. 159.
"Vigil for a Small Sonata." AntR (37:3) Sum 79, p. 324.

PEATTIE, Noel
"The Flight Home." SeC (6:1) 78, p. 41.
"Second Coming." SeC (6:1) 78, p. 43.

PECK, John
"Jonathan." ParisR (75) Spr 79, pp. 90-91.
"King David." ParisR (75) Spr 79, pp. 88-89.
"A Poem from Graduals." Salm (46) Aut 79, p. 95.

PEECH, Emilie
"View" (tr. of Christian J. Van Geel w. W. S. DiPiero). PoNow
(24) 79, p. 61.
"Wind is always driving, wind" (tr. of Christian J. Van Geel w.
W. S. DiPiero). PoNow (24) 79, p. 61.

PEECH, John
"The Hardness of the Wind. " ParisR (75) Spr 79, pp. 83-85.

PEFFER, George
"Insomnia. " Pig (6) 79, p. 31.
"Nothing Translates Well. " Pig (6) 79, p. 93.

PEHRSON, Dale
"The Doe. " EngJ (68:5) My 79, p. 32.

PEHRSON, Peter
"In Reply to a Solicitation for Poetry: Tricks of the Mind. "
Mouth (2:2) Je 79, p. 22.
"Lyrics for Clerks of Chic. " Mouth (2:3) N 79, p. 12.

PELLETIER, Marianne
"Night Rider. " HangL (36) Aut 79, p. 75.

PELLICER, Carlos
"The Hills" (tr. by Sister Miriam Daniel Fahey). MalR (49) Ja
79, p. 92.

PENNA, Sandro
"The businessman strolled toward his house" (tr. by M. J.
Shakely and Ian Young). PoNow (24) 79, p. 44.
Fifteen Poems (tr. by W. S. DiPiero). PoNow (24) 79, pp. 42-44.
"A glass of milk, a square" (tr. by M. J. Shakely and Ian Young).
PoNow (24) 79, p. 44.
"In a dingy theatre pit" (tr. by M. J. Shakely and Ian Young).
PoNow (24) 79, p. 44.
"It was September. People were back" (tr. by W. S. DiPiero).
PoNow (21) 79, p. 45.
"My Poetry" (tr. by Jan Pallister). PoNow (24) 79, p. 45.
"O cemetery lights, don't tell me" (tr. by W. S. DiPiero).
PoNow (21) 79, p. 45.
"The ship arrives. The cheery passengers" (tr. by M. J.
Shakely and Ian Young). PoNow (24) 79, p. 44.
"Silently, the summer went away" (tr. by M. J. Shakely and Ian
Young). PoNow (24) 79, p. 44.
"Still it is sweet to find yourself" (tr. by M. J. Shakely and Ian
Young). PoNow (24) 79, p. 44.
"There was no one in the porter's lodge" (tr. by W. S. DiPiero).
PoNow (21) 79, p. 45.
"Under the April sky this peace of mine" (tr. by W. S. DiPiero).
PoNow (21) 79, p. 45.
"Was he whistling at his door, or did he wish" (tr. by M. J.
Shakely and Ian Young). PoNow (24) 79, p. 44.

PENCE, Susan
"Idols of the Tribe. " DenQ (14:2) Sum 79, p. 42.

PENFOLD, Gerda
"We Were Twins in The. " Vaga (29) 79, p. 44.

PENZAVECCHIA, James
"The Invisible Man Takes a Mistress. " GreenfieldR (7:3/4) Spr-
Sum 79, p. 259.
"The Man with Glass Hands. " GreenfieldR (7:3/4) Spr-Sum 79,
p. 257.
"Missing. " GreenfieldR (7:3/4) Spr-Sum 79, p. 258.
"Thirst. " LittleM (12:1/2) Spr-Sum 78(79), p. 79.

PENZI, J.
"Cyclone. " Mund (11:1) 79, p. 47.
"The Voice. " Mund (11:1) 79, p. 47.

PERCHIK, Simon
"Adrienne. " NewL (46:1) Aut 79, p. 28.
"Door Edge Dark. " PoetryNW (20:4) Wint 79-80, p. 30.
"No Question Has That Many Words. " NewL (46:1) Aut 79, p.
29.
"Room. " NewL (46:1) Aut 79, p. 28.
"Rose's Wedding. " NewL (46:1) Aut 79, p. 29.

PERELMAN, Bob
"At It" (for Steve Benson). SunM (8) Aut 79, p. 157.
"Photo Finish. " SunM (8) Aut 79, p. 159.
"Socialist Realism" (for Bruce Andrews). SunM (8) Aut 79, p.
160.

PERET, Benjamin
"Five Portraits" (tr. by Byron Leonard). MalR (51) Jl 79, p.
54.
"Having Grown Old the Devil Became a Hermit" (tr. by Byron
Leonard). Chelsea (38) 79, p. 26.
"My Latest Misfortunes" (tr. by Byron Leonard). Chelsea (38)
79, p. 25.
"Reform" (tr. by Byron Leonard). Chelsea (38) 79, p. 24.
"A Thousand Times" (tr. by Keith Hollaman). Kayak (50) My 79,
p. 55.
"To Wait on the Street Corner" (tr. by Keith Hollaman). Field
(20) Spr 79, p. 20.
"Tortured Girls" (tr. by Keith Hollaman). Kayak (50) My 79, p.
54.

PEREZ, Gail Adrianne
"The Roadside Chapel. " SoDakR (17:1) Spr 79, p. 82.

PERLBERG, Mark
"When at Night. " Poetry (134:4) Jl 79, pp. 216-217.

PERLMAN, John
  "Brian McInerney's High School Photo. " SunM (8) Aut 79, p. 122.
  "North Lake. " SunM (8) Aut 79, p. 121.

PERREAULT, Ellen
  "Fourth of July Cookout. " GreenfieldR (7:3/4) Spr-Sum 79, p.
     106.
  "Those Trees That Line the Northway. " GreenfieldR (7:3/4)
     Spr-Sum 79, p. 107.

PERRIN, Jane
  Poem.   St. AR (5:2) 79, p. 109.
  Poem.   St. AR (5:2) 79, p. 110.
  Poem.   St. AR (5:2) 79, p. 111.

PERRY, Robyn Renea
  "texas night snake. " BelPoJ (30:2) Wint 79, p. 20.
  "to my grandfather. " BelPoJ (30:2) Wint 79-80, p. 20.

PERSLEY, Thomas
  "Being Born. " EngJ (68:5) My 79, p. 44.

PESCHEL, Enid Rhodes
  "Hope Shines" (tr. of Paul Verlaine). GRR (10:1) 79, p. 87.
  "Streets" (tr. of Paul Verlaine). GRR (10:1) 79, p. 89.
  "Venus Anadyomene" (tr. of Arthur Rimbaud). GRR (10:1) 79,
     p. 91.

PESEROFF, Joyce E.
  "After Dickinson. " NewRep (181:13) 29 S 79, p. 39.
  "April to May. " ParisR (75) Spr 79, pp. 92-94.
  "Orange. " Ploughs (5:2) 79, p. 119.
  "Refuge. " Ploughs (5:2) 79, p. 118.

PETACCIA, Mario A.
  "Vigil for Dominic. " PikeR (1) Sum 79, pp. 2-3.

PETERS, Robert
  "Carnival Man. " Mouth (2:3) N 79, p. 37.
  "He'll see violets from his upstairs bedroom window--it's. "
     Mouth (2:3) N 79, p. 13.
  "In the Woods. " Mouth (2:3) N 79, p. 37.
  "Old Carlson. " Mouth (2:3) N 79, p. 35.
  from The Picnic in the Snow: "Anatomy of Love. " Bachy (14)
     Spr/Sum 79, p. 76.
  from The Picnic in the Snow: "Love Poem for Paul. " Bachy
     (14) Spr/Sum 79, p. 75.
  from The Picnic in the Snow: "Loving Friend. " Bachy (14)
     Spr/Sum 79, p. 75.
  from The Picnic in the Snow: "Max Von Thurn und Taxis. "
     Bachy (14) Spr/Sum 79, p. 76.
  from The Picnic in the Snow: "Paul Taxis Enacts Lohengrin. "
     Bachy (14) Spr/Sum 79, p. 75.

from The Picnic in the Snow: "The Day's Log. " Bachy (14)
  Spr/Sum 79, p. 76.
"Seurat. " PoNow (23) 79, p. 42.
"Snapshots with Buck, Model-A Ford, and Kitchen. " Im (6:1)
  79, p. 6.

PETERSON, Elizabeth
  "The Lesson. " KanQ (11:1/2) Wint-Spr 79, p. 180.

PETERSON, Jim
  "aspirant. " St. AR (5:3) Aut-Wint 79, p. 36.
  "four dark walls. " St. AR (5:3) Aut-Wint 79, p. 38.
  "Linda and the Cowboy. " CutB (12) Spr-Sum 79, p. 58.
  "Notes. " GreenfieldR (7:3/4) Spr-Sum 79, p. 217.
  "Surprise. " St. AR (5:3) Aut-Wint 79, p. 37.

PETERSON, Karla
  "The Unicorn Club" (for Nancey).   Poem (36) Jl 79, p. 7.

PETERSON, Marsha
  "Mime, to While Away. " WebR (4:4) Aut 79, p. 32.
  "The Wooden Coat. " WebR (4:4) Aut 79, p. 32.
  "Sledge Diary. " WebR (4:4) Aut 79, p. 33.
  "Young Couple: versions of an etching by Kaethe Kollwitz. "
    WebR (4:4) Aut 79, p. 34.

PETESCH, Donald A.
  "Cotton Mather on Witches. " WestHR (33:1) Wint 79, p. 62.
  "Father Working on His Books. " KanQ (11:3) Sum 79, p. 100.

PETRAKOS, Chris
  "What Shakes Us. " HangL (35) Spr 79, p. 52.

PETRIE, Paul
  "The Burning Nightmare. " SewanR (87:2) Spr 79, p. 227.
  "Fantasia on the Deaths of Mallory and Irvine. " SouthernR (15:2)
    Spr 79, pp. 402-407.
  "From the Point. " KanQ (11:1/2) Wint-Spr 79, p. 62.
  "Guy Fawkes Night, Lynmouth. " LitR (22:3) Spr 79, p. 355.

PETROPOULOS, Yiannis
  "Isle of Purbeck. " HarvAd (112:4) My 79, p. 25.
  "Medical Examiner's Report" (for Pasos Lignades) (tr. of Odys-
    seus Elytes).   HarvAd (112:4) My 79, p. 16.

PETROSKI, Henry
  "Failure Criterion. " PoNow (25) 79, p. 33.
  "Professor Z Introduces Professor A. " Poetry (133:5) F 79, p.
    278.
  "So This Is Poetry. " PoNow (25) 79, p. 32.

PFINGSTON, Roger
  "April in Indiana. " PoNow (25) 79, p. 28.

"Atlantic Snapshots. " Im (6:1) 79, p. 12.
"Bones. " NewL (46:1) Aut 79, p. 77.
"A Few Weeks after Christmas. " Im (6:1) 79, p. 12.
"Nesting. " PoNow (25) 79, p. 28.
"State Fair Pigs. " PoNow (25) 79, p. 28.
"Tuesday Afternoon, Three Sheets to the Wind. " Im (6:1) 79, p. 12.
"Wind. " Im (6:1) 79, p. 12.

PHARR, Emory C.
"Lightning Bug. " ChrC (96:25) 1-8 Ag 79, p. 750.

PHELPS, Dean
"The Graves at Junction City. " MalR (49) Ja 79, p. 48.

PHILIPS, Carol
"Man Talk. " Tendril (5) Sum 79, p. 41.

PHILLIPS, Ainsley Jo
"Life Analysis # 1. " BallSUF (20:4) Aut 79, p. 79.

PHILLIPS, Dennis
from The Frontier: "Part Three: Fulcrum, A Merging. " Bachy
    (14) Spr/Sum 79, pp. 108-119.
from The Frontier: "Part Four: Frontier, I. " Bachy (15) Aut
    79, pp. 124-34.

PHILLIPS, Frances
"For a Living. " HangL (36) Aut 79, pp. 49-56.

PHILLIPS, James
"departure lounge" (for Scott). Wind (32) 79, p. 29.

PHILLIPS, Jayne Anne
"Asleep in the Past. " Epoch (29:1) Aut 79, p. 19.
"Country. " OP (27) Spr 79, pp. 28-29.
"Cracks. " OP (27) Spr 79, p. 26.
"Happy. " ParisR (75) Spr 79, p. 201.
"Heat. " OP (27) Spr 79, p. 24.
"Port Arthur" (for Janis Joplin). OP (27) Spr 79, p. 30.
"Sanitive. " OP (27) Spr 79, p. 27.
"The Village Girl. " ParisR (75) Spr 79, p. 200.
"The West Texas Farm Bureau Show. " OP (27) Spr 79, p. 31.

PHILLIPS, Louis
"Portrait of a College Administrator. " Academe (65:6) O 79, p. 412.
"The Revolt of the Tuba Players. " CimR (47) Ap 79, p. 15.
"Socrates among the Athenians. " Academe (65:1) F 79, p. 48.

PHILLIPS, Max
"Thalidomide. " Atl (244:1) Jl 79, p. 59.

PHILLIPS, Robert
'The Mole. " NewYorker (55:26) 13 Ag 79, p. 62.
'The Pruned Tree. " PoNow (21) 79, p. 13.

PHILLIS, Yannis
"A Drunken Man. " StoneC (6:3) O 79, p. 30.

PHOCAS, Nikos
"Imitation of Cephalonia" (tr. by Kimon Friar).   Durak (3) 79,
    p. 51.

PICCONE, Sandi
'The Flower Lady. " PoNow (25) 79, p. 33.

PICHON, Ulysses A.
"(I'm the One). " Obs (4:3) Wint 78, pp. 77-79.
"(In the Winter). " Obs (4:3) Wint 78, pp. 76-77.

PIERCY, Marge
"Agitprop. " PoNow (23) 79, p. 28.
'The Cast Off. " Spirit (3:3) Sum 78, p. 4.
'The engulfing garden. " PoNow (23) 79, p. 28.
'The Longest Night. " OP (28) Aut 79, pp. 46-48.
"Loose Woman. " Paint (11) Spr 79, p. 64.
'The market economy. " PoNow (23) 79, p. 28.
'May Apple. " Paint (11) Spr 79, p. 62.
'Morning Athletes" (for Gloria).   OP (28) Aut 79, pp. 44-45.

PIERMAN, Carol J.
"A Criminal Element. " Tele (15) Spr 79, p. 45.
"Cubism. " Tele (15) Spr 79, p. 45.
'The Day You Burned the I Ching. " Tele (15) Spr 79, p. 44.
'Deja Vu. " Ascent (5:1) 79, p. 37.
'The Magician's Props. " Tele (15) Spr 79, p. 44.
"A Memory of Railroads. " Ascent (5:1) 79, p. 36.
'Snow, Snow, Snow--Where will it all End?" Tele (15) Spr 79,
    p. 45.
'Visiting the Shedd Aquarium. " Ascent (5:1) 79, p. 24.

PIERSON, Philip
'Catfish. " GeoR (33:2) Sum 79, p. 413.
"Errands of Mercy. " CarolQ (31:3) Aut 79, p. 85.
'Horsehairs into Eels into Horsehairs. " SouthernPR (19:1) Spr
    79, p. 47.
'In the Slave Cemetery. " Iowa (10:2) Spr 79, p. 91.
'The Monster's Photo Album. " Poetry (133:6) Mr 79, pp. 323-
    325.
"Schooled in Dance" (for Jim Reiss).   CarolQ (31:3) Aut 79, p.
    84.

PIJEWSKI, John
"Beautiful Ruta. " Ploughs (5:2) 79, p. 159.
"Before Dawn in March" (tr. of Jerzy Harasymowicz).   Field

(20) Spr 79, p. 13.
"Burying My Father. " Durak (2) 79, p. 18.
"The Hat. " Poultry (1) 79, p. 3.
"Here's for Everyone. " Durak (2) 79, p. 19.
"The Land of November" (tr. of Jerzy Harasymowicz). Field
    (20) Spr 79, p. 14.
"Looking for Something. " Ploughs (5:2) 79, p. 160.
"The Myth of St. George" (tr. of Jerzy Harasymowicz). Field
    (20) Spr 79, p. 11.
"Twilight" (tr. of Jerzy Harasymowicz). Field (20) Spr 79, p.
    15.

PIKE, Lawrence
    "How to Get Thought and Feeling Out of the Way and Become a
    Poet" (for Frank O'Hara). Poultry (1) 79, p. 11.
    "How to Make a Sow's Ear Out of a Sow's Ear" (for Richard
    Brautigan). Poultry (1) 79, p. 11.

PILKINGTON, Kevin
    "Asleep in the Park. " Ur (2) 79, p. 93.
    "Carlos and Lina. " Ur (2) 79, p. 94.
    "East Haven. " Ur (2) 79, p. 95.
    "Playground. " Ur (2) 79, p. 96.

PILLIN, William
    "Dreams. " Durak (3) 79, p. 54.
    "Sequence: To the End of Time. " Kayak (50) My 79, p. 18.
    "Singers. " Durak (3) 79, p. 55.

PINDAR
    "Isthmian 5" (for Phylákidas of Aigína) (tr. by Elroy L. Bundy).
    SouthernR (15:4) Aut 79, p. 1022.
    "Olympian 4" (for Psaumis of Kamarina) (tr. by Elroy L. Bundy).
    SouthernR (15:5) Aut 79, p. 1017.
    "Olympian 11" (for Hagesidámos of Epizephyrian Lokris) (tr. by
    Elroy L. Bundy). SouthernR (15:4) Aut 79, p. 1019.
    "Olympian 12" (for Ergóteles of Hímera) (tr. by Elroy L. Bundy).
    SouthernR (15:4) Aut 79, p. 1020.
    "Olympian 14" (for Asópikhos of Orchómenus) (tr. by Elroy L.
    Bundy). SouthernR (15:4) Aut 79, p. 1021.

PINES, Paul
    "Bird Poem for Ilyse. " Pequod (3:1) 79, pp. 36-37.
    "Keeping Time. " Confr (18) Spr-Sum 79, p. 96.
    from Ossabaw Island Dream: "As a child my dreams. " Pequod
    (3:1) 79, pp. 32-36.

PINSKER, Sanford
    "Belly Song, for Etheridge Knight. " GreenfieldR (7:3/4) Spr-Sum
    79, p. 234.
    "Icarus, After. " CentR (23:1) Wint 79, p. 68.
    "In Endless Praise of Summer. " Confr (18) Spr-Sum 79, p. 54.
    "Meditations" (for Harry Roskolenko). CharR (5:1) Spr 79, p. 26.

"Note, Left on My Office Door. " ColEng (40:8) Ap 79, p. 929.
"Wearing White Trousers, After Labor Day. " CentR (23:1) Wint
    79, p. 68.

PINSKY, Lawrence
"Dawn. " Tele (15) Spr 79, p. 122.
"I Remember My Grandfather's Chickens. " Tele (15) Spr 79, p.
    122.

PINSKY, Robert
"The Cold. " NewYorker (55:42) 3 D 79, p. 44.
"Stanzas from Valéry. " Ploughs (5:2) 79, pp. 165-166.

PITKIN, Anne
"Kalaloch, 1975. " CarolQ (31:1) Wint 79, p. 34.
"The Skater. " CarolQ (31:1) Wint 79, p. 35.

PITTS, George
"There We Held Duet and Duel. " PartR (46:4) 79, pp. 604-610.

PIZARNIK, Alejandra
"Deaf Lantern" (tr. by Alina Rivero). AmerPoR (8:2) Mr-Ap 79,
    p. 47.
"Encounter" (tr. by Alina Rivero). AmerPoR (8:2) Mr-Ap 79, p.
    47.
"From the Other Side" (tr. by Alina Rivero). AmerPoR (8:2)
    Mr-Ap 79, p. 47.
"Girl in the Garden" (tr. by Alina Rivero). AmerPoR (8:2) Mr-
    Ap 79, p. 47.
"Signals" (tr. by Alina Rivero). AmerPoR (8:2) Mr-Ap 79, p.
    47.

PIZZARELLI, Alan
"Passing Thru Paterson VIII. " JnlONJP (4:1) 79, p. 21.

PLANTENGA, Bart
"Fire. 10/78. " CarolQ (31:2) Spr-Sum 79, p. 8.

PLANTIER, Therese
"The Track" (tr. by Maxine Kumin and Judith Kumin). PoNow
    (24) 79, p. 45.

PLEASANTS, Ben
"The Running Dogs of Buddha. " WormR (74) 79, p. 41.

PLUMLY, Stanley
"Summer Celestial. " NewYorker (55:24) 30 Jl 79, p. 26.
"Tree Ferns. " NewYorker (55:20) 2 Jl 79, p. 42.

PLUMPP, Sterling D.
"Allen" (for the OBAC poets). GreenfieldR (7:3/4) Spr-Sum 79,
    p. 169.
"Exile" (for Amus Mor). Ur (2) 79, p. 98.

PLYMELL, Charles
"Chicken Mantra. " PoNow (21) 79, p. 40.
"Cows. " Aspect (74/75) Ja-Ag 79, p. 78.
"Hey Ray" (for Ray Bremser). SeC (6:1) 78, p. 75.

POBO, Kenneth
"Canterbury Bells. " WindO (34) Spr-Sum 79, p. 35.
"Helen Traubel Rose. " WindO (34) Spr-Sum 79, p. 36.
"Lamplight. " Ur (2) 79, p. 97.
"Stars. " Wind (33) 79, p. 53.

POE, John Troy
"(Crying Drums). " GreenfieldR (7:3/4) Spr-Sum 79, p. 225.
"Unmarked Path. " GreenfieldR (7:3/4) Spr-Sum 79, p. 224.

POLCOVAR, Carol
"Drought. " PartR (46:2) 79, p. 260.

POLIKOFF, Joan
"Late September, 1976. " HangL (36) Aut 79, p. 76.
"Once, very late. " HangL (36) Aut 79, p. 77.
"Stillness. " HangL (36) Aut 79, p. 77.
"Wyoming. " HangL (36) Aut 79, p. 76.

POLITO, Robert
"Spring Training. " Ploughs (5:2) 79, pp. 140-142.
"Those Fireflies, for Instance. " Ploughs (5:2) 79, pp. 143-144.

POLLAK, Felix
"A Triumph Revisited. " Chowder (13) Aut-Wint 79, p. 74.
"Winter Landscape. " PoNow (23) 79, p. 34.

POLLENS, David
"Yard Talk in Summer. " NewRep (181:7) 18 Ag 79, p. 39.

POLLET, Sylvester
"love poem for a cousin-in-law. " St. AR (5:3) Aut-Wint 79, p.
    125.
"xiv arrondissement. " St. AR (5:3) Aut-Wint 79, p. 125.
"30 today. " St. AR (5:3) Aut-Wint 79, p. 125.

POLLITT, Katha
"Ballet Blanc. " NewYorker (55:1) 19 F 79, p. 44.
"Pygmalion. " Poetry (134:1) Ap 79, p. 14.
"Riverside Drive, November Fifth. " Poetry (135:2) N 79, p. 91.
"A Screen Depicting the Fifty-four Episodes of the Tale of Genji
    on a Background of Gold Leaf. " Poetry (134:1) Ap 79, p.
    13.
"Tomato. " Poetry (134:1) Ap 79, p. 12.

POLYAENUS, Julius of Sardis
"Hope is forever stealing the little" (tr. by I. F. Stone).
    NewYRB (26:2) 22 F 79, p. 10.

PONDER, Leanne
"Looking up from Paradise (Notes from Jamaica). " PoetC (11:1)
    79, p. 12.

PONGER, Edward
"A Salesman's Fear. " JnlONJP (3:2) 79, p. 9.

PONSOT, Marie
"Discovery. " Shen (30:2) Wint 79, p. 44.

PONTILLO, Patrick Anthony
"Bleeding on the Edges of Autumn. " UTR (6:3/4) 79, pp. 34-40.

POOLAW, Etheleen
"Deep River Wide with Hands. " BelPoJ (30:2) Wint 79-80, p. 19.
"Stories My Grandmother Told. " BelPoJ (30:2) Wint 79-80, p.
    18.

POOLE, Thomas
"what could be farther from saturday night. " CentR (23:4) Aut
    79, p. 424.

POPA, Vasko
"At the Crossroads" (tr. by George Jevremovic). Durak (2) 79,
    p. 46.
"Lifting Our Arms" (tr. by George Jevremovic). Durak (2) 79,
    p. 45.

POPE, Deborah
"Harvest. " Poem (36) Jl 79, p. 12.
"Rape. " CutB (12) Spr-Sum 79, p. 23.
"What We Say. " Poem (36) Jl 79, p. 13.
"Wisconsin, Late Winter. " Poem (36) Jl 79, p. 14.

PORTER, Anne
"The Weihnachts-Historie. " Comm (106:23) 21 D 79, p. 726.

PORTER, Kenneth
"The Beachcombers. " ChrC (96:19) 23 My 79, p. 588.

PORTUGILL, Jestyn
"Charleston Morning. " NewRep (180:1) 6 Ja 79, p. 31.

POSNER, David
"The Beasts. " Chelsea (38) 79, p. 165.
"Hyena. " Chelsea (38) 79, p. 225.
"Motel Sepulveda. " PoetryNW (20:3) Aut 79, pp. 41-42.

POSTER, Carol
"Brendan Galvin Tries a Contemporary American Translation of
    Crow, Changing Some Names Around to Avoid Paying the
    Royalties. " Poultry (1) 79, p. 4.
"The Cottage. " Poultry (1) 79, p. 4.

"George Garrett Enthusiastically Recalls an Unusual and Extreme-
ly Athletic Sort of Female. " Poultry (1) 79, p. 4.
"The Parody. " Poultry (1) 79, p. 4.
"The Predator. " Poultry (1) 79, p. 4.
"Swamp. " Poultry (1) 79, p. 4.
"Wind Breaks. " Poultry (1) 79, p. 4.

POTTLE, Kathy
"Untitled: Lucy, there will be time to read to you. " Antaeus
(32) Wint 79, p. 53.
"With Cattle Staunton, Virginia. " Antaeus (32) Wint 79, p. 55.

POULIOS, Leftéris
"Erotic Tank" (tr. by Kimon Friar). Durak (3) 79, p. 56.

POUND, Omar
"Carmina Burana. " Montra (5) 79, p. 17.

POWELL, Enid Levinger
"Check Point. " CarlMis (18:1) Wint 79-80, p. 72.
"Dependence. " CarlMis (18:1) Wint 79-80, p. 72.

POWELL, Leslie
"Semantics. " Chomo (6:1) Sum 79, p. 61.

POWELL, Lynn
"Bloodroot. " SmF (7/8) Spr-Aut 78, p. 39.
"Late. " SmF (7/8) Spr-Aut 78, p. 40.
"Photograph/An Early Conversation. " SouthernPR (19:1) Spr 79,
p. 13.

POWERS, Jessica
from "Scivias" of St. Hildegarde: "Wanderer. " Comm (106:5)
16 Mr 79, p. 140.

PRATOR, Vincent T.
"Satisfaction. " BlackF (3:1) Aut-Wint 79, p. 27.

PRATT, Charles W.
"The Cat Outside the Window. " AndR (6:1) Spr 79, p. 50.

PREVERT, Jacques
"Family Portrait" (tr. by Harriet Zinnes). PoNow (24) 79, p.
45.
"Immense and Red" (tr. by Harriet Zinnes). PoNow (24) 79, p.
45.

PRICE, Alice L.
"Finding Salvation. " GreenfieldR (7:3/4) Spr-Sum 79, p. 101.
"Our Dismembered Shadow. " GreenfieldR (7:3/4) Spr-Sum 79, p.
102.

PRICE, Bonni
"After Parra. " Pequod (3:2) 79, p. 19.

"Agoraphobic. " Pequod (3:2) 79, p. 16.
"Lovetalk. " Pequod (3:2) 79, p. 17.
"Nail Biter. " Pequod (3:2) 79, p. 15.
"Prove It. " Pequod (3:2) 79, p. 18.

PRICE, Charles
  "The Creative Process" (for Gene Ruggles). SeC (7:1) 79, p. 43.
  "A Night on the Town. " SeC (7:1) 79, p. 45.
  "A Poem for Captain Cool. " SeC (7:1) 79, p. 46.
  "Present Shock. " SeC (7:1) 79, p. 49.
  "Rhythms. " SeC (7:1) 79, p. 51.
  "Richard Strauss' Dirty Underwear. " SeC (7:1) 79, p. 47.
  "Sailing to Byzantium. " SeC (7:1) 79, p. 50.

PRICE, Reynolds
  "The Annual Heron. " Poetry (135:3) D 79, pp. 154-160.
  "The Dream of Lee. " MassR (20:3) Aut 79, p. 468.
  "Naked Bay (Mark 14:50-52). " CarolQ (31:1) Wint 79, p. 13.

PRICE, V. B.
  "And Other Heroes" (for George Catlin). SoDakR (17:4) Wint 79-
    80, pp. 45-50.

PRINTZ-PAHLSON, Goran
  "Broendal" (tr. by John Matthias). GreenfieldR (7:3/4) Spr-Sum
    79, p. 121.
  "Man Made Monster Surreptitiously Regarding Idyllic Scene in
    Swiss Hermitage, a Copy of Goethe's "Werther" Resting in
    Its Lap" (tr. by John Matthias). GreenfieldR (7:3/4) Spr-
    Sum 79, p. 122.

PRIOR, Matthew
  "The Rude Response. " Playb (26:1) Ja 79, p. 256.

PRIVETT, Katharine
  "Billy Whiskers. " Wind (34) 79, p. 50.
  "Elegy for Theodore Roethke. " StoneC (6:1) F 79, p. 20.
  "A Mourning; for Malcolm Lowrey. " Wind (34) 79, p. 50.
  "The Young Farm-Wife. " Wind (34) 79, p. 51.

PROCTOR, James W.
  "The Nursing Home Lobby. " Wind (33) 79, p. 44.

PROPP, Karen
  "Worms. " CutB (12) Spr-Sum 79, p. 60.

PROPPER, Dan
  "The Annihilation of Jail. " SeC (6:1) 78, p. 46.
  "A Chagall (#1). " SeC (6:2) 78, p. 100.
  "Constructionist Garbage, II. " SeC (6:1) 78, p. 73.
  "Deaths. " SeC (6:2) 78, p. 95.
  "Message to the United Nations. " SeC (6:2) 78, p. 97.
  "Modern Times. " SeC (6:1) 78, p. 45.
  "The Rape of South America, or, Terminal Symbolism" (for

Judith Abrahms).   SeC (6:2) 78, p. 98.
"Song for Alan Watts. " SeC (6:2) 78, p. 99.

PROVENCHER, James
"Proposal. " Wind (35) 79, p. 56.

PROVOST, Sarah
"Bedtime Story. " HolCrit (16:5) D 79, p. 13.
"Rumor. " NewOR (6:2) 79, p. 131.
"The Wrong People. " CharR (5:2) Aut 79, p. 56.

PRUNTY, Wyatt
"Another Apollo and Daphne" (for Robert Graves).   SouthernR
    (15:3) Sum 79, p. 636.
"The Downhill Dream. " SouthernR (15:3) Sum 79, p. 635.
"The Flood. " LitR (22:3) Spr 79, p. 301.
"The Florist's Daughters. " DenQ (14:2) Sum 79, p. 103.
"For Unk. " Poem (35) Mr 79, p. 40.
"gulls at evening. " St. AR (5:3) Aut-Wint 79, p. 23.
"The Janus. " LitR (22:3) Spr 79, p. 302.
"The Man of Pure Aspirin. " Poem (35) Mr 79, p. 43.
"Miniature. " Poem (35) Mr 79, p. 41.
"Miss Ida, the Parrot and the Cat. " Poem (35) Mr 79, p. 42.
"Repetition. " DenQ (14:2) Sum 79, p. 102.
"The Wake. " SouthernR (15:3) Sum 79, p. 637.

PRYOR, Douglas N.
"Alabama Puberty. " SouthernHR (13:3) Sum 79, p. 197.
"The Dead Man. " SouthernHR (13:3) Sum 79, p. 197.

PRYOR, Mary
"Cosmoba Alley Off Queen Square. " DacTerr (16) 79, p. 50.

PUPKO, Maria
"I will not tell you anything" (tr. of Afanasii Fet).   AmerPoR
    (8:3) My-Je 79, p. 27.

PURENS, Ilmars
"Admonition. " PoNow (22) 79, p. 37.
"Before a Storm. " PoNow (22) 79, p. 38.
"Palm Sunday on East 9th. " PoNow (22) 79, p. 37.
"Red Sports Dream. " PoNow (22) 79, p. 37.
"Roll Up Your Sleeves. " PoNow (22) 79, p. 37.
"Small Miracles. " PoNow (22) 79, p. 37.

PUZISS, Marla
"the women at the well. " SmF (7/8) Spr-Aut 78, p. 38.

PYBUS, Rodney
"Loveless at Sea. " Stand (20:2) 79, p. 6.
"Loveless Attent. " Stand (20:2) 79, p. 8.
"Loveless Husband. " Stand (20:2) 79, p. 9.
"Loveless Labours. " Stand (20:2) 79, p. 8.
"Newcoming South. " Stand (20:2) 79, p. 7.

QABBANI, Rana
"Untitled: if a wild green horse. " Paint (11) Spr 79, p. 66.
"Untitled: I've been broken by waiting. " Paint (11) Spr 79, p. 65.

QUASIMODO, Salvatore
Eight Poems (tr. by Rina Ferrarelli). PoNow (24) 79, pp. 46-47.

QUERTERMOUS, Max
"Do Dolphins, Like Seasons?" Poem (36) Jl 79, p. 3.
"Sacrifice: That the Sun May Rise. " Poem (36) Jl 79, p. 5.
"She. " Poem (36) Jl 79, p. 4.
"To Exorcists. " Poem (36) Jl 79, p. 6.

QUINLAN, Magdaline
"Ice Fishing. " GeoR (33:4) Wint 79, p. 880.

QUINN, John
"Buck. " CutB (12) Spr-Sum 79, p. 25.
"Ring-Necked Parakeet. " CutB (12) Spr-Sum 79, p. 27.

QUINN, John Robert
"At Times I Feel Like a Quince Tree. " KanQ (11:4) Aut 79, p. 48.
"On Re-Reading James Joyce. " Wind (33) 79, p. 59.
"The Shape of a Poem. " Wind (33) 79, p. 59.
"To Maybelle, Dusting. " Wind (33) 79, p. 14.

QUIXLEY, Jim
"The Motion. " Mouth (2:2) Je 79, p. 28.

RAAB, Lawrence
"Disappointment. " Poetry (133:5) F 79, p. 265.
"Familiar Landscapes. " Poetry (133:5) F 79, pp. 270-271.
"In a Southern Garden. " Atl (243:1) Ja 79, p. 52.
"The Professional. " MichQR (18:1) Wint 79, p. 24.
"The Rest. " Poetry (133:5) F 79, p. 267.
"The Room. " Poetry (133:5) F 79, p. 268.
"Two Clouds (for Jennifer, March 20, 1977). " MichQR (18:1) Wint 79, p. 26.
"The Window. " Poetry (133:5) F 79, p. 269.
"You Would Know. " Poetry (133:5) F 79, p. 266.

RA'AV, Ester
"Etruscan Statue" (tr. by Bernhard Frank). PoNow (24) 79, p. 47.

RABONI, Giovanni
Ten Poems (tr. by Stuart Friebert and Vinio Rossi). QW (8) Wint 79, pp. 72-76.

RACANELLI, Vita
"Observation of Snow at Four P. M. " Tele (15) Spr 79, p. 6.
"A Rhapsody of Sorts. " Tele (15) Spr 79, p. 6.

RACHAL, Patricia
"For Anne. " SouthernR (15:2) Spr 79, p. 387.
"From a Bestiary. " SouthernR (15:2) Spr 79, p. 392.
"Lake Michigan in Fall. " SouthernR (15:2) Spr 79, p. 390.

RACHEL, Naomi
"Be Forewarned. " Paint (12) Aut 79, p. 19.
"Frat Rats. " PoNow (25) 79, p. 33.
"the image. " Wind (33) 79, p. 45.
"in the wrong. " Confr (18) Spr-Sum 79, p. 124.
"a myth. " Wind (33) 79, p. 46.
"The Poem. " MalR (52) O 79, p. 117.
"7 proofs for theorem # 13: God Is Not and Never Was an Art
    Patron. " Wind (33) 79, p. 45.

RADHUBER, Stanley
"The Coming of Clouds. " GRR (10:1) 79, p. 145.

RADIN, Doris
"The Exhibition. " PoNow (21) 79, p. 18.
"From the Ice House. " Chelsea (38) 79, p. 224.

RADNOTI, Miklos
"Circling, the eagle plies his trade in the sky; deep down on the"
    (tr. by Emery George). PoNow (23) 79, p. 45.
"Elegy" (tr. by Emery George). MinnR (NS 12) Spr 79, p. 22.
"Friday" (tr. by Emery George). Spirit (3:3) Sum 78, p. 32.
"Letter to My Wife" (tr. by Clive Wilmer and George Gömöri).
    SouthernR (15:1) Wint 79, p. 143.
"Montenegro Elegy" (tr. by Emery George). PoNow (23) 79, p.
    45.
"On the Way Home" (tr. by Emery George). MinnR (NS 12) Spr
    79, p. 23.
"Poem in Autumn" (tr. by Emery George). PoNow (24) 79, p.
    47.
"The Ragged Robin Opens" (tr. by Emery George). MichQR
    (18:3) Sum 79, p. 408.
"Root" (tr. by Jascha Kessler). MichQR (18:3) Sum 79, p. 407.
"The Third Eclogue" (tr. by Clive Wilmer and George Gömöri).
    SouthernR (15:1) Wint 79, p. 144.
"Twenty-Eight Years" (tr. by Emery George). MinnR (NS 12)
    Spr 79, p. 20.
"Youth" (tr. by Emery George). MichQR (18:3) Sum 79, p. 408.

RADTKE, Rosetta
"Advent. " SoDakR (17:2) Sum 79, p. 85.

RAFFEL, Burton
"Creation Myths. " MichQR (18:1) Wint 79, p. 99.
"Philadelphia. " MichQR (18:1) Wint 79, p. 96.

RAIL, DeWayne
"The Dispossessed" (for Richard Hugo). Wind (32) 79, p. 38.
"The Dying Man. " Wind (32) 79, p. 37.

RAINE, Carl
"The Train Set. " AmerS (48:3) Sum 79, p. 342.

RAINE, Craig
"Facts of Life. " SewanR (87:4) Aut 79, p. 540.

RAIZISS, Sonia
"Adam" (tr. of David Maria Turoldo). PoNow (24) 79, p. 60.
"The Heart Always Colder" (tr. of David Maria Turoldo). PoNow
    (24) 79, p. 60.
"Modigliani" (tr. of Arnaldo di Benedetto). PoNow (24) 79, p. 5.
"The moth staggers against the glass panes" (tr. of Alfredo de
    Palchi). PoNow (24) 79, p. 41.
"O My Days" (tr. of David Maria Turoldo). PoNow (24) 79, p.
    60.
"Return" (tr. of Vittorio Seveni). PoNow (24) 79, p. 54.
"Spring is a pigeon picking at" (tr. of Alfredo de Palchi). PoNow
    (24) 79, p. 41.

RAKOSI, Carl
Nine poems. Montra (5) 79, p. 46.

RALPH, Marshall
"A Curious Phenomenon. " Poetry (135:2) N 79, p. 92.

RAMEY, Jack
"Satyr. " Poem (37) N 79, p. 1.

RAMINGTON, John
"Theological Reflections at Roger's Tavern. " ParisR (75) Spr 79,
    p. 240.

RAMIREZ, Miguel Flores
"Guernica" (tr. by Linda Scheer). PoNow (24) 79, p. 15.
"One Day Mirrors Will Have Aged" (tr. by Linda Scheer). PoNow
    (24) 79, p. 15.

RAMKE, Bin
"Biography of a Strangler. " PoNow (25) 79, p. 28.
"The Concert for Bangladesh. " GeoR (33:2) Sum 79, p. 392.
"The Magician. " Agni (10/11) 79, p. 144.
"Mater Dolorosa. " GeoR (33:3) Aut 79, p. 566.
"The Object of the Dispute. " Poetry (134:3) Je 79, pp. 139-141.
"Obscurantism. " Poetry (134:3) Je 79, p. 142.
"On Living the Rich, Full Life. " OhioR (20:2) Spr-Sum 79, p.
    7.
"To Bury a Horse in Texas. " PoNow (25) 79, p. 28.
"Victory Drive, Near Fort Benning, Georgia. " Poetry (134:3)
    Je 79, p. 143.
"Westminster Chimes. " OhioR (20:2) Spr-Sum 79, pp. 6-7.

RAMSEY, Jarold
"Going and Coming. " PraS (53:2) Sum 79, p. 173.
"Lupine Dew" (for Sophia). PoNow (23) 79, p. 11.

RAMSEY, Paul
"The Burden. " SmF (7/8) Spr-Aut 78, p. 12.
"A Leaf Fire Seen. " SmF (7/8) Spr-Aut 78, p. 13.
"Roulette. " Bits (9) Ja 79.

RANDALL, Julia
"Monet at Giverny. " AmerPoR (8:1) Ja-F 79, p. 30.
"The Trackers. " AmerPoR (8:1) Ja-F 79, p. 30.

RANDALL, Margaret
"Home. " FourQt (28:2) Wint 79, p. 14.
"In a Plastic Bag. " PoNow (22) 79, p. 26.
"Nothing Was the Way It Was. " PoNow (22) 79, p. 26.

RANDALL, Paula
"All Things Exist in Order to End. " StoneC (6:1) F 79, p. 15.

RANKIN, Jennifer
"From the Mud Hut: Section II. " NoAmR (264:2) Sum 79, pp.
   10-17.

RANKIN, Paula
"Bedtime Story. " CarolQ (31:1) Wint 79, p. 47.
"Callers. " OhioR (20:2) Spr-Sum 79, pp. 64-65.
"For the Child Drowned in the Well of Black Water. " QW (7)
   Aut 78, p. 122.
"Getting the Truth to Come Clear. " ArkRiv (4:3) 79, p. 16.
"In the Calendar Square of the Dream. " Ploughs (5:1) 79, p.
   105.
"Losing Rings. " Chowder (13) Aut-Wint 79, p. 10.
"Love in Magnolia Cemetery. " KanQ (11:1/2) Wint-Spr 79, p.
   92.
"Poem for Exchange of Habitat. " Ploughs (5:1) 79, p. 104.
"Provisions: For a Book of Poems Received on New Year's
   Eve" (for David). KanQ (11:1/2) Wint-Spr 79, p. 91.
"Shared Visions. " GeoR (33:4) Wint 79, p. 915.
"Something Good on the Heels of Something Bad. " NewOR (6:2)
   79, p. 174.
"Tenants: To Keep Us Carefully Moving. " KanQ (11:1/2) Wint-
   Spr 79, p. 93.
"Thinking of Others. " Chowder (13) Aut-Wint 79, p. 11.
"Two Lovers on Bridge in Winter. " Ascent (5:1) 79, p. 35.

RANKIN, Rush
"Albert Camus. " SenR (10:1) Spr 79, p. 95.
"Baroque Friends. " SenR (10:1) Spr 79, p. 99.
"Descendants. " SenR (10:1) Spr 79, p. 102.
"Glee. " SenR (10:1) Spr 79, p. 97.
"Snails, Octopus, Doves. " SenR (10:1) Spr 79, p. 105.
"The Woman Who Combed. " NewL (46:1) Aut 79, p. 35.

RANSMEIER, J. C.
"tahiti: for p. gauguin. " St. AR (5:3) Aut-Wint 79, p. 15.

RAPHAEL, Dan
"i step-dive in a growing tree. " Tele (15) Spr 79, p. 135.

RAS, Barbara
"First Quarter Moon: Something Animal. " DenQ (14:2) Sum 79, p. 60.
"Letter to a Friend Growing Feathers in a Bar. " DenQ (14:2) Sum 79, p. 62.
"Two Flights. " DenQ (14:2) Sum 79, p. 58.
"Visiting the Grave. " DenQ (14:2) Sum 79, p. 59.

RASOF, Henry
"The Fourth Option. " KanQ (11:1/2) Wint-Spr 79, p. 193.

RATCLIFFE, Stephen
"Air. " Poetry (133:6) Mr 79, p. 321.
"Pacheteau's Calistoga Hot Springs. " MassR (20:2) Sum 79, p. 208.
"Postscript, on a Name. " Poetry (133:6) Mr 79, p. 321.
"Star Route Farm. " PraS (53:1) Spr 79, p. 76.

RATINER, Steven
"Dead Bodies. " CalQ (15) Wint 79, p. 64.
"making magic. " Tendril (4) Wint 79, p. 42.
"Marriage at Midnight. " CalQ (15) Wint 79, p. 66.

RATTI, John
"Inside, Outside, and Beyond. " Salm (43) Wint 79, p. 98.
"My Mother Remembers Spanish Influenza. " NewYorker (55:31) 17 S 79, p. 42.
"You See?" NewYorker (55:26) 13 Ag 79, p. 36.

RAVIKOVITCH, Dahlia
"Deep Calleth unto Deep" (tr. by Chana Bloch). PoNow (24) 79, p. 33.
"The Tearing" (tr. by Chana Bloch). PoNow (24) 79, p. 33.

RAVNDAL, Janeal Turnbull
"Grace. " ChrC (96:37) 14 N 79, p. 1124.

RAWLEY, James M.
"Ryder Runs. " BelPoJ (29:3) Spr 79, p. 4.

RAWLINGS, Doug
"Prometheus Again. " Sam (79) 79, p. 58.

RAY, David
"At the Nelson Gallery" (for Samuel). PoNow (21) 79, p. 15.
"Beatrice. " QW (8) Wint 79, p. 95.
"The Cenote at Chichen Itza. " Harp (258:1546) Mr 79, p. 103.
"A Dream of Valentino. " PoNow (22) 79, p. 38.
"Extreme Unction in Pa. " NewL (46:2) Wint 79-80, p. 106.
"The Factories in the Fields" (for Cesar Chavez). Mund (11:1)

79, p. 39.
"The Father. " Spirit (3:3) Sum 78, p. 7.
"For Gary Gilmore. " GreenfieldR (7:3/4) Spr-Sum 79, p. 163.
Fifteen Poems. CharR (5:SI) 79, pp. 33-51.
"The Great American Poem. " Antaeus (32) Wint 79, pp. 82-86.
"A Gypsy Lady in Mexico. " Spirit (3:3) Sum 78, p. 5.
"Heaven with a Gun" (for Frank & Lucy Sibley). GreenfieldR
    (7:3/4) Spr-Sum 79, p. 164.
"In Victoria Station. " Spirit (3:3) Sum 78, p. 6.
"Lewis Hine's Photographs of the Empire State. " GeoR (33:3)
    Aut 79, p. 661.
"Mulberries. " PoNow (21) 79, p. 40.
"The Rivals. " PoNow (22) 79, p. 38.
"Sonnet to Seabrook. " MassR (20:2) Sum 79, p. 258.
"Stopping at Muna. " VirQR (55:2) Spr 79, p. 301.
"The Sun's Eye: Monument Valley. " Mund (11:1) 79, p. 38.
"The Thirties. " VirQR (55:2) Spr 79, p. 301.
"The Training Bra. " Harp (258:1546) Mr 79, p. 103.
"The Tourist. " Mund (11:1) 79, p. 39.
"Vivian. " MissouriR (3:1) Aut 79, p. 27.
"The Woman Who Is Like a Pepper. " GeoR (33:3) Aut 79, p.
    660.

RAY, Grayce
"Poem for Some Small Cafe. " DacTerr (16) 79, p. 51.
from Poems from a Residential Hotel, Room 609: 'The Priest
    in the Window Well. " DacTerr (16) 79, p. 52.

RAY, Judy
"Beethoven. " GreenfieldR (7:3/4) Spr-Sum 79, p. 166.
"Drinking in Africa. " WestB (5) 79, p. 31.
"A Fire in Wales. " GreenfieldR (7:3/4) Spr-Sum 79, p. 168.
"Flamingoes. " GreenfieldR (7:3/4) Spr-Sum 79, p. 167.
"For My Mother. " WestB (5) 79, p. 32.
"Rose Bay Willow Herb. " NewL (46:2) Wint 79-80, p. 100.

RAY, Robert Beverley
"June 21. " Poetry (134:3) Je 79, pp. 158-159.
"On My 35th Birthday. " Poetry (134:3) Je 79, pp. 163-166.
"Pachelbel's Canon in D Major" (for James O. Naremore).
    Poetry (134:3) Je 79, pp. 160-162.

RAY, S. Judy
"The Nun on the Train. " PoNow (25) 79, p. 33.

RAY, Shreela
"The First Thunderstorm. " PoNow (25) 79, p. 34.
"for Margaret Bourke-White. " Focus (13:81) My-Je 79, p. 31.
"Games. " Focus (13:82) Ag 79, p. 31.
"A Gang of Saints. " Focus (13:83) O 79, p. 20.
"the excuse is a circle. " Ur (2) 79, p. 100.
Twenty-nine Poems. Falcon (18) Spr 79, pp. 18-49.

RAYMOND, Monica
"The Advisor. " Aspect (74/75) Ja-Ag 79, p. 5.

REA, Susan Irene
"In Your Own House. " Northeast (3:7) Spr 79, p. 28.
"Love Poem. " Ploughs (5:1) 79, p. 106.
"Poem for Dorothy Holt (1905-1967). " PikeR (1) Sum 79, p. 1.

REA, Tom
"To Her Son on Mother's Day. " QW (8) Wint 79, p. 114.

RECCARDI, Joe
"Remembering Him. " KanQ (11:1/2) Wint-Spr 79, p. 192.

RECTOR, Liam
"Edward Munch" (to Jordan Smith). ParisR (75) Spr 79, pp. 204-
    205.
"The Eventual Music" (for David St. John). Shen (30:1) Aut 78,
    p. 90.
"In Snow. " CimR (49) O 79, p. 47.
"Passing Cards. " AmerPoR (8:2) Mr-Ap 79, p. 15.
"When Down by Long Boy's Lane. " ParisR (75) Spr 79, pp. 206-
    207.
"Where You Get Off. " PartR (46:2) 79, p. 249.

REDSHAW, Thomas Dillon
"Wild Thyme. " CarlMis (17:2/3) Spr 79, p. 45.
"Yarrow Charm. " CarlMis (17:2/3) Spr 79, p. 44.

REED, James
Morning Notes to a Nighttime Diary. Bits (chapbook) 79. En-
    tire issue.
"Taking a Break from the Study of English, I Watch the World
    Series. " PoNow (25) 79, p. 34.

REED, Jeremy
"How Much Longer. " Kayak (52) D 79, p. 28.
"Missing. " Kayak (52) D 79, p. 27.
"Notes Afterward. " Kayak (52) D 79, p. 29.
"Owls and Hands. " Kayak (52) D 79, p. 28.
"Swimming Without Head" (for John Digby). Kayak (52) D 79,
    p. 26.

REED, John R.
"Historical Piece: Florence at Siena. " TexQ (21:3) Aut 78, p.
    34.
"Lay Brother at the Siena Bus Stop. " TexQ (21:3) Aut 78, p.
    33.
"Il museo dell' opera del duomo, Florence. " TexQ (21:3) Aut
    78, p. 33.
"The Pazzi Conspiracy. " TexQ (21:3) Aut 78, p. 34.

REED, Sharon
"As the state line comes closer, ". HangL (35) Spr 79, p. 73.

REED, Thomas
"A Change of Feeling, a Change of Form. " Epoch (28:3) Spr-
Sum 79, p. 252.
"Evaporating Unevenly. " Tendril (5) Sum 79, p. 42.
"For Howard Wong Who Talks to Himself Loudly and Angrily
Downstairs. " Epoch (28:3) Spr-Sum 79, p. 253.

REES, Daniel G.
"Blood and Rock and Ink and Wood. " KanQ (11:1/2) Wint-Spr
79, p. 105.
"Humbug for All Seasons. " KanQ (11:1/2) Wint-Spr 79, p. 106.
"Much to My Credit. " KanQ (11:3) Sum 79, p. 99.

REES, Ennis
"The Salmon Poacher. " NewRep (180:18) 5 My 79, p. 30.

REEVE, F. D.
"Late Autumn in Walpole. " NewEngR (1:3) Spr 79, p. 357.

REGISTER, W. Raymond
"The Preview. " SouthernHR (13:2) Spr 79, p. 138.

REIBETANZ, John
"Sam Appleby, Horseman. " Poetry (133:4) Ja 79, pp. 218-219.

REICH, Heather Tosteson
"Tonight. " SouthernPR (19:1) Spr 79, p. 12.
"Waltz. " SouthernPR (19:1) Spr 79, p. 12.

REID, Alastair
"Chronicle from the Indies" (tr. of José Emilio Pacheco).
PoNow (24) 79, p. 33.
"A Dream" (tr. of Jorge Luis Borges). NewEngR (2:1) Aut 79,
p. 118.
"The Human Condition" (tr. of Pablo Neruda). NewEngR (2:1)
Aut 79, p. 119.
"Mosquitoes" (tr. of José Emilio Pacheco). PoNow (24) 79, p.
33.
"Overboard" (tr. of Heberto Padilla). NewYRB (26:16) 25 O 79,
p. 16.
"The School of Winter" (tr. of Pablo Neruda). NewEngR (2:1)
Aut 79, p. 118.
"Self-Portrait of the Other" (tr. of Heberto Padilla). NewYRB
(26:16) 25 O 79, p. 16.
"Things That Might Have Been" (tr. of Jorge Luis Borges).
NewEngR (1:4) Sum 79, p. 468.
"To Pablo Armando Fernandez" (tr. of Heberto Padilla).
NewYRB (26:16) 25 O 79, p. 16.
"Turner's Landscape" (tr. of José Emilio Pacheco). PoNow (24)
79, p. 33.

REID, P. C.
"Scene. " PoetC (11:3) 79, p. 25.

REID, Robert F. III
    "Heart of Light. " WindO (34) Spr-Sum 79, p. 15.
    "Night Game. " SmPd (46) 79, p. 12.

REID, Robert Sims
    "Monday, the First Hour" (for Gayle). CutB (12) Spr-Sum 79,
       p. 13.

REILLY, Robert T.
    "All Hallow's Eve. " ChrC (96:35) 31 O 79, p. 1059.

REINER, Lois
    "Father. " ChrC (96:21) 6-13 Je 79, p. 637.
    "Mother. " ChrC (96:17) 9 My 79, p. 522.

REINERT, Mike
    "First the Clouds. " EngJ (68:5) My 79, p. 38.

REISS, James
    "Brothers (I). " OhioR (20:2) Spr-Sum 79, p. 34.
    "Brothers (II). " OhioR (20:2) Spr-Sum 79, p. 35.
    "The Mittenleaf Tree. " Iowa (10:2) Spr 79, p. 93.
    "On Learning the People's Republic of China Has Lifted Its Ban
      on Beethoven. " Poetry (134:6) S 79, pp. 322-325.
    "Pumas. " VirQR (55:1) Wint 79, p. 111.

REITER, Lora
    Poem. St. AR (5:2) 79, p. 26.
    Poem. St. AR (5:2) 79, p. 36.

REITER, Thomas
    "The Air We Breathe, Angels" (for Peter). QW (6) Spr-Sum 78,
      p. 113.
    "Bait Shop. " QW (6) Spr-Sum 78, p. 116.
    "Candids" (for J. M.). QW (6) Spr-Sum 78, p. 113.
    "A Charm for Your Doorstep. " PoetryNW (20:3) Aut 79, pp. 31-
      32.
    "The First Lesson. " QW (7) Aut 78, p. 48.
    "Hellbenders. " QW (9) Spr-Sum 79, p. 30.
    "Ice Fishing Above the Dam. " MassR (20:4) Wint 79, p. 687.
    "The Knife & Scissors Man. " KanQ (11:1/2) Wint-Spr 79, p. 10.
    "Pickup Games. " QW (6) Spr-Sum 78, p. 114.
    "Regatta. " QW (9) Spr-Sum 79, p. 31.
    "Seeding Quail Hollow Creek. " QW (7) Aut 78, p. 50.
    "Zalenka, Bait Gathering. " CimR (49) O 79, p. 30.

REITTER, Rose
    "Here There Be Dragons. " StoneC (6:1) F 79, p. 6.

RENSBERGER, David
    "Christmas. " Poem (36) Jl 79, p. 17.
    "November. " Poem (36) Jl 79, p. 18.
    "Three Sonnets, with Prelude and Close. " Poem (36) Jl 79, pp.

20-21.
"Within the Day. " Poem (36) Jl 79, p. 19.

REPP, John
 "Age" (for Ken). SmPd (45) 79, p. 20.
 "Ascent" (for Grant Hackett). EnPas (8) 79, p. 36.
 "bee. " GRR (10:1) 79, p. 129.
 "The Bridge. " GRR (10:1) 79, p. 118.

RETALLACK, Joan
 "The Adventure of Dialectic. " MassR (20:1) Spr 79, p. 161.
 "The New Realism. " MassR (20:1) Spr 79, p. 162.
 "To Those Who Have Abandoned Words. " CarlMis (17:2/3) Spr
   79, p. 107.

REVARD, Carter
 "Minor Cadences. " Chelsea (38) 79, p. 205.

REVELL, Donald
 "A Few Discretions. " Poem (37) N 79, pp. 50-52.
 "No Moment. " Poem (37) N 79, pp. 48-49.
 "Satiesme. " Poem (37) N 79, p. 47.

REVERDY, Pierre
 "Apres-midi" (tr. by R. W. Stedingh). NowestR (18:2) 79, p. 70.
 "Chacun sa part" (tr. by R. W. Stedingh). NowestR (18:2) 79,
   p. 72.
 "Saltimanques" (tr. by R. W. Stedingh). NowestR (18:2) 79, p.
   72.

REWAK, William J.
 "Illusion. " CEACritic (41:4) My 79, p. 17.

REYES, Ellen
 "The Trodden Path. " Wind (33) 79, p. 47.

REZMERSKI, John Calvin
 "Account. " PoNow (21) 79, p. 28.
 "A Dream of Indians. " PoNow (21) 79, p. 28.
 "Miracle. " PoNow (21) 79, p. 28.
 "Willmar at Night. " PoNow (21) 79, p. 28.

RIBOVICH, John
 "As Arm Encircled Waist. " Poem (37) N 79, p. 2.
 "Succession. " Poem (37) N 79, p. 3.

RICAPITO, Joseph V.
 "Surrendered Hand" (tr. of Vicente Aleixandre). PoNow (24) 79,
   p. 2.

RICE, Chris
 "Wedding Dress on a Wire Coat-Hanger. " GRR (10:3) 79, p. 107.

RICE, Clayton
"The Call of the Colonel. " PoNow (25) 79, p. 34.

RICE, Pamela
"This Morning's Tornado. " CutB (13) Aut-Wint 79, p. 46.

RICE, Stan
"Anne's Curls. " SeC (6:2) 78, p. 164.
"Four Wolves. " SeC (6:2) 78, p. 162.
"In the Hospital Courtyard. " SeC (6:2) 78, p. 161.

RICHARDS, Elizabeth
"Apartment on 63rd. " HarvAd (112:3) Ap 79, p. 23.

RICHARDS, Melanie
"Pomegranates. " Aspen (8) Aut 79, p. 65.
"Thistles. " Aspen (8) Aut 79, p. 65.

RICHARDS, Peggy
"Death Watch. " ChrC (96:17) 9 My 79, p. 516.

RICHARDS, Vincent
"I'm Gonna Write a Poem. " HangL (35) Spr 79, p. 74.

RICHARDSON, Dorothy Lee
"Trail. " TexQ (21:4) Wint 78, p. 117.

RICHARDSON, James
"Neutral Territory. " Shen (30:1) Aut 78, pp. 16-20.

RICHARDSON, James M.
"The Jook Joint. " BlackF (3:1) Aut-Wint 79, p. 23.

RICHARDSON, Verlena Orr
"John Emerson. " PortR (25) 79, p. 37.
"Notes Without Envelopes. " PortR (25) 79, p. 36.

RICKARD, Paul
from The Paumonak Dialogues: (V). GreenfieldR (7:3/4) Spr-
Sum 79, p. 183.

RICKEL, Boyer
"The Boy. " Iowa (10:2) Spr 79, p. 94.

RIDEOUT, Darryl
"Harper Falls in Love. " SmPd (46) 79, p. 34.

RIEMAN, Michael
"Eyes of the Fish" (tr. of Jose Emilio Pacheco). PoNow (24)
79, p. 40.

RIEMER, Ruby
"Avian Hours. " SouthernPR (19:2) Aut 79, p. 52.

RIGGS, Dionis Coffin
"From a Hill in Anatolia. " StoneC (6:1) F 79, p. 26.
"Holiday Visit" (tr. of Behcet Necatigil w. Ozcan Yalim and William A. Fiedler). StoneC (6:1) F 79, p. 28.

RIGSBEE, David
"The Loneliness of Animals. " Iowa (10:1) Wint 79, p. 55.
"Vanishing Point. " Iowa (10:1) Wint 79, p. 53.

RILEY, Beau
"I am a dabbler why not. " Mouth (2:2) Je 79, p. 30.
"I Saw in San Francisco. " Mouth (2:2) Je 79, p. 12.
"Retirement. " Mouth (2:2) Je 79, p. 47.
"Salesmen smile they. " Mouth (2:2) Je 79, p. 26.
"Sauna Sequence. " Mouth (2:2) Je 79, p. 21.
"25 July 1966. " Mouth (2:2) Je 79, Front cover.

RILEY, Joanne M.
"Fable. " Poem (35) Mr 79, p. 13.
"Folk-Dance. " Poem (35) Mr 79, p. 16.
"Great Spirit. " Poem (35) Mr 79, pp. 14-15.
Poem. St. AR (5:2) 79, p. 60.
"Snowstorm. " WestHR (33:3) Sum 79, p. 238.
"The Woman. " GreenfieldR (7:3/4) Spr-Sum 79, p. 223.

RILKE, Rainer Maria
"The Carousel" (tr. by Norbert Krapf). PoNow (24) 79, p. 48.
Eight Poems (tr. by Steven Lautermilch). TexQ (21:4) Wint 78, pp. 22-26.
"Entrance" (tr. by Norbert Krapf). PoNow (21) 79, p. 44.
"Evening" (tr. by Norbert Krapf). PoNow (21) 79, p. 44.
"Fall Day" (tr. by Norbert Krapf). PoNow (21) 79, p. 44.
"From a Childhood" (tr. by Norbert Krapf). PoNow (24) 79, p. 48.
"From a Childhood" (tr. by Franz Wright). QW (9) Spr-Sum 79, p. 10.
"Grieving" (tr. by Franz Wright). QW (9) Spr-Sum 79, p. 11.
"Last Evening" (tr. by Franz Wright). QW (9) Spr-Sum 79, p. 9.
"Orpheus, Eurydice, Hermes" (tr. by Franz Wright). Durak (2) 79, p. 14.
"Rilke's Complaint. " Spirit (3:1/2) Aut-Wint 77-78, p. 6.
"Les Roses. " GRR (10:1) 79, p. 98.
from Sonnets to Orpheus Part Two: Twenty-nine Poems (tr. by David Young). Field (20) Spr 79, pp. 65-95.
"The Swan" (tr. by Franz Wright). QW (9) Spr-Sum 79, p. 10.
"Washing the Corpse" (tr. by Paul Morris). WebR (4:3) Spr 79, p. 7.

RIMBAUD, Arthur
"Comedy of Thirst. " Durak (3) 79, pp. 44-48.
"sensation. " St. AR (5:3) Aut-Wint 79, p. 16.
"Vénus Anadyomène. " GRR (10:1) 79, p. 90.

RIMMON, Shlomith
    from Gazelle, I'll Send You: "A bouquet--to scatter its flowers
        on the floor and the table" (tr. of Amir Gilboa w. Shirley
        Kaufman). WebR (4:3) Spr 79, p. 9.
    from Gazelle, I'll Send You: "Finally I go to the man who set
        traps for the birds" (tr. of Amir Gilboa w. Shirley Kauf-
        man). WebR (4:3) Spr 79, p. 8.
    from Gazelle, I'll Send You: "How would I stand then, what side
        of my face expose to the light" (tr. of Amir Gilboa w. Shir-
        ley Kaufman). WebR (4:3) Spr 79, p. 8.
    from Gazelle, I'll Send You: "Standing on tiptoe shutting my
        eyes so I won't see what's going on in the yard" (tr. of
        Amir Gilboa w. Shirley Kaufman). WebR (4:3) Spr 79, p. 8.

RINALDI, Nicholas
    "Everything Humanly Possible Was Tried and We Failed." LitR
        (22:3) Spr 79, p. 303.
    "My Time." LitR (22:3) Spr 79, p. 306.
    "Scenes of Violence." LitR (22:3) Spr 79, p. 304.
    "Shadow of the Crow." LitR (22:3) Spr 79, p. 305.

RIND, Sherry
    "A Private Ceremony." SouthernPR (19:2) Aut 79, p. 15.
    "The Ugly Sister." PoetryNW (20:3) Aut 79, pp. 17-18.

RINGOLD, Francine Leffler
    "Chagall: Sometimes a Painting Speaks My Mind." GreenfieldR
        (7:3/4) Spr-Sum 79, p. 103.
    "Woman Walking Away." GreenfieldR (7:3/4) Spr-Sum 79, p.
        104.

RIOS, Alberto
    "The Man Who Named Children." CutB (12) Spr-Sum 79, p. 78.
    "Morning." Spirit (4:1) Aut-Wint 78-79, p. 11.
    "Second Grade." LittleM (12:1/2) Spr-Sum 78 (79), p. 56.
    "Yaqui." Spirit (4:1) Aut-Wint 78-79, p. 15.

RISI, Nelo
    "Apple Trees Apple Trees Apple Trees" (tr. by Lawrence R.
        Smith). PoNow (24) 79, p. 48.
    "The Other Side" (tr. by Lawrence R. Smith). PoNow (24) 79,
        p. 48.

RISTAU, Harland
    "5th Seat, 3rd Row." Northeast (3:7) Spr 79, p. 23.
    "Pastel." ChrC (96:29) 19 S 79, p. 887.

RISTEEN, Eleanor
    "Naming the Colors." Sky (9) Aut 79, pp. 43-44.
    "Synthesis." Sky (9) Aut 79, p. 42.

RITCHIE, Elisavietta
    "Picnic Down St. Mary's County." PoNow (23) 79, p. 36.

from Through the River of Corals: "Curfew Poem. " Wind (34)
79, p. 52.
from Through the River of Corals: "Marigolds: Malaysia: Jan-
uary. " Wind (34) 79, p. 52.

RITSOS, Yannis
"After Each Death" (tr. by Edmund Keeley). AmerPoR (8:2) Mr-
Ap 79, p. 33.
"Attack" (tr. by Edmund Keeley). AmerPoR (8:2) Mr-Ap 79, p.
33.
"Current Events" (tr. by Edmund Keeley). Pequod (3:1) 79, p.
81.
"Diary of Exile III" (tr. by Anthony Tsirantonakis). PoNow (24)
79, p. 49.
"Doubtful Stature" (tr. by Edmund Keeley). Pequod (3:1) 79, p.
81.
"The Earth's Attraction" (tr. by Kimon Friar and Kostas Myrsi-
ades). Chelsea (38) 79, p. 82.
"First Rain" (tr. by Rae Dalven). PoNow (24) 79, p. 34.
"The Heard and the Unheard" (tr. by Rae Dalven). PoNow (24)
79, p. 34.
"In the Barracks" (tr. by Rae Dalven). PoNow (24) 79, p. 34.
"Insomnia" (tr. by Edmund Keeley). AmerPoR (8:2) Mr-Ap 79,
p. 33.
"Lightless" (tr. by Kimon Friar and Kostas Myrsiades). Chelsea
(38) 79, p. 81.
"The Moonlight Sonata" (tr. by Peter Bien). NewEngR (1:3) Spr
79, p. 301.
"The Only" (tr. by Edmund Keeley). Pequod (3:1) 79, p. 80.
"Secret Audience" (tr. by Kimon Friar and Kostas Myrsiades).
Chelsea (38) 79, p. 83.
"Sketch" (tr. by Edmund Keeley). Pequod (3:1) 79, p. 80.
"Triplet" (tr. by Edmund Keeley). Pequod (3:1) 79, p. 80.
"The Two Sides" (tr. by Edmund Keeley). AmerPoR (8:2) Mr-
Ap 79, p. 33.
"With the Unapproachable" (tr. by Edmund Keeley). Pequod (3:1)
79, p. 81.
"A Wreath" (tr. by Edmund Keeley). Pequod (3:1) 79, p. 80.

RIVERO, Alina
"Deaf Lantern" (tr. of Alejandra Pizarnik). AmerPoR (8:2) Mr-
Ap 79, p. 47.
"Encounter" (tr. of Alejandra Pizarnik). AmerPoR (8:2) Mr-Ap
79, p. 47.
"From the Other Side" (tr. of Alejandra Pizarnik). AmerPoR
(8:2) Mr-Ap 79, p. 47.
"Girl in the Garden" (tr. of Alejandra Pizarnik). AmerPoR
(8:2) Mr-Ap 79, p. 47.
"Signals" (tr. of Alejandra Pizarnik). AmerPoR (8:2) Mr-Ap 79,
p. 47.

RIVERS, J. W.
from The Chicago Notebook: "Memories of the South Side. "

PikeR (1) Sum 79, pp. 13-25.
"Garrison. " PoetC (10:3) 79, p. 33.
"Getting Ready for Football in July. " WindO (34) Spr-Sum 79,
    p. 16.
"Prayer. " PoetC (10:3) 79, p. 33.
"Raid. " StoneC (6:3) O 79, p. 32.

ROBBINS, Anthony
"Divorce. " NewL (46:1) Aut 79, p. 53.

ROBBINS, Doren
"Princess Hollywood and the Vagabond. " Ur (2) 79, p. 102.
"You Float Down My Eyes. " Ur (2) 79, p. 104.

ROBBINS, Martin
"And I Understood" (tr. of Gevorg Emin). PoNow (24) 79, p.
    13.
"The Compass" (tr. of Luciano Marrucci w. Ruth Feldman).
    PoNow (24) 79, p. 25.
"Dialogue" (tr. of Gevorg Emin). PoNow (23) 79, p. 46.
"Doesn't It Seem to You, " (tr. of Gevorg Emin). PoNow (24)
    79, p. 14.
"Flashback. " GreenfieldR (7:3/4) Spr-Sum 79, p. 232.
"From My August Armory. " Os (9) 79, p. 5.
"Halloween. " EnPas (9) 79, p. 20.
"Late Winter Rain." StoneC (6:1) F 79, p. 9.
"Mother" (tr. of Luciano Marrucci w. Ruth Feldman). PoNow
    (24) 79, p. 25.
"Night/Late August. " FourQt (28:4) Sum 79, p. 18.
"Night Trees" (tr. of Luciano Marrucci w. Ruth Feldman).
    PoNow (24) 79, p. 25.
"The Piano" (tr. of Gevorg Emin). PoNow (24) 79, pp. 13-14.
"Savings and Loan Associations. " Os (8) 79, p. 25.
"Snapshot/Glacial Lake. " Im (5:3) 79, p. 6.
"Spring Rites. " GreenfieldR (7:3/4) Spr-Sum 79, p. 233.
"Summer Solstice/New Neighborhood. " StoneC (6:1) F 79, p. 9.
"Winter Scene" (tr. of Gevorg Emin). PoNow (24) 79, p. 13.

ROBBINS, Sheryl
"Swimming with Teresa. " Salm (43) Wint 79, p. 106.

ROBERT, Tracy
"Age. " DenQ (14:2) Sum 79, p. 72.
"Even No Noise. " DenQ (14:2) Sum 79, p. 74.
"Intemperate Roses." DenQ (14:2) Sum 79, p. 75.
"The Projectionist's Room." DenQ (14:2) Sum 79, p. 73.

ROBERTS, George
"Hotel Athena. " DacTerr (16) 79, p. 54.

ROBERTS, Len
"Beauty and the Nuclear Reactor at Three-Mile Island. " WestB
    (5) 79, p. 6.

"Cellars. " WestB (5) 79, p. 7.
"Clicking. " WestB (5) 79, p. 8.
"Earth Blue and Brown and Silent Now. " Spirit (3:1/2) Aut-Wint
    77-78, p. 13.
"Fighting. " HangL (35) Spr 79, p. 54.
"Some Things Have Not Changed. " HangL (35) Spr 79, p. 53.
"You Know I Didn't Mean It. " HangL (35) Spr 79, p. 56.

ROBERTS, Percival
"love's diminution. " St. AR (5:3) Aut-Wint 79, p. 90.
"variation on catullus' theme. " St. AR (5:3) Aut-Wint 79, p. 87.

ROBERTSON, Kell
"For Hank Williams. " SeC (6:2) 78, p. 119.
"Merlene. " SeC (6:2) 78, p. 124.
"Rules and Men and Boundaries. " SeC (6:2) 78, p. 123.
"Song. " SeC (6:2) 78, p. 122.
"A Victory. " SeC (7:1) 79, p. 9.

ROBERTSON, Kirk
"Almost Equinoctal Agony. " Wind (32) 79, p. 41.
"Cultural Insight. " PikeF (2) Wint 78-79, p. 22.
"election night. " Wind (32) 79, p. 40.
"He Was a Guest. " SeC (6:1) 78, p. 52.
"The Indian Lid Is Not Tilted--newspaper headline. " Wind (32)
    79, p. 40.
"Nevada. " PoNow (21) 79, p. 17.

ROBIN, Ralph
"Original Glow. " SouthwR (64:2) Spr 79, p. 130.

ROBINSON, David
"Awakening. " ConcPo (12:1) Spr 79, p. 79.

ROBINSON, James Miller
"The Choice. " Sam (79) 79, p. 68.
"Dallas. " Poem (35) Mr 79, p. 60.
"Journey to the Border. " Sam (79) 79, p. 69.
"Seattle. " Poem (35) Mr 79, p. 61.
"That Day. " Sam (72) 79, p. 32.

ROBINSON, Leonard Wallace
"Squalor and Early Sorrow. " NewL (46:1) Aut 79, p. 80.

ROBINSON, Peter
"Dirty Language. " Stand (20:3) 79, p. 18.

ROCHE, Paul
"The Tearing-up of the Epiphyllums. " Confr (18) Spr-Sum 79,
    p. 22.

ROCKWELL, Glen
"Keys. " MassR (20:4) Wint 79, p. 686.

RODGERS, James
"Eloping. " GreenfieldR (7:3/4) Spr-Sum 79, p. 228.

RODRIGUEZ, Aleida
"Above: The abysmal, water
Below: The joyous, lake. " Bachy (14) Spr-Sum 79, p. 79.
"Moving to Allesandro. " Bachy (14) Spr-Sum 79, p. 78.
"Night Work" (for Eloise). Bachy (14) Spr-Sum 79, p. 80.
"A Personal Alphabet. " Bachy (14) Spr-Sum 79, p. 78.
"What Has Remained on Suellen's Postcard from Mexico After the
    Rain. " Bachy (14) Spr-Sum 79, p. 80.

ROETHKE, Theodore
from Cuttings: "One nub of growth. " Tendril (5) Sum 79, p. 5.

ROGERS, Bruce P.
"July 1977 A Hunger Demonstration in Cuzco. " Aspen (8) Aut
    79, pp. 37-41.

ROGERS, David
"The Poet Gives Thanks. " PoetC (11:1) 79, p. 2.
"Sowing. " PoetC (11:1) 79, p. 5.

ROGERS, Del Marie
"I Am Waiting for a Magical Animal. " Epoch (28:2) Wint 79, p.
    166.

ROGERS, Pattiann
"All the Elements of the Scene. " PoetryNW (20:1) Spr 79, pp.
    16-17.
"Capturing the Scene. " PoetryNW (20:4) Wint 79-80, p. 47.
"A Giant Has Swallowed the Earth for a Pill. " Poetry (134:4)
    Jl 79, p. 207.
"How to Stay Safe in the City. " BelPoJ (29:4) Sum 79, p. 13.
"The Literary Man. " PoetryNW (20:1) Spr 79, p. 17.
"The Man Hidden Behind the Drapes. " PoetryNW (20:4) Wint 79-
    80, pp. 44-45.
"Seeds. " PoetC (10:3) 79, p. 38.
"The Success of the Hunt. " Iowa (10:3) Sum 79, p. 111.
"Synthesising the Word. " Poetry (134:4) Jl 79, p. 206.
"What the Body Means to Belief. " PoetryNW (20:4) Wint 79-80,
    pp. 45-46.

ROGERS, Stephanie
"Nights Departure. " BlackF (3:1) Aut-Wint 79, p. 35.

ROKWAHO
from The Poet's Analyst: "weightless reality. " BelPoJ (30:2)
    Wint 79-80, p. 23.

ROLLINGS, Alane
"And in Return. " SenR (10:1) Spr 79, p. 116.
"Doing Time. " CarlMis (17:2/3) Spr 79, p. 32.

"For Robert, Leaving Home." CarlMis (17:2/3) Spr 79, p. 30.
"For the People Who Will Never Be Born." SenR (10:1) Spr 79,
    p. 123.
"In Unassuming Colors." SenR (10:1) Spr 79, p. 110.
"Love and Fantasy." SenR (10:1) Spr 79, p. 114.
"Love and Terror" (for E. W.). SenR (10:1) Spr 79, p. 112.
"Making Fortunes." CarlMis (17:2/3) Spr 79, p. 31.
"Political Despair and that Last Moment." SenR (10:1) Spr 79,
    p. 121.
"Take It from Me." SenR (10:1) Spr 79, p. 119.

ROMAN, Howard
"Invitation to the Seashore." LitR (22:3) Spr 79, p. 364.

ROMER, Stephen
"Notes for an Exhibition" (for B.). HarvAd (112:1) Mr 79, p.
    11.

ROMINES, Ann
"Grading Papers: No Lunch." EngJ (68:5) My 79, p. 33.

ROMTVEDT, David
"Famous People." Aspen (7) Spr 79, p. 63.
"Formal Setting." Aspen (7) Spr 79, p. 62.
"Moon." AmerPoR (8:3) My-Je 79, p. 28.
"Private Practice." PoNow (22) 79, p. 38.
"Tropical Madness." Aspen (7) Spr 79, p. 61.

RONAH, John
"Pigeon Images." Sam (79) 79, p. 37.

RONAN, John J.
"The Habits of the Rat." AndR (6:1) Spr 79, p. 65.

RONAN, Richard
"The Agony in the Garden." AmerPoR (8:2) Mr-Ap 79, p. 29.
"The Beekeeper's Sister" (for Jane J. C.). HangL (36) Aut 79,
    pp. 57-62.
"The Light House." SmPd (46) 79, p. 36.

RONCI, Ray
"Building Her House." Ploughs (5:3) 79, p. 134.
"In the Livingroom." Ploughs (5:3) 79, p. 135-136.

RONEY, Anne
"November, Four Years After My Father's Death." SmF (7/8)
    Spr-Aut 78, p. 20.
"Spring Leaffall." SmF (7/8) Spr-Aut 78, p. 19.

RONSARD, Pierre de
"Invective Against Denise, a Witch" (tr. by Anthony Hecht).
    AmerS (48:4) Aut 79, p. 499.
Ten poems. Montra (5) 79, p. 162.

ROOT, Judith C.
"Blackberries Live Here. " KanQ (11:4) Aut 79, p. 130.
"Driving Home. " PoNow (25) 79, p. 34.
"Winter in California. " KanQ (11:4) Aut 79, p. 131.

ROOT, William Pitt
"Anamax Open Pit. " QW (9) Spr-Sum 79, p. 51.
"A Step in the Dance. " PoNow (23) 79, p. 9.

ROSBERG, Rose
"Conversation. " SouthernHR (13:2) Spr 79, p. 163.
"Disguises. " SouthernHR (13:2) Spr 79, p. 163.
"Silver Is Meant for Distances. " Sam (79) 79, p. 2.

ROSE, Craig
"Doomed to Ignorance. " JnlONJP (3:2) 79, p. 19.

ROSE, Gonzalo
"Watchword. " LitR (23:2) Wint 80, p. 275.

ROSE, Lynne Carol
"Because the Night Goes on Forever. " GRR (10:1) 79, p. 12.
"In the Sharp Square of the Window. " GRR (10:1) 79, p. 8.
"The Man Called John. " GRR (10:1) 79, p. 9.
"The Revenants. " SmPd (45) 79, p. 28.
"The Sad Man's Kingdom. " GRR (10:1) 79, p. 5.
"Sybil. " GRR (10:1) 79, p. 10.
"Sybil and the Sad Man. " GRR (10:1) 79, p. 11.
"Tending to the Emptiness. " GRR (10:1) 79, p. 14.

ROSE, Wendy
"The Day I Was Conceived. " BelPoJ (30:2) Wint 79-80, p. 42.
"Indian People: don't get it mixed up--this is all for you. "
     BelPoJ (30:2) Wint 79-80, p. 44.
"Naming Power. " BelPoJ (30:2) Wint 79-80, p. 43.

ROSELIEP, Raymond
"Adieu. " ChrC (96:18) 16 My 79, p. 552.
"all day. " WindO (34) Spr-Sum 79, p. 5.
"Audience. " ChrC (96:16) 2 My 79, p. 493.
"Fair. " ChrC (96:27) 29 Ag-5 S 79, p. 818.
"Family Album. " PikeR (1) Sum 79, p. 26.
"Haiku. " PikeR (1) Sum 79, p. 27.
"in the lettuce core. " Bits (9) Ja 79.
"Spouse. " ChrC (96:32) 10 O 79, p. 967.
"the wren. " WindO (34) Spr-Sum 79, p. 5.

ROSEN, Kenneth
"Arrowhead. " Antaeus (32) Wint 79, p. 64.
"In Egypt Land. " SouthernR (15:2) Spr 79, p. 408.
"Kingdom Come. " SoCaR (11:2) Spr 79, p. 27.
"A Laughable Party. " ArkRiv (4:3) 79, p. 42.
"Nova Scotia. " Shen (30:2) Wint 79, p. 92.
"The Red Windmill. " ArkRiv (4:3) 79, p. 44.

ROSENBAUM, Harriet
"The Sound of Silence." StoneC (6:1) F 79, p. 14.

ROSENBERG, Chuck
"Louisiana Hayride Appearance." SunM (8) Aut 79, p. 28.

ROSENBERG, L. M.
"Gathering Chestnuts." SouthwR (64:4) Aut 79, p. 323.
"Saint Guthlac." SouthwR (64:4) Aut 79, p. 324.

ROSENBERGER, F. C.
"Poets Observed." ArizQ (35:2) Sum 79, p. 152.

ROSENFELD, Irma
"Antique." ChiR (30:4) Spr 79, p. 80.

ROSENFELD, Marjorie Stamm
"David Hominidae." SouthwR (64:3) Sum 79, p. 237.

ROSENFIELD, Patricia B.
"Ventress Library." SouthernPR (19:1) Spr 79, p. 61.

ROSENTHAL, Abby
"The Child's Lullaby." Tendril (4) Wint 79, p. 44.
"The Garden." CarolQ (31:3) Aut 79, p. 14.
"La Salsa Picante." CarolQ (31:3) Aut 79, p. 12.
"Three Dangerous Sleeps." Tendril (4) Wint 79, p. 43.

ROSS, Carolyn
"Diving." Salm (46) Aut 79, p. 101.
"Katherine's Hands." Salm (46) Aut 79, p. 100.

ROSS, Gary
"Himself Within." MalR (51) Jl 79, p. 47.

ROSS, Marty
"Bo Diddley at Forty-seven." Spirit (4:1) Aut-Wint 78-79, p. 18.

ROSS, Mary Beth
"Love Poem." Chomo (5:3) Spr 79, p. 24.

ROSS, Sherman
"My Reincarnation." BlackF (3:1) Aut-Wint 79, p. 37.

ROSSI, Vinio
Ten Poems (tr. of Giovanni Raboni w. Stuart Friebert). QW (8) Wint 79, pp. 72-76.

ROSSINI, Frank
"according to the baltimore catechism." GreenfieldR (7:3/4) Spr-Sum 79, p. 254.

ROSTON, Ruth
"Cleanliness, Compassion. " SmPd (45) 79, p. 24.
"The Dream Collector. " SmPd (45) 79, p. 18.
"Fortieth Reunion. " SmPd (45) 79, p. 18.

ROTHFORK, John
"Attachments. " CharR (5:1) Spr 79, p. 92.
"Take the Name War Eagle. " SoDakR (17:4) Wint 79-80, p. 51.

ROTTENBERG, Dorian
"The Ugly Girl" (tr. of Nikolay Zabolotsky). PoNow (24) 79, p.
   63.

RUARK, Gibbons
"A Brief Gratitude Exhaled in a Roman Theater. " AmerPoR (8:1)
   Ja-F 79, p. 39.
"Brunelleschi and Esposito: Thinking Aloud in the Pazzi Chapel. "
   AmerPoR (8:1) Ja-F 79, p. 40.
"For a Suicide, A Little Early Morning Music. " AmerPoR (8:1)
   Ja-F 79, p. 41.
"In the City Without Wings. " AmerPoR (8:1) Ja-F 79, p. 39.
"Italian Bells. " AmerPoR (8:1) Ja-F 79, p. 40.
"On Hearing My Father's Voice in a Dead Sleep. " AmerPoR
   (8:1) Ja-F 79, p. 39.
"A Title and a Preface for Convenevole Da Prato, Who Pawned
   a Rare Book Belonging to a Student. " AmerPoR (8:1) Ja-F
   79, p. 40.

RUBENFELD, Andrew
"The Pier" (for Valden Madsen). Mouth (2:3) N 79, pp. 14-18.

RUBENFELD, Florence
"Circling the Wagons. " ParisR (75) Spr 79, p. 210.
"The Little Rivals. " ParisR (75) Spr 79, p. 212.
"The Powerful Remove. " ParisR (75) Spr 79, p. 211.

RUBENSTEIN, Carol
"No Blame. " Tele (15) Spr 79, p. 140.

RUBENSTEIN, Roberta
"Lifelines. " CEACritic (41:4) My 79, p. 40.

RUBIN, Barry
"San Pietro" (tr. of Joseph Brodsky). NewYorker (55:11) 30 Ap
   79, p. 38.

RUBIN, Larry
"Amid the Pines. " SouthwR (64:4) Aut 79, p. 354.
"Biorhythm: One Part of the Cycle. " NewOR (6:3) 79, p. 265.
"Fraternity Ghosts. " FourQt (28:4) Sum 79, p. 32.
"The Great American Poem. " Antaeus (32) Wint 79, pp. 82-86.
"Lines for My Father, Who Died Too Soon. " SouthernPR (19:2)
   Aut 79, p. 23.

"Studying Old Photographs: The Unknown Grandmother. " Chowder
(12) Spr-Sum 79, p. 28.
"Veteran, in Transit. " PoNow (23) 79, p. 13.

RUBIN, Mark
"Again. " CutB (12) Spr-Sum 79, p. 14.
"Again. " CutB (13) Aut-Wint 79, p. 13.
"Should the Moons Come Over. " Nat (228:7) 24 F 79, p. 216.
"Stepping Out. " CutB (12) Spr-Sum 79, p. 15.
"Stepping Out. " CutB (13) Aut-Wint 79, p. 12.
"The Swans in Missouri. " Nat (228:16) 28 Ap 79, p. 472.

RUBIN, Stan Sanvel
"Tourist. " GreenfieldR (7:3/4) Spr-Sum 79, p. 213.

RUBY, Michael
"The Sense of Failure" (for M). HarvAd (112:2) Mr 79, p. 20.

RUCHERT, Wallace Jr.
"At a Writers' Conference. " PoNow (25) 79, p. 34.

RUDMAN, Mark
"Family Romance. " Atl (243:1) Ja 79, p. 72.
"My Sister, Life" (tr. of Boris Pasternak w. Bohdan Boychuk).
PoNow (24) 79, p. 42.
"The Purpose of Soul" (tr. of Boris Pasternak w. Bohdan Boy-
chuk). PoNow (24) 79, p. 42.

RUDNIK, Raphael
"Amsterdam Street Scene, 1972. " OP (28) Aut 79, p. 26.
"Copyboy. " OP (28) Aut 79, pp. 27-28.
"Frank 207. " OP (28) Aut 79, p. 25.

RUDOLF, Anthony
"Water" (tr. of Edmond Jabès). Stand (20:2) 79, p. 45.

RUEF, Joseph A.
"Obituary. " SmPd (46) 79, p. 19.

RUEFLE, Mary
"The Blue of October. " Epoch (28:3) Spr-Sum 79, p. 248.
"Dance" (for Christina Svane). MissR (24) Aut 79, p. 96.
"Entry. " MissR (24) Aut 79, p. 98.
"In a Foreign Country" (for Aki Busch). MissR (24) Aut 79, p.
95.
"In the Night Blackness. " MissR (24) Aut 79, p. 94.
"Lake. " MissR (24) Aut 79, p. 97.
"Mathew Brady Arranging the Bodies. " MissR (24) Aut 79, p. 93.
"The Perfection of Clouds. " Epoch (28:3) Spr-Sum 79, p. 247.
"Repeating Herself. " HolCrit (16:3) Je 79, p. 7.

RUETTIMANN, Donna
"The Clearing" (for Michael). Poem (37) N 79, pp. 56-57.

"From the First Book of a Modern Testament. " Poem (37) N
  79, p. 55.
"Unicorns in the Surf. " Poem (37) N 79, p. 58.

RUFFIN, Paul
"The Dream. " KanQ (11:1/2) Wint-Spr 79, p. 7.
"Landing Through Fog. " TexQ (21:3) Aut 78, p. 126.

RUFFUS, Stephen
"Borderline. " QW (6) Spr-Sum 78, p. 73.
"Karl Wallenda. " QW (8) Wint 79, p. 37.

RUGGIERI, Helen
"Concrete Madonna Discovers the Virtue of Rejection. " Poultry
  (1) 79, p. 10.
"Concrete Madonna Explains Her Marketing Techniques. " Poultry
  (1) 79, p. 10.
"Concrete Madonna Has a Nightmare. " Poultry (1) 79, p. 10.
"Concrete Madonna Has a Reading. " Poultry (1) 79, p. 10.

RUGGLES, Eugene
"Back Inside the Crowd. " Sky (9) Aut 79, pp. 28-29.
"Black Elk Steps Upon Alcatraz. " SeC (6:2) 78, p. 16.
"Children Without Fathers" (for George Gilder). Sky (9) Aut 79,
  p. 32.
"The Lifeguard in the Snow. " SeC (6:2) 78, p. 14.
"Lighting the Oceans. " Sky (9) Aut 79, pp. 30-31.
"Lines from an Alcoholic Ward. " SeC (6:2) 78, p. 13.
"Masses. " SeC (6:2) 78, p. 17.
"Night Visit. " SeC (6:2) 78, p. 15.
"Toward the Muse. " Sky (9) Aut 79, p. 33.

RUGO, Mariève
"Double Exposure. " PoetryNW (20:4) Wint 79-80, pp. 13-14.
"Home. " PoetryNW (20:4) Wint 79-80, pp. 11-13.
"Poem for My Daughters. " Tendril (5) Sum 79, p. 45.
"Surviving the Jungle. " PoetryNW (20:4) Wint 79-80, p. 14.
"To Be a Hawk. " Tendril (5) Sum 79, p. 44.
"The Widow. " SouthernHR (13:4) Aut 79, p. 308.

RULE, Danjal
"Carmilla. " Mouth (2:3) N 79, p. 28.

RUMENS, Carol
"Chess Players. " Stand (20:1) 78-79, p. 60.

RUSHIN, Donna K.
"The Tired Poem Last Letter from a Typical Unemployed Black
  Professional Woman. " Cond (5) 79, pp. 72-76.

RUSS, Lawrence
"The Price of Paper. " GreenfieldR (7:3/4) Spr-Sum 79, p. 214.

RUSSELL, Carol Ann
"Fishing. " Ploughs (5:1) 79, pp. 107-108.
"A Real Man of No Titles. " PortR (25) 79, p. 58.
"So Long. " PoetryNW (20:2) Sum 79, pp. 36-37.

RUSSELL, Hilary
"Three Carp in Idella Gregg's Pond. " EnPas (8) 79, p. 26.

RUSSELL, Norman H.
"By the Fire. " BelPoJ (30:2) Wint 79-80, p. 4.

RUSSELL, Peter
"Orders of Space. " MalR (51) Jl 79, p. 139.

RUSSELL, R. Stephen
"Comings Home, 1883. " CarlMis (18:1) Wint 79-80, p. 159.
"How to Survive Late-Night Driving. " DenQ (14:3) Aut 79, p.
   89.

RUSSELL, Richard
   from O My Darling O My Darling: "Sesame. " StoneC (6:3) O
      79, p. 16.
   from O My Darling O My Darling: "Blest. " StoneC (6:3) O 79,
      p. 16.

RUTH, Fern Pankratz
"Guyana. " ChrC (96:7) 28 F 79, p. 211.

RUTSALA, Vern
"The Death Committee. " Poetry (134:3) Je 79, pp. 152-153.
"East Wind. " Poetry (134:3) Je 79, p. 155.
"Farming Poetry. " PortR (25) 79, p. 75.
"Fog. " PoNow (23) 79, p. 15.
"Further Reasons. " PoNow (22) 79, p. 39.
"The Ghost on the Second Floor. " PoNow (21) 79, p. 36.
"The Great American Poem. " Antaeus (32) Wint 79, pp. 82-86.
"Grief. " PoNow (23) 79, p. 15.
"Guilt. " PoNow (22) 79, p. 27.
"In the Natural History Museum. " PoNow (22) 79, p. 39.
"Less Is More.... " Poetry (134:3) Je 79, p. 154.
"Living C. P. Snow" (for Joan). PortR (25) 79, p. 74.
"The Lonely Man Writes. " PoNow (22) 79, p. 27.
"Monsters. " PoNow (22) 79, p. 39.
"The Other Place. " AmerS (48:3) Sum 79, p. 364.
"O Tannenbaum. " PoNow (22) 79, p. 27.
"The Photographer. " PoNow (22) 79, p. 39.
"Public Appearances. " PoNow (22) 79, p. 39.
"A Snapshot. " PoNow (22) 79, p. 39.
"The Talent Hunt. " PoNow (22) 79, p. 27.
"Time. " Poetry (134:3) Je 79, pp. 150-151.

RYAN, Florence Holmes
"Image of Adam. " Poem (36) Jl 79, p. 41.
"Our Landscapes Change. " Poem (36) Jl 79, p. 40.

RYAN, Heather A.
"Angelica's Bath. " HangL (35) Spr 79, p. 76.

RYAN, Kay
"Albert Einstein's Mustache." WormR (73) 79, p. 8.
"Albert Schweitzer's Mustache. " WormR (73) 79, p. 8.
"Janitor, at Four Stations. " PikeR (1) Sum 79, pp. 28-29.
"Some Famous People Dancing." PikeF (2) Wint 78-79, pp. 4-5.

RYAN, Michael
"All the Time. " Ploughs (5:1) 79, p. 109.
"A Changed Season. " Harp (258:1545) F 79, p. 95.

RYAN, Patrick R.
"Gravy Joe's" (A Self-Portraint in Verse). Kayak (52) D 79, p.
3.

RYAN, R. M.
"And Who Is Your Partner for This Evening's Dance?" PoNow
(21) 79, p. 39.
"Delphi. " PoNow (25) 79, p. 34.
"The Disappearance of America. " PoNow (23) 79, p. 37.
"Grief. " PoNow (25) 79, p. 35.
"My Former Muse. " PoNow (25) 79, p. 35.
"A Warning from the Novelist. " DenQ (14:2) Sum 79, p. 27.

SAARI, Patrick
"Ghandi. " SunM (8) Aut 79, p. 70.

SAAVEDRA, Carlos Castro
"Unemployed. " LitR (23:2) Wint 80, p. 221.

SABA, Umberto
"The Edge" (tr. by Lawrence Venuti). PoNow (24) 79, p. 49.
"I Loved" (tr. by Felix Stefanile). PoNow (24) 79, p. 34.
"Lake" (tr. by Lawrence Venuti). PoNow (23) 79, p. 44.
"The Mirror" (tr. by Lawrence Venuti). PoNow (24) 79, p. 50.
"Portrait of My Daughter" (tr. by Lawrence Venuti). PoNow (23)
79, p. 44.
"Smoke" (tr. by Lawrence Venuti). PoNow (23) 79, p. 44.
"Ulysses" (tr. by Felix Stefanile). PoNow (24) 79, p. 34.
"Winter Noon" (tr. by Felix Stefanile). PoNow (24) 79, p. 34.
"Woman" (tr. by Lawrence Venuti). PoNow (23) 79, p. 45.
"Work" (tr. by Lawrence Venuti). PoNow (23) 79, p. 45.
"Young Girl" (tr. by Lawrence Venuti). PoNow (24) 79, p. 50.

SABATIER, Robert
"The Miracles" (tr. by Maxine Kumin and Judith Kumin). PoNow
(24) 79, p. 50.

SABINES, Jaime
"Amen" (tr. by Steve Kowit). PoNow (24) 79, p. 51.
"Candle" (tr. by Ameen Alwan). VirQR (55:2) Spr 79, p. 307.
"Close by in the night, just a little off" (tr. by Naomi Lindstrom).

CharR (5:1) Spr 79, p. 19.
"I Stuck a Head on Your Shoulders" (tr. by Naomi Lindstrom).
CharR (5:1) Spr 79, p. 18.
"If Someone Tells You It Isn't True" (tr. by Naomi Lindstrom).
CharR (5:1) Spr 79, p. 19.
"No quiero decir nada" (tr. by Ameen Alwan). VirQR (55:2) Spr
79, p. 308.
"The noise from the heater in the next room is like an army"
(tr. by Naomi Lindstrom). CharR (5:1) Spr 79, p. 20.
"Poemas de unas horas misticas" (tr. by Ameen Alwan). VirQR
(55:2) Spr 79, p. 310.
"Si uno pudiera encontrar" (tr. by Ameen Alwan). VirQR (55:2)
Spr 79, p. 309.
"To turn on the stars, press the blue button" (tr. by Naomi
Lindstrom). CharR (5:1) Spr 79, p. 20.

SACHS, Elizabeth Newton
"Celebration. " Paint (11) Spr 79, p. 67.

SADIN, Marjorie
"Hot Coals. " LittleM (12:1/2) Spr-Sum 78 (79), p. 107.

SADOFF, Ira
"Bleak House" (for Dianne). Poetry (135:1) O 79, p. 27.
"The Drive Through Tulsa: August, 1936. " Aspen (8) Aut 79,
p. 35.
"Dursu Uzala. " AmerPoR (8:4) Jl-Ag 79, p. 11.
"Entry. " NewRep (181:18) 3 N 79, p. 26.
"My Wife's Upstairs. " Poetry (135:1) O 79, p. 26.
"Poem after Wang-Wei. " NewEngR (1:4) Sum 79, p. 470.
"The Subject Matter. " Poetry (135:1) O 79, p. 28.

SAGAN, Miriam
"Ariadne. " StoneC (6:2) My 79, p. 29.
"Invocation. " Tele (15) Spr 79, p. 27.
"Montage for Jill. " Tendril (5) Sum 79, p. 46.
"Mother of Multitudes" (after Kathe Kollwitz). Tele (15) Spr 79,
p. 27.

SAHIAN, Hamo
"Burst if you wish, cry if you will" (tr. by Diana Der Hovanes-
sian). PoNow (24) 79, p. 51.
"My ideas" (tr. by Diana Der Hovanessian). PoNow (24) 79, p.
51.
"Vision" (tr. by Diana Der Hovanessian). PoNow (24) 79, p. 51.

ST. CYR, Napoleon
"Inheritance. " SmPd (45) 79, p. 5.

ST. JOHN, David
"The Avenues. " Poetry (134:4) Jl 79, p. 203.
"The Boathouse. " Poetry (134:4) Jl 79, p. 204.
"Casino. " Antaeus (33) Spr 79, p. 93.

"Homage to Robert Johnson. " Antaeus (33) Spr 79, p. 92.
"Hotel Sierra. " NewYorker (55:40) 19 N 79, p. 46.
"Lunch. " ParisR (75) Spr 79, p. 214.

ST. JOHN, Noah Eagleon
"The Death of Innocence. " Wind (32) 79, p. 44.

ST. JOHN, Primus
"Lyrics. " PortR (25) 79, p. 133.

ST VINCENT, Paul
"Philpot. " MinnR (NS 12) Spr 79, p. 14.
"philpot observed: Fourteen Poems. " WormR (74) 79, pp. 55-66.
"Philpot Unfit for Active Service. " MinnR (NS 12) Spr 79, p. 15.

SAISER, Marge
"Three Love Poems. " KanQ (11:1/2) Wint-Spr 79, p. 163.

SAKANOUE, Lady Otomo No
"For a Religious Service to a God" (tr. by Hiroaki Sato).
    Montra (5) 79, p. 119.
"Grieving over the Death of the Nun Rigan, in 735" (tr. by Hiro-
    aki Sato). Montra (5) 79, p. 120.
"Love's Complaint" (tr. by Hiroaki Sato). Montra (5) 79, p. 121.
"A Tanka" (tr. by Hiroaki Sato). Montra (5) 79, p. 121.

SALAS, Katherine
"Making Distinctions. " QW (8) Wint 78, p. 13.

SALASIN, R.
"The Drowned Boy. " WebR (4:3) Spr 79, p. 62.

SALEH, Dennis
"Chameleon Errant. " Poetry (135:1) O 79, pp. 14-15.
"Prodigal Sun. " Poetry (135:1) O 79, pp. 16-17.
"Zippers. " MissouriR (2:2/3) Spr 79, p. 34.

SALERNO, Salvatore Jr.
"The Flicker. " Poem (36) Jl 79, pp. 50-51.
"Moon. " Poem (36) Jl 79, p. 49.

SALINAS, Pedro
"The Absent" (tr. by Harry Thomas). MichQR (18:1) Wint 79,
    p. 118.
"If You Called Me" (tr. by Harry Thomas). MichQR (18:1) Wint
    79, p. 117.

SALISBURY, Ralph
"Another Waiting. " NewL (45:3) Spr 79, p. 98.
"For Years and Years. " CharR (5:1) Spr 79, p. 23.
"An Inspiring Resurrection in the Age of Detente. " CharR (5:1)
    Spr 79, p. 22.

SALKEY, Andrew
"The Remote Collector" (for Cecil Rajendra).   MassR (20:2) Sum
    79, p. 308.

SALLAH, Tijan M.
"Why Come You Yaadicone?"   Wind (34) 79, p. 46.

SALTER, Mary Jo
"Love Poem for a Poet. "   Atl (244:3) S 79, p. 49.

SAMPLE, John Davis
"Quail. "   Poem (37) N 79, p. 64.

SANCHEZ, Carol Lee
"The Old Ones. "   BelPoJ (30:2) Wint 79-80, p. 46.

SANDERS, Scott Patrick
"Instructions for a Big Dream. "   WestB (4) 79, p. 22.

SANDERS, Thomas E.   (Nippawanock)
"The Hippies and the Hopi. "   SoDakR (17:4) Wint 79-80, p. 5.
"Machine out of the God. "   SoDakR (17:4) Wint 79-80, p. 3.

SANDLER, Linda
"Blindsight. "   MalR (49) Ja 79, p. 47.

SANDY, David
"The Bridge Operator. "   Poem (35) Mr 79, pp. 10-11.
"Learning to Swim. "   Poem (35) Mr 79, p. 12.

SANDY, Stephen
"After the Hunt. "   MichQR (18:4) Aut 79, p. 633.
"Balance. "   Poetry (135:1) O 79, pp. 30-31.
"Den. "   MichQR (18:4) Aut 79, p. 632.
"Groupings. "   MichQR (18:4) Aut 79, p. 631.
"A Little Yard. "   Poetry (135:1) O 79, p. 33.
"Oyster Cove. "   NewYorker (55:25) 6 Ag 79, p. 42.
"Pardon. "   PoNow (21) 79, p. 35.
"Sterling Mountain. "   Poetry (135:1) O 79, pp. 32-33.

SANER, Reg
"Congregation, Tableau. "   PoNow (23) 79, p. 10.
"Dear Icarus. "   Bits (10) Jl 79.
"Dear Petrarch:".   Bits (10) Jl 79.
"Nostalgia for Earth" (tr. of Jules Supervielle).   NowestR (18:2)
    79, p. 69.
"Orchestra. "   GeoR (32:2) Sum 79, p. 328.
"Packing In. "   PoNow (23) 79, p. 10.
"Prospectus. "   SouthernPR (19:2) Aut 79, p. 69.

SANESI, Roberto
"Swansea" (tr. by William Alexander).   PoNow (24) 79, p. 51.
"Toward Winter" (tr. by William Alexander).   PoNow (24) 79, p. 51.

SANGE, Gary
"For Good" (and my friends at the Virginia State Penitentiary).
KanQ (11:1/2) Wint-Spr 79, p. 166.

SANTOS, Sherod
"Accidental Weather. "   MissouriR (2:2/3) Spr 79, p. 41.
"Autumn Landscape Viewed from the Study. " Antaeus (32) Wint
     79, p. 51.
"Begin Distance. " Poetry (134:1) Ap 79, pp. 28-29.
"Country Landscape. " Poetry (134:1) Ap 79, pp. 30-31.
"Difficult Place. " ParisR (75) Spr 79, pp. 202-203.
"Love and Neglect: A Dialectical Landscape. " VirQR (55:3)
     Sum 79, p. 509.
"The Maple Trees. " QW (9) Spr-Sum 79, p. 119.
"Melancholy Divorcée" (for MDM). Poetry (134:1) Ap 79, pp.
     26-27.
"On the First Anniversary of Your Departure. " Antaeus (34)
     Sum 79, p. 69.
"Theophile Gautier. " QW (7) Aut 78, p. 61.
"This Quiet Snow. " QW (9) Spr-Sum 79, p. 118.
"An Unknown Man Begins Writing His Auto Biography. " Poetry
     (134:1) Ap 79, pp. 32-33.
"Winter Landscape with a Girl in Brown Shoes. " Antaeus (32)
     Wint 79, p. 49.

SANZARI, Sylvester
"The Emperor's New Clothes. " StoneC (6:2) My 79, p. 27.

SAPPHO
"The Evening Star restores all that the" (tr. by I. F. Stone).
     NewYRB (26:2) 22 F 79, p. 10.
"The moon sets" (tr. by I. F. Stone). NewYRB (26:2) 22 F 79,
     p. 10.

SARAH
"hegira. " Ur (2) 79, p. 106.
"imposter. " Ur (2) 79, p. 110.
"March. " SeC (7:1) 79, p. 14.
"till the constant strain of birth is enough. " Ur (2) 79, p. 108.
"To an Un-married Woman" (for h.). SeC (7:1) 79, p. 12.

SARAH, Robyn
"Old Honesty. " MalR (49) Ja 79, p. 121.
"The Trees. " MalR (49) Ja 79, p. 121.

SARGENT, Dana
"The Courage of the Oven-Tenders. " Mouth (2:3) N 79, p. 48.
"First Name Basis. " Mouth (2:3) N 79, p. 29.
"Judas. " ChrC (96:13) 11 Ap 79, p. 402.

SARGENT, Robert
Poem. St. AR (5:2) 79, p. 25.

SARVING, Ole
"Lances" (tr. by Ole Sarving and Alexander Taylor). <u>PoNow</u> (24) 79, p. 35.
"The Sea" (tr. by Ole Sarving and Alexander Taylor). <u>PoNow</u> (24) 79, p. 35.
"Wild Fear" (tr. by Ole Sarving and Alexander Taylor). <u>PoNow</u> (24) 79, p. 35.

SASSO, Laurence J. Jr.
"Random Reunion. " <u>Confr</u> (19) Aut 79-Wint 80, p. 114.
"Where Ends Must Touch. " <u>Wind</u> (32) 79, p. 43.

SATO, Hiroaki
"Autumn" (tr. of Princess Shikishi). <u>Montra</u> (5) 79, p. 144.
"Big Sky" (tr. of Hōsai Ozaki). <u>Pequod</u> (3:2) 79, pp. 85-86.
"Elegies for Her Daughter, Ko-Shikibu, Who Died in November 1025" (tr. of Lady Izumi). <u>Montra</u> (5) 79, p. 140.
"Elegies for Prince Atsumichi, Who Died on October 2, 1007" (tr. of Lady Izumi). <u>Montra</u> (5) 79, p. 139.
"For a Religious Service to a God" (tr. of Lady Otomo No Sakanoue). <u>Montra</u> (5) 79, p. 119.
Free Verse <u>Haiku</u> from Big Sky: "At Shodo Island" (tr. of Hōsai Ozaki). <u>PartR</u> (46:1) 79, pp. 92-101.
"Grieving over the Death of the Nun Rigan, in 735" (tr. of Lady Otomo No Sakanoue). <u>Montra</u> (5) 79, p. 120.
"Love" (tr. of Princess Shikishi). <u>Montra</u> (5) 79, p. 146.
"Love's Complaint" (tr. of Lady Otomo No Sakanoue). <u>Montra</u> (5) 79, p. 121.
"Miscellany" (tr. of Princess Shikishi). <u>Montra</u> (5) 79, p. 147.
"On Love" (tr. of Lady Izumi). <u>Montra</u> (5) 79, p. 137.
"Other Subjects" (tr. of Lady Izumi). <u>Montra</u> (5) 79, p. 141.
"Spring" (tr. of Princess Shikishi). <u>Montra</u> (5) 79, p. 142.
"Summer" (tr. of Princess Shikishi). <u>Montra</u> (5) 79, p. 143.
"A Tanka" (tr. of Lady Otomo No Sakanoue). <u>Montra</u> (5) 79, p. 121.
Twenty-five poems (tr. of Kotaro Takamura). <u>Montra</u> (6) 79, pp. 103-133.
"Winter" (tr. of Princess Shikishi). <u>Montra</u> (5) 79, p. 145.

SAUL, George Brandon
"By Winter Seas. " <u>ArizQ</u> (35:2) Sum 79, p. 100.

SAVAGE, Tom
"Memoirs of a Viaduct. " <u>Tele</u> (15) Spr 79, p. 62.

SAVITT, Lynne
"June 24, 1977 Thirtieth Birthday Poem. " <u>SeC</u> (6:1) 78, p. 26.
Lust in 28 Flavors. <u>SeC</u> (8:1) 79. Entire issue.

SAVOIE, Terrence M.
"The Far North. " <u>FourQt</u> (28:2) Wint 79, p. 4.
"Stray. " <u>ArkRiv</u> (4:3) 79, p. 37.
"Thaw. " <u>Nimrod</u> (23:1) Aut-Wint 79, p. 14.

SAX, Boria
"The Moth. " PoetC (11:1) 79, p. 17.
'Two in the Morning. " PoetC (11:2) 79, p. 32.

SAYLOR, Mark
"Hello Sister. " PikeF (2) Wint 78-79, p. 7.

SCAMMELL, William
"Above Thirlmere. " Poetry (133:5) F 79, p. 272.
"Aunt Jenny. " Poetry (133:5) F 79, pp. 276-277.
"High Summer. " Poetry (133:5) F 79, p. 274.
"Night Piece. " Poetry (133:5) F 79, p. 275.
"St. Bees in Winter. " Poetry (133:5) F 79, p. 273.

SCANLON, Dennice
"Leaving South Sixth East. " Ur (2) 79, p. 111.
"Skunked. " PoetC (11:1) 79, p. 32.

SCANNELL, Vernon
"Reformed Drunkard. " AmerS (48:2) Spr 79, p. 210.

SCARBROUGH, George
"A Death in the Family. " SmF (7/8) Spr-Aut 78, p. 21.

SCEVE, Maurice
"XLIV" (tr. by Paul Auster). Pequod (3:1) 79, p. 60.
"LIX" (tr. by Paul Auster). Pequod (3:1) 79, p. 60.
"LXXIX" (tr. by Paul Auster). Pequod (3:1) 79, p. 61.

SCHAEFER, Ted
'The Estuary. " KanQ (11:3) Sum 79, p. 38.
"Grapefruit. " KanQ (11:3) Sum 79, p. 39.
"Lake Geneva in Spring. " NewL (46:1) Aut 79, p. 72.
"The Mermaid in the Water Tower. " CharR (5:1) Spr 79, p. 68.
"O'Hare. " NewL (46:1) Aut 79, p. 72.
"Panorama of Illinois and Imaginary Scenes. " PoNow (25) 79, p.
    35.
'The President Contemplates Firepower. " NewL (46:1) Aut 79,
    p. 71.
'The Refugees. " NewL (46:1) Aut 79, p. 71.
"Vet to the V.A. Shrink. " KanQ (11:3) Sum 79, p. 39.

SCHAEFFER, Susan Fromberg
'The Angel. " MidwQ (20:4) Sum 79, p. 368.
"Away. " MidwQ (20:4) Sum 79, p. 375.
"City. " CentR (23:1) Wint 79, p. 63.
'The Day in Its Parts. " AntR (37:2) Spr 79, pp. 195-208.
'The Days of Heaven. " CharR (5:2) Aut 79, p. 53.
'The Exit. " MidwQ (20:4) Sum 79, p. 373.
"Fable. " Chelsea (38) 79, p. 166.
'The Garden. " LittleM (12:1/2) Spr-Sum 78 (79), p. 66.
'The King's Destinies. " MidwQ (20:4) Sum 79, p. 370.
'The King's Melancholy. " MidwQ (20:4) Sum 79, p. 371.

"Letter to Albuquerque" (for E. E. H.). KanQ (11:3) Sum 79, p. 28.
"Signs. " MinnR (NS 12) Spr 79, p. 16.

SCHAPER, Jo
"Predawn Train. " Sam (72) 79, p. 31.
"Promontory # 108. " Sam (72) 79, p. 30.
W. A. M. &T. Tracks Back to Tranquility, Texas (for Pat Burge). Sam (76) 79. Entire issue.

SCHAUBROECK, Beth
"Signs. " PoNow (25) 79, p. 35.

SCHEDLER, Gilbert
"A Spring Day on Campus. " ChrC (96:14) 18 Ap 79, p. 437.

SCHEELE, Roy
"A Clutch of Roots for Arbor Day. " HolCrit (16:2) Ap 79, p. 16.
"Dakota Burial. " PraS (53:3) Aut 79, p. 272.
"Ice Storm in Late November. " PraS (53:3) Aut 79, p. 271.
"Up Early One October Morning. " Comm (106:17) 28 S 79, p. 530.

SCHEER, Linda
"The Dinosaur" (tr. of Augusto Monterroso). Chelsea (38) 79, p. 231.
"(The Drowned)" (tr. of Jose Carlos Becerra). PoNow (24) 79, p. 5.
"Guernica" (tr. of Miguel Flores Ramirez). PoNow (24) 79, p. 15.
"Negative" (tr. of Francisco Hernandez). PoNow (24) 79, p. 19.
"The Old Man and the Gunpowder" (tr. of Francisco Hernandez). PoNow (24) 79, p. 19.
"One Day Mirrors Will Have Aged" (tr. of Miguel Flores Ramirez). PoNow (24) 79, p. 15.
"Street" (tr. of Francisco Hernandez). PoNow (24) 79, p. 19.

SCHEIBLI, Silvia
"Conception. " UTR (6:3) 79, p. 43.
"Death. " UTR (6:3/4) 79, p. 41.
"Letters from the Mojave Desert. " UTR (6:3/4) 79, p. 76.
"The Poet. " UTR (6:3/4) 79, p. 44.

SCHELL, Gary
"Sorrow Cemetery. " PoNow (25) 79, p. 36.
"The Carp. " PoNow (25) 79, p. 36.
"The Rider. " PoNow (25) 79, p. 36.
"Twig. " PoNow (25) 79, p. 36.

SCHELLING, Andrew
"The next morning" (tr. of "anonymous"). ChiR (31:2) Aut 79, p. 109.
"Set beside a fawn-eyed lady" (tr. of "anonymous"). ChiR (31:2)

Aut 79, p. 110.
"Unable to cast a likeness" (tr. of "anonymous").   ChiR (31:2)
  Aut 79, p. 111.
"You are rich, that you can chatter" (tr. of Vidyā).   ChiR (31:2)
  Aut 79, p. 108.

SCHENK, Leslie
  "Glossy Print. "   Paint (12) Aut 79, p. 17.
  "Set Off by Two Words in a Novel. "   BelPoJ (29:3) Spr 79, p.
  24.

SCHEVILL, James
  "The Cenote at Chichen Itza. "   PoNow (21) 79, p. 11.
  "On the Style of Ascending Indian Pyramids. "   PoNow (21) 79,
  pp. 10-11.
  "Tourists at Palenque. "   PoNow (21) 79, p. 11.
  "Two Visions. "   PoNow (21) 79, p. 11.
  "Vision of a Mayan Lord. "   PoNow (21) 79, p. 10.

SCHIFF, Jeff
  "After Childhood. "   SouthernHR (13:4) Aut 79, p. 311.
  "The Fields in Sweden Township. "   SouthernHR (13:4) Aut 79, p.
  343.
  "Five Arks. "   CutB (13) Aut-Wint 79, p. 40.
  "The Flood. "   GreenfieldR (7:3/4) Spr-Sum 79, p. 235.
  "Listening to the Night Chant. "   GreenfieldR (7:3/4) Spr-Sum 79,
  p. 235.
  "The Story of Coal. "   FourQt (28:2) Wint 79, p. 32.
  "Wading Across. "   SouthernPR (19:1) Spr 79, p. 11.

SCHLAGER, Barry
  "There is nothing like the silence. "   EngJ (68:5) My 79, p. 36.

SCHLOSSER, Robert
  "Wing of the Winter Monarch. "   Sam (79) 79, p. 27.

SCHMID, Vernon
  "The Drowning. "   ChrC (96:27) 29 Ag-5 S 79, p. 819.

SCHMITZ, Dennis
  "Building on Farmer Creek" (to Tom Crawford).   Columbia (3)
  79, p. 44.
  "City Ginkgos. "   Field (20) Spr 79, p. 59.
  "Coma. "   Iowa (10:3) Sum 79, p. 106.
  "Cutting Out a Dress. "   Field (21) Aut 79, p. 59.
  "The Great American Poem. "   Antaeus (32) Wint 79, pp. 82-86.
  "The History of Armor. "   Iowa (10:3) Sum 79, p. 105.
  "Leaving the Palace. "   Antaeus (32) Wint 79, p. 44.
  "Making Chicago. "   Antaeus (34) Sum 79, p. 48.
  "On the Fifth Day. "   QW (8) Wint 79, p. 82.
  "Oregon. "   QW (8) Wint 79, p. 81.
  "A Picture of Okinawa. "   Field (21) Aut 79, p. 58.
  "A Rabbit's Death. "   Antaeus (32) Wint 79, p. 45.

"Skinning the Cat. " Antaeus (35) Aut 79, p. 88.
"Soup. " Antaeus (32) Wint 79, p. 43.

SCHNEIDER, Laurie
    "Mr. Cogito and the Pearl" (tr. of Herbert Zbigniew). QW (7)
        Aut 78, p. 112.
    "The twolegs of Mr. Cogito" (tr. of Herbert Zbigniew). QW (7)
        Aut 78, p. 111.

SCHNEIDER, Pat
    "In a Maple Wood. " SmPd (47) 79, p. 4.

SCHNEIDERMAN, Leo
    "At the Mouth of Ash Creek. " SoDakR (17:4) 79, p. 22.
    "Black Kettle Slain. " SoDakR (17:4) Wint 79-80, p. 21.
    "The Texans Try to Conquer Santa Fe a Second Time. " SoDakR
        (17:4) Wint 79-80, p. 19.

SCHNEIDRE, P.
    "Aphorisms. " Shen (30:1) Aut 78, p. 85.
    "Cafe L. A. " Shen (30:2) Wint 79, p. 24.

SCHOLL, Betsy
    "Breathing Shallow. " GreenfieldR (7:3/4) Spr-Sum 79, p. 8.
    "Celia. " GreenfieldR (7:3/4) Spr-Sum 79, p. 5.
    "Returning (1). " GreenfieldR (7:3/4) Spr-Sum 79, p. 10.
    "Returning (2). " GreenfieldR (7:3/4) Spr-Sum 79, p. 11.
    "Spring Fragments. " BelPoJ (29:3) Spr 79, p. 33.
    "The Stutterer. " GreenfieldR (7:3/4) Spr-Sum 79, p. 7.

SCHOR, Sandra
    "In the Best of Health. " CentR (23:4) Aut 79, p. 429.
    "A Priest's Mind. " CentR (23:4) Aut 79, p. 428.
    "Small Consolation. " BelPoJ (29:4) Sum 79, p. 35.

SCHORB, E. M.
    "The Applicant. " SouthernPR (19:1) Spr 79, p. 58.

SCHOTT, Penelope
    "Charm Against Grieving. " SouthernPR (19:2) Aut 79, p. 64.
    "The Collaborators. " AmerPoR (8:5) S-O 79, p. 45.
    "On This Cold October Dawn. " SouthernPR (19:2) Aut 79, p. 65.

SCHRAMM, Darrell G. H.
    "Gerardo's Poem. " Mouth (2:1) F 79, p. 43.
    "Grey Watercolor. " Mouth (2:1) F 79, p. 43.
    "Sphinx. " Mouth (2:1) F 79, p. 48.

SCHRAMM, Richard
    "Between Us. " QW (9) Spr-Sum 79, p. 126.
    "Letters from Another World. " WestHR (33:2) Spr 79, p. 131.

SCHREIBER, Laura
"A Delicate Balance. " SouthernR (15:1) Wint 79, p. 111.
"Seals at Monterey. " SouthernR (15:1) Wint 79, p. 110.

SCHREIBER, Ron
"as if there were time. " Wind (34) 79, p. 54.
"before the Celtics game. " PoNow (23) 79, p. 28.
"the crows of March. " HangL (35) Spr 79, p. 62.
"departure" (for Mary). Wind (34) 79, p. 55.
"dreaming of Ohio. " PoNow (23) 79, p. 28.
"false clues. " PoNow (23) 79, p. 28.
"January, 1978. " HangL (35) Spr 79, p. 58.
"learning the way. " PoNow (23) 79, p. 28.
"Linaria Candles. " Mouth (2:2) Je 79, p. 33.
"May tenth. " HangL (35) Spr 79, p. 57.
"midsummer. " HangL (35) Spr 79, p. 64.
"news from the pigpen (a poem for bosses). " HangL (35) Spr
  79, p. 60.
"september. " Wind (34) 79, p. 55.
"Trientalis Borealis. " Mouth (2:2) Je 79, p. 33.

SCHREINER, Mary L.
"Cancion Primera" (tr. of Miguel Hernandez). MalR (49) Ja 79,
  p. 99.
"Cancion Ultima" (tr. of Miguel Hernandez). MalR (49) Ja 79,
  p. 100.
"Casida del Sediento" (tr. of Miguel Hernandez). MalR (49) Ja
  79, p. 98.

SCHROEER, Willie
"Ingredients for a Year. " PikeF (2) Wint 78-79, p. 18.

SCHUCHMAN, Dorothy
"Star Roses: A Warming from the Nurseries at Quiet Grove,
  Pa. " DenQ (14:2) Sum 79, p. 88.
"Two Up: On Stein. " DenQ (14:2) Sum 79, p. 89.

SCHULER, Bob
"for Raymond Roseliep. " Northeast (3:7) Spr 79, p. 19.

SCHULER, Ruth Wildes
"Old Lady. " Sam (79) 79, p. 81.

SCHULMAN, Grace
"Easy as Wind. " NewYorker (55:21) 9 Jl 79, p. 38.
"That Day's Fire. " Nat (228:5) 10 F 79, p. 150.

SCHURING, Robert
"Winds of Fortune. " EngJ (68:5) My 79, p. 39.

SCHWABSKY, Barry
"Arthur: Perdido. " Poetry (134:2) My 79, p. 78.
"Fragment of a Pastoral. " Poetry (134:2) My 79, p. 82.
"Now I'm Feeling Blue. " Poetry (134:2) My 79, pp. 79-80.

SCHWARTZ, Hillel
"Highwire. " CutB (12) Spr-Sum 79, p. 5.
"Rules of Auction. " DenQ (14:3) Aut 79, p. 107.
"With Cockle Shells. " SouthernHR (13:3) Sum 79, p. 198.

SCHWARTZ, Howard
"Black Holes. " PoNow (22) 79, p. 27.
"From Afar" (tr. of Carmen Orrego). WebR (4:3) Spr 79, p. 40.
"Lament" (tr. of Yehuda Amichai w. Shlomo Vinner). AmerPoR
    (8:3) My-Je 79, p. 43.
"A Latter-Day History of the Castle. " PoNow (22) 79, p. 27.
"Since Then" (tr. of Yehuda Amichai w. Shlomo Vinner).
    AmerPoR (8:3) My-Je 79, p. 43.
Twenty Poems. CharR (5:SI) 79, pp. 55-79.

SCHWARTZ, Lee
"Apparition. " Chomo (5:3) Spr 79, p. 27.

SCHWARTZ, Lloyd
"Mug Shots. " Ploughs (5:2) 79, pp. 113-117.
"Self-Portrait" (for Ralph Hamilton). NewRep (180:8) 24 F 79,
    p. 30.
"Yeats' Prayer. " MassR (20:2) Sum 79, p. 260.

SCHWARTZ, Marian
"Keeping Abreast. " Confr (18) Spr-Sum 79, p. 25.

SCHWARTZ, S. G.
"Amour de Voyage. " MichQR (18:2) Spr 79, p. 266.

SCOTELLARO, Robert
"end of the trail. " Tele (15) Spr 79, p. 131.

SCOTELLARO, Rocco
"For a Foreign Woman Who Is Leaving" (tr. by Ruth Feldman
    and Brian Swann). PoNow (21) 79, p. 46.
"The Friar's Boundary-Wall" (tr. by Ruth Feldman and Brian
    Swann). PoNow (21) 79, p. 46.
"La Gronda. " Os (8) 79, p. 2.
"Natale. " Os (8) 79, p. 4.
Twenty-two Poems (tr. by Ruth Feldman and Brian Swann).
    PoNow (24) 79, pp. 52-54.

SCOTT, Herbert
"Achilles' Heel. " MissR (24) Aut 79, p. 104.
"Boss's Dream. " PoNow (21) 79, p. 29.
"Breakfast at Aunt Hattie's. " DacTerr (16) 79, p. 56.
"Dinosaurs. " QW (7) Aut 78, pp. 5-25.
"Fermata. " MissR (24) Aut 79, p. 101.
"The Grocer's Children. " PoNow (21) 79, p. 29.
"Pension Day. " PoNow (21) 79, p. 29.
"The Present. " MissR (24) Aut 79, p. 107.
"Produce and Relief. " PoNow (21) 79, p. 29.

"The Story of Bread. " Ploughs (5:1) 79, pp. 110-111.
"Travelers. " MissR (24) Aut 79, p. 105.

SCROGGINS, Daryl
"Over the Rooftops. " PoNow (25) 79, p. 36.

SCULLY, James
"Esperanza. " NewYorker (55:3) 5 Mr 79, p. 33.
"May Day. " MinnR (NS 13) Aut 79, p. 5.

SEABURG, Alan
Poem. St.AR (5:2) 79, p. 63.

SEALE, Jan
"Things I Did Not Say at a Junior High Poetry Workshop. " PikeF
    (2) Wint 78-79, p. 27.
"Triptych. " PikeR (1) Sum 79, p. 56.

SEARS, Peter
"He Comes as Wind. " PoNow (23) 79, p. 31.
"I First Practiced Picking Up Small Things. " PortR (25) 79, p.
    56.
"Moon Gliding. " PoNow (23) 79, p. 31.
"Night Beach. " PortR (25) 79, p. 57.
"Rain. " PortR (25) 79, p. 57.
"Slack Tide. " PoNow (23) 79, p. 31.

SEBENTHALL, R. E.
"Potentials. " PoNow (21) 79, p. 39.
"Private Collections. " PoNow (21) 79, p. 39.

SEDGWICK, Eve Kosofsky
"Sexual Hum. " Salm (43) Wint 79, p. 102.

SEIDEL, Frederick
"Death Valley. " AmerPoR (8:5) S-O 79, p. 48.
"Homage to Cicero. " NewYRB (26:21/22) 24 Ja 80, p. 30.
"Men and Woman. " NewYRB (26:4) 22 Mr 79, p. 29.
"The Room and the Cloud. " AmerPoR (8:5) S-O 79, p. 48.
"To Robert Lowell and Osip Mandelstam. " HarvAd (113:1/2) N
    79, p. 19.
"The Trip. " AmerPoR (8:5) S-O 79, p. 48.

SEIDMAN, Hugh
"The Great American Poem. " Antaeus (32) Wint 79, pp. 82-86.

SEILER, Barry
"Fathers and Hearts. " PoNow (25) 79, p. 37.

SELDITZ, Nikki
"Ever Nearer the Gutter. " Ur (2) 79, p. 112.

SELLERS, Bettie M.
"Bluegrass Interval. " GRR (10:3) 79, p. 59.

"Cat for a Neutered Lady. " GRR (10:3) 79, p. 55.
"Discovered at Marblehead. " GRR (10:3) 79, p. 58.
"A Great Plan Backfired" (for Lee Davis). GRR (10:2) 79, p.
   173.
"Having Heard a Woman Preach in Dwight Chapel. " GRR (10:3)
   79, p. 57.
"If Justice Moved. " GeoR (33:4) Wint 79, p. 875.
"The Jilted Bride. " GRR (10:2) 79, p. 174.
"The Morning of the Red-Tailed Hawk. " BelPoJ (29:3) Spr 79,
   p. 35.
"South Georgia Lady. " GRR (10:3) 79, p. 54.
"Whence Cometh My Help?" GRR (10:3) 79, p. 56.

SELVAGGIO, Leni
"Learning to Move" (for Reen Morrison). SlowLR (3) 79, p. 59.

SELVAGGIO, Marc
"The Sound in the Basement. " Nat (229:19) 8 D 79, p. 598.
"Zimmer Among the Chickens. " Poultry (1) 79, p. 10.

SELZER, Richard
"Tumors. " NewEngR (2:1) Aut 79, p. 63.

SERENI, Vittorio
"Return" (tr. by Sonia Raiziss). PoNow (24) 79, p. 54.

SEVAK, Payour
"Your Unripe Love" (tr. by Diana Der Hovanessian). PoNow (24)
   79, p. 54.

SEVERY, Bruce
"Jean Irene. " Wind (32) 79, p. 5.

SEYFRIED, Robin
"Song for what Fell to the Floor. " PoetryNW (20:1) Spr 79, p.
   14.

SHABO, Gary
"The King of Boredom. " PoetryNW (20:4) Wint 79-80, pp. 39-40.

SHAFER, Margaret
"Migrant. " Confr (19) Aut 79-Wint 80, p. 163.
"The Romance of a Hundred Walks in Palestine. " Os (9) 79, p.
   3.

SHAFNER, R. L.
"Getting Back What You Once Lost. " DenQ (14:2) Sum 79, p.
   35.
"Results of an Amateur Graphologist. " DenQ (14:2) Sum 79, p.
   34.
"Two Wives Do Not Always Make a Whole (For JV). " DenQ
   (14:2) Sum 79, p. 36.
"A Woman Is Awake at Night. " DenQ (14:2) Sum 79, p. 37.

SHAKELY, Lauren
"Another Fire. " OhioR (20:2) Spr-Sum 79, p. 10.
"Cleaning House. " OhioR (20:2) Spr-Sum 79, p. 11.
"The Four O'Clocks. " VirQR (55:1) Wint 79, p. 106.

SHAKELY, M. J.
"The businessman strolled toward his house" (tr. of Sandro Pen-
na w. Ian Young). PoNow (24) 79, p. 44.
"A glass of milk" (tr. of Sandro Penna w. Ian Young). PoNow
(24) 79, p. 44.
"In a dingy theatre pit" (tr. of Sandro Penna w. Ian Young).
PoNow (24) 79, p. 44.
"The ship arrives. The cheery passengers" (tr. of Sandro Penna
w. Ian Young). PoNow (24) 79, p. 44.
"Silently, the summer went away" (tr. of Sandro Penna w. Ian
Young). PoNow (24) 79, p. 44.
"Still it is sweet to find yourself" (tr. of Sandro Penna w. Ian
Young). PoNow (24) 79, p. 44.
"Was he whistling at his door, or did he wish" (tr. of Sandro
Penna w. Ian Young). PoNow (24) 79, p. 44.

SHAKESPEARE
"Ophelia's Song. " Playb (26:1) Ja 79, p. 257.

SHAPIRO, Alan
"Captain Wynne to Randolf Routh. " Poetry (134:6) S 79, pp. 337-
338.
"The Dublin Evening Mail. " Poetry (134:6) S 79, p. 336.
"Mezuzah. " Ploughs (5:1) 79, p. 112.
"Randolf Routh to Charles Trevelyan. " Poetry (134:6) S 79, pp.
334-335.
"The Slaughterhouse 1935-1959. " QW (6) Spr-Sum 78, p. 120.

SHAPIRO, Daniel E.
"San Diego Depot. " CutB (13) Aut-Wint 79, p. 51.

SHAPIRO, David
"A Song. " Iowa (10:1) Wint 79, pp. 48-52.

SHAPIRO, E. B.
"Taking Them Back. " SmPd (45) 79, p. 27.

SHAPIRO, Harvey
"Cummings. " Nat (229:17) 24 N 79, p. 534.

SHARBROUGH, David
"Well, Boss. " Tele (15) Spr 79, p. 98.

SHARPE, Peter
"Clefless. " Tendril (5) Sum 79, p. 48.
"Cold Front. " Tendril (5) Sum 79, p. 47.

SHARPS, Samuel M. Jr.
"Young Black Poet. " BlackF (3:1) Aut-Wint 79, p. 26.

SHASTRI, Miriam
"Old Rose" (tr. by Mario Fratti). Wind (33) 79, p. 48.

SHAVER, Shelley
"Judgement Day. " PraS (53:3) Aut 79, p. 261.

SHAW, Robert B.
"Moss. " Poetry (135:1) O 79, p. 20.
"Partial Draft. " Poetry (135:1) O 79, p. 19.

SHECK, Laurie
"Amaranth. " Iowa (10:3) Sum 79, p. 101.
"The Cruise. " Ploughs (5:1) 79, pp. 113-114.
"The Deer. " Poetry (134:2) My 79, p. 83.
"The Land. " PoetryNW (20:1) Spr 79, p. 39.
"Love Poem. " Poetry (134:2) My 79, p. 84.
"Psyche. " Ploughs (5:1) 79, pp. 114-115.
"Sleeping Beauty. " PoetryNW (20:1) Spr 79, pp. 38-39.

SHEEHAN, Timothy
"Tuiska. " Chowder (12) Spr-Sum 79, p. 29.

SHEFLER, Roni
"Many Moons. " Tendril (4) Wint 79, p. 45.

SHEINBERG, Claire
"My Mother. " PikeF (2) Wint 78-79, p. 22.

SHELTON, Richard
"How to Amuse a Stone. " Poetry (134:5) Ag 79, pp. 262-263.
"Point of View. " Poetry (134:5) Ag 79, pp. 266-267.
"The Ship in a Bottle. " Poetry (134:5) Ag 79, pp. 264-265.

SHENTIRIS, Kita
"The Laundromat on the Road to Nirvana. " QW (9) Spr-Sum 79,
p. 122.

SHEPPARD, Patricia
"The Enlightenment. " Hudson (32:3) Aut 79, p. 402.

SHEPPARD, Simon
"Prisoner of Love. " Mouth (2:3) N 79, p. 3.

SHEPPARD, Susan
"Liverwurst, I Presume. " Wind (35) 79, p. 56.
"Transference. " Wind (35) 79, p. 55.

SHEPHERD, J. Barrie
"Bach Wakens Sleepers. " ChrC (96:40) 5 D 79, p. 1202.
"Hindsight. " ChrC (96:13) 11 Ap 79, p. 402.
"Manger Scene: Joseph. " ChrC (96:42) 19 D 79, p. 1261.
"Pawning. " ChrC (96:10) 21 Mr 79, p. 309.
"Prospects. " ChrC (96:34) 24 O 79, p. 1034.

355 SHEPPARD

"Re-petition. " ChrC (96:41) 12 D 79, p. 1240.
"Thanksgiving Wish. " ChrC (96:38) 21 N 79, p. 1161.
"Today's Question. " ChrC (96:12) 4 Ap 79, p. 366.

SHEPPARD, Susan
"Sleeping. " StoneC (6:2) My 79, p. 24.

SHER, Steven
"The Groundhog Foreshadowed. " KanQ (11:1/2) Wint-Spr 79, p. 94.
"To Our Decadence. " KanQ (11:1/2) Wint-Spr 79, p. 94.

SHERIDAN, Michael
"Festival in Nauvoo, Illinois. " PoNow (25) 79, p. 29.
"Pensioners. " PoNow (25) 79, p. 29.
"Warm Spell. " PoNow (25) 79, p. 29.

SHERMAN, Joe
"Songbird Barn. " NewEngR (2:1) Aut 79, p. 120.

SHERRARD, Philip
"Aphrodite Rising" (tr. of Angelos Sikelianos, w. Edmund Keeley). MalR (52) O 79, p. 98.
"Because I Deeply Praised" (tr. of Angelos Sikelianos, w. Edmund Keeley). MalR (52) O 79, p. 100.
"Daedalus" (tr. of Angelos Sikelianos, w. Edmund Keeley). MalR (52) O 79, p. 101.
"Prayer" (tr. of Angelos Sikelianos, w. Edmund Keeley). MalR (52) O 79, p. 99.

SHERWIN, Judith Johnson
"Analysis. " PoNow (21) 79, p. 37.
"Ballade of the Grindstones. " NewYorker (55:31) 17 S 79, p. 48.
"Before the Recovery. " VirQR (55:3) Sum 79, p. 507.
"Count Dracula. " PoNow (21) 79, p. 37.
"Creeley's 'The Dishonest Mailman' by Robert Bly. " Poultry (1) 79, p. 3.

SHEVIN, David
"An Amble. " Confr (19) Aut 79-Wint 80, p. 162.
"The Call. " BelPoJ (29:4) Sum 79, p. 14.
"17V78. " PoNow (25) 79, p. 37.

SHIDELER, Ross
"After Darwin. " Chelsea (38) 79, p. 169.
"On the Purpose of Experiments. " Chelsea (38) 79, p. 168.

SHIELDS, James W.
"January 6, 5:18 A. M. : Before Taking Down the Christmas Tree. " StoneC (6:3) O 79, p. 29.

SHIKISHI, Princess
"Autumn" (tr. by Hiroaki Sato). Montra (5) 79, p. 144.

"Love" (tr. by Hiroaki Sato). Montra (5) 79, p. 146.
"Miscellany" (tr. by Hiroaki Sato). Montra (5) 79, p. 147.
"Spring" (tr. by Hiroaki Sato). Montra (5) 79, p. 142.
"Summer" (tr. by Hiroaki Sato). Montra (5) 79, p. 143.
"Winter" (tr. by Hiroaki Sato). Montra (5) 79, p. 145.

SHINDER, Jason
"Doppelganger. " CalQ (15) Wint 79, p. 48.

SHIRAZI, Hafiz-i
"Ghazal I" (tr. by Elizabeth Gray). Antaeus (33) Spr 79, p. 138.
"Ghazal II" (tr. by Elizabeth Gray). Antaeus (33) Spr 79, p.
    139.
"Ghazal III" (tr. by Elizabeth Gray). Antaeus (33) Spr 79, p.
    140.
"Ghazal IV" (tr. by Elizabeth Gray). Antaeus (33) Spr 79, p.
    141.
"Ghazal V" (tr. by Elizabeth Gray). Antaeus (33) Spr 79, p.
    142.
"Ghazal VI" (tr. by Elizabeth Gray). Antaeus (33) Spr 79, p.
    143.
"Ghazal 10. " Agni (10/11) 79, p. 41.
"Ghazal 36. " Agni (10/11) 79, p. 42.
"Ghazal 37. " Agni (10/11) 79, p. 43.
Ten Ghazals (tr. by Elizabeth Gray). Falcon (18) Spr 79, pp.
    3-14.

SHIRLEY, Aleda
"Bronze. " CutB (13) Aut-Wint 79, p. 26.

SHIRLEY, Phillip
"The Emergency Room Lounge. " Poem (37) N 79, p. 30.
"The Husband and the Wife. " WormR (76) 79, p. 128.
"The Multi-Colored Couple. " WormR (76) 79, p. 128.

SHISLER, Barbara Esch
"The Monarch. " ChrC (96:26) 15-22 Ag 79, p. 783.

SHLONSKY, Avraham
"A Citizen's Dissertation on His Neighborhood" (tr. by Bernhard
    Frank). PoNow (24) 79, p. 55.

SHOEMAKER, Lynn
"Birmingham Sunday. " HangL (36) Aut 79, p. 63.
"First Lesson: The Hanging Flower. " Bachy (15) Aut 79, p. 95.
"Love Poem. " Bachy (15) Aut 79, p. 95.
"Mountain Man Pull High. " Epoch (28:2) Wint 79, p. 161.
"The Storyteller. " Bachy (15) Aut 79, p. 95.

SHOHER, Jessica
"Melancholia. " Ploughs (5:2) 79, p. 146.

SHOLL, Betsy
"Eyewitness. " WestB (4) 79, p. 48.

"How Dreams Come True. " NewOR (6:2) 79, p. 173.
"The Pond. " WestB (4) 79, p. 49.
"Urgency. " NewOR (6:2) 79, p. 172.

SHORE, Jane
"Narcissus. " Aspen (8) Aut 79, p. 34.
"Persian Miniature. " NewRep (181:3/4) 21-28 Jl 79, p. 30.
"Shuttle. " NewRep (181:17) 27 O 79, p. 36.

SHORT, Frank
"Friction. " Bits (10) Jl 79.
"Vermont in April. " PoNow (23) 79, p. 34.

SHOWS, Hal Steven
"In Imitation of a Dead Child's Poem. " Kayak (51) S 79, p. 42.

SHRIVER, Peggy
"The Spirit of 34th Street. " ChrC (96:3) 24 Ja 79, p. 74.

SHUMWAY, Mary
"Burial Ground. " Northeast (3:7) Spr 79, p. 14.
"Not Your Rose, Mr. Eliot. " Northeast (3:7) Spr 79, p. 15.

SHURIN, Aaron
"Cretan Boy. " Mouth (2:1) F 79, p. 18.
"Raving # 16. " Mouth (2:1) F 79, p. 30.

SHURMANTINE, Brad
"Rivalry. " Sam (72) 79, p. 53.

SHURTLEFF, Hillary
"To Jeff. " PortR (25) 79, p. 89.

SHUTTLEWORTH, Paul
"Moonlight on Three Faces. " PoNow (22) 79, p. 39.
"Tornado Watch. " SouthwR (64:3) Sum 79, p. 263.

SIEGEL, Julie
from Lily's Venetian Passion: Part III: "Taking the Frame
    Off. " ChiR (31:1) Sum 79, pp. 69-82.
"So. The moon. " Wind (34) 79, p. 25.
"Winter After Daley. " Wind (34) 79, p. 25.

SIEGEL, Robert
"Jill. " CarolQ (31:1) Wint 79, p. 84.
"Kilmartin Stones. " PraS (53:3) Aut 79, p. 220.
"Mound. " PraS (53:3) Aut 79, p. 221.
"Peonies. " PraS (53:3) Aut 79, p. 219.
"Sumac. " PraS (53:3) Aut 79, p. 222.

SIKELIANOS, Angelos
"Aphrodite Rising" (tr. by Edmund Keeley and Philip Sherrard).
    MalR (52) O 79, p. 98.
"Because I Deeply Praised" (tr. by Edmund Keeley and Philip

Sherrard). MalR (52) O 79, p. 100.
"Daedalus" (tr. by Edmund Keeley and Philip Sherrard). MalR (52) O 79, p. 101.
"Prayer" (tr. by Edmund Keeley and Philip Sherrard). MalR (52) O 79, p. 99.

SILBERSHER, Marvin
"and they did. " JnlONJP (3:2) 79, p. 29.
"approaching short hills. " JnlONJP (3:2) 79, p. 29.
"3. " JnlONJP (3:2) 79, p. 31.

SILBERT, Layle
"Bequeathal. " Confr (18) Spr-Sum 79, p. 95.

SILER, Jocelyn
"The Ladies. " KanQ (11:1/2) Wint-Spr 79, p. 181.
"A Little While Away. " KanQ (11:1/2) Wint-Spr 79, p. 181.

SILESKY, Barry
"History. " PoNow (22) 79, p. 40.

SILKIN, Jon
"The chisel grows heavy. " Stand (20:4) 79, p. 5.
"Going on. " Iowa (10:3) Sum 79, p. 95.
"Jerusalem. " Iowa (10:3) Sum 79, p. 93.
"The Lapidary Poems" (to the memory and work of Merle Brown). Iowa (10:3) Sum 79, p. 91.
"The Lapidary Style. " Stand (20:4) 79, p. 5.
"Lapidary words. " Stand (20:4) 79, p. 5.

SILLIMAN, Ron
"3 Fifths Equals" (w. Charles Bernstein and Steve McCaffery). SunM (8) Aut 79, pp. 162-169.

SILVA, Beverly
"The Man I Love. " PikeF (2) Wint 78-79, p. 7.

SILVA, Gary
"Goneril's Letter to Regan. " PoetC (11:3) 79, p. 26.

SILVA, Jeff
"The Poem of Dead Things. " GreenfieldR (7:3/4) Spr-Sum 79, p. 230.
"The Stunt Man. " CharR (5:1) Spr 79, p. 91.
"Toward Spring. " Chelsea (38) 79, p. 185.
"A Way to Work. " GreenfieldR (7:3/4) Spr-Sum 79, p. 229.
"Wild Life. " Chelsea (38) 79, p. 202.

SILVERSTEIN, Shel
"The Devil & Billy Markham. " Playb (26:1) Ja 79, p. 311.
"The Diet. " Playb (26:10) O 79, p. 149.
"Numbers. " Playb (26:9) S 79, p. 157.
"The Perfect High, or The Quest of Gimmesome Roy. " Playb

(26:7) Jl 79, p. 93.
"The Winner. " Playb (26:12) D 79, p. 193.

SILVERTON, Michael
"Her Rosy Ass Glimps'd. " PoNow (23) 79, p. 12.
"Memorial Day. " PoNow (23) 79, p. 12.

SIMAS, Joey
"Imagine. " Mouth (2:2) Je 79, p. 42.

SIMIC, Charles
"Classic Ballroom Dances. " QW (7) Aut 78, p. 37.
"Crepuscular. " Poetry (135:3) D 79, p. 132.
"Furniture Mover. " Poetry (135:3) D 79, pp. 130-132.
"The Great American Poem. " Antaeus (32) Wint 79, pp. 82-86.
"The Great Horned Owl. " Durak (2) 79, p. 6.
"Green Lampshade. " Poetry (135:3) D 79, p. 129.
"Harsh Climate. " NewYorker (54:49) 22 Ja 79, p. 40.
"Old Couple. " QW (7) Aut 78, p. 35.
"Prodigy. " Field (21) Aut 79, p. 66.
"Rosalie. " QW (7) Aut 78, p. 34.
"Spoons with Realistic Dead Flies on Them" (for T. S.). QW
    (7) Aut 78, p. 36.
"A Suitcase Strapped with a Rope. " Durak (2) 79, p. 5.

SIMMER, Scott
"Flying. " CutB (12) Spr-Sum 79, p. 51.
"Fourth of July Address. Deserted Railroad Tunnel, Colorado.
    Continental Divide. " Spirit (4:1) Aut-Wint 78-79, p. 22.
"Scene from a Farmyard Before Sunrise. " PoNow (25) 79, p.
    37.
"We Were New in the Neighborhood so We Invited Him In. "
    Bits (10) Jl 79.
"Window Washing. " PoNow (25) 79, p. 37.

SIMMERMAN, Jim
"Places. " CarolQ (31:3) Aut 79, p. 87.
"Leaving. " CarolQ (31:3) Aut 79, p. 89.

SIMMONS, Judy
"Minority. " Cond (5) 79, p. 93.

SIMMONS, Sara
"Fudge Cookies. " PikeF (2) Wint 78-79, p. 18.
"Landslide. " PikeF (2) Wint 78-79, p. 18.

SIMMS, Michael
"Marseille" (after Jean Cocteau). WestB (5) 79, p. 66.
"Meditations in Galveston. " WestB (5) 79, p. 67.

SIMON, Marjorie
"Foreplay" (from Modern Bookbinding Practically Considered by
    Wm. Matthews). Kayak (50) My 79, p. 35.

SIMPSON, Louis
"The Art of Story Telling. " AmerPoR (8:1) Ja-F 79, p. 9.
"Caviare at the Funeral. " AmerPoR (8:1) Ja-F 79, p. 9.
"The Liberated Characters' Ball. " AmerPoR (8:1) Ja-F 79, p. 9.
"Sway. " ParisR (76) Aut 79, pp. 110-113.
"Typhus. " AmerPoR (8:1) Ja-F 79, p. 8.
"Unfinished Life. " AmerPoR (8:3) My-Je 79, p. 46.
"Working Late. " NewYorker (55:35) 15 O 79, p. 46.

SIMPSON, Nancy
"Water on the Highway. " GeoR (33:2) Sum 79, p. 394.

SINGER, Burns
"Poem Without a Title. " Stand (20:1) 78-79, p. 71.

SINGER, Davida
"Before Touch, Song of the Romantic. " Mouth (2:1) F 79, p. 7.
"Letters to Women: Dear Carolyn. " Mouth (2:1) F 79, p. 32.
"New Moon. " Mouth (2:1) F 79, p. 5.
"What You Did. " Mouth (2:1) F 79, p. 34.
"Wings" (for C. K.). Mouth (2:1) F 79, p. 1.

SINISGALLI, Leonardo
Nine Poems (tr. by W. S. DiPiero). PoNow (24) 79, pp. 55-56.

SISSON, C. H.
"Autumn Poems. " Stand (20:2) 79, p. 21.

SISSON, Jonathan
"Gazetteer. " Antaeus (34) Sum 79, p. 80.

SJOBERG, John
"A Selection from the Living Sea Scroll. " Spirit (4:2/3) Spr-Sum 79, p. 61.

SKACEL, Jan
from Prohibited Man: "Again I am inaudible, inaudible as light" (tr. by Ewald Osers). Stand (20:1) 78-79, p. 21.

SKEEN, Anita
"conscious of angles. " Nimrod (23:1) Aut-Wint 79, p. 87.
"entering the north field" (w. Carol Barrett). Nimrod (23:1) Aut-Wint 79, p. 57.
"the last link. " Nimrod (23:1) Aut-Wint 79, p. 88.
"rites of access" (w. Carol Barrett). Nimrod (23:1) Aut-Wint 79, p. 58.
"trying to get home. " Nimrod (23:1) Aut-Wint 79, p. 86.

SKINNER, Jeff
"Elizabeth and the Blizzard. " PoetryNW (20:2) Sum 79, pp. 32-33.

SKINNER, Knute
"A Preference. " PoNow (21) 79, p. 34.

SKLAR, Morty
"A Man Lies in White Linen. " NewL (45:3) Spr 79, p. 36.
"McDonald's. " Spirit (3:3) Sum 78, p. 8.
"Poem to the Sun. " NewL (46:2) Wint 79-80, p. 103.

SKLAREW, Deborah
"Sightseer. " PoNow (25) 79, p. 38.

SKLAREW, Myra
"In Bed. " CarolQ (31:3) Aut 79, p. 25.

SKLOOT, Floyd
"Brooklyn Sundays. " Vaga (29) 79, p. 30.
"Executive Search. " Spirit (3:1/2) Aut-Wint 77-78, p. 51.
"Hartstene Island. " Vaga (29) 79, p. 32.
"Home. " Wind (35) 79, p. 17.
"the lesson of the auditors. " St. AR (5:3) Aut-Wint 79, p. 98.
"My Daughter Considers Her Body. " SouthernPR (19:2) Aut 79,
    p. 72.
"office emergency procedures. " St. AR (5:3) Aut-Wint 79, p. 98.
"Windowfans. " Wind (35) 79, p. 18.

SKOYLES, John
"Hard Work. " MissouriR (2:2/3) Spr 79, p. 7.

SLATE, Ron
"The Accomplice. " Antaeus (34) Sum 79, p. 76.
"Invalid. " Antaeus (34) Sum 79, p. 78.
"The Magnifying Glass. " MidwQ (20:2) Wint 79, p. 199.
"The Purple Light. " GeoR (33:3) Aut 79, p. 658.

SLATER, David
"Jean-Louis. " SeC (6:1) 78, p. 68.

SLAVITT, David R.
"Broads. " Poultry (1) 79, p. 2.
"Going West. " Harp (258:1545) F 79, p. 40.
"The Great American Poem. " Antaeus (32) Wint 79, pp. 82-86.

SLEBODA, Steve
Wedding. UTR (6:1) 79. Entire issue.

SLESINGER, Warren
"Morning-Gift, Morning-Glory, Morning Gown. " GeoR (33:2)
    Sum 79, p. 342.
"Sandpaper, Sandpiper, Sandpit. " GeoR (33:2) Sum 79, p. 343.

SLOAN, Benjamin
"The Corpse in the Airplane Luggage Compartment. " Mouth
    (2:2) Je 79, p. 6.
"Home. " Mouth (2:2) Je 79, p. 48.

"Margaret. " Mouth (2:2) Je 79, p. 6.
"Prostitution II. " Mouth (2:2) Je 79, p. 25.

SLOAN, Devillo (Bill)
"three related poems. " Wind (34) 79, p. 56.

SLOTZNICK, M.
Industrial Stuff. QRL (21:1/2) 78, pp. 75-128.

SLUTSKY, Boris
"Horses in the Ocean" (to Ilya Ehrenburg) (tr. by Irina Zhelez-
nova). PoNow (24) 79, p. 56.

SMETZER, Michael
"A Man with Boxes. " WestB (5) 79, p. 70.
"A Naked Man. " PoNow (25) 79, p. 38.
"Report to the Air. " PoNow (25) 79, p. 47.

SMITH, Annette
"Notebook of a Return to the Native Land" (tr. of Aimé Césaire,
w. Clayton Eshleman). Montra (6) 79, pp. 7-37.

SMITH, Arthur
"Coal. " Stand (20:1) 78-79, p. 6.

SMITH, Barbara
"Physical for My Son. " KanQ (11:3) Sum 79, p. 62.

SMITH, Bruce
"Belongings. " CutB (12) Spr-Sum 79, p. 68.
"Late Winter Equivalents and a Prophecy. " GreenfieldR (7:3/4)
Spr-Sum 79, p. 28.
"Mill Running, 1909. " CutB (12) Spr-Sum 79, p. 70.
"Pelvic Meditation. " WestB (4) 79, p. 11.
"Returning to Ask Questions. " WestB (4) 79, p. 12.
"What I Brought Back with the Harrow. " GreenfieldR (7:3/4)
Spr-Sum 79, p. 29.

SMITH, Claude Clayton
"Blueprint. " Ur (2) 79, p. 114.
"From the Basement. " Ur (2) 79, p. 115.

SMITH, Dave
"Backyard, Under the Wasatch Ridge, the Crackle of Dust, Down-
flaming" (for Bruce Weigl). Agni (10/11) 79, p. 46.
"Breech: Birth: Dream" (for Dee). Ploughs (5:1) 79, pp. 116-
123.
"Cabin, Ruined, Oncoming Night. " PraS (53:4) Wint 79-80, p.
315.
"The Colors of Our Age: Pink and Black. " NewYorker (55:41)
26 N 79, p. 46.
from Dandelions: "If, face down in the soft huzzahing of
grasses. " Tendril (6) Aut 79, p. 5.

"Doves Flying. " AmerPoR (8:1) Ja-F 79, p. 16.
"From Salt Lake City, a Report to Those of You Who Have Writ-
    ten for the Pertinent Facts, the Program, the Climate, the
    Future of Our Stars. " QW (6) Spr-Sum 78, p. 13.
"Hawktree. " AmerPoR (8:1) Ja-F 79, p. 15.
"Homecoming Parade. " QW (6) Spr-Sum 78, p. 11.
"Juniper, Wyoming. " Agni (10/11) 79, p. 49.
"Lovers, September. " AmerPoR (8:1) Ja-F 79, p. 17.
"A Man's Daughter. " AmerPoR (8:1) Ja-F 79, p. 16.
"A Moment of Small Pillagers. " AmerPoR (8:1) Ja-F 79, p. 15.
"Morning Light at Wanship, Utah. " AmerPoR (8:1) Ja-F 79, p.
    16.
Nine Poems.   Ascent (4:2) 79, pp. 1-11.
"Pickles. " NoAmR (264:3) Aut 79, p. 37.
"Playing Ball. " QW (6) Spr-Sum 78, p. 10.
"The Plum Tree. " CimR (48) Jl 79, p. 52.
"Reading the Books Our Children Have Written. " PraS (53:4)
    Wint 79-80, p. 316.
"Red-Headed Woodpecker: Ben's Church Virginia. " PraS (53:4)
    Wint 79-80, p. 314.
"The Roundhouse Voices. " NewYorker (54:47) 8 Ja 79, p. 32.
"Running Back. " QW (6) Spr-Sum 78, p. 14.
"Sister Celia" (for John and Jeri Speers). QW (9) Spr-Sum 79,
    p. 68.
"Southern History: Some Snapshots" (for Primus St. John).
    PortR (25) 79, p. 84.
"Suburban Flight. " PraS (53:4) Wint 79-80, p. 312.
"A Sudden Stillness in the Heart. " CimR (48) Jl 79, p. 12.
"These Promises, These Lost, in Sleep Remain to Us. " NoAmR
    (264:1) Spr 79, p. 42.
"Thinking of What You Have Been Through" (to Patricia Goe-
    dicke). AmerPoR (8:1) Ja-F 79, p. 17.
"To My God in Sickness: Spring Diabetes. " Agni (10/11) 79,
    p. 47.

SMITH, David Jeddie
"The Great American Poem. " Antaeus (32) Wint 79, pp. 82-86.

SMITH, Frances Dean
"For Bob Flanagan. " Bachy (15) Aut 79, p. 91.
"For Jane Newton. " Bachy (15) Aut 79, p. 90.
"For Lynne Bronstein. " Bachy (15) Aut 79, p. 90.
"For Robert Greenfield. " Bachy (15) Aut 79, p. 90.
"Free Jazz. " Bachy (15) Aut 79, p. 91.
"Magician. " Bachy (15) Aut 79, p. 91.
"A Short Life of the Poet. " Bachy (15) Aut 79, p. 90.

SMITH, Gerald W. Jr.
"Carpe Diem. " FourQt (28:3) Spr 79, p. 27.

SMITH, Harry
from Two Friends: "Return to Genesis" (w. Menke Katz).
    KanQ (11:1/2) Wint-Spr 79, p. 142.

from Two Friends: "To Genesis and Back" (w. Menke Katz).
KanQ (11:1/2) Wint-Spr 79, p. 143.

SMITH, Jared
"Elegy to a Beetfield." Tele (15) Spr 79, p. 132.
"An Erosion." UTR (6:3/4) 79, pp. 48-54.
"The Only Man Who Lives." SeC (7:1) 79, p. 30.
"Promontory." StoneC (6:2) My 79, p. 16.
"Things to Remember." GreenfieldR (7:3/4) Spr-Sum 79, p. 244.

SMITH, Jordan
"Baraka Bashad" (for Jon Lang). Antaeus (32) Wint 79, p. 62.
"A Lost Sonata." Shen (30:4) 79, pp. 18-22.

SMITH, Ken
"Moiré effect." Stand (20:1) 78-79, p. 16.

SMITH, Larry
"Birds Are Tying Themselves in Knots." PoNow (22) 79, p. 40.
"Drain." PoNow (22) 79, p. 40.
"The Haircut Story." WormR (73) 79, p. 2.
"An Old Story." WormR (73) 79, p. 1.

SMITH, Lawrence R.
"Apple Trees Apple Trees Apple Trees" (tr. of Nelo Risi).
   PoNow (24) 79, p. 48.
"The Comet" (tr. of Paolo Volponi). PoNow (24) 79, p. 62.
"The English Cemetery" (tr. of Franco Fortini). PoNow (24)
   79, p. 15.
"La Grande Jeanne" (tr. of Luciano Erba). PoNow (24) 79, p.
   14.
"He Was Always Nursing Some Human Wound of His" (tr. of
   Giancarlo Marmori). PoNow (24) 79, p. 25.
"Iron and Air." PoNow (25) 79, p. 38.
"The Other Side" (tr. of Nelo Risi). PoNow (24) 79, p. 48.

SMITH, LeRoy Jr.
"The Last Impertinence." Comm (106:23) 21 D 79, p. 726.

SMITH, Margaret
"Landscape." YaleR (68:3) Spr 79, p. 394.

SMITH, Nathaniel B.
"Sure Prey" (tr. of Salvador Espriu). Paint (12) Aut 79, p. 30.

SMITH, Norma
"1. Father." Tele (15) Spr 79, p. 129.
"2. Mother." Tele (15) Spr 79, p. 130.
"Note." Tele (15) Spr 79, p. 131.
"Springtime in Cithaera." Tele (15) Spr 79, p. 130.

SMITH, R. T.
"Bucket." Tendril (6) Aut 79, p. 35.

"Fleeting." SouthernPR (19:1) Spr 79, p. 56.
"On Saturday I Shot a Photograph." SouthernPR (19:2) Aut 79,
    p. 16.
Poem. St. AR (5:2) 79, p. 89.
Poem. St. AR (5:2) 79, p. 117.
"Third Class Carriage." SouthernHR (13:2) Spr 79, p. 100.

SMITH, Ray
"Old Possum." SouthernHR (13:1) Wint 79, p. 77.

SMITH, Rick
"hills (gayle's poem)." Aspect (74/75) Ja-Ag 79, p. 4.
"the lake" (for arbus). Aspect (74/75) Ja-Ag 79, p. 4.

SMITH, Robert L.
"Atelier." Tele (15) Spr 79, p. 101.

SMITH, Ronnie
"Hey You Dig This." BlackF (3:1) Aut-Wint 79, p. 25.

SMITH, Stephen E.
    from The Bushnell Hamp Poems: "A Sinner Struck by Light-
        ning." GRR (10:3) 79, pp. 68-72.
    from The Bushnell Hamp Poems: "Bushnell Hamp Tells What
        Went Wrong." GRR (10:3) 79, p. 66.
    from The Bushnell Hamp Poems: "Gettin Even." GRR (10:3)
        79, p. 64.
    from The Bushnell Hamp Poems: "How Is It." GRR (10:3) 79,
        p. 67.
    from The Bushnell Hamp Poems: "Red's Letter." GRR (10:3)
        79, p. 63.
    from The Bushnell Hamp Poems: "Slow Leak." GRR (10:3) 79,
        p. 65.
    from The Bushnell Hamp Poems: "Spring at Red's Carolina
        Citgo." GRR (10:3) 79, p. 62.
    "A Carolina Drought." GRR (10:1) 79, p. 36.
    "Fluid Drive." GRR (10:1) 79, p. 38.
    "Getting by on Honesty." GRR (10:1) 79, p. 35.
    "Slow Leak." GRR (10:1) 79, p. 37.

SMITH, Stevie
    from The Penguin Book of Women Poets: "The River God."
        NewRep (180:16) 21 Ap 79, p. 29.

SMITH, Sybil
"Conversation Over a Dying Woman." 13thM (4:2) 79, p. 87.

SMITH, Tom
"Fox and Bee." CarolQ (31:1) Wint 79, p. 62.

SMITH, William Jay
"Epitaph of a Stripper." Bits (10) Jl 79.
"Family Graveyard" (tr. of Andrei Voznesensky w. Fred Starr).

HarvAd (113:1/2) N 79, p. 15.
"Saga" (tr. of Andrei Voznesensky w. Vera Dunham). PoNow
(24) 79, p. 36.

SMYTH, Laura
"Poem for a Seagull I Met Twice. " PortR (25) 79, p. 142.

SMYTH, Paul
"Elements of Dying. " EnPas (9) 79, p. 8.
"Erik Satie: Trois gymnopédies. " EnPas (9) 79, p. 7.
"The Head of a Woman. " EnPas (9) 79, p. 5.
"The Longing. " EnPas (9) 79, p. 4.
"Poetics. " Poetry (134:4) Jl 79, pp. 208-209.
"Vigil. " EnPas (9) 79, p. 6.

SNEYD, Steve
"Middleham Castle. " WindO (35) Aut-Wint 79-80, p. 17.

SNIDER, Clifton
"Jesse Rama on Physical Love. " Mouth (2:2) Je 79, p. 45.
"Song of the Night. " PoNow (25) 79, p. 38.

SNODGRASS, W. D.
"The Great American Poem. " Antaeus (32) Wint 79, pp. 82-86.

SNOW, Karen
"Two Sons. " BelPoJ (29:4) Sum 79, pp. 22-29.

SNYDER, Gary
"Axe Handles. " Field (20) Spr 79, p. 37.
"For All. " Field (20) Spr 79, p. 36.
"Old Rotting Tree Trunk Down. " Field (20) Spr 79, p. 38.

SO Chongju
"New Year's Prayer: 1976" (tr. by David McCann). NewL
(46:1) Aut 79, p. 68.

SOBIN, Anthony
"The Diet. " KanQ (11:1/2) Wint-Spr 79, p. 48.
"Eating the Bowfin. " Poetry (134:3) Je 79, pp. 147-148.
"Fecund Poem. " BelPoJ (30:1) Aut 79, p. 36.
"The Stinkhorn. " Poetry (134:3) Je 79, p. 149.
"The Strawberry Hunters. " PoNow (21) 79, p. 43.
"We Decide to Do a Porno Movie. " PoNow (21) 79, p. 43.

SOBIN, Gustaf
"Animalian Eve. " Montra (5) 79, p. 239.
"Cà D'Oro. " Montra (5) 79, p. 240.
"Caesurae: Mid Summer. " Montra (5) 79, p. 230.
"Lagoon. " Montra (5) 79, p. 241.
"Pastorale. " Montra (5) 79, p. 241.
"Voice. " Montra (5) 79, p. 238.
"Written in the Rings (Catullus 11). " Montra (5) 79, p. 242.

SOCOLOW, Liz
"The Laughing Angel: Reims. " Ploughs (5:2) 79, p. 105.
"Taint. " Ploughs (5:2) 79, pp. 103-104.

SOFIELD, David
"In Slow Motion. " NewRep (180:22) 2 Je 79, p. 26.

SOHN, David A.
"Letter to May. " Focus (13:80) Mr-Ap 79, p. 37.

SOLENSTEN, John M.
"The Pelicans on Lake Wanamingo. " CarlMis (17:2/3) Spr 79,
    p. 29.

SOLOMON, Robert
"The Shroud. " SmPd (46) 79, p. 11.

SOLOWEY, E. M.
"Desert Song. " Os (9) 79, p. 2.

SOLWAY, Arthur
"Answers to the Snails. " Chelsea (38) 79, p. 176.
"In this Way I Live. " Chelsea (38) 79, p. 119.

SOMERVILLE, Jane
"Parabola. " NewRena (11) 79, p. 92.
"The Wishing War. " Spirit (3:3) Sum 78, p. 35.

SONIAT, Katherine
"Double-Vision. " Paint (12) Aut 79, p. 20.
"Initial Response. " AmerS (48:3) Sum 79, p. 390.
"Kaleidoscoping. " PoetryNW (20:3) Aut 79, p. 23.
"Mardi Gras Reverie. " GeoR (33:4) Wint 79, p. 895.
"A Season of Unicorn. " Wind (33) 79, p. 49.
"Split Season. " Wind (33) 79, p. 49.
"State Prison Farm: The First Rodeo. " PoNow (25) 79, p. 39.
"A Window of Southern Exposure Gathers Night to the Boarding-
    house. " SouthernHR (13:2) Spr 79, p. 114.

SONNEVI, Goran
    from The Impossible: (50) (tr. by Lennart Bruce). PoNow (24)
        79, p. 57.
    from The Impossible: (76) (tr. by Lennart Bruce). PoNow (24)
        79, p. 57.
    from The Impossible: (82) (tr. by Lennart Bruce). PoNow (24)
        79, p. 57.
    from The Impossible: (83) (tr. by Lennart Bruce). PoNow (24)
        79, p. 57.
    from The Impossible: (90) (tr. by Lennart Bruce). PoNow (24)
        79, p. 57.
    from The Impossible: (180) (tr. by Lennart Bruce). PoNow
        (24) 79, p. 57.

SORRELLS, Helen
"Sky in August. " PraS (53:2) Sum 79, p. 172.

SORRENTINO, Gilbert
"Miss and Hit. " MissR (22/23) Wint-Spr 79, p. 37.
"Post-Modernism Explained. " MissR (22/23) Wint-Spr 79, p.
   36.
Twelve Poems. SunM (8) Aut 79, pp. 81-96.

SOSA, Roberto
"The Poor. " LitR (23:2) Wint 80, p. 190.

SOTO, Gary
"Angel. " NoAmR (264:1) Spr 79, p. 16.
"Bulosan, 1935. " Antaeus (32) Wint 79, p. 57.
"Camilo. " QW (7) Aut 78, p. 89.
"Chiapas. " Poetry (133:4) Ja 79, pp. 213-214.
"Chuy Sends Messages to the Stars. " AmerPoR (8:5) S-O 79, p.
   17.
"Concha. " NoAmR (264:1) Spr 79, p. 14.
"The Drought. " PoNow (23) 79, p. 29.
"La Familia de Lopez, 1901. " Poetry (133:4) Ja 79, p. 215.
"The Map. " PoNow (23) 79, p. 29.
"The Street. " MissouriR (2:2/3) Spr 79, p. 10.
"The Summer. " QW (7) Aut 78, p. 90.
"The Thirtieth Year" (for Buckley). NoAmR (264:1) Spr 79, p.
   17.
"TV in Black and White. " MissouriR (2:2/3) Spr 79, p. 13.

SOULES, Terrill Shephard
"Space-Ship Marriage: 200000-Mile Checkup. " Kayak (52) D 79,
   p. 58.

SOUTHWICK, Marcia
"A Burial, Green. " GeoR (33:1) Spr 79, p. 152.
"Dusk. " Ploughs (5:3) 79, p. 151.
Eight Poems. CharR (5:SI) 79, pp. 83-100.
"Finches. " Ploughs (5:3) 79, p. 152.
"Owning a Dead Man. " Poetry (133:4) Ja 79, p. 197.
"Vasilisa the Beautiful. " CarolQ (31:3) Aut 79, p. 72.
"Winter Gulls. " Poetry (133:4) Ja 79, p. 196.

SPACKS, Barry
"Affair. " PraS (53:1) Spr 79, p. 31.
"The Assimilation. " Poetry (134:5) Ag 79, p. 255.
"Down on Gurney's Farm. " Tendril (4) Wint 79, p. 46.
"Forced Forsythia. " MichQR (18:3) Sum 79, p. 494.
"Instructions for a Trooper. " CarlMis (17:2/3) Spr 79, p. 131.
"Long Day. " PraS (53:1) Spr 79, p. 31.
"Spanish Traffic. " Poetry (134:5) Ag 79, p. 254.
"The Summer Weight of Lemons. " Poetry (134:5) Ag 79, pp.
   253-254.
"Visions of Animals. " PoNow (23) 79, p. 37.
"Watching the Soaps. " PoetryNW (20:3) Aut 79, p. 26.

SPANOS, William V.
"A Meditation on Place. " Chelsea (38) 79, p. 65.

SPARK, Muriel
"Created and Abandoned. " NewYorker (55:39) 12 N 79, p. 60.

SPARROW, Philip
"Eyes that Blink, Eyes that Do Not Blink. " Poultry (1) 79, p. 8.
"Marmalade. " Poultry (1) 79, p. 8.

SPATOLA, Adriano
"Hamlet, Clowns" (tr. by Paul Vangelisti). PoNow (24) 79, p.
   35.
"Rosa in Luxembourg" (above all for Gigia and Marcello) (tr. by
   Paul Vangelisti). PoNow (24) 79, p. 35.

SPEAKES, Richard
"In the Trenches. " PoetryNW (20:3) Aut 79, pp. 33-34.
"Scrimshaw. " Columbia (3) 79, p. 22.
"Weatherman. " GeoR (33:1) Spr 79, p. 194.

SPEAR, Roberta
"The Anniversary. " Nat (228:15) 21 Ap 79, p. 442.
"Building a Small House. " SenR (10:1) Spr 79, p. 50.
"Eclipse. " QW (6) Spr-Sum 78, p. 94.
"The Fiddler's Wife. " SenR (10:1) Spr 79, p. 54.
"In Your Next Life" (for Michael). QW (6) Spr-Sum 78, p. 93.
"The Lust of Clouds. " SenR (10:1) Spr 79, p. 52.
"Nightfall on Pacheco. " SenR (10:1) Spr 79, p. 44.
"Silks. " SenR (10:1) Spr 79, p. 57.
"The Trees Began to Speak. " SenR (10:1) Spr 79, p. 46.
"The White Dress. " NewYorker (55:31) 17 S 79, p. 153.

SPEECE, Merry
"By the Well Pit. " Bits (10) Jl 79.
"Detail from an American Landscape. " Bits (10) Jl 79.

SPEER, Laurel
"Birth Day. " Vaga (29) 79, p. 33.
"The Famous Greyhound Bus Hijack. " PoNow (25) 79, p. 47.
"Going to the Mattresses. " WestB (4) 79, p. 55.
"Late News. " Ur (2) 79, p. 101.
"Lovers at Separate Addresses. " SouthernHR (13:2) Spr 79, p.
   138.
"Outlines. " PikeF (2) Wint 78-79, p. 3.
"Rose Red to Lenny Bruce. " Im (5:3) 79, p. 8.
"The Writer's Night. " PoNow (25) 79, p. 39.

SPEIKERS, P. J.
"(Long Distance). " WestB (5) 79, p. 59.
"(Snowblind). " WestB (5) 79, p. 60.
"(Specimen-I). " WestB (5) 79, p. 63.
"(A Strain of Notes). " WestB (5) 79, p. 61.
"(Three Horses). " WestB (5) 79, p. 59.

SPELLER, Judith
"Richard Drafted (A Fantasy). " BlackALF (13:4) Wint 79, p. 151.

SPENCE, Michael
"The Bengal Tiger. " CharR (5:1) Spr 79, p. 59.
"Neopark. " KanQ (11:1/2) Wint-Spr 79, p. 114.
"Prisoner. " Poem (35) Mr 79, p. 54.
"A Town Facing Night. " Poem (35) Mr 79, p. 55.
"Your Leaving. " CharR (5:1) Spr 79, p. 59.

SPETHMAN, Betsy
"Whose Team Are You On?" EngJ (68:5) My 79, p. 36.

SPICER, David
"Poem to a Prick Teaser. " PoNow (25) 79, p. 39.

SPIEGEL, Robert
"Bedini was hugging Ann. " WormR (74) 79, p. 47.
"Closing Time. " WormR (74) 79, p. 47.
"A Local Legend. " WormR (74) 79, p. 47.
"Rain. " Wind (35) 79, p. 57.
"The Sparrows. " WormR (74) 79, p. 47.

SPINGARN, Lawrence P.
"The Reservation. " PoNow (23) 79, p. 43.

SPIRES, Elizabeth
"At the Bambi Motel. " Poetry (134:4) Jl 79, pp. 194-195.
"Last Night Here or Anywhere. " MissouriR (2:2/3) Spr 79, p. 30.

SPIVACK, Kathleen
"Bashing Myself. " Paint (12) Aut 79, p. 11.
"The Dark. " PoNow (21) 79, p. 39.
"Fugue. " AmerPoR (8:4) Jl-Ag 79, p. 13.
"loving you is. " Tendril (5) Sum 79, p. 49.
"Wild animals in houses. " AmerPoR (8:1) Ja-F 79, p. 27.

SPRINGER, Cathy Davis
"I have returned to the sea alone, ". Nimrod (23:1) Aut-Wint 79, p. 22.

SQUIRES, Radcliffe
"News from the Island Where Executioners Are Exiled. " SewanR (87:3) Sum 79, p. 382.

STACH, Carl
"When I Leave You Today. " KanQ (11:3) Sum 79, p. 73.

STACK, John N. Jr.
"Deaf and Dumb Days. " Wind (33) 79, p. 51.

STACK, Peter
"Poem Called a Story That Begins at the End. " Kayak (51) S

79, p. 56.
"Poem Called Elegy to the Girl Who Drowned Off Point Arena. "
  PoNow (25) 79, p. 39.
"Poem Called Man Looking at Woman. " Kayak (51) S 79, p. 55.
"Poem Called Song for Guitars. " Kayak (51) S 79, p. 54.
"Poem Called the Man in the Polka-Dot Prairie. " Kayak (51) S
  79, p. 54.
"Poem Called Triad. " Kayak (51) S 79, p. 55.

STAFFORD, Kim Robert
"Heartwood. " PoetryNW (20:4) Wint 79-80, pp. 28-29.
"The Lighthouse. " Hudson (32:1) Spr 79, p. 75.
"Near Minerva. " Stand (20:1) 78-79, p. 63.
"The Rocking Chair. " PoetryNW (20:4) Wint 79-80, pp. 27-28.

STAFFORD, William
"About These Poems. " Field (20) Spr 79, p. 40.
"About Yesterday. " PoNow (21) 79, p. 5.
"Absences. " Field (20) Spr 79, p. 41.
"Being Sorry. " GreenfieldR (7:3/4) Spr-Sum 79, p. 99.
"Being Still. " QW (7) Aut 78, p. 134.
"A Certain Gate. " Field (20) Spr 79, p. 43.
"Contributor's Note. " QW (7) Aut 78, p. 135.
"Definitions. " Paint (12) Aut 79, p. 6.
"Glimpses. " AmerPoR (8:3) My-Je 79, p. 48.
"The Great American Poem. " Antaeus (32) Wint 79, pp. 82-86.
"Incident. " SlowLR (3) 79, p. 78.
"A Journey. " Chowder (12) Spr-Sum 79, p. 12.
"Letting You Go. " CarolQ (31:1) Wint 79, p. 33.
"Letting Them Have It. " DacTerr (16) 79, p. 58.
"Little Fictions, Little Truths. " AmerS (48:1) Wint 78-79, p.
  80.
"Making the Scene at a Writers' Conference. " CharR (5:1) Spr
  79, p. 9.
"A Midnight Service for a Friend Now Gone" (for Tony). PortR
  (25) 79, p. 7.
"Murder Bridge. " Field (20) Spr 79, p. 42.
"My Life. " Paint (12) Aut 79, p. 7.
"My Mother Was a Soldier. " CharR (5:1) Spr 79, p. 11.
"Near Dawn Some Time. " GreenfieldR (7:3/4) Spr-Sum 79, p.
  98.
"Not Very Loud. " Nat (228:19) 19 My 79, p. 578.
"Once in the 40's. " CharR (5:1) Spr 79, p. 9.
"One of the Fathers. " Poetry (135:2) N 79, p. 87.
"Out Here Everyone Knows. " PoNow (23) 79, p. 7.
"Out by Keith and Shirley's. " CharR (5:1) Spr 79, p. 10.
"Passing a Pile of Stones. " CimR (48) Jl 79, p. 31.
"Places. " QW (7) Aut 78, p. 134.
"A Scene. " CharR (5:1) Spr 79, p. 9.
"A Talk at the Beginning of Class. " CharR (5:1) Spr 79, p. 10.
"Texas Still Life. " DacTerr (16) 79, p. 57.
"This Time. " CimR (48) Jl 79, p. 20.
"Today. " GreenfieldR (7:3/4) Spr-Sum 79, p. 98.

"Torque. " SlowR (3) 79, p. 79.
Twenty five poems. SmF (9/10) Spr-Aut 79, pp. 3-28. Issue
   devoted to William Stafford.

STALLWORTHY, Jon
"Great Britain. " CornellR (7) Aut 79, p. 75.

STAMBLER, Peter
"Efficacy. " Shen (30:4) 79, p. 98.
"God Invents Faith. " Shen (30:4) 79, p. 98.
"Views from the Temple. " Shen (30:1) Aut 78, pp. 57-62.

STANDING, Sue
"Dead Neck. " AmerS (48:4) Aut 79, p. 456.
"June 21. " Wind (33) 79, p. 50.
"No News, No Weather. " Wind (33) 79, p. 50.
"Returning the Evidence. " OhioR (20:2) Spr-Sum 79, pp. 68-69.
"Standing Still. " QW (8) Wint 79, p. 35.
"Steptoe Butte. " HarvAd (112:4) My 79, p. 24.
"What Can Be Changed. " Confr (19) Aut 79-Wint 80, p. 132.

STANFORD, Ann
"Dreaming of Foxes. " PoNow (21) 79, p. 29.
"Dreaming the Garden. " NewYorker (55:12) 7 My 79, p. 42.
"The Great American Poem. " Antaeus (32) Wint 79, pp. 82-86.
"Listening to Color. " PoNow (21) 79, p. 29.
"Our Town. " PoNow (21) 79, p. 29.

STANFORD, Frank
"The Angel of Death. " SunM (8) Aut 79, p. 24.
"Death and Memory. " AmerPoR (8:2) Mr-Ap 79, p. 17.
"Freedom, Revolt, and Love. " SunM (8) Aut 79, p. 26.
"The History of John Stoss. " AmerPoR (8:2) Mr-Ap 79, p. 16.
"Light Blue. " AmerPoR (8:2) Mr-Ap 79, p. 17.
"Source. " AmerPoR (8:2) Mr-Ap 79, p. 17.
"Starving to Death. " AmerPoR (8:2) Mr-Ap 79, p. 17.
Ten Poems. NewOR (6:4) 79, pp. 366-376. Retrospective.

STANHOPE, Rosamund
"At Eighty. " WebR (4:3) Spr 79, p. 10.

STANTON, Joseph
"Bunraku. " ConcPo (12:1) Spr 79, p. 34.
"Hiroshige. " Ur (2) 79, p. 116.
"Koyasan. " ConcPo (12:1) Spr 79, p. 33.
"Koyasan. " Ur (2) 79, p. 117.

STANTON, Maura
"The Dimestore Clerk. " Aspen (7) Spr 79, p. 27.
"Houses. " Aspen (7) Spr 79, p. 26.
"Palinode. " Iowa (10:3) Sum 79, p. 104.

STAP, Don
"Fall Weather. " QW (7) Aut 78, p. 47.
"First Night of Summer. " QW (7) Aut 78, p. 48.

STARBUCK, George
"A Fold-out Poem. " OhioR (20:2) Spr-Sum 79, between pp. 32-33.
"The Great Dam Disaster a Ballad" (to Kathy). CarolQ (31:3) Aut 79, p. 74.

STARK, David
"After Appomatox. " QW (8) Wint 79, p. 118.
"A Photograph. " PoNow (25) 79, p. 40.

STARR, Fred
"Family Graveyard" (tr. of Andrei Voznesensky w. William Jay Smith). HarvAd (113:1/2) N 79, p. 15.

STEDINGH, R. W.
"Afternoon" (tr. of Pierre Reverdy). NowestR (18:2) 79, p. 71.
"Jugglers" (tr. of Pierre Reverdy). NowestR (18:2) 79, p. 73.
"To Each His Own" (tr. of Pierre Reverdy). NowestR (18:2) 79, p. 73.

STEDMAN, Anne Bradstreet
"Vista. " StoneC (6:1) F 79, p. 21.

STEELE, Timothy
"Border Tramp. " SouthernR (15:4) Aut 79, p. 1003.
"From the Point. " SouthernR (15:4) Aut 79, p. 1005.
"In the King's Rooms. " SouthernR (15:4) Aut 79, p. 1004.
"Murder Mystery. " SouthernR (15:4) Aut 79, p. 1002.

STEFANILE, Felix
"I Loved" (tr. of Umberto Saba). PoNow (24) 79, p. 34.
"Ulysses" (tr. of Umberto Saba). PoNow (24) 79, p. 34.
"Winter Noon" (tr. of Umberto Saba). PoNow (24) 79, p. 34.

STEFFEN, Timothy W.
"I am my own man. " Mouth (2:3) N 79, p. 34.

STEHMAN, John
from Etudes: (1).   GreenfieldR (7:3/4) Spr-Sum 79, p. 181.
from Etudes: (6).   GreenfieldR (7:3/4) Spr-Sum 79, p. 181.
"For Harold. " GreenfieldR (7:3/4) Spr-Sum 79, p. 182.

STEIN, Dona
"Le déjeuner sur l'herbe. " Aspect (74/75) Ja-Ag 79, p. 78.
"I Gathered up Thousands of Leaves" (for Muriel). StoneC (6:3) O 79, p. 14.
"Landscape with Bride. " Ploughs (5:1) 79, pp. 127-128.
"Shovels. " Ploughs (5:1) 79, p. 129.

STEIN, Hesiod
"The Figure." Poultry (1) 79, p. 8.

STEINBERG, Alan
"The Grand Pianist." PortR (25) 79, p. 116.

STEINBERGH, Judith W.
"Lillian's Daughter Pulls Up Her Mother's Garden." AndR (6:1)
Spr 79, p. 25.

STEINGASS, David
"April in Suring Wisconsin." PoNow (22) 79, p. 40.
"In the Hotel Palomar." DacTerr (16) 79, p. 59.
"Lifeguard." PoNow (21) 79, p. 35.
"Paella." NewL (46:1) Aut 79, p. 16.
"The Poet in a Child." PoNow (22) 79, p. 40.

STEINMAN, Lisa
"My Dreams Always Contain Marginalia." ChiR (30:4) Spr 79, p.
32.

STEIR, Vivian
"Sinai." HarvAd (112:3) Ap 79, p. 17.

STEPHENS, Alan
"The Career." DenQ (14:2) Sum 79, p. 39.
"Meeting Old Mr. Jim Porcupine." DenQ (14:2) Sum 79, p.
38.
"A Puff of Smoke." SouthernR (15:3) Sum 79, pp. 627-631.

STERLING, Phillip
"Half-Brave Challenge to a Winter Song." StoneC (6:1) F 79, p.
21.
"Songs for an Unstrung Banjo." GRR (10:2) 79, p. 182.

STERN, Gerald
"Dangerous Cooks." NowestR (18:2) 79, p. 34.
"Good Friday, 1977." NowestR (18:2) 79, p. 36.
"I Remember Galileo." Poetry (134:4) Jl 79, p. 221.
"Joseph Pockets." NowestR (18:2) 79, p. 37.
"Little Did the Junco Know." Poetry (135:3) D 79, p. 125.
"Little White Sister." NewYorker (55:16) 4 Je 79, p. 87.
"Lord, Forgive a Spirit." Pequod (3:1) 79, p. 94.
"Magritte Dancing." Poetry (134:4) Jl 79, p. 224.
"No Wind." NowestR (18:2) 79, p. 33.
"Phipps Conservatory." Pequod (3:1) 79, p. 95.
"Potpourri." Poetry (134:4) Jl 79, pp. 222-223.
"Royal Manor Road." NowestR (18:2) 79, p. 35.
"Waving Goodbye." Poetry (134:4) Jl 79, p. 225.

STERN, Robert
"this is a difficult age for a genie." SouthernPR (19:2) Aut 79,
p. 63.

STERNBERG, Ricardo
"The Alchemist. " Ploughs (5:2) 79, pp. 161-162.
"No Wonder the Wood. "   Ploughs (5:2) 79, p. 163.
"A Small Spider. " Ploughs (5:2) 79, p. 164.

STERNBERGS, Judy
"The Urgent Tree Chopper. " ChrC (96:3) 24 Ja 79, p. 76.

STERNLIEB, Barry
"For a Winemaker. " Wind (34) 79, p. 57.
"Moon Snail. " PoetryNW (20:4) Wint 79-80, p. 37.
"Photograph of Geronimo, 1906. " PoNow (25) 79, p. 40.
"Return to the Photograph. " Wind (34) 79, p. 57.
"Richmond Landfill. " HiramPoR (26) Spr-Sum 79, p. 34.

STEVENS, Alex
"The Patient. " NewYorker (54:52) 12 F 79, p. 115.
"The Turner. " NewYorker (55:19) 25 Je 79, p. 94.

STEVENS, Wallace
Eleven Poems. Field (21) Aut 79, pp. 8-50.   Prose responses
   to the poems written by thirteen contemporary poets.

STEVENSON, Anne
"Charm. " NewYorker (55:20) 2 Jl 79, p. 36.

STEVENSON, Shelby
Poem. St.AR (5:2) 79, p. 103.
Poem. St.AR (5:2) 79, p. 104.

STEWARD, Carl
"Maybe Next Time. " BlackF (3:1) Aut-Wint 79, p. 22.

STEWARD, D. E.
"Tanker. " WebR (4:3) Spr 79, p. 35.

STEWART, Dolores
"Whales Are Out, Cats Are In. " BelPoJ (29:3) Spr 79, p. 12.

STEWART, Frank
"Another Color. " Tendril (6) Aut 79, p. 37.
"Learning to Flower. " Epoch (28:3) Spr-Sum 79, p. 263.
"Letter Written to San Francisco But Never Mailed" (for Peggy
   Campbell). Epoch (28:3) Spr-Sum 79, p. 262.
"Winter Garden. " Tendril (6) Aut 79, p. 36.

STEWART, Jean
"november. " HangL (35) Spr 79, p. 65.

STEWART, Marie Vogl
"My Son Brings Butterflies. " CarlMis (18:1) Wint 79-80, p. 54.

STEWART, Maril Hope
"Decision. " Paint (11) Spr 79, p. 71.

STEWART, Pamela
"A First Divination for H. D. " Paint (11) Spr 79, p. 73.
"For February's Dark Simple. " NewYorker (54:51) 5 F 79, p.
36.
"Ghost Pantoum. " QW (9) Spr-Sum 79, p. 5.
"A Holiday in Chaos." QW (9) Spr-Sum 79, p. 7.
"It Comes. " QW (9) Spr-Sum 79, p. 8.
"Silentia Lunae." MissouriR (2:2/3) Spr 79, p. 37.
"The Undying. " QW (9) Spr-Sum 79, p. 6.

STEWART, Robert
"European Style Hotel. " DacTerr (16) 79, p. 60.
"A Flow Behind the Walls." CharR (5:2) Aut 79, p. 26.
"The Plumber Arrives at Three Mile Island. " NewL (46:2) Wint
79-80, p. 101.
"We Wake. " PoetryNW (20:1) Spr 79, p. 35.
"What It Takes to Be a Plumber. " CharR (5:2) Aut 79, p. 27.

STEWART, Ronald
"Anita Bryant Enters the Kingdom of God. " Mouth (2:1) F 79,
p. 40.
"The Men Who Are Not You. " Mouth (2:1) F 79, p. 26.

STEWART, Susan
"At Six" (for Edward Hirsch). PoetryNW (20:1) Spr 79, p. 11.
"The Delta Parade. " Ploughs (5:1) 79, pp. 124-126.
"The Drowned. " AmerPoR (8:2) Mr-Ap 79, p. 28.
"If I'm Homesick." PoetryNW (20:4) Wint 79-80, pp. 9-10.
"Letter Full of Blue Dresses." PraS (53:4) Wint 79-80, p. 359.
"The Long Boats of the Afternoon." PoetryNW (20:1) Spr 79, p.
10.
"Meaning to Drop You a Line. " Kayak (51) S 79, p. 50.
"My City Knows How to Carry the Sky." PoetryNW (20:4) Wint
79-80, pp. 8-9.
"Neighbors. " PoetryNW (20:1) Spr 79, pp. 11-12.
"The Summons." Kayak (51) S 79, p. 51.
"Yellow Stars and Ice." PoetryNW (20:4) Wint 79-80, pp. 7-8.

STEWART, Wayne
"The Nightraven. " Poem (35) Mr 79, p. 57.
"Twilight at Amerada--Hess Oil Refinery. " Poem (35) Mr 79,
p. 56.

STIBER, Alex
"Another Coming. " StoneC (6:3) O 79, p. 28.
"Stripping Away the Skin. " StoneC (6:3) O 79, p. 28.

STILES, Ward
"The Southern Girl You Didn't Marry. " SouthwR (64:2) Spr 79,
p. 161.

STILL, Gloria
"Ghazal XII: After Ghalib. " Tendril (4) Wint 79, p. 47.

STILLWELL, Elizabeth
"Hallways. " BallSUF (20:1) Wint 79, p. 52.

STILLWELL, Mary Kathryn
"Holding at Flint. " KanQ (11:1/2) Wint-Spr 79, p. 117.
"In the Morning in Morocco. " Confr (19) Aut 79-Wint 80, p.
    186.

STOCK, Bud
"The Kinship. " Poem (37) N 79, p. 54.

STOCK, Robert
"Alternatives in Costa Rica. " Aspect (74/75) Ja-Ag 79, p. 61.
"The Bats. " Aspect (74/75) Ja-Ag 79, p. 61.
"Easter. " PoNow (22) 79, p. 41.
"Life on a Möbius Strip. " KanQ (11:4) Aut 79, p. 10.
"The Medium. " GreenfieldR (7:3/4) Spr-Sum 79, p. 31.
"More Honest Than Iago. " PoNow (22) 79, p. 41.
"Rush Hour at South Ferry. " GreenfieldR (7:3/4) Spr-Sum 79,
    p. 32.

STOKELY, James R. Jr.
"August, Carson Springs. " SmF (7/8) Spr-Aut 78, p. 50.
"June 20, Clifton Heights. " SmF (7/8) Spr-Aut 78, p. 49.
"Molly Mooneyham. " SmF (7/8) Spr-Aut 78, p. 4.

STOKES, Terry
"Are the Stars Out Tonight?" PoNow (21) 79, p. 16.
"The Last Few Days of My Life. " PoNow (22) 79, p. 41.
"My Mother Lies. " Shen (30:2) Wint 79, p. 43.
"Song for the Bleak Morning. " PoNow (21) 79, p. 16.
"They Are Trying Their Best. " Confr (19) Aut 79-Wint 80, p.
    25.

STOKESBURY, Leon
"The Drifting Away of All We Once Held Essential. " QW (7)
    Aut 78, p. 31.
"Morning Song. " QW (9) Spr-Sum 79, p. 123.
"A Review of That Which Contains Both the Night and the Pain. "
    CimR (48) Jl 79, p. 63.

STOLOFF, Carolyn
"Around Once Again. " PoNow (21) 79, p. 31.
"The Building. " SouthernPR (19:1) Spr 79, p. 20.
"The Lifeline. " Agni (10/11) 79, p. 56.
"Truck Farmer. " PraS (53:1) Spr 79, p. 73.
"Under the Cherry Trees. " Bits (9) Ja 79.

STONE, Arlene
"Feeling. " PoNow (21) 79, p. 39.
"From the Mouth of the Poet. " PoNow (22) 79, p. 41.
"The Mammaday. " PoNow (22) 79, p. 41.
"Oedipus the Dark Corona. " Im (6:1) 79, p. 5.

STONE, Carole
"Eulogy. " Wind (33) 79, p. 52.
"Matins. " Wind (33) 79, p. 52.

STONE, I. F.
"Aeschylus, son of Euphorion, " (tr. of Aeschylus). NewYRB
(26:2) 22 F 79, p. 10.
"The Evening Star restores all that the" (tr. of Sappho).
NewYRB (26:2) 22 F 79, p. 10.
"Hope is forever stealing the little" (tr. of Julius Polyaenus of
Sardis). NewYRB (26:2) 22 F 79, p. 10.
"The moon sets" (tr. of Sappho). NewYRB (26:2) 22 F 79, p.
10.
"This, noble Sabinus, is but a stone" (tr. of Greek poet un-
known). NewYRB (26:2) 22 F 79, p. 10.

STONE, Joan
"Drowning. " BelPoJ (30:1) Aut 79, p. 38.
"Finally a Room of One's Own. " WebR (4:3) Spr 79, p. 56.
"Letter from Japan. " PortR (25) 79, p. 91.
"A Question for My Brother Who Knows the Weather. " PortR
(25) 79, p. 90.
"The Weaver" (for Maria). StoneC (6:2) My 79, p. 17.

STONEBURNER, Tony
"The Underlying Body. " ChrC (96:1) 3-10 Ja 79, p. 15.

STORNI, Alfonsina
"Ancestral Burden" (tr. by Dorothy Scott Loos). PoNow (24)
79, p. 58.
"Eye" (tr. by Norma Cantú). PraS (53:3) Aut 79, p. 207.
"Fishermen" (tr. by Norma Cantú). PraS (53:3) Aut 79, p. 207.
"Funeral Notices" (tr. by Dorothy Scott Loos). PoNow (24) 79,
p. 58.
"The Hoax" (tr. by Dorothy Scott Loos). PoNow (24) 79, p. 58.
"Tear" (tr. by Dorothy Scott Loos). PoNow (24) 79, p. 58.
"The Train" (tr. by Dorothy Scott Loos). PoNow (24) 79, p. 58.

STOUT, Liz
"The Fragile Mold. " Salm (44/45) Spr-Sum 79, p. 163.
"This Winter. " Salm (44/45) Spr-Sum 79, p. 164.

STOUTENBURG, Adrien
"The Great American Poem. " Antaeus (32) Wint 79, pp. 82-86.
"Next-Door to the Rest Home Laundry. " PoetryNW (20:1) Spr
79, pp. 31-32.

STRAHAN, Bradley R.
"Old Rambler Blues. " Wind (32) 79, p. 45.

STRAND, Mark
"Between Leaving and Staying" (tr. of Octavio Paz). NewYorker
(55:10) 23 Ap 79, p. 43.

"Light Holds" (to the Painter, Balthus) (tr. of Octavio Paz).
　NewYorker (55:10) 23 Ap 79, p. 42.
"A Morning." Durak (3) 79, p. 39.
"The Return." Durak (3) 79, p. 38.
"Shooting Whales." NewYorker (55:26) 13 Ag 79, p. 30.
"Small Variation" (tr. of Octavio Paz). NewYorker (55:10) 23
　Ap 79, p. 42.
"Waking" (tr. of Octavio Paz). NewYorker (55:10) 23 Ap 79, p.
　42.
"Wind and Water and Stone" (tr. of Octavio Paz). NewYorker
　(55:10) 23 Ap 79, p. 42.

STRATTON, Kip
"Answer." GreenfieldR (7:3/4) Spr-Sum 79, p. 100.
"Proper." GreenfieldR (7:3/4) Spr-Sum 79, p. 100.

STRAUS, Austin
"The Dump." PoNow (25) 79, p. 40.

STREAMAS, John
"Death of Complications." NewL (46:1) Aut 79, p. 52.
"A Sonnet for the Society for the Preservation of Successful
　Kamikaze Pilots." NewL (46:1) Aut 79, p. 52.

STRICKLAND, Stephanie
"Leaving." PoNow (25) 79, p. 40.
"Lives of the Saints." Columbia (3) 79, p. 46.

STRICKLIN, Robert
"Capistrano." Poem (35) Mr 79, p. 35.

STRINGER, Chip
"Eye Level." Antaeus (33) Spr 79, p. 135.
"Where the Hay Is Now Comes to Me." Antaeus (33) Spr 79, p.
　134.

STRIPLING, Kathryn
"Empty Glass." GeoR (33:4) Wint 79, p. 914.
"Lullabye." CarolQ (31:2) Spr-Sum 79, p. 7.

STROUD, Dean
"Carpenter Hymn." ChrC (96:13) 11 Ap 79, p. 406.

STRUTHERS, Ann
"The Cars in the Air." GreenfieldR (7:3/4) Spr-Sum 79, p. 252.
"The Dance." Spirit (3:3) Sum 78, p. 46.
"The Lean Cats of Izmar." PoetC (11:3) 79, p. 30.
"Oyster Shell." PoetC (11:3) 79, p. 31.
"Picking Corn in Persia, Iowa." GreenfieldR (7:3/4) Spr-Sum
　79, p. 251.
"Watching the Out-door Movie Show." NewL (46:1) Aut 79, p.
　41.

STRYK, Dan
"On Taking My Old Father to the Chicago Aquarium. " CharR
(5:1) Spr 79, p. 58.
"Sunday. " PoNow (25) 79, p. 40.
"Vacancies. " KanQ (11:1/2) Wint-Spr 79, p. 52.

STRYK, Lucien
"Siberia. " QW (7) Aut 78, p. 120.
"You Must Change Your Life. " QW (7) Aut 78, p. 121.

STUART, Dabney
"Baby and Child Care. " Ploughs (5:1) 79, p. 131.
"A Figure on the Ice. " Ploughs (5:1) 79, pp. 132-133.
"The Great American Poem. " Antaeus (32) Wint 79, pp. 82-86.
"On the Street Where You Live" (for J. M. M.). MalR (51) Jl
79, p. 40.
"Turntables" (for Darren). Ploughs (5:1) 79, p. 130.

STUART, Floyd C.
"Gravestones. " BallSUF (20:2) Spr 79, p. 80.
"To an Indian Woman. " BallSUF (20:2) Spr 79, p. 72.
"The Wives. " Spirit (3:1/2) Aut-Wint 77-78, p. 52.

STULL, Jonathan
"Blackberry Winter. " Poem (37) N 79, p. 27.

STUMP, Roger
"Fear. " KanQ (11:3) Sum 79, p. 21.

STYLE, Colin
"The Bride's Home. " SewanR (87:1) Wint 79, p. 53.
"Matron 1918. " SewanR (87:1) Wint 79, p. 54.

SUARDIAZ, Luis
"Pedemonte Taught Philosophy" (tr. by Steve Kowit). PoNow (24)
79, p. 58.

SUAREZ, Kristine Cummings
"Shower" (tr. of Nicomedes Suarez). UTR (6:3/4) 79, p. 57.
"South Wind" (tr. of Nicomedes Suarez). UTR (6:3/4) 79, p.
57.
"Torn Fireflies" (tr. of Nicomedes Suarez). UTR (6:3/4) 79,
p. 59.
"White Horse" (tr. of Nicomedes Suarez). UTR (6:3/4) 79, p.
55.

SUAREZ, Nicomedes
"Shower" (tr. by author and Kristine Cummings Suarez). UTR
(6:3/4) 79, p. 56.
"South Wind" (tr. by author and Kristine Cummings Suarez).
UTR (6:3/4) 79, p. 57.
"Torn Fireflies" (tr. by author and Kristine Cummings Suarez).
UTR (6:3/4) 79, p. 59.

'White Horse" (tr. by author and Kristine Cummings Suarez).
   UTR (6:3/4) 79, p. 55.

SUCKLING, Sir John
   "The Rejected Offer. "   Playb (26:1) Ja 79, p. 257.

SUCRE, Guillermo
   "Atlantico abril. "   Mund (11:1) 79, p. 56.
   "En el ocio. "   Mund (11:1) 79, p. 56.
   "El otro sol. "   Mund (11:1) 79, p. 58.
   "Piedra de escandalo. "   Mund (11:1) 79, p. 54.
   "El proscrito, 1930" (a G. Y. B.).   Mund (11:1) 79, p. 58.
   "Sino silencio. "   Mund (11:1) 79, p. 54.

SUK, Julie
   "Dogs Do Bark. "   Spirit (3:1/2) Aut-Wint 77-78, p. 55.
   "Voyager. "   SouthernPR (19:2) Aut 79, p. 59.

SUKENICK, Lynn
   "Beatrice Remembers. "   OP (28) Aut 79, p. 4.
   "Bess Tells Him. "   OP (28) Aut 79, p. 13.
   'He Dreams He Talks to Bess About Emily Dickinson. "   OP (28)
      Aut 79, p. 5.
   'He Dreams of Alice. "   OP (28) Aut 79, pp. 6-12.
   'Houdini Meets Beatrice. "   OP (28) Aut 79, p. 3.
   'Houdini Panics. "   OP (28) Aut 79, p. 14.

SULKIN, Sidney
   "Knowing. "   SouthwR (64:2) Spr 79, p. 166.

SULLIVAN, Francis
   "Ars Amatoria. "   LittleM (12:1/2) Spr-Sum 78 (79), p. 39.
   "Enigma #21. "   LittleM (12:1/2) Spr-Sum 78 (79), p. 42.
   "Psalm. "   LittleM (12:1/2) Spr-Sum 78 (79), p. 41.
   "Psalm. "   SouthernPR (19:2) Aut 79, p. 68.

SULLIVAN, James
   "As Sun, as Sea. "   Comm (106:23) 21 D 79, p. 726.

SULLIVAN, M. J.
   "Bridge Walk. "   StoneC (6:2) My 79, p. 23.

SULLY, Nancy
   'I Am Frugal. "   SouthwR (64:3) Sum 79, p. 264.

SUMMERS, David
   "Glenogle Baths, Edinburgh. "   MalR (51) Jl 79, p. 96.
   'Rhododendrons. "   MalR (51) Jl 79, p. 97.
   'Toronto Y. M. C. A. "   MalR (51) Jl 79, p. 98.

SUMMERS, Hollis
   "Brother Clark. "   OhioR (20:2) Spr-Sum 79, pp. 75-86.

SUPERVIELLE, Jules
  "The Fawn" (tr. by Jan Pallister). PoNow (24) 79, p. 59.
  "The First Dog" (tr. by Andrew Grossbardt and Quinton Duval).
    QW (8) Wint 79, p. 83.
  "Prophecy" (for Jean Cassou). PoNow (24) 79, p. 59.
  "Un regret de la terre" (tr. by Reg Saner). NowestR (18:2) 79,
    p. 69.
  "Seizure" (tr. by Daniel J. Langton). Spirit (3:3) Sum 78, p. 10.
  "Sonnet to Pilar" (tr. by Andrew Grossbardt and Quinton Duval).
    QW (8) Wint 79, p. 82.

SUTER, Linda
  "Luciano Pavarotti Sings 'O Holy Night.'" Atl (244:1) Jl 79, p.
    58.
  "Les vignobles de France." CentR (23:2) Spr 79, p. 153.

SUTHERLAND, Gray
  "A Visitor." Os (8) 79, p. 26.

SUTHERLAND, Joan Iten
  "Gazing at the Clear Evening After Snow" (tr. of Chia Tao w.
    Peter Levitt). Bachy (15) Aut 79, p. 28.
  "Spending the Night on Wu-Yang Stream" (tr. of Meng Hao-Jan
    w. Peter Levitt). Bachy (15) Aut 79, p. 28.
  "To the Tune: Hsiao Ch'ung" (tr. of Li Ch'ing-Chao w. Peter
    Levitt). Bachy (15) Aut 79, p. 29.
  "To the Tune: Ju Meng Ling" (tr. of Li Ch'ing-Chao w. Peter
    Levitt). Bachy (15) Aut 79, p. 29.
  "To the Tune: P'u Sa Man" (tr. of Li Ch'ing-Chao w. Peter
    Levitt). Bachy (15) Aut 79, p. 29.

SUTTER, Barton
  "Korean Porcelain." CarolQ (31:3) Aut 79, p. 10.
  "Swedish Lesson." CarolQ (31:3) Aut 79, p. 9.

SUTTLE, Sandra
  "The City Beneath." Wind (34) 79, p. 40.

SVEHLA, John
  "Spring." Wind (33) 79, p. 29.

SVOBODA, Robert J.
  "Chase Lounges Revisited." SmPd (45) 79, p. 22.
  "O What the Heck!" SmPd (45) 79, p. 23.

SVOBODA, Terese
  "Arbor Day." Columbia (3) 79, p. 71.
  "Asleep at the Center of a Continent." BelPoJ (29:4) Sum 79, p.
    20.
  "Long Distance." PoetryNW (20:3) Aut 79, pp. 29-30.

SWADOS, Bette Beller
  "Listen" (for H. S.). MassR (20:1) Spr 79, p. 76.

SWAIM, Alice Mackenzie
"A Poem Waiting. " Wind (33) 79, p. 54.

SWAN, Jon
"Heaven and Earth. " NewYorker (54:52) 12 F 79, p. 38.

SWANDER, Mary
"Currach" (for my brother). PortR (25) 79, p. 127.
"For Marcus Lynch. " Ploughs (5:1) 79, pp. 134-135.
"Lynch's Window. " PortR (25) 79, p. 126.
"Quay. " MissouriR (2:2/3) Spr 79, p. 27.

SWANGER, David
"Jalisco. " PoetC (11:3) 79, p. 33.
"Lament of the Winged Horse. " Nimrod (23:1) Aut-Wint 79, p.
    17.
"Legacy. " Nimrod (23:1) Aut-Wint 79, p. 18.
"Life Saving Class. " Nimrod (23:1) Aut-Wint 79, p. 16.
"Old Argument. " Nimrod (23:1) Aut-Wint 79, p. 17.
"The Orange Tree. " PoetC (11:3) 79, p. 32.

SWANN, Brian
"Ah, Wilderness! " SouthernPR (19:2) Aut 79, p. 61.
"Back. " NewYorker (55:28) 27 Ag 79, p. 97.
"Before the Kingdom" (tr. of Homero Aridjis). PoNow (24) 79,
    p. 4.
"Bread. " YaleR (68:4) Sum 79, p. 548.
"The Bridge of Breasts" (tr. of Rafael Alberti). PoNow (24) 79,
    p. 1.
"Christmas" (tr. of Rocco Scotellaro w. Ruth Feldman). Os (8)
    79, p. 5.
"The Conquest of Wandlebury. " CarlMis (18:1) Wint 79-80, p.
    56.
"Cousin Annie. " MissR (24) Aut 79, p. 113.
"Driving Off. " AntR (37:3) Sum 79, p. 314.
"The Eaves" (tr. of Rocco Scotellaro w. Ruth Feldman). Os (8)
    79, p. 3.
"Fast by North. " AntR (37:3) Sum 79, p. 312.
"Father F. Blanchet S. J. to the Rev. Father Provincial F. J. N.
    in St. Louis. " BelPoJ (29:4) Sum 79, p. 30.
"For a Foreign Woman Who Is Leaving" (tr. of Rocco Scotellaro
    w. Ruth Feldman). PoNow (21) 79, p. 46.
"Fossil Moves. " NoAmR (264:4) Wint 79, p. 73.
"The Friar's Boundary-Wall" (tr. of Rocco Scotellaro w. Ruth
    Feldman). PoNow (21) 79, p. 46.
"the full moon rises. " SouthernPR (19:2) Aut 79, p. 60.
"Hawk Seasons. " SoDakR (17:1) Spr 79, p. 83.
"The Hockey-Coach's Daughter. " PoNow (22) 79, p. 42.
"Holmes at the Zoo. " PoNow (22) 79, p. 42.
Living Time (for Roberta). QRL (21:1/2) 78, pp. 1-72.
"Masks. " YaleR (69:2) Wint 80, p. 261.
Nine Poems (tr. of Bartolo Cattafi w. Ruth Feldman). PoNow
    (24) 79, pp. 8-9.

"Nocturne" (tr. of Rafael Alberti). PoNow (24) 79, p. 1.
"Our Lady of the Chickens. " CentR (23:2) Spr 79, p. 153.
Poem. St. AR (5:2) 79, p. 76.
Poem. St. AR (5:2) 79, p. 113.
"Potlach." BelPoJ (29:4) Sum 79, p. 31.
"Primal Scene." SouthwR (64:1) Wint 79, p. 61.
"Red Umbrella. " AmerS (48:4) Aut 79, p. 486.
"Red Umbrella. " MissR (24) Aut 79, p. 111.
"Second Hand. " MissR (24) Aut 79, p. 115.
"Set Up. " PoNow (22) 79, p. 42.
"Song of the Sky. " Nat (228:13) 7 Ap 79, p. 379.
"Spider Woman. " AntR (37:3) Sum 79, p. 316.
"Stag. " BelPoJ (29:4) Sum 79, p. 31.
"The Stain. " PoNow (22) 79, p. 42.
"Tashtego's Nightmare. " CharR (5:1) Spr 79, p. 90.
"Touch. " PoNow (22) 79, p. 42.
"The Truth. " MissR (24) Aut 79, p. 117.
Twenty-two Poems (tr. of Rocco Scotellaro w. Ruth Feldman).
     PoNow (24) 79, pp. 52-54.
"What the Grandfathers Told Me. " Agni (10/11) 79, p. 150.
"You Could Drive All the Way to Alaska. " PraS (53:4) Wint 79-
     80, p. 355.

SWANSON, Robert
     "Getting Out of a Pawnshop. " CalQ (15) Wint 79, p. 20.
     "Into the North. " CalQ (15) Wint 79, p. 19.
     "My Ancestor. " CalQ (15) Wint 79, p. 21.

SWARD, Robert
     "The Great American Poem. " Antaeus (32) Wint 79, pp. 82-86.

SWARTS, Helene
     "Medicine. " ChrC (96:37) 14 N 79, p. 1123.

SWARTZ, David
     "Loon Lake. " PikeF (2) Wint 78-79, p. 3.

SWEDE, George
     Eight Poems. WindO (35) Aut-Wint 79-80.

SWEENEY, Barbara
     "For We Are All Madwomen. " MalR (52) O 79, p. 96.
     "Leavetaking /July 4. " MalR (52) O 79, p. 94.
     "On the Boat to Avallon." MalR (52) O 79, p. 92.

SWEENEY, Gael
     "After Hearing Bombs: Dublin, May, 1974. " NewL (46:1) Aut
          79, p. 54.
     "Williamsburg: Digging Up the Insane Asylum. " HiramPoR (26)
          Spr-Sum 79, p. 33.

SWEENEY, Michael
     "Alone with the Dawn. " GRR (10:1) 79, p. 15.

"Eclipses. " GRR (10:1) 79, p. 143.
"Late. " GRR (10:1) 79, p. 16.
"Opening Day. " PikeF (2) Wint 78-79, p. 16.
Twelve Poems. GRR (10:3) 79, pp. 73-86.
"Writer. " GRR (10:1) 79, p. 142.

SWENSON, Karen
"The Accounting. " PraS (53:1) Spr 79, p. 58.
"Chador. " PraS (53:1) Spr 79, p. 59.
"The Daddy Strain. " TexQ (21:4) Wint 78, p. 150.
"Every Woman Holds. " TexQ (21:4) Wint 78, p. 151.
"Good-Bye Dorothy Gayle. " PraS (53:1) Spr 79, pp. 53-57.
"The Millennium. " TexQ (21:4) Wint 78, p. 149.
"The Puppeteers. " CarlMis (17:2/3) Spr 79, p. 94.
"Starvation. " VirQR (55:2) Spr 79, p. 300.
"The Transients. " PraS (53:1) Spr 79, p. 60.
"The Wife of Bath. " TexQ (21:4) Wint 78, p. 152.
"The X Ray. " Salm (43) Wint 79, p. 96.

SWETS, Robert D.
"First Things. " KanQ (11:1/2) Wint-Spr 79, p. 194.

SWIFT, Jonathan
"Phyllis. " Playb (26:8) Ag 79, p. 153.

SWIFT, Michael
"John Higgins. " Mouth (2:3) N 79, p. 6.

SWISS, Thom
"Festival Profile. " Agni (10/11) 79, p. 68.
"A Virtue of Shape. " Agni (10/11) 79, p. 67.

SWIST, Wally
"All the Green Lights Going Home. " Tele (15) Spr 79, p. 105.
"Moment. " StoneC (6:2) My 79, p. 25.
"The Neighbors. " Tele (15) Spr 79, p. 104.
"The Virgin. " Tele (15) Spr 79, p. 105.

SWOPE, Lucy
"At the Edge. " WestB (4) 79, p. 5.
"The Gazette. " WestB (4) 79, p. 9.
"The White Mare and the Man. " WestB (4) 79, p. 6.

SYLVESTER, Nigel Grant
"Beth" (tr. of Carlos Montemayor). DenQ (14:1) Spr 79, p. 63.
"Fifth Ode, Broken" (tr. of Carlos Montemayor). DenQ (14:1)
    Spr 79, p. 66.
"Heth" (tr. of Carlos Montemayor). DenQ (14:1) Spr 79, p. 64.
"Teth" (tr. of Carlos Montemayor). DenQ (14:1) Spr 79, p. 65.

SYMMONS, Prof James
"Give Me This Day. " BlackF (3:1) Aut-Wint 79, p. 27.

SZABO, Lörinc
"Foolish Mirror" (tr. by Nicholas Kolumban).   TexQ (21:4) Wint
    78, p. 35.

SZAFRANSKI, Bernadette
"The Japanese. " CalQ (15) Wint 79, p. 70.

SZE, Arthur
"Dazzled. " NewL (45:3) Spr 79, p. 19.
"listening to a broken radio. " GreenfieldR (7:3/4) Spr-Sum 79,
    p. 12.
"the moon is a diamond. " GreenfieldR (7:3/4) Spr-Sum 79, p.
    13.
"olive night. " GreenfieldR (7:3/4) Spr-Sum 79, p. 13.

SZUMIGALSKI, Anne
"For Padmanab (who may not like it). " MalR (52) O 79, p. 46.
"The Portrait of E. " MalR (52) O 79, p. 44.

TAGLIABUE, John
"Don't Think I'm Mad at You. " GreenfieldR (7:3/4) Spr-Sum 79,
    p. 77.
from Exotic Thoughts in Vacationland: "So many yawns like so
    many lions. " Chelsea (38) 79, p. 219.
"For a Blond Fellow Who Saw Them in Africa--Bill McDiarmid. "
    Chelsea (38) 79, p. 221.
"I Have Caught On: You Have Caught On. " PoNow (23) 79, p.
    33.
"Notebook Reactions to the Computer. " GreenfieldR (7:3/4) Spr-
    Sum 79, p. 78.
"notes in Asia House/NYC. " Chelsea (38) 79, p. 220.
"Pastoral. " AndR (6:2) Aut 79, p. 48.
"Poem: He went. " AndR (6:2) Aut 79, p. 49.
"A Sort of Lecture.... " CentR (23:1) Wint 79, p. 69.
"3 Poems on Tomatoes & Immortality. " Kayak (51) S 79, p. 13.
"The Underground Pressure. " Chelsea (38) 79, p. 219.
"Yes, We Can Stand All These Nobel Prizes, Comets, Universes,
    Epics, They Keep Coming Our Way. " Harp (258:1548) My
    79, p. 105.

TAKACS, Nancy
"For the Old Woman. " HolCrit (16:4) O 79, p. 12.

TAKAMURA, Kotaro
Twenty-five Poems (tr. by Hiroaki Sato). Montra (6) 79, pp.
    103-133.

TAKVAM, Marie
"The Deepest Bow" (tr. by Harold P. Hanson). Paint (11) Spr
    79, p. 75.

TALARICO, Ross
"Discovering Mobility" (To My First Child). QW (6) Spr-Sum

78, p. 121.
"Leisure. " CarlMis (18:1) Wint 79-80, p. 103.
"Looking for Socrates. " PraS (53:2) Sum 79, p. 176.
"Petty Cash, Petty Thieves" (for Gary Snyder).   PraS (53:2)
    Sum 79, p. 175.
"Poem to Be Read at My Wake. " PoetryNW (20:2) Sum 79, pp.
    31-32.

TALL, Deborah
"Bishop's Rock. " Poetry (135:1) O 79, p. 23.
"Crossing. " Iowa (10:2) Spr 79, p. 95.
"Interlude. " Poetry (135:1) O 79, p. 21.
"Scheherezade. " Poetry (135:1) O 79, pp. 24-25.
"The Suicide. " Iowa (10:2) Spr 79, p. 96.
"The Widow's Letter. " Ploughs (5:3) 79, p. 88.
"Yearning. " Poetry (135:1) O 79, p. 22.

TALLENT, Elizabeth
"Circles Around the Sun. " PikeF (2) Wint 78-79, p. 3.
"What It Is Like: For Bar. " PikeR (1) Sum 79, pp. 68-69.

TAMBUZI
"Abstractions. " NewRena (11) 79, p. 78.
"Defiance. " NewRena (11) 79, p. 78.

TAN, Bee Bee
"Embroidering Mandarin Ducks. " 13thM (4:2) 79, p. 5.

TANGREDI, Sam J.
"Ex Libris. " Wind (35) 79, p. 54.

TAPAHONSO, Luci
"For my brother, who was shot defending a friend, on a Decem-
    ber night in 1966. " BelPoJ (30:2) Wint 79-80, p. 31.
"Rose Ann Tso. " BelPoJ (30:2) Wint 79-80, p. 30.

TAPP, Gary
"Dead Dogs and Honeybees. " CimR (47) Ap 79, p. 16.
"The Insect Shuffle Method. " CimR (46) Ja 79, p. 16.

TAPSCOTT, Stephen
"Gallinules. " CarolQ (31:3) Aut 79, p. 81.

TARLEN, Carol
"To a Young Dancer. " Spirit (4:1) Aut-Wint 78-79, p. 42.

TARN, Nathaniel
"Journal of the Laguna de San Ignacio. " Montra (5) 79, p. 176.

TARWOOD, James A.
"The Wrongs. " Wind (35) 79, p. 59.

TATE, Allen
"The Swimmers. " Poetry (135:2) N 79, pp. 67-75.

TATE, James
"Across the Heavens. " PoNow (23) 79, p. 15.
"Bee Keeping, Home Birth, and Foreign Car Repair. " Durak (2)
    79, p. 39.
"Considering the Loss. " PoNow (22) 79, p. 43.
"Detective Shoes. " Durak (2) 79, p. 44.
"Disturbing Islands: Promise to Write. " Antaeus (32) Wint 79,
    p. 46.
"The Great American Poem. " Antaeus (32) Wint 79, pp. 82-86.
"Holiday on an Antfarm. " Durak (2) 79, p. 43.
"In the Realm of the Ignition. " Antaeus (32) Wint 79, p. 48.
"Lousy in Centerfield. " Durak (2) 79, p. 40.
from Missionwork: (1). PoNow (22) 79, p. 43.
from Missionwork: (2). PoNow (22) 79, p. 43.
from Missionwork: (3). PoNow (22) 79, p. 43.
from Missionwork: (4). PoNow (22) 79, p. 43.
from Missionwork: (5). PoNow (22) 79, p. 43.
"Nausea, Coincidence. " Durak (2) 79, p. 42.
"The Powder of Sympathy. " Antaeus (33) Spr 79, p. 94.
"Recurring Highway. " PoNow (22) 79, p. 43.
"The Rustling of Foliage The Memory of Caresses": Fifteen
    Poems. MassR (20:4) Wint 79, pp. 705-720.
"Sloops in the Bay. " Antaeus (32) Wint 79, p. 47.

TAYLOR, Alexander
"Gesture" (tr. of Henrik Nordbrandt). PoNow (24) 79, p. 37.
"Just to Be Sure" (tr. of Benny Anderson). PoNow (24) 79, p.
    30.
"Lances" (tr. of Ole Sarving). PoNow (24) 79, p. 35.
"The Pampered Mermaid" (tr. of Benny Anderson). PoNow (24)
    79, p. 30.
"Photographs" (tr. of Benny Anderson). PoNow (24) 79, p. 30.
"Roads" (tr. of Henrik Nordbrandt). PoNow (24) 79, p. 37.
"The Sea" (tr. of Ole Sarving). PoNow (24) 79, p. 35.
"Wild Fear" (tr. of Ole Sarving). PoNow (24) 79, p. 35.

TAYLOR, Archie V.
"Darkness of Light. " Im (5:3) 79, p. 3.

TAYLOR, Benjamin
"The Perseids This Time" (for Thomas Tatemichi). Shen (30:2)
    Wint 79, p. 41.

TAYLOR, Brian
"Furnished Rooms: Cripple Creek. " Stand (20:4) 79, p. 15.
"Towards Dawn. " Stand (20:4) 79, p. 14.

TAYLOR, Davis
"Occupied. " CarlMis (17:2/3) Spr 79, p. 37.

TAYLOR, Henry
"At the Swings. " VirQR (55:1) Wint 79, p. 107.

TAYLOR, Jeffrey
"Lesson, on the Meramec. " QW (7) Aut 78, p. 82.

TAYLOR, John
"The Deeps. " WestB (5) 79, p. 44.
"The Egg of Nothing. " WestB (5) 79, p. 45.
"End of the Line. " NewL (46:2) Wint 79-80, p. 13.
"The Godhead Celebrating Itself. " WestB (5) 79, p. 45.
"Property. " WestB (5) 79, p. 44.
"Singing Breathing. " GreenfieldR (7:3/4) Spr-Sum 79, p. 62.
"Something You Missed. " GreenfieldR (7:3/4) Spr-Sum 79, p. 61.
"A Text from Isaiah. " WestB (5) 79, p. 45.
"Zombis on Every Channel. " GreenfieldR (7:3/4) Spr-Sum 79,
    p. 61.

TAYLOR, Keith
"The Holy Dance. " BelPoJ (29:3) Spr 79, p. 36.

TAYLOR, Kent
"10-21-78. " Vaga (29) 79, p. 56.
"10-24-78. " Vaga (29) 79, p. 57.

TAYLOR, Laurie
"Isphahan. " WebR (4:3) Spr 79, p. 34.
"Medicine Wheel. " Sam (79) 79, p. 79.

TAYLOR, Marcella
"Mr. World at the Junkanoo Parade. " CarlMis (18:1) Wint 79,
    p. 84.

TAYLOR, Martha
"A Lesson in History. " HangL (35) Spr 79, p. 77.

TAYLOR, Peter
"Five Miles from Home. " Ploughs (5:2) 79, pp. 82-84.

TAYLOR, Robert Jr.
"Caveat Emptor. " PoetryNW (20:1) Spr 79, pp. 34-35.

TEDARDS, Douglas
"The Mothers of Fruitation. " GeoR (33:1) Spr 79, p. 166.

TEKEYAN, Vahan
"The Hanum" (tr. by Diana Der Hovanessian). PoNow (24) 79,
    p. 59.
"The Poet to His Nation" (tr. by Diana Der Hovanessian).
    PoNow (21) 79, p. 45.

TenBERGE, H. C.
"Albi" (tr. by Theo Hermans and Paul Vincent). ChiR (31:2)
    Aut 79, p. 27.
"Andes" (tr. by Theo Hermans and Paul Vincent). ChiR (31:2)
    Aut 79, p. 25.

"Brassem pouy" (tr. by Theo Hermans and Paul Vincent). ChiR
(31:2) Aut 79, p. 21.
"Lübeck" (tr. by Theo Hermans and Paul Vincent). ChiR (31:2)
Aut 79, p. 22.
"Nemrud dagh" (tr. by Theo Hermans and Paul Vincent). ChiR
(31:2) Aut 79, p. 24.
"Swartkrans" (tr. by Theo Hermans and Paul Vincent). ChiR
(31:2) Aut 79, p. 20.
"Water and shadow, shadow and water" (tr. by Theo Hermans
and Paul Vincent). ChiR (31:2) Aut 79, p. 28.

Ten BRINK, Carole L.
Poem. St. AR (5:2) 79, p. 45.
Poem. St. AR (5:2) 79, p. 90.

TENNYSON, Lucy
"Winter Food." BelPoJ (30:2) Wint 79-80, p. 4.

TERRANOVA, Elaine
"Alcestis." Ploughs (5:1) 79, p. 137.
"Summer in Bodines" (for Brenda and Jerry). Ploughs (5:1) 79,
p. 136.
"The Walk to the Castle." Ploughs (5:1) 79, p. 138.

TERRILL, Kathryn
"Iguanas" (for Karen Blixen). ThRiPo (13/14) 79, p. 29.

TERRIS, Virginia R.
"The Cat's View." NewYorker (55:23) 23 Jl 79, p. 38.
"Drinking." NewL (46:1) Aut 79, p. 75.
"Touring." PoNow (23) 79, p. 35.
"Unbuckling Poem." PoNow (23) 79, p. 35.
"The Usual." PoNow (23) 79, p. 35.

THADDEUS, Janice
"Sestina for Mary Shelley." Shen (30:4) 79, p. 92.

THALES
from The Book of Light/The Book of Water (tr. by Keith Gunder-
son). CarlMis (17:2/3) Spr 79, p. 14.

THALMAN, Mark
"Thawing Out." CharR (5:2) Aut 79, p. 55.

THARP, Roland
"Cabin at Bread Loaf Mountain." PoNow (25) 79, p. 41.
"Stony Littleton." PoNow (25) 79, p. 41.

THIEL, Troy
"The Daisy Garden." PikeF (2) Wint 78-79, p. 18.

THOMAS, Debra
"Urania." Hudson (32:1) Spr 79, p. 69.

THOMAS, Harry
"The Absent" (tr. of Pedro Salinas). MichQR (18:1) Wint 79, p. 118.
"If You Called Me" (tr. of Pedro Salinas). MichQR (18:1) Wint 79, p. 117.

THOMAS, J. M.
"April. " Wind (33) 79, p. 55.
"Jennie Copeland. " Wind (33) 79, p. 55.

THOMAS, Kate K.
Poem. St. AR (5:2) 79, p. 112.

THOMAS, Lisa
"Sound. " KanQ (11:3) Sum 79, p. 112.

THOMAS, Lorenzo
from Screen Test: "Consider thoughts to live. " PartR (46:4) 79, pp. 593-596.

THOMAS, Michael
"Prison. " EngJ (68:5) My 79, p. 37.

THOMAS, Peter
"Cache Valley Quartet. " GRR (10:1) 79, pp. 51-55.

THOMPSON, Gary
"Boat Poem. " CutB (13) Aut-Wint 79, p. 25.
"Neighbors. " CutB (13) Aut-Wint 79, p. 24.
"When Are We Really Alive?" QW (7) Aut 78, p. 127.

THOMPSON, Joanna
"Gone. " KanQ (11:1/2) Wint-Spr 79, p. 127.
"Grandmother. " AmerS (48:1) Wint 78-79, p. 106.
"Photo Album with Waterstains. " Im (6:1) 79, p. 3.
Poem. St. AR (5:2) 79, p. 107.

THOMPSON, Judith
"Immediately Upon Landing. " Ploughs (5:3) 79, pp. 68-69.

THOMPSON, N. S.
Eight Poems (tr. of Tristan Tzara). SunM (8) Aut 79, p. 64.

THOMPSON, Phyllis
"The Chill of Distance. " NewL (46:2) Wint 79-80, p. 30.
"Home. " PraS (53:1) Spr 79, p. 36.
"Taking Our Time. " PraS (53:1) Spr 79, p. 37.
"The Wind of the Cliff Ka Hea. " NewL (46:2) Wint 79-80, p. 32.

THOMSON, Sharon
"Community Life. " Pequod (3:2) 79, pp. 56-62.

THORNE, Evelyn
"Never-the-less It Is So. " GRR (10:1) 79, p. 137.

THORPE 392

THORPE, Dwayne
"The Country at the End of the Gong's Last Throb. " WestB (4)
    79, p. 79.
"Night Falls. " WestB (4) 79, p. 77.
"Rooftop Winter." MichQR (18:1) Wint 79, p. 95.
"Snail. " WestB (4) 79, p. 78.
"To Iselin, for Her Nighttime Fear. " WestB (4) 79, p. 78.

THORPE, Peter
"After Visiting the State Prison. " ColEng (41:1) S 79, p. 79.
"Curly Fat Cherubic Visiting Poet. " ColEng (41:1) S 79, p. 79.

TIBULLUS
"Elegy 1. 10" (tr. by Fred Beake). Stand (20:3) 79, p. 7.

TIFFT, Ellen
"Nuclear Land. " NewL (46:2) Wint 79-80, p. 104.

TIKKANEN, Märta
from Love Story of the Century: "No one" (tr. by Thomas and
    Vera Vance). Paint (12) Aut 79, p. 29.
from Love Story of the Century: "She curls up in my arms"
    (tr. by Thomas and Vera Vance). Paint (12) Aut 79, p. 28.

TILL, David
"Panhandle. " DacTerr (16) 79, p. 61.

TILLINGHAST, Richard
"Shooting Ducks in South Louisiana. " NewL (46:1) Aut 79, p. 38.
"Sovereigns" (after Rilke). ParisR (75) Spr 79, p. 241.
"Things Past. " Ploughs (5:3) 79, pp. 79-80.

TINGLEY, Cindy
"Insomnia on a Hot Night. " QW (6) Spr-Sum 78, p. 50.
"This Time. " QW (8) Wint 79, p. 113.

TISDALE, Charles
"Kite Flying. " DenQ (14:3) Aut 79, p. 88.
"Shadowdance. " SoCaR (12:1) Aut 79, p. 33.

TODD, Theodora
"Sleep. " MidwQ (20:4) Sum 79, p. 377.

TOFFLER, Alvin
"The League of Selves. " AntR (37:2) Spr 79, p. 182.

TOLNAY, Thomas
"The Basement Watch. " SouthwR (64:1) Wint 79, p. 17.

TOLTZIS, Alan
"Snow Poem. " Focus (13:81) My-Je 79, p. 31.

TOMKIW, Lydia
"At Sunrise. " WormR (76) 79, p. 122.

"The Bread Boy. " WormR (76) 79, p. 122.
"Forehead. " WormR (76) 79, p. 121.
"The Late Show. " WormR (76) 79, p. 122.

TOMLINSON, Rawdon
"A Room, A Window. " PoNow (22) 79, p. 44.

TONG, Raymond
"Personal Mythology. " WormR (73) 79, p. 30.

TORGERSEN, Eric
"Dear Friend. " PoNow (22) 79, p. 44.
"The Fish. " PoNow (21) 79, p. 34.
"Shannon's Dream. " Spirit (3:1/2) Aut-Wint 77-78, p. 45.
"Thinking About the Basketball Team. " PoNow (22) 79, p. 44.
"Two Home Pieces. " PoNow (21) 79, p. 41.

TORNES, Beth
"Small Fears. " QW (7) Aut 78, p. 45.

TOULET, Jean-Paul
"In Arles" (tr. by Jan Pallister). PoNow (24) 79, p. 59.

TOWLE, Tony
"Postlude. " PartR (46:2) 79, p. 258.

TOWNER, Daniel
"Maid of the Mist. " Wind (32) 79, p. 46.

TRANSTROMER, Tomas
"Baltic Seas III" (tr. by John Matthias). GreenfieldR (7:3/4)
Spr-Sum 79, p. 123.
"Schubertiana" (tr. by Samuel Charters). VirQR (55:1) Wint 79,
p. 115.

TRAWICK, Leonard
"Erlking. " QW (9) Spr-Sum 79, p. 125.
"Father's Dog. " PoNow (25) 79, p. 41.

TREADWELL, George
"Dreaming of Autumn. " Wind (33) 79, p. 12.
"Elmer Fudd's Odyessy. " Wind (33) 79, p. 18.

TRECHOCK, Mark
"Pietà. " ChrC (96:15) 25 Ap 79, p. 470.

TREGEBOV, Rhea
"Foreigners. " CarlMis (18:1) Wint 79, p. 161.

TREITEL, Margot
"Building the Board Up. " PortR (25) 79, p. 122.
"Composition by Mondrian. " Chomo (5:3) Spr 79, p. 5.
"Drop This Poem into the River Neva. " ColEng (41:4) D 79, p.

409.
"Matisse's Danse. " Chomo (5:3) Spr 79, p. 4.
"Minimal Lines. " Chomo (5:3) Spr 79, p. 3.
"Not Speaking the Language. " PortR (25) 79, p. 123.
"The Skeptic's Act of Faith. " Nimrod (23:1) Aut-Wint 79, p. 89.

TREJO, Ernesto
"E. at the Zocalo. " Kayak (51) S 79, p. 48.
"E. Gives a Name. " Kayak (51) S 79, p. 49.
"A Lecture on Crabs" (tr. of José Emilio Pacheco). Chelsea
    (38) 79, p. 178.
"Physiology of the Slug" (tr. of José Emilio Pacheco). Chelsea
    (38) 79, p. 177.

TREJO, Mario
"Champions of the Night. " LitR (23:2) Wint 80, p. 203.

TRELAWNY, Victor
"Campground in Neutral Shades. " PortR (25) 79, p. 160.
"How to Build a Boat. " Bits (9) Ja 79.
"Purge. " PortR (25) 79, p. 161.
"Waterhole. " Wind (32) 79, p. 47.
"Words for Huck Finn. " ConcPo (12:1) Spr 79, p. 12.
"X_____. " Wind (32) 79, p. 47.

TREMBLAY, Bill
"Dream Whispering to the Best Intent of Your Left Wing. " PikeF
    (2) Wint 78-79, p. 13.
"Weeds. " PikeR (1) Sum 79, p. 70.
"Winter Sun. " PikeF (2) Wint 78-79, p. 13.

TREVOR, Stan
"Outside the Crowd Is Stirring. " MalR (49) Ja 79, p. 52.
"Poem for My Mother. " MalR (49) Ja 79, p. 50.
"Poem for My Mother. " MalR (51) Jl 79, p. 118. Corrected
    version.
"To Think That I Once Thought. " MalR (51) Jl 79, p. 119.

TRIEM, Eve
"The Cries of Autumn. " Wind (34) 79, p. 60.
"Dark Sisters. " Wind (34) 79, p. 60.
"Gnarled Bough Blossoming. " Wind (34) 79, p. 61.
"Second Wife. " Wind (34) 79, p. 59.
"The Summingup. " Wind (34) 79, p. 60.
"Travelling. " Wind (34) 79, p. 61.
"Waltz of the Toreadors. " Wind (34) 79, p. 62.

TRIFANOV, Gennady
"Letter from Prison" (tr. by Simon Karlinsky). PoNow (24) 79,
    p. 60.

TRIMPI, Alison A.
"The Skull in the Desert. " SouthernR (15:4) Aut 79, p. 1016.

TRITEL, Barbara
"The Law of Adaptation" (for Louisa Putnam). KanQ (11:1/2)
    Wint-Spr 79, p. 204.

TROWBRIDGE, William
"Stones River Battleground. " PoNow (25) 79, p. 41.

TRUDELL, Dennis
"Among the Consenting Adults. " PoetryNW (20:1) Spr 79, pp.
    42-43.
"The Light in Our Bodies. " GeoR (33:2) Sum 79, p. 279.
"Nobody's Perfect. " GeoR (33:2) Sum 79, p. 278.
"La Vida. " Bits (10) Jl 79.

TRUESDALE, C. W.
"Dragonfly. " Chelsea (38) 79, p. 208.
"Little Roach Poem for Bliem. " Chelsea (38) 79, p. 208.

TSABA, Niobeh
"Song of a Sister's Freedom. " Cond (5) 79, p. 150.
"The Yaller Gal. " Cond (5) 79, p. 149.

TSIRANTONAKIS, Anthony
"Diary of Exile III" (tr. of Yannis Ritsos). PoNow (24) 79, p.
    49.

TSONGAS, George
"Out to Lunch. " SeC (6:2) 78, p. 105.
"20 Years of Irreversible Brain Damage. " SeC (6:2) 78, p. 103.

TSUKIMURA, Reiko
"Four Tanka Poems" (tr. of Miyoko Goto). MalR (52) O 79, p.
    24.
"Seasons. " MalR (52) O 79, p. 88.

TSURUTA, Dorothy Randall
"An African-American in Ghana in Visit. " NegroHB (42:2) Ap-
    My-Je 79, p. 54.
"Grandma. " NegroHB (42:2) Ap-My-Je 79, p. 54.
"'Grandmaw' 1889-1976. " NegroHB (42:2) Ap-My-Je 79, p. 54.

TUCKER, Martin
"The Jaguar in the Tree. " Spirit (3:1/2) Aut-Wint 77-78, p. 12.

TUCKER, Robert
"Summer and Winter. " NewL (46:1) Aut 79, p. 30.
"Told in Weather. " NewL (46:1) Aut 79, p. 30.

TUDOR, Stephen
"Bench Vice. " KanQ (11:3) Sum 79, p. 27.
"Classroom. " OP (27) Spr 79, pp. 42-45.
"The House of Your Head. " OP (27) Spr 79, p. 38.
"Lines. " OP (27) Spr 79, p. 46.

"Message. " OP (27) Spr 79, p. 41.
"The Purchase. " OP (27) Spr 79, p. 40.

TULLOSS, Rod
"The Jewish Orthopaedic Nurse. " PoNow (23) 79, p. 43.
"Speed. " Spirit (3:1/2) Aut-Wint 77-78, p. 48.
"York Pa June 12 1 A. M. 1914. " Spirit (3:1/2) Aut-Wint 77-78, p. 48.

TUÑON, Raúl González
"The Moon with Trigger" (fragment). LitR (23:2) Wint 80, p. 274.

TURCO, Lewis
"Bell Weather. " Comm (106:13) 6 Jl 79, p. 405.
"The Ferry. " Hudson (32:3) Aut 79, p. 400.
"Poem. " PoetryNW (20:3) Aut 79, pp. 30-31.
"Spiders. " CentR (23:4) Aut 79, p. 425.
"Vigilance. " Ploughs (5:3) 79, pp. 29-30.

TURGEON, Gregoire
"February. " Epoch (28:3) Spr-Sum 79, p. 261.
"How It Is Out There. " CarlMis (18:1) Wint 79-80, p. 145.
"Walker Evans. " SouthernPR (19:2) Aut 79, p. 33.

TURNBULL, Gael
"The Best. " Montra (5) 79, p. 174.
"What Makes the Weeds Grow Tall. " Montra (5) 79, p. 172.
"You Are. " Montra (5) 79, p. 173.

TURNER, Alberta T.
"The Angel of ____. " PoNow (21) 79, p. 5.
"Birthing. " Paint (11) Spr 79, p. 76.
"Clothe. " QW (9) Spr-Sum 79, p. 48.
"Work. " QW (9) Spr-Sum 79, p. 49.

TURNER, Alison
"An Afternoon in Santa Cruz. " Nimrod (23:1) Aut-Wint 79, p. 82.
"Housesitting for a Former Mate. " Nimrod (23:1) Aut-Wint 79, p. 79.

TURNER, Doug
"The Spirit. " MalR (52) O 79, p. 86.

TURNER, Samuel S.
"February. " SouthernR (15:1) Wint 79, p. 119.
"Jedediah Smith. " SouthernR (15:1) Wint 79, p. 119.
"November. " SouthernR (15:1) Wint 79, p. 118.

TUROLDO, David Maria
"Adam" (tr. by Sonia Raiziss). PoNow (24) 79, p. 60.
"The Heart Always Colder" (tr. by Sonia Raiziss). PoNow (24) 79, p. 60.
"O My Days" (tr. by Sonia Raiziss). PoNow (24) 79, p. 60.

TUTOR, GlennRay
"Buying Holes." NewOR (6:4) 79, p. 359.

TWICHELL, Chase
"The Dark Hinges" (for H. C.). GeoR (33:4) Wint 79, p. 878.
"Geode." CharR (5:1) Spr 79, p. 59.
"An Orchard Door." PortR (25) 79, p. 107.

TYLER, Robert L.
"My Love Doesn't Like Poetry." KanQ (11:3) Sum 79, p. 98.
"Shaggy Dog." Wind (33) 79, p. 31.

TZARA, Tristan
Eight Poems (tr. by N. S. Thompson). SunM (8) Aut 79, p. 64.

UHER, Lorna
"Alice." MalR (49) Ja 79, p. 102.
"City Trip." MalR (49) Ja 79, p. 103.
"Hands of Absence." MalR (49) Ja 79, p. 104.

ULLMAN, Leslie
"Last Night They Heard the Woman Upstairs." Madem (85:4) Ap
    79, p. 114.
Sixteen Poems. CharR (5:SI) 79, pp. 105-124.

UNGARETTI, Giuseppe
"Calm" (tr. by Jan Pallister and Arthur Neisberg). PoNow (24)
    79, p. 61.
"Night" (tr. by Jan Pallister and Arthur Neisberg). PoNow (24)
    79, p. 61.
"Nostalgia" (tr. by Jan Pallister and Arthur Neisberg). PoNow
    (24) 79, p. 61.

UNGER, Barbara
"Riding the Penn Central Railroad into New York City." Spirit
    (3:3) Sum 78, p. 33.

UNGER, David
"Close to Death" (tr. of Vicente Aleixandre w. Lewis Hyde).
    PoNow (24) 79, p. 29.
"The Entomologist." PoNow (23) 79, p. 39.
"Guitar or Moon" (tr. of Vicente Aleixandre w. Lewis Hyde).
    PoNow (24) 79, p. 29.

UNTERECKER, John
"Bruises." ArkRiv (4:3) 79, p. 39.
"The Envelope." ArkRiv (4:3) 79, p. 38.
"Rivers, Roads, Blood Vessels." ArkRiv (4:3) 79, p. 40.

UPDIKE, John
"Energy: A Villanelle." NewYorker (55:16) 4 Je 79, p. 44.
"On the Way to Delphi." NewRep (180:25) 23 Je 79, p. 34.
"Self-Service." Atl (244:4) O 79, p. 82.

"The Visions of Mackenzie King. " NewRep (180:17) 28 Ap 79, p. 28.

UPHAM, Irvine Frost
"Benares" (tr. of Jorge Luis Borges). TexQ (21:4) Wint 78, p. 7.
"Of Heaven and Hell" (tr. of Jorge Luis Borges). TexQ (21:4) Wint 78, p. 9.
"A Prospect (Un Mañana)" (tr. of Jorge Luis Borges). TexQ (21:4) Wint 78, p. 12.
"Rosas" (tr. of Jorge Luis Borges). TexQ (21:4) Wint 78, p. 6.
"Simón Carbajal" (tr. of Jorge Luis Borges). TexQ (21:4) Wint 78, p. 10.
"To a Caesar" (tr. of Jorge Luis Borges). TexQ (21:4) Wint 78, p. 11.
"To Francisco López Merino" (tr. of Jorge Luis Borges). TexQ (21:4) Wint 78, p. 8.

UPTON, Lee
"The Losses of the Gardener. " DenQ (14:3) Aut 79, p. 47.
"Sleeping in a Cellar. " LittleM (12:1/2) Spr-Sum 78 (79), p. 90.
"The Upton Toe. " GRR (10:2) 79, p. 184.

URDANG, Constance
"Archaeology. " PoNow (23) 79, p. 9.
"The Brother Poems: The Secret. " PoNow (23) 79, p. 9.
"Exercise for the Left Hand. " Paint (11) Spr 79, p. 77.
"Feme Sole. " NewEngR (1:4) Sum 79, p. 426.
"The Great American Poem. " Antaeus (32) Wint 79, pp. 82-86.
"The Invention of Zero. " NewEngR (1:4) Sum 79, p. 426.
"The Invisible Woman. " PoNow (21) 79, p. 5.
"Pity. " NewEngR (1:4) Sum 79, p. 427.
"Somebody's Life. " MissouriR (3:1) Aut 79, p. 29.
"Witch Song. " PoNow (21) 79, p. 5.

VAJDA, David
"Laughter in the City Is Such a Sad Thing. " PikeF (2) Wint 78-79, p. 19.

VALAORITIS, Nanos
"Amusement Park. " Kayak (52) D 79, p. 24.
"The Voice of Artaud. " Kayak (52) D 79, p. 24.

VALEN, Nanine
"Night Circus. " FourQt (29:1) Aut 79, p. 11.
"The River of Lace. " WestB (4) 79, p. 62.

VALENTINE, Jean
"After Elegies (3). " Pequod (3:1) 79, p. 99.
"The Great American Poem. " Antaeus (32) Wint 79, pp. 82-86.
"394" (tr. of Osip Mandelstam w. Anne Frydman). AmerPoR (8:2) Mr-Ap 79, p. 11.
"Working" (in memory of Robert Lowell). HarvAd (113:1/2) N 79, p. 44.

VALIAN, Maxine Kent
"Blessing at Kellenberger Road. " KanQ (11:1/2) Wint-Spr 79, p.
128.

VALIN, Wayne R.
"Ginseng. " TexQ (21:2) Sum 78, p. 24.

VALIS, Noël Maureen
"Black Horse Running. " BallSUF (20:1) Wint 79, p. 32.

VALLEE, Lillian
"Readings" (tr. of Czeslaw Milosz). PoNow (24) 79, p. 31.
"Study of Loneliness" (tr. of Czeslaw Milosz). PoNow (24) 79,
p. 31.

VALLEJO, Cesar
"confusion" (tr. by Joel Zeltzer). Wind (34) 79, p. 64.
"Funeral Train Following the Taking of Bilbao" (tr. by Alvaro
Cardona-Hine). PoNow (24) 79, p. 36.
"Masses" (tr. by Alvaro Cardona-Hine). PoNow (24) 79, p. 36.

Van BRUNT, H. L.
"Ossabaw Suite-IV. " GreenfieldR (7:3/4) Spr-Sum 79, p. 180.

VANCE, Ronald
"Speed Reading. " SunM (8) Aut 79, p. 128.

VANCE, Thomas
from Love Story of the Century: "No one" (tr. of Märta Tik-
kanen w. Vera Vance). Paint (12) Aut 79, p. 29.
from Love Story of the Century: "She curls up in my arms" (tr.
of Märta Tikkanen w. Vera Vance). Paint (12) Aut 79, p.
28.

VANCE, Vera
"The First Time. " Paint (11) Spr 79, p. 78.
from Love Story of the Century: "No one" (tr. of Märta Tik-
kanen w. Thomas Vance). Paint (12) Aut 79, p. 29.
from Love Story of the Century: "She curls up in my arms" (tr.
of Märta Tikkanen w. Thomas Vance). Paint (12) Aut 79, p.
28.
"Woman Combing the Lexicons. " NewEngR (1:3) Spr 79, p. 266.

Van DEMARR, Lee
"Anonymous. " Iowa (10:1) Wint 79, p. 45.
"In the Orchard. " Iowa (10:1) Wint 79, p. 44.

VANDER MOLEN, Robert
"Fog. " Epoch (28:2) Wint 79, pp. 193-201.
"Georgia. " Epoch (29:1) Aut 79, p. 9.
"A Story. " Epoch (28:2) Wint 79, p. 192.

VANDERSEE, Charles
"Summer as the Growing Season. " PoNow (22) 79, p. 44.

Van De WOESTIJNE, Karel
   "Fever Tune" (tr. by André Lefevere).   Paint (12) Aut 79, p. 26.

Van DUYN, Mona
   "The Ballad of Blossom. "   Poetry (134:5) Ag 79, pp. 287-291.
   "The Great American Poem. "   Antaeus (32) Wint 79, pp. 82-86.
   "Moose in the Morning, Northern Maine. "   NewYorker (55:32) 24
      S 79, p. 44.

Van GEEL, Christian J.
   "Wind is always driving, wind" (tr. by Emilie Peech and W. S.
      DiPiero).   PoNow (24) 79, p. 61.
   "View" (tr. by Emilie Peech and W. S. DiPiero).   PoNow (24)
      79, p. 61.

VANGELISTI, Paul
   "Hamlet, Clowns" (tr. of Adriano Spatola).   PoNow (24) 79, p.
      35.
   "Rosa in Luxembourg" (above all for Gigia and Marcello) (tr. of
      Adriano Spatola).   PoNow (24) 79, p. 35.
   "Yes. "   Bachy (15) Aut 79, p. 118.

Van KEUREN, Luise
   "A Woman on the Porch the Day of the Annual Meeting of the
      Thoreau Society. "   EnPas (8) 79, p. 27.

VANN, Anne
   "Epoch in Erie County. "   SmPd (46) 79, p. 6.
   "Still Life. "   SmPd (46) 79, p. 7.

Van OSTAIJEN, Paul
   "Homage to Singer" (tr. by Peter Nijmeijer).   Montra (5) 79, p.
      149.
Van REE, G.
   "white kite flying high. ... "   WindO (34) Spr-Sum 79, p. 7.

Van TASSEL, Katrina
   "The Old Mother. "   StoneC (6:3) O 79, p. 26.

Van WALLEGHEN, Michael
   "Crabapples. "   Ploughs (5:1) 79, pp. 142-143.
   "Do Not Dump Dead Animals. "   Hudson (32:4) Wint 79-80, p.
      527.
   "Driving into Enid" (for Louis Jenkins).   Hudson (32:4) Wint 79-
      80, p. 525.
   "The Fisherman. "   Ascent (4:2) 79, p. 59.
   "How the Fireman's Widow Became a Wasp. "   Ascent (4:2) 79, p.
      61.
   "More Trouble with the Obvious. "   Hudson (32:4) Wint 79-80, p.
      526.
   "Painting the Picture" (for James G. Davis).   Ploughs (5:1) 79,
      p. 140-141.
   "Reading the I Ching. "   Ascent (4:2) 79, p. 60.

"Some Observations by a Newlywed. " Ploughs (5:1) 79, pp. 139-140.

"Walking the Baby to the Liquor Store. " Hudson (32:4) Wint 79-80, p. 528.

Van WINCKEL, Nance
"Paradise in Bronze" (for Lorenzo Ghiberti). Chowder (13) Aut-Wint 79, p. 16.

VARELA, Beatriz
"After Such Pleasures" (tr. of Julio Cortázar w. Calvin Harlan and Manuel Menán). NewOR (6:2) 79, p. 103.
"Commission" (tr. of Julio Cortázar w. Calvin Harlan and Manuel Menán). NewOR (6:2) 79, p. 105.
"Gains and Losses" (tr. of Julio Cortázar w. Calvin Harlan and Manuel Menán). NewOR (6:2) 79, p. 104.
"Happy New Year" (tr. of Julio Cortázar w. Calvin Harlan and Manuel Menán). NewOR (6:2) 79, p. 104.
"Restitution" (tr. of Julio Cortázar w. Calvin Harlan and Manuel Menán). NewOR (6:2) 79, p. 102.

VARELA, Blanca
"Canto villano" (tr. by Elizabeth Hamilton). Field (21) Aut 79, p. 54.
"A Game" (tr. by Elizabeth Hamilton). Field (21) Aut 79, p. 51.
"Persona" (tr. by Elizabeth Hamilton). Field (21) Aut 79, p. 53.

VARGAS, Roberto
Tequila Bird Poems: Nineteen Poems. WormR (73) 79, pp. 15-26.
"Three ... retarded men who disappeared in. " Vaga (29) 79, p. 29.

VAS, István
"One of Us" (tr. by Nicholas Kolumban). TexQ (21:4) Wint 78, p. 29.

VAUGHAN, Frances Downing
"The New Calf. " Tendril (5) Sum 79, p. 50.

VEACH, Cynthia
"The Steer off I-80. " Chelsea (38) 79, p. 214.

VEENENDAAL, Cornelia
"Gate of Horn. " HangL (36) Aut 79, p. 71.
"Kayaks. " HangL (36) Aut 79, p. 70.
"Pancakes. " HangL (36) Aut 79, p. 71.

VEGA, Janine Pommy
"The Bard Owl. " Aspect (74/75) Ja-Ag 79, p. 109.
"Equinox. " Aspect (74/75) Ja-Ag 79, p. 110.
"Jameson's Whiskey. " Aspect (74/75) Ja-Ag 79, p. 108.

VEITCH, Tom
"A Day in the Life of Scrooge McDuck. " SunM (8) Aut 79, p.
57.

VELARDE, Ramon Lopez
"And to Think We Could Have... " (tr. by Douglas Eichhorn).
PoNow (24) 79, p. 23.
"My Heart Is Honored... " (tr. by Douglas Eichhorn). PoNow
(24) 79, p. 23.
"The Purple Blemish" (tr. by Douglas Eichhorn). PoNow (24)
79, p. 23.

VENCLOVA, Tomas
"I Will Mention the Colors" (tr. by Jonas Zdanys). SlowLR (3)
79, p. 72.
"The Room at a Glance" (tr. by Jonas Zdanys). SlowLR (3) 79,
p. 70.
"Slow down and stop. The sentence falls apart" (tr. by Vyt Ba-
kaitis). Pequod (3:1) 79, p. 38.

VENN, George
"Tame Oats. " PortR (25) 79, p. 134.

VENTSIAS, Roberta
"Equilibrium: 16. " ColEng (40:7) Mr 79, p. 785.
"To a Woman of Many Secrets. " ColEng (40:7) Mr 79, p. 786.

VENUTI, Lawrence
"The Edge" (tr. of Umberto Saba). PoNow (24) 79, p. 49.
"Lake" (tr. of Umberto Saba). PoNow (23) 79, p. 44.
"The Man Who Walks in the Woods" (tr. of Giorgio Orelli).
PoNow (24) 79, p. 39.
"The Mirror" (tr. of Umberto Saba). PoNow (24) 79, p. 50.
"Portrait of My Daughter" (tr. of Umberto Saba). PoNow (23)
79, p. 44.
"A Short Walk with Lucia in Autumn" (tr. of Giorgio Orelli).
PoNow (24) 79, p. 39.
"Smoke" (tr. of Umberto Saba). PoNow (23) 79, p. 44.
"Summer" (tr. of Giorgio Orelli). PoNow (24) 79, p. 39.
"To a Philologist" (tr. of Giorgio Orelli). PoNow (24) 79, p.
39.
"Woman" (tr. of Umberto Saba). PoNow (23) 79, p. 45.
"Work" (tr. of Umberto Saba). PoNow (23) 79, p. 45.
"Young Girl" (tr. of Umberto Saba). PoNow (24) 79, p. 50.

VERHAGEN, Hans
"Daydreams" (tr. by Rob Hollis Miller). Durak (3) 79, p. 18.

VERHULST, Pat
"Apocrypha. " LitR (22:3) Spr 79, p. 346.

VERLAINE, Paul
"Crimen Amoris" (to Villiers de l'Isle-Adam). SoDakR (17:1)

"Ode to the Muse on Behalf of a Young Poet. " Atl (243:3) Mr
  79, p. 89.
"Seeds. " NewYorker (55:11) 30 Ap 79, p. 96.
"Shadow. " WestHR (33:3) Sum 79, p. 205.
"The Singers. " PortR (25) 79, p. 103.
"Snow Goose and Southwind's Daughter. " PoNow (21) 79, p. 30.
"Song for the Fishing of the Dead. " PoNow (21) 79, p. 30.
from The Songs of He-Catches-Nothing: Eight Poems. PoNow
  (21) 79, pp. 12-13.
"To a Panhandler Who, for a Quarter, Said 'God Bless You. '"
  Poetry (133:4) Ja 79, p. 189.
"To the Fly in My Drink. " CarolQ (31:2) Spr-Sum 79, p. 84.
"Wading in a Marsh. " Poetry (133:4) Ja 79, pp. 192-193.
"Wild Man. " NowestR (18:1) 79, p. 26.
"Woman-Asleep. " NowestR (18:1) 79, p. 25.
"Your Fortune: A Cold Reading. " Kayak (51) S 79, p. 36.

WAINIO, Ken
"Getting Rid of the Ego. " SeC (6:2) 78, p. 92.
"In a Swoon I Can See It. " SeC (6:2) 78, p. 89.
"Space Age. " SeC (6:2) 78, p. 91.

WAKOSKI, Diane
"Bracelets. " SouthernR (15:1) Wint 79, p. 139.
"Calla Lily. " MissouriR (3:1) Aut 79, p. 13.
"For a Man Who Learned to Swim When He Was Sixty. " NewL
  (45:3) Spr 79, p. 57.
"Measuring. " NewL (45:3) Spr 79, p. 55.
"On the Subject of Roses. " SouthernR (15:1) Wint 79, p. 138.
"Red Runner. " CornellR (7) Aut 79, p. 93.
"Red Runner Again. " CornellR (7) Aut 79, p. 94.

WALCOTT, Derek
"In the Virgins" (for Bill and Pat Strachan). Antaeus (33) Spr
  79, p. 59.

WALD, Diane
"Character. " Pequod (3:1) 79, p. 52.
"Customs. " ArkRiv (4:3) 79, p. 35.
"Edward's Roller Coaster. " ArkRiv (4:3) 79, p. 35.
"The Full Day. " Pequod (3:1) 79, pp. 50-51.
"Magic Almost Makes Me Cry. " Kayak (51) S 79, p. 57.
"Note to Myself. " ArkRiv (4:3) 79, p. 34.

WALDMAN, Anne
"Left Hands. " Paint (11) Spr 79, p. 80.

WALDROP, Keith
"How to Tell Distances. " PartR (46:3) 79, pp. 431-432.
"I Wander Down. " OP (28) Aut 79, pp. 38-39.
"Message. " OP (28) Aut 79, p. 40.
from The Ruins of Providence (for Elsie Michie): "Lullaby in
  January. " Poetry (133:4) Ja 79, p. 194.

from The Ruins of Providence (for Elsie Michie):   "Around the
    Block. " Poetry (133:4) Ja 79, p. 195.
"Signals. " OP (28) Aut 79, p. 43.
"Translation Song. " OP (28) Aut 79, pp. 41-42.

WALDROP, Rosmarie
"Home Drown. " DenQ (14:2) Sum 79, pp. 28-33.
"The Senses Grossly. " Montra (5) 79, p. 158.
from Yael: "Fear of Time" (tr. of Edmond Jabes).   Montra (6)
    79, p. 63.
from Yael: "My Characters In and Outside the Book. " (tr. of
    Edmond Jabes). Montra (6) 79, p. 56.
from Yael: "The Light of the Sea" (tr. of Edmond Jabes).
    Montra (6) 79, p. 61.

WALKER, Brad
"Instructions for a Park. " Shen (30:2) Wint 79, p. 94.

WALKER, David
"The Boy on the Waterville Bridge. " Poetry (133:6) Mr 79, p.
    329.
"An Early Evening in Late Summer. " NewEngR (1:3) Spr 79, p.
    349.
"The Fire in Winter" (for Frances). NewEngR (1:3) Spr 79, p.
    348.
"Fishing the Maze. " NewEngR (1:3) Spr 79, p. 347.
"The Maker of Postcards. " Poetry (133:6) Mr 79, pp. 326-327.
"Message from a Grave. " Poetry (133:6) Mr 79, p. 328.
"Passages" (for F. S. , 1949-1978). GeoR (33:2) Sum 79, p. 298.
"Pigeons, Swallows, and Co. " Poetry (133:6) Mr 79, p. 330.

WALKER, Jeanne Murray
"Deliver me, O Lord from my Daily Bread. " CimR (46) Ja 79,
    p. 38.
"Driving North to the Headwater. " CharR (5:2) Aut 79, p. 31.
"Hand on the Faucet. " CarolQ (31:2) Spr-Sum 79, p. 50.
"On Seeing Children's Snowball Fights: A Conservative Sestina. "
    PoetC (11:1) 79, p. 8.
"The Other. " PoetC (11:1) 79, p. 6.
"Tracking the Sled, Christmas 1951. " CharR (5:2) Aut 79, p.
    28.
"Vespers of a Wall-Paper Stripper. " PoetC (10:3) 79, p. 36.
"Waiting for Midnight in Spring. " CharR (5:2) Aut 79, p. 29.

WALKER, John David
"Fathers and Sons. " PoNow (25) 79, p. 42.

WALKER, Joseph
"Man to Man. " PoNow (25) 79, p. 42.

WALKER, Lawrie
"Landscape. " Stand (20:4) 79, p. 40.
"Old Master. " Stand (20:4) 79, p. 41.

WALKER, Lois V.
"Metaphors." WestB (4) 79, p. 56.

WALLACE, Jon
"Puberty." KanQ (11:1/2) Wint-Spr 79, p. 104.

WALLACE, Robert
"Apartment Hunting." DenQ (14:2) Sum 79, p. 99.
"Dog's Song." PoNow (21) 79, p. 4.
"I Go on Talking to You." DenQ (14:2) Sum 79, p. 101.
"Lucky to Have Warmed Himself." DenQ (14:2) Sum 79, p. 100.
"Monday, the Invention Of." DenQ (14:2) Sum 79, p. 98.
"Starfish." SouthernR (15:1) Wint 79, p. 101.

WALLACE, Ronald
"At the Dolphin Show." Poem (36) Jl 79, p. 2.
"Daybreak." PoetC (10:3) 79, p. 22.
"The Death of the Fat Girl." PoNow (25) 79, p. 29.
"December." Poem (36) Jl 79, p. 1.
"Exhibitionist." CarlMis (17:2/3) Spr 79, p. 170.
"Installing the Bees." PoNow (25) 79, p. 29.
"The Magician's Lunch" (for Dave). CharR (5:2) Aut 79, p. 23.
"On a Morning Like This I Should Have Gone Fishing." HiramPoR
    (26) Spr-Sum 79, p. 35.
"Stillborn." KanQ (11:1/2) Wint-Spr 79, p. 115.
"Trumpeter's Holiday." HiramPoR (26) Spr-Sum 79, p. 35.
"Who Art in Heaven." SouthernPR (19:2) Aut 79, p. 67.
"Winter Song." KanQ (11:1/2) Wint-Spr 79, p. 115.

WALLACH, Yonah
"Stones Are Undone by the River" (tr. by Bernhard Frank).
    PoNow (24) 79, p. 62.

WALLENSTEIN, Barry
"Do It Now." Sky (9) Aut 79, p. 51.

WALLING, Donovan R.
"One Last Dance." Poem (36) Jl 79, p. 22.

WALLS, Doyle Wesley
"The Boy-Jesus." Bits (10) Jl 79.

WALSH, Charlie
"Hymn No. 29." Spirit (3:1/2) Aut-Wint 77-78, p. 11.

WALSH, Joan
"Winter Devotions: Six O'Clock Mass." Comm (106:23) 21 D
    79, p. 726.

WALSH, Marty
"Chrome Faucets." Poem (37) N 79, p. 26.
"Dragonfly." Poem (37) N 79, p. 24.
"His Funerary Throne." Poem (37) N 79, p. 25.
"Hospital Visit." Poem (37) N 79, p. 23.

WALTER, Kenneth
"Holding On." KanQ (11:1/2) Wint-Spr 79, p. 194.

WALTERS, Tim
"The Offering." FourQt (28:3) Spr 79, p. 17.

WALTHALL, Hugh
"Thanksgiving Fantasy." Shen (30:2) Wint 79, p. 93.
"Translation." Shen (30:1) Aut 78, p. 46.

WANEK, Connie
"Lake in February." PraS (53:1) Spr 79, p. 71.

WANG, Karl
"Canary Cage." PikeF (2) Wint 78-79, p. 21.

WANGBERG, Mark
"Morning." PoNow (25) 79, p. 42.
"You." PoNow (25) 79, p. 42.

WANGERIN, Walter Jr.
"Mosquito." ChrC (96:3) 24 Ja 79, p. 71.

WANIEK, Marilyn Nelson
"Herbs in the Attic" (for Amanda Jordan). GeoR (33:4) Wint 79,
p. 898.
"Night Harvest." CarlMis (17:2/3) Spr 79, p. 175.
"Naming the Animal." CarlMis (17:2/3) Spr 79, p. 174.

WANNBERG, Scott D.
"Marriage." Ur (2) 79, p. 122.

WARD, Candice
"The Curse." DenQ (14:3) Aut 79, p. 68.
"The First Hermit." DenQ (14:3) Aut 79, p. 67.
"Hilarious Hilary." DenQ (14:3) Aut 79, p. 66.
"This Window." DenQ (14:3) Aut 79, p. 69.

WARD, Dave
"Sally." Ur (2) 79, p. 124.

WARD, Robert
"Adam." CutB (12) Spr-Sum 79, p. 54.
"Flora in Sparks." QW (9) Spr-Sum 79, p. 112.

WARDEN, Marine Robert
Eight Poems. Bachy (15) Aut 79, pp. 23-27.

WARE, Freddie
"Dreamer." BlackF (3:1) Aut-Wint 79, p. 35.

WARE, Patricia
"The Bones." PortR (25) 79, p. 35.

"The Pig Saga. " CutB (12) Spr-Sum 79, p. 48.
"The Taped Alternative: At the Fillmore" (for Philip Levine).
   PortR (25) 79, p. 34.
"The tide that does not go out. " PortR (25) 79, p. 33.

WARMBROD, Nancy Compton
"Aunt Linie's Harvest. " Poem (35) Mr 79, p. 20.
"Loss. " Poem (35) Mr 79, p. 19.
"Marriage. " Poem (35) Mr 79, p. 17.
"Remembered Essence. " Poem (35) Mr 79, p. 18.

WARREN, Eugene
"Christographia 33. " WebR (4:3) Spr 79, p. 41.

WARREN, Larkin
"Barbara's Hair. " QW (9) Spr-Sum 79, p. 15.
"Misery Loves" (for B. and B.). Tendril (4) Wint 79, p. 49.

WARREN, Lisa
"For a Wizard Lover. " Vaga (29) 79, p. 41.

WARREN, Robert Penn
"Acquaintance with Time in Autumn. " NewYorker (55:30) 10 S
   79, p. 46.
"Aging Man at Noon in Timeless Noon of Summer. " SouthernR
   (15:4) Aut 79, p. 996.
"Antinomy: Time and Identity. " YaleR (68:4) Sum 79, p. 540.
"Aspen Leaf in Windless World. " Poetry (135:2) N 79, pp. 83-
   84.
"August Moon. " NewYorker (55:30) 10 S 79, p. 47.
"Auto-da-fê. " NewYorker (55:46) 31 D 79, p. 28.
"Dreaming in Daylight. " Salm (46) Aut 79, p. 4.
"Filling Night with the Name. " Salm (46) Aut 79, p. 10.
"Globe of Gneiss. " Salm (46) Aut 79, p. 6.
"Grackles, Goodbye! " Salm (46) Aut 79, p. 9.
"Language Problem. " SouthernR (15:4) Aut 79, p. 997.
"Lessons in History. " AmerPoR (8:4) Jl-Ag 79, p. 5.
"The Moonlight's Dream. " Poetry (135:2) N 79, pp. 81-82.
"Night Walking. " AmerPoR (8:4) Jl-Ag 79, p. 48.
"No Bird Does Call. " AmerPoR (8:1) Ja-F 79, p. 3.
"October Picnic Long Ago. " Atl (244:4) O 79, p. 79.
"On into the Night. " Salm (46) Aut 79, p. 11.
"The Only Poem. " AmerPoR (8:4) Jl-Ag 79, p. 5.
"Part of a Short Story. " GeoR (33:1) Spr 79, p. 86.
"Prairie Harvest. " Salm (46) Aut 79, p. 6.
"Preternaturally Early Snowfall in Mating Season. " NewYorker
   (55:30) 10 S 79, p. 46.
"Snowshoeing Back to Camp in Gloaming. " NewEngR (1:3) Spr
   79, p. 263.
"Speleology. " NewYorker (55:30) 10 S 79, p. 47.
"Swimming in the Pacific. " AmerPoR (8:1) Ja-F 79, p. 5.
"Synonyms" (to A. T.). Poetry (135:2) N 79, pp. 76-80.
"Timeless, Twinned. " NewEngR (1:3) Spr 79, p. 265.

"Tires on Wet Asphalt at Night." AmerPoR (8:1) Ja-F 79, p. 4.
"Trips to California." NewYRB (26:12) 19 Jl 79, p. 24.
"Truth." YaleR (68:4) Sum 79, p. 541.
"Weather Report." NewEngR (1:3) Spr 79, p. 262.
"What Is the Voice that Speaks." YaleR (68:4) Sum 79, p. 542.
"When Life Begins." Salm (46) Aut 79, p. 8.

WARREN, Rosanna
"Alps." YaleR (68:4) Sum 79, p. 544.
from Chagall: "The Field." Atl (244:1) Jl 79, p. 58.
"Drowned Son." NewEngR (1:4) Sum 79, p. 442.
"Illustrated History." YaleR (68:4) Sum 79, p. 545.
"Omalos." YaleR (68:4) Sum 79, p. 546.
"Waking." YaleR (68:4) Sum 79, p. 546.

WARSHAWSKI, Morrie
"Dancer Fixing Her Shoulder Strap." Aspect (74/75) Ja-Ag 79,
    p. 6.

WASSON, Audrey
"Going Under." Ascent (4:3) 79, p. 26.
"Pointillism: After a Nightmare." Ascent (4:3) 79, p. 27.

WATERHOUSE, Elizabeth
"The Man in the Common." Ploughs (5:3) 79, pp. 66-67. Cor-
    rected version printed in Ploughs (5:4) 79, p. 171.
"Trick of Turning." HarvAd (112:4) My 79, p. 28.

WATERMAN, Andrew
"Love Sequence" (for V.). Hudson (32:1) Spr 79, pp. 31-35.

WATERMAN, Cary
"Me, Learning to Dance." Tendril (5) Sum 79, p. 51.

WATERS, Michael
"Among Blackberries." GeoR (33:3) Aut 79, p. 532.
"Instinct" (for my uncle). FourQt (29:1) Aut 79, p. 23.

WATKINS, Barbara
"The Previous Tenant." ArkRiv (4:3) 79, p. 36.

WATKINS, Mary
"Come on Home." Cond (5) 79, p. 154.

WATSON, Burton
Eighteen poems (tr. of Lady Kasa). Montra (5) 79, p. 123.
Eleven poems (tr. of Lady Ise). Montra (5) 79, p. 133.
Nineteen poems (tr. of Ono No Komachi). Montra (5) 79, p.
    128.

WATSON, Celia
"Essences" (for John Crowe Ransom). BallSUF (20:4) Aut 79,
    p. 56.

"5th. " LittleM (12:1/2) Spr-Sum 78 (79), p. 5.
"7th. " LittleM (12:1/2) Spr-Sum 78 (79), p. 6.

WATSON, Craig
"June. " MichQR (18:3) Sum 79, p. 409.

WATSON, Ken
"Dreaming. " MalR (49) Ja 79, p. 124.
"Lorelei. " MalR (49) Ja 79, p. 125.

WAUGAMAN, Charles A.
"Day Before Spring. " Wind (32) 79, p. 48.

WAX, Judith
"That Was the Year That Was. " Playb (26:1) Ja 79, p. 260.

WAYMAN, Tom
"Detroit Poem" (for Jim Gustafson). MassR (20:1) Spr 79, p.
   41.
"The Detroit State Poems: A Decade from the Riots. " MinnR
   (NS 13) Aut 79, p. 10.
"The Detroit State Poems: Security. " LittleM (12:1/2) Spr-Sum
   78 (79), p. 9.
"Pickup Cowboy. " Confr (19) Aut 79-Wint 80, p. 175.
"Thinning Carrots. " LittleM (12:1/2) Spr-Sum 78 (79), p. 11.

WEBB, Bernice Larson
"Glass Cage. " StoneC (6:1) F 79, p. 7.
"Snow-Blind. " CEACritic (41:4) My 79, p. 29.
"Span. " KanQ (11:1/2) Wint-Spr 79, p. 144.

WEBB, Charles
"The Bumblebee. " PoNow (22) 79, p. 45.
"Fat Guy. " PoNow (22) 79, p. 45.
"Fish City. " PoNow (25) 79, p. 30.
"The Garbage Lover. " PoNow (25) 79, p. 30.
"The Man-Eating Lake. " PoNow (22) 79, p. 45.
"Return of the Beach Bums. " PoNow (22) 79, p. 45.

WEBB, Martha
"The Bar Downstairs. " Pequod (3:1) 79, p. 79.

WEBBER, Joan Malory
"Wife. " MinnR (NS 12) Spr 79, p. 44.

WEBER, Elizabeth
"Small Mercies. " Tendril (4) Wint 79, p. 48.

WEBER, James
"As Night Begins Her Slow Descent. " Poem (36) Jl 79, p. 24.
"Evening. " Poem (36) Jl 79, p. 26.
"Position. " Poem (36) Jl 79, p. 23.
"A Sound at Morning. " StoneC (6:3) O 79, p. 19.
"Three Poems. " Poem (36) Jl 79, p. 25.

WEBER, R. B.
    "Midwest Directions." PoNow (23) 79, p. 17.

WEBER, Ron
    "The Bicycle Man." PoNow (25) 79, p. 42.

WEBSTER, Lee
    "Warehouse Song." KanQ (11:3) Sum 79, p. 92.

WEEDEN, Craig
    "The Famous Outlaw Returns to His Love." SmPd (45) 79, p.
        12.
    "Moths in the Granola." SouthernPR (19:1) Spr 79, p. 33.
    "A Pizza Joint in Cranston." Poultry (1) 79, p. 3.
    "Yachting in Arkansas." Chowder (12) Spr-Sum 79, p. 28.

WEEKS, James
    "Lepers" (tr. of Aloysius Bertrand). Field (20) Spr 79, p. 48.
    "Messire jean" (tr. of Aloysius Bertrand). Field (20) Spr 79,
        p. 47.

WEEKS, Ramona
    "Glycerine Soap." 13thM (4:2) 79, p. 7.
    "The Necessary Appointment." 13thM (42) 79, p. 6.
    "Second Poem for Clarence." Chelsea (38) 79, p. 120.

WEIDMAN, Phil
    "A Familiar Addiction." WormR (76) 79, p. 130.
    "Fix." WormR (76) 79, p. 129.
    "Four Connections." WormR (76) 79, p. 129.
    "Heading Home." WormR (76) 79, p. 130.
    "Missed Work Friday." WormR (76) 79, p. 129.
    "Short." WormR (76) 79, p. 129.
    "Thanksgiving Morning." WormR (76) 79, p. 129.

WEIGEL, Tom
    "American Way" (to Harns Schiff). Tele (15) Spr 79, p. 70.
    "Audrey Hepburn's Symphonic Salad and the Coming of Autumn"
        (to France). Tele (15) Spr 79, p. 72.
    "Cheers" (for everybody). Tele (15) Spr 79, p. 74.
    "Club 57." Tele (15) Spr 79, p. 73.
    "The Coast Is Clear" (for Rene Ricard) (w. Greg Masters).
        Tele (15) Spr 79, p. 66.
    "To Fritz Lang" (w. Greg Masters). Tele (15) Spr 79, p. 67.
    "Video Bust" (w. Greg Masters). Tele (15) Spr 79, p. 66.

WEIGL, Bruce
    "The Akron, Ohio Limb and Crutch Company." PoNow (22) 79,
        p. 45.
    "A Childhood." Field (21) Aut 79, p. 60.
    "Dorothy Wordsworth" (for B. T.). Field (21) Aut 79, p. 61.
    "Eclipse" (for my father). NewEngR (2:1) Aut 79, p. 88.
    "The Life Before Fear." OhioR (20:2) Spr-Sum 79, p. 89.

"The Limits of Departure. " CimR (49) O 79, p. 48.
"On this Spot. " PoNow (22) 79, p. 45.
"Sailing to Bien Hoa. " WestHR (33:1) Wint 79, p. 56.
"The String Quartet. " WestHR (33:1) Wint 79, p. 18.
"Temple Near Quang Tri, Not on the Map. " NewEngR (2:1) Aut
    79, p. 87.
"The Town Inside. " CimR (49) O 79, p. 64.
"Vaudeville. " CimR (49) O 79, p. 18.

WEINBERG, Cindy
"Summer Solstice. " Chomo (6:1) Sum 79, p. 50.
"Untitled: there are days. " Chomo (6:1) Sum 79, p. 54.
"you give me an iris and propose marriage. " Chomo (6:1) Sum
    79, p. 52.

WEINBERGER, Eliot
"Black and White Stone" (tr. of Octavio Paz). Nat (229:10) 6 O
    79, p. 316.
"Burn the Boats" (tr. of Homero Aridjis). DenQ (14:1) Spr 79,
    p. 41.
"Concert in the Garden" (for Carmen Figueroa de Meyer) (tr. of
    Octavio Paz). Nat (228:23) 16 Je 79, p. 733.
"A Draft of Shadows" (tr. of Octavio Paz). Montra (5) 79, p.
    85.
"Dream in Tenochtitlán" (tr. of Homero Aridjis). DenQ (14:1)
    Spr 79, p. 42.
"Epitaph for No Stone" (tr. of Octavio Paz). DenQ (14:1) Spr
    79, p. 14.
"Golden Lotuses (3)" (tr. of Octavio Paz). Nat (229:9) 29 S 79,
    p. 282.
"Immemorial Landscape" (for José de la Colina) (tr. of Octavio
    Paz). Nat (228:23) 16 Je 79, p. 732.
"In the Middle of This Phrase" (tr. of Octavio Paz). ParisR
    (75) Spr 79, pp. 24-28.
"Ipanema" (tr. of Gabriel Zaid). DenQ (14:1) Spr 79, p. 82.
"Late Again" (tr. of Gabriel Zaid). DenQ (14:1) Spr 79, p. 83.
"Letter from Mexico" (tr. of Homero Aridjis). DenQ (14:1) Spr
    79, p. 44.
"Nightfall" (tr. of Octavio Paz). Nat (228:24) 23 Je 79, p. 764.
"The Prophecy of Man" (tr. of Homero Aridjis). DenQ (14:1)
    Spr 79, p. 47.
"Sun Set" (tr. of Homero Aridjis). DenQ (14:1) Spr 79, p. 46.
"A Tale of Two Gardens" (tr. of Octavio Paz). Montra (5) 79,
    p. 64.
"There Are Birds in this Land" (tr. of Homero Aridjis). DenQ
    (14:1) Spr 79, p. 45.
"With Eyes Closed" (tr. of Octavio Paz). Nat (229:5) 25 Ag-1 S
    79, p. 154.

WEINER, Hannah
"Little Books Indians: Page 2 Numbered. " SunM (8) Aut 79, pp.
    141-153.

WEINGARTEN, Roger
"Memoir." Poetry (133:4) Ja 79, pp. 199-200.
"The Night-Blooming Cereus." Shen (30:1) Aut 78, p. 68.
"Under the Wine Tree at the Edge of Desire." Poetry (133:4) Ja
79, pp. 201-202.
"Victorian Bacchanal." Poetry (133:4) Ja 79, pp. 203-204.

WEINMAN, Paul
"Arms Poised." Chelsea (38) 79, p. 207.
"In the Picture." Chelsea (38) 79, p. 104.

WEINRAUB, Richard
"awake and remember." Mouth (2:1) F 79, p. 35.
"bones." Mouth (2:1) F 79, p. 35.
"Bread Belly." Mouth (2:1) F 79, p. 29.
"untitled: after daniel's gone." Mouth (2:1) F 79, p. 35.

WEISBERG, Eleanor
"Love Poem to My Psychoanalyst--26." AAR (29) 79, p. 121.

WEISS, Irving
from Sens Magique: Fourteen poems (tr. of Malcolm de Chazal).
Chelsea (38) 79, p. 20.

WEISS, Jason
"Epitaph of a Mariner" (tr. of Silvina Ocampo). NewEngR (1:4)
Sum 79, p. 432.
"In Front of the Seine, Recalling the Rio de la Plata" (for Octa-
vio Paz) (tr. of Silvina Ocampo). NewEngR (1:4) Sum 79,
p. 431.
"Infinite Horses" (tr. of Silvina Ocampo). PraS (53:3) Aut 79, p.
210.
"Sleep's Persuasion" (tr. of Silvina Ocampo). PraS (53:3) Aut
79, p. 211.
"To My Desperation" (tr. of Silvina Ocampo). PraS (53:3) Aut
79, p. 209.

WEISS, Ruth
"Anaïs." SeC (6:2) 78, p. 55.
"Coyote" (for John Rampley). SeC (6:2) 78, p. 57.
"Dean Antony." SeC (6:2) 78, p. 59.
"Sena." SeC (6:2) 78, p. 58.
"Tse-Wah-Te-Ay." SeC (6:2) 78, p. 60.

WEISS, Sanford
"His Coming and His Going." Kayak (50) My 79, p. 50.
"Landscape with Cow." Kayak (50) My 79, p. 50.
"Resemblances." Kayak (50) My 79, p. 51.
"Ten Words." Kayak (50) My 79, p. 49.
"Two Things." Kayak (50) My 79, p. 49.

WEISS, Sigmund
"Lack of Advice." Mouth (2:2) Je 79, p. 23.
"Let Madness Rock You." Mouth (2:3) N 79, p. 29.
"An Old Friend." Mouth (2:1) F 79, p. 45.

WEISS, Theodore
"At Any Moment More Than Two Billion Pints of Blood Are Cir-
culating in the United States. '" Nat (229:17) 24 N 79, p.
538.
"En Route" (for Harry and Kathleen). NewRep (180:23) 9 Je 79,
p. 30.
"The Great American Poem. " Antaeus (32) Wint 79, pp. 82-86.

WEITZMAN, Sarah Brown
"Snake Hate. " Tendril (6) Aut 79, p. 38.

WELCH, Don
"The Blind Girl. " PoetC (11:1) 79, p. 26.
"A Portrait of Nuns and Indians. " HiramPoR (26) Spr-Sum 79,
p. 36.
"The Runner. " Ur (2) 79, p. 123.

WELCH, James
"The Great American Poem. " Antaeus (32) Wint 79, pp. 82-86.

WELISH, Marjorie
"Foyer. " SunM (8) Aut 79, p. 98.
"October Screen. " SunM (8) Aut 79, p. 97.

WELLS, Will
"The Aerosol Organ. " HiramPoR (26) Spr-Sum 79, p. 37.
"The River Is Wide. " SouthernPR (19:1) Spr 79, p. 38.
"Two Climbers Dead on the Middle Flatiron. " HiramPoR (26)
Spr-Sum 79, p. 38.

WELSH, William
"The Best Cup of Coffee I Ever Had. " SlowLR (3) 79, p. 33.

WELSH, William
"Carbon. " NewOR (6:3) 79, p. 238.
"Take Five. " NewOR (6:3) 79, p. 239.

WENDT, Ingrid
"Moving the House. " PoNow (25) 79, p. 43.
"Starting from Scratch. " PoNow (25) 79, p. 43.

WENRICH, Douglass
"A Bolt Like Lightning. " PikeF (2) Wint 78-79, p. 7.

WEÖRES, Sandor
"My Poem" (tr. by Nicholas Kolumban). PoNow (24) 79, p. 62.
"One-Liners and Other Aphorisms" (tr. by Robert Zend). MalR
(49) Ja 79, p. 105.
"The Tomb of the Kennedys" (tr. by Nicholas Kolumban). PoNow
(24) 79, p. 62.

WEST, Anthony A.
"Going Places. " Epoch (28:2) Wint 79, p. 167.

WEST, Jon W.
  "B. S. and Fast Facts. " BelPoJ (30:2) Wint 79-80, p. 22.
  "Last Running Man. " BelPoJ (30:2) Wint 79-80, p. 21.

WEST, Michael
  "Propertius 3.13. " MichQR (18:4) Aut 79, p. 606.

WEST, William
  "The Ladies and the Candle. " Playb (26:11) N 79, p. 187.
  "Man's Yard of Stuff. " Playb (26:11) N 79, p. 187.

WESTBROOK, Donna
  "Untitled: Somewhere within you, live I. " BlackF (3:1) Aut-Wint
     79, p. 27.

WESTENHOVER, James Conroy
  "The Log Pond at Sunset. " PoNow (25) 79, p. 43.

WESTERFIELD, Hargis
  "Chapel at Darkfall. " ChrC (96:10) 21 Mr 79, p. 310.

WESTERFIELD, Nancy G.
  "Carolers. " ChrC (96:42) 19 D 79, p. 1261.
  "A Chart Unfiled. " Confr (18) Spr 79, p. 23.
  "Lares and Penates. " WestHR (33:1) Wint 79, p. 61.
  "One Married to Another One. " ColEng (40:5) Ja 79, p. 524.
  "A Slice of Her Life. " ChrC (96:11) 28 Mr 79, p. 347.
  "Where I Walk in Nebraska. " KanQ (11:1/2) Wint-Spr 79, p. 203.

WESTLAKE, Wayne
  "Half My Face Is Falling Off. " EnPas (9) 79, p. 15.

WESTON, Susan
  "Falling in the Dark. " BelPoJ (29:3) Spr 79, p. 22.

WESTWOOD, Norma
  "Castle. " Wind (33) 79, p. 57.
  "The Enclosure. " Wind (33) 79, p. 56.
  "Light Years. " EnPas (9) 79, p. 12.
  "Remember the Painters Who Left. " Wind (33) 79, p. 57.
  "Two Apples. " PraS (53:1) Spr 79, p. 74.
  "The Walnut Tree. " PraS (53:1) Spr 79, p. 74.

WETZEL, Robin
  "Anthem. " KanQ (11:1/2) Wint-Spr 79, p. 182.

WHALEN, Tom
  "Double Head" (tr. of Henri Michaux w. Michelle Benoit).
     Chelsea (38) 79, p. 27.
  "He Writes" (tr. of Henri Michaux w. Michelle Benoit). NewOR
     (6:2) 79, p. 151.
  "The Old Vulture" (tr. of Henri Michaux w. Michelle Benoit).
     Chelsea (38) 79, p. 27.
  "Problems in Space. " Tele (15) Spr 79, p. 120.

WHEALDON, Everett
  Blanket Bill. Sam (73) 79. Entire issue.

WHEATCROFT, John
  "Night Walk." GreenfieldR (7:3/4) Spr-Sum 79, p. 110.
  "The Seers." KanQ (11:3) Sum 79, p. 111.
  "The Ways of Memory." KanQ (11:3) Sum 79, p. 110.

WHEELER, Sylvia
  "Hotel and Cafe Poem." DacTerr (16) 79, p. 64.

WHISLER, Robert F.
  Poem. St.AR (5:2) 79, p. 58.
  "Spaced Out Lady of Leonardo's Unearthly Imago." HolCrit (16:
    5) D 79, p. 15.

WHITE, Gail
  "Return to Astolat." Aspect (74/75) Ja-Ag 79, p. 14.
  "The Wrestlers." ChrC (96:6) 21 F 79, p. 173.

WHITE, J. P.
  "Burning Daylight." KanQ (11:1/2) Wint-Spr 79, p. 126.

WHITE, Jacqueline
  "A Lover's Rebuke." Tele (15) Spr 79, p. 94.
  "27 May 1978." Tele (15) Spr 79, p. 94.

WHITE, James L.
  "The Clay Dancer." DacTerr (16) 79, pp. 65-69.
  "Submission to Death." KanQ (11:3) Sum 79, p. 26.
  "Submission to Silence." KanQ (11:3) Sum 79, p. 26.

WHITE, Mary Jane
  "The Baker on Wednesday." PortR (25) 79, p. 139.
  "Columbus and Isabella." ArkRiv (4:3) 79, p. 15.
  "I Have Stolen Away from the World." ArkRiv (4:3) 79, p. 14.
  "The Men Who Are My Hero." PortR (25) 79, p. 140.

WHITE, William M.
  "Susan's Journey." SouthernR (15:2) Spr 79, pp. 395-399.

WHITEBIRD, J.
  "Lesson." SeC (6:2) 78, p. 129.
  "Shadows." SeC (6:2) 78, p. 131.
  "The View from JB's Window" (for my friend, JB). SeC (6:2)
    78, p. 127.

WHITMAN, Cedric
  "Dissonance." Poetry (134:2) My 79, p. 85.

WHITMAN, Ruth
  "Human Geography." MassR (20:2) Sum 79, p. 336.
  "Traveling." PoNow (23) 79, p. 35.

WHITTEMORE, Reed
"The Great American Poem. " Antaeus (32) Wint 79, pp. 82-86.

WHITTLE, Sister Elizabeth
"at our house. " SmF (7/8) Spr-Aut 78, p. 42.
"plate lunch. " SmF (7/8) Spr-Aut 78, p. 43.

WHYATT, Frances
"Middleton Plantation Gardens, South Carolina. " Chelsea (38)
79, p. 124.
"Shandaken's Widow and the Greening of May. " Chelsea (38) 79,

WHYTE, Robert
"Awake or Asleep. " WormR (73) 79, p. 29.

WICKELHAUS, Martha
"The Nude. " QW (8) Wint 79, p. 36.

WICKERSHAM, Carol
"Making Love to Animals. " Ascent (4:3) 79, p. 9.

WIEDER, Laurance
"Credulous, All Gold. " NewYorker (54:49) 22 Ja 79, p. 32.

WIER, Dara
"Ernie, Lucille, Wanda and Midge Gather Together at the Sea
Train Inn. " QW (6) Spr-Sum 78, p. 49.
"It Wasn't God Who Made Honky Tonk Angels. " QW (6) Spr-Sum
78, p. 47.
"Lucille's Butcher Slaughters a Chicken. " QW (6) Spr-Sum 78,
p. 47.
"On Awakening, Lucille Dresses for Work. " QW (6) Spr-Sum 78,
p. 48.

WIERZYNSKI, Kazimierz
"Art and the Bitch" (tr. by Andrzej Busza and Bogdan Czaykow-
ski). Durak (3) 79, p. 14.

WIGHTMAN, D. D.
"Adult Education. " Wind (35) 79, p. 63.

WILBUR, Richard
"For W. H. Auden. " Atl (244:4) O 79, p. 98.
"The Great American Poem. " Antaeus (32) Wint 79, pp. 82-86.
"Gnomons. " Iowa (10:2) Spr 79, p. 97.
"Icarium Mare. " NewYorker (55:18) 18 Je 79, p. 34.
"Six Years Later" (tr. of Joseph Brodsky). NewYorker (54:46)
1 Ja 79, p. 30.
"Transit. " NewYorker (54:48) 15 Ja 79, p. 38.

WILD, Peter
"Buttercups. " AmerPoR (8:4) Jl-Ag 79, p. 47.
"Cave Moss. " PraS (53:1) Spr 79, p. 68.

"Chestnuts." Aspect (74/75) Ja-Ag 79, p. 3.
"The Clawfoot." PoNow (21) 79, p. 18.
"Coronado." PraS (53:1) Spr 79, p. 69.
"Cousin." AAR (29) 79, p. 50.
"Farmer." NowestR (18:1) 79, p. 73.
"German Shepherds." Ploughs (5:1) 79, pp. 145-146.
"Ice Cream." QW (9) Spr-Sum 79, p. 116.
"Intuition." NowestR (18:2) 79, p. 17.
"John Burroughs on Darwin." Bits (10) Jl 79.
"Maids." CharR (5:2) Aut 79, p. 76.
"Marines." CharR (5:2) Aut 79, p. 76.
"Mayonnaise." SouthernPR (19:2) Aut 79, p. 6.
"My Dog and I Get Chased by a Rainstorm." LittleM (12:1/2)
    Spr-Sum 78 (79), p. 46.
"Navigator." NowestR (18:1) 79, p. 74.
"Paintings." SouthernPR (19:2) Aut 79, p. 7.
"Rapids." Aspect (74/75) Ja-Ag 79, p. 3.
"Reveille." ChiR (31:2) Aut 79, p. 12.
"St. Louis." PortR (25) 79, p. 118.

WILEY, Bennie
"Just Another Bad Ass Day." BlackF (3:1) Aut-Wint 79, p. 23.

WILJER, Robert
"The Equine Spectacle." SouthernR (15:1) Wint 79, p. 136.

WILKINS, W. R.
"for a time." SeC (6:1) 78, p. 53.
"Untitled: swingin' down the street." SeC (6:1) 78, p. 54.

WILKINSON, C. E.
"The Woman of Andahvaylas." HangL (35) Spr 79, p. 66.

WILL, Frederic
"The Discovery of Pain." PoNow (23) 79, p. 15.
"How the Sea and the Dry Land Long for One Another." Spirit
    (3:1/2) Aut-Wint 77-78, p. 32.

WILLARD, Nancy
"The Great American Poem." Antaeus (32) Wint 79, pp. 82-86.

WILLIAMS, Faith
"The day the first glasses came." Nimrod (23:1) Aut-Wint 79,
    p. 23.

WILLIAMS, Gorden
"Peanuts." MalR (49) Ja 79, p. 56.
"Run Around." MalR (49) Ja 79, p. 58.
"The Voices." MalR (49) Ja 79, p. 57.

WILLIAMS, Miller
"Abraham's Sacrifice: I" (tr. of Giuseppe Gioachino Belli).
    NewOR (6:2) 79, p. 122.

"Abraham's Sacrifice: II" (tr. of Giuseppe Gioachino Belli).
   NewOR (6:2) 79, p. 122.
"Abraham's Sacrifice: III" (tr. of Giuseppe Gioachino Belli).
   NewOR (6:2) 79, p. 123.
"The Builders" (tr. of Giuseppe Gioachino Belli). NewOR (6:2)
   79, p. 121.
"The Circumcision of the Lord" (tr. of Giuseppe Gioachino Belli).
   CharR (5:1) Spr 79, p. 7.
"The Creation of the World" (tr. of Giuseppe Gioachino Belli).
   CharR (5:1) Spr 79, p. 5.
"The Flight of the Holy Family" (tr. of Giuseppe Gioachino Belli).
   CharR (5:1) Spr 79, p. 7.
"Form and Theory of Poetry." CimR (48) Jl 79, p. 62.
"The Friend." PoNow (23) 79, p. 30.
"Getting the Message." NewEngR (2:1) Aut 79, p. 85.
"A Good Woman." CimR (48) Jl 79, p. 32.
"Hello." Kayak (52) D 79, p. 39.
"In Scene One Act Two the Blond Boy Falling into Step Beside
   You Says." Kayak (52) D 79, p. 38.
"It's Hard to Think the Brain." PoNow (23) 79, p. 30.
"The Jesus Woman Standing at My Door." PoNow (23) 79, p. 30.
"The Last Person to Speak His Language Is Dying." Kayak (52)
   D 79, p. 38.
"The Letter" (tr. of Giuseppe Gioachino Belli). CharR (5:1) Spr
   79, p. 6.
"Lying." PoetryNW (20:4) Wint 79-80, p. 23.
"On the Last Page of the Last Yellow Legal Pad in Rome Before
   Taking Off for Dacca on Air Bangladesh." CimR (48) Jl 79,
   p. 50.
"The Proper Study." Kayak (52) D 79, p. 39.
"The Slaughter of the Innocents" (tr. of Giuseppe Gioachino Belli).
   CharR (5:1) Spr 79, p. 8.
"The Universal Flood" (tr. of Giuseppe Gioachino Belli). CharR
   (5:1) Spr 79, p. 6.
"The Unknown Sailor." PoNow (23) 79, p. 30.

WILLIAMSON, Alan
   "Bernini's Proserpine." Ploughs (5:2) 79, pp. 91-96.
   "Presence" (for Peter Taylor). Ploughs (5:2) 79, pp. 89-90.

WILLITTS, Martin
   "The Lady Who Wanted Colors." Im (5:3) 79, p. 11.
   "The Operation." Im (5:3) 79, p. 11.

WILLSON, Robert
   "The Last Resort." NewL (46:1) Aut 79, p. 27.

WILMER, Clive
   "Letter to My Wife" (tr. of Miklós Radnóti w. George Gömöri).
      SouthernR (15:1) Wint 79, p. 143.
   "The Third Eclogue" (tr. of Miklós Radnóti w. George Gömöri).
      SouthernR (15:1) Wint 79, p. 144.

WILNER, Eleanor
  "Beyond the Second Landing." NewRep (181:9/10) 1-8 S 79, p.
    32.
  "Laurels." NewRep (180:19) 12 My 79, p. 32.

WILSON, Austin
  "Burning Her Letters." SouthernHR (13:2) Spr 79, p. 136.

WILSON, Edward
  "Fingers." Poetry (133:6) Mr 79, p. 332.

WILSON, Keith
  "Growing Up." PoNow (23) 79, p. 30.
  "In Sere and Twisted Trees." PoNow (23) 79, p. 30.

WILSON, Rob
  "The Rescues." WestHR (33:3) Sum 79, p. 233.

WILSON, Robley Jr.
  "Bears." Atl (243:6) Je 79, p. 81.
  "Bridesmaid." OP (27) Spr 79, p. 18.
  "Crossings." OP (27) Spr 79, p. 23.
  "Demon Lovers." PoetryNW (20:3) Aut 79, p. 42.
  "Love/Love/Love." OP (27) Spr 79, p. 22.
  "On Not Knowing the Names of the Flowers in Montana." Poetry
    (134:5) Ag 79, p. 260.
  "The Persistence of Desire." OP (27) Spr 79, p. 19.
  "Pets." Bits (10) Jl 79.
  "Renting." OP (27) Spr 79, pp. 16-17.
  "The Suspense of Meeting." Poetry (134:5) Ag 79, p. 261.
  "The Wedding Ring." OP (27) Spr 79, pp. 20-21.
  "Yankee Poet." Hudson (32:4) Wint 79-80, p. 530.

WINANS, A. D.
  "America." SeC (6:2) 78, p. 29.
  "carla." Ur (2) 79, p. 126.
  "cavanough's." Ur (2) 79, p. 127.
  "The Dreams." SeC (6:1) 78, p. 9.
  "Excuse the Harshness Excuse the Grime But Seriousness Ain't
    No Crime." SeC (6:2) 78, p. 38.
  The Further Adventures of Crazy John. SeC (7:2) 79. Entire
    issue.
  "I Paid $3.00 to See Bukowski Read." SeC (6:2) 78, pp. 33-37.
  "millie." Ur (2) 79, p. 128.
  "My Woman." SeC (6:1) 78, p. 11.
  "New Breed Author." SeC (6:1) 78, p. 10.
  "Visiting the L.A. Funny Farm." PikeR (1) Sum 79, p. 57.

WINCH, Terence
  "Cigars Make the Body More Interesting" (for Ted Greenwald).
    Tele (15) Spr 79, p. 51.
  from 5 Poems from Famous People: "Real Creeps." Tele (15)
    Spr 79, p. 51.

"Money for Women." Tele (15) Spr 79, p. 52.
"The New York Poem." Tele (15) Spr 79, p. 47.
"Real Rockstar." Tele (15) Spr 79, p. 52.
"Smoke." Tele (15) Spr 79, p. 49.

WINDER, Barbara
"San Pedro Wilderness." PoetC (10:3) 79, p. 42.

WINDHAM, Revish
"Freedom" (to Junior, Mamma and Charles). BlackF (3:1) Aut-
    Wint 79, p. 40.

WINE, James
from Vastansjo: (I). SunM (8) Aut 79, p. 124.
from Vastansjo: (III). SunM (8) Aut 79, p. 126.

WINN, Howard
"Borie in the Vaucluse." GRR (10:2) 79, p. 181.
"Up." Ur (2) 79, p. 129.

WINNER, Robert
"The Chain Gang." AmerPoR (8:2) Mr-Ap 79, p. 32.
"Elegy." AmerPoR (8:2) Mr-Ap 79, p. 32.
"February Morning Through My Kitchen Window." SlowLR (3)
    79, p. 77.

WINSHIP, George P. Jr.
"Dinosaurs at Easter." ChrC (96:13) 11 Ap 79, p. 402.

WINTERS, Anne
"(Detail)." Ploughs (5:2) 79, pp. 45-46.
"Night Wash." NewRep (180:5) 3 F 79, p. 30.
"Royalty" (tr. of Robert Marteau). Poetry (134:1) Ap 79, p. 35.

WINTERS, Nancy
"Kremlin Easter." SouthernR (15:1) Wint 79, p. 146.
"To an Acquaintance." SouthernR (15:1) Wint 79, p. 147.

WISCHNER, Claudia March
"A Riddle." Chowder (13) Aut-Wint 79, p. 25.

WISEMAN, Christopher
"At Filey Brig." MalR (51) Jl 79, p. 94.
"Nocturne for Jean." MalR (51) Jl 79, p. 95.

WITSCHEL, John
"Acute Allergic Reaction Remedied with Epinephrine." Kayak (50)
    My 79, p. 32. Found poem.
"Lying in the Garden at Dawn." Kayak (51) S 79, p. 22.

WITT, Harold
"Among the Cloverleaves." Ur (2) 79, p. 130.
"Bedazzled." GreenfieldR (7:3/4) Spr-Sum 79, p. 56.

"Bus Zaps Plato's Tree. " CarlMis (17:2/3) Spr 79, p. 73.
"Europa. " NewL (46:1) Aut 79, p. 34.
"Frames. " PoetryNW (20:4) Wint 79-80, pp. 10-11.
"Grandma Wylie at the Sunshine Convalescent Hospital. " NewL
    (46:1) Aut 79, p. 34.
"A Necklace of Newport Shells. " GreenfieldR (7:3/4) Spr-Sum 79,
    p. 56.
from Over Fifty: "Conceit. " Confr (19) Aut 79-Wint 80, p. 68.
from Over Fifty: "December First. " StoneC (6:2) My 79, p. 15.
"Save Tilg and Bartell. " Ur (2) 79, p. 131.
"The Way to the Lake. " Wind (32) 79, p. 49.

WITTE, John
"Elegy: Noah's Crow. " Iowa (10:2) Spr 79, p. 98.
"Flight. " Epoch (28:3) Spr-Sum 79, p. 255.
"Leo. " PoetryNW (20:3) Aut 79, pp. 34-35.
"Moth. " AntR (37:3) Sum 79, p. 311.
"Power Failure. " PoNow (25) 79, p. 30.
"Seven of Us Going to Sleep. " Kayak (51) S 79, p. 23.
"Truckstop. " Epoch (28:3) Spr-Sum 79, p. 254.
"Wild Bill at Troy Grove, Ill. " PoNow (25) 79, p. 30.

WITTLINGER, Ellen
"The Knickknack Shelf. " Aspect (74/75) Ja-Ag 79, p. 37.

WOESSNER, Warren
"Buffalo Cliff" (for Bill and Jean). BelPoJ (29:3) Spr 79, p. 3.
"Looking at Power. " BelPoJ (29:3) Spr 79, p. 2.

WOIWODE, Larry
"Neighboring Contrary. " NewYorker (55:27) 20 Ag 79, p. 91.

WOJAHN, David
"The Vigil. " PortR (25) 79, p. 106.
"You Turn. " PortR (25) 79, p. 105.

WOLITZER, Hilma
"People in the News. " PoNow (21) 79, p. 47.

WOLVEN, Fred
After the Death of Theodore Roethke. UTR (6:2) 79. Entire
    issue.
"A Confused Landscape" (for Chris McLelland). UTR (6:3/4) 79,
    p. 60.
"Goldfinches (for Duane Locke). UTR (6:3/4) 79, p. 61.
"Interlude" (for Sharon). UTR (6:3/4) 79, p. 63.
"Interlude. " Wind (32) 79, p. 25.
"Morning Sounds: Grass Stretching, Water Sifting. " UTR (6:3/4)
    79, p. 64.
"Moving Up the Mountain. " Wind (32) 79, p. 24.
"Poetic Directions. " AAR (29) 79, p. 21.
"A Small Gift for Jason. " AAR (29) 79, p. 88.
"Walking Alone in this World" (for Lisa Ritchie). UTR (6:3/4)
    79, p. 62.

WOOD, Amelia
"Extremes. " Chowder (12) Spr-Sum 79, p. 11.
"Unscientific. " SoDakR (17:2) Sum 79, p. 30.

WOOD, Randy
"The Dream. " QW (6) Spr-Sum 78, p. 32.
"The Words. " QW (6) Spr-Sum 78, p. 32.

WOOD, Robert E.
"Deficient. " Wind (32) 79, p. 50.
"Earth Water Air Fire. " Wind (32) 79, p. 50.

WOOD, Susan
"Learning to Live Without You. " NewEngR (2:1) Aut 79, p. 23.

WOOD, Wendy
"between us" (for valery). Tele (15) Spr 79, p. 129.
"i never knew it was you. " Tele (15) Spr 79, p. 129.
"o so to-. " Tele (15) Spr 79, p. 127.
"she-leaves. " Tele (15) Spr 79, p. 128.

WOODCOCK, George
"The Skeena. " MalR (51) Jl 79, p. 50.

WOODFORD, Bruce P.
"The Coming Event. " PoNow (23) 79, p. 37.

WOODS, Carl
"Angelo Lake. " Wind (35) 79, p. 64.
"Biography. " Poem (35) Mr 79, p. 31.
"Forced March. " Wind (33) 79, p. 58.
"Garden. " Poem (36) Jl 79, p. 34.
"Liberation. " Wind (33) 79, p. 58.
"The Power. " Tele (15) Spr 79, p. 119.
"Storm. " Wind (33) 79, p. 59.
"Sycamore Swing. " Poem (35) Mr 79, p. 33.
"The Word. " Poem (35) Mr 79, p. 32.

WOODS, John
"Ahwah (a cheap shot). " Sky (9) Aut 79, pp. 7-8.
"The Cherenkov Variations. " Sky (9) Aut 79, pp. 5-6.
"The Long Marriage. " QW (8) Wint 79, p. 27.
"The Servant of Butterflies. " QW (8) Wint 79, p. 28.
"The Water Poem. " Field (20) Spr 79, p. 60.

WORLEY, James
"Electrolytes. " ChrC (96:36) 7 N 79, p. 1084.
"His Eighty-second Spring. " ChrC (96:19) 23 My 79, p. 580.
"Living Is a Lot. " ChrC (96:9) 14 Mr 79, p. 268.
"Mark Van Doren. " ChrC (96:33) 17 O 79, p. 1006.
"New Year's Eve. " ChrC (96:43) 26 D 79, p. 1287.
"Old Wife, Senile. " ChrC (96:39) 28 N 79, p. 1176.
"Telling the World. " ChrC (96:27) 29 Ag-5 S 79, p. 815.

"To Walden Wherever. " KanQ (11:1/2) Wint-Spr 79, p. 93.
"Touchstone. " ChrC (96:17) 9 My 79, p. 526.

WORLEY, Jeff
"How the Poem Finally Arrives. " PoetryNW (20:1) Spr 79, p.
    21.
"Uncle Matt. " CalQ (15) Wint 79, p. 24.

WORSLEY, Alice
"Eddic Lament. " BelPoJ (29:4) Sum 79, p. 33.
"Recurring Dream" (for Doris Lessing). BelPoJ (29:4) Sum 79,
    p. 34.

WRAY, Elizabeth
"Broken Borders. " Kayak (51) S 79, p. 28.
"A Map of Scars. " PartR (46:2) 79, pp. 250-251.

WRENN, Tom
"Love Song. " Wind (34) 79, p. 65.

WRIGHT, A. J.
"Prelude. " Poem (37) N 79, p. 53.

WRIGHT, C. D.
"Final Paradise for Dead Birds. " QW (8) Wint 79, p. 93.
"Libretto. " Field (21) Aut 79, p. 57.
"Passenger. " QW (8) Wint 79, p. 94.
"Terrorism. " QW (8) Wint 79, p. 93.
"Yellow Dresses. " Field (21) Aut 79, p. 56.

WRIGHT, Carolyne
"Mania Klepto. " Ploughs (5:3) 79, pp. 83-84.
"Rehearsal for a Visit. " Stand (20:1) 78-79, p. 62.
"Returning What We Owed. " PoNow (25) 79, p. 43.
"Two Measures" (for Susan). KanQ (11:1/2) Wint-Spr 79, p. 114.

WRIGHT, Charles
"The Great American Poem. " Antaeus (32) Wint 79, pp. 82-86.
"The Lemon-Yellow Rooster" (tr. of Eugenio Montale). PoNow
    (24) 79, p. 32.
"October. " NewYorker (55:34) 8 O 79, p. 42.
"Portrait of the Artist with Hart Crane. " Durak (3) 79, p. 41.
"Portrait of the Artist with Li Po. " Durak (3) 79, p. 40.
"Seaside" (tr. of Eugenio Montale). PoNow (24) 79, p. 32.
"Self-Portrait. " QW (6) Spr-Sum 78, p. 123.
"Spellbound" (tr. of Eugenio Montale). PoNow (24) 79, p. 32.

WRIGHT, Franz
"At the Grave of Someone Named Emily Snow. " Durak (3) 79,
    p. 16.
"From a Childhood" (tr. of Rainer Maria Rilke). QW (9) Spr-
    Sum 79, p. 10.
"Grieving" (tr. of Rainer Maria Rilke). QW (9) Spr-Sum 79, p.

11.
"Last Evening" (tr. of Rainer Maria Rilke). QW (9) Spr-Sum 79,
    p. 9.
"The Moth. " QW (9) Spr-Sum 79, p. 11.
"Orpheus, Eurydice, Hermes" (tr. of Rainer Maria Rilke). Durak
    (2) 79, p. 14.
"Rene Char. " QW (7) Aut 78, p. 33.
"The Road. " Durak (2) 79, p. 57.
"Sarah Bitterfield: Poem from a Woman's Dream Journal. "
    MissouriR (2:2/3) Spr 79, p. 31.
"The Secret Address. " Durak (2) 79, p. 56.
"The Swan" (tr. of Rainer Maria Rilke). QW (9) Spr-Sum 79, p.
    10.

WRIGHT, James
"Coming Home to Maui. " OhioR (20:2) Spr-Sum 79, pp. 8-9.
"A Flower Passage. " Poetry (133:5) F 79, pp. 288-289.
"The Ice House. " OhioR (20:2) Spr-Sum 79, p. 9.
"Leave Him Alone. " Durak (3) 79, p. 6.
"Lightning Bugs Asleep in the Afternoon. " NewYorker (55:27)
    20 Ag 79, p. 26.
"My Notebook. " Durak (3) 79, p. 7.
"A Rainbow on Garda. " Durak (3) 79, p. 5.
"Sheep in the Rain. " Poetry (133:5) F 79, p. 287.
"With the Gift of an Alabaster Tortoise. " NewYorker (55:43) 10
    D 79, p. 46.
"Young Women at Chartres" (in memory of Jean Garrigue).
    GeoR (33:2) Sum 79, p. 326.
"Your Name in Arezzo. " Poetry (133:5) F 79, p. 286.

WRIGHT, James A.
"In February. " Wind (35) 79, p. 66.

WRIGHT, T. L.
"Avalon" (for Eugene Current-Garcia). SouthernHR (13:1) Wint
    79, p. iii.

WRIGHT, Terry
"(commercialism). " PikeF (2) Wint 78-79, p. 19.
"Moon Walk in the Middle of July. " PikeR (1) Sum 79, p. 59.
"(punk poem). " Pig (6) 79, p. 8.

WRIGLEY, Robert
"The Bees" (for K). WestHR (33:3) Sum 79, p. 234.
"Drowning. " WestHR (33:4) Aut 79, p. 309.
"The Fence. " Chowder (12) Spr-Sum 79, p. 16.
"Fireflies. " QW (9) Spr-Sum 79, p. 33.
"Nightcrawlers. " WestHR (33:3) Sum 79, p. 236.
"The Rattlesnake. " Chowder (12) Spr-Sum 79, p. 17.

WYATT, David
"For the Last Time 'I want no lights in the dusk'--Keats. " Wind
    (32) 79, p. 52.

"In a Cornfield at Dusk 'troubling the dream coast'--Louis Simpson. " Wind (32) 79, p. 52.

WYLIE, Alvin Bennett
"Waiting for a Miracle. " Sam (72) 79, p. 84.

WYMAN, Hastings Jr.
"With Timbrel and Dance. " SouthernPR (19:1) Spr 79, p. 67.

WYNAND, Derk
"Plot of a Belief" (tr. of Friederike Mayrocker). MalR (52) O 79, p. 138.

WYNDHAM, Harald
"Sonnett in Blank Verse. " Ur (2) 79, p. 136.

WYNNE, John
"Two Struggling Actresses. " ParisR (76) Aut 79, pp. 103-109.

YALIM, Ozcan
"Anadlou' Daki Bir Tepeden" (tr. of Dionis Coffin Riggs). StoneC (6:1) F 79, p. 27.
"Holiday Visit" (tr. of Behcet Necatigil w. Dionis Coffin Riggs and William Fiedler). StoneC (6:1) F 79, p. 28.

YA'OZ-KEST, Itamar
"On the River Lookout" (tr. by Bernhard Frank). PoNow (24) 79, p. 63.
"Quarry" (tr. by Bernhard Frank). PoNow (24) 79, p. 63.

YARNALL, Judith
"The Animals. " WestB (5) 79, p. 2.
"Fever. " WestB (5) 79, p. 4.
"Looking at the Rembrandts. " WestB (5) 79, p. 1.
"Totem. " WestB (5) 79, p. 5.

YASHIN, Alexander
"Kind Deeds" (tr. by Irina Zheleznova). PoNow (24) 79, p. 63.

YATES, David C.
"Snickersnee. " PoNow (25) 79, p. 45.
"Two Lions. " GreenfieldR (7:3/4) Spr-Sum 79, p. 239.

YATES, J. Michael
"In Peacetime" (tr. of Karl Krolow). NewOR (6:2) 79, p. 152.

YATES, James
"Barcelona Postcard. " MissR (24) Aut 79, p. 130.
"Burning Abandoned Magazines. " PoNow (25) 79, p. 44.
"Four Elements. " MissR (24) Aut 79, pp. 121-129.
"An Invitation to Dance. " SouthernPR (19:1) Spr 79, p. 74.

YAU, John
"From the Chinese. " Tele (15) Spr 79, p. 42.

"Nine Songs. " Tele (15) Spr 79, p. 43.
"Radio. " Tele (15) Spr 79, p. 43.

YEAGER, Peter E.
"Fear of Falling" (for Jodi). SmPd (45) 79, p. 15.

YEAGLEY, Joan
"Angus Run. " PoNow (25) 79, p. 44.
"The Studs of McDonald County. " PoNow (25) 79, p. 44.

YOTS, Michael
"Edgar Allan Poe I Hate You. " PikeF (2) Wint 78-79, p. 10.
"Points of View. " PikeF (2) Wint 78-79, p. 10.
"What I Said to Prove I Was Sane. " PikeF (2) Wint 78-79, p. 10.

YOUNG, Al
"The Great American Poem. " Antaeus (32) Wint 79, pp. 82-86.

YOUNG, David
"Other Forms Were Near: Five Words. " Durak (3) 79, pp. 57-61.
"The Picture Says. " NewYorker (55:12) 12 My 79, p. 166.
"The Poem of the Cold. " PoNow (22) 79, p. 28.
"Sexual Groans. " PoNow (22) 79, p. 28.
from Sonnets to Orpheus Part Two: Twenty-nine Poems (tr. of Rainer Maria Rilke). Field (20) Spr 79, pp. 65-95.

YOUNG, Ellen R.
"Saints. " ChrC (96:34) 24 O 79, p. 1028.

YOUNG, Gary
"The Doctor Rebuilds a Hand" (for Brad Crenshaw). Antaeus (32) Wint 79, p. 61.
"Starfish. " Chowder (13) Aut-Wint 79, p. 15.

YOUNG, Ian
"Was he whistling at his door, or did he wish" (tr. of Sandro Penna w. M. J. Shakely). PoNow (24) 79, p. 44.
"A glass of milk, a square" (tr. of Sandro Penna w. M. J. Shakely). PoNow (24) 79, p. 44.
"Silently, the summer went away" (tr. of Sandro Penna w. M. J. Shakely). PoNow (24) 79, p. 44.
"The businessman strolled toward his house" (tr. of Sandro Penna w. M. J. Shakely). PoNow (24) 79, p. 44.
"The ship arrives. The cheery passengers" (tr. of Sandro Penna w. M. J. Shakely). PoNow (24) 79, p. 44.
"Still it is sweet to find yourself" (tr. of Sandro Penna w. M. J. Shakely). PoNow (24) 79, p. 44.
"In a dingy theatre pit" (tr. of Sandro Penna w. M. J. Shakely). PoNow (24) 79, p. 44.

YOUNG, Virginia Brady
"Butterfly. " PikeR (1) Sum 79, p. 31.

"The Closed Box. " HiramPoR (26) Spr-Sum 79, p. 39.
"Taught to Be Polite. " PikeR (1) Sum 79, p. 30.

YOURGRAU, Barry
"Aerial. " Tele (15) Spr 79, p. 117.
"Fauve. " Tele (15) Spr 79, p. 117.

YURKIEVICH, Saúl
"Self-Criticism. " LitR (23:2) Wint 80, p. 281.
"Spaces. " LitR (23:2) Wint 80, p. 280.

YURMAN, R.
"What It Does. " ColEng (41:4) D 79, p. 411.

ZABLE, Jeffrey
"Tortured by the Muse. " Wind (35) 79, p. 67.

ZABOLOTSKY, Nikolay
"The Ugly Girl" (tr. by Dorian Rottenberg). PoNow (24) 79, p.
63.

ZACHARY, Frank
"H2Ode. " NewYorker (55:13) 14 My 79, p. 44.

ZADE, Wayne
"The Drowned Man. " NoAmR (264:1) Spr 79, p. 13.

ZADRAVEC, Katherine
"Mad River. " PoNow (23) 79, p. 47.

ZAID, Gabriel
"Ipanema" (tr. by Eliot Weinberger). DenQ (14:1) Spr 79, p.
82.
"Late Again" (tr. by Eliot Weinberger). DenQ (14:1) Spr 79, p.
83.

ZAMBARAS, Vassilis
"Crow's-Foot. " Spirit (3:1/2) Aut-Wint 77-78, p. 37.
"The Poet as Archaeologist. " Spirit (3:1/2) Aut-Wint 77-78, p.
37.
"Poetry Lesson. " Spirit (3:1/2) Aut-Wint 77-78, p. 37.

ZARANKA, William
"The Cook's Tale" (parody of Chaucer, w. David Cummings).
PoetC (10:3) 79, pp. 4-21.
"'If You Ever Write a Book, Put Me in It. '" SoCaR (11:2) Spr
79, p. 2.
"Sauna. " PoNow (25) 79, p. 44.
"Sitfast Acres. " Paint (12) Aut 79, p. 22.

ZARIN, Cynthia
"Charlottesville, August. " Poetry (134:5) Ag 79, pp. 272-273.

ZARZYSKI, Paul
"Instant Replay" (for Doc Odorizzi). Chowder (13) Aut-Wint 79,
  p. 44.
"The Late Long Haul of Hay. " PoNow (25) 79, p. 44.
"Nightcrawlers. " QW (6) Spr-Sum 78, p. 7.
"On the Way to the Blind" (for Dave and Curt). PortR (25) 79,
  p. 119.
"Partner" (for Kim Zupan). CutB (13) Aut-Wint 79, p. 48.
"Take-Home Pay. " QW (6) Spr-Sum 78, p. 8.
"Trying One Outside. " CutB (13) Aut-Wint 79, p. 47.
"Vischio. " QW (6) Spr-Sum 78, p. 5.

ZAWADIWSKY, Christine
"Lost. " Im (6:1) 79, p. 10.
"Not for Me. " Vaga (29) 79, p. 42.
"The Nurse with White Hair and Her Slow Poisons. " MissouriR
  (2:2/3) Spr 79, p. 23.
"Soundless Compartment. " Im (6:1) 79, p. 10.
"Your Body Is a Uniform. " Im (6:1) 79, p. 10.

ZDANYS, Jonas
"I Will Mention the Colors" (tr. of Tomas Venclova). SlowLR
  (3) 79, p. 72.
"The Room at a Glance" (tr. of Tomas Venclova). SlowLR (3)
  79, p. 70.

ZEIDNER, Lisa
"Diner. " MissR (22/23) Wint-Spr 79, p. 176.
"God's Jukebox. " MissR (22/23) Wint-Spr 79, p. 175.
"The Madonna Has That Look Again. " WestB (5) 79, p. 28.
"Mind the Quiet. " MissR (22/23) Wint-Spr 79, p. 174.
"Skinner Remembers a Fall. " Shen (30:1) Aut 78, p. 66.
"Tornado Warning. " MissR (22/23) Wint-Spr 79, p. 173.

ZEIGER, L. L.
"Spider-Part One. " PoNow (22) 79, p. 46.
"Statues. " PoNow (22) 79, p. 46.

ZIEGLER, Alan
"The Last Act. " PoNow (22) 79, p. 47.
"The Pusher. " PoNow (22) 79, p. 46.
"Take-out Order. " PoNow (22) 79, p. 47.
"Talent. " PoNow (22) 79, p. 47.

al-ZEIN, Amira
"Color of Memory: Color of Blood" (tr. by Kamal J. Boullata).
  Paint (12) Aut 79, p. 31.

ZELMAN, Anita
"Tone. " Sam (79) 79, p. 78.

ZELTZER, Joel
"adolescence" (tr. of Juan Ramon Jiminez). Wind (34) 79, p. 31.

"confusion" (tr. of Cesar Vallejo). Wind (34) 79, p. 64.
"the cradling" (tr. of Gabriela Mistral). Wind (34) 79, p. 44.
"pompeii" (tr. of Jose Emilio Pacheco). Wind (34) 79, p. 47.

ZELVIN, Elizabeth
"Denise at Twenty-Nine." 13thM (4:2) 79, p. 23.

ZEND, Robert
"One-Liners and Other Aphorisms" (tr. of Sandor Weores).
MalR (49) Ja 79, p. 105.

ZEPEDA, Rafael
"Doctor Locklin and Mr. Hyde." WormR (76) 79, p. 132.
"Jalapeno Peppers." WormR (76) 79, p. 130.
"Wittgenstein, Jasper, Johns, and Me." WormR (76) 79, p. 131.

ZHELEZNOVA, Irina
"Do Not Speak..." (tr. of Anna Akhmatova). PoNow (24) 79, p.
1.
"Horses in the Ocean" (to Ilya Ehrenburg) (tr. of Boris Slutsky).
PoNow (24) 79, p. 56.
"The Goths of old at baptism meekly wore" (tr. of Yevgeny
Vinokurov). PoNow (24) 79, p. 62.
"Kind Deeds" (tr. of Alexander Yashin). PoNow (24) 79, p. 63.

ZIEGER, L. L.
"The Snack." Poultry (1) 79, p. 11.

ZIENTARA, Jerry
"Bell." Mouth (2:2) Je 79, p. 37.
"Buzz." Mouth (2:2) Je 79, p. 38.
"When the lightning hit, when the lightning up." Mouth (2:2) Je
79, p. 13.

ZIMAN, Larry
"Freed." Ur (2) 79, p. 137.

ZIMMER, Paul
"Danse Zimmer." PoetryNW (20:4) Wint 79-80, p. 42.
"The Duke Ellington Dream." PoetryNW (20:4) Wint 79-80, pp.
43-44.
"The Great American Poem." Antaeus (32) Wint 79, pp. 82-86.
"The Great House." PoetryNW (20:1) Spr 79, p. 18.
"The History of Bears." MissouriR (3:1) Aut 79, p. 34.
"Irene Gogle" (for Erik). PoetryNW (20:1) Spr 79, pp. 18-19.
"Zimmer the Goat Boy." Poultry (1) 79, p. 10.
"Zimmer's Last Gig." Harp (258:1548) My 79, p. 102.

ZIMROTH, Evan
"Eutrophication." Poetry (134:2) My 79, pp. 74-75.

ZINNES, Harriet
"Away from You" (tr. of Cecilia Meireles). PoNow (24) 79, p.

25.

"Dialogues." Paint (11) Spr 79, p. 81.

"Family Portrait" (tr. of Jacques Prevert). PoNow (24) 79, p.
    45.

"Horse, in Old Brookville." Chelsea (38) 79, p. 188.

"Immense and Red" (tr. of Jacques Prevert). PoNow (24) 79, p.
    45.

"The loft was lived in. The brick unshapely sagged from ceil-
    ings." PoNow (22) 79, p. 47.

"Not to be undone, he unlaced his shoes and walked down to the."
    PoNow (22) 79, p. 28. Thirteen selections from Entropisms.

"Sleepless Palinurus" (tr. of Silvina Ocampo). PoNow (24) 79,
    p. 38.

"Tomorrow the trains may not run. Not because of a strike but."
    PoNow (22) 79, p. 47.

"Turn." PoNow (22) 79, p. 47.

"Wallace Stevens Gives a Reading." CentR (23:3) Sum 79, p. 289.

ZITO, Eleanor Shiel
    "The Fallen Woman." FourQt (28:2) Wint 79, p. 12.

ZUBER, Isabel
    "Come to See Me." Im (5:3) 79, p. 10.

ZU-BOLTON, Ahmos II
    "The Basketball Star." Spirit (3:1/2) Aut-Wint 77-78, p. 16.
    "In Our Love(ing)." BlackALF (13:1) Spr 79, p. 34.
    "Open Letter." BlackALF (13:1) Spr 79, p. 34.

ZURCHER, Susan
    "the Woolworth heir." Im (5:3) 79, p. 5.

ZWEIG, Ellen
    "The Woman Has a Green Stone." Chelsea (38) 79, p. 127.
    "The Women of Paris." Chelsea (38) 79, p. 125.

ZWICKER, Katrina L.
    "for Georgia O'Keeffe." Chomo (5:3) Spr 79, p. 22.

ZWICKY, Fay
    "Emily Dickinson Judges the Bread Division at the Amherst Cattle
        Show, 1858." Pequod (3:1) 79, pp. 11-12.
    "Fungus Epidemic." Pequod (3:1) 79, p. 10.

ZYDEK, Frederick
    "Dark Room" (for M. D.). SouthwR (64:3) Sum 79, p. 280.
    "Incubus Hominus Sanctorium." Poem (35) Mr 79, p. 39.

ZYNE, R. Gordon
    "No Legged Man." Wind (33) 79, p. 60.